Sisters in Crime
Revisited

Sisters in Crime Revisited

Bringing Gender into Criminology

IN HONOR OF FREDA ADLER

FRANCIS T. CULLEN
University of Cincinnati

PAMELA WILCOX
University of Cincinnati

JENNIFER L. LUX
University of Cincinnati

CHERYL LERO JONSON
Xavier University

New York   Oxford

OXFORD UNIVERSITY PRESS

Oxford University Press is a department of the University of Oxford.
It furthers the University's objective of excellence in research,
scholarship, and education by publishing worldwide.

Oxford   New York
Auckland   Cape Town   Dar es Salaam   Hong Kong   Karachi
Kuala Lumpur   Madrid   Melbourne   Mexico City   Nairobi
New Delhi   Shanghai   Taipei   Toronto

With offices in
Argentina   Austria   Brazil   Chile   Czech Republic   France   Greece
Guatemala   Hungary   Italy   Japan   Poland   Portugal   Singapore
South Korea   Switzerland   Thailand   Turkey   Ukraine   Vietnam

For titles covered by Section 112 of the US Higher Education Opportunity Act,
please visit www.oup.com/us/he for the latest information about pricing and
alternate formats.

Published by Oxford University Press
198 Madison Avenue, New York, New York 10016
http://www.oup.com

Library of Congress Cataloging-in-Publication Data
Cullen, Francis T.
  Sisters in crime revisited : bringing gender into criminology : in honor of Freda
  Adler / Francis T. Cullen, University of Cincinnati, Pamela Wilcox,
  University of Cincinnati, Jennifer L. Lux, University of Cincinnati,
  Cheryl Lero Jonson, Xavier University.—First Edition.
     pages cm
  Includes index.
  ISBN 978-0-19-931118-7
  1. Feminist criminology. 2. Women criminal justice personnel. 3. Female offenders.
  4. Women—Crimes against. 5. Adler, Freda. I. Title.
  HV6030.C84 2014
  364.3'74—dc23
                                                        2014010619

Printing number: 9 8 7 6 5 4 3 2 1
Printed in the United States of America
on acid-free paper

Zoë Knijff

Freda Adler

Author:
Sisters in Crime: The Rise of the New Female Criminal

CONTENTS

CONTRIBUTORS

Leanne Fiftal Alarid is Associate Professor of Criminal Justice at the University of Texas at El Paso.

Danielle L. Boisvert is Assistant Professor and Director of Criminal Justice and Criminology Graduate Programs at Sam Houston State University.

Sandra Lee Browning is Associate Professor of Criminal Justice at the University of Cincinnati.

Meda Chesney-Lind is Professor and Department Chair of Women's Studies at the University of Hawaii at Manoa.

Nicholas Corsaro is Assistant Professor of Criminal Justice at the University of Cincinnati.

Francis T. Cullen is Distinguished Research Professor of Criminal Justice and Sociology at the University of Cincinnati.

Walter S. DeKeseredy is the Anna Deane Carlson Endowed Chair of Social Sciences and Professor of Sociology at West Virginia University.

Mary Dodge is Professor of Criminal Justice at the University of Colorado Denver.

Bonnie S. Fisher is Professor of Criminal Justice at the University of Cincinnati.

Dana L. Haynie is Professor of Sociology and Director of the Criminal Justice Research Center at The Ohio State University.

Candace Kruttschnitt is Professor of Sociology at the University of Toronto.

Cheryl Lero Jonson is Assistant Professor of Criminal Justice at Xavier University.

Nicole V. Lasky is a Ph.D. Candidate in Criminal Justice at the University of Cincinnati.

Jennifer L. Lux is a Ph.D. Candidate in Criminal Justice and a Research Associate in the Corrections Institute at the University of Cincinnati.

Sarah M. Manchak is Assistant Professor of Criminal Justice at the University of Cincinnati.

Alida V. Merlo is Professor of Criminology at Indiana University of Pennsylvania.

James W. Messerschmidt is Professor of Sociology and Women and Gender Studies and Chair of the Criminology Department at the University of Southern Maine.

Jody Miller is Professor of Criminal Justice at Rutgers University.

Madeleine Novich is a Ph.D. Candidate in Criminal Justice at Rutgers University.

Alex R. Piquero is Ashbel Smith Professor of Criminology at the University of Texas at Dallas.

Nicole Leeper Piquero is Professor of Criminology and Associate Dean for Graduate Programs at the University of Texas at Dallas.

Joycelyn M. Pollock is Distinguished Professor of Criminal Justice at Texas State University.

Amanda M. Petersen is a Ph.D. Student in Criminology, Law and Society at the University of California, Irvine.

Jesenia M. Pizarro is Associate Professor of Criminal Justice at Michigan State University.

Emily J. Salisbury is Associate Professor of Criminal Justice at the University of Nevada, Las Vegas.

Jennifer Schwartz is Associate Professor of Sociology at Washington State University.

Martin D. Schwartz is Visiting Professor of Sociology at George Washington University.

Sally S. Simpson is Professor of Criminology and Criminal Justice and Director for the Center for the Study of Business Ethics, Regulation, and Crime at the University of Maryland.

Paula Smith is Associate Professor of Criminal Justice at the University of Cincinnati.

Brian Soller is Assistant Professor of Sociology at the University of New Mexico.

Darrell Steffensmeier is Professor of Sociology and Criminology at Pennsylvania State University.

Mary K. Stohr is Professor of Criminal Justice and Criminology at Washington State University.

Jody Sundt is Associate Dean for Graduate and Executive Education and Associate Professor in the School of Public and Environmental Affairs at Indiana University—Purdue University Indianapolis.

Stephen Tomsen is Professor of Criminology at the University of Western Sydney.

Jamie C. Vaske is Assistant Professor of Criminology and Criminal Justice at Western Carolina University.

Emily M. Wright is Associate Professor of Criminology and Criminal Justice at the University of Nebraska, Omaha.

Pamela Wilcox is Professor of Criminal Justice at the University of Cincinnati.

John Paul Wright is Professor of Criminal Justice at the University of Cincinnati and Research Professor in the Center for Social and Humanities Research at King Abdulaziz University in Jedda, Saudi Arabia.

ACKNOWLEDGMENTS

This project has been a labor of love—a way of honoring and expressing our affection for Freda Adler, our "sister in crime." We thus want to start by stating our collective gratitude to Freda, for her sustained contributions both to criminology and to the careers and personal well-being of many of us in the discipline.

Sisters in Crime Revisited would not have been possible without an outpouring of good will. Those asked to author chapters for this volume had one thing in common: They were all very busy and had no time to take on yet another scholarly obligation. Despite daunting workloads and a tight submission deadline, they agreed enthusiastically to write the chapters requested of them. Their generosity was inspired not by the prospect of another line on their vitas (which they certainly did not need!) but by their heartfelt desire to join in a long-overdue celebration of a cherished colleague. They have done so marvelously, crafting a set of essays that provides a fascinating tour through the many facets of the study of women and crime. Their efforts have resulted in a book of scholarly consequence, revealing why it is essential to bring gender into the core of criminology and offering a fitting tribute to Freda Adler.

Special praise must also be extended to Sarah Calabi, our initial editor at Oxford University Press, who showed inordinate faith in the project. We were disappointed for her to leave the press, but this special volume will be one enduring mark, among others, that she will leave on the field of criminology.

Following Sarah's departure, we received unwavering support from Sherith Pankratz. During the project, Caroline Osborne and Olivia Caroline Geraci at Oxford University Press supplied invaluable assistance. We also must note the fine work of Oxford's production staff, especially Roxanne Klaas. And we would be remiss if we did not express our appreciation to the scholars whose constructive reviews made this volume both possible and much improved: Irshad Altheimer, Rochester Institute of Technology; Dawn Beichner, Illinois State University; Jennifer L. Hartman, University of North Carolina at Charlotte; Kristen Kuehnle, Salem State University; and Christina Mancini, Virginia Commonwealth University.

We must highlight as well the support that we have received from those in our academic homes, the School of Criminal Justice at the University of Cincinnati and the Department of Criminal Justice at Xavier University. Victoria Chamberlin was particularly helpful in bring this volume to press.

Finally, a book-length project is a complex undertaking with many tasks that must be addressed sooner rather than later. In our case, our writing and editorial duties often intruded into time that perhaps should have been devoted to our private lives. Accordingly, for their continued understanding, we wish to express our love and gratitude to those closest to us who have helped make this tribute to Freda possible: Paula Dubeck (from Francis T. Cullen), Michael Rosenberg (from Pamela Wilcox), T. J. Brown (from Jennifer Lux), and Paul Jonson (from Cheryl Lero Jonson).

PART I

Celebrating Freda Adler

CHAPTER 1

Introduction:
Sisters in Crime as a Criminological Classic

Francis T. Cullen and Pamela Wilcox

In 1975, after three years of work, Freda Adler published what would become a criminological classic: *Sisters in Crime: The Rise of the New Female Criminal.* The title was significant for two reasons. First, this volume was preceded by Clifford Shaw's 1938 study of delinquents in Chicago, *Brothers in Crime.* The title, *Sisters in Crime,* thus suggested that crime was no longer a male preserve. Women might also be involved in the criminal enterprise, not only as consorts to men but also with other women—their sisters! Second, the book's subtitle, *The Rise of the New Female Criminal,* indicated that something new was afoot—that women's roles in society were being transformed not only in the conventional world but also in the criminal world. These were bold claims for a time period in which women were just beginning to break down the barriers in a variety of domains—whether in education, sports, the workplace, or the home. At that historical moment, no act could seem more unfeminine or unnatural for women than to break the law in some purposeful, wanton way. Could this really be happening?

As her book was brought to press by McGraw–Hill—the paperback edition sold for $3.95—Freda could not have anticipated the remarkable reception it would receive. (We will call Dr. Adler "Freda" because this is how she is known to everyone—to family, friends, students, and professional colleagues.) She would eventually have "over 300 interviews to newspapers, news magazines, television (her first television interview was with Barbara Walters), and radio networks" (Flynn, 1998, p. 3). She would appear on *Face the Nation* and on the game shows *What's My Line?* and *To Tell the Truth* (Hartman & Sundt, 2011). Our favorite is that she was a guest on the *Johnny Carson Show*—something reserved for true celebrities! For today's younger generation, this would be akin to an appearance on the *David Letterman Show.*

What would lead a book by a social scientist, writing in relative obscurity when she authored *Sisters in Crime*, to receive such attention, if not celebrity status? Three factors, we believe, played a role. First, as hinted above, there was a striking convergence of the book's message with the prevailing social context that had arisen in the 1960s and extended into the 1970s. For the decade preceding the book's publication, the United States had been in a period marked by political turmoil, calls for expanded civil rights, and a cultural revolution. One product of these times was a growing women's movement. The book's message was that the emerging transformation of women's roles in society would occur not only in the legitimate but also in the illegitimate domain. Freda's nuanced statement of this thesis would be reduced by others to the provocative contention, "Women's liberation causes female crime." Although she never made such a crude claim, Freda would nonetheless be blamed for supposedly casting a dark shadow over women's equality. Still, the slogan likening liberation to crime also had the advantage of imprinting *Sisters in Crime* with a clear identity that, in those changing times, could not be ignored.

Second, *Sisters in Crime* was written in prose that was provocative and evocative. It was literary in quality and thus was authored to be read by all. This style allowed McGraw–Hill to market it as a trade book. But underlying the edginess of the book was a foundation of solid scholarship, which cited and used the writings of the leading criminologists of the day. Citations to these social scientists were sequestered in the footnotes at the book's end, but even a cursory glace at these notes reveals that the argument was informed by cutting-edge criminology available in the early 1970s. Embedded in the text, moreover, was the thorough use of what C. Wright Mills (1959) called the "sociological imagination." Freda used biographical accounts to give the book a vivid sense of reality. But as Mills had urged, she linked the personal to the structural or, in today's terms, she linked the micro to the macro. Thus, she noted how modernization, urbanization, industrialization, family fragmentation, affluence, technological inventions, educational access, and medical advances were combining to transform women's roles in society and to create fresh behavioral options, including the choice of crime. In short, Freda's capacity for easily understood erudition made the book special—accessible to all and respectable to her scholarly peers.

Indeed, the scholarly merits of *Sisters in Crime* did not stop with an analysis of "changing patterns" in female crime, the subject of the first and last chapters. Although her book was often reduced to the so-called liberation thesis, it contained so much more. Various chapters, for example, examined controversial issues that would inform the study of women and crime for the next generation and beyond. Thus, Freda anticipated the interest that subsequent scholars would have in the intersection of race, class, and gender (Chapter 6), in how gender shapes involvement in drugs and sex-related crimes (Chapters 3 and 5), in female delinquency and white-collar crime (Chapters 4 and 7), and in the differential and sexist treatment of women before the law and in the correctional system (Chapters 8 and 9).

Third, the book proved to be a classic because it served a core function of any work hoping to establish a new theoretical and research paradigm: to provide puzzles or questions for scholars to solve, secure publications, and earn tenure and other professional rewards (Cole, 1975; Kuhn, 1970). In fact, one of this chapter's authors earned, early in his career, his first publication in the prominent journal *Criminology* by testing Freda's "masculinity thesis" (see Cullen, Golden, & Cullen, 1979)! Notably, a recent check of Google Scholar shows that *Sisters in Crime* has received over 1,000 citations!

Our book, *Sisters in Crime Revisited: Bringing Gender into Criminology*, is intended to honor Freda Adler. As a result, in this chapter, we focus on four interrelated topics in the sections to follow: (1) how Freda became a criminologist; (2) the central criminological thesis of *Sisters in Crime*; (3) three major criticisms of *Sisters in Crime*, all of which have value but merit continued reconsideration today; and (4) the legacy of Freda's criminological classic, *Sisters in Crime*.

However, *Sisters in Crime Revisited* is not intended to look back 40 years to 1975 and to relive a period that has long since passed. This volume is not a historical work but a scientific work—a focus that Freda has always embraced in her criminological investigations. As we will argue, the enduring value of Freda's *Sisters in Crime* was not so much the book's specifics (however important they were) but its role in inspiring subsequent scholars to *bring gender into criminology*. In this context, we believed that a tribute to Freda would have most integrity not by trumpeting all that she has personally contributed but by pulling together under one cover the best scientific information *currently* available on the diverse aspects of women, crime, and justice—issues that Freda illuminated in *Sisters in Crime*.

Our introductory chapter thus will end by providing a roadmap to follow—which we call the "plan of the book"—as readers take an exciting excursion across the contemporary landscape of the criminological study of gender and crime. But as promised, we begin by briefly recounting the story of Freda's entrance into criminology, of her classic book and the debates it sparked, and of the role of *Sisters in Crime* in shaping the criminological enterprise.

Becoming a Criminologist

Freda Adler's entrance into criminology is best understood in the context of America 50 years past: This decision was both pathbreaking for a woman and constrained by traditional role expectations. Thus, born on November 21, 1934, Freda grew up in a household that encouraged her to pursue her education and to engage in a variety of activities, from equestrianism to swimming competitively (the information in this section is drawn largely from the excellent biographic accounts of Freda by Flynn, 1998, and by Hartman & Sundt, 2010, 2011). After high school, she enrolled in the University of Pennsylvania, where she studied sociology and was often one the few women in her courses.

She earned her B.A. degree in 1956, but did not immediately go on to graduate school—which might be a common career path today. Instead, the next decade of her life was devoted to motherhood, as she gave birth to and raised three wonderful children (all of whom would later receive medical or academic doctorates). Many women of her generation would have remained homemakers and forfeited an academic career. In 1965, however, Freda took the uncommon path at that time by retuning to Penn and entering the graduate program in sociology. She would receive her master's degree in 1968 and her doctoral degree in 1971.

So much has changed in the ensuing years that readers now would have difficulty truly appreciating the challenges posed by Freda's career choice. She was the only woman in a cohort of scholars who would later have important impacts on the field (her classmates included Robert Figlio, Marc Riedel, Robert Silverman, Terence Thornberry, and Charles Welford). Early in her career, she would receive mail addressed to Fred A. Adler. (Paula Dubeck, Francis Cullen's spouse, arrived at the University of Cincinnati in 1974 to find the nameplate on her door inscribed with Paul A. Dubeck!) Freda's singular status, at Penn and beyond, did not seem to faze her, one suspects, because she did not look for or pay much attention to any sexist slight she might have received. The work was too important, the experience too much fun, and her purpose too directed to waste time on the foolishness of others. This orientation did not blind her to the sexism permeating society, including the justice system—as many passages in *Sisters in Crime* reveal. It was just that she would not allow such things to weigh her down or impede her goals. She was always, as the phrase goes, "leaning forward."

Freda's entry into criminology was not foreordained but was contingent on living in the Philadelphia area and near the University of Pennsylvania. What if she had lived in New York and, because of family reasons and propinquity, attended Columbia University, where little criminology was undertaken?

By contrast, Freda entered at Penn what Robert Merton (1995) has called a "cognitive micro-environment" (p. 5) in which multiple scholars, including graduate students, were devoted to a particular way of thinking or paradigm. Thus, from her undergraduate days onward, Freda had taken courses and been guided by such luminaries as Otto Pollak, Thorsten Sellin, and Marvin Wolfgang—scholars who intended to make criminology a scientific enterprise. Ironically, Freda's perspectives on women and crime were shaped by these scholars in two ways—in terms of what she rejected (the perspective of Pollak) and what she embraced (the sociology of Sellin and Wolfgang).

Thus, she rejected the more psychiatric approach of Otto Pollak who, at least in part, linked females' criminality to their biology—disagreeing with him in class where she was the only female student when he would discuss whether women's offending was the result of penis envy! Pollak argued that female crime was more plentiful than commonly believed, in part because women selected family members for victims and thus were more able to keep it hidden. But he also asserted that females had culled a special talent for deceitfulness that could be used to conceal their illegalities. This skill at deceit could be traced to experiences unique to women, such as concealing their discomfort during menstruation and faking orgasms (Gunnison, 2010; Pollak, 1950). Freda rejected this "essentialist" view of females in which their crime was linked to their biological differences from men.

Instead, Freda adopted the thoroughly sociological approach espoused by other Penn criminologists, Thorsten Sellin and especially Marvin Wolfgang (she dedicated *Sisters in Crime* "To Marvin E. Wolfgang—Kind friend and wise mentor"). The embrace of sociology permeates the pages of *Sisters in Crime*; this perspective led Freda to reject the idea that female offenders were somehow psychiatrically or biologically defective creatures whose pathology had caused them to depart from a woman's "natural" role as a caretaker to men and children. Rather, she came to see crime as having general social causes—that men and women are more alike than different and typically enter crime for similar reasons. Thus, in *Sisters in Crime*, Freda notes that "criminal women are first human, second female, and third criminal" (Adler, 1975, p. 22). She observes that the "incidence and kinds of crimes are more closely associated with social than sexual factors" (p. 27). She further contends, "Until there is complete social equality it will not be possible to tell with any certainty which of the demonstrated differences between the sexes are biological and which cultural. But what is clear is that as the position of women approximates the position of men, so does the frequency and type of their criminal activity" (p. 251). And she offers in summary, "what we have described is a gradual but accelerating social revolution in which women are closing many of the gaps, social and criminal, that have separated them from men. The closer they get, the more alike they look and act" (p. 30). We return to this theme in the following section.

Sisters in Crime

Freda did not write *Sisters in Crime* out of the clear blue sky. Rather, the book was the culmination of two prior research projects that focused her attention on women law-breakers. The first project was her 1971 doctoral dissertation, *The Female Offender in Philadelphia*, which explored sentencing disparities between Black and White women in the justice system (Hartman & Sundt, 2011). The second project, following the receipt of her doctorate, was her role in a research team evaluating drug treatment programs that involved interviewing staff and offenders of both genders, initially across Pennsylvania and then into other states (Flynn, 1998, p. 5). Freda drew a key insight from this experience: "When I was out in the field, the female interviewees reported committing crimes to support their habit that were similar to those men were committing" (Hartman & Sundt, 2011, p. 212). But was this insight idiosyncratic or did it point to a larger trend in society?

When Freda examined data from the Federal Bureau of Investigation (FBI) in the *Uniform Crime Reports*, something clearly seemed afoot. Thus, in *Sisters in Crime*, she would observe that percentage increases in female arrests dwarfed those of males:

> During the twelve-year period between 1960 and 1972 the number of women arrested for robbery rose by 277 per cent, while the male figure rose 169 per cent. Dramatic differences are found in embezzlement (up 280 per cent for women, 50 per cent for men), larceny (up 303 per cent for women, 82 per cent for men), and burglary (up 168 per cent for women, 63 per cent for men). (Adler, 1975, p. 16)

Only murder and aggravated assault seemed immune from this trend. Further, the same picture emerged for juveniles:

> During the period between 1960 and 1972 the number of females under eighteen arrested for robbery jumped by 508 per cent, while the juvenile male figure rose 250 per cent. Likewise, other figures mounted: larceny (up 334 per cent for girls, 84 per cent for boys), burglary (up 177 per cent for girls, 70 per cent for boys), auto theft (up 110 per cent for girls, 38 per cent for boys). (1975, pp. 17–18)

What accounted for this apparent convergence in offending? Again, in *Sisters in Crime*, Freda stopped short of setting forth a set of propositions or drawing a causal diagram that specified the details of her theory of female criminality. Still, her main line of argument was clear. She asserted that the effects of crime are general, not gender specific, and that the causal forces that underlie crime are overwhelmingly rooted in social roles and the experiences they bring. In turn, because gender roles were being socially transformed in America—a transformation rooted in broad structural changes and not simply hurried along by the women's movement—women's exposure to criminogenic risk factors was becoming more similar to men's. And so too was their criminal involvement. Women's criminality thus was not etched either in the stone of biology or in the stone of gender roles that could never be transformed. In short, Freda rejected biological essentialism and the permanency of female oppression. As women's lives changed, she asserted, so too would their criminality.

Beyond this general observation that role shifts caused crime shifts, it is possible to extract from the pages of *Sisters in Crime* an integrated causal model. This theoretical perspective has three components. Thus, Freda suggests that criminal involvement is a by-product of the following:

- Criminal motivations, substantially due to the stresses that modern life imposes on individuals;
- The strength of informal social controls or "restraints";
- Access to illegitimate means, which involves both the sheer opportunity to perform a crime and the cognitions or identity needed to see this opportunity as "possible."

In her view, women in the 1960s and 1970s were beginning to experience increases in these components. Thus, as a result of social change, women were exposed to increased stresses and to weakening social controls (especially younger women). More controversially, Freda claimed that women were gaining access to greater illegitimate means, either in the workplace (for white-collar crime) or in the streets. Importantly, illegitimate means involve not only the sheer opportunity to offend but also facilitative cognitions (see also Cloward, 1959; Cloward & Piven, 1979). What changed thus was not simply that women *could* commit more traditionally male crimes but that they *saw themselves as able to do so.* If women could imagine becoming doctors, lawyers, or politicians, if they could imagine playing soccer and basketball, then they could imagine using illicit substances, joining a gang, and stealing while at work. This transformation in cognition—in the script for what one's life could now become—is often what is omitted in an understanding of *Sisters in Crime*.

Three Criticisms

A sign of any work's vitality is that others take the ideas seriously enough to devote their time to assessing them. No matter how appealing, provocative ideas should not simply be accepted—as some have been, much to the detriment of criminological knowledge and of crime policy (see Cullen & Gendreau, 2001; Finckenauer, 1982). As Robert Merton (1973) pointed out long ago, a core norm of science is what he called "organized skepticism" (p. 277), which involves the scientific community rigorously examining all claims to truth.

Notably, *Sisters in Crime* proved to be a formidable work that inspired sustained assessment. A number of scholars read Freda's book and derived testable hypotheses. As noted, one of these was by an author of the current chapter, who published a "partial test of the masculinity hypothesis" (Cullen et al., 1979). This body of research leveled three main criticisms at *Sisters in Crime*, which in some ways are continuing points of debate even today. Each of these appraisals has merit but also limitations.

First, there was the *liberation critique*. At its simplest level, Freda was accused of blaming women's liberation for crime. Some prominent activists excoriated Freda, because they believed that linking liberation to crime might be used by traditionalists as an argument against women's rights. However, the charge that Freda proposed that offenders were somehow politically liberated is absurd. In *Sisters in Crime*, female offenders are quoted as saying that they do not embrace "women's lib." As Freda wrote about her interviewee named Marge:

> She, like the majority of incarcerated women throughout the country, comes from a lower socioeconomic level and tends to identify with a value code embracing the "traditional" image of women. . . . Marge will not tolerate the mention of women's liberation, she considers it synonymous with lesbian. (Adler, 1975, pp. 7–8)

Freda's perspective thus was far more nuanced than the liberation critique suggested. Her concern was with shifting gender roles that allowed females not to join the women's lib political movement but to break through the structural and perceptual barriers that had placed "masculine" crimes off limits to women. Although the women's liberation movement might have contributed to such emancipation, changes in gender roles were part of a broader social revolution that started in the 1960s and gained impetus in the 1970s as battles over civil rights—over achieving equality for all—were fought (see Adler, 1975, p. 25). Thus, Freda was not referring to women's liberation per se but to what she preferred to call a "new feminism":

> The new feminism is not an organized movement, it does not hold meetings or press conferences. It is an all-pervasive consciousness which has permeated virtually every level of womanhood in America. The new feminism pertains to the women who may deny any sympathy for formalized [political] action, but who have recently secured their first job since marriage or decided to go back to school. . . . It also means sexually honest women who expect the same orgastic satisfaction as men, and who are requiring that men do something about it. And most relevant to our subject, it describes the women who have concluded that prostitution and shoplifting are not their style; embezzlement, robbery, and assault are more congenial to their self-image. (1975, pp. 26–27)

In fairness to critics, Freda did imply that more female offenders might be drawn from the middle and upper classes as women entered the world of work and had access to white-collar crimes. Although (as noted above) Freda was well aware that most females in the justice system came from the lower echelons of society, critics perhaps had a point in reminding us that offenders who enjoyed the fruits of liberation remained the exception. Regardless of the rise of some "new" female offenders, the typical offender still lived at the margins of society (Giordano, Kerbel, & Dudley, 1981; Wolfe, Cullen, & Cullen, 1984). As Wilson and Herrnstein noted, "The typical female offender is poor, undereducated, disproportionately a member of a minority group, and dependent on her limited resources for her own support and often the support of her children" (1985, p. 124).

Second, there was the *stability of sex differences* critique. Darrell Steffensmeier (1978, 1980) was most effective in developing the argument that sex differences in crime were stubbornly persistent and not as malleable as Freda had suggested. Steffensmeier presented carefully analyzed empirical data showing that, although property crime was rising more rapidly for women, the absolute difference in the number of crimes committed by the sexes was not narrowing. Further, he revealed that there was not much evidence that the gender gap was narrowing in serious and masculine forms of crime. In many ways, he argued that equality in the criminal world might be harder to attain than in the conventional world (Steffensmeier, 1982).

Notably, Freda did not have the advantage of the insights produced by subsequent research on how male gender shapes criminal involvement, both through identities and through peer networks (see, e.g., DeKeseredy & Schwartz, 2013; Messerschmidt, 1993). As such, gender might involve more than changes in motivations, controls, and illegitimate opportunity. It might also involve fundamental conceptions of what it means to be a "man" and to have male peer support groups. This aspect of gender might be more male specific and thus more difficult for women to experience.

Although Steffensmeier's critique still holds in many ways, gender convergence has occurred. It just may have taken longer than Freda anticipated. For one thing, men's and women's crime seems to rise and fall in concert, suggesting that they are affected by the same social forces. For another thing, according to compiled statistics, the arrest ratio for male to female crimes is narrowing. In 1976, men outdistanced women in violent crime arrests by an 8.4:1 ratio (176,284 male arrests to 20,953 female arrests) and in property crime arrests by a 3.3:1 ratio (672,750 to 205,507 arrests) (FBI, 1977, p. 176, Table 27). By 2012, the male:female ratio for violent crime arrests had shrunk to 4.0:1 (278,167 male arrests to 69,074 female arrests). The property crime ratio was only 1.7:1 (694,051 to 417,083 arrests) (FBI, 2013, Table 33).

We also found the crime of embezzlement fascinating—in part because, as we prepared this chapter, a report appeared in the *Cincinnati Enquirer* on a female who had embezzled $1 million as the chief financial officer for a computer consulting company (Kelly, 2013). Around the time Freda was writing, the male:female ratio in embezzlement had narrowed from 3.8:1 (in 1967) to 1.9:1 (in 1976) (FBI, 1977, p. 176, Table 27). Notably, in 2003, FBI statistics showed that *more women* than men had been arrested for embezzlement (6,426 to 6,301). By 2012, men had edged ahead in such arrests, but only by a negligible margin (5,603 for men to 5,376 for women). It appears that Freda was prescient in predicting this development:

> As women invade the business world, there is no reason to expect them to be any more honest than men, and to the extent that crime is related to motivation and opportunity, the incidence of such white-collar crime as embezzlement and fraud should achieve par with men. (Adler, 1975, p. 252)

Third, there was the *gender-specificity critique*. In disputing previous attempts to attribute female criminality to some inherent gender-specific biological or psycho-logical pathology, Freda argued that the causes of crime were general—the same for men and women. Again, if women's social roles and thus experiences approximated those of men, then so too would the nature and amount of their criminality. Schooled in criminology, including the perspectives that prevailed in the cognitive micro-environment of the University of Pennsylvania, Freda was comfortable asserting this fundamentally sociological understanding of crime.

Other female scholars, however, have proposed a revised gender-specific perspec-tive. Similar to Freda, they reject the notion that any pathology inherent in being female was connected to crime. Instead, they argue that there are other psychological conditions (e.g., depression) and social experiences (e.g., sexual abuse)—not rooted in women's pathology but in their patriarchal oppression—that lead females to enter crime through distinct "gendered pathways." And there is evidence supportive of this revised gender-specific view (Miller & Mullins, 2006). Still, consistent with the generality approach taken by Freda, there is also evidence that the risk factors for males and females are similar (Moffitt, Caspi, Rutter, & Silva, 2001) or, in the least, overlapping with one another (Alarid, Burton, & Cullen, 2000; Daigle, Cullen, & Wright, 2007; Hartman, Turner, Daigle, Exum, & Cullen, 2009). Research from corrections also indicates a substantial overlap across men and women in predictors of recidivism (Andrews & Bonta, 2010, p. 62; Smith, Cullen, & Latessa, 2009; Vose, Lowenkamp, Smith, & Cullen, 2009).

Freda Adler's Legacy: Bringing Gender Into Criminology

Freda Adler's career did not begin and end with *Sisters in Crime*. She was not a one-hit wonder! She went on to publish "25 books as author or coauthor, 13 books as editor or co-editor, and over 100 journal articles" (Hartman & Sundt, 2011, p. 218). She made important contributions not only to the study of women and crime but also to comparative criminology, to theoretical criminology, and to maritime criminology (presciently focusing on the problem of piracy). She has done much to preserve the discipline's ideas through her 25-year editorship of the *Advances in Criminological Theory* series and her rescuing of the Oral History Criminology Project (whose interviews are now online via the website of the American Society of Criminology). Her service to the United Nations and to the field is too extensive to list here. And, of course, Freda was honored as the 47th president of the American Society of Criminology—and the 3rd female president (Flynn, 1998; Petersen, 2006). Through much of this professional journey she was accompanied by her beloved late husband, Gerhard Mueller, a criminologist of remarkable competence and accomplishment and a man of culture and honor.

Still, although it would be reductionist to see Freda's career as synonymous with *Sisters in Crime*, it is still important to admit that this volume was, and remains, a criminological classic. To be sure, other female scholars writing at this time made essential contributions—those who might be considered her "sisters in criminology" (see Chapter 2). But it is still the case that *Sisters in Crime* was a special book that transformed so much thinking when it was published and in the years that followed. Indeed, it succeeded in bringing gender into criminology so that it could never again be ignored.

Plan of the Book

Sisters in Crime Revisited was written *in honor of Freda Adler*. But to understand the origins and nature of this enterprise, two considerations must be shared with the book's readers.

First, *Sisters in Crime* was published in 1975—40 years ago. The 38 authors who have combined their inordinate talents to honor Freda in the current volume have done so in part in recognition of her authoring a criminological classic and, more generally, in having had a scholarly career that had a defining influence on the field of criminology. But truth be told, we are honoring Freda not only for her criminological contributions but also for her personal integrity, good humor, and unfailing generosity. It may sound trite, but this is a project inspired by our respect and love of Freda the person—not just a celebration of Freda the scholar.

Second, as editors, we can praise the chapters' authors by noting that the list of contributors is similar to the roster at an annual all-star game for professional baseball. The diversity and depth of scholarship found in the pages to follow are remarkable. Importantly, however, the authors were not recruited to celebrate Freda by commenting on a specific aspect of *Sisters in Crime*. As noted above, doing so would not be an authentic way to honor her.

In the end, Freda is a University of Pennsylvania criminologist who believes in a scientific approach to the study of crime and justice. Science should not view 40-year-old works—even classics such as *Sisters in Crime*—as sacred texts to be paid homage and treated as sacrosanct. Instead, science should treat important books as creating fresh but provisional paradigms that should be studied, revised, and perhaps supplanted. We thus honor Freda by embracing what she most values—this scientific ethos. Our book thus does not look backward to relive what Freda wrote in 1975, but rather conveys what the 40-year research agenda inspired by *Sisters in Crime* now tells us about gender and crime.

Perhaps the most important contribution of *Sisters in Crime* is that it made it impossible for subsequent generations to ignore women. By itself and by what it inspired, the true value of her classic work is captured by its subtitle: *Bringing Gender into Criminology*. Consistent with this theme, the chapters to follow are organized to provide systematic coverage of how taking gender seriously enriches our contemporary understanding of crime and justice.

Sisters in Crime Revisited is divided into seven parts. Part I is composed of the current chapter and then a second chapter authored by two scholars, Alida Merlo and Joycelyn Pollock, who experienced and contributed to the development of feminist criminology. They discuss how a group of scholars—which included but was not limited to Freda—combined to illuminate the importance of gender to the study of crime. These sisters in criminology were writing at a time when few women were in academia and showed their courage and brilliance in writings that transformed thinking about women's involvement in crime and in the justice system.

In the past decade or so, life-course or developmental criminology has emerged as a major paradigm that is reshaping our understanding of the onset, persistence, and desistance of criminal careers (Cullen, 2011). Reflecting this line of inquiry, Part II presents chapters that explore "the development of offending." Meda Chesney-Lind, who offered perhaps the first major theory of gendered pathways into crime (1989), contributes an essay on this very topic (Chapter 5). Three other chapters also explore the factors—both unique to females and general to all offenders—that lead women into offending and serious crime. Thus, in Chapter 3, Jamie Vaske, Danielle Boisvert, and John Paul Wright provide an innovative analysis showing how "biosocial criminology" can contribute to the study of gender and crime. In Chapter 4, Nicole Leeper Piquero and Alex Piquero use their insights on life-course criminology to illuminate persistent female offending. And in Chapter 6, Leanne Fiftal Alarid and Emily Wright reveal how women become felony offenders.

Part III seeks to build on an insight from *Sisters in Crime* that female criminality is intimately shaped by the social contexts in which women are, or are not, enmeshed. This part thus explores how female crime is influenced by the contexts of gangs (Madeleine Novich and Jody Miller in Chapter 7), social networks (Dana Haynie and Brian Soller in Chapter 8), and the workplace (Mary Dodge in Chapter 9).

Part IV extends this line of analysis by exploring how social context affects harms that might be visited upon women. In Chapter 10, Pamela Wilcox, Bonnie Fisher, and Nicole Lasky examine an issue that was not central to *Sisters in Crime* but has since become a major concern in the field: how "gendered opportunity" influences women's *victimization*. And in Chapter 11, Sally Simpson and Candace Kruttschnitt explore evidence, including innovative data drawn from Baltimore, on whether neighborhood context intersects with gender to affect experiences with violent victimization.

Part V focuses on two important theoretical issues. In Chapter 12, Jennifer Schwartz and Darrell Steffensmeier tackle the sticky problem of the capacity of criminology to explain the "gender gap" in crime—or why, despite many changes, men still tend to commit more crimes than women. This analysis explores the causal importance of gendered opportunity, a construct central to *Sisters in Crime*. In Chapter 13, Amanda Petersen, Emily Salisbury, and Jody Sundt discuss whether feminist theory—which was initiated by the sisters in criminology starting in the 1970s—continues to have relevance today.

Part VI focuses on the important issue of how the *gender of men* might affect their involvement in crime. *Sisters in Crime* focused on how roles—what it means to be female—were changing and might affect women's criminality. James Messerschmidt (1993), however, made the important insight that male gender—what it means to be a man—also merits consideration. Might not crime be a form of "doing masculinity"? In Chapter 14, he and Stephen Tomsen revisit this insight and explore the relationship between masculinities and crime. Similarly, in Chapter 15, Walter DeKeseredy and Martin Schwartz illuminate the unique nature of male peer groups and how they might encourage the victimization of women.

Part VII addresses another issue explored by Freda in *Sisters in Crime*: the differential experiences of female offenders in the justice system. Thus, in Chapter 16, Nicholas Corsaro, Jesenia Pizarro, and Sandra Lee Browning examine how gender might affect criminal justice processing. In Chapter 17, Mary Stohr, Cheryl Lero Jonson, and Jennifer Lux illuminate how gender shapes offenders' prison experiences. Finally, in Chapter 18, Paula Smith and Sarah Manchak set forth a gendered theory of offender rehabilitation.

We reiterate that all contributors to this volume are delighted to honor Freda Adler—an innovative and consequential scholar and a caring and supportive colleague, mentor, and friend. We trust that we have succeeded in providing chapters that live up to Freda's own high standards. If so, then *Sisters in Crime Revisited* will be a fitting tribute to Freda, a gift not only to Freda but also to what she has always deeply cherished—the field of criminology.

References

Adler, F. (1975). *Sisters in crime: The rise of the new female criminal*. New York, NY: McGraw-Hill.

Alarid, L. F., Burton, V. S., Jr., & Cullen, F. T. (2000). Gender and crime among felony offenders: Assessing the generality of social control and differential association theories. *Journal of Research in Crime and Delinquency, 37*, 171–199.

Andrews, D. A., & Bonta, J. (2010). *The psychology of criminal conduct* (5th ed.). New Providence, NJ: Anderson/LexisNexis.

Chesney-Lind, M. (1989). Girls' crime and women's place: Toward a feminist model of female delinquency. *Crime and Delinquency, 35,* 5–29.

Cloward, R. A. (1959). Illegitimate means, anomie, and deviant behavior. *American Sociological Review, 24,* 164–176.

Cloward, R. A., & Piven, F. F. (1979). Hidden protest: The channeling of female innovation and resistance. *Signs, 4,* 651–669.

Cole, S. (1975). The growth of scientific knowledge: Theories of deviance as a case study. In L. A. Coser (Ed.), *The idea of social structure: Papers in honor of Robert K. Merton* (pp. 175–200). New York, NY: Harcourt Brace Jovanovich.

Cullen, F. T. (2011). Beyond adolescence-limited criminology: Choosing our future—The American Society of Criminology 2010 Sutherland Address. *Criminology, 49,* 287–330.

Cullen, F. T., & Gendreau, P. (2001). From nothing works to what works: Changing professional ideology in the 21st century. *The Prison Journal, 81,* 313–338.

Cullen, F. T., Golden, K. M., & Cullen, J. B. (1979). Sex and delinquency: A partial test of the masculinity hypothesis. *Criminology, 17,* 301–310.

Daigle, L. E., Cullen, F. T., & Wright, J. P. (2007). Gender differences in the predictors of juvenile delinquency: Assessing the generality–specificity debate. *Youth Violence and Juvenile Justice, 5,* 254–286.

DeKeseredy, W. S., & Schwartz, M. D. (2013). *Male peer support and violence against women.* Boston, MA: Northeastern University Press.

Federal Bureau of Investigation. (1977). *Crime in the United States 1976: Uniform crime reports.* Washington, DC: U.S. Government Printing Office.

Federal Bureau of Investigation. (2013). *Crime in the United States 2012: Uniform crime reports.* Retrieved from http://www.fbi.gov/about-us/cjis/ucr/crime-in-the-u.s./2012/crime-in-the-u.s.-2012/tables

Finckenauer, J. O. (1982). *Scared straight! and the panacea phenomenon.* Englewood Cliffs, NJ: Prentice Hall.

Flynn, E. E. (1998). Freda Adler: A portrait of a pioneer. *Women and Criminal Justice, 10,* 1–26.

Giordano, P. C., Kerbel, S., & Dudley, S. (1981). The economics of female criminality: An analysis of police blotters, 1890–1975. In L. H. Bowker (Ed.), *Women and crime in America.* New York, NY: Macmillan.

Gunnison, E. (2010). Pollak, Otto: The hidden female offender. In F. T. Cullen & P. Wilcox (Eds.), *Encyclopedia of criminological theory* (pp. 722–724). Thousand Oaks, CA: Sage.

Hartman, J. L., & Sundt, J. L. (2010). Adler, Freda: Sisters in Crime. In F. T. Cullen & P. Wilcox (Eds.), *Encyclopedia of criminological theory* (pp. 3–6). Thousand Oaks, CA: Sage.

Hartman, J. L., & Sundt, J. L. (2011). The rise of feminist criminology: Freda Adler. In F. T. Cullen, C. L. Jonson, A. J. Myer, & F. Adler (Eds.), *The origins of American criminology: Advances in criminological theory* (Vol. 16, pp. 205–220). New Brunswick, NJ: Transaction.

Hartman, J. L., Turner, M. G., Daigle, L. E., Exum, M. L., & Cullen, F. T. (2009). Exploring the gender differences in protective factors: Implications for understanding resiliency. *International Journal of Offender Therapy and Comparative Criminology, 53,* 249–277.

Kelly, B. R. (2013, November 15). Woman sentenced for stealing from business. *Cincinnati Enquirer*, p. C5.

Kuhn, T. S. (1970). *The structure of scientific revolutions* (2nd ed.). Chicago, IL: University of Chicago Press.

Merton, R. K. (1973). *The sociology of science: Theoretical and empirical investigations* (N. K. Storer, Ed.). Chicago, IL: University of Chicago Press.

Merton, R. K. (1995). Opportunity structure: The emergence, diffusion, and differentiation of a sociological concept, 1930s–1950s. In F. Adler & W. S. Laufer (Eds.), *The legacy of anomie theory: Advances in criminological theory* (Vol. 6, pp. 3–78). New Brunswick, NJ: Transaction.

Messerschmidt, J. (1993). *Masculinities and crime: Critique and reconceptualization of theory*. Totowa, NJ: Rowman & Littlefield.

Miller, J., & Mullins, C. W. (2006). The status of feminist theories in criminology. In F. T. Cullen, J. P. Wright, & K. R. Blevins (Eds.), *Taking stock: The status of criminological theory—Advances in criminological theory* (Vol. 15, pp. 217–249). New Brunswick, NJ: Transaction.

Mills, C. W. (1959). *The sociological imagination*. New York, NY: Oxford University Press.

Moffitt, T. E., Caspi, A., Rutter, M., & Silva, P. A. (2001). *Sex differences in antisocial behavior: Conduct disorder, delinquency, and violence in the Dunedin Longitudinal Study*. Cambridge, UK: Cambridge University Press.

Petersen, R. D. (2006). The female presidents of the American Society of Criminology. *Feminist Criminology*, *1*, 147–168.

Pollak, O. (1950). *The criminality of women*. Philadelphia: University of Pennsylvania Press.

Shaw, C. R. (1938). *Brothers in crime*. Chicago, IL: University of Chicago Press (with the assistance of H. D. McKay & J. F. McDonald).

Smith, P., Cullen, F. T., & Latessa, E. J. (2009). Can 14,737 women be wrong? A meta-analysis of the LSI-R and recidivism for female offenders. *Criminology and Public Policy*, *8*, 183–208.

Steffensmeier, D. J. (1978). Crime and the contemporary woman: An analysis of the changing levels of female property crime, 1960–75. *Social Forces*, *57*, 556–584.

Steffensmeier, D. J. (1980). Sex differences in patterns of adult crime, 1965–1978. *Social Forces*, *58*, 1080–1108.

Steffensmeier, D. J. (1982). Organization properties and sex-segregation in the underworld: Building a sociological theory of sex differences in crime. *Social Forces*, *61*, 1010–1032.

Vose, B., Lowenkamp, C. T., Smith, P., & Cullen, F. T. (2009). Gender and the predictive validity of the LSI-R: A study of parolees and probationers. *Journal of Contemporary Criminal Justice*, *25*, 459–471.

Wilson, J. Q., & Herrnstein, R. J. (1985). *Crime and human nature*. New York, NY: Simon & Schuster.

Wolfe, N. T., Cullen, F. T., & Cullen, J. B. (1984). Describing the female offender: A note on the demographics of arrests. *Journal of Criminal Justice*, *12*, 483–492.

CHAPTER 2

Sisters in Criminology:
The Origins of Feminist Criminology

Alida V. Merlo and Joycelyn M. Pollock

The United Nations declared 1975 to be "International Women's Year," and the first World Conference on Women was held in Mexico City. Indeed, the United Nations then declared 1976–1985 to be the "Decade of Women." This attention reflected the rapid social changes that were taking place regarding the role of women in society. In the late 1970s, Sally K. Ride was accepted by NASA into the astronaut training program and later became the first American woman in space. In the 1970s, the National Organization for Women was growing, and the Equal Rights Amendment was passed by both houses of Congress (in 1972), although ultimately failing to achieve the majority necessary for passing the constitutional amendment. Women were entering nontraditional occupations, including politics, in record numbers. Indira Gandhi, Margaret Thatcher, Shirley Chisholm, and Barbara Jordan were powerful leaders in their own right, but even more powerful as symbols of women's growing freedom to challenge men's monopoly of social and economic power.

There was also a darker side of women's prominence in the news. The decade opened with the trial of Charles Manson and his female followers (including Susan Atkins and Leslie van Houten) for the Tate–LaBianca slayings. Also in the 1970s, Lynnette Fromme (another "Manson girl") and Sara Jane Moore tried, at different times, to assassinate President Gerald Ford. Female terrorists received as much or more press than their male conspirators. Leila Khaled (Popular Front for the Liberation of Palestine), Gudrun Ensslin (Baader-Meinhof Gang in Germany), and Emily Harris (Symbionese Liberation Army) in the United States employed terroristic tactics that appalled and astonished readers—how could women do such things? Patty Hearst, the pretty blonde co-ed heiress—a Symbionese Liberation Army kidnapping victim who turned gun-toting, bank-robbing terrorist herself—seemed to epitomize the era's perception of the "dark side of liberation."

17

Against this backdrop was a growing interest in female criminality in the academic world. Freda Adler's *Sisters in Crime*, published in 1975, was not the only, nor was it the first academic contribution to our understanding of female criminality from this time period. However, it did become a clarion call for others to take up the question of whether women were indeed becoming more violent, as the evening news seemed to indicate. Her work echoed some but challenged others' views on female criminality, and her central thesis that women are not inherently different from men in any way that affects their criminal choices still engenders healthy discussion and inquiry that continue 40 years later.

Freda Adler and her colleagues ushered in a new era for feminist criminology in the 1970s and 1980s. Together, Freda Adler, Rita Simon, Eileen Leonard, Christine Rasche, Carol Smart, and many other "sisters" brought "gender into criminology" and forged a path for criminologists to challenge the previous work, explore new areas of research, and establish feminist criminology. Their influence was extraordinary, and their contributions are significant.

There were theories of female criminality before the 1970s. A sprinkling of early writings attempted to explain why women committed so much less crime than men, but also why certain women committed crime, such as (in chronological order) Kellor (1900), Adams (1914), Weidensall (1916), Davis (1937), Bishop (1931), Glueck and Glueck (1934), Thomas (1937), and Tappan (1947). Some journal articles in the 1960s and early 1970s also showed the gender disparity in official crime reports, some of which also presented findings from self-report studies to compare to official reports (e.g., Barker & Adams, 1962; Clark & Haurek, 1966; Hindelang, 1971; Rosenblatt & Greenland, 1974).

The major theories of crime, however, virtually ignored women, and when women were mentioned, it was to note simply that they were different. Criminologists literally did not know what to say about the gender disparity in crime or the female offenders who committed crime. But this was about to change. In the 1960s and early 1970s, women were beginning to enter the previously all-male academic field of criminology, then mostly a subunit in sociology. Ruth Morris, Marguerite (Rita) Warren, Joan McCord, Freda Adler, Rita Simon, Natalie Sokoloff, Barbara Raffel Price, Nicole Hahn Rafter, Dorothy Bracey, Margaret Zahn, Christine Rasche, Edith Flynn, and several others received degrees in the 1960s or early 1970s. They would become, in essence, *sisters in criminology*—a set of remarkable scholars whose very presence and scholarship would bring gender into the field of criminology in an enduring way.

Empirical evidence shows that, in fact, attention given to women and crime in journals increased in the 1970s. Thus, Wright (1987) examined publications that were indexed in *Sociological Abstracts* from 1956 to 1960 and compared them to the number that appeared in the same index between 1976 and 1980. He found that the percentage of published articles dealing with women as offenders, victims, and professionals increased from 7% (of 328 articles) in the first time period to over 22% (of 1,943 articles) from 1976 to 1980. Wright's study demonstrated that there was a greater emphasis on women and crime during the latter part of the 1970s.

Still, efforts to bring gender into criminology were not uniformly successful. Wright (1987) also examined criminology textbooks from two different time periods: 1956–1965 and 1976–1985. Although the number of textbooks increased from 14 to 38, the actual mean number of pages devoted to women and crime remained static, with about 14 pages in both time periods (Wright, 1987). He contended that the textbook authors did not keep pace with the enhanced coverage of women and crime research that appeared in contemporary journals and that the topics associated with offending, victimization, and professional positions in the field were largely "overlooked" (Wright, 1987, p. 421).

Notably, not all of the early sisters in criminology investigated women and crime or did so exclusively. Nonetheless, many did and their scholarship did much to bring gender into criminology. So, when the early sisters in criminology studied female offenders, what occupied their attention? The journal and book publications focusing on women in this time period can be categorized into four general areas: (1) critiques of traditional criminology; (2) theoretical analyses, including the emancipation/liberation theory; (3) rebuttals to the liberation theory; and (4) later theories and feminist criminology during the 1970s and 1980s. In the remainder of this chapter, we consider, in turn, the contributions made in each of these four scholarly areas.

The Critiques

Dorie Klein (1973), Meda Chesney-Lind (1973), Carol Smart (1977), and others provided extensive critiques of traditional criminology. Their points, summarized, were as follows:

- Theoretical approaches to women were reductionist and deterministic to a greater extent than those being developed to understand male criminality;
- Theories were based on sexual stereotypes assumed to be fact (women were more passive, manipulative, emotional, and deceptive than men);
- Theories were more likely to focus solely on perceived biological traits, to the exclusion of the social, cultural, and economic factors present in theories of male criminality;
- Female offenders were "pathologized" in a way dissimilar to male offenders (criminality was perceived as more normal for men and boys; therefore, female offenders were described as more masculine or as more disturbed than male offenders); and
- The system focused disproportionately on sexual deviance of girls or women.

Dorie Klein (1973) reviewed the writings of Cesare Lombroso (1835–1909), W. I. Thomas (1863–1947), Otto Pollak (1908–1998), and other early theorists who sought to explain female criminality, and she concluded that such theories were largely classist, racist, and sexist. Klein showed how these theorists assumed stereotypes as facts and reduced women's actions to biological or psychological traits supposedly determined by their sex, thus ignoring the role of socialization. Lombroso had proposed that women were more primitive than men and amoral, but that their inherent traits, including passivity, stopped them from committing crime. Thomas identified women's trait of "adornment" (to make themselves attractive to men) that encouraged theft. Pollak disagreed with Lombroso and Thomas that women actually committed less crime than men. He believed that women's inherent trait of deceptiveness and the criminal justice system's chivalry were the reasons women did not appear in official arrest statistics as often as men. Klein identified other 1970s-era writers who, like Lombroso, focused on physiological or psychological characteristics of women to explain criminality (whereas theories of men's criminality were more sophisticated and multifaceted). Klein also noted that theorists presumed the criminal woman was abnormal in that she was more masculine than a "normal" woman, pointing out that "normal femininity" was defined as "masochistic, passive and sexually indifferent" (Klein, 1973, p. 18). Klein singled out Konopka (1966), Vedder and Somerville (1970), and Cowie, Cowie, and Slater (1968) as examples of the attempt to pathologize and sexualize female delinquents.

In the same special issue of *Issues in Criminology* in which Klein published her critique, Meda Chesney-Lind (1973) set forth her early research showing that the juvenile justice system focused on girls' sexuality. She presented the research from self-report studies that indicated girls committed the same patterns of offenses as boys, just at much lower levels. Yet, official reports and the crimes for which girls found themselves in detention were primarily concerned with running away or sexual promiscuity. Of course, what official reports showed was the system's focus on the sexuality of girls, not necessarily reflecting their actual patterns of behavior.

Rasche (1975) linked the lack of criminological research on women to the fact that women represented a small proportion of arrestees, as documented in 1972, when male arrests outpaced female arrests six to one. She noted that females comprised such a small percentage of incarcerated offenders (less than 5% of prison inmates in 1975) that correctional authorities tended to exclude them from newer rehabilitation programs, which were primarily targeted for the majority population (male inmates). Female offenders' small numbers also made it difficult to show statistical significance in evaluations of various treatment approaches. Unfortunately, this "underrepresentation" affected women's ability to access innovative programs on both the federal and the state level (Rasche, 1975, p. 11). Furthermore, Rasche noted that "women themselves have been disregarded as important or as fit topics of research" (p. 12). Cumulatively, Rasche contended that these factors perpetuated our lack of knowledge of female offenders (p. 11).

However, Rasche advocated for new scientific research on women and crime not only because of the dearth of prior research that focused on women but also because arrests reported by the FBI were increasing. Using these data, Rasche illustrated the dramatic uptick in the percentage of women arrested and girls referred to the juvenile justice system in the late 1960s and early 1970s, the long-term consequences these arrests would have on the incarceration of women and girls necessitating new or expanded institutions, and the effect of the mother's criminality on children who remained with their mothers and those who were separated because of incarceration (Rasche, 1975, p. 14).

Brodsky (1975) observed that opportunities for women and perceptions of their competence were expanding, but these social changes would be accompanied by possibilities for new criminal activities. "Thus, the advantages of more independence in the work world also bring greater risk and responsibility for which many women are not prepared" (Brodsky, 1975, p. 101). Brodsky noted that research did not support the hypothesis that women fared better than men in terms of greater leniency by law enforcement. Specifically, she advocated for more flexible alternative sanctions in the handling of female offenders because many of them had dependent children. She stressed the importance of developing programs that reflected the needs of offenders who were not necessarily similar to other inmates historically incarcerated in prison or jail (p. 102).

Smart (1976, 1977) also exposed the dearth of early theories that focused on factors other than inherent characteristics of women to explain their criminality. She called such theories sexist because they attributed negative traits to women without questioning social and cultural influences or stereotypes. Smart pointed as well to the then-current theories identifying the premenstrual syndrome as a causal factor for violent crime by women as an example of biological reductionism. She noted that Holloway Prison for women in England developed into an institution where those inside were presumed "sick" because of the prevalent view that female offenders were abnormal. The focus on individual factors ignored the social and economic elements of crime. Further, the presumption of chivalry of the system (referring to Otto Pollak's belief that the system "protected" women by not arresting them) was based on the inequality of women and their dependence on men for protection. She pointed out that, in practice, women had to "earn" this favored status by meeting the ideal of femininity and that those who did not were treated as "evil" or "bad."

Norland and Shover (1977) identified then-current theorists (e.g., Morris, 1964; Payak, 1963; Sandhu & Allen, 1969) who described females as "naturally" dependent, passive, and emotional, noting that these researchers never attempted to prove or even provide any evidence for such assumptions. They argued that official statistics and the use of incarcerated samples biased their views and that these authors made no attempt to document the supposed sex differences.

Pollock (1978) also reviewed early theories, noting that "women were defined by their sexual behavior . . . [and] influenced by psychological or biological drives to a greater extent than [men]. The theories on female criminality were generally contaminated by popular stereotypes and myths regarding women" (p. 51). One example provided was Sheldon and Eleanor Glueck, who published *Five Hundred Delinquent Women* in 1934. They collected data on both individual and environmental factors, but their conclusions led them to advocate the sterilization of female offenders as the solution to intergenerational crime, blaming the woman, as many did, for being the genesis of the "bad seed" in families, while ignoring the economic challenges of single, unmarried women in that time period.

Similarly, in a review of the published literature, Horney (1978) challenged findings reported by Dalton (1961, p. 28), who contended that there was evidence of a connection between criminal behavior and the menstrual cycle. By contrast, Horney explained that the symptoms reportedly associated with menstruation were more likely symptoms that both men and women had in response to stress (p. 26). Furthermore, Horney cautioned that the limited number of studies dealing specifically with women and crime and the menstrual cycle and the impetus to use this as a possible explanation of the insanity defense for women were problematic. She advocated for more empirical research before any changes regarding the legal definition of insanity were introduced. These kinds of biological explanations demonstrate the approaches taken in this time period to explain female criminality.

Kruttschnitt (1980–1981) conducted a different kind of inquiry that focused on the legal system's conduct toward women (specifically sentencing) rather than trying to explain the offender's behavior (p. 249). Using a sample of 1,034 female defendants from California between 1972 and 1976, she found "that economic rank, respectability, and social integration all have a significant bearing . . . on the sentences that women offenders receive" (Kruttschnitt, 1980–1981, p. 262). In brief, those offenders who were economically marginalized, who were unemployed, who received welfare, and who had previous experience with the justice system were more likely to receive harsher sanctions in court. Kruttschnitt's research refuted the notion that women were more likely to be treated leniently by the courts.

These critiques laid bare the sexist presumptions of early writers and questioned what was believed to be true of not only female offenders, but also women in general. The idea that femininity was merely a socially manufactured construct was a paradigm shift that undercut most, if not all, of the theories that came before. Enter new theories of female crime.

The Theories of the 1970s and Early 1980s

The Changing Role of Women: The Rise of Emancipation Theory

The second category of writing in the 1970s through the early 1980s was composed of theories that either supplanted or elaborated on the then-current theories of crime developed to explain male criminality (e.g., differential association, social control, strain, labeling theory).

There were still many examples of the sexist approaches that pathologized female offenders and garnered the extreme criticism of Smart, Klein, and others (e.g., Vedder and Somerville, 1970). Other theorists, however, presented more multifaceted theories, based on sex-role theory—the idea that women's crime was shaped by the cultural beliefs and opportunities that were attached to being a female. A prominent example of this approach was articulated by Dale Hoffman-Bustamante (1973).

Hoffman-Bustamante's work, like that of Klein and Chesney-Lind, was published in a 1973 special edition of *Issues in Criminology* that focused on female criminality. She criticized earlier "moralistic" theorizing and proposed that female criminality could be explained by these factors:

- Differential role expectations for men and women;
- Sex differences in socialization patterns and application of social control;
- Structurally determined differences in opportunities to commit particular offenses;
- Differential access or pressures toward criminally oriented subcultures and careers; and
- Sex differences built into the crime categories themselves.

She noted that these factors explained not only why women committed less crime, but also why gender disparity was smaller in some crimes. Hoffman-Bustamante (1973) wrote:

> Females are more closely supervised and more strictly disciplined in our society . . . females have been taught to conform to more rigid standards and rewarded for such behavior, whereas males are told to conform, yet rewarded for flaunting many conventional standards. (p. 120)

Hoffman-Bustamante (1973) noted that women's increased numbers in forgery, counterfeiting, fraud, and embezzlement could be explained by their role in society and attendant access and opportunity. Her sex-role/opportunity theory foreshadowed many of the sex role–based theories that came later (such as John Hagan's power-control theory).

Hoffman-Bustamante's approach also anticipated pathbreaking books that were later published in 1975—*Sisters in Crime* by Freda Adler and *Women in Crime* by Rita Simon. In articulating their two perspectives, Adler and Simon raised awareness of the issue of female criminality and offered new and contemporary explanations. They invited other researchers to explore the extent to which women engaged in crime and the causes of female criminality. Together, they forged a path for the emergence of feminist criminology and enhanced its status.

Simon (1975b) and Adler (1975) based their theories on the premise that societal restrictions and cultural mores had confined women to the home and excluded them from engaging in "masculine" crimes such as auto theft and burglary. The difference between these theories and Hoffman-Bustamante's (1973) perspective, however, is that Simon and Adler wrote that the growing social and economic freedoms of women had led to criminal, as well as legitimate opportunities. They used percentage increases to show that women were escalating their participation in all areas of the criminal enterprise. Females, Adler (1975) noted, "are now being found not only robbing banks single handedly, but also committing assorted armed robberies, muggings, loan-sharking operations, extortion, murders, and a wide variety of other aggressive, violence-oriented crimes" (p. 14).

In short, Adler (1975) and Simon (1975a, 1975b) proposed theories that were in agreement with other criminologists but that also "pushed the envelope" when they observed that what was popularly called "women's liberation" was having an effect on women's behavior.

In light both of historical factors that were changing sex roles and of recent social developments and events, Adler (1975) observed that women were becomingly increasingly violent. She postulated that as women became more liberated, they would also engage in more criminal behavior, including violent behavior. For example, Adler (1975) wrote, "In the same way that women are demanding equal opportunity in fields of legitimate endeavor, a similar number of determined women are forcing their way into the world of major crimes" (p. 13). Although not ignoring jumps in other offenses, Simon (1975a) predicted increases in property crimes. She contended that as more women became employed outside the home, their opportunities to commit certain economic offenses such as embezzlement and fraud would rise. Together, then, Adler and Simon set forth versions of female emancipation theory that forced scholars to take notice. Their perspectives are examined in more detail in the following sections.

Freda Adler's Perspective

Freda Adler sparked controversy, critiques, and counterarguments about the validity of female emancipation or liberation as an explanation of female criminality. She helped shepherd the development of feminist criminology.

In *Sisters in Crime*, Adler (1975) noted some of the changes that occurred as a result of women's liberation and suggested that these changes would make women as likely as men to participate in historically male-dominated crimes. This "emancipation hypothesis" helped explain the rise in officially reported female crime. Female offenders portrayed in the media armed with machine guns (e.g., Patty Hearst) or as drug-addled murderers (e.g., the "Manson" girls) seemed to confirm that the world was, in fact, changing. Such depictions and evidence illustrated that women's roles in society and their likelihood to pursue criminality were forever altered.

Adler contended that liberation would free women and that women had the same basic tendencies or characteristics as men. They were perceived as no more law abiding than their male counterparts. Once liberated, women would participate in crimes analogous to those committed by their male brethren, and they would also experience comparable health issues like high blood pressure, heart disease, and stress. The changes for women included a more masculine role in society and a more masculine identity. As a result, girls would become more masculinized earlier in the socialization process; and they would emulate boys' involvement in delinquent and criminal behavior. Ultimately, women would be equal to men and their involvement in criminal activity and in business would increase.

With respect to chivalrous treatment, Adler (1975) noted that police were less likely to arrest women and that female offenders historically had an advantage because of their (the officers') "deeply ingrained prejudices" (p. 49). She discussed the paternalistic tendencies of police officers (which mirror other parts of society) to treat women (offenders as well as nonoffenders) differently. The belief that the attitude persisted at various levels of policing despite the rising crime rate of women "puts it in the category of a prejudice" (Adler, 1975, p. 49).

Similarly, Adler noted that police officers were also less likely to accept their female colleagues. Part of their reluctance, she hypothesized, was because of the women who were entering the ranks of patrol officer. Rather than resembling an officer's wife, the new recruits were more like a male officer. In brief, Adler postulated that male officers' resistance to female patrol officers was not that female officers were weak, but rather that they demonstrated the same masculine traits as their fellow officers and thus potentially diminished the officers' status (Adler, 1975, p. 50). Despite officers' apprehensions, Adler cited anecdotal evidence from police officers in New York and Washington who reported that their female colleagues were highly effective on patrol.

Rita Simon's Perspective

Simon (1976) reviewed demographic data concerning women's participation in employment and education and then presented percentages of total arrest numbers for women from the 1930s through the 1970s. These arrest data showed that women's arrests for all crimes doubled (from 7.4% in 1932 to 15.3% in 1972), but had quadrupled for property crimes (from 5.3% to 21.4%) (Simon, 1976, p. 36). She wrote, "If present trends in these crimes persist, approximately equal numbers of men and women will be arrested for fraud and embezzlement by the 1990s, and for forgery and counterfeiting the proportions should be equal by the 2010s" (Simon, 1976, p. 39). And she was almost correct: Women's percentage of total arrests in 2012 was 41% for fraud, 48% for embezzlement, and 37.5% for forgery/counterfeiting (FBI, 2013, Table 42).

In discussing women's involvement in auto theft and burglary, Simon (1975a) also compared arrest data from 1953 to 1972 collected by the FBI and published in their Uniform Crime Reports (UCR). She noted that male offenders continued to dominate in these two crime categories during the 20-year period. Simon (1975a) hypothesized that these crimes typically require skills that are learned in a criminal subculture and that historically women had not been integrated into such networks (p. 42). As a result, women have more limited opportunities than men to obtain such skills. In the 2012 UCR data, women continued to be underrepresented in these two crime categories, with men accounting for 84% of the arrests for burglary and 81% of the arrests for auto theft (FBI, 2013, Table 42). Although these data do not emulate the 1972 data that Simon referenced (women comprised 5% of burglary and slightly over 5% of auto theft arrests), they do suggest that Simon was correct in her rationale that women did not have access to the requisite connections and specific skills to engage in these two crime categories.

Importantly, Simon (1975a) also considered alternative explanations for the increase in women's involvement in certain kinds of crime as evidenced in arrest data. First, she noted that:

> It is plausible to assume that the police are becoming less "chivalrous" to women suspects and that women are beginning to receive more "equal" treatment; two, police behavior alone cannot account for the large increases in larceny, fraud, embezzlement and forgery by women that have occurred over the last half dozen years and the absence of increases in homicide, aggravated assaults, and other violent crimes. (p. 47)

In brief, Simon (1975a) focused on crime as a matter of opportunity and specifically theorized how it would affect women's involvement in property crimes. Women could not commit white-collar crimes when they did not have access to these opportunities. As more women entered the labor force outside the home, Simon (1975a) predicted that their involvement in criminal activity not only would increase but also would be reflected in the crimes that men traditionally committed (p. 47). She cautioned, however, that the increases reported in serious crimes by the media reflected women's greater involvement in larceny, fraud, and embezzlement rather than in violent crimes such as homicide. For violent offenses, there had been little change in female arrests over the two decades (Simon, 1975a, p. 46).

Simon warned that her predictions applied only if women's opportunities increased in the ensuing years. Simon (1975a) noted that women's representation in the higher status professions was not evident from the employment data that she reviewed and that women were more concentrated in traditional female occupations in the 1970s than at any other time. Without access to the kinds of professions where they would be able to commit white-collar and other occupational crimes, Simon (1975a) contended that women's involvement in these offenses would not increase dramatically (pp. 106–107). Simon's hypothesis was thus contingent on women having more opportunities in employment. Without access to the bank or the corporate world, women still would be relegated to engaging in lower level economic crimes such as fraud or shoplifting.

The Criminology of Deviant Women

In 1979, Adler and Simon collaborated on an edited book entitled *The Criminology of Deviant Women*. Although some chapters were reprints or adaptations from their earlier works, this co-edited work also included contributors who researched women being processed across the criminal justice system, as well as a cross-cultural perspective of female offending. In one of the chapters, Adler (1979a, p. 93) discussed the arrest rates of women. She observed that, with the exception of arrests for murder, women were engaging in more crime and that for specific crimes such as forgery and counterfeiting and fraud and embezzlement their arrest rates were 80% to 100% higher in 1972 than in 1960. She reiterated her earlier hypothesis that major changes were occurring in society and that "women are closing many of the gaps, social and criminal, that have separated them from men. The closer they get, the more alike they look and act" (Adler, 1979a, p. 94).

In the final chapter, Adler revisited the emancipation/liberation hypothesis and its applicability to other countries. She identified a number of changes occurring in various countries (both established and developing) regarding the role of women, their opportunities, and their involvement in crime. For example, Adler (1979b) noted that, "Although universally, males continue to commit the greatest number of offenses, women are beginning to emulate their patterns in both forms and dimensions of criminality, and worldwide statistics are indicative of these trends" (p. 409). However, she qualified this statement with the caveat that few cross-cultural data were available to verify the trend of female criminality. Still, she maintained "most of the scant statistical evidence demonstrates that the increasing crime rate is a universal phenomenon" (Adler, 1979b, p. 409).

Notably, with additional data (1959–1978), Austin (1982) subsequently found empirical support for the correlation between the female emancipation hypothesis (Adler, 1975; Simon, 1975a) and crime. Austin noted that the increase in female participation in the labor market and the uptick in divorce rates were indicators of female emancipation. Austin concluded that the women's movement may be able to partly explain increased involvement of women and crime (p. 428). Although Austin found that the increases were primarily for the less serious offenses, he noted that rather than embezzlement (as Simon predicted), the effects of female emancipation were detected with more certainty with regard to two specific offenses, robbery and auto theft (p. 427).

Adler and Simon highlighted the gains that occurred during the late 1960s and early 1970s because of women's increasing liberation as an explanation of female criminality. They viewed this social change as creating opportunities for crime. As Weisheit (1984) noted, "Adler (1975) synthesized the opportunity and socialization approaches and argued that changing perceptions of opportunity should lead to increases in female crime" (p. 570). Provided the chance, women were as likely to engage in crime as men. Crime was a manifestation of women realizing their capabilities. Furthermore, societal changes resulted in girls and women becoming more masculine and, subsequently, more criminal.

The Rebuttals

The third category of writings in this time period can be categorized as rebuttals to the emancipation theory. Clearly energized by the new paradigm that women were just as criminal as men given the same opportunities, many scholars were spurred to explore this line of inquiry. Freda Adler had illuminated an area of study that previously had not received much attention. Furthermore, her work inspired developments in the field in feminist criminology and prompted other scholars to investigate alternative explanations. She prioritized gender and she initiated a conversation nationally in mainstream media and in academia. Nonetheless, it did not take long before Adler's theory (and Simon's perspective as well) received criticism. Researchers argued against the liberation theory along two lines: that female offenders did not express particularly "liberated" attitudes and that statistics did not support increasing levels of violent crime by women (although property crime was rising) (see, e.g., Crites, 1976; Steffensmeier, 1978). Several prominent studies are reviewed below to illustrate the genre of research that emerged in response to the views expressed by Freda Adler and other sisters in criminology such as Rita Simon.

Leventhal (1977) assessed whether female offenders were more likely to embody or demonstrate liberated attitudes. To address this issue, he compared the views of female inmates and college girls. Contrary to the liberation thesis, he discovered that it was college students, not inmates, who were more favorable to equal roles for women or possessed more favorable attitudes toward women. Leventhal (1977) found that female inmates viewed women as weak, less capable than men, and unable to control their emotions, and the respondents believed that women should be submissive and not drink, curse, or smoke. Similarly, Widom (1981) reported that female inmates demonstrated similar conservative views when compared to the control group (Morris, 1987). Certainly, these studies' findings were not supportive of the idea that women's liberation led to their criminality.

Researchers also tested the hypothesis that women's crimes, especially violent crimes, increased as a result of women's liberation. When Steffensmeier (1978) examined the UCR arrest data from 1960 to 1975, he noted an increase in arrest rates for female offenders, but then pointed out that the male–female gender gap that was apparent in 1960 had either widened or remained the same in 1975 (p. 567). When he analyzed the property crime data from the UCR, he observed that women were not making rapid increases in traditional male offenses (e.g., burglary). Rather, women's largest increase was for larceny-theft, and women were "catching up" to men only in larceny and fraud/embezzlement (Steffensmeier, 1978, pp. 577–578). Furthermore, Steffensmeier (1978) contended that the women's movement could not explain the increases in property crimes for women. The increase preceded the advent of the women's movement (identified as occurring in the late 1960s) and "other forces in society already were providing the impetus for changing patterns of female crime well before the initial rise of the women's movement" (Steffensmeier, 1978, p. 579). Contrary to the hypothesis that women were holding jobs in corporate America and interacting on a level playing field with their male counterparts in business and finance, Steffensmeier (1978) noted that larceny was most commonly associated with shoplifting, and fraud usually referred to either passing checks without sufficient funds to cover them or engaging in welfare fraud. Rather than signaling a new era, these crimes reflected women's traditional sex roles in society and affected lower class and minority women who were not typically influenced by the women's movement (Steffensmeier, 1978, p. 580, 1982).

Similarly, Norland and Shover (1977) reviewed over 100 research articles and concluded that there was little evidence that female offenders were becoming more violent. They also noted that the media seemed to be fixated on the "new violent criminal" in the 1970s, but it was an echo of what Otto Pollak had said in 1950. Norland and Shover noted that "criminologists had been predicting for the past 80 years that . . . [the] equalization between the sexes . . . would lead to an increase in the volume of female crime" (p. 90). Furthermore, whether for juveniles or for adults, Norland and Shover found no data to substantiate the claim that girls and women were involved increasingly in aggressive offenses or that they were displaying aggressive tendencies (p. 99).

Subsequently, Shover, Norland, James, and Thornton (1979) tested two related theories using a sample of 1,002 public school students in grades 8 through 12 during 1976–1977. The first theory was that higher delinquency rates among girls would be associated with higher scores on a measurement tool of traditional masculinity/ femininity; the second theory was that sex-role socialization would be related to females' greater attachment to others, belief in rules and law, and opportunity. They found that the second theory had more empirical evidence, although their findings were not fully supportive of either theory. They concluded that when the feminine role is modified, there is an increase in female property crime. However, Shover et al. (1979) found no support for the premise that increased opportunity for girls and women resulted in greater participation in aggressive crime. Furthermore, they predicted that if there were a weakening of traditional gender roles in the future, the rate of female involvement in property and violent crime would increase. However, these increases would be neither large nor dramatic (Shover et al., 1979, p. 174).

Cullen, Golden, and Cullen (1979) explored Adler's (1975) contention that individuals with traits associated with male aggressiveness would be more likely to engage in violent offending. They noted that because Adler had relied on group-level data, her analysis precluded determining whether such a trait was statistically related to greater involvement in serious crime (Cullen et al., 1979, p. 303). With a sample of 182 college students enrolled in a social science class who self-reported prior delinquent behavior, they tested the aggressiveness and criminal/delinquent involvement of the participants. Cullen et al. found "that independent of sex, male traits increase a person's propensity to engage in various forms of delinquency" (p. 307).

Furthermore, although the effects of this masculinity hypothesis seemed to affect both male and female college students' participation in delinquency/criminality, Cullen et al. (1979) found a greater effect on male young adults than on female young adults (p. 307). Although their data provided some support to the masculinity hypothesis, they concluded that young men were still more likely to be involved in delinquency than young women and that those young men who demonstrated greater male aggressive characteristics were the most likely to participate in delinquent or criminal activities (p. 308). They suggested that there must be other variables, including structural and psychological factors, that were related to gender and resulted in greater involvement of men in deviant behaviors than women (p. 308).

In a subsequent survey of 1,002 high school students, Norland, Wessel, and Shover (1981) refuted Adler's (1975) hypothesis that major changes that were occurring in society were causing women and girls to become more masculine. Their analysis found that masculine characteristics among the girls in their sample "indirectly reduce their extent of involvement in delinquent conduct" (Norland et al., 1981, p. 430). In their sample, girls with more masculine characteristics reported less involvement in delinquent conduct than girls with fewer masculine characteristics (p. 430). They found no positive relationship between masculine characteristics and any status offending, property, or violent offending. Rather than a straightforward relationship, they concluded that the link between gender and behavior was more complicated than originally envisioned. Norland et al. suggested "that account be taken of the social and affiliational [sic] nature of the offenses in explaining the relationship between masculine characteristics and delinquent conduct" (p. 431).

Leonard (1982) offered a detailed critique of existing theories in criminology and their applicability to male behavior. She noted that "a single theoretical canopy has been assumed for men and women, although their social realities are extremely diverse" (Leonard, 1982, p. xii). She analyzed male and female arrest data from 1955 to 1970 as well as arrest data from 1979 and challenged two of Adler's (1975) hypotheses: (1) the rapid increase in women's equality with men and (2) the definition and scope of liberation, which Leonard contended focused too much on crime (p. 10). Leonard argued that Adler's "new woman criminal is more a myth than a reality" (p. 43), that data can be interpreted in various ways, and that percentage increases are not a valid predictor of female criminality. Rather, she contended that women's involvement in crime has increased in some areas but that this increase was primarily in property crime (Leonard, 1982, p. 31). By contrast, Leonard suggested that official statistics demonstrated women's lack of involvement in criminality and "that the most challenging and unexplained issue is the astonishing absence of criminality within the female population" (p. 43).

In analyzing specific violent and property crime conviction data on women in England and Wales from 1951 to 1980, Box and Hale (1984) also questioned the emancipation hypothesis of female criminality. They contended that indicators that had been used to ascertain female liberation, such as labor force participation, might be inadequate. Rather than assume that women who were in the labor force were achieving parity with men, it was more likely that women working outside the home were in low-paying jobs where there was not much chance of equal pay. They concluded that with the exception of one property crime, theft from employers, "no clear and unambiguous relationship is apparent between emancipation and other crimes" in these data (Box & Hale, 1984, p. 484). Although women may have had an opportunity to engage in criminal behavior, such an explanation did not inform us about the offender's motivation. They posited that when theorists link emancipation and crime, "women are reduced to mere imitators or mindless hedonists" (Box & Hale, 1984, p. 494).

Post-Adler Contributions to Feminist Criminology: 1970s and 1980s

Clearly, Adler and Simon spurred future research and the interest and passion for the study of female crime can be attributed to these two scholars and their prominence. Furthermore, through their individual and collaborative approaches, they moved the agenda in a dramatic and historical manner. During the mid-1970s and the decade of the 1980s, more studies on female criminality were conducted, and there was an increase in the number of papers presented on women and crime at the major conferences in the discipline, specifically the annual meetings of the American Society of Criminology and the Academy of Criminal Justice Sciences. Scholars continued to employ empirical research to test the hypotheses of Adler and Simon, publishing their findings in the major journals as well as in books devoted to women and crime. Our thinking about female criminality was undergoing a transformation, and gradually the discussion and debate about its causes, as well as its prevention and treatment, moved away from what Leonard (1982) referred to as "an addendum to the study of male criminality" (p. 184). By contrast, we had begun to witness what Leonard had advocated: "The subject of women and crime . . . studied in its own right as a separate and distinct phenomenon" (p. 184). Many scholars hastened to fill the void in the literature on women and crime, and their efforts were impressive. As explored below, some of these topics included women offenders' differential experiences in the justice system, more details on how females' perceptions affect their decisions to offend, female youth, correlations of arrest and victimization data, and the initial study of the intersection of race, class, and gender.

According to Anderson (1976), it was W. I. Thomas (1937) who first discussed the issue of chivalry, and it has emerged repeatedly in references or studies on female criminality. Chivalry is the theory that the justice system "protects" women with favorable treatment at each decision stage of the system. Summarizing the literature from 1907 to 1975, Anderson concluded that a chivalrous criminal justice system was a "myth" (p. 355). She advocated for more research on women offenders devoid of the myth. In addition, she noted that chivalry is not uniform in its application and that future research should focus on it systematically. Anderson cited the research (including Adler, 1975) that demonstrated that Black women have fared worse in the justice system than White women. Finally, she contended that sexist definitions of crime must be altered before an understanding of female criminality can emerge (Anderson, 1976, p. 355).

Scutt (1976, 1978) also proposed a type of sex-role theory that pointed to societal expectations of women as inhibiting criminal choices. She observed that women's liberation may increase criminality among women; however, she also noted that changing attitudes may affect definitions of crime. The focus on how social changes might affect official counting of female-perpetrated crime was an early forerunner to the "greater formalization" theory that came much later, arguing that women's increased numbers were a result of system changes in definition more than actual changes in women's behavior (Chesney-Lind, 1997; Steffensmeier, 1980). Scutt (1976, 1978) also presented the possibility that women's increased economic responsibilities might lead to more crime; this is a forerunner to Steffensmeier and Streifel's (1992) economic marginalization theory.

In addition, studies explored differences in Black and White youth processed by the system compared to those who had no contact with the system. Using a sample of 3,200 youths, Datesman, Scarpitti, and Stephenson (1975) contrasted youth who were handled by family court with students in public school. For this study, Datesman et al. (1975) explored whether there was a relationship between delinquent behavior and self-concept and between delinquent acts and perceptions of opportunity among female respondents to the survey (p. 119). They found that delinquent and nondelinquent White girls had similar self-concept scores, but that Black female delinquents had lower levels of self-esteem than both their White counterparts and their Black female nondelinquents. Both White and Black delinquent girls perceived their opportunities as less positive than did the nondelinquent respondents. Datesman et al. concluded that their sample of Black female delinquent youth was more likely to have had previous contact with the juvenile court in the previous year than their White female counterparts. In addition, the authors noted that subcultural support for female delinquency might be absent among girls because "female delinquency is largely individualistic, and not buttressed by the support and approval to as great an extent as male delinquency" (Datesman et al., 1975, p. 112).

Giordano (1978) also utilized two samples of girls, those in a juvenile institution and those in high school, to determine the connection between delinquent behavior and friendship patterns. Rather than maladjustment on the part of the girls who engaged in delinquent and status-offending behaviors, Giordano found a relationship between group association and self-reported delinquent activity (p. 132). For both Black and White adolescent girls, their perceptions of other girlfriends' approval were related to their delinquent behavior. Rather than being different in this regard, girls and boys shared certain similarities in that they compared themselves to their same-sex peers (Giordano, 1978, p. 132).

Giordano, Kerbel, and Dudley (1981) recognized some of the limitations of contemporary FBI data and thus chose to examine police blotters in Toledo, Ohio, from 1890 to 1975. Their goal was to assess changes in female offending. Their research indicated that rather than "new opportunities" (Giordano et al., 1981, p. 80), crime data must be considered from an "economic marginalization" (p. 80) view. They proposed studying female crime in the same way that male crime had been explored— that is, by investigating the structural and economic conditions in society. They noted that when data from 1930 were examined, the impact of the Depression on the economic conditions of women was obvious. Women who were married were working to feed their families and survive, rather than because they had achieved equality with men or to free themselves from domestic life. Women's involvement in property offenses such as burglary, theft, embezzlement, and robbery significantly increased when compared to earlier years (Giordano et al., 1981, p. 81). However, Giordano et al. did not attribute this increase to female liberation. Rather, they found that when employment data were available from the police blotters, unemployed women were more likely to be arrested. Furthermore, these women tended to be single, divorced, or separated (Giordano et al., 1981, p. 81). In brief, the most disadvantaged women were arrested predominantly for property crimes (Giordano et al., 1981, p. 81).

Some scholars employed various methodologies and compared arrest data on men and women with victimization data to determine whether official arrest data on female involvement in crime were consistent with victim reports. Recognizing the limitations of arrest data, Hindelang (1979) used the National Crime Survey victimization data available from 1972 to 1976 to assess women's involvement in index (i.e., serious) crimes. His analysis indicated that female involvement in such offenses was relatively stable during this time frame, except for larceny, which had increased. The victimization data correlated with the arrest data. In addition, no evidence of a gender-based chivalry appeared: Male victims were more likely than female victims to report female offenders to the police. Although limited by the years of his analysis, Hindelang (1979) noted that these data did not support a hypothesis that victims' reporting behavior was changing; that is, women were not more likely to be reported for criminal behavior than in previous years.

Research also compared adult Black and White female offenders' involvement in crime by race. Young (1980) used National Crime Survey data from 1972 to 1975 in 26 of the largest cities to examine Black and White female crime. In her study, she employed personal victimization reports for rape, robbery, assault, and larceny from the person (Young, 1980, p. 28). For offenders acting alone, Young found that the victimizations committed by White and Black female offenders had comparable patterns. However, the victimization patterns for multiple offenders differed by race. Thus, when multiple offenders were involved in a victimization incident, Young found that the crime patterns of Black female offenders were more similar to those of multiple White male offenders than to those of White female offenders (p. 31).

In assessing alternative explanations for women's involvement in crime, Richards and Tittle (1981) attempted to determine whether differences in crime rates between men and women could be explained by their perceived risk of apprehension. Using 1972 interview data from New Jersey, Iowa, and Oregon, Richards and Tittle investigated six variables that might explain differences between men and women regarding their perceptions of risk. They found that gender differences in perceived visibility best accounted for the lower crime rates of women versus men (p. 1194). The visibility variable suggested that women thought that their behavior was more likely to be monitored than that of their male counterparts and that they were more likely to be apprehended (p. 1188). Richards and Tittle noted that a person's position in the social structure may influence his or her perception of risk and visibility. Rather than high-status actors being deterred from criminal behavior, they contended that lower status actors, such as women, may be more susceptible to deterrence because they have fewer resources to insulate themselves from public review and less power than other members of society. In brief, the offender's position and role affected one's perception of risk (Richards & Tittle, 1981, p. 1194).

In *Judge, Lawyer, Victim, Thief,* Nicole Hahn Rafter and Elizabeth Stanko (1982) elaborated on the images of women (i.e., "passive and weak, masculine, impulsive and nonanalytic, purely evil," pp. 2–3) and how they affected the perception and treatment of women offenders, victims, and professionals in the system. Despite the absence of scientific evidence, they noted that the assumptions about gender wielded a "powerful influence on theories about women involved with the criminal justice system" (Rafter & Stanko, 1982, p. 4).

Researchers continued to study female offenders at various stages of the criminal justice system. For example, to gain a better understanding of female inmates, Mahan (1982) interviewed women in New Mexico prisons. Feinman (1980) and Baunach (1979, 1985) employed questionnaires and interviews to examine and understand the experiences of female inmates and inmate mothers in a number of states. Moyer (1984) elaborated on female offenders' difficulties with parenting while in prison and lack of economic opportunities. Pollock (1986) examined correctional officer perceptions of female and male inmates and how sex stereotypes influenced their perception that female inmates were much more difficult to supervise, a theme that persists in corrections today. Clearly, feminist criminology was expanding.

Clarice Feinman (1980, 1986) furthered the study of female criminality in her books and in her role as the founding editor of the journal *Women and Criminal Justice*. In an examination of FBI arrest data at various times between 1960 and 1983, she concluded that female offenders were largely the same over the decades of her study. Specifically, they "[are] uneducated, unskilled, and disproportionately from ethnic and racial minority groups; commit crimes yielding small rewards; and more often than not, are arrested for behaving in a manner that is not socially acceptable for women" (Feinman, 1986, p. 32). Feinman (1986) also noted the discrimination women faced in the economic sphere and its effects in various aspects of their lives as offenders and professionals.

Feminist criminology clearly gained a foothold in the discipline during this era. These researchers and their work represent a sampling of some of the studies and books that appeared in the 1970s and 1980s. Far from exhaustive, the studies summarized offer a glimpse of the work published and the expansion of feminist criminology in the study of female offenders, victims, and professionals. These scholars helped to inspire the next generation of feminist criminologists. In 1982, Eileen Leonard advocated for the separate study of women, but with the ultimate goal of a "unitary science, with unitary theories that no longer ignore vast segments of society" (p. 185). The published literature and conference presentations on female crime and victimization demonstrated significant progress in attaining that goal.

Conclusion

In the 1970s the social roles of women were changing rapidly and academic interest in women extended to female offenders. Theoretical work targeted and critiqued the unquestioning acceptance of sexual stereotypes rampant in earlier theories of female criminality. Theories were developed that sought to explain the increasing criminality of women, focusing not on internal, inherent traits of women, but rather on sex roles and the influence of changing societal expectations and opportunities. Even in 1986, Chesney-Lind noted that the serious study of female criminology and how society responds to it was still in its "infancy" (p. 95). Although we have transcended the infancy period, research continues to evolve. Our understanding of correlates of delinquency and crime has increased, but research on brain development, pathways to deviant behavior, abuse and maltreatment, and the gendered nature of the criminal justice system is ongoing.

This review of academic activity 40 years ago provides us with several interesting observations that point out the dynamic nature of the academic enterprise. For instance, some of the feminist critiques criticized earlier writings for describing female delinquents as coming from more dysfunctional families, being more relationship oriented, and having more mental health issues. Smart (1977), Klein (1973), Morris (1965), and others viewed these descriptions as stereotypical and reductionist; however, more current research continues to find that there are differences between female and male delinquents and offenders and there is empirical support that the "pathways" of women to prison differ from those of men (see Arnold, 1990; Bottcher, 1993; Chesney-Lind, 1997; Chesney-Lind & Rodriguez, 1983; Gaarder & Belknap, 2002; Daly, 1992; Maher, 1997; Owen, 1998; Pollock, 1998; Richie, 1996; Silbert & Pines, 1981). Interestingly, some of these early critiques seem to have been without merit. Thus, Norland and Shover (1977) suggested that the idea that female delinquents were more likely to come from dysfunctional homes (citing Morris, 1964) was a misconception derived from the fact that parents were more likely to report girls than boys for incorrigibility. In fact, longitudinal studies now provide fairly good evidence that female offenders are more likely than male offenders to come from more severely dysfunctional families.

Adler's liberation hypothesis was preceded by earlier observations that women were becoming more violent as a result of emancipation (see, e.g., Pollak, 1950), and there have also been subsequent predictions that women's roles in violent crime were becoming equal to men's (e.g., Baskin & Sommers, 1993). The empirical support for such a proposition continues to be equivocal. In 1932, women comprised about 8.7% of murder and nonnegligent manslaughter arrests and, today, 80 years later, they still comprise only about 11%. Further, whether official arrest statistics are measuring an increase in violent activity or a change in formal processing is still a hotly contested issue.

Freda Adler and Rita Simon ignited the contemporary study of female criminology. Their research prompted critiques, facilitated further research, and contributed to a significant body of literature (Merlo, 1995). As Weisheit and Mahan (1988) noted, Freda Adler's "work was instrumental in drawing attention to the issue of female criminality" (p. 3). Moyer (1992) contended that feminists concluded that Adler and Simon's publications contributed to the "development of research interest in the woman offender" (p. 8). In fact, Moyer (1992) reminds us that the first women and crime classes were taught by Freda Adler and her contemporaries in the first half of the 1970s. Even more important, Freda Adler and colleagues, including both those who preceded her and the scholarly sisters who followed her, "opened the door of credibility for criminologists to study women" (Moyer, 1992, p. 8).

One important difference between Adler's work and that of earlier theorists was the notoriety it attained. When *Sisters in Crime* was published, it moved the agenda on female criminality in ways that had not previously occurred. Whether it was television appearances and radio interviews in mainstream media outlets like the *Today Show* or WNYC or in publications like *Psychology Today*, Freda Adler represented women who were engaged in research in our discipline and she gave voice to the study of female criminality. She enhanced the stature of research on the criminology of women for the field and the public. For that contribution and all the subsequent research that followed, the discipline of criminology has been enriched.

References

Adams, H. (1914). *Women and crime*. London, UK: T. Warner Laurie.

Adler, F. (1975). *Sisters in crime: The rise of the new female criminal*. New York, NY: McGraw–Hill.

Adler, F. (1979a). Changing patterns. In F. Adler & R. J. Simon (Eds.), *The criminology of deviant women* (pp. 91–94). Boston, MA: Houghton Mifflin.

Adler, F. (1979b). The interaction between women's emancipation and female criminality: A cross-cultural perspective. In F. Adler & R. J. Simon (Eds.), *The criminology of deviant women* (pp. 407–418). Boston, MA: Houghton Mifflin.

Adler, F., & Simon, R. J. (Eds.). (1979). *The criminology of deviant women*. Boston, MA: Houghton Mifflin.

Anderson, E. A. (1976). The "chivalrous" treatment of the female offender in the arms of the criminal justice system. *Social Problems, 23,* 350–357.

Arnold, R. A. (1990). Women of color: Processes of victimization and criminalization of Black women. *Social Justice, 17,* 153–166.

Austin, R. L. (1982). Women's liberation and increases in minor, major, and occupational offenses. *Criminology, 20,* 407–430.

Barker, G. H., & Adams, W. T. (1962). Comparisons of delinquencies of boys and girls. *Journal of Criminal Law, Criminology and Police Science, 53,* 470–475.

Baskin, D. R., & Sommers, I. (1993). Females' initiation into violent street crime. *Justice Quarterly, 10,* 559–583.

Baunach, P. J. (1979). Mothering from behind prison walls. Paper presented at the Annual Meeting of the American Society of Criminology, Philadelphia, PA.

Baunach, P. J. (1985). *Mothers in prison*. New Brunswick, NJ: Transaction Books.

Bishop, C. (1931). *Women and crime*. London, UK: Chatto & Windus.

Bottcher, J. (1993). Gender as social control: A qualitative study of incarcerated youths and their siblings in greater Sacramento. *Justice Quarterly, 12,* 33–57.

Box, S., & Hale, C. (1984). Liberation/emancipation, economic marginalization, or less chivalry: The relevance of three theoretical arguments to female crime patterns in England and Wales, 1051–1980. *Criminology, 22,* 473–497.

Brodsky, A. M. (1975). Planning for the female offender: Directions for the future. In A. M. Brodsky (Ed.), *The female offender* (pp. 100–108). Beverly Hills, CA: Sage.

Chesney-Lind, M. (1973). Judicial enforcement of the female sex role: The family court and the female delinquent. *Issues in Criminology, 8*(2), 51–69.

Chesney-Lind, M. (1986). Women and crime: The female offender. *Journal of Women in Culture and Society, 12,* 78–96.

Chesney-Lind, M. (1997). *The female offender: Girls, women and crime.* Thousand Oaks, CA: Sage.

Chesney-Lind, M., & Rodriguez, N. (1983). Women under lock and key: A view from the inside. *The Prison Journal, 63,* 47–65.

Clark, J. P., & Haurek, E. (1966). Age and sex roles of adolescents and their involvement in misconduct. *Sociology and Social Research, 50,* 495–508.

Cowie, J., Cowie, V., & Slater, E. (1968). *Delinquency in girls.* London, UK: Heinemann.

Crites, L. (1976). *The female offender.* Lexington, MA: Heath.

Cullen, F. T., Golden, K. M., & Cullen, J. B. (1979). Sex and delinquency: A partial test of the masculinity hypothesis. *Criminology, 17,* 301–310.

Dalton, K. (1961). Menstruation and crime. *British Medical Journal, 2,* 1752–1753.

Daly, K. (1992). Women's pathways to felony court: Feminist theories of lawbreaking and problems of representation. *Southern California Review of Law and Women's Studies, 2,* 11–52.

Datesman, S. K., Scarpitti, F. R., & Stephenson, R. M. (1975). Female delinquency: An application of self and opportunity theories. *Journal of Research in Crime and Delinquency, 12,* 107–123.

Davis, K. (1937). The sociology of prostitution. *American Sociological Review, 2,* 744–755.

Federal Bureau of Investigation. (2013). *Crime in the United States 2012: Arrests by sex, 2012* [Data file]. Retrieved from http://www.fbi.gov/about-us/cjis/ucr/crime-in-the-u.s/2012/crime-in-the-u.s.-2012/tables/42tabledatadecoverviewpdf

Feinman, C. (1980). *Women in the criminal justice system.* New York, NY: Praeger.

Feinman, C. (1986). *Women in the criminal justice system* (2nd ed.). New York, NY: Praeger.

Gaarder, E., & Belknap, J. (2002). Tenuous borders: Girls transferred to adult court. *Criminology, 40,* 481–517.

Giordano, P. C. (1978). Girls, guys, and gangs: The changing social context of female delinquency. *Journal of Criminal Law and Criminology, 69,* 126–134.

Giordano, P. C., Kerbel, S., & Dudley, S. (1981). The economics of female criminality: An analysis of police blotters, 1890–1975. In L. H. Bowker (Ed.), *Women and crime in America* (pp. 65–82). New York, NY: Macmillan.

Glueck, S., & Glueck, E. (1934). *Five hundred delinquent women.* New York, NY: Knopf.

Hindelang, M. J. (1971). Age, sex, and the versatility of delinquent involvement. *Social Problems, 18,* 522–535.

Hindelang, M. J. (1979). Sex differences in criminal activity. *Social Problems, 27,* 143–156.

Hoffman-Bustamante, D. (1973). Nature of female criminality. *Issues in Criminology, 8*(2), 117–136.

Horney, J. (1978). Menstrual cycles and criminal responsibility. *Law and Human Behavior, 2,* 25–36.

Kellor, F. (1900). Psychological and environmental study of women criminals. *American Journal of Sociology, 5,* 527–543.

Klein, D. (1973). The etiology of female crime: A review of the literature. *Issues in Criminology*, *8*(2), 3–30.

Konopka, C. (1966). *The adolescent girl in conflict*. Englewood Cliffs, NJ: Prentice Hall.

Kruttschnitt, C. (1980–1981). Social status and sentences of female offenders. *Law and Society Review*, *15*, 247–266.

Leonard, E. (1982). *Women, crime and society: A critique of theoretical criminology*. New York, NY: Longman.

Leventhal, G. (1977). Female criminality: Is "women's lib" to blame? *Psychological Reports*, *41*, 1179–1182.

Mahan, S. (1982). *Unfit mothers*. Saratoga, CA: R&E Research Associates.

Maher, L. (1997). *Sexed work: Gender, race, and resistance in a Brooklyn drug market*. New York, NY: Oxford University Press.

Merlo, A. V. (1995). Female criminality in the 1990s. In A. V. Merlo & J. M. Pollock (Eds.), *Women, law, and social control* (pp. 119–134). Boston, MA: Allyn & Bacon.

Morris, A. (1987). *Women, crime and criminal justice*. Oxford, UK: Basil Blackwell.

Morris, R. R. (1964). Female delinquency and relational problems. *Social Forces*, *43*, 82–89.

Morris, R. R. (1965). Attitudes toward delinquency by delinquents, non-delinquents and their friends. *British Journal of Criminology*, *5*, 254–265.

Moyer, I. L. (1984). Deceptions and realities of life in women's prisons. *The Prison Journal*, *24*, 45–56.

Moyer, I. L. (1992). Crime, conflict theory, and the patriarchal society. In I. L. Moyer (Ed.), *The changing roles of women in the criminal justice system: Offenders, victims, and professionals* (pp. 1–24). Long Grove, IL: Waveland.

Norland, S., & Shover, N. (1977). Gender roles and female criminality. *Criminology*, *15*, 87–104.

Norland, S., Wessel, R. C., & Shover, N. (1981). Masculinity and delinquency. *Criminology*, *19*, 421–433.

Owen, B. (1998). *"In the mix": Struggle and survival in a women's prison*. Albany, NY: State University of Albany Press.

Payak, B. J. (1963). Understanding the female offender. *Federal Probation*, *27*(4), 11–12.

Pollak, O. (1950). *The criminality of women*. Philadelphia: University of Pennsylvania Press.

Pollock, J. M. (1978). Early theories of female criminality. In L. H. Bowker (Ed.), *Women, crime, and the criminal justice system* (pp. 25–50). Lexington, MA: Lexington Books.

Pollock, J. M. (1986). *Sex and supervision: Guarding female inmates in prison*. Westport, CT: Greenwood.

Pollock, J. M. (1998). *Criminal women*. Cincinnati, OH: Anderson.

Rafter, N. H., & Stanko, E. A. (Eds.). (1982). *Judge, lawyer, victim, thief: Women, gender roles, and criminal justice*. Boston, MA: Northeastern University Press.

Rasche, C. E. (1975). The female offender as an object of criminological research. In A. M. Brodsky (Ed.), *The female offender* (pp. 9–28). Beverly Hills, CA: Sage.

Richards, P., & Tittle, C. R. (1981). Gender and perceived chances of arrest. *Social Forces*, *59*, 1182–1199.

Richie, B. (1996). *Compelled to crime: The gender entrapment of battered Black women*. New York, NY: Routledge.

Rosenblatt, E., & Greenland, C. (1974). Female crimes of violence. *Canadian Journal of Criminology and Corrections, 16*, 173–180.

Sandhu, H. S., & Allen, D. E. (1969). Female delinquency: Goal obstruction and anomie. *Canadian Review of Sociology/Revue canadienne de sociologie, 6*, 107–110.

Scutt, J. A. (1976). Role conditioning theory: An explanation for disparity in male and female criminality? *Australian and New Zealand Journal of Criminology, 9*, 25–35.

Scutt, J. A. (1978). Toward the liberation of the female lawbreaker. *International Journal of Criminology and Penology, 6*, 5–18.

Shover, N., Norland, S., James, J., & Thornton, W. E. (1979). Gender roles and delinquency. *Social Forces, 58*, 162–175.

Silbert, M. & Pines, A. (1981). Sexual child abuse as an antecedent to prostitution. *Child Abuse & Neglect, 5*, 407–411.

Simon, R. J. (1975a). *The contemporary woman and crime.* Washington, DC: National Institute of Mental Health.

Simon, R. J. (1975b). *Women and crime.* Lexington, MA: Heath.

Simon, R. J. (1976). American women and crime. *Annals of the American Academy of Political and Social Science, 423*, 31–46.

Smart, C. (1976). *Women, crime and criminology: A feminist critique.* Boston, MA: Routledge & Kegan Paul.

Smart, C. (1977). Criminology theory: Its ideology and implications concerning women. *British Journal of Sociology, 28*, 89–100.

Steffensmeier, D. J. (1978). Crime and the contemporary woman: An analysis of changing levels of female property crime, 1960–75. *Social Forces, 57*, 566–584.

Steffensmeier, D. J. (1980). Sex differences in patterns of adult crime, 1965–1977: A review and assessment. *Social Forces, 58*, 1080–1108.

Steffensmeier, D. J. (1982). Trends in female crime: It's still a man's world. In B. R. Price & N. Sokoloff (Eds.), *The criminal justice system and women* (pp. 117–129). New York, NY: Clark Boardman.

Steffensmeier, D., & Streifel, C. (1992). Time-series analysis of female-to-male arrests for property crimes, 1960–1985: A test of alternative explanations. *Justice Quarterly, 9*, 78–103.

Tappan, P. (1947). *Delinquent girls in court.* New York, NY: Columbia University Press.

Thomas, W. I. (1937). *The unadjusted girl.* Boston, MA: Little, Brown.

Vedder, C. B., & Somerville, D. B. (1970). *The delinquent girl.* Springfield, IL: Thomas.

Weidensall, J. (1916). *The mentality of the criminal woman.* Baltimore, MD: Warwick & York.

Weisheit, R. A. (1984). Women and crime: Issues and perspectives. *Sex Roles, 11*, 567–581.

Weisheit, R., & Mahan, S. (1988). *Women, crime, and criminal justice.* Cincinnati, OH: Anderson.

Widom, C. (1981). Perspectives of female criminality: A critical examination of assumptions. In A. Morris & I. Gelsthorpe (Eds.), *Women and crime.* Cambridge, UK: Institute of Criminology.

Wright, R. A. (1987). Are "sisters in crime" finally being booked? The coverage of women and crime in journals and textbooks. *Teaching Sociology, 15*, 418–422.

Young, V. D. (1980). Women, race, and crime. *Criminology, 18*, 26–34.

PART II

The Development of Offending

CHAPTER 3

A Biosocial Perspective
of Female Offending

Jamie C. Vaske, Danielle L. Boisvert, and John Paul Wright

When criminologists discuss gender and crime, they often do so through a sociological lens, explaining female offending through environmental pressures such as patriarchy, economic marginalization, or victimization. They also apply traditional criminological theories to the gender gap in crime, arguing that males have greater involvement in criminal conduct because they are more likely to have delinquent peers or poor supervision by their parents. Yet, these explanations ignore other risk factors—namely biological and psychological factors—that may be important to the etiology of offending for both genders.

It is understandable why many contemporary criminologists remain hesitant to discuss biological and psychological risk factors for offending: Biological theorizing had a sordid history. Early theorists who employed multifactor or biosocial explanations of criminality claimed that women were biologically inferior to men, were "big children" (Lombroso & Ferrero, 2004, p. 8), and were a "swarm of defected, diseased, antisocial misfits" (Glueck & Glueck, 1934, p. 303). However, although exceptions perhaps exist, such biased thinking no longer characterizes biosocial criminology. Current biosocial research takes a more neutral position in its discussion of offenders. Thus, it avoids sexist ideology and casts biological risk factors as increasing a person's *probability* of offending rather than as an essential trait that leads ineluctably to deviant conduct.

Although the fields of psychology and biosocial criminology have investigated the biopsychosocial reasons for offending among females and males, much of this literature is not discussed in mainstream criminology texts or journals. To fill this gap, the current chapter reviews the empirical evidence on the biosocial risk factors for antisocial behavior between and within genders. First, it discusses the potential biosocial reasons for the gender differences in antisocial and criminal behavior. That is, the first section addresses the question: Why are males more antisocial than females? Second, it reviews the evidence on the biological, psychological, and sociological risk factors for female offending. In particular, it highlights the interplay between biopsychosocial factors and how this intersection may explain female offending, especially the increase in female antisocial behavior during adolescence. Finally, the chapter sets forth an explanation for why females' antisocial behavior is predominantly covert in nature, but also for why females may drift into overt antisocial behavior given specific circumstances.

It is important to note that the chapter focuses on the broader construct of antisocial behavior rather than on criminal behavior specifically. Antisocial behavior is a heterogeneous construct that includes a variety of behaviors, such as verbal aggression, defying authority, lying, engaging in delinquency or crime, and other behaviors that conflict with societal norms. This approach is taken for two reasons. First, many offenders experience the "generality of deviance," in which they engage not only in crime but also in an array of deviant behaviors. Thus, the sources of crime are also the sources of other types of deviance—to explain one is to explain the other (Gottfredson & Hirschi, 1990). Second and more important, the chapter examines the development of females' risk factors through a life-course perspective. Early manifestations of conduct problems, which would not be considered crimes per se, may be connected to later involvement in delinquency and in adult criminality. That is, antisocial behavior in childhood is potentially inextricably related to persistent criminal behavior across the life course.

Explaining the Gender Gap: Why Are Males More Antisocial?

Research on the topic of gender and antisocial behavior has typically focused on addressing two questions: (1) are the risk factors for criminal and antisocial behavior the same for males and females, and (2) what risk factors explain the gender gap in criminal and antisocial behavior? A number of scholars have addressed the first question (Daigle, Cullen, & Wright, 2007; Moffitt, Caspi, Rutter, & Silva, 2001; Smith & Paternoster, 1987), with results suggesting that there are many gender similarities in the risk factors for crime. Some risk factors, however (such as social bond/control variables, depression), explain more variation in females' crime and delinquency (Krohn & Massey, 1980), whereas other factors (such as social learning variables and low self-control) are more relevant to explaining males' antisocial behavior (Alarid, Burton, & Cullen, 2000; Mazerolle, 1998; Moffitt et al., 2001; Smith & Paternoster, 1987). Further, the general causes of crime may be the same, but the specific variables within that theory of crime may differ for males and females. For example, general strain theorists have argued that strain theory explains offending for both males and females. But some research suggests that the specific types of strain differ between the sexes, with males experiencing strains related to financial success, violent victimization, and negative school experiences and females experiencing strains related to maintaining social relationships (Broidy & Agnew, 1997; Mazerolle, 1998). Overall, the empirical evidence seems to support both sides by demonstrating that some causes of crime and antisocial behavior are the same for males and females, whereas others have shown that there are important gender differences in risk factors.

The topic of this chapter concerns the second research question: Why are males more likely to engage in most forms of crime and antisocial behavior than females? Scholars have put forth two explanations for the gender gap in crime and antisocial behavior (Rutter, Caspi, & Moffitt, 2003). First, researchers argue that males have greater exposure to risk factors than females, and this greater exposure to risk factors translates into greater involvement in antisocial behavior. For instance, because males may have higher levels of certain biological (e.g., testosterone), psychological (e.g., antisocial attitudes), and sociological risk factors (e.g., delinquent peers), they are more likely than females to engage in delinquent and antisocial behavior. Second, scholars assert that males may be more sensitive to the effects of certain biological, psychological, and sociological risk factors than females. Thus, even if males and females are exposed to the same risk factor, that risk factor would have a greater impact on antisocial behavior for males than for females. The next sections review the empirical evidence concerning both of these explanations for the gender gap in antisocial behavior.

Males' Exposure to Risk Factors

One reason why males engage in more antisocial behavior than females is their greater exposure to risk factors and their lower exposure to factors that prevent antisocial behavior. Thus, it is the combination of too many risk factors and too few inhibitory mechanisms that facilitate males' antisocial behavior. The overrepresentation of risk and underrepresentation of inhibition in males can be found at the biological, psychological, and sociological levels of analysis. At the psychological level, studies have shown that males exhibit greater risk taking, hyperactivity, negative emotionality (i.e., willing to take advantage of others, feel mistreated, suspicious), antisocial attitudes, lower self-regulation, less aversion to risk, and lower levels of moral beliefs than females (Heimer & De Coster, 1999; Mazerolle, 1998; Moffitt et al., 2001). Furthermore, the gender gap in antisocial behavior may be explained by these psychological risk factors (Burton, Cullen, Evans, Alarid, & Dunaway, 1998; LaGrange & Silverman, 1999). Moffitt et al.'s (2001) analysis of youth from the Dunedin Longitudinal Study revealed that 96% of the gender gap in antisocial behavior was explained by males' higher levels of negative emotionality and lower levels of constraint. Similarly, Heimer and De Coster found that males were more likely to engage in violent delinquency than females because males were more likely to endorse attitudes favorable to violent behavior (i.e., "It is alright to beat up another person if he/she called you a dirty name or if he/she started the fight"). These results show that males may engage in higher levels of antisocial behavior because males and females think differently about the world and social situations.

These gender differences in psychology may exist because of gender differences in biology. For example, Lombroso and Ferrero (2004) suggested that women were less likely to engage in crime because they had fewer biological and physiological abnormalities than men. More recent studies have shown that, compared to females, males may be less risk averse, have lower levels of self-control, and exhibit higher levels of negative emotionality because males (on average) have a smaller orbitofrontal cortex (Gur, Gunning-Dixon, Bilker, & Gur, 2002), less activity in the insula and frontal lobes when presented with risky decisions (Lee, Chan, Leung, Fox, & Gao, 2009), higher levels of testosterone (Walsh, 2011), and lower levels of corticotrophin-releasing hormone and adrenocorticotropic hormone (Young, Korszun, Figueiredo, Banks-Solomon, & Herman, 2008). Males' smaller orbitofrontal cortex may translate into higher levels of negative emotionality and biases in risky decision making. The orbitofrontal cortex is responsible for the regulation of negative emotion from the amygdala and the anticipation of rewards and punishments. That is, males may be less neurobiologically sensitive to situations where costs and rewards are uncertain (i.e., uncertainty produces avoidance behaviors or hesitation), they are less sensitive to punishment, and they may be less likely to integrate information about costs into their decision making (Lee et al., 2009). Furthermore, studies have shown that females are more likely to hesitate when taking risks, especially after being punished for previously engaging in risky behavior. Females may be more reflective and cautious because they experience greater activity in inhibitory and rational parts of the brain (i.e., insula, frontal lobes) when confronting the possibility of making risky decisions (Lee et al., 2009).

Increases in testosterone—for both males and females—have also been linked with aggression, antisocial behavior, violent behavior, lower sensitivity to punishment, greater sensitivity to reward, and greater risk taking (Stanton, Liening, & Schultheiss, 2011; van Goozen, Fairchild, Snoek, & Harold, 2007). In an innovative study, Vermeersch, T'sjoen, Kaufman, and Vincke (2008) found that males with higher levels of testosterone were more likely to be risk taking and were more likely to surround themselves with peers who were risk taking. Subsequently, associating with more risk-seeking peers increased the respondents' own risk-taking behavior. These findings indicate that biology may influence behavior because it shapes people's decisions about their environment (testosterone → decision to associate with risky peers → increased risk-taking behavior).

Finally, males and females differ on a host of sociological risk and inhibitory factors. On average, males report higher levels of harsh discipline, violent victimization, delinquent peer association, negative experiences in school and with adults, weaker attachments to peers, lower levels of supervision, and lower involvement in school activities (Agnew, 2009; Daigle et al., 2007; Mazerolle, 1998). The gender gap in these sociological risk factors may partially explain males' greater involvement in antisocial behavior. Indeed, Moffitt et al.'s (2001) analysis found that weak attachment to peers and delinquent peer association explained 25% of the gender differences in antisocial behavior, whereas family risk factors explained 9% of the gender gap. In sum, a large body of research shows that males may have more exposure to biological, psychological, and sociological risk factors and less exposure to biological, psychological, and sociological inhibitory factors than females. These gender differences in risk and inhibitory factors have been shown to explain a moderate to large portion of the gender gap in antisocial behavior.

Males' Sensitivity to Risk Factors

A second explanation for the gender gap in antisocial behavior is that certain biological, psychological, and sociological risk factors may have a stronger impact on males than on females. This hypothesis suggests that males and females may be exposed to the same risk factor, but that it would lead to antisocial behavior for males more so than for females; thus, males may be less resilient to certain risk factors than females. At the biological level, this hypothesis may be true for a number of genetic and biological risks (Lombroso & Ferrero, 2004). For instance, Vaske, Wright, Boisvert, and Beaver (2011) found that small increases in genetic risk lead to criminal behavior for males, but that females had to experience large increases in genetic risk before they offended. More specifically, females who were in the highest genetic risk group had the same odds of offending as males who were in the lowest genetic risk group.

Studies have also identified specific genetic risk factors that may have a stronger impact on males than on females. One of the genetic risk factors identified is the low-activity variant of the monoamine oxidase A (*MAOA*) gene. MAOA is an enzyme that is responsible for degrading excess neurotransmitters during neurotransmission, and a low level of MAOA has been linked to higher levels of aggression and hypersensitivity to negative stimuli. The activity of the MAOA enzyme is partially controlled through the *MAOA* gene on the X chromosome. A case study of a Dutch family and control subjects revealed that males with the low-activity variant of the *MAOA* gene exhibited problems of severe mental retardation and aggression, as well as various forms of impulsive behavior including exhibitionism, arson, and attempted rape. By contrast, females with the low-activity variant were of normal intelligence and did not exhibit severe behavioral problems (Brunner et al., 1993). Along similar lines, Meyer-Lindenberg and his colleagues (2006) revealed that males with the low-activity variant of the *MAOA* gene had less connection between the orbitofrontal cortex and amygdala than females with the low-activity variant. This finding is interesting because it may point to genetic (i.e., *MAOA*) and biological (i.e., connection between orbitofrontal cortex and amygdala) reasons for why some males score higher on inventories of negative emotionality and poor self-regulation.

Two considerations may explain why the low-activity allele on the *MAOA* gene may be particularly detrimental for males: (1) the *MAOA* gene is located on the X chromosome; and (2) increases in testosterone may decrease activity of the *MAOA* gene. Each of these possibilities is discussed in order.

First, it is important to recognize that for a single gene, people typically inherit one allele (or genetic variant) from their mother and one variant from their father; therefore, if a person inherits a "bad" variant from one parent, it is possible that this person will inherit a "good" variant from the other parent to offset the risk from the bad variant. This is not the case for genes that are located on the X chromosome, because males only inherit one X chromosome from their mother, whereas females inherit two X chromosomes (one from their mother and one from their father); thus, males can only have one allele of the *MAOA* gene (either the low-activity allele or the high-activity allele from their mother), whereas females have two alleles (either two low-activity alleles, a low- and a high-activity allele, or two high-activity alleles). If a male receives the low-activity variant from his mother, there is no way that he can inherit a second high-activity allele to act as a "backup" to offset the risk of the low-activity variant; females, however, have the possibility of receiving a high-activity allele to protect them. Also, even if females receive two low-activity alleles, it is possible that one of the alleles will be silenced or inactivated by the *XIST* gene, a gene that randomly silences one of the X chromosomes to prevent genetic overload in females. If a female has a low-activity allele and a high-activity allele, one would expect (in evolutionary terms) that the low-activity allele would be silenced, leaving the female with the high-activity variant and unscathed in genetic terms. The *XIST* gene does not activate if there is only one X chromosome, and thus inactivation does not occur in men. Finally, studies have shown that genetic "risks" tend to occur on the maternal X chromosome more so than on the paternal X chromosome, a process referred to as genomic imprinting (Ostrer, 2001). Because males receive only one X chromosome, which is from their mother, they are more likely to inherit and be affected by genetic risks on the X chromosome than their sisters. It is for these reasons—only one X chromosome for boys, the X chromosome is maternally inherited, X inactivation for females but not for males—that one would expect genes on the X chromosome to have a particularly detrimental impact on boys. Indeed, Bainbridge (2003) explains how these processes lead to the concentration of particular diseases (hemophilia, Duchenne muscular dystrophy, color blindness) in males compared to females. Given the evidence from Meyer-Lindenberg et al. (2006) and others, we can see how X-linked genes, such as *MAOA*, can have a greater impact on antisocial behavior for males than for females.

Second, problems associated with the low-activity allele of the *MAOA* gene can also be exacerbated by increased levels of testosterone. Testosterone has been shown to decrease expression of the *MAOA* gene. If an individual already has the low-activity variant, increasing his testosterone can further suppress activity of the *MAOA* gene—creating a "double whammy"—and lead to behavioral problems for the individual. Results from Sjöberg et al. (2008) suggest that high testosterone leads to lower levels of MAOA enzyme activity for males with the low-activity allele compared to males with the high-activity allele. As a result, males with high testosterone and the low-activity allele of MAOA reported more aggressive behavior than males with low testosterone and the low-activity allele. Thus, some genes may have a disproportionate impact on males' antisocial behavior because they are on the X chromosome and testosterone can affect expression of some X-linked genes.

In addition to males' sensitivity to genetic risk factors, some research suggests that males with particular psychological diagnoses may have worse outcomes in terms of externalizing behaviors than females with the same diagnosis (Gaub & Carlson, 1997). For example, Gershon and Gershon's (2002) meta-analysis of 21 studies found that males with attention deficit hyperactivity disorder (ADHD) were more likely to exhibit externalizing behavior problems than females with ADHD. Similarly, Christie et al. (1988) reported that the odds of developing a drug-use disorder were higher for males diagnosed with major depressive disorder than for females with major depressive disorder. Importantly, however, a number of studies show that females with psychological diagnoses may have worse outcomes in terms of internalizing behaviors (depression, suicide attempts) and substance-use disorders than males (Gershon & Gershon, 2002; Loeber, Burke, Lahey, Winters, & Zera, 2000).

Finally, a number of researchers have suggested that males may be more sensitive to environmental risk factors than females (Cowie, Cowie, & Slater, 1968; Rutter et al., 2003). That is, males who are exposed to an environmental risk factor may exhibit more behavioral problems than females who are exposed to the same risk factor. There is some evidence to support this hypothesis as it pertains to childhood maltreatment and victimization. An analysis of 676 abused and neglected youths showed that abused males were more likely to be unemployed, to be homeless, to fail to graduate high school, to have a substance-use disorder, to have been arrested, and to engage in violent behavior than abused females (McGloin & Widom, 2001). Similar results were garnered from Vaske's (2011) analysis of young adults, which showed that males who experienced childhood abuse or neglect, adolescent violent victimization, or adolescent intimate-partner violence were generally more likely to engage in violent offending, property offending, marijuana use, or alcohol abuse than females who experienced the same type of victimization. Approximately 30% of males who were physically or psychologically victimized by their partners during adolescence reported adulthood violent offending and marijuana use. Comparatively, 7.9% of female intimate-partner victims engaged in violent offending and 22.1% of female intimate-partner victims used marijuana during emerging adulthood. These results suggest that males may be less resilient to the effects of victimization than females. Other studies on resilience have found that males may be more sensitive to the effects of family poverty and conflict than females (Werner & Smith, 1982).

In conclusion, research has shown that males are more likely to engage in antisocial behavior, especially violent behavior. Part of the reason why males may exhibit higher levels of antisocial behavior is that they have greater exposure to risk factors than females. That is, males may have higher levels of psychological (i.e., low self-control, preference for risk, negative emotionality, antisocial attitudes), biological (i.e., smaller orbitofrontal cortex, less activity in inhibitory regions during risky decision making, higher testosterone), and sociological risk factors (i.e., poor family environment, weaker attachments to school, delinquent peers, violent victimization) than females, which translates into greater antisocial behavior among males. Furthermore, even when males and females are exposed to similar risk factors, males may be more sensitive to certain risk factors than females. These perspectives explain why males are more likely to engage in crime and antisocial behavior than females, but there remain at least two important questions regarding the intersection of gender and crime: (1) are biological, psychological, and sociological risk factors important to female offending, especially the increase in antisocial behavior during adolescence, and (2) why do females typically choose crimes that are covert and social in nature rather than overt? Both questions are addressed in the subsequent sections.

Explaining Females' Antisocial Behavior

Similar to the research on males, studies have also shown that a range of factors are relevant to the etiology of female antisocial behavior. Stated differently, genetic, biological, psychological, and sociological factors may explain why some females engage in high levels of antisocial behavior and other females do not (i.e., they help to account for *within-group* differences among women). It is important to recognize that these risk factors often work together to influence behavior and that the relevance of some factors (e.g., genetics) may wax and wane as females move through the life course.

Genetic Factors

Until recently, few criminologists believed that genetic factors were important for explaining variation in delinquent or criminal behavior. This situation has changed, however, with the growing number of studies demonstrating a genetic contribution to delinquent and criminal involvement. A number of these studies have looked specifically at females and have shown that the average heritability estimate for antisocial behavior is between 40% and 50%. Others have suggested that genetic factors may be less important to the etiology of antisocial behavior as females move from early adolescence into adulthood (Boisvert, Vaske, Wright, & Knopik, 2012; Hicks et al., 2007; Wang, Niv, Tuvblad, Raine, & Baker, 2013), with environmental factors (e.g., peers, romantic partners) playing a greater role in antisocial behavior during late adolescence and early adulthood. (The importance of romantic partners and peers in female adolescent antisocial behavior will be discussed later in the chapter.) Also, research indicates that genetic factors may explain less variation in alcohol and drug use than in other measures of antisocial behavior for females (Dick et al., 2009; Hicks et al., 2007; Knopik, Heath, Bucholz, Madden, & Waldron, 2009). Despite these caveats, genetic factors seem to be important for understanding why some females are more likely to engage in antisocial behavior than others.

Genetic factors may be relevant for female antisocial behavior, but the research on *which* specific genetic factors are of causal importance is less conclusive. The majority of the current research examines genetic factors related to the dopamine, serotonin, and neurotransmitter enzyme systems (e.g., MAOA). For instance, investigations of the National Longitudinal Study of Adolescent Health sample have revealed that: (1) variants in the dopamine transporter *DAT1* and in the serotonin transporter *5HTTLPR* genes were related to alcohol abuse in adulthood for females; (2) adulthood marijuana use was higher among females with the 7R allele of the *DRD4* gene; (3) the TaqIA polymorphism was associated with violent delinquency in females; and (4) property offending was higher among females with the low/low variant of the *MAOA* gene than among females with the high/high variant (DeLisi, Beaver, Vaughn, & Wright, 2009; Vaske, 2011; Vaske, Beaver, Wright, Boisvert, & Schnupp, 2009). Other studies have also found that the low/low genotype of the *MAOA* gene is associated with higher levels of conduct disorder, stealing, vandalism, and overall offending in adolescent and adult females (Prom-Wormley et al., 2009; Sjöberg et al., 2007). Although a number of studies identify the low-activity allele as the risk-conferring variant of the *MAOA* gene, some researchers have found that the high-activity variant is associated with alcohol problems among females in adolescence and adulthood (Gokturk et al., 2008; Nilsson, Wargelius, Sjöberg, Leppert, & Oreland, 2008). Similar issues arise when considering the associations between maladaptive behaviors and variants in the *DAT1* and *5HTTLPR* genes (Gelernter, Kranzler, Coccaro, Siever, & New, 1998; Vaske et al., 2011). It appears that specific genes are important for antisocial behavior among females, but the research is inconclusive on which variant within the genetic factor is problematic. One explanation for these mixed results is that a particular variant (i.e., the low-activity allele of *MAOA*) may be important for certain behaviors, such as covert behaviors, whereas the other variant (i.e., the high-activity allele) is related to different behaviors (e.g., alcohol use). That is, both variants may be risk conferring, but they may increase risk for different behaviors.

Another explanation for these mixed results is that the genetic factor may lead to antisocial behavior only when it is paired with particular environments. This phenomenon, known as a gene–environment interaction, states that the effect of a genetic factor on antisocial behavior is contingent on the type of environment a person is in (and vice versa). For instance, a host of studies have found that genetic variants increase the risk of antisocial behavior among females who experience childhood abuse, but the same variants do not lead to higher levels of antisocial behavior among females who report no childhood abuse (Vaske, 2011; Widom & Brzustowicz, 2006). Thus, it is the exposure to both genetic and environmental risks (i.e., dual hazards) that promotes antisocial behavior, whereas exposure to only one risk factor may not significantly increase the likelihood of antisocial behavior.

Gene–environment interactions occur when environmental factors exacerbate the effects of genetic risks. There is another way, however, that biological and social factors work together to promote offending: gene–environment correlations. A gene–environment correlation is described as when genetic propensities increase the likelihood that an individual will experience a particular environment. That is, a parent's genetics may influence his or her parenting behaviors, or people's genetics may impact how they view the world and cause them to select themselves into environments that are most consistent with their personality. An example of a gene–environment correlation comes from Comings, Muhleman, Johnson, and MacMurray (2002). They found that a variant in the androgen receptor gene was linked to males' impulsivity and number of sexual partners, as well as to father abandonment and early menarche among females. The authors concluded that father abandonment may correlate with early menarche for females because the androgen receptor gene causes both risky and promiscuous behaviors for fathers and the onset of early menarche among daughters.

The above literature shows that genetic factors are important for antisocial behavior for females, yet genetic factors do not work alone to increase risk. Instead, genetic variants often combine with environmental factors in a variety of ways to influence females' behavior. The next section expands on the interplay of environment and biology to describe how early childhood environments may influence biological and psychological functioning and ultimately lead to antisocial behavior for females.

Early Childhood Environments

Terrie Moffitt and Avshalom Caspi's work on life course–persistent offenders has shed light onto the early childhood risk factors for persistent antisocial behavior among females. In their study of youths from birth to adulthood, they found that life-course offending among females was linked to several early childhood risk factors, including harsh discipline, inconsistent discipline, family conflict, undercontrolled temperament, and poor receptive vocabulary at age 3 (Moffitt & Caspi, 2001). One explanation for these effects is a transactional model where parents and children influence each others' behavior. For instance, difficult children—those who are continually fussy, noncompliant, and coercive—may evoke negative responses from their parents, and these negative parental responses in turn exacerbate their child's problem behavior. Indeed, some evidence exists that supports the existence of this cycle of negative child–parent interaction (Jaffee et al., 2004). Thus, experimental and observational studies show that defiant children can elicit verbal and physical discipline from parents (↑ youth defiance, ↑ physical discipline), whereas decreases in youths' problematic behavior (either through pharmacological or through behavioral interventions) result in fewer instances of harsh discipline from parents (↓ youth defiance, ↓ physical discipline) (Lytton, 1990). Furthermore, parents may respond more rapidly and with more concern to antisocial behavior among girls than among boys (Kerr, Stattin, & Burk, 2010). Gender norms may shape how parents perceive their child's antisocial behavior. That is, parents may worry more if they observe their daughter engaging in antisocial behavior based on the belief that she will place herself in a risky situation that she cannot control (e.g., be more vulnerable to physical or sexual abuse) or that her early misbehavior is more likely lead to later antisocial behavior (e.g., the belief that "boys will be boys" and thus that some trouble is "normal" for them). This is merely speculation, but it may explain the relationship between parenting and problematic behavior among girls.

Although the transactional model assumes that there is a reciprocal relationship between parents' and girls' behavior, there are other situations where a parent's (or an adult's) behavior has a direct, negative impact on girls' development. These situations often include childhood sexual abuse, physical abuse, and neglect. Numerous studies have shown that childhood maltreatment is related to females' psychological functioning, running away, early sexual behavior, delinquency, violent offending, alcohol problems, substance use, relational aggression, prostitution or sex work, and adulthood offending (Chesney-Lind, 1986; Miller, 1986; Salisbury & VanVoorhis, 2009; Widom, Schuck, & White, 2006; Wilson & Widom, 2010). For example, Chesney-Lind and Shelden's (1998) ethnographic study of juvenile girls revealed that 100% of the delinquent girls reported childhood sexual or physical abuse. Studies using a variety of methodologies (i.e., matched control, prospective, and meta-analyses) have consistently found that females who are maltreated exhibit antisocial behaviors in adolescence and adulthood (Hubbard & Pratt, 2002; Widom & Maxfield, 2001). Various pathways linking these behaviors together have been proposed, but the basic hypothesis is as follows: childhood maltreatment → psychological functioning/attitudes → early aggression/running away/substance use/early onset of sexual behavior → offending or sex work.

Social science research has clearly articulated the psychological and behavioral consequences of childhood maltreatment, but less discussion has been devoted to the neurobiological consequences of abuse and neglect. There are reasons to believe, however, that childhood abuse increases the likelihood of psychological and behavioral problems because abuse sets in motion a series of neurobiological changes. Studies from neuroscience and biopsychiatry have shown that childhood abuse and neglect can have far-reaching effects on biological functioning, all the way to changing how an individual's genes are expressed. For example, research has revealed that the expression of glucocorticoid and estrogen receptor genes in the hippocampus and hypothalamus (respectively) is inhibited among those who experience neglect or physical abuse during early childhood (Champagne et al., 2006; Weaver et al., 2004). The glucocorticoid and estrogen receptor genes code for neurohormones that are involved in regulating a person's stress response and increasing social bonding. Thus changes in the expression of these genes may be part of the explanation for why we see higher levels of stress reactivity, anxiety disorders, depression, and weak or inconsistent social attachments among abused females.

Childhood abuse can also influence other biological systems in females, such as triggering an early onset of puberty and menarche (Fishbein, Miller, Winn, & Dakof, 2009). Andersen and Teicher's (2009) review of the empirical evidence shows that abused offspring often have higher levels of arousal or reward-related chemicals in the brain (i.e., corticotropin-releasing hormone, adrenocorticotropic hormone, dopamine) and deficits in many inhibitory neurotransmitters and regions (i.e., benzodiazepine receptors, GABA receptors, serotonin, glucocorticoids, prefrontal cortex). These neurobiological changes may create a state where females are highly sensitive to stress and engage in sensation-seeking or compulsive behaviors, such as drug use or risky sexual behavior. Furthermore, respondents who are separated from or neglected by their mothers during early childhood may be more sensitive to the pleasurable effects of drugs in adolescence than respondents who were not separated from their mothers (Marco, Adriani, Llorente, Laviola, & Viveros, 2009). These findings indicate that abuse may lead to biochemical changes that promote not only the onset but also the continued use of illicit substances. Although abuse often occurs in childhood, many of these changes and behaviors may not emerge until adolescence, indicating that adolescence is a critical period for the expression of risk and the development of antisocial behavior among females.

Adolescence

Relative to childhood and adulthood, research shows that adolescence is a time for increased sensation seeking, greater sensitivity to rewards (especially alcohol, drugs, and peers), higher negative emotional arousal and reactivity, increased salience and time with peers, less supervision and involvement with parents, and more conflict with parents (Schepis, Adinoff, & Rao, 2008; Steinberg, 2008). These findings coincide with the everyday observation that adolescents prefer their peers over their parents, often conflict with parents regarding rules, are moody and unpredictable, and experiment with risky behaviors. What is less obvious, however, are the biological reasons why these processes occur. The answer to this question lies in developmental changes in hormones, neurotransmitters, and brain structures and connections.

Menarche has been emphasized as the main biological impetus for the onset of females' maladaptive and antisocial behavior in adolescence. The actual event of menarche is not hypothesized to increase girls' risk of maladaptive behavior; rather it is the physiological changes leading up to menarche that are believed to influence the brain and behavior. These physiological changes include changes in the distribution of fat, breast development, increase in height, activation of the hypothalamic–pituitary–gonadal axis, and secretion of follicle-stimulating hormone, luteinizing hormone, estrogen, and progesterone. Activation of the hypothalamic–pituitary–gonadal axis and increases in pubertal hormones have been linked to decreases in gray-matter density in the frontal lobe, parietal lobe, and parahippocampal gyri in females (Lenroot & Giedd, 2010; Peper et al., 2009). Thus, the physiological events of puberty may lead to changes in the brain and perhaps influence how girls think, feel, and behave.

Indeed, there is some evidence that menarche may have an impact on girls' psychological functioning and behavior. Among girls within the United States, the average age for menarche is 12 to 13 (Cairns & Cairns, 1994). Around these ages, there begins to be a decrease in the gender gap for delinquent behavior and an increase among females in a host of psychological and sociological risk factors. Research has shown that the onset of puberty and menarche in girls often results in significant increases in depressive symptoms (Nolen-Hoeksema & Girgus, 1994), sensation or excitement seeking, feelings of wanting to be part of a social group (Forbes & Dahl, 2010), conflict with parents, and association with older peers, deviant peers, and romantic partners (Haynie, 2003; Westling, Andrews, Hampson, & Peterson, 2008). The culmination of these factors creates a situation where females are experiencing new emotional or psychological needs, and they enter into their social environment to fulfill their needs. This environment is often characterized by lower levels of parental supervision, greater association with peers and romantic partners, and a greater salience of peers and romantic partners. For example, female participants of ethnographic studies have said that they began engaging in antisocial behavior during adolescence because "The shoplifting was for the excitement. . . . I got a lot of attention from these friends" (pp. 73–74), "I wanted to be a part of it, you know. I wanted to be accepted, to be part of a crowd" (p. 77), and there was "a gradual replacement of prosocial peers with delinquent ones that occurred over a 1–2 year period of time, during the middle stages of adolescence" (p. 73) (Baskin & Sommers, 1998). Together, these pieces of evidence show that biological, psychological, and sociological risk factors converge to "push" and "pull" females toward antisocial behavior in adolescence.

In addition to menarche, a number of other biopsychosocial changes that occur during adolescence increase the risk of antisocial behavior for females (and males). One of these changes is alterations in the reward-processing circuits, whereby adolescents become more sensitive to rewards. For instance, studies have shown that adolescents exhibit higher levels of activity in the nucleus accumbens—a brain area responsible for anticipating and evaluating reward—during a rewarding task than children and adults (Galvan et al., 2006). The increased blood flow in the nucleus accumbens may be exacerbated by increased dopamine activity and a greater density of dopamine receptors in the striatum and nucleus accumbens during adolescence relative to childhood and adulthood (Andersen, Rutstein, Benzo, Hostetter, & Teicher, 1997; Andersen & Teicher, 2000; Schepis et al., 2008). These changes in the brain regions and neurotransmitters that are involved in reward processing may correspond to adolescent females experiencing greater pleasure from risky behaviors and drug use at this stage of development.

Changes in the brain may also explain why peers become very important to youths during adolescence. In particular, oxytocin—the hormone responsible for social bonding—increases during adolescence (Steinberg, 2008). Increases in the chemicals for social bonding, coupled with youth's greater involvement with peers and romantic partners, may explain the salience of peers and romantic relationships during adolescence. The brain may also be changing in ways that make adolescents sensitive to their peers' approval and rejection. Studies have shown that agreement with peers and acceptance by peers activates the reward systems of the brain for adolescents more so than for adults. Furthermore, disagreement with peers and peer rejection activate youths' pain centers (Berns, Capra, More, & Noussair, 2010; Campbell-Meiklejohn, Bach, Roepstorff, Dolan, & Frith, 2010). Given youth's greater sensitivity to reward, it is understandable why adolescents value their peers' and partners' approval more so than children or adults.

Research has highlighted the effects of peers and romantic partners on antisocial behavior for females. First, opposite-sex peers appear to play a significant role in the onset and continuation of delinquency among females. A number of studies have shown that, as females move into adolescence, their peer groups become more mixed sex than same sex (Cairns & Cairns, 1994) and that mixed-sex peer groups are associated with higher levels of property and violent delinquency for females (Haynie, Steffensmeier, & Bell, 2007; McCarthy, Felmlee, & Hagan, 2004). For example, adolescent girls have reported that they were more likely to be in a group of males or in a mixed-sex group when they got into trouble than in a group that consisted solely of girls (Giordano, 1978). Antisocial male peers may increase females' involvement in delinquency by merely suggesting involvement in the crime (i.e., instigation), more forcefully using peer pressure (through ridicule or demands), exposing females to opportunities for delinquency, or providing reinforcement for engaging in antisocial behavior (Alarid, Marquart, Burton, Cullen, & Cuvelier, 1996; Warr, 1996). Furthermore, it is likely that females' involvement with opposite-sex peers, especially those who are engaging in antisocial behavior, increases conflict between girls and their parents, thus further eroding parents' social control during adolescence. Parents may have less concern about male peers when girls are in middle childhood, but once girls move into adolescence, opposite-sex peers may be seen as a risk factor for deviance and risky sexual behavior. Indeed, there is some evidence that opposite-sex peers may have a particularly strong impact on delinquency for females once they reach puberty (Caspi, Lynam, Moffitt, & Silva, 1993).

Second, antisocial romantic partners may also contribute to females' delinquency in adolescence. For instance, Haynie, Giordano, Manning, and Longmore (2005) found that adolescent females with delinquent romantic partners engaged in higher levels of minor delinquency (i.e., drinking, smoking, fighting, truancy) than adolescent females with nondelinquent partners. Similar to peer influences, antisocial romantic partners may increase the likelihood of deviance for girls by introducing them to criminal behavior, providing opportunities for deviance, and reinforcing their antisocial behavior. Yet, the quality of a romantic relationship may have unique effects on girls' antisocial behavior above and beyond the effects of social learning factors. For example, Simons, Stewart, Gordon, Conger, and Elder (2002) found that the quality of the romantic relationship was lower among females who had a deviant romantic partner. In turn, a relationship characterized by a lack of warmth, communication, and responsiveness increased females' likelihood of engaging in criminal behavior. Poor romantic relationships could promote antisocial behavior because deviant partners are not serving as a social control against antisocial behavior, females are attempting to cope with relationship problems through drug use, or females may be actively using violence to sanction their partners for cheating or other forms of misbehavior (Giordano, 2009). The role of romantic relationships may also become more salient as females move into early adulthood and romantic relationships begin to replace the importance of peers. These romantic relationships may then promote continuity in antisocial behavior. Moffitt et al. (2001) found that antisocial females who selected antisocial mates in early adulthood experienced significant increases in their level of offending from adolescence into adulthood. In contrast, the level of self-reported crime remained unchanged from adolescence to adulthood for females who did not select an antisocial mate. Thus, antisocial romantic partners may introduce females to delinquency as well as promote stability and deeper involvement in offending.

Overall, the above evidence suggests that females' antisocial behavior is a function of genetic, biological, psychological, and sociological factors across the life course. These risk factors may have reciprocal effects on one another, as well as exacerbate the effects of each other. Furthermore, it is important to consider these risk factors in a longitudinal context. Some risk factors, such as genetics, appear to have a stronger impact on antisocial behavior in childhood and early adolescence than in adulthood. Other risk factors (i.e., abuse) may emerge during childhood, but do not impact antisocial behavior until adolescence or adulthood, whereas additional sets of factors (i.e., menarche, biological changes, opposite-sex peers, romantic partners) emerge during adolescence and influence behavior during adolescence and perhaps adulthood. There has been some theorizing on changes in biopsychosocial factors and changes in antisocial behavior among females in a longitudinal framework (Javdani, Sadeh, & Verona, 2011), but currently there is little empirical investigation in this area.

Females' Choice of Antisocial Behaviors

Official, victim, and self-report surveys show that the gender gap is widest for behaviors that involve physical confrontation or can harm others, whereas males and females are more similar for behaviors that do not directly harm others and are "victimless" in nature. For example, analysis of data from the National Longitudinal Survey of Youth 1979: Children and Young Adults shows that the gender gap in physical aggression or violent delinquency (the male:female odds ratio) increases from ages 10–12 (odds ratio = 1.67) to ages 16–18 (odds ratio = 2.22) (see Table 3.1). In contrast, the gender difference in theft and alcohol use disappears as youths move from ages 10–12 to 12–16 (see Table 3.1). These data show that the gender gap in general antisocial behavior may narrow during adolescence because females increase their involvement in property and substance-use offenses, but not in violent offenses. Furthermore, when females do engage in violent behavior, it is likely to be against those who are close to the female (i.e., a partner or child) or in a social setting (Snell & Morton, 1994). This leads to the question: Why are females just as likely to choose property and drug offending as males, but less likely to choose violent offending?

Little to no research exists on this topic, but it is possible to infer an explanation based on the nature of the crimes and the research on gender and aggression. First, property and drug crimes tend to be covert and have low visibility, which means that only a few people (if any) may know that the perpetrator committed the offense. By contrast, violent crimes cannot be easily concealed; the offenses involve direct contact and thus are obvious to the victim (and perhaps to others). Furthermore, compared to males, females may be generally less likely to physically assault others because they (1) anticipate that they will feel guilt and anxiety from their physical aggression, (2) perceive that they will cause more harm to the victim, and (3) are

TABLE 3.1   **Prevalence of Physical Aggression, Theft, and Alcohol Use from Ages 10 to 18 for Males and Females**

HURT SOMEONE BADLY ENOUGH TO NEED A DOCTOR	AGE 10	AGE 12	AGE 14	AGE 16
Male	26.50%*	25.00%*	18.70%*	15.10%*
Female	16.30%	14.00%	9.50%	6.80%
Odds ratio of male:female	1.62	1.81	1.97	2.22
THEFT	AGE 10	AGE 12	AGE 14	AGE 16
Male	13.90%*	10.30%	11.00%	11.70%*
Female	7.60%	9.50%	9.70%	5.00%
Odds ratio of male:female	1.83	1.08	1.09	2.34
GOTTEN DRUNK	AGE 10	AGE 12	AGE 14	AGE 16
Male	6.10%*	9.20%	19.60%	30.90%
Female	2.70%	8.60%	18.10%	25.20%
Odds ratio of male:female	2.26	1.06	1.08	1.22

*Significant difference ($p \leq .05$) between male and female percentages.

more likely to believe that the victim will retaliate, thus placing themselves in danger (Eagly & Steffen, 1986). A study of 120 youths in grades 4 through 7 showed that girls were more likely to feel guilty or upset over behaving aggressively toward a classmate compared to boys, and they expected more disapproval from their parents for their aggressive behavior (Perry, Perry, & Weiss, 1989). Similarly, even if females experience more anger or emotional response to provocation than males, they are likely not to react aggressively toward the provoker for fear of retaliation or injury (Winstok, 2007). These perceived internal and external negative consequences may cause females to exclude physical aggression from their list of possible antisocial behaviors. This explanation is consistent with Anne Campbell's (1999) staying-alive hypothesis, which states that evolutionary forces have shaped females to be more fearful of risky situations, especially those that may lessen their chances of survival.

If females are frustrated or upset by someone, they may be much more likely first to use indirect social aggression (e.g., gossiping, eye rolling, or "*the look*") or to covertly steal something (e.g., boyfriend, material goods) from that person. These indirect methods, however, often escalate the situation and could ultimately lead to physical violence. For example, Miller and Mullins's (2006) ethnographic study of 35 African American adolescent girls revealed that the most common reasons for physical violence between girls were girls spreading rumors about each other, stealing one another's boyfriends, perceived signs of disrespect (e.g., eye rolling, staring), and insulting one's appearance. Other ethnographic research suggests that the social context, social norms, and personal identity dictate what is valued and how physical violence is instigated and played out. For instance, a girl may fight if others indicate that she does not fit the stereotype of femininity, if she wants to portray herself as tough or a "bitch," if she is bored and the culture allows fighting as one way to have fun, or as a way to cope with victimization within the home (Morash & Chesney-Lind, 2009). The motivation to resort to physical violence may also be heightened by the presence of others. As Baskin and Sommers (1998) explain, retaliation in the presence of third parties allows females to "save face" and "is an attempt to regulate other people's knowledge and opinions about oneself and one's friends" (p. 117); thus, physical violence is a way to control their identity and others' perceptions.

Adult female offenders may also engage in violence and property offending as a way to support a drug addiction. Studies of adult female robbers report that females may initially begin robbing people for fun or to get material goods, but then females may use robbery as a way to obtain drugs (Baskin & Sommers, 1998; Miller, 1998). As Denise, a female offender from Baskin and Sommers' study, states:

> So, yeah, it started as fun. But then I got into drugs and I did it to get money to party and get high. So it then became both—fun and drug money. But then I got a habit and I did robberies in order to take care of my habit—for nothing else. (p. 105)

A study of 422 burglars from North Carolina, Kentucky, and Ohio also showed that "money for drugs" was the top reason for committing a burglary for adult females, whereas males reported that their top reason for committing burglaries was to get money (Blevins, Kuhns, & Lee, 2012). Together, these studies reveal that women who are entrenched in criminal lifestyles may use violence and property offending as a means to acquire drugs.

In sum, the above literature shows that females may be less likely to use violence because they expect to feel guiltier over their violent behavior and are more afraid of retaliation or injury than males. Property and drug offending may be less likely to be detected, and thus a girl's sense of identity or reputation may be left undamaged. Also, females are more sensitive to punishment and have a greater commitment to school and prosocial institutions. Thus, engaging in antisocial behavior, especially violent behavior, may threaten those connections and cause females to feel guilty. This is not always the case, however. Females may engage in violent behavior when they feel provoked and when they perceive that other methods of dealing with a situation have failed; thus, they may engage in violence when they feel like they have been "pushed to their limits." As the ethnographic research suggests, females may first deal with conflict and problems through covert methods, but as the situation escalates, they are likely to resort to physical violence, especially if one's culture or identity supports such an action.

Conclusion

The current chapter reviewed the biological, psychological, and sociological explanations for the gender gap in antisocial behavior, as well as biosocial explanations for why females may engage in antisocial behavior. The biosocial perspective of female offending is a unique area of inquiry that a growing number of scholars are beginning to investigate, although it has traditionally received little attention from mainstream criminology. Notably, there are several compelling reasons why the biosocial perspective should be considered when scholars seek to explain variation in antisocial behavior.

First, the biosocial perspective is a holistic approach that recognizes that our brains and physiology influence how we perceive the world, the choices we make, and how behaviors are played out in a social context. To ignore the impact of our brains in our decisions is to ignore a significant part of the explanation for why people behave badly. Similarly, studying human genetics and neurobiology provides insight into the complexity of our decision making, the irrationality of our thinking and decisions, and the automatic nature of many unconscious thoughts and processes that foster maladaptive behavior.

Second, the promise of biosocial criminology is that it can help researchers understand how and why environmental risk factors impact behavior. Investigators can address questions regarding how people learn a certain behavior, why peers are such salient role models during adolescence, why some people always end up in high-risk situations, how stressful life events and weak social bonds lead to psychological changes and antisocial behavior, and whether there are gender differences in each of these processes. Thus, biosocial criminology does not seek to reduce antisocial behavior or gender differences merely to brains, genes, or biological traits. Instead, it acts to complement traditional criminological theory by helping us to better understand the multisystemic processes that produce deviant behavior within both genders and to better understand the gender differences (or similarities) in antisocial behavior.

The current chapter reviewed a biosocial perspective on gender and antisocial behavior, but a number of questions remain unanswered regarding the intersection of gender and offending. For example, if the gender gap is partially explained by males' increased exposure to risk factors, why are males exposed to more risk than females? Is this differential exposure a product of evolutionary forces as early theorists hypothesized (see Thomas, 1903)? Also, why do females increase their involvement in covert antisocial behaviors during adolescence but not in overt antisocial behaviors? If females are less likely to engage in violent behaviors because of greater guilt and fear of retaliation than males, does this mean that females experience little guilt and fear of retaliation for property and drug crimes? Is this pattern of offending and set of feelings consistent across ethnic groups and social classes? Do these psychological processes explain the changes in property and drug offending for females in adolescence and early adulthood? If so, what explains changes in the psychological processes: genetics, biology, environment, or all three?

There are a host of additional questions to be answered regarding gender and antisocial behavior, especially as it pertains to the biosocial perspective of crime. Researchers such as Anne Campbell and others have advanced the biosocial explanations of female offending, but much remains to be done. It is our hope that readers of this volume and this chapter will walk away with questions they can research and contribute to the development of a biosocial perspective of female offending.

References

Agnew, R. (2009). The contribution of "mainstream" theories to the explanation of female delinquency. In M. Zahn (Ed.), *The delinquent girl* (pp. 7–29). Philadelphia, PA: Temple University Press.

Alarid, L. F., Burton, V. S., Jr., & Cullen, F. T. (2000). Gender and crime among felony offenders: Assessing the generality of social control and differential association theories. *Journal of Research in Crime and Delinquency, 37*, 171–199.

Alarid, L. F., Marquart, J. W., Burton, V. S., Jr., Cullen, F. T., & Cuvelier, S. J. (1996). Women's roles in serious offenses: A study of adult felons. *Justice Quarterly, 13*, 431–454.

Andersen, S. L., Rutstein, M., Benzo, J. M., Hostetter, J. C., & Teicher, M. H. (1997). Sex differences in dopamine receptor overproduction and elimination. *NeuroReport, 8*, 1495–1498.

Andersen, S. L., & Teicher, M. H. (2000). Sex differences in dopamine receptors and their relevance to ADHD. *Neuroscience and Biobehavioral Reviews, 24*(1), 137–141.

Andersen, S. L., & Teicher, M. H. (2009). Desperately driven and no brakes: Developmental stress exposure and subsequent risk for substance abuse. *Neuroscience and Biobehavioral Reviews, 33*, 516–524.

Bainbridge, D. (2003). *The X in sex*. Cambridge, MA: Harvard University Press.

Baskin, D. R., & Sommers, I. B. (1998). *Casualties of community disorder: Women's careers in violent crime*. Boulder, CO: Westview Press.

Berns, G. S., Capra, C. M., Moore, S., & Noussair, C. (2010). Neural mechanisms of the influence of popularity on adolescent ratings of music. *Neuroimage, 49*, 2687–2696.

Blevins, K. R., Kuhns, J. B., & Lee, S. Z. (2012). *Understanding decisions to burglarize from the offender's perspective*. Charlotte: University of North Carolina at Charlotte, Department of Criminal Justice and Criminology.

Boisvert, D., Vaske, J., Wright, J. P., & Knopik, V. (2012). Sex differences in criminal behavior: A genetic analysis. *Journal of Contemporary Criminal Justice, 28*, 293–313.

Broidy, L., & Agnew, R. (1997). Gender and crime: A general strain theory perspective. *Journal of Research in Crime and Delinquency, 34*, 275–306.

Brunner, H. G., Nelen, M. R., van Zandvoort, P., Abeling, N. G., van Gennip, A. H., Wolters, E. C., . . . & van Oost, B. A. (1993). X-linked borderline mental retardation with prominent behavioral disturbance: Phenotype, genetic localization, and evidence for disturbed monoamine metabolism. *American Journal of Human Genetics, 52*, 1032–1039.

Burton, V. S., Jr., Cullen, F. T., Evans, T. D., Alarid, L. F., & Dunaway, R. G. (1998). Gender, self-control, and crime. *Journal of Research in Crime and Delinquency, 35*(2), 123–147.

Cairns, R. B., & Cairns, B. D. (1994). *Lifelines and risks: Paths of youth in our times*. Cambridge, UK: Cambridge University Press.

Campbell, A. (1999). Staying alive: Evolution, culture, and women's intra-sexual aggression. *Behavioral and Brain Sciences, 22*, 203–214.

Campbell-Meiklejohn, D. K., Bach, D. R., Roepstorff, A., Dolan, R. J., & Frith, C. D. (2010). How the opinion of others affects our valuation of objects. *Current Biology, 20*, 1165–1170.

Caspi, A., Lynam, D., Moffitt, T. E., & Silva, P. A. (1993). Unraveling girls' delinquency: Biological, dispositional, and contextual contributions to adolescent misbehavior. *Developmental Psychology, 29*, 19–30.

Champagne, F. A., Weaver, I. C. G., Diorio, J., Dymov, S., Szyf, M., & Meaney, M. J. (2006). Maternal care associated with methylation of the estrogen receptor-α1b promoter and estrogen receptor-α expression in the medial preoptic area of female offspring. *Endocrinology, 147*, 2909–2915.

Chesney-Lind, M. (1986). "Women and crime": The female offender. *Signs, 12*, 78–96.

Chesney-Lind, M., & Shelden, R. G. (1998). *Girls, delinquency, and juvenile justice*. Belmont, CA: Wadsworth.

Christie, K. A., Burke, J. D., Regier, D. A., Rae, D. S., Boyd, J. H., & Locke, B. Z. (1988). Epidemiologic evidence for early onset of mental disorders and higher risk of drug abuse in young adults. *American Journal of Psychiatry, 145*, 971–975.

Comings, D. E., Muhleman, D., Johnson, J. P., & MacMurray, J. P. (2002). Parent–daughter transmission of the androgen receptor gene as an explanation of the effect of father absence on age of menarche. *Child Development, 73*, 1046–1051.

Cowie, J., Cowie, V. A., & Slater, E. (1968). *Delinquency in girls*. London, UK: Heinemann.

Daigle, L. E., Cullen, F. T., & Wright, J. P. (2007). Gender differences in the predictors of juvenile delinquency. *Youth Violence and Juvenile Justice, 5*, 254–286.

DeLisi, M., Beaver, K. M., Vaughn, M. G., & Wright, J. P. (2009). All in the family: Gene × environment interaction between *DRD2* and criminal father is associated with five antisocial phenotypes. *Criminal Justice and Behavior, 36*, 1187–1197.

Dick, D. M., Bernard, M., Aliev, F., Viken, R., Pulkkinen, L., Kaprio, J., & Rose, R. J. (2009). The role of socioregional factors in moderating genetic influences on early adolescent behavior problems and alcohol use. *Alcoholism: Clinical and Experimental Research, 33*, 1739–1748.

Eagly, A. H., & Steffen, V. J. (1986). Gender and aggressive behavior: A meta-analytic review of the social psychological literature. *Psychological Bulletin, 100*, 309–330.

Fishbein, D., Miller, S., Winn, D. M., & Dakof, G. (2009). Biopsychological factors, gender, and delinquency. In M. Zahn (Ed.), *The delinquent girl* (pp. 84–106). Philadelphia, PA: Temple University Press.

Forbes, E. E., & Dahl, R. E. (2010). Pubertal development and behavior: Hormonal activation of social and motivational tendencies. *Brain and Cognition, 72*, 66–72.

Galvan, A., Hare, T. A., Parra, C. E., Penn, J., Voss, H., Glover, G., & Casey, B. J. (2006). Earlier development of the accumbens relative to orbitofrontal cortex might underlie risk-taking behavior in adolescents. *Journal of Neuroscience, 26*, 6885–6892.

Gaub, M., & Carlson, C. L. (1997). Gender differences in ADHD: A meta-analysis and critical review. *Journal of the American Academy of Child and Adolescent Psychiatry, 36*, 1036–1045.

Gelernter, J., Kranzler, H., Coccaro, E. F., Siever, L. J., & New, A. S. (1998). Serotonin transporter protein gene polymorphism and personality measures in African American and European American subjects. *American Journal of Psychiatry, 155,* 1332–1338.

Gershon, J., & Gershon, J. (2002). A meta-analytic review of gender differences in ADHD. *Journal of Attention Disorders, 5,* 143–154.

Giordano, P. C. (1978). Girls, guys and gangs: The changing social context of female delinquency. *Journal of Criminal Law and Criminology, 69,* 126–132.

Giordano, P. C. (2009). Peer influences on girls' delinquency. In M. Zahn (Ed.), *The delinquent girl* (pp. 127–145). Philadelphia, PA: Temple University Press.

Glueck, S., & Glueck, E. T. (1934). *500 delinquent women.* New York, NY: Knopf.

Gokturk, C., Schultze, S., Nilsson, K. W., von Knorring, L., Oreland, L., & Hallman, J. (2008). Serotonin transporter (5-HTTLPR) and monoamine oxidase (MAOA) promoter polymorphisms in women with severe alcoholism. *Archives of Women's Mental Health, 11,* 347–355.

Gottfredson, M. R., & Hirschi, T. (1990). *A general theory of crime.* Stanford, CA: Stanford University Press.

Gur, R. C., Gunning-Dixon, F., Bilker, W. B., & Gur, R. E. (2002). Sex differences in temporo-limbic and frontal brain volumes of healthy adults. *Cerebral Cortex, 12,* 998–1003.

Haynie, D. L. (2003). Contexts of risk? Explaining the link between girls' pubertal development and their delinquency involvement. *Social Forces, 82,* 355–397.

Haynie, D. L., Giordano, P. C., Manning, W. D., & Longmore, M. A. (2005). Adolescent romantic relationships and delinquency involvement. *Criminology, 43,* 177–210.

Haynie, D. L., Steffensmeier, D., & Bell, K. E. (2007). Gender and serious violence: Untangling the role of friendship sex composition and peer violence. *Youth Violence and Juvenile Justice, 5,* 235–253.

Heimer, K., & De Coster, S. D. (1999). The gendering of violent delinquency. *Criminology, 37,* 277–318.

Hicks, B. M., Blonigen, D. M., Kramer, M. D., Krueger, R. F., Patrick, C. J., Iacono, W. G., & McGue, M. (2007). Gender differences and developmental change in externalizing disorders from late adolescence to early adulthood: A longitudinal twin study. *Journal of Abnormal Psychology, 116,* 433–447.

Hubbard, D. J., & Pratt, T. C. (2002). A meta-analysis of the predictors of delinquency among girls. *Journal of Offender Rehabilitation, 34,* 1–14.

Jaffee, S. R., Caspi, A., Moffitt, T. E., Polo-Tomas, M., Price, T. S., & Taylor, A. (2004). The limits of child effects: Evidence for genetically mediated child effects on corporal punishment but not on physical maltreatment. *Developmental Psychology, 40,* 1047–1058.

Javdani, S., Sadeh, N., & Verona, E. (2011). Expanding our lens: Female pathways to antisocial behavior in adolescence and adulthood. *Clinical Psychology Review, 31,* 1324–1348.

Kerr, M., Stattin, H., & Burk, W. J. (2010). A reinterpretation of parental monitoring in longitudinal perspective. *Journal of Research on Adolescence, 20,* 39–64.

Knopik, V. S., Heath, A. C., Bucholz, K. K., Madden, P. A., & Waldron, M. (2009). Genetic and environmental influences on externalizing behavior and alcohol problems in adolescence: A female twin study. *Pharmacology Biochemistry and Behavior, 93,* 313–321.

Krohn, M. D., & Massey, J. L. (1980). Social control and delinquent behavior: An examination of the elements of the social bond. *Sociological Quarterly*, *21*, 529–543.

LaGrange, T. C., & Silverman, R. A. (1999). Low self-control and opportunity: Testing the general theory of crime as an explanation for gender differences in delinquency. *Criminology*, *37*, 41–72.

Lee, T. M. C., Chan, C. C. H., Leung, A. W. S., Fox, P. T., & Gao, J. (2009). Sex related differences in neural activity during risk taking: An fMRI study. *Cerebral Cortex*, *19*, 1303–1312.

Lenroot, R. K., & Giedd, J. N. (2010). Sex differences in the adolescent brain. *Brain and Cognition*, *72*, 46–55.

Loeber, R., Burke, J. D., Lahey, B. B., Winters, A., & Zera, M. (2000). Oppositional defiant and conduct disorder: A review of the past 10 years, part I. *Journal of the American Academy of Child and Adolescent Psychiatry*, *39*, 1468–1484.

Lombroso, C., & Ferrero, G. (2004). *Criminal woman, the prostitute, and the normal woman* (N. H. Rafter & M. Gibson, Trans.). Durham, NC: Duke University Press. (Original published in 1893).

Lytton, H. (1990). Child and parent effects in boys' conduct disorder: A reinterpretation. *Developmental Psychology*, *26*, 683–697.

Marco, E. M., Adriani, W., Llorente, R., Laviola, G., & Viveros, M. P. (2009). Detrimental psychophysiological effects of early maternal deprivation in adolescent and adult rodents: Altered responses to cannabinoid exposure. *Neuroscience and Biobehavioral Reviews*, *33*, 498–507.

Mazerolle, P. (1998). Gender, general strain, and delinquency: An empirical examination. *Justice Quarterly*, *15*, 65–91.

McCarthy, B., Felmlee, D., & Hagan, J. (2004). Girl friends are better: Gender, friends, and crime among school and street youth. *Criminology*, *42*, 805–835.

McGloin, J. M., & Widom, C. S. (2001). Resilience among abused and neglected children grown up. *Development and Psychopathology*, *13*, 1021–1038.

Meyer-Lindenberg, A., Buckholtz, J. W., Kolachana, B., Hariri, A. R., Pezawas, L., Blasi, G., . . . & Weinberger, D. R. (2006). Neural mechanisms of genetic risk for impulsivity and violence in humans. *Proceedings of the National Academy of Sciences*, *103*, 6269–6274.

Miller, E. M. (1986). *Street woman*. Philadelphia, PA: Temple University Press.

Miller, J. (1998). Up it up: Gender and the accomplishment of street robbery. *Criminology*, *36*, 37–66.

Miller, J., & Mullins, C. W. (2006). Stuck up, telling lies, and talking too much: The gendered context of young women's violence. In K. Heimer and C. Kruttschnitt (Eds.), *Gender and crime: Patterns in victimization and offending* (pp. 41–66). New York: New York University Press.

Moffitt, T. E., & Caspi, A. (2001). Childhood predictors differentiate life-course persistent and adolescence-limited antisocial pathways among males and females. *Development and Psychopathology*, *13*, 355–375.

Moffitt, T. E., Caspi, A., Rutter, M., & Silva, P. A. (2001). *Sex differences in antisocial behaviour: Conduct disorder, delinquency, and violence in the Dunedin Longitudinal Study*. New York, NY: Cambridge University Press.

Morash, M., & Chesney-Lind, M. (2009). The context of girls' violence: Peer groups, families, schools, and communities. In M. Zahn (Ed.), *The delinquent girl* (pp. 182–206). Philadelphia, PA: Temple University Press.

Nilsson, K. W., Wargelius, H. L., Sjöberg, R. L., Leppert, J., & Oreland, L. (2008). The *MAO-A* gene, platelet MAO-B activity and psychosocial environment in adolescent female alcohol-related problem behaviour. *Drug and Alcohol Dependence, 93*, 51–62.

Nolen-Hoeksema, S., & Girgus, J. S. (1994). The emergence of gender differences in depression during adolescence. *Psychological Bulletin, 115*, 424–443.

Ostrer, H. (2001). Invited review: Sex-based differences in gene expression. *Journal of Applied Physiology, 91*, 2384–2388.

Peper, J. S., Brouwer, R. M., Schnack, H. G., van Baal, G. C., van Leeuwen, M., van den Berg, S. M., . . . & Hulshoff Pol, H. E. (2009). Sex steroids and brain structure in pubertal boys and girls. *Psychoneuroendocrinology, 34*, 332–342.

Perry, D. G., Perry, L. C., & Weiss, R. J. (1989). Sex differences in the consequences that children anticipate for aggression. *Developmental Psychology, 25*, 312–319.

Prom-Wormley, E. C., Eaves, L. J., Foley, D. L., Gardner, C. O., Archer, K. J., Wormley, B. K., . . . & Silberg, J. L. (2009). Monoamine oxidase A and childhood adversity as risk factors for conduct disorder in females. *Psychological Medicine, 39*, 579–590.

Rutter, M., Caspi, A., & Moffitt, T. E. (2003). Using sex differences in psychopathology to study causal mechanisms: Unifying issues and research strategies. *Journal of Child Psychology and Psychiatry, 44*, 1092–1115.

Salisbury, E. J., & Van Voorhis, P. (2009). Gendered pathways: A quantitative investigation of women probationers' paths to incarceration. *Criminal Justice and Behavior, 36*, 541–566.

Schepis, T. S., Adinoff, B., & Rao, U. (2008). Neurobiological processes in adolescent addictive disorders. *American Journal of Addictions, 17*, 6–23.

Simons, R. L., Stewart, E., Gordon, L. C., Conger, R. D., & Elder, G. H., Jr. (2002). Test of life-course explanations for stability and change in antisocial behavior from adolescence to young adulthood. *Criminology, 40*, 401–434.

Sjöberg, R. L., Ducci, F., Barr, C. S., Newman, T. K., Dell'Osso, L., Virkkunen, M., & Goldman, D. (2008). A non-additive interaction of a functional MAO-A VNTR and testosterone predicts antisocial behavior. *Neuropsychopharmacology, 33*, 425–430.

Sjöberg, R. L., Nilsson, K. W., Wargelius, H. L., Leppert, J., Lindström, L., & Oreland, L. (2007). Adolescent girls and criminal activity: Role of MAOA-LPR genotype and psychosocial factors. *American Journal of Medical Genetics Part B; Neuropsychiatric Genetics, 144*, 159–164.

Smith, D. A., & Paternoster, R. (1987). The gender gap in theories of deviance: Issues and evidence. *Journal of Research in Crime and Delinquency, 24*, 140–172.

Snell, T. L., & Morton, D. C. (1994). *Women in prison.* Washington, DC: U.S. Department of Justice, Bureau of Justice Statistics.

Stanton, S. J., Liening, S. H., & Schultheiss, O. C. (2011). Testosterone is positively associated with risk taking in the Iowa Gambling Task. *Hormones and Behavior, 59*, 252–256.

Steinberg, L. (2008). A social neuroscience perspective on adolescent risk-taking. *Developmental Review, 28*, 78–106.

Thomas, W. I. (1903). *Sex and society: Studies in the social psychology of sex.* New York, NY: Arno Press.

van Goozen, S. H., Fairchild, G., Snoek, H., & Harold, G. T. (2007). The evidence for a neurobiological model of childhood antisocial behavior. *Psychological Bulletin, 133*, 149–182.

Vaske, J. (2011). *Genes and abuse as causes of offending*. El Paso, TX: LFB.

Vaske, J., Beaver, K. M., Wright, J. P., Boisvert, D., & Schnupp, R. (2009). An interaction between DAT1 and having an alcoholic father predicts serious alcohol problems in a sample of males. *Drug and Alcohol Dependence, 104*, 17–22.

Vaske, J., Wright, J. P., Boisvert, D., & Beaver, K. M. (2011). Gender, genetic risk, and criminal behavior. *Psychiatry Research, 185*, 376–381.

Vermeersch, H., T'sjoen, G., Kaufman, J. M., & Vincke, J. (2008). The role of testosterone in aggressive and non-aggressive risk-taking in adolescent boys. *Hormones and Behavior, 53*, 463–471.

Walsh, A. (2011). *Feminist criminology through a biosocial lens*. Durham, NC: Carolina Academic Press.

Wang, P., Niv, S., Tuvblad, C., Raine, A., & Baker, L. A. (2013). The genetic and environmental overlap between aggressive and non-aggressive antisocial behavior in children and adolescents using the self-report delinquency interview (SR-DI). *Journal of Criminal Justice, 41*, 277–284.

Warr, M. (1996). Organization and instigation in delinquent groups. *Criminology, 34*, 11–37.

Weaver, I. C. G., Cervoni, N., Champagne, F. A., D'Alessio, A. C., Sharma, S., Seckl, J. R., . . . Meaney, M. J. (2004). Epigenetic programming by maternal behavior. *Nature Neuroscience, 7*, 847–854.

Werner, E. E., & Smith, R. S. (1982). *Vulnerable, but invincible: A longitudinal study of resilient children and youth*. New York, NY: McGraw–Hill.

Westling, E., Andrews, J. A., Hampson, S. E., & Peterson, M. (2008). Pubertal timing and substance use: The effects of gender, parental monitoring and deviant peers. *Journal of Adolescent Health, 42*, 555–563.

Widom, C. S., & Brzustowicz, L. M. (2006). MAOA and the "cycle of violence": Childhood abuse and neglect, MAOA genotype, and risk for violent and antisocial behavior. *Biological Psychiatry, 60*, 684–689.

Widom, C. S., & Maxfield, M. G. (2001). *An update on the "cycle of violence."* Washington, DC: National Institute of Justice, Research in Brief.

Widom, C. S., Schuck, A. M., & White, H. R. (2006). An examination of pathways from childhood victimization to violence: The role of early aggression and problematic alcohol use. *Violence and Victims, 21*, 675–690.

Wilson, H. W., & Widom, C. S. (2010). The role of youth problem behaviors in the path from child abuse and neglect to prostitution: A prospective examination. *Journal of Research on Adolescence, 20*, 210–236.

Winstok, Z. (2007). Perceptions, emotions, and behavioral decisions in conflicts that escalate to violence. *Motivation and Emotion, 31*, 125–136.

Young, E. A., Korszun, A., Figueiredo, H. F., Banks-Solomon, M., & Herman, J. P. (2008). Sex differences in HPA axis regulation. In J. B. Becker, K. J. Berkley, N. Geary, E. Hampson, J. P. Herman, & E. A. Young (Eds.), *Sex differences in the brain: From genes to behaviour* (pp. 95–105). New York, NY: Oxford University Press.

CHAPTER 4

Life-Course-Persistent Offending

Nicole Leeper Piquero and Alex R. Piquero

Research on female offenders, however, is lacking, and some question whether a comparable group of persistent female offenders exists . . . evidence consistently documents a small but observable group of persistent female offenders whose pathways into and out of offending both mirror and diverge from those of their male counterparts in notable ways. (Goldweber, Broidy, & Cauffman, 2009, p. 205)

The relationship between gender and crime has long been of interest to criminologists. In the late 19th century, Cesare Lombroso published one of the first statements about female offending in the field of criminology, *La donna delinquente, la prostitute e la donna normale* (or *Criminal Woman, the Prostitute, and the Normal Woman*). In it, he argued that the criminal woman was a cunning and dangerous criminal—much more so than the criminal male. Since then, there have been other works, but none has been more groundbreaking and trendsetting than Adler's (1975) *Sisters in Crime* (see also Simon, 1975).

Departing from Lombroso's view that females were innately more pathological than men, Adler viewed the rise in female offending primarily as a result of the women's liberation movement and the opportunities that came along with it. Writing in the early 1970s, during a period of much social change, Adler (1975) noted:

Female delinquency today is a serious social problem not only because of its capacity for social disruption but because it often leads to future adult criminality. Although it is not a new problem, it is far more prevalent and has undergone ominous qualitative changes in recent years. The rapid growth of the juvenile population, the equal-rights movement, changes in laws governing females and juveniles, prolonged education, altered job opportunities, urbanization, industrialization, family fragmentation, and the perennial generation gap contribute to its rapid expansion. With the growing emphasis on competition and individual rights rather than social duties, the increasing stress on affluent goals rather than stable employment or ethical means, the growth of nonproductive leisure, longer postponements of adult responsibility, and greater dependency on peers rather than family for role models, young people have been treated and traumatized by a bewildering variety of often contradictory forces. When we add to this the current tendency for public agencies to manage minor difficulties which would formerly have been handled privately, it is not surprising that female delinquency is growing and changing. (p. 108)

And although there have been many other important theoretical contributions about the origins, nature, and patterning of female delinquency and criminal activity (Colvin & Pauly, 1983; Daly & Chesney-Lind, 1988; Hagan, Gillis, & Simpson, 1985; Messerschmidt, 1993; Simpson, 1989; Zahn, 2009), none of them clashed more with the prevailing view of the time that girls' offending was not of much concern because, after all, "boys collect stamps, girls collect boys" (Cohen, 1955, pp. 142–143).

Using Adler's pioneering work as a springboard, this chapter considers one specific contemporary explanation of female offending, Moffitt's (1993) developmental taxonomy and its specific life-course-persistent (LCP) offending hypothesis. In so doing, we review Moffitt's theory as well as an alternative conception of female offending proposed by Silverthorn and Frick (1999), the empirical research that has accumulated assessing these two theoretical frameworks, and then outline a theoretical and empirical research agenda that continues in the spirit of Adler's call for attention to female offending. Before we do so, we provide some summary observations regarding what is known more generally about the development of offending.

Development of Offending

Although there has long been an interest in comparing officially based arrest trends across gender (Schwartz & Steffensmeier, 2011; Schwartz, Steffensmeier, & Feldmeyer, 2009), there has been much less attention paid toward longitudinal offending patterns across gender, primarily because of the lack of longitudinal data on female offenders and female offending. For the most part, what had been known in criminology about the long-term development of offending has emerged from longitudinal investigations of male offending (see Farrington, Piquero, & Jennings, 2013; Laub & Sampson, 2003; Piquero, Farrington, & Blumstein, 2007). Many of the available analyses of long-term offending patterns uncover important heterogeneity in offending patterns, such that offenders tend to follow offending trajectories that do not necessarily comport with what is routinely demonstrated by the aggregate age–crime curve. That is, some offenders begin offending in late childhood or early adolescence and do not desist in late adolescence—oftentimes continuing well into their 30s and 40s, whereas other offenders begin their offending in late adolescence or early adulthood. Even further, some offenders offend routinely but do so at a very low level (see reviews in Jennings & Reingle, 2012; Piquero, 2008).

As the number of longitudinal studies have increased and researchers have started to pay more attention to gender and included females in their samples and analyses (Baskin & Sommers, 1998; Broidy et al., 2003; D'Unger, Land, & McCall, 2002; Fergusson & Horwood, 2002; Giordano, 2010; Piquero, Brame, & Moffitt, 2005; Tracy & Kempf-Leonard, 1996), there has been a renewed interest in exploring sex differences in antisocial and criminal behavior over the life course. Those longitudinal studies that have tracked female and male offending patterns over the life course tend to indicate that, with some exceptions, the majority of female offenders do not offend at the high-frequency rates that men do, nor is their involvement in offending of long duration (e.g., Piquero et al., 2005).

In part spurred by the purported increase in female offending, interest about female offenders, their offending patterns, and the system's response to their behavior led the Office of Juvenile Justice and Delinquency Prevention to form the Girls Study Group to compare offending trends between males and females, to examine the causes and correlates of female delinquency and offending, and to consider the various justice-oriented, social, and health system responses for such delinquency, as well as the consequences of those responses (Zahn, Hawkins, Chiancone, & Whitworth, 2008). Among the Girls Study Group's most important findings were the following: (1) girls were not necessarily more violent than in previous years (as had been believed) and any purported increase was instead a result of how the juvenile justice system responded to girls' behavior; (2) although some risk factors were gender sensitive, many of the same risk factors were related to delinquency among boys and girls; and (3) there remains a lack of evidence-based research on successful prevention and intervention programming for girls (Zahn et al., 2008, pp. 6–7).

On the heels of the Girls Study Group and its findings, two recent reviews of the literature on persistent female offenders and persistent female offending nicely summarize the scholarly literature on this issue. In their review of the literature on persistent female offenders, Goldweber et al. (2009) conclude that: (1) there is evidence documenting a small group of early-onset female offenders whose offending is chronic and persistent; (2) female offenders tend to become involved in antisocial behavior for many of the same reasons as do male offenders, but there may be some gender-specific differences in the risk factors for females (e.g., adverse interpersonal relationships and early puberty, which opens doors for association with [typically older] male peers) (Haynie & Piquero, 2006); and (3) the consequences of female offending, especially serious female offending and incarceration, are little understood, but no less important, with some consequences being potentially female specific (e.g., mental health issues, child rearing) (see, e.g., Lanctôt, Cernkovich, & Giordano, 2007).

Further, and picking up on some of these themes, Russell and his colleagues' (Russell, Robins, & Odgers, 2014) recent review of how antisocial behavior from childhood to adulthood is patterned across gender revealed three important conclusions: (1) males and females appear to follow similar antisocial and offending pathways, but males are more likely to have offending patterns that are characterized by frequent, diverse, and violent behavior and tend to desist much later than females; (2) sex differences in neuropsychological and social risk factors influence the observed sex differences in antisocial behavior, as males tend to have "more" of the same risk factors than females; and (3) the antisocial and criminal trajectories of females appear to be more similar than different when compared to males, but with the exception that the female trajectories are of a higher magnitude and longer duration—especially when behavior is measured through self-reports as opposed to official records. Much less is known about the correlates that distinguish between unique female offending trajectories, although the few studies that have assessed correlates show that the less-chronic offending of females is, in large part, a result of their faster cognitive and emotional development, their lower levels of neuropsychological deficits, and their stronger prosocial socialization experiences (Russell et al., 2014, p. 4; see also Moffitt, Caspi, Rutter, & Silva, 2001).

With this brief background in hand, we next turn to a review of Moffitt's developmental taxonomy and its explicit LCP offender hypothesis, as well as an alternative theoretical framework offered by Silverthorn and Frick. Importantly, Moffitt's LCP theory was designed to be relevant across genders, with some female-specific nuances, whereas Silverthorn and Frick's perspective was developed primarily for the population of female offenders.

LCP Offender Theories

One of the fundamental facts in criminology concerns the relationship between age and crime. It seems that everywhere, and at all times, criminal activity rises in early adolescence, peaks in late adolescence, and then decreases quickly in early adulthood (Hirschi & Gottfredson, 1983). An important caveat about this pattern, however, is the recognition that this relationship is routinely observed in the aggregate; that is, it is always produced using a cross-sectional time period and summarizes the ages of those individuals involved in crime (typically arrested). Although such depictions are important, it does not readily and always follow that what is true at the aggregate level is also true at the individual level.

Moffitt's Taxonomy of Offending Theory

On this score, the developmental psychologist Terrie Moffitt (1993) hypothesized that this aggregate curve hides variation in the longitudinal patterning of antisocial behavior such that there are two distinct offender typologies underlying the aggregate relationship. The first group, adolescence limited (AL), characterizes the majority of offenders and the majority of offending. According to Moffitt, AL offenders are caught in a "maturity gap," which is a time period in adolescence where persons are biologically advanced (physically resembling adults) but are not yet permitted adult social status and behaviors that come along with being an adult. Faced with a desire for autonomy but an inability to legally engage in adult-like behaviors, similarly situated AL offenders turn to the peer social context around them and engage in adult-like behaviors that they believe offer them adult-like status, such as drug use, promiscuous sexual activity, and theft. Yet, as AL offenders age and enter their early adult years, they are legally permitted many of the behaviors that they once coveted, and desistance from crime is the modal outcome. Only a select few AL offenders persist in criminal activity as a result of being ensnared by some of the possible negative outcomes of their previous delinquent behaviors (e.g., drug addiction, incarceration) (see Hussong, Curran, Moffitt, Caspi, & Carrig, 2004).

The second typology in Moffitt's taxonomy is composed of a small number of persons, and the risk factors and offending careers for these persons are drastically different from those exhibited by AL offenders. Denoted as LCP offenders, these individuals begin their antisocial behavior early in the life course (childhood), continue them throughout adolescence, and then persist into and throughout adulthood. Although the manifestation of their antisocial acts may vary depending upon their age (temper tantrums and lying in childhood, theft and substance use in adolescence, domestic violence and fraud in adulthood), the common themes underlying the nature of LCP offending are involvement in a variety of antisocial acts and an inclusion of person-oriented offenses—neither of which characterizes AL offending. Importantly, and unlike the correlates associated with AL offending, LCP offenders suffer injurious childhoods, which are often left unattended. Specifically, before they exhibit LCP-style antisociality, persons at high risk for becoming LCP offenders are born more often with neuropsychological deficits and into deficient familial and socioeconomic environments that are not equipped with the resources to help them overcome their injurious entry into the world. As a result, and in part because of their antisociality, their behavior negatively influences parental socialization efforts, has the potential to emote harsh discipline upon the child, and hampers the development of self-control. Left uncorrected, their hampered personalities and antisocial lifestyles combine to form a process of "cumulative continuity" and increase the likelihood of failure in a variety of other life domains including failed education, diminished employment, and inadequate interpersonal relationships. Thus, unlike the more positive adulthood envisioned among AL offenders, the likelihood of change among LCP offenders is slim.

In the original statement of her dual taxonomy, Moffitt (1993) did not articulate any gender-specific expectations regarding how males and females would sort into the two offender trajectories. In a subsequent book chapter, she outlined a more specific set of expectations regarding gender and offending. Specifically, Moffitt (1994) noted:

> The crime rate for females is lower than for males [citations omitted]. In this developmental taxonomy, much of the gender difference is attributed to sex differences in the risk factors for *life-course-persistent* antisocial behavior. Little girls are less likely than little boys to encounter all of the putative initial links in the causal chain. Research has shown that girls have lower rates of symptoms of nervous system dysfunction,

difficult temperament, late milestones in verbal and motor development, hyperactivity, learning disabilities, reading failure, and childhood conduct problems [citations omitted]. Thus, the consequent processes of cumulative continuity do not ensue for most girls. Girls lack the personal diathesis elements of the evocative, reactive, and proactive person/environment interactions that initiate and maintain *life-course-persistent* antisocial behavior. *Adolescence-limited* delinquency, on the other hand, is open to girls as well as boys. According to the theory advanced here, girls, like boys, should begin delinquency soon after puberty, to the extent that they (1) have access to antisocial models, and (2) perceive the consequences of delinquency as reinforcing. Girls should partake of *adolescence-limited* delinquency to the extent that they partake of its etiological elements. (p. 39, emphasis in original)

Thus, although Moffitt (1994) hypothesizes that males and females will be found within each of the two offending trajectories, males should be overrepresented among LCP offenders because they have higher (but not necessarily different) levels of LCP-style risk factors (i.e., neuropsychological deficits), whereas AL offending should be similarly open to both males and females virtually equally.

Silverthorn and Frick's Delayed-Onset Pathway Theory

Moffitt's gender-based hypotheses were not equally accepted by the entire academic community. Most notably, Silverthorn and Frick (1999) argued that girls' antisocial behavior does not begin in childhood as Moffitt proffers, but instead develops in adolescence. They propose a "delayed-onset" pathway. This single pathway for girls is similar to Moffitt's early-childhood-originating LCP trajectory in that key risk factors such as family dysfunction and childhood abuse, coupled with individual factors like cognitive or neurological deficits, poor impulse control, and unemotional personality, are present during childhood. However, the pathway differs from the LCP trajectory in arguing that female antisocial behavior begins in—or is delayed until—adolescence largely because females experience a series of protective factors that insulate them until adolescence. Silverthorn and Frick suggest that parental monitoring and socialization to adhere to gender stereotypes, as well as the prosocial experience of elementary school, may help to explain the lack of antisocial behaviors in childhood for girls.

However, the onset of antisocial behavior for girls occurs in adolescence because it coincides with "biological (e.g., hormonal changes associated with puberty) and psychosocial (e.g., less parental monitoring and supervision; greater contact with deviant peers) changes that encourage antisocial behavior in girls with predisposing vulnerabilities (e.g., [Callous-Unemotional traits]; problems in emotional regulation)" (Frick & Viding, 2009, p. 1118). Thus, the key distinction between Silverthorn and Frick's delayed-onset model and Moffitt's dual taxonomy is that for Silverthorn and Frick, adolescent-onset females resemble LCP males in terms of risk factors but do not resemble AL males. There is, then, only one pathway of female antisocial behavior in Silverthorn and Frick's model, an adolescent-onset pathway, the behavior of which is defined by individual and familial risk factors similar to that of a LCP trajectory.

Empirical Research on Gender and LCP Offending

As recently reviewed by Russell et al. (2014), a sizeable number of studies have been carried out on gender differences in longitudinal offending patterns. Because a detailed review of this literature is beyond the scope of this chapter, we focus here on those studies that have specifically assessed Moffitt's LCP hypothesis and Silverthorn and Frick's delayed-onset hypothesis.

One of the first studies to test Moffitt's developmental taxonomy across gender used data from a Swedish cohort born in 1953 and followed to age 30. Specifically, Kratzer and Hodgins (1999) divided the sample into five groups: (1) stable early starters, who were convicted for an offense both before and after age 18 and who committed at least one crime during each of three or more age periods (441 males, 30 females); (2) an AL group, who were convicted for an offense before age 18 but not after (703 males, 148 females); (3) an adult-starter group, who were convicted for an offense after age 18 but not before (907 males, 237 females); (4) a discontinuous offender group, who were registered for at least one crime during two age periods (at least one of the convictions occurred before age 18 and another after age 18) (294 males, 39 females); and (5) a no-crime group, who had never been convicted (4,756 males, 6,297 females). When comparing these groups, Kratzer and Hodgins found mixed evidence regarding Moffitt's taxonomy.

For example, in support of Moffitt, they found that early starters (regardless of gender) committed more crimes, exhibited a more diverse pattern of offending, and had lower composite intelligence scores. Further, and as Moffitt anticipated, early starters as a group were composed of a higher percentage of males (6.2%) than females (0.4%). Several results were contradictory to Moffitt's theory, namely that whereas 33% of the crimes committed by females were committed by early starters, 45% were committed by adult starters (Kratzer & Hodgins, 1999, p. 68). Also unexpected was the finding that among females, several childhood variables (e.g., socioeconomic status, global IQ, school performance, school conduct problems) were important in the offending of both the early-starter and the AL groups.

Moffitt and her colleagues (2001) conducted one of the most comprehensive analyses of sex differences in antisocial behavior using self-report and official records in the Dunedin Birth Cohort to age 21. Although a complete review of their findings is beyond the scope of this chapter, we provide a summary of those results that are directly relevant to the LCP hypothesis across gender. First, although males were observed to be more antisocial than females—especially for violence—there were some exceptions, including the similarities with respect to drug use, as well as involvement in domestic violence. Relatedly, during adolescence, sex differences were minimal with respect to most forms of antisocial behavior. Second, although the risk factors that predicted LCP antisocial behavior were similar across gender (suggesting that Moffitt's taxonomy describes offending patterns in girls as well as in boys; Moffitt et al., 2001, p. 8), there were substantially fewer females in the LCP group primarily because they do not have the same level of risk factors for it, suggesting "remarkable similarities between males and females with respect to risk factors for antisocial behaviour" (p. 6). Further, although LCP was rare in the Dunedin data overall, both genders who were involved in antisocial behavior evidenced similarity on both stability and onset age—regardless of the measurement used to assess antisocial behavior (Moffitt et al., 2001, p. 5). Third, although LCP-style offending appears reserved primarily for males, the antisocial behavior of females seems to be strongly related to situations and circumstances. As Moffitt and her colleagues summarize, the:

> variety of antisocial involvement that is more typical of females is particularly influenced by social factors. Indeed, in contrast to the assumption that socialization generates sex differences, we found evidence that socialization effects may generate sex similarities in antisocial behaviour. In particular, the findings point to the conclusion that, with regard to socialization influences, male peers play a prominent role in shaping the antisocial behaviour of females. (p. 8)

In short, the authors summarize their collective findings as indicating that the antisocial behavior of females follows the same causal laws as the antisocial behavior of males:

> Females are unlikely to develop the neuro-developmental form [LCP offending] because they are unlikely to have the risk factors for it, whereas they are as likely as males to develop the socially influenced form [AL offending] because they share with males the risk factors for it. (p. xvi)

The Dunedin data have also been helpful in studying whether Moffitt's taxonomy applies to females and males (see, e.g., Moffitt & Caspi, 2001; Piquero et al., 2005). In one of these studies, Odgers et al. (2008) investigated the childhood origins and adult outcomes of conduct problem trajectories measured between ages 7 and 26 (LCP, adolescent onset, childhood limited, and low). The results were largely supportive of Moffitt's expectations regarding LCP offending. First, there were more males than females who were following the LCP trajectory pathway. Second, as children, LCPs were characterized by social, familial (e.g., harsh and inconsistent discipline, much family conflict), and neurodevelopmental (e.g., low intellectual ability, reading difficulties, hyperactivity) risk factors, whereas as adults, individuals on the LCP pathway were involved in serious violence and also suffered mental and physical health problems as well as economic problems. Importantly, not only were both of these findings observed among males and females, but also these authors also reported that the number of trajectories, as well as their shapes, was remarkably similar across females and males (Odgers et al., 2008, pp. 690–691). There is a sizable empirical literature assessing the various hypotheses put forth in Moffitt's developmental taxonomy, and several of these studies offer important challenges and potential modifications to the two-group model (see Laub & Sampson, 2003; McCabe, Hough, Wood, & Yeh, 2001). Although these details are beyond the current review, Moffitt (2006) summarizes much of this literature.

There have been several empirical investigations of Silverthorn and Frick's (1999) delayed-onset pathway model. In an initial empirical examination using data from a sample of 72 adjudicated adolescent girls from Alabama, Silverthorn and her colleagues (Silverthorn, Frick, & Reynolds, 2001) found support for the delayed-onset framework. Specifically, their findings showed that adolescent-onset girls also had high levels of callous-unemotional traits, impulse-control problems, and other vulnerabilities that were more similar to those of boys with a childhood onset than to those of boys with an adolescent onset. Other studies assessing the delayed-onset model, however, have generated a more mixed set of findings.

Lahey et al. (2006) used data from the National Longitudinal Survey of Youth 1979 to examine sex differences in antisocial behavior within the context of both Moffitt's dual taxonomy and Silverthorn and Frick's delayed-onset model. Although a detailed review of their findings is beyond the scope of this chapter, findings tended to provide more support for Moffitt's dual taxonomy and less support for Silverthorn and Frick's delayed-onset model. In particular, Lahey et al. found that girls in the AL group did not exhibit the early risk factors that were characteristic of LCP males, that there were a nontrivial number of girls in the LCP group (although there were many more men, as Moffitt anticipates), and that:

> the LCP group of females had deviant levels of all of the early risk variables attributed to the LCP trajectory by Moffitt (1993) for males, and there were no significant differences in the associations of these risk variables with the LCP group (i.e., no significant LCP-by-sex interactions), except for maternal delinquency. (p. 753)

In a study using data from the Philadelphia Perinatal Project, White and Piquero (2004) undertook a specific analysis of the delayed-onset model with an African American birth cohort followed into their 30s. Several key findings emerged from their study. First, there were no gender differences with respect to early-onset offending, measured as a police contact by age 13. Second, consistent with Silverthorn and Frick, results showed that female late-onset offenders scored similar to male early-onset offenders on 9 of 10 risk factors. Third, not surprisingly, early-onset males had worse criminal outcomes than male and female late-onset offenders but did not differ from early-onset females. Finally, a comparison of various risk factors among late-onset female and late-onset male offenders indicated more similarities than differences.

Leve and Chamberlain (2004) used a small ($n = 62$) sample of girls who were referred for placement and treatment from the Oregon Youth Authority for serious delinquency to examine the various background factors that may be related to an early onset. Their analysis showed the following: (1) child (e.g., IQ) and family (e.g., biological parent criminality) factors were strong predictors of early onset; (2) onset age was predictive of participation in risky sexual behavior as well as antisocial behavior more generally; and (3) there were a nontrivial number of early-onset girls—with 23% of the sample arrested before age 11.

Summary of Existing Research

As noted earlier, Russell et al. (2014) recently conducted a review of sex differences in antisocial behavior from childhood to adulthood in studies using the group-based trajectory methodology. One finding to emerge from their review of 47 studies was that although there seemed to be support for offending patterns that resembled the pathways as put forth by both Moffitt and Silverthorn and Frick, the trajectory studies also showed that there were other offending patterns that were not anticipated by the theory, such as moderate antisocial and early-onset desister pathways (Russell et al., 2014, p. 13). That said, it still remains the case that most studies show that childhood onset of antisocial behavior—especially the form that continues well into adulthood—is much more common among boys and less common among girls (see Hipwell et al., 2002; Moffitt & Caspi, 2001). At the same time, it seems that strong support does not yet exist for Silverthorn and Frick's model, but this conclusion remains guarded because there are only a handful of empirical studies.

Conclusion

Much of criminology's early history was focused on male offenders—and much of what was written on the topic of crime was also produced by male scholars. Interest in female offenders waxed and waned throughout much of the 20th century, but the work of Freda Adler provided an important reminder to the field that female offenders and female offending were important criminological topics. An increase in theoretical work ensued and data collection efforts followed that provided some important baseline information regarding the nature of female offending. Until recently, however, there had been little theoretical, and especially empirical, work that considered and described females' longitudinal offending patterns. In this chapter, we have provided a review of two specific theoretical frameworks designed to explain LCP offending among females and highlighted some of the studies that have sought to examine these models. Here, we identify a series of theoretical and empirical topics that we believe are worthy of attention to move forward our understanding of LCP female offenders.

First, with the exception of Moffitt and Silverthorn and Frick, there does not exist much more by way of theory with respect to LCP offending among females. Although this may have something to do with the observation that persistent or chronic female offenders are the exception and not the norm, it does not follow that the field should abandon consideration of why LCP females may exist and how they may be similar to—or different from—their male LCP counterparts. In short, there is a need to better theorize female offenders and their offending (see Kruttschnitt, 1996; Lanctôt & Le Blanc, 2002), and in this regard there must be consideration not only to shared risk factors but also to potentially female-specific risk factors or gender-specific reactions to those risk factors. Notably, researchers have identified potentially important gender-specific pathways into offending (Chesney-Lind & Pasko, 2004; Sommers & Baskin, 1994) and, in turn, the juvenile justice system (Odgers, Robins, & Russell, 2011).

Second, and recognizing that theory can also be informed and built through basic descriptive data, we believe that there needs to be much more research that simply documents female offending over the life course, and we list four specific data needs here.

1. Not only is the collection of traditional forms of antisocial, delinquent, and criminal behavior important, but also there is an important need to consider measuring different forms of antisocial behavior, especially indirect and relational forms of aggression, which girls are involved in (see Crick & Grotpeter, 1995; Lagerspetz & Björkqvist, 1994; Underwood, 2003). Little research has been conducted on whether indirect or relational aggression patterns continue into adulthood or whether the nature of antisocial behavior among females changes in manifestation throughout the life course and whether it does so in different ways compared to males. In this regard, it is also important to consider how males and females become involved in antisocial behavior in the preadolescence years and to include investigation of the nature, type, and frequency of such behavior (e.g., Loeber, Stouthamer-Loeber, Hipwell, Burke, & Battista, 2013).

2. It may be helpful to also consider the expansion of qualitative data collection efforts among female offenders to get a sense, in their own words, of why they may persistently offend as well as why they stop. On this latter point, the role of marriage seems relevant because there is consistent evidence that marriage inhibits offending, but that it does so primarily and more so for males than for females (see review in Craig, Diamond, & Piquero, 2014).

3. There have been few investigations of Moffitt's prediction that males on the LCP trajectory have "more" or a "higher level of" risk factors than the smaller number of females on the LCP trajectory. One recent study examining whether boys and girls had different risk thresholds for delinquency showed that although there were similarities in many risk and promotive factors, there were some sex differences as well as differences between age periods (Wong et al., 2013, p. 648). Another investigation that examined sex differences in the predictors of violent and nonviolent juvenile offending among British juvenile offenders found that although female violent offenders were more likely to self-harm than male violent offenders, virtually none

of the risk factors tested via a standardized assessment profile tool differed across genders (Stephenson, Woodhams, & Cooke, 2014). Much more work is needed on the extent to which the predictors of distinct offending styles and types are more similar or different across genders (e.g., Archer, 2004; Harachi et al., 2006).

4. Consideration of different life outcomes of LCP offending among females is also important. Recent work by Henneberger, Oudekerk, Repucci, and Odgers (2014) shows that even with a sample of criminal justice–involved adolescent girls, there is a subgroup of violent and delinquent girls who experience more severe health and crime problems in adulthood, and some later-life outcomes may be more salient for persistent female offenders (see Goldweber et al., 2009, p. 223).

Third, there remains a contention in the literature as to whether female offenders who are in the juvenile and adult justice systems require different interventions and whether they respond differently to interventions that may be more appropriate for males (Cauffman, 2008; Hipwell & Loeber, 2006). Although this debate will not be settled here, the takeaway is that several intervention programs have shown success in reducing delinquency among female offenders (Chamberlain, Leve, & DeGarmo, 2007). Researchers should continue to develop and evaluate theory and evidence-based prevention and intervention programs that focus on reducing delinquency and antisocial behavior. They should also pay considerable attention to any potential differences in the risk and protective factors associated with female LCP offending that may be measured using current classification tools and, in turn, integrated into service delivery (see Reisig, Holtfreter, & Morash, 2006).

In closing, we state that the field of criminology owes a debt of gratitude to Freda Adler for her many contributions, but without question, *Sisters in Crime* occupies a central place as one pivotal scholarly effort that influenced a field and generation of criminologists. Within that spirit, we hope that in the decades to come the field of criminology redoubles theoretical and empirical efforts that seek to describe the points of similarity and difference between male and female offenders, to include their onset, persistence, and desistance, as well as to consider a wide range of potential correlates and manifestations of antisocial behavior over the life course.

References

Adler, F. (1975). *Sisters in crime: The rise of the new female criminal*. New York, NY: McGraw–Hill.

Archer, J. (2004). Sex differences in aggression in real-world settings: A meta-analytic review. *Review of General Psychology, 8*, 291–322.

Baskin, D., & Sommers, I. (1998). *Casualties of community disorder: Women's careers in violent crime*. Boulder, CO: Westview Press.

Broidy, L. M., Nagin, D. S., Tremblay, R. E., Bates, J. E., Brame, B., Dodge, K., . . . Vitaro, F. (2003). Developmental trajectories of childhood disruptive behaviours and adolescent delinquency: A six site, cross-national study. *Developmental Psychology, 39*, 222–245.

Cauffman, E. (2008). Understanding the female offender. *Future of Children, 18*, 119–142.

Chamberlain, P., Leve L. D., & DeGarmo, D. S. (2007). Multidimensional treatment foster care for girls in the juvenile justice system: 2-year follow-up of a randomized clinical trial. *Journal of Consulting and Clinical Psychology, 75*, 187–193.

Chesney-Lind, M., & Pasko, L. (2004). *The female offender: Girls, women, and crime.* Thousand Oaks, CA: Sage.

Cohen, A. K. (1955). *Delinquent boys: The culture of the gang.* New York, NY: The Free Press.

Colvin, M., & Pauly, J. (1983). A critique of criminology: Toward an integrated structural-Marxist theory of delinquent production. *American Journal of Sociology, 89*, 513–551.

Craig, J. M., Diamond, B., & Piquero, A. R. (2014). Marriage as an intervention in the lives of criminal offenders. In J. A. Humphrey & P. Cordella (Eds.), *Effective interventions in the lives of criminal offenders* (pp. 19–37). New York, NY: Springer.

Crick, N. R., & Grotpeter, J. K. (1995). Relational aggression, gender, and social–psychological adjustment. *Child Development, 66*, 710–722.

Daly, K., & Chesney-Lind, M. (1988). Feminism and criminology. *Justice Quarterly, 5*, 497–538.

D'Unger, A. V., Land, K. C., & McCall, P. (2002). Sex differences in age patterns of delinquent/criminal careers: Results from Poisson latent class analyses of the Philadelphia cohort study. *Journal of Quantitative Criminology, 18*, 349–375.

Farrington, D. P., Piquero, A. R., & Jennings, W. G. (2013). *Offending from childhood to late middle age: Recent results from the Cambridge Study in Delinquent Development.* New York, NY: Springer.

Fergusson, D. M., & Horwood, L. J. (2002). Male and female offending trajectories. *Development and Psychopathology, 14*, 159–177.

Frick, P. J., & Viding, E. (2009). Antisocial behavior from a developmental psychopathology perspective. *Development and Psychopathology, 21*, 1111–1131.

Giordano, P. C. (2010). *Legacies of crime: A follow-up of the children of highly delinquent girls and boys.* Cambridge, UK: Cambridge University Press.

Goldweber, A., Broidy, L. M., & Cauffman, E. (2009). Interdisciplinary perspectives on persistent female offending: A review of theory and research. In J. Savage (Ed.), *The development of persistent criminality* (pp. 205–230). New York, NY: Oxford University Press.

Hagan, J., Gillis, A. R., & Simpson, J. (1985). The class structure of gender and delinquency: Toward a power-control theory of common delinquent behavior. *American Journal of Sociology, 90*, 1151–1178.

Harachi, T., Fleming, C., White, H., Ensminger, R., Abbott, R., Catalano, R., & Haggerty, K. (2006). Aggressive behavior among girls and boys during middle childhood: Predictors and sequel of trajectory group membership. *Aggressive Behavior, 32*, 279–293.

Haynie, D. L., & Piquero, A. R. (2006). Pubertal development and physical victimization in adolescence. *Journal of Research in Crime and Delinquency, 43*, 3–35.

Henneberger, A. K., Oudekerk, B. A., Repucci, N. D., & Odgers, C. L. (2014). Differential subtypes of offending among adolescent girls predict health and criminality in adulthood. *Criminal Justice and Behavior, 41*, 181–195.

Hipwell, A. E., & Loeber, R. (2006). Do we know which interventions are effective for disruptive and delinquent girls? *Clinical Child and Family Psychological Review, 9*, 221–255.

Hipwell, A. E., Loeber, R., Stouthamer-Loeber, M., Kennan, K., White, H. R., & Kroneman, L. (2002). Characteristics of girls with early onset disruptive and antisocial behaviour. *Criminal Behavior and Mental Health, 12,* 99–118.

Hirschi, T., & Gottfredson, M. R. (1983). Age and the explanation of crime. *American Journal of Sociology, 89,* 552–584.

Hussong, A. M., Curran, P. J., Moffitt, T. E., Caspi, A., & Carrig, M. M. (2004). Substance abuse hinders desistance in young adult's antisocial behavior. *Development and Psychopathology, 16,* 1029–1046.

Jennings, W. G., & Reingle, J. M. (2012). On the shape of developmental/life-course violence, aggression, and delinquency trajectories: A state-of-the-art review. *Journal of Criminal Justice, 40,* 472–489.

Kratzer, L., & Hodgins, S. (1999). A typology of offenders: A test of Moffitt's theory among males and females from childhood to age 30. *Criminal Behaviour and Mental Health, 9,* 57–73.

Kruttschnitt, C. (1996). Contributions of quantitative methods to the study of gender and crime, or bootstrapping our way into the theoretical thicket. *Journal of Quantitative Criminology, 12,* 135–161.

Lagerspetz, K. M. J., & Björkqvist, K. (1994). Indirect aggression in boys and girls. In L. R. Huesmann (Ed.), *Aggressive behavior: Current perspectives* (pp. 131–150). New York, NY: Plenum Press.

Lahey, B. B., VanHulle, C. A., Waldman, I. D., Rodgers, J. L., D'Onofrio, B. M., Pedlow, S., . . . Keenan, K. (2006). Testing descriptive hypotheses regarding sex differences in the development of conduct problems and delinquency. *Journal of Abnormal Child Psychology, 34,* 737–755.

Lanctôt, N., Cernkovich, S. A., & Giordano, P. C. (2007). Delinquent behavior, official delinquency, and gender: Consequences for adulthood functioning and well-being. *Criminology, 45,* 131–157.

Lanctôt, N., & Le Blanc, M. (2002). Explaining deviance by adolescent females. In M. Tonry (Ed.), *Crime and justice: A review of research* (Vol. 29, pp. 113–202). Chicago, IL: University of Chicago Press.

Laub, J. H., & Sampson, R. J. (2003). *Shared beginnings, divergent lives: Delinquent boys to age 70.* Cambridge, MA: Harvard University Press.

Leve, L. D., & Chamberlain, P. (2004). Female juvenile offenders: Defining an early-onset pathway for delinquency. *Journal of Child and Family Studies, 13,* 439–452.

Loeber, R., Stouthamer-Loeber, M., Hipwell, A. E., Burke, J. D., & Battista, D. (2013). Some key issues in the early development of aggression in girls. In D. Pepler & W. Craig (Eds.), *A focus on relationships: Understanding and addressing aggressive behavior problems* (pp. 55–71). Waterloo, ON: Wilfrid Laurier University Press.

McCabe, K. M., Hough, R., Wood, P. A., & Yeh, M. (2001). Childhood and adolescent onset conduct disorder: A test of the developmental taxonomy. *Journal of Abnormal Child Psychology, 29,* 305–316.

Messerschmidt, J. W. (1993). *Masculinities and crime.* Lanham, MD: Rowman & Littlefield.

Moffitt, T. E. (1993). Adolescence-limited and life-course-persistent antisocial behavior: A developmental taxonomy. *Psychological Review, 100,* 674–701.

Moffitt, T. E. (1994). Natural histories of delinquency. In H. J. Kerner & E. Weitekamp (Eds.), *Cross-national longitudinal research on human development and criminal behavior* (pp. 3–61). Dordrecht, The Netherlands: Kluwer Academic Press.

Moffitt, T. E. (2006). Life-course persistent versus adolescence-limited antisocial behavior: Research review. In D. Cicchetti & D. J. Cohen (Eds.), *Developmental psychopathology, risk, disorder, and adaptation* (2nd ed., Vol. 3, pp. 570–598). New York, NY: Wiley.

Moffitt, T. E., & Caspi, A. (2001). Childhood predictors differentiate life-course persistent and adolescence-limited antisocial pathways in males and females. *Development and Psychopathology, 13*, 355–376.

Moffitt, T. E., Caspi, A., Rutter, M., & Silva, P. A. (2001). *Sex differences in antisocial behaviour.* Cambridge, UK: Cambridge University Press.

Odgers, C. L., Moffitt, T. E., Broadbent, J. M., Dickson, N., Hancox, R. J., Harrington, H., . . . Caspi, A. (2008). Female and male antisocial trajectories: From childhood origins to adult outcomes. *Development and Psychopathology, 20*, 673–716.

Odgers, C. L., Robins, S. J., & Russell, M. A. (2011). Morbidity and mortality risk among the "forgotten few": Why are girls in the justice system in such poor health? *Law and Human Behavior, 34*, 429–444.

Piquero, A. R. (2008). Taking stock of developmental trajectories of criminal activity over the life course. In A. M. Liberman (Ed.), *The long view of crime: A syntheses of longitudinal research* (pp. 23–78). New York, NY: Springer.

Piquero, A. R., Brame, R., & Moffitt, T. E. (2005). Extending the study of continuity and change: Gender differences in the linkage between adolescent and adult offending. *Journal of Quantitative Criminology, 21*, 219–243.

Piquero, A. R., Farrington, D. P., & Blumstein, A. (2007). *Key issues in criminal career research: New analyses of the Cambridge Study in Delinquent Development.* New York, NY: Cambridge University Press.

Reisig, M. D., Holtfreter, K., & Morash, M. (2006). Assessing recidivism risk across female pathways to crime. *Justice Quarterly, 23*, 384–405.

Russell, M. A., Robins, S., & Odgers, C. L. (2014). Developmental perspectives: Sex differences in antisocial behavior from childhood to adulthood. In R. Gartner & B. McCarthy (Eds.), *Oxford handbook on gender, sex, and crime.* New York. NY: Oxford University Press (forthcoming).

Schwartz, J., & Steffensmeier, D. (2011). Stability and change in girls' delinquency and the gender gap: Trends in violence and alcohol offending across multiple sources of evidence. In S. Miller, S. Leve, & P. Kerig (Eds.), *Delinquent girls: Contexts, relationships, and adaptation* (pp. 3–23). New York, NY: Springer.

Schwartz, J., Steffensmeier, D., & Feldmeyer, B. (2009). Assessing trends in women's violence via data triangulation: Arrests, convictions, incarcerations, and victim reports. *Social Problems, 56*, 494–525.

Silverthorn, P., & Frick, P. J. (1999). Developmental pathways to antisocial behavior: The delayed-onset pathway in girls. *Development and Psychopathology, 11*, 101–126.

Silverthorn, P., Frick, P. J., & Reynolds, R. (2001). Timing of onset and correlates of severe conduct problems in adjudicated girls and boys. *Journal of Psychopathology and Behavioral Assessment, 23*, 171–181.

Simon, R. J. (1975). *Women and crime*. Lexington, MA: Lexington Books.

Simpson, S. S. (1989). Feminist theory, crime, and justice. *Criminology, 27*, 605–631.

Sommers, I., & Baskin, D. (1994). Factors related to female adolescent initiation into violence crime. *Youth and Society, 24*, 468–489.

Stephenson, Z., Woodhams, J., & Cooke, C. (2014). Sex differences in predictors of violent and non-violent juvenile offending. *Aggressive Behavior, 40*, 165–177.

Tracy, P., & Kempf-Leonard, K. (1996). *Continuity and discontinuity in criminal careers*. New York, NY: Plenum.

Underwood, M. K. (2003). *Social aggression among girls*. New York, NY: Guilford Press.

White, N., & Piquero, A. R. (2004). A preliminary empirical test of Silverthorn and Frick's delayed-onset pathway in girls using an urban, African-American, US-based sample. *Criminal Behavior and Mental Health, 14*, 291–309.

Wong, T., Loeber, R., Slotboom, A. -M., Bijleveld, C., Hipwell, A. E., Stepp, S., & Koot, H. (2013). Sex and age differences in the risk threshold for delinquency. *Journal of Abnormal Child Psychology, 41*, 641–652.

Zahn, M. A. (Ed.). (2009). *The delinquent girl*. Philadelphia, PA: Temple University Press.

Zahn, M. A., Hawkins, S. R., Chiancone, J., & Whitworth, A. (2008). *Girls Study Group: Understanding and responding to girls' delinquency*. Washington, DC: Office of Juvenile Justice and Delinquency Prevention.

CHAPTER 5

Gendered Pathways Into Delinquency

Meda Chesney-Lind

Prior to the mid-1970s, theorizing about delinquency was actually theorizing about *male* delinquency, although the myopic theoretical and research focus on boys was largely seen as unproblematic or even easily defensible. To those who might be skeptical, perhaps it is relevant to review the origins and extensiveness of androcentric thinking of classic delinquency researchers and the intellectual legacy (and voids) this thinking produced and still produces. After a review of this issue, the chapter will then turn to the earliest feminist research on girls' delinquency, which reveals strong evidence that gender matters in delinquency. A discussion of girls' pathways into the justice system follows, with a focus on the role of girls' victimization in girl's delinquency. Finally, current trends in female delinquency will be considered, including a critical review of evidence that girls are going "wild" as well as what the current focus on the trafficking of girls might mean for the "victims" of that trafficking.

Ignoring Female Offenders

In the early 19th century, public and governmental interest in youthful misbehavior in the United States was directly tied to the explosive immigration and population growth that the country was experiencing. Between 1750 and 1850, the population of the United States went from 1.25 million to 23 million (Empey, 1982, p. 59). Cities such as Chicago not only were experiencing massive immigration and growth, but also were creating a new urban environment based on manufacturing as well as trade—unlike the cities of the Eastern seaboard that were largely commercial ports.

Chicago would also serve as an important setting for the emerging fields of sociology (particularly urban sociology), criminology, and social work (Deegan, 1988). For early crime researchers at the University of Chicago such as Clifford Shaw and Henry McKay, delinquency and crime research provided the perfect venue to develop and demonstrate the utility of positivist criminology to solve social problems. Members of what came to be known as the Chicago School borrowed from ecological approaches and specifically rejected notions of ethnicity or race playing a particular role in the generation of delinquency (a pattern often adopted by the often nativist and anti-immigrant political leaders of the day). They noted, instead, that behaviors tended to cluster in particular low-income neighborhoods and stay there through several different ethnic groups (i.e., much like is seen in nature in ecological succession) (Park & Burgess, 1925).

This same group of researchers assumed that aspects of the social world could be precisely measured and clearly linked as causes and effects. This positivist perspective emphasized the researcher as objective and detached from both the data collection process and the use of the findings, although with hindsight we can see the androcentric assumptions that undergirded much of the work done. As an example, it is valuable to take a closer look at the research of Shaw and McKay on the juvenile crime problem in Chicago. Their classic work, *Juvenile Delinquency in Urban Areas* (Shaw & McKay, 1942), focused almost exclusively on male delinquents in Chicago (more than 60,000), and they repeatedly referred to the rates associated with this group as "delinquency rates" (although they occasionally make parenthetical reference to data on female delinquency). Similarly, landmark case studies like *The Jack-Roller* (first published in 1930) (Shaw, 1966) and *Brothers in Crime* (Shaw et al., 1938) traced only male experiences with the law.

Nor was their work unique in this regard. Early fieldwork on delinquent gangs in Chicago set the stage for another important type of delinquency research—subcultural theory. Yet here, too, researchers focused almost exclusively on males and male groups. Thrasher (1963) studied over 1,000 juvenile gangs in Chicago during roughly the same period that Shaw and McKay's more quantitative work was being done. Thrasher devoted approximately 1 page in a book of 300 or so pages to a discussion of the five or six female gangs he encountered in his field observations. Thrasher did mention, in passing, two factors he believed accounted for the smaller number of girl gangs:

> first, the social patterns for the behavior of girls, powerfully backed by the great weight of tradition and custom, are contrary to the gang and its activities; and secondly, girls, even in urban disorganized areas, are much more closely supervised and guarded than boys and are usually well incorporated into the family groups or some other social structure. (p. 228)

In this work, no consideration was given to the effect of field researchers on study participants or the potential that social phenomenon are given their meaning by individuals, and these meanings are as important as precisely measured "realities." Instead, Thrasher and Shaw failed to understand how their own gender colored their view of the world, which meant they completely ignored or sexualized girls and talked almost exclusively to boys and young men about gangs and delinquency.

The Chicago School did come upon some key insights—ones that might travel well into the 21st century. Notably, a focus on subcultures, the social organization of urban neighborhoods, and the role played by class and inequality in the production of crime are important ideas. Many other influential delinquency researchers who would follow specifically noted that masculinity was at the core of many delinquent acts (often in rebellion about the confines of their circumscribed world, which often included a rejection of things feminine) (Cloward & Ohlin, 1966; Cohen, 1955). Overall, however, this literature produced delinquency theories that were curiously untethered from the real consequences of boys' and men's violence. There was also the fact that not only other boys but also girls were among their victims. Oddly, even the work that was initially done on women's victimizations during the second wave of feminism (which began in the 1960s) largely left the delinquency literature more or less untouched, primarily because the earliest work on women's victimizations focused on adult women, not girls.

Meanwhile, thinking about girls and their misbehavior, if it occurred at all, was left to an intellectually isolated collection of researchers. Many of these researchers assumed that most female misbehavior was almost unimaginable, so they believed that such conduct was likely produced by extreme maladjustment. Therefore, if female crime existed at all, it was either expressive of women's deep venality (Lombroso & Ferrero, 1895) or shaped by girls' and women's anatomies, particularly their sexuality, and their ability to be devious (Pollak, 1950).

In contrast, the earliest feminist work on female delinquency focused on exactly what *had* been happening to the girls during the same historic period that shaped the classic legal and social responses to the delinquency problem. Although the earliest researchers had clearly ignored girls, the same could not be said of the founders of the juvenile justice system. Literature critically analyzing the activities of the earliest years of the juvenile court would find evidence of the intense focus in the policing of young girls' sexuality (Chesney-Lind, 1973; Odem, 1995; Schlossman & Wallach, 1978). This work would reveal evidence of considerable discrimination against girls charged with such offenses as "sexual immorality," "waywardness," and later "incorrigibility," the status offenses of that day—noncriminal offenses that would result in the incarcerations of vast numbers of young girls during most of the 20th century (Chesney-Lind & Shelden, 2003).

Studies of early family court activity reveal that almost all of the girls who appeared in these courts were charged with immorality or waywardness (Chesney-Lind, 1971; Schlossman & Wallach, 1978; Shelden, 1981). The charge of immorality is critical to understand in this context because it almost always applied to girls. A detailed study of the nation's first juvenile court in Cook County shows that between 1906 and 1927, the two most common charges against girls were immorality and incorrigibility. The proportion of total charges that were immorality ranged from a low of 15% to a high of 55%; the proportion of charges that were incorrigibility ranged from a low of 33% to a high of 73%. The third most common charge was larceny (ranging from 6% to 17%) (Knupfer, 2001, p. 199). The sanctions for such misbehavior were extremely severe. For example, the Chicago family court sent half the girl delinquents but only one fifth of the boy delinquents to reformatories between 1899 and 1909 (Schlossman & Wallach, 1978, p. 72). Similarly, in Memphis, females were twice as likely as males to be committed to training schools (Shelden, 1981, p. 70).

Curiously, classic midcentury academic efforts to explain delinquent behavior ignored these patterns and were, instead, clear and unapologetic efforts to study male delinquents. "The delinquent is a rogue male," declared Albert Cohen in his influential book on gang delinquency written in 1956 (p. 140). More than a decade later, Travis Hirschi (1969), in his equally important book titled *Causes of Delinquency*, relegated women to a footnote that suggested, somewhat apologetically, that "in the analysis that follows, the 'non-Negro' becomes 'White,' and the girls disappear" (pp. 35–36).

One might want to believe that such cavalier androcentrism is no longer found in academic approaches to delinquency. For this reason, two more relatively recent examples are instructive. In *Delinquency Careers in Two Birth Cohorts*, Tracy, Wolfgang, and Figlio (1990) revisit the practice of including only boys in their delinquency cohort:

> The decision was made, therefore, to study delinquency and its absence in a cohort consisting of all boys born in 1945 and residing in Philadelphia from a date no later than their tenth birthday until at least their eighteenth. Girls were excluded, partly because of their low delinquency, and partly because the presence of the boys in the city at the terminal age mentioned could be conclusively established from the record of their registration for military service. (p. 9)

Classic sociological and criminological paradigms of crime and delinquency (including most of the key theories of crime) were deeply affected by the grinding poverty the researchers observed in the urban slums of Northern cities such as Chicago (see Chesney-Lind & Shelden, 2003). Their early research and theorizing documented inequality's social effects both numerically and qualitatively, and their theories also pushed back against the anti-immigrant bias of many in the political establishment of the day by downplaying the role of ethnicity (and implicitly race) in crime generation.

The real limitations of this legacy of theorizing youthful defiance are twofold. Despite the deeply problematic role of race in U.S. history, no classic delinquency theories thoughtfully engaged the role of race and racism. These theories also stereotyped and celebrated masculinity while ignoring girls, gender violence, and sexism. Finally, there is no mention of sexual orientation or homophobia, although some of the early ethnographies clearly document extreme forms of gender violence. In short, classic delinquency theory tended to normalize male violence, ignore delinquent girls while trivializing their victimizations, and privilege class over other forms of oppression—particularly racial oppression and homophobia.

Remember the Ladies

The women's movement has traditionally been divided into two historic "waves," although work on the status of women can be dated well before the first of these events and continued in a rather clear form after the first wave had passed. Generally, however, the first wave is recognized as starting with the Seneca Falls Convention in 1848, and the second wave is dated to the publication of Betty Friedan's influential book, *The Feminine Mystique*, in 1963.

In this context, the inclusion of women in criminological research and theorizing was catalyzed by the second wave of the feminist movement in the late 1960s and early 1970s. Freda Adler's studies of women offenders and women addicted to drugs documented issues related to their children, their needs, inadequacies of the justice system, and their uniqueness from male offenders (Flynn, 1998). Adler's (1975) book, *Sisters in Crime*, preceded several essays she wrote on women offenders as well as other scholars' research and critiques concerning the changing patterns of women's criminality.

Simon's book, *Women and Crime*, published the same year (1975), generated interest in women offenders. Adler drew on the work of the sociologist Durkheim, whereas Simon pointed to the women's movement to explain the empirical findings about women, the justice system, and crime.

As might be expected, many feminist criminologists of this period brought the insights of other feminist theorists into their groundbreaking work and focused on women's oppression as a key cause of injustice and victimization. In the United States, Dorie Klein and June Kress (1973) edited a classic special volume of *Issues in Criminology* on women and crime. The scope and significance of women's victimization was then explored in two influential books: Susan Brownmiller's exposure of the extent of rape in *Against Our Will* (1975) and Del Martin's *Battered Wives* (1976). British feminists were early to spark the development of criminological theory with the appearance of Heidensohn's pathbreaking paper, "The Deviance of Women," in 1968 and of Smart's *Women, Crime, and Criminology* in 1976. Clearly, a signal event was the founding of the Women and Crime Division of the American Society of Criminology in 1982 (Rafter, 2000, p. 9).

Girls' Lives and the Criminal System

The amount of violence against girls and women worldwide is truly staggering. The World Health Organization (2013) recently reported that "overall, 35% of women worldwide have experienced either physical and/or sexual intimate partner violence or non-partner sexual violence" (p. 2) and that globally "as many as 38% of all murders of women are committed by intimate partners" (p. 2). Because violence against girls and women is such a vast problem and the site of such violence is frequently the home, one wonders whether classic theorizing about delinquency and crime applies at all to girls' and women's victimization, let alone girls' and women's offending.

Recall that much of this theory and research was really built upon notions of urban youth subculture, the slum, and the streets—so the field saw its role as basically predicting and explaining public male crime and mostly male victimization.

Because the abuse of such a vast number of girls and women persists, hard questions should be asked not only of crime researchers but also of the system that promises justice and the prevention of victimization—the police, the courts, and the prisons. Certainly, if the goal of criminal justice systems worldwide is safety and the prevention of criminal victimization, they have failed girls and women spectacularly. Although there are some encouraging signs globally (Hadi & Chesney-Lind, 2014), there is mounting evidence that girls and women cannot count on the criminal justice system to provide them with protection from male violence, let alone stay out of the endorsement of male privilege in patriarchy.

Instead, there is evidence globally that many girls and women who start off as victims are often punished as criminals, particularly when they are victimized within the family. In Afghanistan, for example, approximately 600 women and girls are imprisoned for "moral crimes"; according to a report by the Human Rights Watch (2013), this represents a 50% increase in the past year and a half. The report indicated that almost all girls in juvenile detention and about half of the women in Afghan prisons had been arrested for moral crimes. These crimes usually involved flight from unlawful forced marriage, domestic violence, or an alleged relationship outside of marriage when, in reality, the women had been raped or forced into prostitution.

The Human Rights Watch study (2013) reported that when girls and women went to the police in need of immediate help or protection, they were instead often arrested. Running away from a forced marriage (often to much older men), an abusive relationship, physical violence, rape, or forced prostitution should clearly not be criminal acts, but the report documents the fact that police often arrest the women based on complaints filed by their husbands or relatives. Prosecutors routinely ignore evidence that supports the women's accounts of their situations and the logic behind their running away or fleeing abuse. Finally, judges often convict solely on the basis of "confessions" given by the women in the absence of their lawyers and "signed" without having been read to the women, who cannot read or write. After conviction, women routinely face long prison sentences, in some cases more than 10 years (Human Rights Watch, 2013).

One might assume that such blatant judicial involvement in the enforcement of male privilege and female subjugation can only be found in extremely conservative and religious societies such as those mentioned above, but that would be incorrect. As noted previously, the earliest history of the juvenile justice system in the United States clearly shows that this "justice" system was heavily involved in punishing girls for parental defiance and sexual expression. Nor is this a pattern that is clearly relegated to the past. Currently, in the United States, arrests of girls account for nearly one third of all arrests of young people (Federal Bureau of Investigation, 2012), and many of these girls are being held for a wide range of behaviors that violate parental authority: "running away from home"; being "a person in need of supervision," "a minor in need of supervision," "incorrigible," "beyond control," "truant"; or being in need of "care and protection." Although not technically crimes, these offenses can result in a youth's arrest and involvement in the criminal justice system. In 2009 (the last year for which we have complete data on runaway arrests), status offenses account for 15% of arrests for girls—with the offense of runaway alone accounting for 10% of girls' offenses. Comparatively, status offenses account for only 9% of boys' arrests and runways for only 3% of boys' arrests.

Criminalizing Girls' Survival: Girls' Pathways to Arrest

For many years, statistics showing large numbers of girls arrested for status offenses were taken to be representative of the different types of male and female delinquency in the United States (and elsewhere in the global north). However, the results of self-report studies of male and female delinquency (which ask school-age youth whether they have committed delinquent acts) do not indicate the same dramatic gender differences in misbehavior found in official statistics. Specifically, girls charged with these noncriminal status offenses appear to have been, and continue to be, significantly overrepresented in court populations (Chesney-Lind & Pasko, 2013).

It has long been known that a major reason for the presence of many girls in the juvenile justice system was because their parents insisted on their arrest. After all, who else would report a youth as having "run away" from home? In the early years of the juvenile justice system, parents were the most significant referral source; in Honolulu, for example, nearly half (44%) of the girls who appeared in court in the 1920s and 1930s were referred by parents (Chesney-Lind, 1971).

The fact that parents are often committed to two standards of adolescent behavior is one explanation for these disparities—one that should not be discounted as a major source of tension, even in modern families. Despite expectations to the contrary, gender-specific socialization patterns have not changed much, and this is especially true for parents' relationships with their daughters (Ianni, 1989; Kamler, 1999; Katz, 1979; Orenstein, 2000; Thorne, 1993). Even parents who oppose sexism in general feel "uncomfortable tampering with existing traditions" (Katz, 1979, p. 24) and "do not want to risk their children becoming misfits" (p. 24). Girls can also clash with their parents around issues of gender identity in families committed to heteronormative sexuality, a concern that is surfacing in recent research on girls on the streets in the juvenile justice system (Irvine, 2010; Schaffner, 2006).

Whatever the reason, parental attempts to adhere to and enforce the sexual double standard will continue to be a source of conflict between them and their daughters. Another important explanation for girls' problems with their parents that has received attention only in more recent years is that of physical and sexual abuse. Looking specifically at the problem of childhood sexual abuse, it is increasingly clear that this form of abuse is a particular problem for girls.

Reviewing the limited research on girls' pathways into official delinquency suggests that life experiences, particularly childhood ones, play a unique role in girls' risk of offending. Focusing mostly on female offending, the "pathways" research indicates that childhood trauma is a defining feature in the lives of many female offenders, and it is often related to one's likelihood of committing crimes (to name a few, Belknap & Holsinger, 2006; Bloom, Owen, Deschenes, & Rosenbaum, 2002; Gaarder & Belknap, 2002; Chesney-Lind & Pasko, 2013; Schaffner, 2006; Zahn, 2009). Female offenders are more likely than their male counterparts to come from troubled families and negative peer groups, to have chemically dependent or criminally involved parents, and to suffer from sexual, emotional, and physical abuse in their homes (Acoca, 1998; Giordano, 2010; Leve & Chamberlain, 2004; Piquero, Gover, MacDonald, & Piquero, 2005; Riehman, Blutenthal, Juvonen, & Morrall, 2003). Not surprising then, these volatile relationships and abusive experiences precipitate running away (their escape strategy) and increase exposure to criminal opportunities and further victimization on the streets (Acoca, 1998; Brannigan & Van Brunschot, 1997; Chen, Tyler, Whitbeck, & Hoyt, 2004; Flowers, 2001). They also underscore female juvenile offenders' high rates of coexisting mental health and substance-abuse disorders (Abram et al., 2008; Bailey & McCloskey, 2005; Fishbein, Miller, Winn, Dakof, & Zahn, 2009; Liu, 2004; Schaffner, 2006).

Indeed, the pathways literature shows a strong connection between sexual abuse and girls' delinquency. Girls are three times more likely than boys to be the victims of child sexual abuse (Sedlak & Broadhurst, 1996); such abuse tends to be intrafamilial and their sexual victimization tends to last longer and have more serious consequences than stranger abuse (Bergen, Martin, Richardson, Allison, & Roeger, 2004; Finkelhor, 1994; Jacobs, 1993). The imposition of adult sexuality on children disrupts psychosexual development, and among its effects are promiscuity, rebellion, feelings of shame and guilt, and a loss of self-esteem. Once girls reach puberty, they often come to the realization that their experiences are different from those of their peers and they begin to withdraw. Many "hold a distorted image of their own bodies" (Boyer & James, 1982, pp. 79–80), which may "lead them to expect that their worth will only be acknowledged when they permit sexual access" (pp. 79–80). Further, the girls may learn "that the most effective way to communicate with adults is through sex" (Campagna & Poffenberger, 1988, p. 66) and view themselves as commodities. Boyer (2008), in her research on female prostitution in Seattle, found a direct relationship between sexual abuse of girls and their subsequent involvement in prostitution. Widom (1995) also found that victims of child sexual abuse are 27.7 times more likely to be arrested for prostitution as adults than are nonvictims.

Some Rescue: The FBI's Dubious War on Street Girls[1]

One new risk that runaway girls must contend with is being "rescued" by police and other law enforcement agencies as "victims" of being sexually trafficked. Although sexual exploitation of girls is a serious problem globally, some of the ways these issues are politically and legally framed are extremely problematic (see Berman, 2003). This distortion is particularly acute with regard to the issue of juvenile runaways and the survival sex that often accompanies girls' lives on the streets. For example, the FBI recently announced with great fanfare that it had rescued 105 youth and arrested 150 "pimps" for prostitution in 76 cities, including Boston, Denver, and San Francisco (Yost, 2013). The three-day raid, dubbed "Operation Cross Country," was the largest in a decade-long FBI initiative aimed at what they called the persistent threat of child prostitution (Yost, 2013). But when viewed closely, the FBI's rescues look less like real heroism and more like a photo op.

First, the people rescued were not small children. They were almost all teens, girls and young women, 13 to 17 years old. According to the FBI's lead investigator, virtually all "come from runaway or group homes, and they feel like this [prostitution] is the only way for them to survive on the street" (Yost, 2013).

Second, the girls would almost certainly not characterize what was happening as a rescue. Images on the video accompanying the FBI's press release showed girls in handcuffs. As noted earlier, for centuries, law enforcement and other elements of the juvenile justice system have sought to eliminate prostitution, often incarcerating young women for long terms for "sexual immorality" or "for their own protection." Now, they are being rescued and offered services of dubious quality that typically involve social stigma and detention.

In fact, many of these girls have already experienced the woefully inadequate services available to runaway youth. Girls who are on the streets usually have suffered sexual and other violent abuses in their homes and in alternative settings such as foster homes. The journal *Child Maltreatment* reports there are some 100,000 substantiated cases a year. Sexual abuse of girls occurs at earlier ages and for longer periods than boys' abuse, and girls' abusers are more likely to be family members. It is no surprise that some run away from home.

Once girls run away, as noted previously, they sometimes turn to teen prostitution to survive. The social context that produces teen prostitution and survival sex is a sad mix of broken and dysfunctional families, abused and traumatized youth, defunded social services, adults willing to exploit desperate youth, and privileged older, wealthier men who have absorbed the cultural idea that they should buy sex. It is worth noting that although the FBI proudly reported on rounding up over 100 women and 100 pimps—often men of color—they made no similar mention of any broad effort to arrest the thousands of clients, or "johns," who make the whole system function financially.

Government leaders and police often fail to acknowledge their own complicity in further stigmatizing girls engaged in survival sex. The FBI's multicity raid involved officers enforcing standard laws related to prostitution or solicitation, meaning that many of these so-called rescues involved little more than "rounding up the usual suspects."

Periodic law enforcement raids change none of these realities, nor do they change the fact that crucial local, state, and federal dollars used to fund services for girls on the run from abusive families have been devastated by draconian budget cuts. Federal sequestration alone is predicted to bring a 56% cumulative reduction in juvenile justice funds that once provided states with vital community-based services for troubled families and alternative care.

Oakland, California police lieutenant Kevin Wiley declared, "They [girls] usually get into this because they are running away from something else" (as cited in Yost, 2013). He noted, "It goes way beyond law enforcement to solve this epidemic" (as cited in Yost, 2013). The Trafficking Victims Protection Act of 2000 and its reauthorizations define commercially sold girls as victims (Department of State, Office of Website Management, 2006), but most state laws allow for girls under the age of 18 to be charged as prostitutes. Advocacy groups have tried to pass safe-harbor laws, which mandate that any girl under 18 who has been sexually exploited be treated as a victim, not a criminal, and placed in safe treatment facilities that provide medical and mental health services. Only 25% of states have passed such legislation. Even then, victims in these states often find their rescue home is a shelter or detention facility. With no system for helping teens put their lives on track, putting handcuffed girls in patrol cars is far from a rescue. It is more like a round-trip ticket to a visit with a broken detention system, followed by a return to the street.

Protection or Punishment? Girls' Experiences After Arrest

Although not great in number, a few studies have examined how gender and risk factors matter in juvenile court processing. Focusing mostly on gender bias, MacDonald and Chesney-Lind (2001) found that gender did not have a significant impact on early stages of court processing; at sentencing, however, girls received harsher penalties than did boys. Alternatively, McGuire (2002) found that sex (male) seemed to be the most influential factor when minor offenses are considered as a basis for detainment, whereas race was the significant factor when considering serious offenses. McGuire also found, however, that girls experienced differential pathways to juvenile court, often marked by sexuality issues, poor school performance, drug use, and family conflict. Accordingly, Mallicoat (2007) found that although probation officers understood such risk factors in girls' lives and deemed them "not criminally dangerous" (p. 25), they often concentrated on girls' "sexually inappropriate behaviors from which they needed to be saved" (p. 25). Other research also found that probation officers and other court officials frequently assume girl offenders to be "out of control" and engage a similar "child-saving" technique to "protect" girls from their own choices (Baines, 1997; Bloom et al., 2002; Feld, 2009; Gaarder, Rodriguez, & Zatz, 2004; Inderbitzin, 2007; Miller, 1994). With a focus on their physical appearance and sexuality, research has found that the characterization of girls in their case files regularly obscures girls' agency and deems them to be manipulative, hysterical, and verbally abusive (Bloom et al., 2002; Gaarder, 2004; Goodkind, 2005).

Accordingly, Kempf-Leonard and Sample's (2000) survey of juvenile court judges found that deceitful, manipulative actions led to more punitive case processing for girls, but not for boys. Consistent with these findings, Gaarder et al.'s (2004) study of 174 girls' case files and 14 interviews with probation officers in Arizona found that stereotypical images of girls outweighed any realities. Girls in their study were labeled as sexually promiscuous, untrustworthy, trashy, needy, whiny, manipulative, and irresponsible, while connections to their life histories and contexts were lost. Girls' character flaws were conceived as negative internal attributes and independent certainties, divorced from their victimization experiences and current needs. Although probation officers and court psychologists seemed sympathetic to girls' plights, girls were still blamed for their troubles and "their pasts that were catching up to" them (Gaarder et al., p. 558).

Upcriming Girls' Defiance?

Although arrest statistics still reflect the importance of status and other trivial offenses in official female delinquency, the 1990s saw a curious surge of interest in girls, often girls of color, engaged in nontraditional, masculine behavior—notably joining gangs, carrying guns, and fighting with other girls. The beginning of the 21st century continued this "bad girl" discourse, with an added focus on White girls' relational aggression and bullying as an undiscovered, concealed culture.

The increase in the arrests of girls for "other assaults" added fuel to this fire. Since the mid-1980s, arrests of girls for this offense have increased by nearly 200%, and by 2011, more than one of three juveniles arrested for other assaults was female (Federal Bureau of Investigation, 2012). What is going on? Are we seeing a major shift in the behavior of girls and an entry of girls into violent behaviors, including gang violence, that were once the nearly exclusive domain of young boys? As we shall see, this is the conclusion one would draw from the papers and television, but a closer look at the trends presents a more complex view.

Certainly, all forms of media have been obsessed with the "bad," "wild," and "violent" girl. Whether it was the female revolutionary of the 1970s, the girl gang-banger of the 1980s, the violent girl of the 1990s, or the mean girl at the turn of the 21st century, the past few decades have seen a cavalcade of girls acting out in ways that seem far worse than merely unfeminine (see Chesney-Lind & Irwin, 2007). Often, the media frame is one that juxtaposes girls' aggression or violence with stereotypical images of a girlhood devoid of behavior of this sort. The *Newsweek* issue on youth violence, as an example, included an insert on girls' violence complete with a picture of an African American girl wearing a bandanna over her face, peering at the camera over the barrel of a gun, with the headline "Girls Will Be Girls" (Leslie, Biddle, Rosenberg, & Wayne, 1993, p. 44). In many ways, this gender juxtaposition makes sense in a country that grew up reading Longfellow's poem about his daughter: "When she was good, she was very, very good, but when she was bad she was horrid" (Longfellow, 2013).

Well into the 21st century's first decade such stories continued. On May 16, 2006, the *Toronto Star* reported that although no all-female gangs existed in Toronto and girls only comprised 6% of known gang members, female violence was on the rise as "more and more, girls are becoming involved in youth gangs in Canada—a trend that was virtually unheard of just five years ago" (Edwards, 2006). On July 28, 2009, New Jersey Attorney General Anne Milgram announced that law enforcement officials dismantled an all female–led gang-involved narcotics ring. Dubbing the investigation "Operation Bloodette," Milgram went on to state that she wished "this was not one (glass) ceiling women were breaking" and that "women are taking over dominant roles in traditionally male-dominated gangs" (Read, 2009). And on August 25, 2010, the *Las Vegas Review–Journal* reported that "ten members of an all-female gang were arrested on robbery and burglary charges" (Blaskey, 2010). The article opens with the catchy line, "Girls just want to have fun. But girls in gangs—well, apparently they'll rob you blind" (Blaskey, 2010). Later, however, the article noted that the young women mostly stole shoes and clothes and that no one was seriously hurt; it nonetheless pointed out that attempted murder charges were expected against at least one of the women.

Many journalists who wrote about these trends relied almost exclusively on arrest data to justify their focus on girls and violence. Certainly, a quick look at these data leaves one with the impression that delinquency in girls is on the increase, particularly in nontraditional areas (like violence). In 1983, girls accounted for roughly one in five arrests (21.4%), but by 2011 girls comprised nearly one in three juvenile arrests (29.7%) (Federal Bureau of Investigation, 2012). And although both male and female arrests have been declining in recent years, arrests of juvenile boys declined far more steeply, decreasing 26.5% during the first decade of the 21st century compared to a decrease in girls' arrests of only 15.4%. The same trend was seen in the arrest of girls for simple assault, where the 10-year period showed a decrease in boys' arrests of 21.7%, whereas arrests of girls for the same offense dropped by only 7.5% (Federal Bureau of Investigation, 2012). In short, the much vaulted "crime drop" was really a crime drop in boys' official delinquency, not girls'.

What about the actual data on girls' violence? The picture is decidedly mixed. Most importantly, as noted previously, although official court populations often contained large numbers of girls charged with status offenses, particularly running away from home, it turns out that self-report data routinely show that girls act out violently and have been doing so since the earliest self-report data were published (Elliott & Voss, 1974). Second, there appears to be little evidence that these patterns have changed in the past few decades, despite the media frenzy on the topic.

The Centers for Disease Control and Prevention in Atlanta has monitored youthful behavior in a national sample of school-age youth in a number of domains (including violence) at regular intervals since 1991 in a biennial survey entitled the Youth Risk Behavior Survey. As an example, a review of the data collected over the 1990s and into the 21st century reveals that, although 34.4% of girls surveyed in 1991 said that they had been in a physical fight in the previous year, by 2001 that figure had dropped to 23.9%, a 30.5% decrease in girls' fighting; boys' violence also decreased during the same period but less dramatically—from 50.2% to 43.1%, a 14.1% drop (Centers for Disease Control and Prevention, 1992–2002). Since that time, if anything, the decline has continued. In 2011, 24.4% of girls and 40.7% of boys said they had been in a physical fight in the past year (Centers for Disease Control and Prevention, 1992–2012).

To further explore these issues, Stevens, Morash, and Chesney-Lind (2011) used two national self-report data sets to compare self-reported behavior with self-reported arrests in two different time periods (1980 and 2000). This research found that girls in 1980 had about a one in four chance of having been charged with a crime compared to girls in 2000, who had about a three in four chance of arrest. Furthermore, Black girls in 2000 were nearly seven times more likely than their 1980 counterparts to have been charged with a crime (see also Steffensmeier, Schwartz, Zhong, & Ackerman, 2005).

In short, although girls had long reported that they were acting out violently, their arrests, particularly in the 1960s and 1970s, did not necessarily reflect that reality. Instead, girls' arrests tended to emphasize petty and status offenses; by the 1990s, that had changed dramatically, as more girls were arrested, particularly for such seemingly "masculine" offenses as simple assault—and this pattern was particularly pronounced among African American girls.

Research such as the studies referenced above increasingly suggests that these shifts in girls' arrest patterns are not products of a change in behavior, with girls getting "more" violent, but of the process of "upcriming." Not only do other measures of girls' criminality fail to show an increase in girls' violence, but also there is ample evidence that girls are being more heavily policed, particularly at home and in school (Chesney-Lind & Irwin, 2007). Specifically, girls are being arrested for assault because of arguments with their parents, often their mothers (see Buzawa & Hotaling, 2006), or for other assault for fighting in school because of new zero-tolerance policies enacted after the Columbine shootings (see New York ACLU, 2007). In decades past, this violence would have been ignored or labeled a status offense, like being "incorrigible" or a "person in need of supervision." Now, an arrest is made.

Girls are also staying in the system after being arrested for these new "violent" offenses. The National Center for Juvenile Justice noted that between 1985 and 1997, the growth in the female caseload "outpaced" the growth in the male caseload (101% compared to 54%). Between 1997 and 2009, the male delinquency caseload declined by 24% compared to a female caseload that decreased by only 1%. As a result, in 2009 females accounted for 28% of the delinquency caseload, up from only 19% in 1985 (Puzzanchera, Adams, & Hockenberry, 2012, pp. 12–14).

And although the steep increases in girls' detention and incarceration rates that occurred at the turn of the century have stabilized and even declined in recent years, girls are now *more* likely than boys to be detained for "person offenses" (with 36% of girls compared to 30% of boys held for these types of offenses) (Puzzanchera et al., 2012, p. 34). Finally, there has actually been an increase in the proportion of youth of color in those systems (from 60.3% in 2001 to 67.6% in 2010) (Bradford, 2013, p. 10). These two patterns again focus on the need to consider the role of both race and gender in girls' experiences of the juvenile justice system, particularly their experiences in custody.

Jailing Girls

Conditions for girls held in the juvenile equivalents of jail and prison are also a sub-stantial problem because there is little effective monitoring of the conditions of youthful confinement in the United States. A Department of Justice investigation of the Mississippi training schools holding girls, 75% of whom were committed for status offenses, probation violations, or contempt of court, provides horrific evidence of abuse (Boyd, 2003). In their letter to the governor of Mississippi, the investigators detail the conditions they found at Columbia Training School. They specifically detailed "unconstitutionally abusive practices such as hog-tying, pole-shackling, improper use and over use of restraints and isolation, staff assaulting youth, and OC spray abuse" (Boyd, 2003, p. 5). Hog-tying was described in detail in the report:

> Approximately 10–15 boys and girls consistently described the practice, where youth are placed face down on the floor with their hands and feet shackled and drawn together. That is, youths' hands are handcuffed behind their backs. Their feet are shackled together and then belts or metal chains are wrapped around the two sets of restraints, pulling them together . . . several girls in Hammond Cottage told us that either they had been hog-tied or they had witnessed other girls being hog-tied. They reported that girls are typically tied for three hour periods in the corners of the cottage and stated that girls are also hog-tied in the SIU [Special Intervention Unit]. Girls also reported being hog-tied in a SIU cell called the "dark room." (Boyd, 2003, p. 7)

The report also detailed examples of girls being "shackled to poles in public places" if they were "noncompliant" during military exercise (Mississippi uses a "military model for delinquent youth" stressing "vigorous physical fitness") (Boyd, 2003, p. 2). Girls at Columbia reported being placed in the dark room for "acting out or being suicidal" (Boyd, 2003, p. 7). The windowless isolation cell has lighting controlled by staff; it is also stripped of everything but a drain in the floor, which serves as a toilet. When in use, the room is completely dark, and the girls are placed in the room naked. One girl reported being placed in the room for three days with "little access to water as her requests for water were largely ignored" (Boyd, 2003, p. 7). The report concluded that "the conditions in the SIU are particularly inhumane. The cells are extremely hot with inadequate ventilation. Some girls are naked in a dark room where they must urinate and defecate in a hole that they cannot flush" (Boyd, 2003, p. 10).

Such horrific conditions are particularly ironic because the defense offered by most juvenile court judges until very recently was that they were jailing or incarcer-ating girls for "their own protection." Race also matters in girls' placement in such facilities. In 2011, African American girls and Native American adolescents had the highest rates of placement in residential detention (123 and 179 per 100,000) (Child Trends, 2014). White females were also less likely to be in residential placement

(37 per 100,000 in 2011) than were Hispanic females (47 per 100,000) (Child Trends, 2014). Asian females were the least likely to be in residential placement, with a rate of 11 per 100,000 (Child Trends, 2014).

Conclusion

This chapter has explored both the historic roots of classic delinquency theory and the key voids that developed as a result of that history. The great strength of this theoretical legacy was a focus on the role played by inequality, poverty, and subculture in the generation of crime and delinquency. That said, the criminogenic aspects of other forms of oppression and inequality were largely ignored or trivialized (particularly in the case of gender). Also missed was the juvenile justice system's complicity with patriarchy, its role in continuing aspects of the toxic legacy of slavery and White privilege, and its unquestioned endorsement (particularly in juvenile detention centers and training schools) of "normalcy" of heterosexuality and the need to police girl's sexuality to prevent homosexuality. Although this discussion of girls' pathways into delinquency, particularly official delinquency, has focused largely on gender, it has also attempted to call attention to other forms of inequality where possible, and it has tried to place the patterns found in the United States into a more global framework.

In reviewing girls' pathways into delinquency, particularly the kind of delinquent behavior that gets girls arrested, a key theme is that gender matters in girls' delinquency and the official responses to that behavior. The theoretical neglect of the causes of female delinquency meant that the crucial role played by victimization in girls acting out (particularly running away) was missed. Also missed was the crucial role that the juvenile justice system has played in backstopping patriarchal systems of control. Although such complicity has long been present in the U.S. juvenile justice system, it is perhaps far clearer in global systems of jurisprudence, particularly in religiously conservative countries. A key theme in this discussion was the long-standing interest of the court in the policing of girls, particularly with reference to girls' sexuality. In the court's early years, such an interest was easy to detect because girls were incarcerated for sexual immorality in large numbers. In later decades, this interest was often masked by less explicit offense categories, like runaway, but the interest was often just below the surface.

The turn of the century was accompanied by a new focus on girls, apparently policing "girls' violence." Careful research on these offenses, however, revealed the shifts as thinly veiled efforts to relabel girls' arguments with their parents as crimes rather than status offenses. Also apparent was the upcriming of minor forms of school violence, which swept large numbers of youth, particularly youth of color, into the juvenile justice system.

In sum, classic delinquency theory focused more or less exclusively on the role of class and urban subculture as the generating milieu of delinquency. This focus had the effect of normalizing male violence, missing racism, and ignoring both girls' victimization and the role it plays in traditional female "delinquency." Such a myopic focus on the misbehavior of boys also permitted researchers to miss completely the racism and sexism that permeated the juvenile justice system. The insights of critical feminist criminology point to the need for a delinquency theory that consciously theorizes both gender and patriarchy and on a more global stage. Hopefully, this modest effort has begun that important conversation.

NOTE

[1]This section of the chapter is adapted from an op ed that first appeared on the blog *Feministing* on August 26, 2013. The coauthor on the op ed is Lisa Pasko. http://feministing .com/2013/08/26/some-rescue-the-fbis-dubious-war-on-street-girls/

References

Abram, K. M., Choe, J. Y., Washburn, J. J., Teplin, L. A., King, D. C., & Dulcan, M. K. (2008). Suicidal ideation and behaviors among youths in juvenile detention. *Journal of the American Academy of Child and Adolescent Psychiatry, 47,* 291–300.

Acoca, L. (1998). Outside/inside: The violation of American girls at home, on the streets, and in the juvenile justice system. *Crime and Delinquency, 44,* 561–589.

Adler, F. S. (1975). *Sisters in crime: The rise of the new female criminal.* New York, NY: McGraw–Hill.

Bailey, J. A., & McCloskey, L. A. (2005). Pathways to adolescent substance use among sexually abused girls. *Journal of Abnormal Child Psychology, 33,* 39–53.

Baines, M. (1997). Mad, bad or angry? Gender, sexual abuse and the pathologising of young women's behaviour. *Youth Studies Australia, 16,* 19–23.

Belknap, J., & Holsinger, K. (2006). The gendered nature of risk factors for delinquency. *Feminist Criminology, 1,* 48–71.

Bergen, H. A., Martin, G., Richardson, A. S., Allison, S., & Roeger, L. (2004). Sexual abuse, antisocial behaviour and substance use: Gender differences in young community adolescents. *Australian and New Zealand Journal of Psychiatry, 38,* 34–41.

Berman, J. (2003). (Un)popular strangers and crises (un)bounded: Discourses of sex-trafficking, the European political community and the panicked state of the modern state. *European Journal of International Relations, 9,* 37–86.

Blaskey, M. (2010). Ten members of all-female gang arrested on robbery, burglary charges. *Las Vegas Review–Journal.* Retrieved from http://www.reviewjournal.com/news/ten-members-all-female-gang-arrested-robbery-burglary-charges/

Bloom, B., Owen, B., Deschenes, E. P., & Rosenbaum, J. (2002). Improving juvenile justice for females: A statewide assessment in California. *Crime and Delinquency, 48,* 526–552.

Boyd, R. (2003). *CRIPA investigation of Oakley and Columbia training schools in Raymond and Columbia, Mississippi. Turner Broadcasting Systems.* Retrieved from http://i.cdn.turner.com/cnn/2008/images/04/01/oak.colu.miss.findinglet.pdf/

Boyer, D. (2008). *Who pays the price? An assessment of youth involvement in prostitution in Seattle.* Seattle, WA: Human Services Department.

Boyer, D., & James, J. (1982). Easy money: Adolescent involvement in prostitution. In S. Davidson (Ed.), *Justice for young women*. Seattle, WA: New Directions for Young Women.

Bradford, S. (2013). *Common ground: Lessons learned from five states that reduced juvenile confinement by more than half*. Washington, DC: Justice Policy Institute.

Brannigan, A., & Van Brunschot, E. G. (1997). Youthful prostitution and child sexual trauma. *International Journal of Law and Psychiatry, 20*, 337–354.

Buzawa, E. S., & Hotaling, G. T. (2006). The impact of relationship status, gender, and minor status in the police response to domestic assaults. *Victims and Offenders, 1*, 323–360.

Campagna, D. S., & Poffenberger, D. L. (1988). *The sexual trafficking in children: An investigation of the child sex trade*. Dover, MA: Auburn House.

Centers for Disease Control and Prevention, Youth Risk Behavior Surveillance System. (1992–2012). *CDC–YRBSS—Youth risk behavior surveillance system—Adolescent and school health. Centers for Disease Control and Prevention*. Retrieved from http://www.cdc.gov/HealthyYouth/yrbs/index.htm/

Chen, X., Tyler, K., Whitbeck, L., & Hoyt, D. (2004). Early sexual abuse, street adversity, and drug use among female homeless and runaway adolescents in the Midwest. *Journal of Drug Issues, 34*, 1–22.

Chesney-Lind, M. (1971). *Female juvenile delinquency in Hawaii*. Honolulu: University of Hawai'i at Manoa.

Chesney-Lind, M. (1973). Judicial enforcement of the female sex role: The family court and the female delinquent. *Issues in Criminology, 8*(2), 51–69.

Chesney-Lind, M., & Irwin, K. (2007). *Beyond bad girls: Gender, violence and hype*. New York, NY: Routledge.

Chesney-Lind, M., & Pasko, L. (2013). *The female offender: Girls, women, and crime*. Thousand Oaks, CA: Sage.

Chesney-Lind, M., & Shelden, R. G. (2003). *Girls, delinquency, and juvenile justice* (3rd ed.). Belmont, CA: Wadsworth.

Child Trends. (2014). *Juvenile detention*. Retrieved from http://www.childtrends.org/?indicators=juvenile-detention/

Cloward, R., & Ohlin, L. E. (1966). *Delinquency and opportunity: A theory of delinquent gangs*. Glencoe, IL: The Free Press.

Cohen, A. K. (1956). *Delinquent boys: The culture of the gang*. New York, NY: The Free Press.

Deegan, M. J. (1988). *Jane Addams and the men of the Chicago School, 1892–1918*. New Brunswick, NJ: Transaction Books.

Department of State, Office of Website Management, Bureau of Public Affairs. (2006). *U.S. laws on trafficking in persons*. Retrieved from http://www.state.gov/j/tip/laws/

Edwards, P. (2006, May 17). Number of female gang members on the rise: Police. *Toronto Star*.

Elliott, D. S., & Voss, H. L. (1974). *Delinquency and dropout*. Lexington, MA: Lexington Books.

Empey, L. T. (1982). *American delinquency, its meaning and construction*. Chicago, IL: Dorsey Press.

Federal Bureau of Investigation. (2012). *Crime in the U.S. 2011*. Retrieved from http://www.fbi.gov/about-us/cjis/ucr/crime-in-the-u.s/2011/crime-in-the-u.s.-2011/

Feld, B. C. (2009). Violent girls or relabeled status offenders? An alternative interpretation of the data. *Crime and Delinquency, 55*, 241–265.

Finkelhor, D. (1994). The international epidemiology of child sexual abuse. *Child Abuse and Neglect, 18*, 409–417.

Fishbein, D., Miller, S., Winn, D. M., Dakof, G., & Zahn, M. A. (2009). *Biopsychological factors, gender, and delinquency.* Retrieved from http://www.rti.org/publications/abstract.cfm?pubid=13583/

Flowers, B. R. (2001). *Runaway kids and teenage prostitution: America's lost, abandoned, and sexually exploited children.* Westport, CT: Greenwood Press.

Flynn, E. E. (1998). Freda Adler: A portrait of a pioneer. *Women and Criminal Justice, 10*(1), 1–26.

Gaarder, E., & Belknap, J. (2002). Tenuous borders: Girls transferred to adult court. *Criminology, 40*, 481–517.

Gaarder, E., Rodriguez, N., & Zatz, M. S. (2004). Criers, liars, and manipulators: Probation officers' views of girls. *Justice Quarterly, 21*, 547–578.

Giordano, P. C. (2010). *Legacies of crime: A follow-up of the children of highly delinquent girls and boys.* Cambridge, NY: Cambridge University Press.

Goodkind, S. (2005). Gender-specific services in the juvenile justice system: A critical examination. *Affilia, 20*, 52–70.

Hadi, S. T., & Chesney-Lind, M. (2014). Silence and the criminalization of victimization: On the need for an international feminist criminology. In H. Bershot & Arrigo (Eds.), *Routledge handbook on international crime and justice studies* (pp. 33–52). London, UK: Routledge.

Heidensohn, F. (1968). The deviance of women: A critique and an enquiry. *British Journal of Sociology, 61*(Suppl. 1), 111–126.

Hirschi, T. (1969). *Causes of delinquency.* Berkeley: University of California Press.

Human Rights Watch. (2013, May 21). *Afghanistan: Surge in women jailed for "moral crimes": Prosecute abusers, not women fleeing abuse.* Retrieved from http://www.hrw.org/news/2013/05/21/afghanistan-surge-women-jailed-moral-crimes/

Ianni, F. A. J. (1989). *The search for structure: A report on American youth today.* New York, NY: The Free Press.

Inderbitzin, M. (2007). The impact of gender on juvenile justice decisions. In R. Muraskin (Ed.), *It's a crime: Women and justice* (4th ed., pp. 782–791). Upper Saddle River, NJ: Prentice Hall.

Irvine, A. (2010). We've had three of them: Addressing the invisibility of lesbian, gay, bisexual, and gender nonconforming youths in the juvenile justice system. *Columbia Journal of Gender and Law, 19*, 675–701.

Jacobs, J. L. (1993). Victimized daughters: Sexual violence and the empathic female self. *Signs, 19*, 126–145.

Kamler, B. (1999). *Constructing gender and difference: Critical research perspectives on early childhood.* Cresskill, NJ: Hampton Press.

Katz, P. A. (1979). The development of female identity. *Sex Roles, 5*, 155–178.

Kempf-Leonard, K., & Sample, L. L. (2000). Disparity based on sex: Is gender-specific treatment warranted? *Justice Quarterly, 17*, 89–128.

Klein, D., & Kress, J. (Eds.). (1973). Women, crime and criminology [Special issue]. *Issues in Criminology, 8*(3).

Knupfer, A. M. (2001). *Reform and resistance: Gender, delinquency, and America's first juvenile court.* New York, NY: Routledge.

Leslie, C., Biddle, N., Rosenberg, D., & Wayne, J. (1993, August 2). Girls will be girls. *Newsweek Magazine*, p. 44.

Leve, L., & Chamberlain, P. (2004). Female juvenile offenders: Defining an early-onset pathway for delinquency. *Journal of Child and Family Studies, 13*, 439–452.

Liu, R. X. (2004). The conditional effects of gender and delinquency on the relationship between emotional distress and suicidal ideation or attempt among youth. *Journal of Adolescent Research, 19*, 698–715.

Lombroso, C., & Ferrero, G. (1895). *The female offender*. Buffalo, NY: Hein.

Longfellow, H. (2013). *There was a little girl*. *Poetry Foundation*. Retrieved from http://www.poetryfoundation.org/poem/173916/

MacDonald, J. M., & Chesney-Lind, M. (2001). Gender bias and juvenile justice revisited: A multiyear analysis. *Crime and Delinquency, 47*, 173–195.

Mallicoat, S. L. (2007). Gendered justice attributional differences between males and females in the juvenile courts. *Feminist Criminology, 2*, 4–30.

Martin, D. (1976). *Battered wives*. San Francisco, CA: Glide.

McGuire, D. (2002). The interactive effects of race, sex and offense severity on detention processing decisions. *Journal for Juvenile Justice and Detention Services, 17*, 59–78.

Miller, J. (1994). Race, gender, and juvenile justice: An examination of disposition decision-making for delinquent girls. In M. D. Schwartz and D. Milovanovic (Eds.), *The intersection of race, gender and class in criminology* (pp. 219–246). New York, NY: Garland.

New York ACLU. (2007). *Criminalizing the classroom: The over-policing of New York City schools*. Retrieved from https://www.aclu.org/racial-justice/criminalizing-classroom-over-policing-new-york-city-schools/

Odem, M. E. (1995). *Delinquent daughters: Protecting and policing adolescent female sexuality in the United States, 1885–1920*. Chapel Hill: University of North Carolina Press.

Orenstein, P. (2000). *Schoolgirls: Young women, self-esteem, and the confidence gap*. New York, NY: Anchor Books.

Park, R. E., & Burgess, E. W. (1925). *The city*. Chicago, IL: University of Chicago Press.

Piquero, N. L., Gover, A. R., MacDonald, J. M., & Piquero, A. R. (2005). The influence of delinquent peers on delinquency: Does gender matter? *Youth and Society, 36*, 251–275.

Pollak, O. (1950). *The criminality of women*. Philadelphia: University of Pennsylvania Press.

Puzzanchera, C., Adams, B., & Hockenberry, S. (2012). *Juvenile court statistics 2009*. Pittsburgh, PA: National Center for Juvenile Justice. Retrieved from http://www.ojjdp.gov/ojstatbb/njcda/pdf/jcs2009.pdf/

Rafter, N. H. (2000). *Encyclopedia of women and crime*. Phoenix, AZ: Oryx Press.

Read, P. (2009). *"Operation Bloodette" nets 43 members of female-led drug ring*. Retrieved from http://www.nj.com/news/index.ssf/2009/07/operation_bloodette_nets_43_me.html/

Riehman, K., Blutenthal, R., Juvonen, J., & Morral, A. (2003). Adolescent social relationships and the treatment process: Findings from quantitative and qualitative analyses. *Journal of Drug Issues, 33*, 865–896.

Schaffner, L. (2006). *Girls in trouble with the law*. New Brunswick, NJ: Rutgers University Press. Retrieved from http://site.ebrary.com/id/10167787/

Schlossman, S., & Wallach, S. (1978). *The crime of precocious sexuality: Female juvenile delinquency in the progressive era.* Retrieved from http://www.eric.ed.gov/ERICWebPortal/detail?accno=EJ180904/

Sedlak, A., & Broadhurst, D. (1996). *National study of the incidence of child abuse and neglect.* Rockville, MD: Westat.

Shaw, C., & McKay, H. D. (1942). *Juvenile delinquency and urban areas.* Chicago, IL: University of Chicago Press.

Shaw, C. R. (1966). *The jack-roller: A delinquent boy's own story.* Chicago, IL: University of Chicago Press.

Shaw, C. R., McKay, H. D., McDonald, J. E., McDonald, J. F., Hanson, H. B., & Burgess, E. W. (1938). *Brothers in crime.* Chicago, IL: University of Chicago Press.

Shelden, R. G. (1981). Sex discrimination in the juvenile justice system: Memphis, Tennessee, 1900–1917. In M. Q. Warren (Ed.), *Comparing male and female offenders* (pp. 55–72). Newbury Park, CA: Sage.

Simon, R. J. (1975). *Women and crime.* Lexington, MA: Lexington Books.

Smart, C. (1976). *Women, crime, and criminology: A feminist critique.* London: Routledge & Kegan Paul.

Steffensmeier, D., Schwartz, J., Zhong, H., & Ackerman, J. (2005). An assessment of recent trends in girls' violence using diverse longitudinal sources: Is the gender gap closing? *Criminology, 43,* 355–406.

Stevens, T., Morash, M., & Chesney-Lind, M. (2011). Are girls getting tougher, or are we tougher on girls? Probability of arrest and juvenile court oversight in 1980 and 2000. *Justice Quarterly, 28,* 719–744.

Thorne, B. (1993). *Gender play: Girls and boys in school.* New Brunswick, NJ: Rutgers University Press.

Thrasher, F. M. (1963). *The gang: A study of 1,313 gangs in Chicago.* Chicago, IL: University of Chicago Press.

Tracy, P. E., Wolfgang, M. E., & Figlio, R. M. (1990). *Delinquency careers in two birth cohorts.* New York, NY: Plenum Press.

Widom, C. (1995). *Victims of childhood sexual abuse—Later criminal consequences.* Washington, DC: Office of Juvenile Justice and Delinquency Prevention.

World Health Organization. (2013). *Global and regional estimates of violence against women: Prevalence and health effects of intimate partner violence and non-partner sexual violence.* Retrieved from http://www.who.int/reproductivehealth/publications/violence/9789241564625/en/index.html/

Yost, P. (2013). *Child prostitution: Raids rescue 105 young people. The Big Story.* Retrieved from http://bigstory.ap.org/article/fbi-raids-rescue-105-kids-forced-prostitution/

Zahn, M. A. (2009). *The delinquent girl.* Philadelphia, PA: Temple University Press.

CHAPTER 6

Becoming a Female Felony Offender

Leanne Fiftal Alarid and Emily M. Wright

Freda Adler's 1975 work, entitled *Sisters in Crime*, examined the rates of serious violent offending of adult women and determined that in the 1970s, the rate of serious crime committed by women was outpacing the rise in the crime rate for men. Adler's ideas coalesced at the beginning of the women's liberation movement, at the time when women were starting to make strides in professional and financial worlds and becoming more socially independent. In a theory that became better known as the "liberation hypothesis" or the "emancipation hypothesis," it was thought that opportunities for women would increase and, simultaneously, that women would experience more freedom and be subjected to fewer informal controls on their behavior. The crux of Adler's theory was that violent offending rates and types of crime that involved coercion and confrontation would continue to increase over time. If true, this increase in rates of women's serious crime compared to men's rates would slowly narrow the gender gap that has always existed, where men have committed the vast majority of serious and violent forms of crime.

Empirical research on crime trends over time has failed to support the liberation hypothesis. Nonetheless, this hypothesis succeeded in challenging nearly a century of ideas regarding why women committed crime. It was traditionally assumed that women became involved in serious criminality because of biological abnormalities or psychological defects (Freud, 1933; Lombroso & Ferrero, 1895/1959; Pollack, 1950). In contrast, Freda Adler's work helped to spur theory regarding the sociological factors (e.g., opportunities) that influence women's crime. Most crimes committed by women have been and still are today of a less serious nature. However, Adler's observations concerning the gender gap in violent and serious offending behavior have sustained a great deal of attention in the literature and sparked debate over the past 40 years (e.g., Lauritsen, Heimer, & Lynch, 2009; Schwartz, Steffensmeier, Zhong, & Ackerman, 2009). Scholars remain interested not only in why females remain disproportionately less involved in violence and serious criminality than males, but also in what theories better explain why women become involved in such criminality, their roles in the criminal event, and how women criminals perceive themselves—all of which comprise the subject matter addressed in this chapter.

Serious/Felony/Index Crime Rates Over Time

The FBI has identified eight felony offenses as Type I index crimes that are uniformly considered serious crimes. These crimes are homicide/murder, forcible rape/sexual assault, aggravated assault, robbery, arson, burglary, larceny/felony theft, and motor vehicle theft. The UCR allows index crime rates to be examined over time by way of arrests that are known to the police and reported to the FBI. The UCR trends are commonly compared to National Crime Victimization Survey (NCVS) data for the same time period. The NCVS data are collected by the U.S. Bureau of the Census by asking a nationally representative sample of households to self-report incidents in which they have been victimized by crime. The NCVS captures criminal events that have been reported to the police as well as incidents that have not been reported to the police. The proportionate increases and decreases over time have remained fairly consistent between the two sources. For instance, both the UCR and the NCVS indicate that violent crime and victimization rates across the United States decreased by approximately 13% between 2001 and 2010 (FBI, 2011; Lauritsen & Rezey, 2013).

The data show that the proportion of women's involvement in some index offenses, such as larceny, has risen proportionately faster than that for men. Since 2002, the population of sentenced female inmates in state or federal institutions has increased 1.6% compared to 1.1% for males (Carson & Golineli, 2013). However, Darrell Steffensmeier (1995) argued that these numbers may be a bit misleading for a number of reasons. First, women have always constituted a disproportionately lower percentage of arrests and convictions than men, for every type of serious crime. A small gain in the raw numbers of women being arrested will appear as a larger percentage. For example, it takes only 10 women to register a 10% increase in an existing group of 100, whereas it takes 100 people to register the same 10% increase if the initial group was already larger (such as what you might find with the male population in a group of 1,000). Nonetheless, raw numbers show that the number of sentenced female inmates has increased by over 12,000 in a 10-year span (Carson & Golineli, 2013).

Notably, the most recent statistics on state prison populations show that a higher proportion of male inmates (54.3%) than female inmates (36.8%) were incarcerated for violent offenses in 2011. By contrast, a higher proportion of female (27.8%; 25.1%) than male (17.7%; 16.2%) inmates were locked up for property offenses and drug offenses, respectively (Carson & Golineli, 2013). Much of the growth in arrest and incarceration rates for women since the 1980s thus has been attributed to the change in laws and system responses that set stiffer punishments for nonserious crimes, such as drug crimes, or regulated responses to crimes that disproportionately impact women, such as domestic violence. For example, the war on drugs affected longer sentences for drug use, possession, and sales from 1982 to the present. Bloom, Owen, and Covington (2004), among others, have contended that women's numbers in the criminal justice system suffered disproportionately compared to men's as a result. Tougher arrest policies and laws requiring prison sentences in response to nonviolent crimes related to drugs increased the number of women who went to prison instead of receiving community sanctions (Bloom et al., 2004). These policies had a net-widening effect for women, especially given their disproportionate involvement in drug offenses (Javdani, Sadeh, & Verona, 2011), leading some to suggest that the war on drugs is a "war on women" (Chesney-Lind & Pasko, 2004). Similarly, bringing more girls into the juvenile justice system as a result of status offenses, such as running away, has also tended to increase females' numbers in the criminal justice system (Chesney-Lind & Pasko, 2004; Chesney-Lind & Shelden, 2004; Javdani et al., 2011).

Another example of a system response that may have differentially impacted females was mandatory dual-arrest policies for assault and aggravated assault (Steffensmeier, Zhong, Ackerman, Schwartz, & Agha, 2006). In such dual-arrest policies, it is mandatory for police officers to arrest both parties in a domestic violence dispute, regardless of who was the "instigator" and who was the "victim" within the dispute. Many scholars suggest that women are overwhelmingly the victims in domestic violence cases, particularly those which involve the criminal justice system (Johnson, 2008), and a policy that treats victims and perpetrators "equally" does not necessarily account for their different roles. In fact, arresting women in these circumstances is a practice that does not reflect their actual violence levels (Chesney-Lind, 2002) and appears to have disproportionately increased women's arrest rates compared to their male counterparts (Javdani et al., 2011).

For these reasons, some researchers maintain that actual *levels* of violent crime committed by women have changed very little, but the debate continues. According to Steffensmeier (1995):

> For masculine and serious violent crimes, then, females have made small gains in arrests for masculine crimes (mainly in arrests for minor assaults) but have not gained ground on males in arrests for serious violent crimes like murder, aggravated assault, and robbery. (p. 96)

More recently, scholars have examined UCR arrest data and NCVS victimization data to determine the trends in men and women's crime over a 30-year period and to examine whether the gender gap in offending has changed. Although some argue that the gender gap has changed little between the 1970s and 2005 (Schwartz et al., 2009; Steffensmeier et al., 2006), others maintain that long-term declines are present for both women and men, but that the gender gap appears to be narrowing because the decline for violent crime was greater for men (Heimer, Lauritsen, & Lynch, 2009; Lauritsen et al., 2009). Women's violent crime rates have always been lower than men's violent crime rates, but Lauritsen and her colleagues suggest a "civilizing hypothesis," where the presence of women in public and work spheres has reduced men's interpersonal violence, which has led to a narrowing gender gap in offending. They argue that although decreases in *male* offending have been the primary factor driving the narrowing gender gap between men and women, by no means does this suggest that female offending has increased (Heimer et al., 2009). Perhaps the reason why some scholars find little to no difference in the gender gap in offending whereas others do is the way in which their rates are calculated. Thus, whereas Schwartz and her colleagues counted individual *offenders*, Lauritsen and her colleagues counted criminal *incidents*.

The differences between criminal incidents and criminal offenders differ widely. Whereas one criminal offender can be involved in multiple incidents, one criminal incident more often involves more than one offender. When criminal incidents involve accomplices, co-defendants may be charged with the same criminal incident without paying detailed attention to the role each accomplice played in the incident. Thus, the more important question becomes, to what degree did women's involvement in serious crime constitute a solo act, and to what degree did serious crime involve accomplices? If women committed an act alone, to what degree was she the aggressor or did she respond in self-defense? If women committed the crime with others, who were these accomplices and what role in serious crime did she play in the group?

How Criminological Theories Explain Women's Involvement in Felony Offending

Criminological theories were created to help explain why people commit crimes and deviate from the norm. In this section, we discuss how traditional criminological theories, feminist criminological theory, and the pathways-to-crime approaches explain serious and violent female criminal behavior.

Traditional Criminological Theories

In early criminological theories, women's involvement in serious offending was typically linked to traditional role expectations or mental health problems. Given that women were expected to be the kinder and gentler sex, women who engaged in criminal behavior were considered abnormal and more masculine because they broke traditional gender role expectations (Ogle, Maier-Katkin, & Bernard, 1995). Other explanations tended to pathologize women's criminal behavior, suggesting that their behavior was the result of some mental disease or illness. However, as Ogle and her colleagues suggest, the social structural context in which human behavior occurs is important to consider to more fully understand women's behavior. Freda Adler was one of the first to argue this point with regard to female criminality.

Freda Adler suggested new ways of thinking about female criminality that had not yet been widely communicated in criminology—that social experiences, not biological factors such as sex, influenced behavior and that violent crimes were associated with the liberation of women away from their traditional gender roles. Freda Adler (1975) argued that one's social position and social role expectations were more important than sex in determining criminal behavior. She suggested that aggression and dominance, characteristics more often seen among offenders and males in general, were socially learned and that the reason why more males were offenders was because they were socially shaped to be aggressive, dominating, and risky to achieve their goals. The assumption is that if females were raised like males and had the same opportunities as males, their behavior would be more like that of males. Notably, Adler was not alone in challenging traditional thinking about women and crime. For example, Rita Simon (1975) also endorsed a widely read version of the liberation or emancipation thesis in that she linked women's liberation to a rise in property crime.

In a sense, the liberation thesis shares similar assumptions to Cloward and Ohlin's (1960) theory of differential opportunity. Both theories predict that certain forms of crime are tied to legitimate and illegitimate opportunities available for each sex and that as a woman's position in the public sphere increases, so too do her opportunities for both legitimate advancement and illegitimate behavior. Thus, instead of pathologizing women's crime, Freda Adler and other scholars, such as Simon, borrowed elements from traditional criminological theories designed to explain male offending (e.g., opportunities for deviance, learned aggressiveness, social status) and applied them to women's offending.

Other traditional theories of crime have also been used to account for serious crime committed by women. For example, Travis Hirschi's (1969) theory of social control was tested with young adult women, aged 18 to 24, convicted of felony crimes. Conventional social bonds, specifically parental attachment, reduced crime for adult females, but being married or attached to a male significant other *increased* property and drug crime (Alarid, Burton, & Cullen, 2000). This same study found that differential association theory can account for women's serious offending behaviors, in that crime is learned in a process of exposure to persons and definitions favorable to lawbreaking. Procriminal definitions include repeated exposure to crime from family members and significant others for extended time periods. This research supports the notion that like that of male offenders, serious crime by females is impacted by bonds to others and definitions or beliefs that are favorable to violating the law.

Gottfredson and Hirschi's theory of low self-control (1990) has been used as well to explain female offending. Researchers have found that when an opportunity presents itself, women who already lack the ability to control themselves will be more likely to commit criminal behavior (Burton, Cullen, Evans, Alarid, & Dunaway, 1998). Although Burton et al. assessed both violent (e.g., felonious assault) and nonviolent (e.g., stolen items) acts in their study, others have found that low self-control is a strong risk factor for chronic, serious, and violent criminal behavior among women (Brennan, Breitenbach, Dieterich, Salisbury, & Van Voorhis, 2012).

Some scholars have examined whether traditional theories can be "gendered" or tweaked to make them more applicable to female crime (e.g., Heimer & De Coster, 1999). Studies suggest that some elements of traditional criminological theories—such as low self-control, learning processes and beliefs, strain, peer association, opportunities, family processes, and perceived costs or benefits of crime—are evident in women's lives and may be risk factors for their criminal behavior (e.g., Brennan et al., 2012; De Coster, Heimer, & Cumley, 2012; Heimer & De Coster, 1999; Simpson, Yaher, & Dugan, 2008). However, the debate over the generality or specificity of criminological theories for females continues (Daigle, Cullen, & Wright, 2007; Mullins & Miller, 2008). On one hand, it has been suggested not only that traditional theoretical concepts have a different impact for women, but also that these concepts influence criminality differently for women than they do for men. For example, although females experience different early socialization, higher levels of parental control, different forms of strain, and fewer delinquent friendships than males, each of these factors influences women differently (compared to men) with respect to their involvement in crime (De Coster et al., 2012). On the other hand, feminist theorists consistently argue that simply "adding gender" into traditional theories does little to help us understand how gender interacts with race and social and economic marginalization across the life course to impact women's serious and violent crime.

Feminist Criminological Theory

Feminist theories generally attempt to bring women into the forefront of intellectual inquiry by examining how the construction of masculinity, femininity, and gender inequality defines who individuals are and how they behave. One of the key ideas in feminist theory is that women (and men) behave according to the way others see as acceptable for their gender. Liberal and socialist theories focus on the salience of sex-role socialization and equality of opportunities for women compared to men. They argue that females may be oppressed by social norms that foster unequal opportunities. Liberal feminist theories suggest that women are socialized to accept subservient positions in society and that even if women had equal opportunities for work as men do, they would be placed into work that meets their gendered roles, such as being a caregiver or a homemaker. In essence, women are kept oppressed by these social norms. Radical feminist theories also agree that women are oppressed, but these theories argue that such oppression is the result of structural inequality in power between men and women. They assert that male and female crime is fundamentally linked to patriarchy, which is a sexist system of power dominated by males; because males possess most of the political and economic power, their dominance in society is fostered through politics, culture, and the legal system or laws (Cullen & Agnew, 2011).

Feminist theories have been critical of traditional criminological theories, arguing that traditional theories themselves used male-offender data to derive theories that explained male behavior without considering how the "lived experiences" of being female differ from that of males and how gendered realities are fundamentally tied to race or ethnicity and social and economic marginalization. For example, Chesney-Lind (1997) argues that females' criminal behaviors often start out as survival strategies to escape abusive homes. As opposed to males, females are much more likely to experience abuse, particularly sexual abuse, early in their lives. They often seek to escape this abuse by running away from home. Because of their marginal economic status, female runaways are forced to resort to gendered criminal behavior (e.g., prostitution) for survival, which in turn can further ensnare them into a life of crime and drug dependency. Largely because of arguments from feminist criminologists that traditional theories neglected important facets of life among females, such as early abuse and victimization, and their calls to look at female criminality through a different (gendered) lens, another feminist theory—the pathways perspective—became popular.

Pathways to Crime

The pathways-to-crime approach is the most recent advancement of feminist theories of crime. This feminist approach argues that women offenders engage in qualitatively different offenses than men (primarily nonviolent), do so for different reasons, and, in particular, come into the criminal justice system via different paths than men (Wright, Van Voorhis, Salisbury, & Bauman, 2012). In short, the pathways perspective argues that the confluence of trauma, substance abuse, and mental health problems puts women on paths to crime that are inherently different from the paths into crime and the criminal justice system taken by men (Salisbury & Van Voorhis, 2009; Wright, Salisbury, & Van Voorhis, 2007). For example, early victimization and abuse by family members or friends may lead to later depression or drug use, both of which can increase women's serious and violent felony behavior (Salisbury & Van Voorhis, 2009). Additionally, women's relationships with others are considered potential motivators for or inhibitors against their criminal behavior, given that women are typically more relational than men and tend to measure themselves by their relationships with others (Miller, 1976). In fact, Wright and her colleagues (Wright, DeHart, Koons-Witt, & Crittenden, 2013) suggest that many times, women's serious crime is committed "as a response to, a reason for, or an element of relationships with other people" (p. 73), for instance, as violence against an abusive significant other, forgery or fraud committed to provide for their own family members, or as co-offending within an intimate relationship. By placing high importance on these core issues, the pathways approach thus uses elements of earlier feminist theories (e.g., early victimization, drug use) as factors that create the unique paths women take into serious crime.

The pathways perspective began with various qualitative studies that explored, primarily from women's perspectives, how they had become entrenched in a criminal lifestyle. From her analysis of 40 presentence investigation reports, Daly (1992) was able to identify five different paths women took in getting to court for a felony charge: First, as a direct result from parents who were addicted to drugs, incarcerated, or had died, *harmed and harming women* had experienced childhood neglect or had experienced physical, sexual, or emotional abuse. They were typically impoverished, had developed drug problems and mental health issues of their own, and reported problems with managing their anger. Daly suggested that the early abuse they had endured greatly affected their menial coping skills; it is possible that as a result of their traumatic and disorganized early home life, they turned to drugs or developed mental health problems (e.g., depression), which further contributed to their criminal behavior. Second, *battered women* seemed almost like a subset of harmed and harming women, but women in this group had committed assault or murder against an abusive man. This incident was typically their sole violent offense. Third, *street women* also suffered neglect or abuse as children, but usually ran away from home to escape the abuse. While living on the street, they reported being taken in by an older man, becoming addicted to drugs, and supporting their drug habit through property and vice crime. Fourth, *drug-connected women* were likely to become involved in the drug market through a male family member or friend. They may have used drugs but did not display the same level of problems with drugs, mental illness, or anger as the previous three groups. Fifth, *other women* came from working-class or middle-class backgrounds and committed felony offenses because of socioeconomic circumstances or the desire for money. They had a higher level of education and employment record and little to no histories of abuse, addiction, or violence.

Scholars have since looked at pathways leading women into the criminal justice system using various methodologies, samples, and techniques. This research has continued to identify the salience of early victimization and abuse among women offenders in combination with their often dysfunctional family origins, economic and social marginality, and negative influences of family and romantic partners. For instance, childhood abuse has been linked to higher rates of violent and property crime among women (Teague, Mazerolle, Legosz, & Sanderson, 2008). The experience of being abused or neglected as a child has been shown to affect females differently than males. Thus, Rivera and Widom (1990) found that abused or neglected girls were more likely than girls who were not abused or neglected to have arrests for violent delinquency, but childhood abuse did not seem to be a contributing factor for later violence for boys. Abuse and victimization may also persist over a longer period of time for females, leading to further negative outcomes. For example, being involved in an intimate but abusive relationship has been linked to increased incidences of violent crime and drug use for women (Moe, 2006; Richie, 1996). In all, abuse and victimization have significant long-lasting effects on women's serious and violent criminal behavior, with females in prison significantly more likely to experience both childhood sexual abuse and adult intimate partner violence than women with no criminal history (Severson, Postmus, & Berry, 2005).

Qualitative and quantitative work has largely replicated Daly's typologies of women's pathways into crime; although they received different names, many of the core characteristics of each pathway have remained the same (see, e.g., Brennan et al., 2012; Chesney-Lind, 1997; Gilfus, 1992; Owen, 1998; Richie, 1996; Salisbury & Van Voorhis, 2009; Shechory, Perry, & Addad, 2011; Simpson et al., 2008). Thus, Simpson et al. (2008) largely replicated Daly's pathways in a study of women in jail, most of whom were African American. Similarly, Brennan and his colleagues (2012) summarized the various pathways that have been identified in the literature regarding women offenders (using different samples and methods and naming the pathways differently). Brennan et al. concluded that this literature revealed five "types" of women that follow various pathways into serious criminal behavior (i.e., crimes that often resulted in criminal justice sanctions or imprisonment).

First, Brennan and his colleagues (2012) noted that the literature base has generally identified *normal or situational female offenders*, who are characterized by an absence of risk factors, late onset into crime, and minor offenses. Shechory et al. (2011) describe these women as low crime offenders, who largely engage in minor and nonserious forms of crime. Second, *adolescence-limited female offenders* typically engage in minor crimes and desist by adulthood. Third, *victimized, socially withdrawn, and depressed female offenders* experienced early abuse and trauma, leading to withdrawn behaviors, mistrust of others, hostility, drug use, and eventually crime (Brennan et al., 2012). In fact, Salisbury and Van Voorhis (2009) found support for a pathway between childhood victimization and mental illness (depression and anxiety) and then to substance use, which led to recidivism among female offenders. These women might also encompass Shechory et al.'s drug-offending women, who were characterized by chronic delinquency, early criminal behavior, vast criminal history, unstable childhood, family conflict, drug use, and abuse, or Richie's (1996) battered women. Fourth, *chronic serious female offenders* have been characterized as high-risk women who endured early abuse and reported school and family-related problems, low self-control, and aggressive personality (Brennan et al., 2012). This pathway seems to typify Daly's harmed and harming women. Finally, *socialized or socially marginalized female offenders* have been characterized throughout the literature as poor, marginalized, undereducated women with criminal families and friends (Brennan et al., 2012). For instance, Salisbury and Van Voorhis (2009) found evidence of a pathway among relationship dysfunction with significant others, adult victimization, mental health problems, and substance use among female recidivists.

Using various methodological techniques, Brennan and his colleagues (2012) found evidence for four of the aforementioned five pathways: the *normal functioning drug or property offenders*, characterized by few risk factors and possible "snares" like drug use, which kept them involved in criminal lifestyles; the *battered women/victimization pathway*, characterized by extreme and lifelong abuse and victimization from others; the *poor marginalized socialized offenders*, characterized by low self-efficacy, poverty, marginalized status, and antisocial friends, family, or significant others; and the *antisocial aggressive women offenders*, characterized by low self-control, antisocial personality, histories of abuse, and various problems in childhood leading to adult crime and drug use. Thus, the core components of the pathways-to-crime perspective appear to be quite robust and have been replicated among several studies. The salience of abuse, unhealthy relationships with others, social and economic marginalization, drug use, and mental health problems as primary ways in which women proceed into serious crime cannot be ignored. Many of these themes become evident when discussing women's roles in and motivations for serious criminal behavior.

Women's Involvement in Serious Felony Offenses

As noted above, many scholars suggest that serious misbehavior among females is more likely to occur with others, such as friends, family, or, in particular, male significant others, whereas women are more likely to engage in nonserious and nonviolent behavior alone; however, female offenders overwhelmingly commit nonserious and nonviolent forms of crime (Bloom, Owen, & Covington, 2003). Serious or persistent offending behavior is defined by the magnitude of harm that the crime causes other people, such as crimes of violence (murder, assault, and robbery), as well as felony property crimes and drug crimes, and constitutes a small proportion of the total amount of crimes known or reported. In 2011, approximately 52% of female prisoners committed nonviolent property and drug crimes, such as larceny, motor vehicle theft, fraud, drug trafficking, or drug possession (Carson & Golineli, 2013). About 37% committed violent offenses such as murder (10.7%), robbery (8.9%), or assault (8.5%) during that same year (Carson & Golineli, 2013). More serious or violent criminal behavior tends to be correlated with co-offending among women, in part because some crimes require specialized knowledge or skills or networking with other accomplices to complete the job.

For instance, Richard Cloward's (1959) theory of illegitimate opportunity highlights how access to social networks in the criminal underworld might be shaped by gender differences. Researchers noted that sex segregation existed in both professional criminal enterprises that were organized and more profitable (Adler, 1993; Steffensmeier, 1983) and in unorganized mixed-gender, criminal partnerships involved in typical street crime (Alarid, Marquart, Burton, Cullen, & Cuvelier, 1996). Based on interviews with young women aged 18 to 24, Leanne Alarid and her colleagues (1996) found that women acted alongside male partners as accomplices when the crime was particularly dangerous or high risk, such as robbery, burglary, and some drug deals. In these cases, men took leadership roles and women acted in secondary roles. In contrast, women tended to act alone when committing forgery, theft, driving while intoxicated, and assault (Alarid et al., 1996). Additionally, using a larger sample, Koons-Witt and Schram (2003) found that African American females committed violent crimes most often alone (60%) compared to White women, who committed solo crimes only 40% of the time. White women were more likely to commit violent offenses with men (55%) compared to only 30% of African American women (Koons-Witt & Schram, 2003). Supporting the notion that women's serious crime is often influenced by males, they also found that only a small percentage of violent crimes were committed with all-female accomplices—5% for White women and 9% for African American women (Koons-Witt & Schram, 2003).

Felony Drug Dealing and Trafficking

It has also been argued that women engage in crime for different reasons than men, and when they engage in crime, they likely fulfill different roles than males do. Many women report engaging in drug crime for various reasons, including to support their own (or a loved one's) drug habit, to provide monetarily for their family, or simply for the power or thrill of it (e.g., Wright et al., 2013). The division of labor in the drug trade, however, is defined first by gender and second by race or ethnicity, with women again likely taking a secondary, and potentially less profitable, role. In a detailed qualitative analysis of key themes from 15 studies that other researchers conducted regarding women's roles in the drug economy over nearly three decades, Maher and Hudson (2007) found that most women remain relegated to subordinate or second-ary roles, which are less profitable. For example, women may sell drugs on the side as a way to support their own or their partner's addiction, but Moe (2006) found that this was primarily for a short time and it never yielded enough to support other financial needs such as rent or food.

Others suggest that more women are drug couriers or "mules" than actual deal-ers. Women's courier status may be preferred by drug dealers because women may be viewed by the law enforcement community as less likely to be carrying drugs and therefore less likely to be searched than males. In a rare study of drug traffickers who were convicted of smuggling drugs through London's Heathrow airport over a six-year period, women comprised 28% ($n = 471$) of a total of 1,715 smugglers (Harper, Harper, & Stockdale, 2002). Researchers found that in smuggling drugs through airports, women were more likely to take greater risks than men with respect to the class of drugs, the quantity of drugs, and the method of concealment. Women were more likely to carry heroin and cocaine, which carried a stiffer sen-tence, than they were to carry marijuana. Although concealing drugs in luggage was the most common method for both women (45%) and men (31%), women were more likely to secure drugs directly to their body as couriers, whereas men were more likely to send drugs by freight. Women who carried drugs as couriers carried more actual weight and value (measured in terms of drug purity) than did men couriers in this study (Harper et al., 2002).

Women may also be introduced to the drug trade by others important to them, such as family members and significant others (Maher & Hudson, 2007). Moe (2006) noted that family was an important resource for helping women learn the drug trade and gain contacts. Some family members provided constant exposure to drugs and helped some women support their addictions (Moe, 2006), such as caring for depen-dent children during drug use or drug-selling activity. Maher and Hudson's (2007) review identified that the few women who were more successful in the drug trade seemed to initially rely on men to facilitate entry into drug networks, have multiple income sources, and function both as a primary caretaker of children and as a drug dealer. Maher and Hudson concluded that:

> little has changed since the first research in this area was conducted during the early 1980s . . . street-based drug markets are gender stratified and hierarchical and that women primarily access and sustain economic roles through their links with men who act as gatekeepers, sponsors, and protectors. Within these markets, female roles continue to be sexualized, but some women utilize "feminine" attributes and institutional sexism to their advantage. (p. 821)

Serious Property Crimes

Drug addiction has also been linked to women's involvement in serious property crimes such as felony theft, embezzlement, and fraud (Miller, 1998; Moe, 2006; Sommers & Baskin, 1993). In general, less social science research has been done with respect to women's involvement in burglary and motor vehicle theft, both of which require establishing criminal networks to fence or sell stolen property. One of the first known studies of this type was conducted with female residential burglars (Decker, Wright, Redfern, & Smith, 1993). This study suggested that women burglars engaged in crime for a variety of reasons—for the thrill or fun of it, to make fast money, or to support substance-use habits (Decker et al., 1993). Similar to their secondary or subservient roles in drug-related crimes, women burglars also reported taking limited roles in burglary, at least initially. Women indicated that they did not necessarily have the skills needed to successfully work alone and instead took opportunities to learn from their friends (or boyfriends) who had expertise in the area (Decker et al., 1993). Eventually, however, women reported becoming integral components of successful burglary collaborations—explaining how they selected target locations and planned the offenses.

Interviews with 18 women who were actively involved in residential burglary and 8 women involved in motor vehicle theft found that gaining initial access and learning techniques limited the opportunities women had for involvement in a type of crime that was dominated by men (Mullins & Cherbonneau, 2011; Mullins & Wright, 2003). Limited opportunities, together with being perceived by male associates as physically and emotionally weak or untrustworthy, explained why so few women pursued this avenue. The women who managed to establish criminal networks and trust of their male accomplices appeared to have an adequate skill set and even acted masculine.

Women perpetrators seemed willing to use gender stereotypes—other people viewing women as sex objects—to their advantage. Women who acted alone or with all-female accomplices tended to use their sexuality or to pretend they needed help so as to catch people off guard or lure in potential targets (Mullins & Cherbonneau, 2011; Mullins & Wright, 2003). Mullins and Wright (2003) made an interesting observation about the differences between how women and men view getting out of the life:

> The female offenders believed that, in order to go straight, they first needed to sever ties with their male associates . . . [in contrast to male offenders who] . . . see

their best hope of going straight as lying in the establishment of an enduring relationship with a "good" woman . . . the men talk about the need to *make* a tie, the
women about the need to *break* one. (p. 835)

Crimes of Violence

Lethal violence by women tends to be more often self-directed through suicide and
self-mutilation than violent behavior against other people (Batton, 2004). Researchers theorize that the low rate of women's violent behavior directed at others occurs,
in part, because women are socialized to control and suppress their anger. This
socialization begins early as girls learn that expressing anger outright is not consistent with femininity. In addition, girls are more strongly influenced by family and
parental bonds and seem to have less experience with violence (De Coster et al.,
2012; Heimer & De Coster, 1999).

As mentioned at the beginning of this chapter, women who are socioeconomi-
cally disadvantaged tend to have higher rates of violence than women of higher social
status. One potential reason for this is that marginalized women experience more
stress and have fewer coping mechanisms for dealing with anger than women with
more social advantages. In fact, women offenders report high levels of financial
strain because they are often the primary caregivers of many or young dependent
children, but they also report low levels of financial or emotional support (Bloom
et al., 2003; Mumola, 2000; Sharp, 2003).

Of all the possible crimes of violence, the official statistics from the UCR indicate that women are most likely to be involved in assault and aggravated assault.
Most women do not usually instigate assaultive behavior unless it is in response to
being battered or abused by domestic partners, family, or acquaintances (Campbell,
1993; Muftic, Bouffard, & Bouffard, 2007) or in self-defense because they see no
other option at the time (Miller & Meloy, 2006). Sommers and Baskin (1993) termed
this behavior as victim precipitated and retaliatory in nature, with little advanced
planning.

In many cases of intimate-partner violence, drug use becomes a coping mechanism for an abusive relationship (Moe, 2004; Richie, 1996). Only about 14% of assault
incidents involving a female perpetrator were related to drug dealing, where violence
was used as an informal method of social control (Sommers & Baskin, 1993). Only
one known study examined retaliatory street violence of men and women. The data
showed that of the few women who resorted to retaliation, women were less likely
than men to use firearms and more likely to use nonviolent and indirect methods of
vengeance (Mullins, Wright, & Jacobs, 2004). More social scientific research exists,
in fact, on the rare instances when women commit murder.

This research reveals that when women kill, it is often because they are reacting
to a victim-precipitated abusive situation from which they have experienced multiple episodes of stress. The power inequality in the relationship, coupled with having
fewer rules for outwardly expressing their anger, leads a small percentage of women
to murder their spouses and significant others (Ogle et al., 1995).

Robbery

When compared to assault and murder, the crime of robbery is more impersonal and planned (Sommers & Baskin, 1993). The motivation to commit robbery for women is about taking money or property by force or the threat of force for noncompliance. When women decide to commit robbery, their actions convey both their own beliefs about gender and others' perceptions about basic differences between women and men. These beliefs will influence how women behave. For example, Jody Miller (1998) found that half of the women robbers she interviewed worked with a male accomplice to rob a male victim—a male accomplice reportedly never robbed a female victim. The other half of the women committed robbery alone—for the same reasons as men; but unlike men, female robbers targeted other women as victims because women are perceived as less likely to be armed and to fight back. Similar results were found by Sommers and Baskin (1993). If women decide to rob men, they report using their sexuality to behave as stereotypical weak and vulnerable females so that they can maximize the most control over their target, who will be caught off guard when the situation quickly changes (Miller, 1998). According to Miller (1998), "A few of the women interviewed appear to have gained access to male privilege by adopting male attitudes about females, constructing their own identities as more masculine, and following through by behaving in masculine ways" (p. 61). Having criminal associates who were part of a violent subculture helped to legitimize and normalize violence. Yet, at the same time, women who committed robberies were not specialists in this type of crime, but were also involved in vice crimes and nonviolent forms of theft, primarily to get money for drugs (Sommers & Baskin, 1993).

How Do Women Convicted of Felony Crimes See Themselves?

The social identity of women remains predominately derived from their reproductive and sexual roles, as well as their marital status related to men. The responsibility of child care lies chiefly with women, who may also be working to contribute to the household. Even so, few women are able to see themselves as autonomous from their relationships (Ogle et al., 1995). Much of the way that women see themselves is likely dependent on age and type of conviction.

For example, Alarid and Vega (2010) interviewed 104 young first-time felons between the ages of 18 and 21. Nearly 8 in 10 young adult women retained a favorable self-identity and did not see themselves as felons or criminals. Establishing that positive postconviction identity as a good mother or person demonstrates that most first-time felons had not yet assumed a deviant or criminal master status in the way they saw themselves (Alarid & Vega, 2010). Not all women defined themselves the same way. Young women convicted of possession or sales of controlled substances were more likely to define themselves as criminal than women who were convicted of other offenses such as burglary, theft, robbery, assault, or injury to a child.

By their late 20s, however, women who stayed tied to the criminal lifestyle seemed to define themselves by their drug addictions, seeing themselves as "junkies," "crackheads," or "cokebitches" (Baskin & Sommers, 1998, p. 125). It is possible that identity may change with age or experience, or it may be more influenced by how the individual views her behavior as departing from traditional gender roles. For example, women who were convicted of robbery and who participated in equal crime partnerships with men appeared to have no issue with seeing themselves as criminal. On the other hand, the women robbers who "accepted not only women's position as secondary, but their own as well . . . used their gender identity to construct themselves as noncriminal" (Miller, 1998, p. 61).

Women who saw themselves relative to societal gender expectations and used these perceptions to justify their own criminal behavior have been observed in social science research (Kruttschnitt & Carbone-Lopez, 2006). This phenomenon likely occurred during Kathryn Whiteley's (2012) interviews of seven Australian women who were serving prison sentences for homicide. Four of the women pled guilty, but provided rationale and attempted to counter the system-imposed murderer label with that of a good and caring mother or an individual who was victimized in her previous relationships. Although court records acknowledged abusive relationships or the presence of mental illness, evidence also pointed to each woman's willful intent to commit murder. Whiteley observed that most women:

> relied on the lesser pathology of addiction as a rationale to explain their offending and avoided at all costs the identity of mental illness. . . . While only two of the women had been diagnosed with a mental illness prior to their offending, six of the seven had since come under the care of mental health experts. (p. 243)

The other three women who pled not guilty at the trial portrayed themselves postconviction as being victims of the system itself, but had no need to reaffirm themselves as being good people. Because the women in this study overwhelmingly defined themselves as victims, they seemed disempowered and unable to see themselves in control over their thoughts, actions, and, ultimately, their futures.

As women become more deeply immersed in criminal activity for longer time periods, it has been suggested that their friends and networks change, as does their commitment to the values, lifestyles, and norms of the criminal subculture. Patricia Adler (1993) discusses the identity shift that occurred over six years as she moved deeper into the world of drug dealing. The identity shift may be necessary indeed for people who move from a largely prosocial life to one that requires repeated exposure to illegal activity. However, most people involved in criminal activity do not report an identity shift per se, but one in which they retain their relationships as a mother or as a member in their family unit.

Conclusion

Our understanding of serious and violent female offenders has evolved in a significant way over the past 40 years. The substantial increases in serious or violent crime committed by women have simply not taken place as originally predicted.

If anything, crime trends over time show that many forms of serious criminality are more strongly linked with inequality and marginalization than with emancipation. Most women do not engage in serious and violent crime, and they often report doing so for very different reasons than men. Additionally, when they do engage in these crimes, women's roles are often secondary and less profitable than males' roles in crime. It appears that the majority of serious offending among women is done in tandem with accomplices. However, exceptions to these circumstances exist, with women engaging in solo violent acts for similar reasons to males; the explanations for such behavior, however, have evolved over the years.

Freda Adler's (1975) *Sisters in Crime* ushered in a new era in thinking about female criminals by questioning what life experiences contribute to serious crime among women. Adler's work, along with that of others, largely moved explanations of female criminality away from intraindividual traits (e.g., biological and psychological pathology) to sociological phenomena. This cognitive transformation allowed subsequent scholars to explore other potential reasons for females' criminal involvement—ranging from societal expectations, social structure, and marginalization to familial violence and abusive relationships. To date, the majority of research indicates that the female felony offenders are socially and economically marginalized, likely survivors of chaotic or abusive family life, and potentially struggle with substance use, mental health problems, or dysfunctional relationships. Scholarly attention to these factors, however, may not have been granted had it not been for Freda Adler and other pioneers like her.

References

Adler, F. (1975). *Sisters in crime: The rise of the new female offender.* New York, NY: McGraw–Hill.

Adler, P. A. (1993). *Wheeling and dealing: An ethnography of an upper-level dealing and smuggling community* (2nd ed.). New York, NY: Columbia University Press.

Alarid, L. F., Burton, V. S., Jr., & Cullen, F. T. (2000). Gender and crime among felony offenders: Assessing the generality of social control and differential association theories. *Journal of Research in Crime and Delinquency, 37,* 171–199.

Alarid, L. F., Marquart, J. W., Burton, V. S., Jr., Cullen, F. T., & Cuvelier, S. J. (1996). Women's roles in serious offenses: A study of adult felons. *Justice Quarterly, 13,* 431–454.

Alarid, L. F., & Vega, O. L. (2010). Identity construction, self perceptions, and criminal behavior of incarcerated women. *Deviant Behavior, 31,* 704–728.

Baskin, D. R., & Sommers, I. B. (1998). *Casualties of community disorder: Women's careers in violent crime.* Boulder, CO: Westview Press.

Batton, C. (2004). Gender differences in lethal violence: Historical trends in the relationship between homicide and suicide rates, 1960–2000. *Justice Quarterly, 21,* 421–461.

Bloom, B., Owen, B., & Covington, S. (2003). *Gender-responsive strategies: Research practice and guiding principles for women offenders.* Washington, DC: U.S. Department of Justice, National Institute of Corrections.

Bloom, B., Owen, B., & Covington, S. (2004). Women offenders and the gendered effects of public policy. *Review of Policy Research, 21*, 31–48.

Brennan, T., Breitenbach, M., Dieterich, W., Salisbury, E. J., & Van Voorhis, P. (2012). Women's pathways to serious and habitual crime: A person-centered analysis incorporating gender responsive factors. *Criminal Justice and Behavior, 39*, 1481–1508.

Burton, V. S., Jr., Cullen, F. T., Evans, T. D., Alarid, L. F., & Dunaway, R. G. (1998). Gender, self-control, and crime. *Journal of Research in Crime and Delinquency, 35*, 123–147.

Campbell, A. (1993). *Men, women and aggression.* New York, NY: Basic Books.

Carson, E. A., & Golineli, D. (2013). *Prisoners in 2012—Advance counts.* Washington, DC: U.S. Department of Justice.

Chesney-Lind, M. (1997). *The female offender: Girls, women, and crime.* Thousand Oaks, CA: Sage.

Chesney-Lind, M. (2002). Criminalizing victimization: The unintended consequences of pro-arrest policies for girls and women. *Criminology and Public Policy, 2*, 81–91.

Chesney-Lind, M., & Pasko, L. (2004). *The female offender: Girls, women and crime* (2nd ed.). Thousand Oaks, CA: Sage.

Chesney-Lind, M., & Shelden, R. G. (2004). *Girls, delinquency, and juvenile justice* (3rd ed.). Belmont, CA: Thomson Wadsworth.

Cloward, R. A. (1959). Illegitimate means, anomie, and deviant behavior. *American Sociological Review, 24*, 164–176.

Cloward, R. A., & Ohlin, L. E. (1960). *Delinquency and opportunity: A theory of delinquent gangs.* New York, NY: The Free Press.

Cullen, F. T., & Agnew, R. (2011). *Criminological theory: Past to present* (4th ed.). New York, NY: Oxford University Press.

Daigle, L. E., Cullen, F. T., & Wright, J. P. (2007). Gender differences in the predictors of juvenile delinquency: Assessing the generality–specificity debate. *Youth Violence and Juvenile Justice, 5*, 254–286.

Daly, K. (1992). Women's pathways to felony court: Feminist theories of lawbreaking and problems of representation. *Southern California Review of Law and Women's Studies, 2*, 11–52.

Decker, S., Wright, R., Redfern, A., & Smith, D. (1993). A woman's place is in the home: Females and residential burglary. *Justice Quarterly, 10*, 143–162.

De Coster, S., Heimer, K., & Cumley, S. R. (2012). In F. T. Cullen and P. Wilcox (Eds.), *The Oxford handbook of criminological theory* (pp. 313–330). New York, NY: Oxford University Press.

Federal Bureau of Investigation. (2011). *Crime in the United States; Uniform Crime Reports.* Washington, DC: U.S. Department of Justice.

Freud, S. (1933). *New introductory lectures on psychoanalysis.* New York, NY: Norton.

Gilfus, M. E. (1992). From victims to survivors to offenders: Women's routes of entry into street crime. *Women and Criminal Justice, 4*, 63–90.

Gottfredson, M. R., & Hirschi, T. (1990). *A general theory of crime.* Stanford, CA: Stanford University Press.

Harper, R. L., Harper, G. C., & Stockdale, J. E. (2002). The role and sentencing of women in drug trafficking crime. *Legal and Criminological Psychology, 7*, 101–114.

Heimer, K., & De Coster, S. (1999). The gendering of violent delinquency. *Criminology*, 37, 277–318.

Heimer, K., Lauritsen, J. L., & Lynch, J. P. (2009). The national crime victimization survey and the gender gap in offending: Redux. *Criminology*, 47, 427–438.

Hirschi, T. (1969). *Causes of delinquency*. Berkeley: University of California Press.

Javdani, S., Sadeh, N., & Verona, E. (2011). Gendered social forces: A review of the impact of institutionalized factors on women and girls' criminal justice trajectories. *Psychology, Public Policy, and Law*, 17, 161–211.

Johnson, M. P. (2008). *A typology of domestic violence: Intimate terrorism, violent resistance, and situational couple violence*. Lebanon, NH: Northeastern University Press.

Koons-Witt, B. A., & Schram, P. J. (2003). The prevalence and nature of violent offending by females. *Journal of Criminal Justice*, 31, 361–371.

Kruttschnitt, C., & Carbone-Lopez, K. (2006). Moving beyond the stereotypes: Women's subjective accounts of their violent crime. *Criminology*, 44, 321–352.

Lauritsen, J. L., Heimer, K., & Lynch, J. P. (2009). Trends in the gender gap in violent offending: New evidence from the national crime victimization survey. *Criminology*, 47, 361–400.

Lauritsen, J. L., & Rezey, M. L. (2013). *Bureau of Justice Statistics Technical Report: Measuring the prevalence of crime with the National Crime Victimization Survey*. Washington, DC: U.S. Department of Justice.

Lombroso, C., & Ferrero, W. (1895/1959). *The female offender*. London, UK: Peter Owen.

Maher, L., & Hudson, S. L. (2007). Women in the drug economy: A metasynthesis of the qualitative literature. *Journal of Drug Issues*, 37, 805–826.

Miller, J. (1998). Up it up: Gender and the accomplishment of street robbery. *Criminology*, 36, 37–66.

Miller, J. B. (1976). *Toward a new psychology of women*. Boston, MA: Beacon Press.

Miller, S. L., & Meloy, M. L. (2006). Women's use of force: Voices of women arrested for domestic violence. *Violence Against Women*, 12, 89–115.

Moe, A. M. (2004). Blurring the boundaries: Women's criminality in the context of abuse. *Women's Studies Quarterly*, 32, 116–138.

Moe, A. M. (2006). Women, drugs, and crime. *Criminal Justice Studies*, 19, 337–352.

Muftic, L. R., Bouffard, J. A., & Bouffard, L. A. (2007). An exploratory study of women arrested for intimate partner violence: Violent women or violent resistance? *Journal of Interpersonal Violence*, 22, 753–774.

Mullins, C. W., & Cherbonneau, M. G. (2011). Establishing connections: Gender, motor vehicle theft, and disposal networks. *Justice Quarterly*, 28, 276–302.

Mullins, C. W., & Miller, J. (2008). Temporal, situational, and interactional features of women's violent conflicts. *Australian and New Zealand Journal of Criminology*, 41, 36–62.

Mullins, C. W., & Wright, R. (2003). Gender, social networks, and residential burglary. *Criminology*, 41, 813–840.

Mullins, C. W., Wright, R., & Jacobs, B. A. (2004). Gender, streetlife and criminal retaliation. *Criminology*, 42, 911–940.

Mumola, C. J. (2000). *Bureau of Justice Statistics special report: Incarcerated mothers and their children*. Washington, DC: U.S. Department of Justice.

Ogle, R. S., Maier-Katkin, D., & Bernard, T. J. (1995). A theory of homicidal behavior among women. *Criminology, 33,* 173–193.

Owen, B. (1998). *In the mix: Struggle and survival in a woman's prison.* Albany: State University of New York Press.

Pollack, O. (1950). *The criminality of women.* Philadelphia: University of Pennsylvania Press.

Richie, B. E. (1996). *Compelled to crime: The gender entrapment of battered Black women.* New York, NY: Routledge & Kegan Paul.

Rivera, B., & Widom, C. S. (1990). Childhood victimization and violent offending. *Violence and Victims, 5,* 19–35.

Salisbury, E. J., & Van Voorhis, P. (2009). Gendered pathways: A qualitative investigation of women probationers' paths to incarceration. *Criminal Justice and Behavior, 36,* 541–566.

Schwartz, J., Steffensmeier, D., Zhong, H., & Ackerman, J. (2009). Trends in the gender gap in violence: Reevaluating NCVS and other evidence. *Criminology, 47,* 401–424.

Severson, M., Postmus, J. L., & Berry, M. (2005). Incarcerated women: Consequences and contributions of victimization and intervention. *International Journal of Prisoner Health 1,* 223–240.

Sharp, S. F. (2003). Mothers in prison: Issues in parent–child contact. In S. F. Sharp (Ed.), *The incarcerated woman: Rehabilitative programming in women's prisons* (pp. 151–166). Upper Saddle River, NJ: Prentice Hall.

Shechory, M., Perry, G., & Addad, M. (2011). Pathways to women's crime: Differences among women convicted of drug, violence and fraud offenses. *Journal of Social Psychology, 151,* 399–416.

Simon, R. J. (1975). *Women and crime.* Lexington, MA: Lexington Press.

Simpson, S. S., Yaher, J. L., & Dugan, L. (2008). Understanding women's pathways to jail: Analyzing the lives of incarcerated women. *Australian and New Zealand Journal of Criminology, 41,* 84–108.

Sommers, I., & Baskin, D. R. (1993). The situational context of violent female offending. *Journal of Research in Crime and Delinquency, 30,* 136–162.

Steffensmeier, D. (1995). Trends in female crime: It's still a man's world. In B. R. Price and N. J. Sokoloff (Eds.), *The criminal justice system and women: Offenders, victims and worker* (2nd ed., pp. 89–104). New York, NY: McGraw–Hill.

Steffensmeier, D. J. (1983). Organization properties and sex-segregation in the underworld: Building a sociological theory of sex differences in crime. *Social Forces, 61,* 1010–1108.

Steffensmeier, D., Zhong, H., Ackerman, J., Schwartz, J., & Agha, S. (2006). Gender gap trends for violent crimes, 1980–2003. *Feminist Criminology, 1,* 72–98.

Teague, R., Mazerolle, P., Legosz, M., & Sanderson, J. (2008). Linking childhood exposure to physical abuse and adult offending: Examining mediating factors and gendered relationships. *Justice Quarterly, 25,* 313–348.

Whiteley, K. M. (2012). *Women as victims and offenders: Incarcerated for murder in the Australian criminal justice system.* Unpublished doctoral dissertation, Queensland University of Technology, Brisbane, Queensland, Australia.

Wright, E. M., DeHart, D. D., Koons-Witt, B. A., & Crittenden, C. A. (2013). "Buffers" against crime? Exploring the roles and limitations of positive relationships among women in prison. *Punishment and Society, 15,* 71–95.

Wright, E. M., Salisbury, E. J., & Van Voorhis, P. (2007). Predicting the prison misconducts of women offenders: The importance of gender-responsive needs. *Journal of Contemporary Criminal Justice, 23*, 310–340.

Wright, E. M., Van Voorhis, P., Salisbury, E. J., & Bauman, A. (2012). Gender-responsive lessons learned and policy implications for women in prison: A review. *Criminal Justice and Behavior, 39*, 1612–1632.

PART III

Social Context of Female Crime

CHAPTER 7

The Social Worlds of Girls in Gangs

Madeleine Novich and Jody Miller

Feminist criminology's attention to the experiences of women and girls, as well as efforts to understand how gender shapes their social worlds, has provided great insights into young women's involvement in gangs (see Campbell, 1984; Chesney-Lind & Hagedorn, 1999; Miller, 2001).[1] Girls' experiences in gangs and the consequences of their gang involvement vary by—among other things—their ethnicity, the gender composition of their gangs, and the community contexts in which their gangs emerge. In this chapter, we investigate the social worlds of girls in gangs within these larger contexts and with specific attention to how gender and gender inequality shape girls' experiences within these groups. We focus on four aspects of the gendered social world of gangs: (1) young women's pathways into these groups; (2) the gendered social organization and activities of gangs; (3) how gender shapes young women's participation in and experiences of crime and violence; and (4) the place of motherhood in girls' participation in and desistance from gangs.[2]

Research on the social worlds of young women in gangs is embedded within larger trends in gang research. The study of gangs has a long history, but one that has waxed and waned depending on the extent to which these groups have been at the forefront of public concerns as a serious social problem. The earliest systematic research on gangs was sociologist Frederic Thrasher's classic study, *The Gang*, published in 1927. His study, and many more following it, assumed that gangs were all male, paying little or no attention to young women (see Cloward & Ohlin, 1960; Cohen, 1955). Gang research picked up again during the turbulent period of the 1960s and early 1970s. Classic studies at that time, including James F. Short and Fred L. Strodtbeck's (1965) *Group Process and Gang Delinquency* and Malcolm W. Klein's (1971) *Street Gangs and Street Workers*, likewise paid little attention to young women's place in gangs. Importantly, however, these studies offered the first glimpse of the presence of young women in gangs, suggesting that they were between a quarter and a third of gang members as early as the mid-20th century. That these scholars ignored such a sizeable proportion of the groups they were studying is a reflection of the androcentric bias that permeated criminology at the time (Daly & Chesney-Lind, 1988).

Research on young women in gangs first appeared in a meaningful way in the 1970s and 1980s (Bowker, Gross, & Klein, 1980; Bowker & Klein, 1983; Brown, 1978; Campbell, 1984; Miller, 1973; Quicker, 1983; see Curry, 1998, for an overview), coinciding with not only the second wave of feminism, but also with the growth of feminist scholarship in the social sciences, including in criminology (Adler, 1975; Smart, 1976). This shift raised awareness in the field of the need to study women and girls, leading to the emergence of research on the topic of gender and gangs. In addition, several scholars worked to reconstruct the "lost" years of research on girls in gangs by returning to the unanalyzed data of prior scholars (Fishman, 1995) and interviewing adult women and men who had been gang members in the 1950s and 1970s (Moore, 1991).

Contemporary scholarship on young women in gangs reflects both the expansion of feminist criminology and its requisite attention to the experiences of women, as well as the tremendous growth in gangs and gang scholarship beginning in the late 1980s and early 1990s. In 1980, fewer than 200 cities reported having gangs, but by 1992 that number had grown to more than 750 (Klein, 1995). The most recent estimates available suggest that as of 2011, a total of 3,300 jurisdictions across the United States have gangs (Egley & Howell, 2013). As a consequence, gangs have remained a consistent topic of scholarly research for the past several decades, and our knowledge about young women's gang involvement has grown considerably. Indeed, the emergence of large-scale longitudinal survey research on gangs—which now regularly includes both young women and young men—confirms the mid-20th-century estimates of girls' presence in gangs, suggesting that young women are anywhere from a fifth to nearly half of all gang youth across communities with these groups (Esbensen & Carson, 2012; Thornberry, Krohn, Lizotte, Smith, & Tobin, 2003).

As we move to our discussion of the social worlds of girls in gangs, two features of this survey research are notable. First, young women's involvement in gangs tends to peak at younger ages than that of their male peers, meaning that they join and exit gangs earlier than young men (Esbensen & Carson, 2012). Indeed, whereas young men are more likely to remain gang involved into young adulthood, gang membership for girls is much more likely to remain a primarily adolescent undertaking (Hunt, Joe-Laidler, & MacKenzie, 2005; Miller, 2001). Second, whereas girls in gangs are more delinquent than their nongang peers—both male and female—male gang members have a much greater likelihood of being involved in serious crime (Esbensen & Carson, 2012). This is an especially important point to keep in mind. Despite a great deal of contemporary concern with perceived increases in young women's delinquency and violence, gang research—like other studies of women, girls, and crime—does not bear out this popular belief (Lauritsen, Heimer, & Lynch, 2009). We discuss some of the reasons for this misconception later in the chapter. But first, we turn our attention to the social contexts associated with young women's pathways into gangs.

Girls' Pathways Into Gangs

To account for the proliferation of gangs across the United States over the past several decades, scholars have focused on two significant issues. First is the deterioration in living conditions for many youth caused by structural changes brought about by deindustrialization (Wilson, 1996). Large numbers of youth, especially racial minorities in urban communities, grow up in neighborhoods in which racial segregation, poverty, social isolation, and violence are commonplace (Peterson & Krivo, 2010). These circumstances are strongly tied to the presence of youth gangs[3] (Durán, 2013; Katz & Schnebly, 2011; Vigil, 2002). Second, scholars point to the diffusion of gang culture, through popular media attention to gangs, and the commercialization of gang style in music, films, the Internet, and other media (Collins, 2006; Klein, 1995; Papachristos, 2005). The popularity of gang style is believed to add to youthful identification with gang culture, increasing the likelihood that groups of youths will adopt gang names, symbols, and style and will be recognized and responded to as gangs. Some scholars suggest that cultural diffusion may help explain the simultaneous growth in gangs so many communities across the United States and western Europe witnessed in the 1990s and 2000s (Klein & Maxson, 2010).

These are important explanations for the proliferation of gangs, yet they are not designed to offer much specific insight into the role gender might play in these processes. Other questions to ask are, What leads young women to join gangs? And how do they describe their decisions to do so? To address these questions, qualitative scholars investigate girls' accounts of why they join and what they gain from their gang participation, as well as their life histories and life contexts prior to and at the time they become gang members. These studies reveal several pertinent factors and contexts: neighborhood conditions, including the presence of gangs and gang-involved peers; family relations, including various forms of family problems such as violence and substance abuse, as well as the influence of gang-involved family members; and factors related to gender inequality, including patriarchal constraints and gender-based victimization.

Growing up poor and in impoverished, racially segregated urban communities often means growing up in neighborhoods where both gangs and violence are commonplace. Consider the description offered by Kristy, a St. Louis gang member in Jody Miller's (2008) study. Asked to describe her neighborhood, she offered one word: "Slum." She then elaborated:

> I mean broken liquor bottles everywhere, people standing on the corner, uh, everybody momma [strung] out on this [drug], everybody daddy's out on this, don't do nuttin, you know. Police harassing you constantly. . . . Don't none of them kids got no positive role model. . . . It's like my street, then there's a street where don't nobody on my street like 'em. And they'll come through shooting, anything. I mean you get jumped for having on a [certain color] hat and stuff. (Miller, 2008, p. 19)

When gangs are a visible presence in girls' neighborhoods, their social networks are more likely to include gang members (Fleisher & Kreinert, 2004), increasing both their opportunity and their desire to join. Chantell, for example, joined her Columbus, Ohio, gang at age 12. She lived with her mother, grandmother, and siblings in a neighborhood where gangs were "just like everywhere," explaining, "when I was young, I grew up around 'em. Just grew up around 'em, basically. Then when you grow up around 'em and you see 'em so much, until you want to get initiated." At the time she joined, many of her neighborhood friends were doing the same, as had her older sister. "It was just like, people were just like gettin' in it and having fun," she explained. Nikki also joined at age 12, explaining, "If you ain't in it you just be . . . you just be feelin' left out. You be like, 'oh they all in a gang and I'm just sittin' here'" (see Miller, 2001, pp. 42–43).

For some inner-city youth—female and male—gangs provide an avenue for adapting to oppressive living conditions imposed by their environments (Fleisher & Kreinert, 2004; Vigil, 2002). As Joe and Chesney-Lind (1995) explain, "the gang assists . . . in coping with their lives in chaotic, violent, and economically marginalized communities" (p. 411). One thing they offer is a way to alleviate boredom and offer an opportunity for "fun," as Chantell put it (see also Quicker, 1983), particularly because urban youth in poor communities often have few options for recreation and entertainment. Moreover, because these neighborhoods are often dangerous, gangs may assist young women by providing opportunities to learn street and fighting skills (Fishman, 1995) and by offering protection and retaliation against victimization in high-crime communities (Miller, 2001).

Although impoverished and dangerous neighborhood conditions help answer the question of why girls come to join gangs, this remains only a partial explanation—particularly because most girls in high-risk neighborhoods do not join gangs (Bjerregaard & Smith, 1993). Qualitative research with young women in gangs consistently finds that there are often myriad problems in their lives growing up, especially those tied to challenges within their families. Joan Moore's (1991) comparison of male and female gang members, for example, indicated that young women recounted more cases of childhood abuse and neglect and more frequently came from homes where wife abuse and other family problems were present. Similarly, Miller (2001) compared female gang members with other at-risk girls from the same communities and also found that gang girls came from more troubled families than their female peers—typically experiencing compound family problems associated with violence, substance abuse, and incarceration.[4]

Consider the example of Felicia, a homegirl interviewed as part of Geoffrey P. Hunt and Karen Joe-Laidler's multiyear collaborative research on gangs in San Francisco:

> Felicia's life up until now has "been pretty crazy." Born in Guatemala and the oldest of four, Felicia was raised in San Francisco's Mission District by her divorced mother who supported the family with welfare, until she got her general equivalency

diploma and a job a couple of years ago. Her mother beat her often and severely, and Felicia cannot recall a single positive memory from her childhood. She did however enjoy elementary school—she had a 4.0 average through fifth grade. Felicia reached a turning point at twelve years of age when she left home "because of my stepfather." She bounced between the streets and relatives—her cousin, her aunt—to return to her mother's home three years later. (Schalet, Hunt, & Joe-Laidler, 2003, p. 122)

Given stories like Felicia's, it is not surprising that scholars suggest that some girls join gangs because they perceive them as a surrogate family. Indeed, Susan, another San Francisco gang member, described her gang as "the family I never had before" (Joe-Laidler & Hunt, 1997, p. 155). This is especially so for girls who have suffered abuse. In her study of girls in gangs and cliques in Boston, for example, Dana Nurge (2003) quotes ZZ, who says:

Half the girls in my clique were abused by somebody . . . we all talk about it together. It's sad sometimes but after we talk about it we're able to laugh and say that it's in the past and behind us. (p. 169)

In Miller's (2001) study, the ways in which family problems facilitated girls' gang involvement were varied, but they shared a common thread—young women began spending time away from home as a result of difficulties or dangers there and sought to meet their social and emotional needs elsewhere (see also Campbell, 1990; Joe & Chesney-Lind, 1995). Gangs may offer a network of friends for girls whose parents are unable to provide stable family relations; moreover, girls' friendships with other gang members may provide a support system for coping with family problems, abuse, and other life problems (Fleisher & Krienert, 2004; Joe & Chesney-Lind, 1995). Regardless of whether gangs actually fulfill these roles in young women's lives, it is clear that many girls believe they will when they become involved.

Erica, for example, was 17 when Miller (2001) interviewed her and had joined her gang when she was 15. She lived with her father and stepmother for most of her childhood, until her father and uncle raped her at the age of 11. Since that time, she had been shuffled back and forth between foster homes, group homes, and residential facilities and had little contact with her family because they turned their backs on her. She explained, "I didn't have *no* family. Because of the incidents with my dad and my uncle. After that, they just deserted me and I didn't, I had nothin' else" (Miller, 2001, p. 49, emphasis in original). Erica's childhood up to that point had been filled with violence. Her father was physically abusive toward her stepmother, toward her, and toward her siblings, and as a young child, Erica had witnessed her biological mother being raped. Both her father and her stepmother had spent time in jail, and there was heavy alcohol and drug use in the home as she was growing up. As a result, she described herself as a physically aggressive child. She explained, "In elementary school before I even knew anything about gangs, I'd just get in a lot of fights" (Miller, 2001, p. 49).

Erica's initial contact with gangs came when she was 14 and living in a foster home. During her stay there, she met a group of kids and began spending time with them:

> I just started talkin' to 'em. And, they always wore them blue rags and black rags and all that. And, I asked them, I said, "well, you part of a gang?" And they tell me what they're a part of. So, it was like, everywhere I went, I was with them. I was never by myself. (Miller, 2001, p. 49)

Erica said she joined the gang "just to be in somethin'" and so that it could be "like a family to me since I don't really have one of my own" (Miller, 2001, p. 49). She felt that being in the gang allowed her to develop meaningful relationships. She explained, "People trust me and I trust them. It's like that bond that we have that some of us don't have outside of that. Or didn't have at all" (p. 49). Nonetheless, Erica expressed some ambivalence about being in a gang, because it involved antisocial attitudes and behaviors that she did not see as being part of who she really was, particularly as she neared adulthood. Her decision to join, however, was in part a search for belonging and attachment. Nurge (2003) likewise reports that the young women she spoke to "explained that they needed to join the gang in order to 'survive'—it provided them with physical, social, and economic security that they deemed necessary and otherwise unavailable at the time of joining" (p. 178).

In addition, some girls who lack close relationships with their primary caregivers can turn to siblings or extended family members for a sense of belonging and attachment. If these family members are gang involved, the likelihood girls will choose to join as well increases. Thirteen-year-old Lisa, for example, joined her older brother's gang "because that's what [he] was so I wanted to be like that too" (Miller, 2001, p. 53). Their mother had died when she was 11, and she described their father as physically abusive and distant. Lisa felt very close to her brother and said her desire to be with him was her primary reason for joining his gang. Even when relationships with parents or other adults are strong, having adolescent or young adult gang members in the family often heightens the appeal of gangs (Hunt, MacKenzie, & Joe-Laidler, 2000). In fact, Miller (2001) found that the themes just reviewed—neighborhood exposure to gangs, family problems, and gang-involved family members—were overlapping in most gang girls' accounts, distinguishing them from the nongang girls she compared them to in her study.

Finally, research with Latina, Chicana, Vietnamese, Filipino, and Samoan young women suggests that gang joining is also sometimes related to their resistance to patriarchal cultural expectations for women and girls within their families and communities (Campbell, 1987; Joe-Laidler & Hunt, 2001; Portillos, Jurik, & Zatz, 1996). In addition to the limited opportunities such girls share with their male counterparts in disadvantaged communities, they also sometimes face stricter parental expectations, the burden of child-care responsibilities, and subordination to men (Campbell, 1990). Cindy, a 16-year-old San Francisco gang member, lamented:

> Parents . . . they think guys can't get pregnant so they get to go out all the time and they don't care. But when a girl goes out they think we're gonna come home pregnant. That is a big discrimination. Like we are all the same. We can't go out because they think girls are suppose to stay home, cook, clean and guys can just go out and have fun. That isn't right. (Joe-Laidler & Hunt, 2001, p. 666)

Likewise, a homegirl interviewed by Anne Campbell (1987) sought to reject the gender oppression she witnessed her mother and other women endure in her community:

> Puerto Rican women they hurt a lot. . . . They suffer a lot because of the man. Or because of their kids. I don't know. Like my mother—I say "Mommy, why don't you leave Poppy?" "Ah, because I love him at the time and I don't want you to have a stepfather." I used to tell her, "Oh man, sometimes you're stupid." (p. 462)

Janet, a Vietnamese gang member interviewed by Joe-Laidler and Hunt (2001), likewise explained, "the more [our parents] tell us what to do, we disobey them more" (p. 666).

In contrast, many of the African American gang girls in San Francisco, as well as some of the Latinas, "reported almost a complete absence of parental expectations or controls" (Joe-Laidler & Hunt, 2001, p. 667). These findings suggest there are meaningful variations across race and ethnicity in young women's motives for gang joining. Regardless, as Nurge (2003) summarizes, "When appropriately contextualized, young women's choices to join gangs often appear to be practical (albeit temporary and limited) solutions to the multiple problems and limitations they face in their homes, schools, and communities" (pp. 178–179).

Gender and the Social Organization of Girls' Gangs

Gang life is attractive to young women because it gives them a source of empowerment and protection in an unsafe environment. Gangs take a variety of organizational forms, however, and these have consequences for the nature of young women's experiences. Researchers have identified several types of gangs with female members, including coed or mixed-gender gangs, female satellites of male gangs, and all-female gangs (Miller, 1975; see also Joe-Laidler & Hunt, 1997). There have been several case studies of all-female gangs (Lauderback, Hansen, & Waldorf, 1992; Venkatesh, 1998), but these groups account for a small percentage of young women's gangs. With the exception of some Latino or Latina gangs—where girls' auxiliary or satellite groups to male gangs are common (Miranda, 2003; Portillos et al., 1996)—coed gangs are the most widespread (Miller, 2001; Nurge, 2003).

Scholars differentiate these mixed-gender groups further based on their gender composition, which can include a majority of males, a balance of males and females, and—much less commonly—a majority of females (Peterson, Miller, & Esbensen, 2001).

Although homegirls generally characterize themselves as equals to their male counterparts, they in fact navigate a social landscape within gangs marked by oppressive, male-dominated structures and gender inequalities, which they sometimes contribute to as well (Miller, 2001; Schalet et al., 2003). Yet, the types of gangs girls join, as well as the ratio of males to females within them, shape the gangs' gender hierarchies and young women's experiences (Joe-Laidler & Hunt, 1997; Miller & Brunson, 2000; Nurge, 2003). The vast majority of girls join coed gangs because male membership is generally seen as necessary for the gang to be recognized and taken seriously on the streets. Several girls in Miller's (2001) study, for instance, characterized all-female gangs as laughable and unable to garner respect on the streets. The few studies of all-female gangs, however, belie this characterization (Lauderback et al., 1992; Venkatesh, 1998).

The number and proportion of female members impact gang members' behaviors and experiences. For example, the gang's gender composition is related to patterns of delinquency among its members (Peterson, 2012). Peterson and her colleagues (2001) compared four compositional types—all male, majority male, gender balanced, and majority- or all female—and found that gang activities and individual delinquency rates for males and females varied across these types. Majority- or all-female gangs were the least delinquent, followed, surprisingly, by all-male gangs. Both gender-balanced and majority-male gangs were similar with regard to male gang members' delinquency, but girls were most delinquent when they were members of majority-male gangs. These findings suggest that having female members increases male gang members' criminal involvement. Despite this possibility, some male members suggest that girls can temper criminal activity. Jon, a St. Louis gang member, explained, "dudes would go places and be the ones that usually fight . . . and sometimes girls usually break it up. If it wasn't for them, we would have gotten in a whole lot of trouble" (Miller & Brunson, 2000, p. 436). The impact of gender organization on gang member behavior, then, is something researchers need to learn more about.

Miller's (2001) study of female gang members in St. Louis and Columbus found that girls in mixed-gender gangs often described themselves as equals to their male counterparts, repeatedly telling her that male and female members were "all the same": "They give every last one of us respect the way they give the males," Sonita explained (p. 179). Yet, so-called equality within the gang was based on a male normative ideal, with girls attempting to construct an identity as "one of the guys." For instance, Latisha explained, "we just like dudes to them. We just like dudes, they treat us like that 'cause we act so much like dudes" (Miller, 2001, p. 180). This depiction may be closest to reality when young women are the sole or one of a handful of girls in otherwise male gangs, where they may be given something like "honorary male" status. James, a male gang member whose gang was almost all male, said of the few young women in his group, "Most people look at the girls in our neighborhood [with respect] because they [are] mostly like us. They don't do mostly things that girls do, they do what we do" (Miller & Brunson, 2000, p. 433). Gang girls also strive for equality by distancing themselves from nongang girls. Brandi, for instance, described how girls in gangs are different from other girls because "we act more, more like guys. Not like guys, guys, guys, but act different from most girls" (Miller, 2001, p. 180). Such characterizations may be more common among African American and White gang members, like the young women Miller interviewed. Studies of Latina gang members are more likely to describe "accomplished femininity" among these homegirls, rather than an orientation favoring masculinity (Joe-Laidler & Hunt, 2001; Portillos et al., 1996).

Regardless of how girls position themselves vis-à-vis the young men in their groups, most gangs have a hierarchical structure in which men are at the top (Miller, 2001; Miller & Brunson, 2000; Nurge, 2003). In Miller's (2001) study, for instance, most Columbus-based girls stated that their gang had one leader (the "OG"), and all except one were male. Although high-ranking females did exist, girls' mobility was limited, and high status was largely a result of girls' connections to high-status male members. Female gang members are generally viewed as lesser and weaker than male members. In fact, male members consistently refer to gang participation as a "male thing" (Miller & Brunson, 2000). Moreover, gang girls navigate a series of gender-based circumstances and contradictions that further render them unequal.

One contradiction is that young women in gangs face the challenge of balancing normative social expectations of femininity with socially desired and rewarded traits in gangs of masculinity, toughness, and aggression. Vashelle, a 14-year-old St. Louis gang member, noted that "some people just don't think it's ladylike, you know what I'm saying . . . people are down on gals as far as being in the gang" (Miller, 2001, p. 181). Twelve-year-old Trina likewise described competing demands resulting from her desire to be a tomboy and familial pressure to be more feminine. Her gang involvement gave her the space to resist her mother's expectations:

> I got to do what dudes usually do. I got to be like dudes. 'Cause my mama used to try everything. My mama used to tell me like that type of stuff. I ain't like to wear earrings and stuff and she say, "Girl, you ain't no boy! Girls got to wear earrings." I say, "I want to be a tomboy." (Miller, 2001, p. 181)

Ironically, however, Joe-Laidler and Hunt (2001) found that although girls saw their gangs as sites for resisting patriarchal family constraints, many still "evaluate themselves in the gendered terms of their parents, striving to be 'good girls' while engaging in more 'liberatin' experiences" (p. 667).

Research also finds that female gang members routinely police the behaviors of their female members, simultaneously holding them accountable for behaviors that they deem "out of bounds" for girls, but also valuing masculinity. Gang girls, especially those in male-dominated groups, sometimes distance themselves from other young women to further align themselves with young men (Miller, 2001;

Miller & Brunson, 2000). By turning on other girls, such young women express loyalty to the group. Miller (2001) found that some girls did this by keeping silent during male gang members' discussions about disrespecting women. For example, Monica, a female member in a male-dominated group, explained:

> At first, when I first ever started listening to them talk, it made me mad and I would jump in and say my little piece. And my brother would look at me like, "Are you going to sit here and join the conversation or just butt in when you get mad?" So I just learned to just sit back and just keep mine to myself. (Miller, 2001, p. 189)

They also reconciled female victimization by placing responsibility on the woman (Miller, 2001). Monica, again, put the fault on her gang peer Andrea for male mistreatment: "I put that on her. They ain't gotta do her like that, but she don't gotta let them do her like that either" (Miller, 2001, p. 189). Another way of maintaining that they were "equals" in the gang, despite evidence to the contrary, was to write off incidents of female victimization as unique. For example, Sonita, who was raped by a member of her gang, felt it was an "isolated incident" and women were not typically in danger (Miller, 2001, p. 191). Yet, research shows that young women in gangs face quite a bit of violence at the hands of their male gang peers, partners, and boyfriends (Joe-Laidler & Hunt, 1997; Schalet et al., 2003). In contrast, young women in gender-balanced gangs, and especially in all-female gangs, are more likely to emphasize the value of their friendships with other girls, even describing them as a surrogate family. Pam, a member of a gender-balanced gang, remarked, "most of the girls for real is family and friends. We went to school together, grew up together" (Miller & Brunson, 2000, p. 434; Hunt & Joe-Laidler, 2001).

Another contradiction young women faced was the sexual double standard and sexual exploitation of women. Gang girls themselves often upheld the sexual double standard, harshly judging those girls who were seen as sexually "loose" (Miller, 2001; Schalet et al., 2003), rather than identifying it as a feature of patriarchal ideology. The clearest illustration of this attribution is the initiation practice of "sexing in" some young women into gangs. Young women who join gangs through this method are viewed as the least reliable members, as sexually available and promiscuous, and are often subject to harsh derogatory mistreatment by both male and female members (Miller, 2001; Schalet et al., 2003). Jermaine, a male gang member, explained, "if they get sexed in, they don't really get no respect" (Miller & Brunson, 2000, p. 439). Benita, a San Francisco homegirl, remarked that women who are sexed in are "more substandard—like we'll treat 'em, like shit" (Schalet et al., 2003, p. 126). Angela described how:

> we had one girl that did that. And she did not get none of her respect. None ah that. And. . . . me and this other dude, we jumped her out. We were always abusing her. . . . And I started to feel bad for her after a while. But she should never got sexed in. That lost her respect right there. (Schalet et al., 2003, p. 126)

Despite the exploitative nature of this practice, female gang members typically do not challenge or speak out against it. Miller (2001) explains:

> Ironically, denigrating girls who were sexed in or exploited, rather than holding the young men accountable, was the key to maintaining the tenuous but vital belief that the male gang members viewed them as equals. Creating this dichotomy allowed girls to conclude that the boys in their gangs treated and discussed *other* young women in sexually derogatory ways—young women who deserved it because they were "nasty." (p. 194)

A final contradiction young women routinely navigated within gangs was the belief that women are weaker and softer than men. Despite gang girls seeking to define themselves as equals, they are routinely excluded—by the young men in their groups and by choice—from more serious, status-building forms of gang crime such as drive-by shootings and, in some gangs, income-generating activities like drug sales (Joe-Laidler & Hunt, 1997; Miller, 2001; Miller & Brunson, 2000). Such a sentiment is commonly expressed by male gang members, for whom the exclusion of girls from status-enhancing activities allows them to maintain such endeavors as a masculine purview and retain the most profitable income-generation strategies for themselves. This sentiment was expressed by Dwayne, a St. Louis gang member: "Robbery and stuff like that, we don't want no girls with us doing stuff like that. . . . We don't want no girls with us, period, when we got to go to work" (Miller & Brunson, 2000, p. 437). Likewise, Ray said, "We do more than all the girls do, but we just give them what they can do. They don't do no hard, you know, shooting nobody or drive-bys" (Miller & Brunson, 2000, p. 437). Despite such sentiments undermining young women's claims to equality, they also provided gang girls with an out for avoiding those activities they found troubling (Miller, 2001).

Ultimately, when homegirls join gangs, they gain certain benefits, such as protection and friendship, but also make a series of compromises that impact their social experiences. Despite viewing the gang as a space of empowerment, these are male-dominated groups and young women must negotiate their place in their groups with care. Often, this means also adhering to beliefs and even contributing to situations that reinforce their unequal status vis-à-vis their male counterparts. Yet, it is through these compromises that they are able to limit their involvement in serious crime and view the gang as a transitory, as opposed to a permanent, aspect of their lives. As Miller (2001) notes:

> Gang girls [strike] a situationally specific 'patriarchal bargain' within their gangs, which allow[s] . . . them to draw many of the social benefits of gang affiliation while avoiding or negotiating which of the gang's riskier sides they [will] partake in. (p. 196)

Delinquency and Violence in Young Women's Gangs

Although generally involved in less serious forms of delinquency than their male counterparts, homegirls participate in a variety of different types of social delinquency—most commonly drinking, drug use, and fighting. Male gang members also talk about serious crime more than they commit it, although they engage in a large and disproportionate amount of the crime committed by adolescents and young adults (Klein & Maxson, 2010). Across gender, gang members are also exposed to a disproportionate amount of violence and victimization (Taylor, 2008), although their experiences of violence are shaped by gender (Cepeda & Valdez, 2003; Joe-Laidler & Hunt, 2001; Miller, 2001). Despite this involvement in violent conduct, most gang members' time is spent engaging in social activities and primarily nonserious forms of delinquency.

Brandi, a Columbus gang girl, explained, "a typical day would be sittin' back at the park or somethin' like that or [at] one of our friend's house, or a gang member's house, gettin' drunk, gettin' high, and you know watchin' TV" (Miller, 2001, p. 84). Likewise, Veronica, another Columbus gang member, remarked, "We just be, like, when we was over at my cousin's house, we just be sittin' there watching TV. . . . Just listen to music, dancin'. They be sitting around playin' with guns, drinkin' and stuff, smokin' weed" (Miller, 2001, p. 84). Substance use within the gang fosters social solidarity. As one San Francisco homegirl explained:

> Like let's say we go out. And some of them just has it on them and they'll be like oh, you know we got some fry. You want to do it or whatever so we just do it. Like if we go to a dance or like if we go to [an amusement park] or something. You know we won't just . . . sit at home and fry. (Hunt, Joe-Laidler, & Evans, 2002, pp. 392–393)

Despite being a common part of their everyday activities, gang girls describe needing to engage in substance use in socially acceptable and gender-normative ways (Cepeda & Valdez, 2003). Hunt et al. (2002) found that gang girls experience a series of social controls governing their behavior vis-à-vis alcohol and drug use (p. 396). These included age restrictions, control by homeboys or boyfriends, and concerns about reputation or respect. When asked about activities that men can do but women cannot, one homegirl responded:

> We can't do drugs a lot . . . they want us to do only one drug, and that's weed. . . . We can't do other stuff 'cause a lot of stuff can happen. . . . They don't like when some of them get drugs 'cause they're all messed up. . . . I think they just don't want to see us all messed up. They wanna see us not drugged. (Hunt et al., 2002, p. 398)

Another homegirl described sniffing glue—a drug women were not supposed to use—and:

> all of a sudden one of the homeboys comes up and he gets my bag and he throws it. And he just smacks me down. And I just fell down. . . . He started hitting on me . . . he had slapped me down. (p. 399)

In other words, homegirls are not "allowed to 'get fucked up'" (p. 398).

Getting high or drinking excessively could signal disrespectability to home-boys and other homegirls alike. "The girls who do a lot of drugs, sometimes the guys call them tecatas," one homegirl explained; "they don't treat them with respect" (Hunt et al., 2002, p. 405). Another remarked:

> To get respect out on the street you should like not get all fucked up with all kinds of guys and do stupid things in front of guys. . . . Make sure you can control your drugs and if you drink, just don't get too fucked up. Don't make a fool of yourself. (Joe-Laidler & Hunt 2001, p. 668)

Gang girls were as judgmental as homeboys about other girls' respectability. As one girl remarked, "I can't respect a female that don't respect herself" (Hunt et al., 2002, p. 406).

The link between substance use and sexual respectability was tied to risks for sexual victimization, for which young women—rather than their victimizers—were blamed (Cepeda & Valdez, 2003; Hunt et al., 2002; Miller, 2008). One homegirl explained, "Some of the other girls that I know, they got a bad reputation like from getting dusted, and you know, they pull chains on them and they get raped by guys, you know" (Hunt et al., 2002, p. 404). Likewise, a gang-associated young woman described how a 17-year-old girl was gang raped after a party:

> Everyone had been drinking and smoking [weed]. She always wanted to be around the guys. After almost everyone had left, three members of the [gang] took her into the back room and "pulled a train" on her. She was all fucked up. She wanted to do it because she did not fight back. Everyone in the neighborhood knows this happened but she still hangs out with them like nothing. (Cepeda & Valdez, 2003, p. 100)

Gender-based violence is a significant risk for female gang members, tied to the sexual double standard, gender inequalities, and the dominance of masculinity in these groups. Notably, recent research suggests that male gang members also have high rates of sexual victimization, although we know little about the social contexts of these events (Gover, Jennings, & Tewksbury, 2009).

In addition, it was not uncommon for drinking and drug use to segue into fight-ing, another common event in homegirls' delinquent social world (Joe-Laidler & Hunt, 2001). Intergang conflicts were a means of building cohesiveness within the group. Miller (2001) explains:

> An important element of gang life involves spending time and energy challenging and fighting with rival gangs; it is often at the level of these antagonisms that youths stake out the identity of their gang in opposition to their enemies . . . having common enemies facilities members' perceptions of themselves as a unified group. (p. 135; see also Klein & Maxson, 2010)

Gang clashes typically occur when one group enters the other's territory seeking to cause trouble or at popular public places where youths gather. Internal conflicts and fights also arise among gang members, although most are intergang conflicts over turf or drugs (Joe-Laidler & Hunt, 1997). One San Fransisco homegirl explained how fights usually start:

> If I would be in [another area] and they would see I am not from [there], and they would ask what I was doing over there, and you know all these girls would come and jump me. And vice versa. That is just like if they come into our turf and we don't know who they are, say for instance they are selling dope or something, they can't just come to our turf and sell dope and don't give us nothing. (Joe-Laidler & Hunt 1997, p. 158)

It was also common for fights to start over men, especially when homeboys "messed around" with girls outside the neighborhood (Schalet et al., 2003). One San Francisco girl explained, "After they fuck them or do whatever they want to do, they bring them down [and] we beat their ass" (Schalet et al., 2003, pp. 123–124).

Like with substance use, there are also gender norms that guide homegirls' participation in intergang fighting (Joe-Laidler & Hunt, 1997; Miller, 2001; Miller & Decker, 2001; Schalet et al., 2003). As noted previously, perceptions of appropriate masculinity and femininity often mean excluding young women from more serious confrontations like drive-bys and homicides, which remain the purview of young men. Veronica, a Columbus-based gang girl, described such a situation: "They went to go do a drive-by on [rival gang members]. . . . They wouldn't let us [females] go. But, we wanted to go, they wouldn't let us" (Miller, 2001, p. 141). Likewise, Sonita explained, "If they wanna go do somethin' bad and they think one of the females gonna get hurt they don't let 'em do it with them. . . . Like if they was involved with a shooting or whatever, [girls] can't go" (Miller, 2001, p. 141). In fact, Miller and Decker (2001) examined the police files for every gang homicide in St. Louis over the six-year period when gang homicides were at their peak in the city, and not one of the 229 incidents had been committed by a female gang member.

Homegirls, instead, are typically expected to fight against other gang girls; these are conflicts homeboys rarely get involved in (Miller, 2001). Here is a typical account of such conflicts: "I had a beef with this girl named Shaunna. . . . I had to go buck her. . . . Punch her, beat her up" (Miller, 2001, p. 138). When women participate in gang confrontations, it is typically expected that they use weapons designated as appropriate for girls, such as their fists and knives, as opposed to guns (Miller & Decker, 2001). Vashelle explained, "Most girls, they ain't gonna do nothing for real but try to stab you, cut you, or something like that. As far as coming shooting and stuff like a dude would do, no" (Miller & Decker, 2001, p. 132). Likewise, Crystal noted, "Girls don't be up there shooting unless they really have to" (Miller & Decker, 2001, p. 127). Homegirls typically do not use guns because, according to Pam, "we ladies, we not dudes for real . . . all we do is fight" (Miller & Decker, 2001, p. 127).

In general, research finds that gang girls do not escalate violent situations. As long as they are not met with a direct challenge, they are content to avoid confrontations (Miller, 2001; Miller & Decker, 2001). For example, Pam explained:

> We going to the show or skating, to the mall. We be seeing some of our enemies too when we do those things, clubs and stuff, we be seeing a lot of our enemies. [If] they don't say nothing to us, we don't say nothing to them. They say something to us, we say something to them. So that way everybody just go they own little way if they don't want nothing to happen. (Miller, 2001, p. 136)

Despite these gender differences, fighting is a means for gang girls to bolster their reputation within their gangs and to build reputations as not to be messed with (Campbell, 1987; Joe-Laidler & Hunt, 1997). Miller (2001) found that fighting helped girls establish a reputation as "one of the guys." Through such conflicts, they could emphasize the importance of being tough, aggressive, and not wrapped up in "feminine" concerns. For example, Veronica explained:

> A lot of girls get scared. Don't wanna break their nails and stuff like that. So, ain't no need for them to try to be in a gang. And the ones that's in it, most of the girls that's in act like boys. They why they in, 'cause they like to fight and stuff. They know how to fight and they use guns and stuff. (pp. 180–183)

Joe-Laidler and Hunt (2001) also report that homegirls establish respectability by being able to stand up for themselves. As one young woman articulated:

> A homegirl has to have a mean head on her shoulders. She has to be responsible or respectable. . . . Keep your head up and watch over the moves of others. You can't let nobody get you or you will be got. (Joe-Laidler & Hunt, 2001, p. 665)

Additionally, fighting could be used to defend one's honor and show others that they are "nobody's fool" (p. 671). One gang girl described how she defended her reputation by beating a girl who had sex with her boyfriend:

> I hit this girl over the head with a bat. She had screwed my dude. I walked in on them. After that, that bitch got up, went outside. That bitch slipped up one day, and I busted her on the head with the bat. (p. 671)

Ultimately, homegirls are deeply entrenched in a male-dominated, delinquent social world and thus it is not surprising that rules about masculinity and femininity dictate their behaviors, interactions, perceptions, and concepts of respect, even when it comes to their involvement in gang crime (Joe-Laidler & Hunt 2001; Miller, 2001).

Motherhood and Gang Participation

The final topic we focus on in exploring the social worlds of girls in gangs is pregnancy and motherhood. We do so because a number of scholars have investigated this topic, it is a common life event among gang members, and it is often a significant turning point for changing young women's ties to their gangs. Motherhood does not affect all girls' involvement in gang activities, but for most it has an important impact, often facilitating their exit from gangs or, at a minimum, drastically curtailing their participation in gang activities such as drinking, drug use, and fighting (Fleisher & Krienert, 2004; Hunt et al., 2005; Miller, 2001). As a result of these life changes, homegirls commonly face a series of challenges in navigating their identities as gang members, respectable women, and "good" mothers.

Many young women who become mothers maintain their gang ties; however, they typically alter their behavior for the benefit of their child. The most dramatic change is the reduction in their social interactions with gang friends coupled with an increase in time spent at home (Hunt et al., 2005; Moloney, Hunt, Joe-Laidler, & MacKenzie, 2011; Miller, 2001). "Before I used to go out a lot with my friends," said Graciela, a 19-year-old member of an all-Latina female gang; "I don't go out no more, and I just stay home with the baby" (Moloney et al., 2011, p. 11). Likewise, 17-year-old Ebony explained:

> I don't have time ta have friends now. . . . I want ta like take care of my son, and just go home and be with my son. . . . Sometimes I do feel like goin' out, but that's kinda like once every six months. (Moloney et al., 2011, p. 11)

Hunt and his colleagues (2005) attribute the decline in gang connectedness to a change in participation in the kinds of gang activities that facilitate social solidarity. Specifically, young mothers are often less interested in partaking in social events that were harmful to their fetuses, infants, or children, such as drinking, drug use, and risk-taking behaviors. Graciela explained:

> I stopped talking to them really because, my friends go out a lot. . . . and I don't want to take my baby out with me and hang around my friends, and drink and hang out on the corner or whatever. . . . I don't want my baby there. (Moloney et al., 2011, p. 13)

Indeed, among the 118 homegirls interviewed by Hunt and his colleagues (2005), 85% reported abstaining from drinking once their pregnancies were confirmed. One mother, who reflected a common sentiment of female gang members, explained, "Even though I was young, I knew what I was supposed to do and what I was not supposed to do. Drinking was something [I was] not supposed to do. It's not good for my daughter, you know" (Hunt et al., 2005, p. 357). Likewise, another stated, "I knew that any kind of drugs or alcohol would affect my sons' births, so I stopped all that" (p. 357).

Hunt and his colleagues (2005) found that some gang girls' substance use resumed postpartum. However, a majority of the mothers consumed a lesser amount, with greater self-regulation, and often in private spaces as opposed to in the streets or parks. "Nothing really changed, except now I just have to be a little more alert because I have my kid, my baby," one mother explained, "I can't get too high, too drunk. I would never let myself get too high" (Hunt et al., 2005, pp. 365–366). Another stated:

> I didn't drink at all when I was pregnant. But now it's just like I drink but, you know, not as much as before. . . . I drink to a certain level where I know I'm not drunk. So I control my drinking. (p. 366)

Moreover, because of its privatization, substance use is less a means for fostering group solidarity and instead is primarily for relaxing at home.

In addition to curtailing social drinking and drug use, pregnancy, motherhood, and increased time spent at home also reduce gang girls' involvement in risk-taking behavior such as drug dealing, shoplifting, and fighting (Fleisher & Kreinhart, 2004; Miller, 2001; Moloney et al., 2011). For example, Monica, a Columbus gang member, described changes in the role of a pregnant young woman in her gang as follows:

> They don't expect her to go out there and sell nothin' like that, or smoke bud or nothing. But if, if she wasn't sick or havin' morning sickness or whatever, she would come out and play cards and play dominos and then get back home when she got tired. (Miller, 2001, p. 89)

Young mothers also avoid "stirring things up" or engaging in violent confrontations with rival gang members because "they don't want nothing to happen around her baby" (Miller, 2001, p. 120). As Tonya, a St. Louis gang member said, "Once a girl get pregnant, she will maybe get out of it. . . . Not get out of it, but you know, she have to chill, she have to stay inside and all that" (Miller, 2001, p. 120).

Pregnancy and motherhood also tend to lead to positive life choices and the adoption of healthier behaviors. This includes desisting from gang involvement entirely (Hunt et al., 2005; Moloney et al., 2011). Of the only gang girl she knew to become pregnant, Veronica said, "She had got pregnant and she had the baby, she ain't never come back around to no sets or nothin'" (Miller, 2001, p. 88). Fleisher and Krienert's (2004) study of 75 gang women in Champaign, Illinois, revealed that 64% of inactive gang members named pregnancy as the primary reason for exiting. According to Miller (2001), two significant reasons young mothers exit their gangs are to avoid exposing their children to gang life and because they believed a child born into a gang is "forever marked as a gang member"—a stigma young mothers did not want their babies to have (p. 88). Leslie, who was pregnant at the time of her interview, explained:

> The leader, he tried to tell you, he tried to tell the guys to get their girls pregnant, so then that would be—'cause they try to say if a child is born into a gang then they're

always going to be [in the] gang from birth to death.... And I mean, I've already told my boyfriend, I said my baby is not gonna have nothin' to do with no gang. You may be in a gang but don't bring it around my kid. (Miller, 2001, pp. 88–89)

Motherhood also inspired some gang girls to seek legitimate employment or return to school (Fleisher & Kreinhart, 2004; Moloney et al., 2011). As one homegirl noted, "That's what got me into school, to go to school and stuff" (Hunt et al., 2005, p. 358).

Although pregnancy and the birth of a child have some positive effects, they also result in some challenges and tensions, especially as young mothers negotiate the contradictions between being "respectable" women, good mothers, and gang members. Prior to motherhood, respectability is based on one's independence and sexual reputation (Joe-Laidler & Hunt, 2001). Postpartum, homegirls are faced with maintaining sexual respectability in light of being young mothers—two identities that are often viewed as contradictory. Moloney and her colleagues (2011) found that young mothers attempt to navigate this challenge in two ways. First, they emphasize that their pregnancy did not result from promiscuity. Sonya, a gang member and mother, explained how she "only had sex with [her boyfriend]. That was it. Nobody else. And he knew that.... He knew I wasn't sluttin' around with no dudes'" (Moloney et al., 2011, p. 8). Second, it was important that young mothers articulate a disinterest in sex. Sonya continued:

I'm not into sex.... I have sex with him because he wants to. I'm even embarrassed.... I'm not that kind of girl.... He's my man and because I got feelings for him [I do it]. (p. 8)

Gang mothers also face the challenge of maintaining their gang identity and exhibiting "good mothering," again two seemingly conflicting identities (Moloney et al., 2011). Although gang activities often involve social drinking, drug use, and delinquency, mothers who engage in this behavior are often looked down upon as undeserving of respect. To negotiate this situation, good mothers emphasize the actions of "bad" mothers, distancing themselves from those who exhibit irresponsible behavior. Giggles, a 16-year-old Latina gang member and mother, said:

There are so many other girls that I know with kids and they're still out there banging with their kids two, three in the morning. So many things have happened to babies because their moms are stupid, taking them out to parties, parks, while they're drunk, drinking in front of them, smoking in front of them. That's something I wouldn't do. (Moloney et al., 2011, p. 10)

Mothers who wish to maintain their gang identity often continue to participate in drinking, selling drugs, and fighting (Hunt et al., 2005; Miller, 2001; Moloney et al., 2011). However, good mothers would only do so once their baby was cared for and out of harm's way. For example, Frosty, a 17-year-old gang mother, said:

> As long as I don't have my baby with me, I'm down [will join in a fight]. If I got my baby with me, I'm a punk [won't join in a fight]. Cuz I'm not gonna do nothing violent with my kid with me. (Moloney et al., 2011, p. 15)

Despite their attempts to keep their children separate from gang life, young gang mothers recognize that gang activities could place them in harm's way. Silvia explained:

> I don't wanna get jumped. Because of the baby. . . . Like for a month, I had to go to [a rival gang's street]. . . . I was confronted. . . . I was like 'I'm with my baby, what the fuck are you coming up ta me? Come up ta me when I'm by myself. I don't care what you do ta me, but with my baby, no. (Moloney et al., 2011, p. 15)

Despite these challenges, gang girls who become mothers generally make significant and positive changes to their lives. Hunt and his colleagues (2005) attribute this to a maturation process, whereby:

> young women begin to consciously control and regulate their risky behaviors, particularly drinking, partying, and associating with gang peers, to protect their children's well-being and at the same time develop plans and aspirations to improve the quality of life for their children and themselves. (p. 336)

As one mother explained, "It leads my life. It changed everything. Matter of fact, I said I do everything for my daughter now. . . . Going to school, working hard, working in the community. Everything I do is for her benefit" (Hunt et al., 2005, p. 369).

Conclusion

In this chapter, we have provided a detailed description of the social worlds of girls in gangs, addressing a number of issues, including how social and environmental contexts impact girls' gang involvement, why they become involved, and what their experiences are like in gangs, including their participation in delinquency and exposure to violence and the role that motherhood plays in changing young women's relationships with their gangs. Girls join gangs in response to a myriad of problems in their lives. In the context of broader economic hardships and tumultuous and violent neighborhoods, gang life can become an attractive option. It affords young women a reprieve from family hardships, a support network, and skills, such as fighting, that are necessary for survival on the streets. Yet gang involvement also exacerbates, rather than improves, many of the problems in homegirls' lives. This occurs not only because of their crime involvement and risks for victimization, but also because of the gender inequalities often replicated within these groups. In the long run, gang involvement has a series of consequences that often narrow young women's life options even further (Moore, 1991).

We conclude with several observations about the direction that research on the social worlds of girls in gangs might fruitfully take. First, despite the dramatic increase in research on girls in gangs beginning in the late 20th century, less of this work has carried forward into the 21st century. The field of gang research, especially its rich qualitative traditions, appears to be at risk of returning to a primary focus on young men. Thus, we need new research to capture homegirls' experiences in an ever-changing world. As importantly, research on female and male gang members alike must be more attentive to gender. According to Maxson, Egley, Miller, and Klein (2014), "Gender is a relational concept; it is not simply about women and girls, but also about men and boys. . . . [It] should not simply apply to studies of women and girls" (p. 270).

Recent research suggests a number of important avenues for such research. As noted, the gendered social organization of gangs appears to impact gang members' behaviors and experiences, but our knowledge of these relationships requires better clarification. In addition, new research suggesting that both female *and* male gang members are at heightened risk for sexual victimization raises key questions about how gender creates risks within gangs (Gover et al., 2009). Finally, recent research investigates additional ways that gender and sexuality intersect in gang members' lives. Vanessa Panfil (2014) is among the first scholars to study the lives of gay men in gangs. Despite the numerous patriarchal constraints homegirls describe in their lives, especially those tied to heterosexual respectability, female and transgender members of the lesbian, gay, bisexual, transgender, and queer community are undoubtedly present in gangs and have unique experiences worth learning more about. Yet, thus far, we do not have the research necessary to address these important questions.

NOTES

[1]We use the terms "girls" and "young women" here interchangeably because the studies we draw from are based on research with female gang members from early adolescence to early adulthood.

[2]Although quantitative research has also investigated young women's experiences in gangs (see Peterson, 2012, for an overview), our primary focus here is on the insights of qualitative studies, the goal of which is to illuminate contextual understandings of social worlds (Decker & Pyrooz, 2012; see Hughes, 2005).

[3]There are gangs in suburban communities and even rural areas, although their numbers are much smaller (Howell, Egley, Tita, & Griffiths, 2011). No systematic research has studied girls' gang involvement in such settings.

[4]Curiously, qualitative and quantitative studies often differ on these fundamental findings (see Maxson & Whitlock, 2001; Thornberry et al., 2003). It may be that measures used in

survey research are less able to capture the nuances that emerge when young women recount their life histories.

References

Adler, F. (1975). *Sisters in crime: The rise of the new female criminal.* New York, NY: McGraw–Hill.

Bjerregaard, B., & Smith, C. (1993). Gender differences in gang participation, delinquency, and substance use. *Journal of Quantitative Criminology, 4,* 329–355.

Bowker, L. H., Gross, H. S., & Klein, M. W. (1980). Female participation in delinquent gang activities. *Adolescence, 15,* 509–519.

Bowker, L. H., & Klein, M. W. (1983). The etiology of female juvenile delinquency and gang membership: A test of psychological and social structural explanations. *Adolescence, 18,* 739–751.

Brown, W. K. (1978). Black female gangs in Philadelphia. *International Journal of Offender Therapy and Comparative Criminology, 21,* 221–228.

Campbell, A. (1984). *The girls in the gang.* New York, NY: Basil Blackwell.

Campbell, A. (1987). Self definition by rejection: The case of gang girls. *Social Problems, 34,* 451–466.

Campbell, A. (1990). Female participation in gangs. In C. R. Huff (Ed.), *Gangs in America* (pp. 163–182). Newbury Park, CA: Sage.

Cepeda, A., & Valdez, A. (2003). Risk behaviors among young Mexican American gang-associated females: Sexual relations, partying, substance use, and crime. *Journal of Adolescent Research, 18,* 90–106.

Chesney-Lind, M., & Hagedorn, J. M. (Eds.). (1999). *Female gangs in America: Essays on girls, gangs and gender.* Chicago, IL: Lakeview Press.

Cloward, R. A., & Ohlin, L. E. (1960). *Delinquency and opportunity: A theory of delinquent gangs.* Glencoe, IL: The Free Press.

Cohen, A. K. (1955). *Delinquent boys: The culture of the gang.* Glencoe, IL: The Free Press.

Collins, P. H. (2006). New commodities, new consumers: Selling blackness in a global market-place. *Ethnicities, 6,* 297–317.

Curry, G. D. (1998). Female gang involvement. *Journal of Research in Crime and Delinquency, 35,* 100–118.

Daly, K., & Chesney-Lind, M. (1988). Feminism and criminology. *Justice Quarterly, 5,* 497–538.

Decker, S. H., & Pyrooz, D. C. (2012). Contemporary gang ethnographies. In F. T. Cullen and P. Wilcox (Eds.), *The Oxford handbook of criminological theory* (pp. 274–293). New York, NY: Oxford University Press.

Durán, R. J. (2013). *Gang life in two cities: An insider's journey.* New York, NY: Columbia University Press.

Egley, A., Jr., & Howell, J. C. (2013). *Highlights of the 2011 National Youth Gang Survey. OJJDP juvenile justice fact sheet.* Washington, DC: U.S. Department of Justice.

Esbensen, F. -A., & Carson, D. C. (2012). Who are the gangsters? An examination of the age, race/ethnicity, sex, and immigration status of self-reported gang members in a seven-city study of American youth. *Journal of Contemporary Criminal Justice, 28,* 465–481.

Fishman, L. T. (1995). The vice queens: An ethnographic study of black female gang behavior. In M. W. Klein, C. L. Maxson, & J. Miller (Eds.), *The modern gang reader* (pp. 83–92). Los Angeles, CA: Roxbury.

Fleisher, M. S., & Krienert, J. L. (2004). Life-course events, social networks, and the emergence of violence among female gang members. *Journal of Community Psychology, 32,* 607–622.

Gover, A. R., Jennings, W. G., & Tewksbury, R. (2009). Adolescent male and female gang members' experiences with violent victimization, dating violence, and sexual assault. *American Journal of Criminal Justice, 34,* 103–115.

Howell, J. C., Egley, A., Jr., Tita, G. E., & Griffiths, E. (2011). U.S. gang problem trends and serious-ness, 1996–2009. *National Gang Center Bulletin, No. 6.* Tallahassee, FL: National Gang Center.

Hughes, L. A. (2005). Studying youth gangs: Alternative methods and conclusions. *Journal of Contemporary Criminal Justice, 21,* 98–119.

Hunt, G. P., & Joe-Laidler, K. (2001). Situations of violence in the lives of girl gang members. *Health Care for Women International, 22,* 363–384.

Hunt, G. P., Joe-Laidler, K., & Evans, K. (2002). The meaning and gendered culture of getting high: Gang girls and drug use issues. *Contemporary Drug Problems, 29,* 375–415.

Hunt, G. P., Joe-Laidler, K., & MacKenzie, K. (2005). Moving into motherhood: Gang girls and controlled risk. *Youth and Society, 36,* 333–373.

Hunt, G. P., MacKenzie, K., & Joe-Laidler, K. (2000). 'I'm calling my mom': The meaning of family and kinship among homegirls. *Justice Quarterly, 17,* 1–31.

Joe, K. A., & Chesney-Lind, M. (1995). "Just every mother's angel": An analysis of gender and ethnic variations in youth gang membership. *Gender and Society, 9,* 408–430.

Joe-Laidler, K., & Hunt, G. P. (1997). Violence and social organization in female gangs. *Social Justice, 24,* 148–169.

Joe-Laidler, K., & Hunt, G. P. (2001). Accomplished femininity among the girls in the gang. *British Journal of Criminology, 41,* 656–678.

Katz, C. M., & Schnebley, S. M. (2011). Neighborhood variations in gang member concentra-tions. *Crime and Delinquency, 57,* 377–407.

Klein, M. W. (1971). *Street gangs and street workers.* Englewood Cliffs, NJ: Prentice Hall.

Klein, M. W. (1995). *The American street gang: Its nature, prevalence and control.* New York, NY: Oxford University Press.

Klein, M. W., & Maxson, C. L. (2010). *Street gang patterns and policies.* New York, NY: Oxford University Press.

Lauderback, D., Hansen, J., & Waldorf, D. (1992). "Sisters are doin' it for themselves": A Black female gang in San Francisco. *Gang Journal, 1,* 57–70.

Lauritsen, J. L., Heimer, K., & Lynch, J. P. (2009). Trends in the gender gap in violent offending: New evidence from the National Crime Victimization Survey. *Criminology, 47,* 361–400.

Maxson, C. L., Egley, A., Miller, J., & Klein, M. W. (Eds.). (2014). *The modern gang reader.* New York, NY: Oxford University Press.

Maxson, C. L., & Whitlock, M. (2001). Joining the gang: Gender differences in risk factors for gang membership. In C. R. Huff (Ed.), *Gangs in America* (3rd ed., pp. 19–36). Thousand Oaks, CA: Sage.

Miller, J. (2001). *One of the guys: Girls, gangs and gender.* New York, NY: Oxford University Press.

Miller, J. (2008). *Getting played: African American girls, urban inequality, and gendered violence.* New York: New York University Press.

Miller, J., & Brunson, R. K. (2000). Gender dynamics in youth gangs: A comparison of male and female accounts. *Justice Quarterly, 17,* 801–830.

Miller, J., & Decker, S. H. (2001). Young women and gang violence: An examination of gender, street offending and violent victimization in gangs. *Justice Quarterly, 18,* 115–140.

Miller, W. B. (1973). The molls. *Society, 2,* 11, 32–35.

Miller, W. B. (1975). *Violence by youth gangs and youth groups as a crime problem in major American cities.* Washington, DC: U.S. Government Printing Office.

Miranda, M. K. (2003). *Homegirls in the public sphere.* Austin: University of Texas Press.

Moloney, M., Hunt, G. P., Joe-Laidler, K., & MacKenzie, K. (2011). Young mother (in the) hood: Gang girls' negotiations of new identities. *Journal of Youth Studies, 14,* 1–19.

Moore, J. W. (1991). *Going down to the barrio: Homeboys and homegirls in change.* Philadelphia, PA: Temple University Press.

Nurge, D. (2003). Liberating yet limiting: The paradox of female gang membership. In L. Contos, D. C. Brotherton, & L. Barrios (Eds.), *Gangs and society: Alternative perspectives* (pp. 161–182). New York, NY: Columbia University Press.

Panfil, V. R. (2014). 'I will fight you like I'm straight': Gay gang- and crime-involved men's participation in violence. In D. Peterson & V. R. Panfil (Eds.), *Handbook of LGBT communities, crime, and justice.* New York, NY: Springer.

Papachristos, A. V. (2005). Gang world. *Foreign Policy,* (March/April), 48–55.

Peterson, D. (2012). Girlfriends, gun-holders, and ghetto-rats? Moving beyond narrow views of girls in gangs. In S. Miller, L. D. Leve, & P. K. Kerig (Eds.), *Delinquent girls: Contexts, relationships, and adaptation* (pp. 71–84). New York, NY: Springer.

Peterson, D., Miller, J., & Esbensen, F. -A. (2001). The impact of sex composition on gangs and gang member delinquency. *Criminology, 39,* 411–439.

Peterson, R. D., & Krivo, L. J. (2010). *Divergent social worlds: Neighborhood crime and the racial-spatial divide.* New York, NY: Russell Sage Foundation.

Portillos, E., Jurik, N., & Zatz, M. (1996). Machismo and Chicano/a gangs: Symbolic resistance or oppression? *Free Inquiry in Creative Sociology, 24,* 175–184.

Quicker, J. C. (1983). *Homegirls: Characterizing Chicana gangs.* San Pedro, CA: International University Press.

Schalet, A., Hunt, G. P., & Joe-Laidler, K. (2003). Respectability and autonomy: The articulation and meaning of sexuality among the girls in the gang. *Journal of Contemporary Ethnography, 32,* 108–143.

Short, J. F., Jr., & Strodtbeck, F. L. (1965). *Group process and gang delinquency.* Chicago, IL: University of Chicago Press.

Smart, C. (1976). *Women, crime and criminology: A feminist critique.* London, UK: Routledge & Kegan Paul.

Taylor, T. J. (2008). The boulevard ain't safe for your kids . . . : Youth gang membership and violent victimization. *Journal of Contemporary Criminal Justice, 24,* 125–136.

Thornberry, T. P., Krohn, M. D., Lizotte, A. J., Smith, C. A., & Tobin, K. (2003). *Gangs and delinquency in developmental perspective.* New York, NY: Cambridge University Press.

Thrasher, F. M. (1927). *The gang: A study of 1,313 gangs in Chicago.* Chicago, IL: University of Chicago Press.

Venkatesh, S. A. (1998). Gender and outlaw capitalism: A historical account of the Black Sisters United "girl gang." *Signs, 23,* 683–709.

Vigil, J. D. (2002). *A rainbow of gangs: Street cultures in the mega-city.* Austin: University of Texas Press.

Wilson, W. J. (1996). *When work disappears: The world of the new urban poor.* New York, NY: Knopf.

CHAPTER 8

A Social Network Perspective of Gender and Crime

Dana L. Haynie and Brian Soller

One of the most vexing issues in criminology is understanding why women and girls engage in much lower levels of criminal behavior than boys and men. Two overarching questions focus on this issue: (1) how can we explain the higher rate of crime among boys and men compared to girls and women, and (2) how can we explain why girls and women engage in crime? Researchers interested in these questions are for the most part divided into two camps. The "gender-neutral" camp argues that traditional theories of crime are equally capable of explaining female involvement as they are of explaining male criminality, whereas the "gender-specific" camp argues that female-centric theories are necessary to account for girls' and women's unique experiences to explain gender variation in crime.

In this chapter, we argue that a social network perspective provides an especially valuable tool for addressing the issue of gender and crime. This is because a social network perspective emphasizes both the structure of social ties among individuals and the meaning attached to those ties. In this way, a social network perspective provides a theoretical "middle ground" that can examine how network structure and behavior may be similar or different across genders and consider how these ties or structure may differently impact males and females to shape the level and type of crime committed by men and women. Those interested in a wider variety of explanations of gender differences in offending may wish to consult review articles by Steffensmeier and Allan (1996) and Kruttschnitt (2013), as well as other chapters in this volume.

Below, we begin by describing a social network perspective and how it has informed research on crime and delinquency. Next, we discuss briefly the topic of gender and crime, describing what is known about the similarities and differences and what remains unclear or unaddressed by research. We then move into a discussion of how a social network approach can better inform criminological explanations of gender and crime. We conclude the chapter by discussing future directions for research.

A Social Network Perspective of Crime

The awareness of the role of social networks in shaping emotions, opinions, behaviors, attitudes, information, and health outcomes has exploded recently with research documenting widespread and often powerful network influences. A network perspective has also recently regained popularity in criminology (Papachristos, 2011) with awareness that many traditional criminological theories (e.g., learning, labeling, control, and opportunity theories) all touch on the topic of the influence and the structure of interpersonal relationships for understanding criminal behavior. Thus, it is no surprise that criminologists are increasingly recognizing that a social network perspective offers a rich theoretical and methodological lens through which a deeper understanding of the relationship between social structures and processes and crime emerges.

The Social Network Perspective

What is a social network perspective? A social network perspective offers a unique view of human behavior in its underlying focus on interdependencies among individuals (i.e., actors in network language) and, more importantly, indicates that these interdependencies have important consequences for individual and collective outcomes. Therefore, it emphasizes both the ties connecting individuals within shared contexts (e.g., schools, neighborhoods, workplaces) and the characteristics of actors (e.g., gender, race, delinquency) in that structure. A social network perspective also views individual behavior as enacted in a social process where interactions among and between network members influence individual behavior and preferences, define situations and behavior, and shape whether behaviors or objects are viewed as desirable or undesirable (Pescosolido, 1992).

An exciting development in the field of criminology is the increased emphasis being placed on social networks and network analysis (Papachristos, 2011). Spurred by recent methodological developments in social network analysis, as well as the availability of a novel dataset, the National Longitudinal Study of Adolescent Health (hereafter, Add Health), researchers now have the tools to more thoroughly examine how social networks factor into delinquent behavior. For instance, when examining the role of peers in delinquent behavior, a network perspective offers a more desirable measurement strategy where friendship networks are carefully mapped out, responses about peer behaviors come directly from friends, and network homogeneity (i.e., attribute similarity among associates) and structure are considered.

Scholars interested in applying a social network perspective to understand criminal behavior require complete (or near complete) data on individuals' ties or connections. Although these ties can take on different forms (e.g., casual acquaintances, romantic attachments, acts of aggression), for researchers interested in adolescent behavior, they often take on the form of friendship ties among adolescents. This suggests that the quantity and structure of friendship ties among adolescents offer explanatory power for a variety of social behaviors, including delinquency. By studying friendship ties among adolescents in a social setting, network perspectives provide an opportunity to test competing theoretical hypotheses for the peer-delinquency association, while also advancing new network concepts—such as centrality and density—and methods that expand our knowledge of delinquent contexts.

Social network methods, concepts, and data also allow researchers to test well-established criminological theories in novel ways. Importantly, prominent criminological theories have long focused on various aspects of social relationships to explain delinquent behavior. For instance, Hirschi's social control theory (1969) extends Durkheim's (1951) notion of social integration to suggest that strong attachments between individuals deter criminal involvement. Hirschi argues that bonds to family members and peers constrain adolescents from acting on natural antisocial impulses. One key expectation of this theory is that compared to those lacking strong friendship bonds, adolescents who maintain affective ties to friends are more behaviorally constrained and are thus less likely to engage in delinquency. To explain females' lower involvement in crime, a social control perspective would emphasize the stronger, prosocial ties girls have with others compared to those of boys. Other criminological theories, such as differential association (Sutherland, 1947) and social learning theory (Akers, 2009), propose that delinquency is learned through peer relationships that expose youth to delinquent acts and social definitions of behavior that are favorable to law and norm violations. Thus, influence and learning theories argue that the manner in which peer relations affect subsequent criminal involvement depends on the delinquency profiles of one's associates.

The Peer-Delinquency Association

Although peer relationships are central to the above theories of delinquency, until recently, researchers have not been able to draw upon detailed social network data to test these theories and ask more varied questions about the role of friendship networks in offending. To do this, work has begun using the detailed school friendship networks available in the Add Health data. Add Health is unique in that it provides an opportunity to analyze complete social networks of adolescents attending a nationally representative sample of schools in the United States. To achieve this sample, researchers collected data on every student attending school on the day the questionnaire was administered. As part of this data collection effort, researchers provided students with rosters listing all schoolmates and asked them to nominate up to 10 of their closest friends (5 males and 5 females). Because nearly every student present completed the questionnaire, it is possible to recreate most friendship ties of the students in the school. This information provides the largest and most comprehensive portrayal of adolescents' school-based friendship networks to date.

The availability of social network data through the Add Health data set has provided criminologists with an unprecedented opportunity to test key principles of criminological theories. For instance, Haynie (2001) integrated insights from control and influence theories to build and empirically test a network theory of adolescent delinquency. Utilizing network data from Add Health, she examined the association between embeddedness in densely connected peer network groups (a marker of social bonds to peers) and delinquent peer associations and adolescent delinquency. In support of both control and influence theories, Haynie (2001) found that on average, being a member of a densely connected peer group was negatively associated with delinquent behavior, whereas attachments to delinquent peers were positively associated with delinquency involvement. However, Haynie (2001) also found that network density accentuates the association between delinquent peer attachments and delinquency. She suggests that network cohesion facilitates a common identity among both delinquent and nondelinquent peer groups and—from a control perspective—constrains the behavior of peer group members to be consistent with the normative behavior of the group. As evidenced by the work of Haynie (2001) and others (Mangino, 2009; McGloin & Shermer, 2009), exactly how peer attachments influence subsequent offending appears to depend on both behavioral and network structural characteristics of one's peer group.

A second common question among network-orientated criminologists concerns whether peer delinquency influences subsequent behavior or, instead, results from "projection," or the tendency for adolescents to overestimate the extent to which their own behavior is similar to their friends' behavior. The issue of projection has long encumbered research on peer influence because most surveys on the matter gather "perceptual" measures of peer delinquency (e.g., "how many of your friends steal?"), rather than network-based measures of peer offending. The Add Health data provide a unique opportunity to address this question because friendship networks can be carefully defined (by having adolescents nominate their closest friends, by having friends' behavior come from friends' responses, and by controlling for adolescents' prior delinquency). Taking this approach, results using the Add Health data suggest that peer delinquency is associated with an adolescent's subsequent delinquency, controlling for prior behavior; however, the effect is much smaller than that estimated by prior research not incorporating network methods and data (Haynie & Osgood, 2005). This finding suggests that relying on adolescent perceptions of friends' behavior introduces substantial same-source bias, which in turn inflates the correlation between friends' and adolescents' behavior.

Peer Influence Versus Self-Selection

Another key issue in the field of criminology has been trying to understand whether adolescents self-select into delinquent peer groups on the basis of their own behavior (as suggested by Gottfredson & Hirschi, 1990), supporting the adage that "birds of a feather flock together." If this idea is true, it suggests that individuals' friendship networks should exhibit predominately delinquent behavior (delinquents flocking together) or nondelinquent behavior (nondelinquents flocking together). Therefore, this raises the question: Do adolescents have homogenous networks in terms of the delinquency of their friends?

Using friendship network information available in the Add Health data set and a dichotomous measure of delinquency (1 = yes, adolescent engaged in delinquency during the past year; 0 = no delinquency), Haynie (2002) found that adolescents are located in rather heterogeneous friendship networks. That is, youth tend to have friends who are both delinquent and nondelinquent. Specifically, she found that 56% of adolescents are in a mixed network with both delinquent and nondelinquent peers, 28% are in an entirely delinquent network, and 16% are in an entirely non-delinquent network.

These findings suggest that peer networks are much more heterogeneous in terms of exposure to delinquent friends. Although there is some evidence that delinquents cluster together, most adolescents in schools have both delinquent and non-delinquent friends in their networks of close acquaintances. This finding is at odds with Gottfredson and Hirschi's (1990) assertion that self-selection is entirely responsible for the peer-delinquency association because the assumption is that there are clearly delineated delinquent or nondelinquent networks that adolescents choose to join. Instead, most adolescents are exposed to both delinquent and nondelinquent patterns and the ratio of these patterns influences behavior. When friendship networks contain access to both delinquent and nondelinquent friends, the network may be less effective in providing clear behavioral guidelines, cohesive norms, and consistent values regarding behavioral expectations.

Recent work interested in untangling self-selection from peer influence has adopted a more sophisticated network approach to better understand the role of peers in criminal and delinquent outcomes. Much of this recent work has been spurred by the development of new stochastic actor–oriented models that allow for the analysis of the coevolution of networks and behavior (Snijders, van de Bunt, & Steglich, 2010). Stochastic actor–oriented models have been particularly useful in the examination of adolescent risk behaviors such as delinquency. For instance, utilizing two waves of data from Dutch high school students, Snijders and Baerveldt (2003) found that similarity in friends' delinquency is a result of two factors: (1) tie formation, which captures selection (e.g., delinquent friends selecting other delinquents as friends); and (2) friendship ties breaking when delinquent behavior among friends becomes dissimilar (referred to as tie dissolution). Although this provides evidence of selection processes operating to make friends similar in terms of their delinquent behavior, the study was not designed to test whether friends also exert influence to change individuals' behavior to be the same as that in the friendship group.

To address the relative importance of self-selection and peer influence, Baerveldt, Völker, and Van Rossem (2008) drew on friendship network data from students in 16 Dutch high schools. Specifically, they found that in every high school, contact with delinquent peers influenced the likelihood that youths would engage in delinquent conduct. Evidence for self-selection (e.g., delinquent adolescents selecting other delinquent adolescents as friends) was only found in 4 of the 16 schools and depended in part on network differences between the schools. Likewise, using comparable data, Weerman (2011) found only limited evidence that selection is the reason why youths have similar levels of delinquency. Rather, he found evidence that peer influence is more important in causing delinquency, although he reports smaller influence effects compared to prior studies that did not use a network-based perspective (Weerman, 2011).[1] Finally, using longitudinal network data from students in Sweden, researchers found evidence of both selection and peer influence playing a role in why friends behave similarly (Burk, Steglich, & Snijders, 2007), with some evidence that peer influence played a larger role in shaping behavioral similarity among friends. In sum, this new and growing body of research provides somewhat mixed evidence regarding the role that selection and influence play in shaping adolescent delinquency. Unfortunately, little is known about the role of selection for explaining gender variation in the peer-delinquency association.

Empirically, it has yet to be determined whether selection processes toward delinquency play a different role among male and female adolescents. However, there is some reason to expect that selection processes may be more important for girls than for boys. The idea that adolescents prefer similar others as friends has a long history in the social sciences (McPherson, Smith-Lovin, & Cook, 2001). Individuals have a tendency to select similar others as friends because those who are similar (e.g., sociodemographic background, attitudes, behaviors) tend to have more common experiences to draw upon and, as a result, can relate more easily to each other. This makes these relationships easier to maintain, more rewarding, and stable. Because girls tend to have smaller and more intimate friendship networks than boys and because they are more likely to disclose intimate feelings, girls may be more discerning about whom they select as friends. In addition, because gender norms are more likely to operate to stigmatize delinquency, especially violence among girls, nondelinquent girls may be especially likely to spurn delinquent adolescents as friends. In contrast, delinquent girls who are engaging in more nonnormative gender behavior may be especially likely to select out other delinquent adolescents as friends because these individuals are likely to also be stigmatized (if girls) or to provide a supportive context in which to engage in delinquent behavior. This implies that the delinquent behavior of a friend may be a critical factor in whether girls select another as a friend.

Boys, in contrast, have larger, more fluid networks of friends that often are organized around shared activities, such as sports and other extracurricular activities, or around spaces in neighborhoods where play takes place, such as a basketball court (e.g., Clampet-Lundquist, Edin, Kling, Jeffrey, & Duncan, 2011). In this sense, the overlap in shared activities or interactional contexts may take precedence over the delinquent behavior of friends among boys. In addition, because delinquency tends to be more overlooked or less stigmatizing among boys (compared to girls), they may be less likely to consider the delinquent behavior of others when selecting friends.

This is why selection factors other than delinquency, such as mutual interest and involvement in sports or other activities, may take center stage for boys' friendship relationships. As a result, selection processes may be more important in explaining delinquency similarity among girls than among boys.

Understanding the Causes of Delinquency

In addition to examining the peer-delinquency association, the Add Health data allow researchers to examine network behaviors and network structures as important mediating and moderating variables with regard to delinquency. For instance, in the criminology and developmental literature, there has been a common finding that girls who experience pubertal development earlier than their peers are at increased risk of engaging in subsequent delinquent behavior. One reason for this increased risk is the differing peer networks that more developed versus less developed females find themselves in. In particular, research from the Add Health data found that females who experience early pubertal development have higher levels of delinquency one year later, but this is because these girls are at heightened risk of being involved in romantic relationships and because their friends are engaging in risky behaviors (Haynie, 2003). This suggests that peer networks serve as a mechanism that differently places certain groups of adolescents at heightened risk of problem behaviors.

Kreager (2007) examined the moderating role of race, socioeconomic status, and school achievement in the association between violence and peer popularity. In so doing, he tested the hypothesis, drawn from the subculture of violence perspective, that the prestige associated with fighting should vary by sociodemographic characteristics. He found little evidence that the violence–popularity relationship varied by race or socioeconomic status, but did find that the relationship varied by school achievement for males. Specifically, violence was associated with substantially higher popularity for boys who performed poorly in school compared to boys who performed well academically in school. No such association was found for girls, however.

The nature of friendship relations in delinquent versus nondelinquent networks was also developed in three influential studies. Giordano, Cernkovich, and Pugh (1986) found that various dimensions of friendship relations did not differ markedly between delinquent and nondelinquent adolescents. Both delinquent and nondelinquent youth reported similar levels of attachment, intimacy, and contact with friends. Kandel and Davies (1991) also found few differences in the quality of friendship relationships among adolescents who did and did not use illicit drugs. More recently, Kreager, Rulison, and Moody (2011) used network clustering methods to identify friendship groups in school-based adolescent peer networks to examine the structural characteristics (e.g., cohesiveness, stability) of delinquent and nondelinquent groups. With network data from the PROSPER school-based program, they found that net of background characteristics, delinquent groups were structurally similar to groups with low levels of delinquency. However, they also found that drinking groups were *more* cohesive, stable, and in more prominent positions in the social network than nondrinking groups. The latter finding is consistent with a "party" subculture commonly found in school ethnographies.

Further Contributions

In addition to the network studies examining adolescent delinquency, network analyses have been frequently used within criminology to study criminal organizations and groups. For example, a number of researchers have created visual graphs, called sociograms, to depict gang members' relationships. By connecting gang members through friendship ties, it is possible to determine whether the gang is cohesive (i.e., members are friends with one another) or whether there are central figures in the gangs (see, e.g., Curry & Decker, 2003). Similarly, recent work by Papachristos (2009) analyzed gang homicide by examining the social networks of homicide incidents among gang members. This innovative approach illustrates how homicide diffuses through gangs via an epidemic-like process of social contagion. Drawing on these approaches, law enforcement investigators are beginning to use network analysis to better understand crime and violence prevention strategies (Braga, Kennedy, Waring, & Piehl, 2001; McGloin, 2005). Other research has incorporated network mapping to describe organized crime (Klerks, 2001), narcotics trafficking patterns (Natarajan, 2006), terrorist organizations (Pedahzur & Perliger, 2006), and white-collar crime (Baker & Faulkner, 1993).

A central focus of work on neighborhoods and crime also emphasizes the role of residents' networks to determine how they impede or facilitate crime (Kornhauser, 1978; Sampson & Groves, 1989). From this perspective, economically disadvantaged neighborhoods have elevated crime rates because they are typically composed of networks of residents who are weakly connected to one another and, subsequently, unable to enforce community standards of social control (Sampson & Groves, 1989). Recent work has expanded this perspective and shows how network ties in neighborhoods can operate to facilitate crime or to shape the type of crime that emerges (Browning, Dietz, & Feinberg, 2004; Schreck, McGloin, & Kirk, 2009).

Despite the increased attention being directed at the role of social network processes for understanding involvement in crime, limited attention has been paid to how a social network approach can help to explain both gender differences in crime and how gender shapes network processes to differentially impact girls' versus boys' involvement in crime. How might a social network perspective illuminate gender differences in crime?

Below we argue that gender socialization patterns shape the structure of networks and drive differences in the social meanings of relationships and behavior among males and females. Integrating insights from criminological theories of gender and offending (e.g., Steffensmeier & Allan, 1996) and sociological theories of gender and interpersonal relationships (e.g., Soller, 2014), we highlight how social networks may differentially affect male and female offending. We also elaborate how gender differences in various social network characteristics potentially contribute to gender variation in offending.

Gender, Crime, and Social Networks

Although recent attention has focused on the changing magnitude of the gender gap in crime over time, it remains undisputed that girls and women commit less crime than boys and men; this is especially so when the focus is on more serious or violent crime (Lauritsen, Heimer, & Lynch, 2009). In part as a response to their lower levels of criminal involvement, early research in criminology largely ignored the importance of gender in explanations of crime.

Although more recent research increasingly considers how gender shapes the nature and pathways toward delinquency and other criminological outcomes (e.g., victimization; see Miller, 2001), gender largely remains overlooked when it comes to the application of a social network perspective to criminal conduct. Almost the entire body of recent research drawing on either a social network perspective or methods has focused either on explaining overall crime rates and levels or solely on the criminal involvement of males. There has been little consideration of how gender shapes the structure and context of social networks and the influence that these characteristics exert on criminal behavior.

Gender, Delinquent Peers, and Crime

The one exception to this oversight is the growing literature on peers and delinquency. Given that exposure to delinquent peers is one of the most robust predictors of involvement in crime and delinquency (Warr, 2002), recent research has begun examining the nature and importance of these peers for boys and girls (McGloin & DiPietro, 2013). Initially, the importance of delinquent peers for girls was believed to be nonexistent because theorists argued that family influence subsumed peer influence for girls, and girls who did engage in delinquency were characterized as defective—either as social isolates or as rejects (Campbell, 1980; Konopka, 1966). In contrast, the importance of peers for male criminal behavior has been emphasized since early in the literature (Cohen, 1955; Thrasher, 1927). Eventually, with more focus being placed on the generalizability of criminological theory to female offending, researchers argued that peers, especially deviant peers, were just as influential for female offending as for male offending. This view led to the conclusion that there was little cause to articulate how gender shapes the nature and importance of deviant peers for girls compared to boys (Gaarder & Belknap, 2002; Miller, 2001).

However, given that females are involved in crime at much lower rates than males, researchers have reconsidered what role delinquent peers may play in explaining this gender gap, focusing in particular on how gender shapes social networks and crime. Many researchers suggest that a large portion of the gender gap in offending can be attributed to the fact that girls and women have lower levels of exposure to delinquent peers than boys and men. This is largely explained by pointing to the greater constraints and social control placed on females that limit their exposure to deviant norms, behavior, and opportunities to commit crime. For instance, boys may have more opportunities to socialize with deviant peers because they are often afforded more autonomy by and receive less social control from parents; in contrast, girls are supervised much more carefully, have greater restrictions placed on them, and may be punished more quickly for minor transgressions by parents (Morash, 1986; Smith & Paternoster, 1987). The result of these gender differences is that, on average, girls associate with fewer delinquent peers relative to boys (Esbensen, Peterson, Taylor, & Freng, 2010).

Notably, this argument points to the role of gender in shaping *exposure* to delinquent peers; peer association is thus an important risk factor for males and females. Such a risk-factor approach, however, overlooks the possibility that peer processes may be gendered. In other words, when exposed to deviant peers, girls may be differentially influenced by their behavior than males. To explain how this might emerge, researchers have examined similarities and differences in girls' and boys' friendship networks. Although many studies find some similarities between girls' and boys' friendships (e.g., they both value trust, authenticity, and similar status in friendships), they also note important gender differences in the nature of friendships. Boys tend to have larger friendship networks, whereas girls have smaller networks with one or a few best friends (Benenson, 1990). Girls are more likely to characterize their friendships as having high intimacy, emotional involvement, and confidentiality compared to boys' characterizations (Waldrop & Halverson, 1975). Girls may also communicate in different ways than boys, exhibiting higher levels of responsiveness, reciprocity, and harmony in their dialog with one another (Piehler & Dishion, 2007). Other research suggests that girls feel more empathy and prosocial feelings toward friends than boys (Rose & Rudolph, 2006). Moreover, boys have friendship networks characterized by more hierarchy, more activity orientation (e.g., sports), and less inclination to discuss intimate matters with friends (Rose & Rudolph, 2006).

As a result of these significant differences in friendship relationships, some researchers have suggested that gender will moderate the impact of peer influence on delinquent behavior. On one hand, girls may be more influenced by friends' behavior (whether prosocial or delinquent) than boys. As noted above, this is because girls are more emotionally invested in their friendships and are more likely to disclose intimate information among friends, including involvement in risky or criminal behavior. This investment is important to consider because research indicates that friends are especially influential when adolescents are especially close to them or spend more time with them (Agnew, 1991). As a result, friends' participation in either prosocial or delinquent behavior may be especially influential in shaping girls' involvement in delinquency if girls are more emotionally invested in these relationships compared to boys. In addition, because delinquency, especially violence, is generally less condoned among girls, girls may need more of a push to engage in this risky behavior. Friends' involvement in delinquency may serve this purpose and act as a more critical factor in determining whether girls become involved in delinquency compared to boys. In contrast, because it is more socially acceptable for boys to engage in delinquency and violence, friends' involvement may matter less. That is, boys may be drawn to risky behavior regardless of their friends' participation. Overall, these gender differences suggest that friends' behavior will be more influential for girls than for boys in shaping their involvement in delinquency.

On the other hand, some researchers argue that girls should be less influenced by friends' delinquent behavior than boys. For instance, Steffensmeier and his colleagues' theory of gendered focal concerns suggests that male and female involvement in delinquency depends on gendered norms and values that inhibit crime among girls and women and encourage involvement among boys and men (Haynie, Steffensmeier, & Bell, 2007; Steffensmeier & Allan, 1996). As Steffensmeier and Allan (1996) note, "the cleavage between what is considered feminine and what is criminal is sharp, while the dividing line between what is considered masculine and what is criminal is often thin" (p. 476). This suggests that girls may be more protected from the negative influence of peers. That is, gendered focal concerns theory suggests that girls tend to have higher (more moral) expectations about their friends' conduct, are more likely to encourage their friends' participation in conventional activities, and are in general less tolerant of delinquent behavior (Haynie et al., 2007; Mears, Ploeger, & Warr, 1998; Steffensmeier & Allan, 1996; Warr, 2002). Moreover, because of the greater emphasis placed on protecting girls' virtue, female friends are more likely to meet in places supervised by parents and other adults, whereas male friends spend more time in public settings away from family and other supervision (McCarthy, Felmlee, & Hagan, 2004).[2] In short, social expectations regarding how to enact, or "do gender" (Connell, 1987; Miller, 2002), may operate to protect girls' from delinquent influence while at the same time serving to encourage boys' responsiveness to delinquent peers.

In addition, boys may face greater pressure to subscribe to friends' behavior because of the greater status hierarchy involved in friendships as well as the more competitive nature of male friendships (Agnew, 2009). Male friendships, also organized around gendered values and norms, are more prone to displays of masculinity, competition, risk taking, flaunting of boundaries, and character contestations that are often associated with delinquent behavior (Steffensmeier & Allan, 1996). Boys are also more often engaged together in activities that are impersonal and physical and that involve interactions with strangers. These friendship dynamics among boys may increase the likelihood both that boys' activities involve delinquency and violence and that boys face more pressure to go along with the group when it comes to participating in risky activities, such as delinquency. In sum, these gender differences in friendship dynamics suggest that boys may be more influenced by friends' delinquency than are girls.

Although few longitudinal analyses have assessed whether girls are more or less influenced by friends' delinquency, several studies have examined the cross-sectional associations. The bulk of this prior work has reported similarly sized correlations between boys' and girls' individual delinquency and that of their friends (Hartjen & Priyardarsini, 1984; Laird, Pettit, Dodge, & Bates, 2005; Mears et al., 1998). Several meta-analyses of gender differences in correlates of delinquency also find that the effects of friends' delinquency on respondent's delinquency are similar for boys and girls (Hubbard & Pratt, 2002; Wong, Slotboom, & Bijleveld, 2010). In general, this body of research finds that although boys are more likely than girls to have delinquent friends, when girls are exposed to delinquent friends, the effects of these peer associations operate similarly across gender.

Although most studies report that the influence of delinquent friends is similar for boys and girls, a few studies have found gender differences in the relationship between friends and individual delinquency. For example, using cross-sectional data, Mears and his colleagues (1998) found that boys were more strongly affected than girls by delinquent friends. Similarly, using longitudinal data, Piquero, Gover, MacDonald, and Piquero (2005) found that friends' delinquency had stronger effects on male delinquency than on female delinquency.[3] In contrast, Zimmerman and Messner (2010) found that friends' violence is more strongly associated with girls' violent behavior than that of boys. The latter authors argue that girls are more influenced by peers than boys because of the more intimate and emotionally invested ties characterizing girls' friendships compared to boys'.

A limitation of all of these studies, however, is that they did not utilize network data. Instead, scholars relied on reports by respondents on the extent to which their friends participate in delinquency. Asking respondents to report on their perceptions of friends' behavior (rather than directly collecting the information from the friends themselves) increases the risk that adolescents will project their own delinquent behavior to their friends. One recent study of gender differences in peer influence, conducted on a sample of students attending secondary schools in a major Dutch city, remedied this methodological limitation (Weerman & Hoeve, 2012). The research design included the collection of network data in which the delinquent involvement of each respondent was measured. Using multivariate analyses and two waves of data, these authors found that the effect of delinquent peers is greater for girls than for boys.[4] In addition, they noted that the effect of a self-report measure of deviant peer pressure was significantly associated with girls' delinquency but not with that of boys. This latter study suggests that friends' behavior is more influential for girls than for boys, supporting the idea that girls' more intimate friendships provide avenues for greater peer influence to operate than they do among boys.

In sum, criminologists offer a mixed picture of whether girls or boys are more influenced by friends' delinquency. On one hand, because girls are socialized to be more law abiding in general than boys and face higher penalties for engaging in delinquency, they may be less influenced by friends' delinquency than boys. Alternatively, because of their greater intimacy with friends, as well as a desire to acquiesce to group norms to avoid conflict, girls may be more influenced by friends' behavior (prosocial or delinquent). Boys, on the other hand, may be drawn to risky behavior such as delinquency regardless of their friends' behavior.

The Importance of Opposite-Sex Friends

Instead of focusing on friends in general, some research has highlighted the importance of opposite-sex friends for shaping delinquent and criminal behavior. In the
case of girls influencing their male friends, because of the greater emphasis placed on
following rules and because they experience considerably more control in their own
lives than males, female friends are likely to introduce similar attitudes and practices
in their opposite-sex friendships. As noted earlier, females are more supportive of
attitudes or beliefs that directly or indirectly discourage illegal activities and especially violent activities, and they are more likely to encourage their friends' participation in conventional activities. Second, female friends may reduce male delinquency
or violence by reducing opportunities for delinquency. This is because female friends
tend to socialize in settings that are supervised by adults, whereas boys more often
congregate in settings lacking in familial or adult supervision (McCarthy et al., 2004).
Third, because they are less attracted to displays of physical prowess and character
contestations, female friends may reduce the motivation or pressure for males to
offend than is the case for boys in relationships with other boys. Last, males may be
reluctant to commit predatory violence (e.g., assault or rob someone) when their
female friends are present because of fear they will snitch or gossip about the event
(Steffensmeier, 1983).

In contrast, males will provide their female friends with messages more favorable
for delinquency and violence, more exposure to situations where the opportunity
for violence is present, and situationally pressuring participation in co-offending
roles as accomplices, lookouts, or decoys. Also, females in cross-sex friendships
might be less deterred from committing violent acts when in the company of male
friends who might provide protection or backup.

Empirical research is consistent with these arguments. Although examinations of
the role of opposite-sex friends in prior studies are typically confounded by the possibility of a romantic attachment being included as a friendship tie, they generally
show that boys are more likely to have a stronger influence on girls' involvement in
delinquency than girls have on boys in mixed-sexed friendships. For example, several
studies have shown that males tend to influence females in drug use (Covington,
1985; Inciardi, Lockwood, & Pottieger, 1993) and in the commission of serious property crime (Steffensmeier & Ulmer, 2005). Other research shows that girls who spend
time in mixed-sex groups are more likely to engage in delinquency than are girls who
participate in same-sex groups (Giordano, 1978); that girls' delinquency was higher if
they affiliated with male friends (Agnew & Brezina, 1997; Caspi, Lynam, Moffitt, &
Silva, 1993); that female youth were much more likely to report that the instigator of
delinquency in their group was of the opposite sex (Warr, 1996); and that criminal
offending, including violence, is lower in all-female gangs and tends to increase as the
proportion of males in the gang increases (Miller & Brunson, 2000; Peterson, Miller, &
Esbensen, 2001).

These observations notwithstanding, evidence also exists showing that females
influence male offending but that their influence tends to be in the direction of

deterring male delinquency as opposed to encouraging it (as does the male effect, which tends to encourage female offending). This finding is supported by many studies that indicate a strong link between reduced recidivism in male offenders and their relational involvement with females (Shover, 1996; Warr, 2002). McCarthy et al. (2004) report that female-dominated friendship networks (compared to male-dominated networks) reduce involvement in property crime among both female and male youths, although the effect is weaker for males. Research using the social network data available in Add Health also supports these ideas, indicating that exposure to opposite-sex friends increases the odds of females engaging in serious violence but actually operates to reduce males' involvement in serious violence (Haynie et al., 2007).

Romantic Relationships and Crime

In addition to a focus on peers and friendship networks, research on gender and crime has also emphasized the role of girls' and women's romantic relationships with boys and men in shaping their criminal involvement. Research by Haynie and her colleague (Haynie & Osgood, 2005), for example, used social network data from Add Health to show how male romantic partners have a unique criminogenic influence on female delinquency, independent of the effect of the friendship network. Similar to research examining the influence of opposite-sex friends for female offending, this vein of research suggests that males are especially "risky" for females, often introducing them to criminal lifestyles and supporting or coercing them in criminal activities (Caspi et al., 1993; Giordano, 1978; Haynie et al., 2007). Indeed, some argue persuasively that relationships with males are the primary pathway toward crime for females (e.g., Jones, 2008). In part, this is attributed to gender socialization and the greater primacy girls and women place on having and maintaining romantic relationships (Giordano, 1978). Because romantic relationships are often central to females' identities (Soller, 2014), associating and forming close emotional relationships with criminal males becomes especially problematic for females. Several qualitative studies illustrate the importance of relationships with men in explaining pathways toward and reasons for involvement in crime (Jones, 2008; Mullins & Wright, 2003). Even more problematic, there is some evidence that deviant males are viewed as more desirable romantic partners by females during adolescence (Rebellon & Manasse, 2004).

"Doing Gender" and Criminal Involvement

Another vein of criminological research that focuses on how gender shapes social networks emphasizes how gender socialization and identity affect how delinquent and criminal behavior is carried out. In the gang literature, for example, Miller and Decker (2001) found that female gang members use gender both to shape and to accomplish their criminal activities, as well as to temper their involvement in gang crime (see also Jacobs & Miller, 1998). For instance, although female gang members may hold guns for male members, they seldom employ guns themselves when participating in violent altercations (Miller & Decker, 2001). Similarly, qualitative work by Mullins and Wright (2003) highlights the role of gender in shaping the offense of residential burglary. Here the authors note several important gender differences between male and female burglars that shape criminal activity: initiation into criminal networks, the motivation for carrying out burglary, the ability and means to select targets, and the commission of the crime. Specifically, women are more likely to be initiated into crime through a relationship with a male romantic partner, to be motivated by fear of losing a valued relationship or the need to provide economically for children, to use their sexuality to target victims, and to be less likely to carry out the actual commission of the crime, instead relying on male partners to do so (Mullins & Wright, 2003). As this work indicates, female crime and delinquency are embedded in social networks, which in turn are shaped by gender processes.

Gender and White-Collar Crime

Similar to the studies on how gender shapes girls' gang involvement, a smaller body of research has focused on the role of gender in shaping white-collar and corporate crime (see Daly, 1989; Zietz, 1981). Most recently, a study by Steffensmeier, Schwartz, and Roche (2013) examined gender differences in recent corporate financial scandals. Although women were less likely to be part of corporate criminal networks, when they were involved, they played more minor roles and made less profit compared to male co-conspirators. In addition, there is evidence that women's involvement in corporate crime was much more likely to come about as a result of a close personal or romantic relationship with a male co-conspirator (Steffensmeier et al., 2013). These findings show how sex typing and exclusionary practices minimize and marginalize women's participation in corporate networks and hence corporate crime, lending further credence to the argument that gender stratification is also a key organizational element of criminal street networks (Miller & Decker, 2001; Steffensmeier, 1983).

Gender, Neighborhoods, and Social Networks

Research focusing on social relationships that are embedded within neighborhoods may also help us understand gender differences in crime and delinquency. For instance, Harding's (2009) mixed-methods study of youth socializing within urban neighborhoods suggests boys' peer relationships within disadvantaged neighborhoods contribute to gender variation in crime and delinquency. In his study, he presents qualitative data that indicate younger boys socialize with older males to help avoid victimization within disadvantaged and violent urban neighborhoods. Although older teens and young adults provide some protection from neighborhood victimization, relationships with these older peers present younger boys with alternative cultural models (Wilson, 1996) that influence their own cultural worldviews and behavior. Harding's work suggests neighborhood-based social networks are an important conduit through which unconventional cultural models that encourage the use of violence are transmitted across age cohorts. However, future research focusing on girls' neighborhood-based social relationships may provide more insight into how girls' social relationships influence their offending patterns because Harding's study only concentrated on the socialization of boys.

Recent research also suggests that variation in exposure to violent peers across neighborhood contexts, coupled with gender variation in peer influence, accounts for the gender gap in violence across neighborhoods. Using data from the Project on Human Development in Chicago Neighborhoods, Zimmerman and Messner (2010) found that the gender gap in violent offending is narrower in disadvantaged neighborhoods than in more advantaged communities. The authors also found that adolescents are exposed to delinquent peers at greater rates in disadvantaged neighborhoods and that girls' violence is more strongly associated with peers' aggressive behavior when compared to boys. Zimmerman and Messner argue that stronger associations between peer violence and personal violence among girls, coupled with increased exposure to delinquent peers among adolescents in disadvantaged neighborhoods, had an impact on the gender gap in offending: Rates of violent behavior among boys and girls were more similar for youngsters living in poor communities as opposed to those from more advantaged residential contexts.

Although research by Harding (2009) and Zimmerman and Messner (2010) has enriched our understanding of how neighborhood-based peer relationships influence adolescent behavioral development, they were unable to measure social ties among them using social network data. In fact, to our knowledge, no network study has measured neighborhood-based friendships among youths for an entire neighborhood in the United States. Measuring a complete adolescent friendship network within a neighborhood (let alone several neighborhoods) would be costly and logistically challenging because it would require responses from nearly every adolescent in the neighborhood. Furthermore, such a study would likely necessitate a roster that includes every adolescent in the neighborhood, from which nominations could be drawn. Compiling such a roster would also present a significant challenge to studying neighborhood-based peer networks. Largely because of such restrictions, most network studies of adolescent offending are school based and therefore fail to account for important nonschool social relationships that could potentially contribute to adolescent offending and gender variation in delinquent behavior.

Gender, Affiliation Networks, and Crime

Still, network-based approaches to adolescent offending and risk taking may advance our understanding of how neighborhoods and other nonschool contexts factor into the gender–crime relationship. Thus far, this chapter has focused on how features of networks composed of individuals and their social ties to one another contribute to gender variation in youthful offending. However, social networks may also be conceptualized as sets of actors who are *indirectly* tied to one another through shared participation in a second "mode," which may be a club, group, social setting, or some other collection of individuals. In network analytic terminology, such networks represent two-mode, or "affiliation" networks (Wasserman & Faust, 1994). Within such social structures, actors (mode 1) are directly tied to memberships in a second mode (mode 2), and entities from the same mode cannot be directly linked to one another, but may be indirectly linked through the other mode. Although most network-based studies of adolescent offending focus on "one-mode" networks, in which actors from a single set are directly tied to one another, two-mode network approaches to adolescent offending provide a potentially useful analytic tool for understanding gender variation in delinquency.

For instance, we noted previously that girls are more likely to socialize in places supervised by adults, whereas boys spend more time in public settings devoid of supervision. From a two-mode network perspective, one may reconstruct affiliation networks, consisting of actors (mode 1) and actors' activity settings (mode 2), to analyze how key differences in adolescents' activity settings (e.g., levels of adult supervision) contribute to the gender gap in offending. Furthermore, the structure of relations *across* activity locations within a two-mode network potentially affects the behavior of actors within the network and contributes to gender variation in delinquency.

An emerging network approach to understanding variation in adolescent risk behavior utilizes a two-mode network framework and focuses on interconnections among individuals and "activity spaces" (Browning & Soller, 2014). Activity spaces are collections of locations and settings to which individuals are regularly exposed throughout their routine activities (e.g., school, "hanging out," sports activities). This contextual model of youth development focuses on the structure and composition of community-based ecological (or eco-) networks, which are two-mode networks composed of individuals who are connected through shared activity settings. According to this perspective, both setting exposures and the patterns of interconnectedness of eco-networks have implications for the social control and socialization of youth and, in turn, delinquent and other risky behavior.

Browning and Soller (2014) suggest interacting within highly structured spaces characterized by adult supervision and conventional activities (e.g., Boy or Girl Scouts, band, youth sports) decreases adolescent offending through conventional socialization and adult monitoring and social control processes. Alternatively, activities within unstructured and unsupervised settings (e.g., hanging out with peers) lack adult monitoring and provide opportunities to engage in delinquency (Osgood, Wilson, O'Malley, Bachman, & Johnston, 1996). Because girls more often socialize with peers in structured and supervised settings compared to boys, gender differences in the extent of adult monitoring within activity settings may account for gender variation in delinquency.

Gender differences with regard to individual positions within eco-networks may contribute to the gender gap in offending. In particular, the nature and location of leisure time preferences tend to be largely gendered (Maccoby, 1988), which may have important implications for gender variation in offending among youth. For instance, males are more likely to spend time in neighborhood streets or parks, whereas girls have a greater tendency to spend time with friends at residences or at shopping malls (Maccoby, 1988). Similarly, boys have been found to engage in activities within more unstructured and unsupervised spaces with peers than do girls (Maimon & Browning, 2010; Osgood et al., 1996). From an opportunity perspective, unstructured peer contexts often lack adequate adult supervision and therefore provide more opportunities for adolescents to engage in delinquent behavior. From an eco-network standpoint, gender differences in the frequency of interaction within unstructured settings may mean boys have more chances than girls to engage in delinquent behavior with peers.

However, girls' delinquency may be more responsive to characteristics of activity settings, including unstructured socialization and lack of adult monitoring, or social disorder (e.g., loitering, hostility among others, drug use). For instance, in a study of African American adolescents in Philadelphia, Mennis and Mason (2011) found girls' substance-using behavior to be more responsive to the level of perceived safety within activity locations than that of boys. Specifically, girls were more likely than boys to engage in substance use when they assessed their activity spaces as unsafe. More recent research corroborates this finding. Browning, Soller, Gardner, and Brooks-Gunn (2013), for example, found that girls' internalizing symptomology (e.g., depressive symptoms, anxiety) was more responsive to features of their local environment (e.g., disorder). Further research may help assess whether gender variation in behavioral responses to activity space characteristics contributes to differences in offending among boys and girls.

Beyond characteristics of particular activity settings, the geographic dispersion and interconnectedness of activity settings within eco-networks potentially contribute to gender differences in delinquent behavior. Browning and Soller (2014) argue that engaging in shared activities across several different locations enhances social control and the conventional socialization of youth within particular settings, as well as the larger community. Additionally participating in structured activities within eco-networks embeds youth in the routine public activities of conventional life and potentially has implications for prosocial behavior among youth. Interestingly, research suggests that urban boys' activity spaces are more geographically dispersed compared to girls' activities, which are relatively spatially constrained and are situated closer to their home residences (Clampet-Lundquist et al., 2011).

Such gender differences in the dispersion of activity spaces may mean that boys share fewer activity spaces with other community residents when engaging in their routine activities. Because sharing several activity settings with others likely enhances adult supervision over adolescents within eco-networks, girls may be subject to more consistent and higher levels of informal social control across their routine activity spaces. Thus gender differences in the geographic dispersion of youths' activity spaces potentially contribute to gender variation in crime because of variation in the levels of adult monitoring among boys' and girls' activity spaces. Future research that attends to gender processes in conceptualizing the effects of eco-networks on youthful offending and risk taking may provide even more insight into how social network processes contribute to variation in delinquency among boys and girls.

Conclusion

We argue in this chapter that a social network perspective provides an especially valuable lens through which girls' and women's lesser and often different involvement in crime and delinquency can be understood. By focusing on the role of gender socialization, focal concerns, expectations, and activity spaces, a social network perspective can help explain both why females are involved in less crime than males and why and how some girls and women engage in criminal behavior. Thus, a network perspective suggests that gender cannot be treated simply as an individual attribute tacked on to existing theories, but rather must be treated as something that is socially constructed and accomplished through interaction with others.

NOTES

[1]However, work by Knecht (2008), which uses Dutch data, finds evidence of selection for delinquency and alcohol use with no significant evidence of influence. Clearly there continues to be mixed evidence regarding the importance of selection and influence for adolescent risky behavior.

[2]In addition, there is some evidence that boys are more likely than girls to engage in "deviancy training" where verbal cues are used to support and amplify delinquent behavior (Brechwald & Prinstein, 2011).

[3]Other studies examining close friend influence effects for substance use (Erickson, Crosnoe, & Dornbusch, 2000) and roommate socialization of binge drinking (Duncan, Boisjoly, Kremer, Levy, & Eccles, 2005) have been found for male but not for female adolescents.

[4]However, they also note that the gender difference is only significant under a one-tailed test of significance.

References

Agnew, R. (1991). The interactive effects of peer variables on delinquency. *Criminology, 29,* 47–72.

Agnew, R. (2009). The contribution of "mainstream" theories to the explanation of female delinquency. In M. A. Zahn (Ed.), *The delinquent girl* (pp. 147–163). Philadelphia, PA: Temple University Press.

Agnew, R., & Brezina, T. (1997). Relational problems with peers, gender, and delinquency. *Youth and Society, 29,* 84–111.

Akers, R. L. (2009). *Social learning and social structure.* New Brunswick, NJ: Transaction.

Baerveldt, C., Völker, B., & Van Rossem, R. (2008). Revisiting selection and influence: An inquiry into the friendship networks of high school students and their association with delinquency. *Canadian Journal of Criminology and Criminal Justice, 50,* 559–587.

Baker, W. E., & Faulkner, R. R. (1993). The social organization of conspiracy: Illegal networks in the heavy electrical equipment industry. *American Sociological Review, 58*, 837–860.

Benenson, J. F. (1990). Gender differences in social networks. *Journal of Early Adolescence, 10*, 472–495.

Braga, A. A., Kennedy, D. M., Waring, E. J., & Piehl, A. M. (2001). Problem-oriented policing, deterrence, and youth violence. *Journal of Research in Crime and Delinquency, 38*, 195–225.

Brechwald, W. A., & Prinstein, M. J. (2011). Beyond homophily: A decade of advances in understanding peer influence processes. *Journal of Research on Adolescence, 21*, 166–179.

Browning, C. R., Dietz, R. D., & Feinberg, S. L. (2004). The paradox of social organization. *Social Forces, 83*, 503–534.

Browning, C. R., & Soller, B. (2014). Moving beyond neighborhood: Activity spaces and ecological networks as contexts for youth development. *Cityscape: A Journal of Policy Development and Research, 16*, 165–196.

Browning, C. R., Soller, B., Gardner, M., & Brooks-Gunn, J. (2013). "Feeling disorder" as a comparative and contingent process: Gender, neighborhood conditions, and adolescent mental health. *Journal of Health and Social Behavior, 54*, 296–314.

Burk, W. J., Steglich, C. E. G., & Snijders, T. A. B. (2007). Beyond dyadic interdependence: Actor-oriented models for co-evolving social networks and individual behaviors. *International Journal of Behavioral Development, 31*, 397–404.

Campbell, A. (1980). *Female delinquency in social context.* Oxford, UK: Blackwell.

Caspi, A., Lynam, D., Moffitt, T. E., & Silva, P. A. (1993). Unraveling girls' delinquency. *Developmental Psychology, 29*, 19–30.

Clampet-Lundquist, S., Edin, K., Kling, J. R., & Duncan, G. J. (2011). Moving teenagers out of high-risk neighborhoods: How girls fare better than boys. *American Journal of Sociology, 116*, 1154–1189.

Cohen, A. K. (1955). *Delinquent boys: The culture of the gang.* New York, NY: The Free Press.

Connell, R. W. (1987). *Gender and power.* Stanford, CA: Stanford University Press.

Covington, J. (1985). Gender differences in criminality among heroin users. *Journal of Research in Crime and Delinquency, 22*, 329–353.

Curry, G. D., & Decker, S. H. (2003). *Confronting gangs* (2nd ed.). Los Angeles, CA: Roxbury.

Daly, K. (1989). Gender and varieties of white-collar crime. *Criminology, 27*, 76–794.

Duncan, G. J., Boisjoly, J., Kremer, M., Levy, D. M., & Eccles, J. (2005). Peer effects in drug use and sex among college students. *Journal of Abnormal Child Psychology, 33*, 375–385.

Durkheim, E. (1951). *Suicide: A study in sociology.* New York, NY: The Free Press.

Erickson, K. G., Crosnoe, R., & Dornbusch, S. M. (2000). A social process model of adolescent deviance: Combining social control and differential association perspectives. *Journal of Youth and Adolescence, 29*, 395–425.

Esbensen, F. A., Peterson, D., Taylor, T. J., &Freng, A. (2010). *Youth violence: Sex and race differences in offending, victimization, and gang membership.* Philadelphia, PA: Temple University Press.

Gaarder, E., & Belknap, J. (2002). Tenuous borders: Girls transferred to adult court. *Criminology, 40*, 481–517.

Giordano, P. C. (1978). Girls, guys and gangs: The changing social context of female delinquency. *Journal of Criminal Law and Criminology, 69*, 126–132.

Giordano, P. C., Cernkovich, S. A., & Pugh, M. D. (1986). Friendships and delinquency. *American Journal of Sociology, 91*, 1170–1202.

Gottfredson, M. R., & Hirschi, T. (1990). *A general theory of crime.* Stanford, CA: Stanford University Press.

Harding, D. J. (2009). Violence, older peers, and the socialization of adolescent boys in disadvantaged neighborhoods. *American Sociological Review, 74*, 445–464.

Hartjen, C. A., & Priyadarsini, S. (1984). *Delinquency in India: A comparative analysis.* New Brunswick, NJ: Rutgers University Press.

Haynie, D. L. (2001). Delinquent peers revisited: Does network structure matter? *American Journal of Sociology, 106*, 1013–1057.

Haynie, D. L. (2002). Friendship networks and delinquency: The relative nature of peer delinquency. *Journal of Quantitative Criminology, 18*, 99–134.

Haynie, D. L. (2003). Contexts of risk? Explaining the link between girls' pubertal development and their delinquency involvement. *Social Forces, 82*, 355–397.

Haynie, D. L., & Osgood, D. W. (2005). Reconsidering peers and delinquency: How do peers matter? *Social Forces, 84*, 1109–1130.

Haynie, D. L., Steffensmeier, D., & Bell, K. E. (2007). Gender and serious violence untangling the role of friendship sex composition and peer violence. *Youth Violence and Juvenile Justice, 5*, 235–253.

Hirschi, T. (1969). *Causes of delinquency.* Berkeley: University of California Press.

Hubbard, D. J., & Pratt, T. C. (2002). A meta-analysis of the predictors of delinquency among girls. *Journal of Offender Rehabilitation, 34*, 1–13.

Inciardi, J. A., Lockwood, D., & Pottieger, A. E. (1993). *Women and crack-cocaine.* New York, NY: Macmillan.

Jacobs, B. A., & Miller, J. (1998). Crack dealing, gender, and arrest avoidance. *Social Problems, 45*, 550–569.

Jones, N. (2008). Working "the code": On girls, gender, and inner-city violence. *Australian and New Zealand Journal of Criminology, 41*, 63–83.

Kandel, D., & Davies, M. (1991). Friendship networks, intimacy, and illicit drug use in young adulthood: A comparison of two competing Theories. *Criminology, 29*, 441–469.

Klerks, P. (2001). The network paradigm applied to criminal organizations. *Connections, 24*, 53–65.

Knecht, A. (2008). *Friendship selection and friends' influence. Dynamics of networks and actor attributes in early adolescence.* Unpublished Ph.D. Dissertation, University of Utrecht, Utrecht, The Netherlands.

Konopka, G. (1966). *The adolescent girl in conflict.* Englewood Cliffs, NJ: Prentice Hall.

Kornhauser, R. R. (1978). *Social sources of delinquency: An appraisal of analytic models.* Chicago, IL: University of Chicago Press.

Kreager, D. A. (2007). When it's good to be "bad": Violence and adolescent peer acceptance. *Criminology, 45*, 893–923.

Kreager, D. A., Rulison, K., & Moody, J. (2011). Delinquency and the structure of adolescent peer groups. *Criminology, 49*, 95–127.

Kruttschnitt, C. (2013). Gender and crime. *Annual Review of Sociology, 39*, 291–308.

Laird, R. D., Pettit, G. S., Dodge, K. A., & Bates, J. E. (2005). Peer relationship antecedents of delinquent behavior in late adolescence. *Development and Psychopathology, 17*, 127–144.

Lauritsen, J. L., Heimer, K., & Lynch, J. P. (2009). Trends in the gender gap in violent offending: New evidence from the national crime victimization survey. *Criminology, 47*, 361–399.

Maccoby, E. E. (1988). Gender as a social category. *Developmental Psychology, 24*, 755–765.

Maimon, D., & Browning, C. R. (2010). Unstructured socializing, collective efficacy, and violent behavior among urban youth. *Criminology, 48*, 443–474.

Mangino, W. (2009). The downside of social closure. *Sociology of Education, 82*, 147–172.

McCarthy, B., Felmlee, D., & Hagan, J. (2004). Girl friends are better: Gender, friends, and crime among school and street youth. *Criminology, 42*, 805–836.

McGloin, J. M. (2005). Policy and intervention considerations of a network analysis of street gangs. *Criminology and Public Policy, 4*, 607–635.

McGloin, J. M., & DiPietro, S. (2013). Girls, friends, and delinquency. In F. T. Cullen & P. Wilcox (Eds.), *The Oxford handbook of criminological theory* (pp. 294–312). New York, NY: Oxford University Press.

McGloin, J. M., & Shermer, L. O. (2009). Self-control and deviant peer network structure. *Journal of Research in Crime and Delinquency, 46*, 35–72.

McPherson, M., Smith-Lovin, L., & Cook, J. M. (2001). Birds of a feather: Homophily in social networks. *Annual Review of Sociology, 27*, 415–444.

Mears, D. P., Ploeger, M., & Warr, M. (1998). Explaining the gender gap in delinquency. *Journal of Research in Crime and Delinquency, 35*, 251–266.

Mennis, J., & Mason, M. J. (2011). People, places, and adolescent substance use. *Annals of the Association of American Geographers, 101*, 272–291.

Miller, J. (2001). *One of the guys: Girls, gangs, and gender.* New York, NY: Oxford University Press.

Miller, J. (2002). The strengths and limits of "doing gender" for understanding street crime. *Theoretical Criminology, 6*, 433–460.

Miller, J. (2008). *Getting played: African American girls, urban inequality, and gendered violence.* New York: New York University Press.

Miller, J., & Brunson, R. K. (2000). Gender dynamics in youth gangs: A comparison of males' and females' accounts. *Justice Quarterly, 17*, 419–448.

Miller, J., & Decker, S. H. (2001). Young women and gang violence: Gender, street offending, and violent victimization in gangs. *Justice Quarterly, 18*, 115–140.

Morash, M. (1986). Gender, peer group experiences, and seriousness of delinquency. *Journal of Research in Crime and Delinquency, 23*, 43–67.

Mullins, C. W., & Wright, R. (2003). Gender, social networks, and residential burglary. *Criminology, 41*, 813–840.

Natarajan, M. (2006). Understanding the structure of a large heroin distribution network: A quantitative analysis of qualitative data. *Journal of Quantitative Criminology, 22*, 171–192.

Osgood, D. W., Wilson, J. K., O'Malley, P. M., Bachman, J. G., & Johnston, L. D. (1996). Routine activities and individual deviant behavior. *American Sociological Review, 61*, 635–655.

Papachristos, A. V. (2009). Murder by structure. *American Journal of Sociology, 115*, 74–128.

Papachristos, A. V. (2011). The coming of a networked criminology? In J. MacDonald (Ed.), *Measuring crime and criminality* (Vol. 17, pp. 101–140). New Brunswick, NJ: Transaction.

Pedahzur, A., & Perliger, A. (2006). The changing nature of suicide attacks: A social network perspective. *Social Forces, 84*, 1987–2008.

Pescosolido, B. A. (1992). Beyond rational choice: The social dynamics of how people seek help. *American Journal of Sociology, 97*, 1096–1138.

Peterson, D., Miller, J., & Esbensen, F. A. (2001). The impact of sex composition on gangs and gang member delinquency. *Criminology, 39*, 411–440.

Piehler, T. F., & Dishion, T. J. (2007). Interpersonal dynamics within adolescent friendships. *Child Development, 78*, 1611–1624.

Piquero, N. L., Gover, A. R., MacDonald, J. M., & Piquero, A. R. (2005). The influence of delinquent peers on delinquency: Does gender matter? *Youth and Society, 36*, 251–275.

Rebellon, C. J., & Manasse, M. (2004). Do "bad boys" really get the girls? Delinquency as a cause and consequence of dating behavior among adolescents. *Justice Quarterly, 21*, 355–389.

Rose, A. J., & Rudolph, K. D. (2006). A review of sex differences in peer relationship processes. *Psychological Bulletin, 132*, 98–131.

Sampson, R. J., & Groves, W. B. (1989). Community structure and crime: Testing social-disorganization theory. *American Journal of Sociology, 94*, 774–802.

Schreck, C. J., McGloin, J. M., & Kirk, D. S. (2009). On the origins of the violent neighborhood: A studying the nature and predictors of crime-type differentiation across Chicago neighborhoods. *Justice Quarterly, 26*, 771–794.

Shover, N. (1996). *Great pretenders: Pursuits and careers of persistent thieves.* Boulder, CO: Westview Press.

Smith, D. A., & Paternoster, R. (1987). The gender gap in theories of deviance: Issues and evidence. *Journal of Research in Crime and Delinquency, 24*, 140–172.

Snijders, T. A. B., & Baerveldt, C. (2003). A multilevel network study of the effects of delinquent behavior on friendship evolution. *Journal of Mathematical Sociology, 27*, 123–151.

Snijders, T. A. B., van de Bunt, G. G., & Steglich, C. E. G. (2010). Introduction to stochastic actor–based models for network dynamics. *Social Networks, 32*, 44–60.

Soller, B. (2014). Caught in a bad romance: Adolescent romantic relationships and mental health. *Journal of Health and Social Behavior, 55*, 56–72.

Steffensmeier, D., & Allan, E. (1996). Gender and crime: Toward a gendered theory of female offending. *Annual Review of Sociology, 22*, 459–487.

Steffensmeier, D. J. (1983). Organization properties and sex-segregation in the underworld. *Social Forces, 61*, 1010–1032.

Steffensmeier, D. J., Schwartz, J., & Roche, M. (2013). Gender and twenty-first-century corporate crime: Female involvement and the gender gap in Enron-era corporate frauds. *American Sociological Review, 78*, 448–476.

Steffensmeier, D. J., & Ulmer, J. T. (2005). *Confessions of a dying thief: Understanding criminal careers and illegal enterprise.* New York, NY: Aldine Transaction.

Sutherland, E. H. (1947). *Principles of criminology* (4th ed.). Philadelphia, PA: Lippincott.

Thrasher, F. M. (1927). *The gang: A study of 1,313 gangs in Chicago.* Chicago, IL: University of Chicago Press.

Waldrop, M. F., & Halverson, C. F., Jr. (1975). Intensive and extensive peer behavior: Longitudinal and cross-sectional analyses. *Child Development, 46*, 19–26.

Warr, M. (1996). Organization and instigation in delinquent groups. *Criminology, 34*, 11–37.

Warr, M. (2002). *Companions in crime.* New York, NY: Cambridge University Press.

Wasserman, S., & Faust, K. (1994). *Social network analysis: Methods and applications*. New York, NY: Cambridge University Press.

Weerman, F. M. (2011). Delinquent peers in context: A longitudinal network analysis of selection and influence effects. *Criminology, 49,* 253–286.

Weerman, F. M., & Hoeve, M. (2012). Peers and delinquency among girls and boys. *European Journal of Criminology, 9,* 228–244.

Wilson, W. J. (1996). *When work disappears*. New York, NY: Random House.

Wong, T. M. L., Slotboom, A. M., & Bijleveld, C. (2010). Risk factors for delinquency in adolescent and young adult females: A European review. *European Journal of Criminology, 7,* 266–284.

Zietz, D. (1981). *Women who embezzle or defraud*. New York, NY: Praeger.

Zimmerman, G. M., & Messner, S. F. (2010). Neighborhood context and the gender gap in adolescent violent crime. *American Sociological Review, 75,* 958–980.

CHAPTER 9

Women, Work,
and White-Collar Crime

Mary Dodge

Revisiting Freda Adler's (1975) *Sisters in Crime* offers us an opportunity to explore the evolution of gender and white-collar crime. Forty years later some things have changed, and some have stayed the same. Adler's work represents a milestone in the history of gender studies and criminology, and her pioneering efforts established a framework for understanding current and future research related to women and crime. Adler's voice and rich narrative continue to influence scholarship that explores the role of gender in criminal behavior. Her words resonate in our historical and present understanding of female criminality and white-collar crime:

> The variety of opportunities that have opened for women in the last decade have multiplied their access to a whole new range of illicit behaviors. It is not that women have replaced one deviant behavior with another; they have merely added new ones to their repertoire. This is particularly true in the area of acquisitive offenses whereby a whole spectrum of white-collar crimes have supplemented shoplifting, the traditional female property offense. (Adler, 1975, p. 164)

Women and white-collar crime is an area of study that has received scant attention in the literature. Prior to 1975, scholars focused on the misconduct of men in corporate and professional occupations because by definition they, almost exclusively, were in positions to commit white-collar crimes. As noted above, Adler (1975) was one of the first scholars to establish a connection between women and white-collar crime. Only in the past 5 to 10 years has a more substantial body of research emerged on women and upper-level crime. Admittedly, females rarely were mentioned in the white-collar crime literature because the offenses they committed failed to rise to the level of Edwin Sutherland's (1945) definition of white-collar crime.

Vande Walle (2002) argued the term itself is entrenched in masculine stereotypes that excluded women from even committing white-collar crime because "their blouses may not be white" (p. 283). The conceptualization of the male white-collar criminal is changing as an increasing number of women move into positions that offer opportunities to engage in corporate and occupational fraud.

This chapter begins by offering an overview of the development and definitional issues related to white-collar crime. As indicated in the chapter, the controversy over what constitutes white-collar crime delineates many stalling points for further examination of the role of women. The next section provides a general background on the gendered nature of criminal activity and the types of crimes women engage in, including evidence of increased financial fraud. The connections between white-collar crime and opportunity are then explored. This discussion illustrates how the glass ceiling limits female access to high-status positions in the workplace and participation in upper level crime. Finally, the chapter examines the intricate connections between legitimate and illegitimate opportunities for women in male-dominated careers, which remain limited, except in cases of embezzlement. Throughout the chapter, the work of Freda Adler is presented as the foundation for current perspectives of women and white-collar crime.

The Concept of White-Collar Crime

In 1939, Sutherland's famous presidential address to the American Society of Sociology and the American Economic Association in Philadelphia garnered substantial attention by scholars and the media. His lecture, later published in the *American Sociological Review*, noted that white-collar criminality existed in every occupation, although he primarily focused on the misdeeds, transgressions, and graft of large corporations, physicians, and politicians (Sutherland, 1949). One important aspect of Sutherland's work was the distinction between street crime and suite crime, which challenged long-standing and accepted notions of criminality as a lower class problem. Since Sutherland introduced the idea of a new and ignored category of criminal offenses and offenders, definitional debates over what constitutes white-collar crime have yet to be settled. Geis (2007) described the ensuing controversies over the definition of upper level crime as "an unending obsession among white-collar-crime-scholars" (p. 4).

Sutherland's (1985) concept of white-collar crime involved an offender of "respectability and high social status who committed offenses in the course of his occupation" (p. 7). In other words, offenders were successful, white, upper class male professionals. Sutherland's definition is criticized for being ambiguous, arbitrary, and dogmatic (Geis, Meier, & Salinger, 1995; Holtfreter, 2005; Tappan, 1947), although fundamental aspects of his lexicon are included in most current descriptions of offenders and offenses. Many researchers adopt a broad definition, which encompasses all types of financial fraud, bribery, corruption, insider trading, price fixing, and similar offense categories. In contrast, other scholars argue that the inclusion of less profitable financial fraud, such as embezzlement, dilutes the true meaning of white-collar crime (Steffensmeier, Schwartz, & Roche, 2013). Among researchers, there is little agreement about the intricacies, depth, and width of what constitutes white-collar crime. Friedrichs (2010), however, noted three general areas of consensus among scholars on the following aspects of white-collar crime: (1) It occurs in a legitimate occupational context; (2) it is motivated by economic gain or occupational success; and (3) it is rarely characterized by direct, intentional violence (p. 5). Although semantics may seem trivial, concepts of what and who might be labeled as white-collar crime have, in many ways, limited research related to the role of gender.

White-collar crime often is categorized as either occupational (i.e., acts committed by individuals for personal gain) or corporate crime (i.e., acts committed to benefit organizations). Occupational fraudsters use their employment position for personal gain by deliberately misusing resources or assets (Association of Certified Fraud Examiners, 2012). Physicians, for example, may charge for more expensive procedures, attorneys may bill clients for hours spent on unrelated tasks, and accountants may pilfer money from clients. Corporate crime involves a wide variety of transgressions such as false advertising, price fixing, corruption, and unsafe products. Research also has distinguished between high-status offenders and middle-class offenders (see e.g., Holtfreter, 2005; Weisburd, Wheeler, Waring, & Bode, 1991). In other words, not all offenders are in prestigious corporate positions and may still engage in a variety of activities considered white-collar crime (Benson & Moore, 1992; Weisburd et al., 1991). A research study of occupational white-collar crimes discovered that high-status offenders were more likely to be involved in fraudulent statements, whereas middle-class offenders committed asset misappropriation or corruption (Holtfreter, 2005). The status of the offender in the occupational frauds committed by individuals in Holtfreter's study clearly differs, but both groups were engaged in white-collar crime. This difference, arguably, holds true for bank tellers who embezzle money or corporate executive officers who engage in a price-fixing conspiracy.

Much of the controversy over definitions of white-collar crime, more often than not, hinges on whether the focus is on the offender or the offense. Previous research in white-collar crime includes a wide variety of people and organizations committing embezzlement, insider trading, medical fraud, Ponzi schemes, and consumer safety violations (see, e.g., Cressey, 1953; Cullen, Maakestad, & Cavender, 1984; Dodge & Geis, 2003; Jesilow, Pontell, & Geis, 1993; Simpson & Elis, 1996; Szockyj & Geis, 2002; Zietz, 1981). David Friedrichs (2010), a notable and prolific scholar, best summarized the difficulty of definition as an unsolvable puzzle, which will likely remain fluid:

> More generally, white collar crime is a generic term for the whole range of illegal, prohibited, and demonstrably harmful activities involving a violation of a private or public trust, committed by institutions and individuals occupying a legitimate, respectable status and directed toward financial advantage or the maintenance and extension of power and privilege. (p. 8)

The Crimes Women Commit

Some criminologists posit that women are just as likely to engage in white-collar crime for the same reasons as men, despite a notable gender gap in almost all categories of offending. Overall, previous research shows that women commit more gender-specific crimes such as prostitution and shoplifting, although participation in other criminal behaviors has increased incrementally. In 2011, the FBI's UCR revealed that almost 26% of all arrests were female. The National Incident-Based Reporting System data for 2012 (FBI, 2012, *National Incident-Based Reporting System*) shows that total female arrests outnumbered that for males only in prostitution and commercialized vice. In the same year, female arrest totals in three white-collar crime areas remained lower compared to the totals for males: 25,885 women and 35,989 men for forgery and counterfeiting; 57,645 women and 86,948 men for fraud; and 8,784 women and 9,455 men for embezzlement (FBI, 2012, *National Incident-Based Reporting System*). Percentage change increases in arrest for females from 2011 to 2012 included the following: murder and nonnegligent manslaughter (+2.0), robbery (+1.0), embezzlement (+7.3), and gambling (+2.6). Arrest statistics, on one hand, are arguably a poor reflection of criminal behavior and often fail to reflect changes in policies and practices in the criminal justice system (Cullen, Agnew, & Wilcox, 2014). Additionally, UCR fraud data include crimes such as confidence games and bad checks, which rarely rise to the level of white-collar crime. Arrest data, on the other hand, are useful for examining crime trends and patterns, despite known limitations.

Differences between male and female offending show a gender gap, despite increased participation by women. Belknap (2001), who noted the inconsistencies in differences of female offenders over time, identified three trends related to women and crime. First, less serious offenses and drug use may show more "gender convergence." Second, fluctuations in empirical findings may be a result of changes in the economy and law enforcement practices. Third, the intersection of race and age is largely ignored, but they represent important variables in "understanding the true nature of female criminality and criminality in general" (Belknap, 2001, p. 117). The differences in female white-collar offending and intersectionality are even less understood, although the low number of minority women in high-status positions limits any empirical efforts to understand relationships among race, gender, and upper level crime.

The prediction that female involvement in white-collar crime would increase, posited by Adler (1975) and Simon (1975), was met with controversy, although the idea that women, like men, would use their positions to commit crimes for economic gain was far from unrealistic. Adler (1975) argued the following:

> In the future a greater proportion of wealth and power will pass through feminine hands, and almost all of it will be wielded responsibly. But it would be an unrealistic reversion to quixotic chivalry to believe that, for better or worse, women will be any more honest than men. (p. 169)

Similarly, Simon (1975) hypothesized an increase in property, financial, and white-collar offenses as women moved into positions more conducive to offending.

Notably, more contemporary arrest data analyzed by Simon and Ahn-Redding (2005) showed an increase in the number of women in high-status positions that resulted in higher incidents of white-collar crime. According to the researchers, in 2000, almost 37% of the employed women held managerial, professional, and technical positions, and 17% held executive or administrative positions. Their data also showed that in 2001 women accounted for more than one third of all arrests for larceny and nearly half of all embezzlement and fraud arrests. Simon and Ahn-Redding concluded that the data supported the hypothesis that women were committing more white-collar crimes because increased participation in the labor force provided greater opportunity.

Other studies lend further credence to the conclusion that women's participation in white-collar crime has increased. In a 1986 Bureau of Justice Statistics report, Manson reported that females were arrested more often for white-collar offenses (i.e., forgery or counterfeiting, fraud, and embezzlement) than for most other types of crime. Data from 1963 to 1998 showed similar rates for males and females arrested for embezzlement, fraud, forgery, and larceny (Small, 2000). Albanese (1993) also found an increase in the number of women involved in white-collar offenses during the 1970s and 1980s. His research showed that the increase in the number of women who were employed in white-collar jobs coincided with high patterns of arrest for fraud, forgery or counterfeiting, and embezzlement. The National White-Collar Crime Center reported a pronounced increase in the number of females engaging in financial fraud, particularly in the number of women arrested for embezzlement from 1980 to 1998 (Haantz, 2002).

Workplace Opportunities

Criminologists have long recognized the role of opportunity in criminal behavior, including white-collar crime (see, e.g., Benson & Simpson, 2009). In fact, Sutherland (1945) emphasized the importance of opportunity in the commission, not only of street offending, but also of upper level wrongdoing. Adler (1975) acknowledged his contribution: "Edwin Sutherland's foresighted recognition that the kind of crime committed depended more on different opportunities than on stereotyped criminal propensities provided the theoretical framework [for further exploration]" (p. 156).

Benson, Madensen, and Eck (2009) presented a persuasive argument for recognizing the importance of opportunity structures in the commission, prevention, and discovery of white-collar crime. Adler offered similar observations with regard to gender: "The kinds of crimes one commits are related to the illegal opportunities to commit them" (as cited in Dodge, 2009, p. 180). Access to opportunities thus might shape the kinds of offenses engaged in by males and females. In this regard, recent empirical research suggests that the higher incidence of misconduct in scientific research by men may be the result of males having more opportunity to commit fraud based on overrepresentation in sheer numbers and dollar amounts of grant awards (Fang, Bennett, & Casadevall, 2013; Kaatz, Vogelman, & Carnes, 2013).

Adler maintained that as women entered the public sphere with fewer social controls, their participation in crime would increase. In a 2009 interview, she explained: "In my day, women didn't go to bars or drive cars; consequently, it's hard to hijack or have a get-away car if you don't know how to drive" (Dodge, 2009, personal communication). On one hand, when women are excluded from corporate positions, they are unlikely participants in large corporate financial fraud, as exemplified by the male-dominated scandals of Enron, Tyco, or Worldcom. In 1975, when *Sisters in Crime* was published, women represented approximately 46% of the labor force and received only 15% of medical, dentistry, and law degrees (Small, 2000). Important changes have taken place. Currently, women represent almost 50% of the workforce and earn the majority of college degrees (Lennon, 2013). Even so, women still confront a glass ceiling in the workplace as they attempt to move up in the organizational hierarchy.

The glass ceiling, a term said to have been first coined by Gay Bryant, a successful magazine editor in an interview with Nora Frenkiel (1984), represents a metaphorical barrier used to describe the obstacles in achieving advancement in the workplace faced by women and minorities. The glass ceiling, according to Longo and Straehley (2008), is a barrier in organizational cultures that favor men: "These cultures often serve to exclude women from the necessary networking and mentoring that are required for promotion to the top positions" (p. 88). The Federal Glass Ceiling Commission (1995) defined the glass ceiling as an "unseen, yet unbreachable barrier that keeps minorities and women from rising to the upper rungs of the corporate ladder, regardless of the qualifications or achievements" (p. 4). Subsequent research by Cotter, Hermsen, Ovadia, and Vanneman (2001) uncovered a distinct gender bias, which prevents women from obtaining high-level, powerful, and prestigious positions. The barrier for African American women may be even more pronounced and often is described as a concrete ceiling (Catalyst, 1999). The glass-ceiling effect is associated with a variety of differential workplace characteristics based on gender and race, including hierarchical positions, authority, professional relationships, and income (Duleep & Sanders, 1992; Fernandez, 1998; Frankforter, 1996; Wright, Baxter, & Birkelund, 2000).

Arguably, the glass ceiling is far from shattered. Women remain marginalized in the workplace in positions and income, particularly in male-dominated or hyper-masculine jobs. Despite education attainment equal to or exceeding that of male counterparts, women are excluded from high-level positions. A national report revealed less than 20% of the top leadership jobs are held by women (Lennon, 2013). Her 2013 report, "Benchmarking Women's Leadership in the United States," shows the following:

- Women in academic positions are underrepresented at almost 30%.
- Women of color in academia account for 11% of assistant professors and 4% of professors.
- Almost half of all law school graduates were women (48%), but only 15% of equity partners and 5% of managing partners in law firms were women.

- Women represented 51% of professional, managerial, and related positions in business and commercial banking, but only 14% to 15% worked in executive positions and Fortune 500 businesses.
- Ten percent of the chief executive officer positions in the top 10 banking companies were women.
- Thirteen percent of boards of director positions in Fortune 500 companies were women and 3% of those were women of color. (Lennon, 2013, pp. 7–9)

The U.S. Bureau of Labor Statistics (2013), based on a national survey of approximately 60,000 households, also portrayed a bleak picture of women in the workforce. According to the report, in the United States, 22 women hold leadership roles in the government. More specifically, only 9% of mayors in the 100 largest U.S. cities are women. As of January 2013, the United States had only five female governors. In 2013, a total of 20 women served as U.S. senators and 78 were members of the U.S. House of Representatives. In professional positions, 34% of physicians and surgeons were women and 14% were architects and engineers. Of the 112 U.S. Supreme Court justices to serve on the highest court, only 4 have been women (National Women's Law Center, 2013). As shown in Table 9.1, a low percentage of women hold positions viewed as high status and many remain in bookkeeping and accounting careers.

Women, on average, earn less than men in comparable jobs, despite better performance in some cases. The U.S. Bureau of Labor Statistics (2013) shows women remain disadvantaged in terms of pay and promotion, although the sheer numbers of women in the workforce are approaching male levels. Female lawyers, for example, earn 25% less than the average male salary. Women physicians earn substantially less and hold positions in lower prestige specialties compared to male colleagues (Dubeck & Borman, 1996; Lim, 2002). "In 1970, American women were paid 59 cents for every dollar their male counterparts made," noted Sheryl Sandberg (2013, p. 5), chief operating officer at Facebook, and "by 2010 . . . the compensation rose to 77 cents for every dollar men made" (p. 5). Clearly, women continue to be marginalized and subordinated at many levels in the workplace.

TABLE 9.1   Occupational Positions and Gender: 2011 Annual Averages

OCCUPATION	TOTAL EMPLOYED	PERCENTAGE WOMEN
Chief executives	1,515	24.2
Financial managers	1,107	54.2
General and operations managers	978	30.4
Bookkeeping, accounting, and auditing clerks	1,300	89.9
Physicians and surgeons	822	33.8
Lawyers	1,085	31.9

Note: Numbers in the thousands.

Source: Adapted from Bureau of Labor Statistics Report (2013).

Women in the workplace also face performance challenges, often based on gendered stereotypes. According to Sandberg (2013), ambition is expected for men, but often is interpreted as a negative quality in women:

> "She is *very* ambitious" is not a compliment in our culture. Aggressive and hard-charging women violate unwritten rules about acceptable social conduct. Men are continually applauded for being ambitious and powerful and successful, but women who display these same traits often pay a social penalty. Female accomplishments come at a cost. (p. 16, emphasis in original)

Women executives often are criticized for failing to conform to gender stereotypes and more assertive women are labeled as "arrogant, aggressive, or abrasive" (Rhode, 1989, p. 170). Previous research found that women who fail to display typical feminine attributes or engage in perceived masculine behaviors in the workplace often are seen as less competent and devoid of social skills; additionally, they are disliked and derogated (Cejka & Eagly, 1999; Heilman, 2001; Heilman & Okimoto, 2007; Heilman, Wallen, Fuchs, & Tamkins, 2004; Rudman & Glick, 2001). Notably, these workplace barriers have implications for how gender affects participation in white-collar crime.

Opportunity and Offense Type

Position in an organization often determines the types of crimes an employee is able to commit, and women who are unable to advance in the organizational hierarchy are less likely to participate in large-scale corporate fraud (Friedrichs, 2010; Holtfreter, 2005; Steffensmeier et al., 2013). Numerous researchers have noted that female involvement in white-collar crime reflects employment status, which may account for the high number of female embezzlers (Croall, 2001; Daly, 1989; Davies, 2003). Sixty-one percent of accountants and auditors are women (Bureau of Labor Statistics Report, 2013). Lower status occupation opportunities limit the involvement of women in white-collar crime. As Adler (1975) observed, "Housewives might pilfer from the supermarket while doing the grocery shopping, but could not embezzle from a corporation unless they work out of the executive office" (p. 28).

Embezzlement is a prevalent problem in the workplace. Writing in 1975, Adler observed that "embezzlement losses for all organizations costs approximately two hundred million dollars per year" (p. 161). Four decades later, the costs of embezzlement are estimated at billions of dollars annually. Adler also noted that, relative to other offenses, women had access to more opportunities to embezzle. Today, studies and crime data tend to show that male involvement in white-collar crime outnumbers female arrests in almost all arrest categories for embezzlement, fraud, and forgery. However, this is not always the case, and the gender gap in this type of offending appears to be narrowing considerably (Holtfreter, 2005; Steffensmeier, 1993).

Several reports provide data on these issues. For example, the 2012 Marquet report on embezzlement shows that of 522 perpetrators in 528 cases, 219 were male (42%) and 303 were female (58%) (Marquet International, 2012). The 2012 Association of Certified Fraud Examiners global fraud study found almost two thirds of all fraud cases were committed by men. However, the results also showed that the ratio of male to female fraudsters varied by region. In Europe, Asia, Africa, and Latin America, 75% or more of the frauds were committed by men. By contrast, Canada (48%) and the United States (55%) evidenced much lower proportions of male fraudsters (and, by implication, more even gender ratios).

FBI data on arrests in the United States are relevant in showing the convergence of the gender gap. In 2000, females accounted for 50% of all arrests for embezzlement; since that time, the annual proportion of embezzlement arrests for females versus males has remained relatively consistent. Simon and Ahn-Redding (2005) discovered a steady increase in total female arrests beginning in 1964. In 2012, estimated embezzlement arrests in the FBI's UCR for males ($n = 6,307$) and females ($n = 5,928$) were only slightly different (FBI, 2012, *Crime in the United States*, Table 37).

One area where gender appears to continue to exert an effect, however, is in the profitability of the crime. For example, recent reports indicate that on average, males embezzle higher dollar amounts than females (Association of Certified Fraud Examiners, 2012; Marquet International, 2012). The Association of Certified Fraud Examiners report gathered data from certified fraud examiners and included 1,388 cases of occupational fraud involving corruption, asset misappropriation, and financial statement fraud. In their study, the median loss in a fraud committed by a male was $200,000 compared to $91,000 for females. This finding of males incurring higher losses holds true across all levels in a company—that is, regardless of whether the offender is an employee, manager, or owner or executive. Thus, although the rates of embezzlement are becoming more similar for females and males, access to large monetary sums by gender remains disparate. As Adler (1975) reminded us, "When, therefore, we find women being convicted of embezzling large sums it is a certain sign that they have become not only more important criminals but also more important people" (p. 163).

Recent research indicates that women represent a small percentage of the known offenders engaging in corporate crime—perhaps because their access to top executive positions is limited (see Table 9.2). Steffensmeier et al. (2013), for example, developed a database of 83 corporate frauds involving 436 defendants. The analyses revealed that only 9% of the corporate crime schemes involve women. The results suggest that women were rarely part of a conspiracy group and when they were involved in the criminal activities, they held minor roles and made less profit. According to the research findings, female involvement follows two trajectories: relational or utility. The majority of women in the sample either had a close personal involvement with a male co-conspirator or held a financial position necessary for commission of the crime. Obviously, as noted by Steffensmeier and his

TABLE 9.2   Executives in Fortune 10 Companies: 2012

COMPANY	NO. OF EXECUTIVE POSITIONS	NO. OF FEMALES IN EXECUTIVE POSITIONS	PERCENTAGE OF FEMALES IN EXECUTIVE POSITIONS
ExxonMobil	5	0	0
Walmart stores	32	7	22
Chevron	18	3	17
ConocoPhillips	9	3	33
General Motors	17	4	24
General Electric	40	7	18
Berkshire Hathaway	20	4	20
Fannie Mae	15	5	33
Ford Motor	34	2	6
Hewlett-Packard	12	3	25
Total/average	202	38	19.8

Source: Lennon (2013).

colleagues (2013), the findings "do not comport with images of highly placed or powerful white-collar female criminals" (p. 448).

Conclusion

In all likelihood, women will continue to hold a higher proportion of powerful corporate, professional, and political positions in the future. Inequality in the workplace and occupational status, as well as the role of females in legal and illegal white-collar crime, remains perplexing. Adler (1975) wrote, "Western history is replete with examples of women who have risen above their cultural stereotype to become leaders of vigor and acclaim. These women have, in fact, displayed a remarkable talent for ruthless and highly aggressive leadership" (p. 45). Case studies of powerful women executives and politicians demonstrate that when females are given the opportunity, behaviors consistent with those of male white-collar crime are possible (Dodge, 2009). Research shows that women commit and justify crimes for different reasons than men; however, the reality is equivocal and may have little relationship to what it means to be male or female. Often, women commit crimes for the same reasons as men, material gain (Davies, 2003). "First, while cupidity may be universal," according to insight provided by Adler (1975, p. 27), "ability and opportunity are less evenly distributed." In other words, criminal activity is a human undertaking shaped by societal structures and processes. Vande Walle (2002) emphasized that gender, race, and class are socially produced categories structured by gendered practices that define power positions and subordination. Similarly,

Adler (1975) stressed, "The entrance of women into the major leagues of crime underscores the point that the incidence and kinds of crime are more closely associated with social than sexual factors" (p. 27).

In the same vein as early feminist scholars, examinations of the changing role of women in the private, public, and criminal spheres indicates an increased pressure to perform in hypermasculine workplaces, which value winning, profiting, and obtaining financial status. Indeed, Martha Stewart is not the poster child for women and white-collar crime and, in fact, was tried and convicted of perjury, not insider trading. Case studies, although anecdotal, demonstrate the potential for narrowing the gender gap (Dodge, 2009):

- The general counsel for Hewlett-Packard, Ann Baskins, resigned after allegations of pretexting (i.e., gaining access to private phone records) and insider trading emerged.
- Harriette Walters and Diane Gustus masterminded a $20 million fraud against the government.
- Betty Loren-Maltese was accused of racketeering and fraud in connection to an insurance scheme that resulted in losses of $12 million.
- Linda Schrenko faced over 40 counts of conspiracy and money laundering in her campaign to become the governor of Georgia.
- Sara Bost, the former mayor of Irvington, New Jersey, was indicted on five felony counts, including taking bribes and witness tampering.
- Enron employee Lea Fastow was indicted on conspiracy to commit wire fraud, money laundering, aiding and abetting, and tax fraud. She and her husband, Andrew Fastow, allegedly laundered money from off-the-book partnerships and secret deals by giving phony gifts to family members.
- Robin Szeliga, former chief financial officer at Qwest, pled guilty to one count of insider trading for her part in a multibillion-dollar accounting scandal.

In the future, the white-collar crimes by women will likely equal those of men in terms of monetary losses and offense types. The number of women involved in white-collar crime will only reach true equity when the glass ceiling no longer blocks occupational opportunity—women have not yet reached the top. Adler's discerning insight into women and white-collar crime is the framework for continued exploration: "It's not about being male or female, it's about money" (personal communication, March 2007). Although written 40 years ago, Adler's (1975) words might well have been published today:

> As women invade the business world, there is no reason to expect them to be any more honest than men, and to the extent that crime is related to motivation and opportunity, the incidence of such white-collar offenses as embezzlement and fraud should achieve par with men. It is not only in men's private clubs and taverns that males are being forced to make way for females. (p. 252)

References

Adler, F. (1975). *Sisters in crime: The rise of the new female criminal.* New York, NY: McGraw–Hill.

Albanese, J. (1993). Women and the newest profession: Females as white-collar criminals. In C. C. Culliver (Ed.), *Female criminality: The state of the art* (pp. 119–131). New York, NY: Garland.

Association of Certified Fraud Examiners. (2012). *Report to the nations on occupational fraud and abuse: 2012 global fraud study.* Austin, TX: Author.

Belknap, J. (2001). *The invisible woman: Gender, crime, and justice* (2nd ed.). Belmont, CA: Wadsworth.

Benson, M. L., Madensen, T. D., & Eck, J. E. (2009). White-collar crime from an opportunity perspective. In S. S. Simpson & D. Weisburd (Eds.), *The criminology of white-collar crime* (pp. 175–193). New York, NY: Springer.

Benson, M. L., & Moore, E. (1992). Are white-collar and common offenders the same? An empirical and theoretical critique of a recently proposed general theory of crime. *Journal of Research in Crime and Delinquency, 29,* 251–272.

Benson, M. L., & Simpson, S. S. (2009). *White-collar crime: An opportunity perspective.* New York, NY: Routledge.

Bureau of Labor Statistics Report. (February 2013). *Women in the labor force: A databook.* U.S. Bureau of Labor Statistics Report 1040. Retrieved from http://www.bls.gov/cps/wlf-databook-2012.pdf

Catalyst, Inc. (1999). *Women of color in corporate management: Opportunities and barriers.* Retrieved from http://www.catalyst.org/knowledge/women-color-corporate-management-opportunities-and-barriers/

Cejka, M. A., & Eagly, A. H. (1999). Gender-stereotypic images of occupations correspond to the sex segregation of employment. *Personality and Social Psychology Bulletin, 25,* 413–423.

Cotter, D. A., Hermsen, J. M., Ovadia, S., & Vanneman, R. (2001). The glass ceiling effect. *Social Forces, 80,* 655–681.

Cressey, D. (1953). *Other people's money: A study of the social psychology of embezzlement.* New York, NY: The Free Press.

Croall, H. (2001). *Understanding white collar crime.* Buckingham, UK: Open University Press.

Cullen, F. T., Agnew, R., & Wilcox, P. (Eds.). (2014). *Criminological theory: Past to present* (5th ed.). New York, NY: Oxford University Press.

Cullen, F. T., Maakestad, W. J., & Cavender, G. (1984). The Ford Pinto case and beyond: Moral boundaries and the criminal sanction. In G. Geis, R. F. Meier, & L. M. Salinger (Eds.), *White-collar crime: Classic and contemporary views* (pp. 280–298). New York, NY: The Free Press.

Daly, K. (1989). Gender and varieties of white-collar crime. *Criminology, 27,* 769–793.

Davies, P. A. (2003). Is economic crime a man's game? *Feminist Theory, 4,* 283–303.

Dodge, M. (2009). *Women and white-collar crime.* Upper Saddle River, NJ: Prentice Hall.

Dodge, M., & Geis, G. (2003). *Stealing dreams: A fertility clinic scandal.* Boston, MA: Northeastern University Press.

Dubeck, P., & Borman, K. (1996). *Women and work.* New York, NY: Garland.

Duleep, H. O., & Sanders, S. (1992). Women above the glass ceiling: Perceptions on corporate mobility and strategies for success. *Gender and Society, 12,* 339–355.

Fang, F. C., Bennett, J. W., & Casadevall, A. (2013). Males are overrepresented among life science researchers committing scientific misconduct. *mBio, 4*, 1–3.

Federal Bureau of Investigation. (2011). *Crime in the United States: Uniform Crime Reports.* Retrieved from http://www.fbi.gov/about-us/cjis/ucr/crime-in-the-u.s/2011/crime-in-the-u.s.-2011/

Federal Bureau of Investigation. (2012). *Crime in the United States: Uniform Crime Reports.* Retrieved from http://www.fbi.gov/about-us/cjis/ucr/crime-in-the-u.s/2012/crime-in-the-u.s.-2012/

Federal Bureau of Investigation. (2012). *National Incident-Based Reporting System.* Retrieved from http://www.fbi.gov/about-us/cjis/ucr/nibrs/2012/table-pdfs/offenders-sex-by-offense-category-2012/

Federal Glass Ceiling Commission. (1995). *Solid investments: Making full use of the nations' human capital.* Washington, DC: U.S. Department of Labor. Retrieved from http://www.dol.gov/oasam/programs/history/reich/reports/ceiling2.pdf/

Fernandez, M. (1998). Asian Indian Americans in the Bay Area and the glass ceiling. *Sociological Perspectives, 41*, 119–149.

Frankforter, S. A. (1996). The progression of women beyond the glass ceiling. *Journal of Social Behavior and Personality, 11*, 121–132.

Frenkiel, N. (March 1984). The up-and-comers: Bryant takes aim at the settlers-in. *Adweek* (*Magazine World*) special report.

Friedrichs, D. O. (2010). *Trusted criminals: White collar crime in contemporary society.* Belmont, CA: Wadsworth Cengage Learning.

Geis, G. (2007). *White-collar and corporate crime.* Upper Saddle River, NJ: Pearson Prentice Hall.

Geis, G., Meier, R. F., & Salinger, L. M. (1995). *White-collar crime: Classic and contemporary views* (3rd ed.). New York, NY: The Free Press.

Haantz, S. (2002). *Women and white collar crime.* National White Collar Crime Center. Retrieved from www.jpsimsconsulting.com/site_media/cms_page_media/44/Women%20and%20White-Collar-Crime.pdf

Heilman, M. E. (2001). Description and prescription: How gender stereotypes prevent women's ascent up the organizational ladder. *Journal of Social Issues, 57*, 657–674.

Heilman, M. E., & Okimoto, T. G. (2007). Why are women penalized for success at male tasks? The implied communality deficit. *Journal of Applied Psychology, 92*, 81–92.

Heilman, M. E., Wallen, A. S., Fuchs, D., & Tamkins, M. M. (2004). Penalties for success: Reactions to women who succeed at male tasks. *Journal of Applied Psychology, 89*, 416–427.

Holtfreter, K. (2005). Is occupation fraud "typical" white-collar crime? A comparison of individual and organizational characteristics. *Journal of Criminal Justice, 33*, 353–365.

Jesilow, P., Pontell, H. N., & Geis, G. (1993). *Prescription for profit: How doctors defraud Medicaid.* Berkeley: University of California Press.

Kaatz, A., Vogelman, P. N., & Carnes, M. (2013). Are men more likely than women to commit scientific misconduct? Maybe, maybe not. *mBio, 4*(2), e00156–13. doi:10.1128/mBio.00156-13.

Lennon, T. (2013). *Benchmarking women's leadership in the United States.* Denver: University of Denver, Colorado Women's College. Retrieved from http://womenscollege.du.edu/bwl/report.pdf/

Lim, H. A. (2002). Women doctors and crime: A review of California physician sanctioning data 1990–1994. *Justice Professional, 15*, 149–167.

Longo, P., & Straehley, C. J. (2008). Whack! I've hit the glass ceiling! Women's efforts to gain status in surgery. *Gender Medicine, 5*, 88–96.

Manson, D. A. (1986). *Tracking offenders: White-collar crime*. Bureau of Justice Statistics Special Report, NCJ-102867. Washington, DC: U.S. Department of Justice.

Marquet International. (2012). *Marquet report on embezzlement*. Retrieved from http://www .marquetinternational.com/

National Women's Law Center. (2013). *Women in the federal judiciary: Still a long way to go*. Retrieved from http://www.nwlc.org/print/resource/women-federal-judiciary-still-long-way-go-1/

Rhode, D. L. (1989). *Justice and gender: Sex discrimination and the law*. Cambridge, MA: Harvard University Press.

Rudman, L. A., & Glick, P. (2001). Prescriptive gender stereotypes and backlash toward agentic women. *Journal of Social Issues, 57*, 743–762.

Sandberg, S. (2013). *Lean in: Women, work, and the will to lead*. New York, NY: Random House.

Simon, R. J. (1975). *Women and crime*. Lexington, MA: Lexington Books.

Simon, R. J., & Ahn-Redding, H. (2005). *The crimes women commit, the punishments they receive* (3rd ed.). Lanham, MD: Lexington Books.

Simpson, S. S., & Elis, L. (1996). Theoretical perspectives on the corporate victimization of women. In E. Szockyj & J. G. Fox (Eds.), *Corporate victimization of women* (pp. 33–58). Boston, MA: Northeastern University Press.

Small, K. (2000). Female crime in the United States, 1963–1998: An update. *Gender Issues, 75*(3), 75–90.

Steffensmeier, D. J. (1993). National trends in female arrests, 1960–1990: Assessment and recommendations for research. *Journal of Quantitative Criminology, 9*, 411–441.

Steffensmeier, D. J., Schwartz, J., & Roche, M. (2013). Gender and twenty-first-century corporate crime: Female involvement and the gender gap in Enron-era corporate frauds. *American Sociological Review, 78*, 448–476.

Sutherland, E. H. (1945). White-collar criminality. *American Sociological Review, 5*, 1–12.

Sutherland, E. H. (1949). *White collar crime*. New York, NY: Holt, Rinehart, and Winston.

Sutherland, E. H. (1985). *White collar crime: The uncut version*. New Haven, CT: Yale University Press.

Szockyj, E., & Geis, G. (2002). Insider trading: Patterns and analysis. *Journal of Criminal Justice, 30*, 273–286.

Tappan, P. W. (1947). Who is the criminal? *American Sociological Review, 12*, 96–102.

U.S. Bureau of Labor Statistics. (2013, October). Retrieved from http://www.bls.gov/cps/wlf-databook-2012.pdf

Vande Walle, G. (2002). "The collar makes the difference": Masculine criminology and its refusal to recognize markets as criminogenic. *Crime, Law and Social Change, 37*, 277–291.

Weisburd, D., Wheeler, S., Waring, E., & Bode, N. (1991). *Crimes of the middle classes: White-collar offenders in the federal courts*. New Haven, CT: Yale University Press.

Wright, E. O., Baxter, J., & Birkelund, G. E. (2000). The glass ceiling hypothesis: A reply to critics. *Gender and Society, 14*, 814–821.

Zietz, D. (1981). *Women who embezzle or defraud: A study of convicted felons*. New York, NY: Praeger.

PART IV

Social Context
of Female Victimization

CHAPTER 10

Gendered Opportunity
and Victimization

Pamela Wilcox, Bonnie S. Fisher, and Nicole V. Lasky

Freda Adler's book *Sisters in Crime: The Rise of the New Female Criminal*, published in 1975, paved the way for a new era in American criminology. Prior to Adler's landmark work, criminologists tended either to ignore female criminality altogether or to view its etiology as completely distinct from that of males. In particular, biological determinism was a popular approach to understanding female criminality, if it was considered at all (Hartman & Sundt, 2011). Adler (1975) challenged these precedents with her "liberation hypothesis." In brief, she hypothesized that women's liberation not only enhanced legitimate opportunities (i.e., in the form of education and employment), but also provided greater access to *illegitimate* opportunity structures (i.e., crime). More specifically, she extended the view that liberation provided women with increasing access to traditionally male-dominated criminal opportunities that could serve as alternative means for achieving goals. She stated:

> Women are no longer indentured to the kitchen, baby carriages, or bedrooms of America. . . . In the same way that women are demanding equal opportunity in fields of legitimate endeavor, a similar number of determined women are forcing their way into the world of major crimes. (Adler, 1975, pp. 12–13)

Adler boldly embraced a unisex theory of crime, but one with an explicit focus on implications for female offending: Women's *and* men's involvement in crime resulted from access to illegitimate opportunity structures, women were gaining greater such access, and thus the nature of women's crime should increasingly become similar to that of men's crime with continued liberation (see also Adler, 1977).

These ideas about opportunity and female's criminality brought Adler fame, but also harsh criticism. At the time of publication, Adler's liberation hypothesis found itself at the nexus of a cultural revolution. It asserted the importance of taking women and gender seriously while simultaneously raising questions and doubts about the social implications of changing gender roles. It was a threat and an opportunity to both traditionalists and feminists. (Hartman & Sundt, 2011, p. 216)

Over time, in fact, empirical evidence has mounted in opposition to the liberation hypothesis (e.g., Schwartz, Steffensmeier, & Feldmeyer, 2009; Steffensmeier, 1978, 1980; Steffensmeier & Allan, 1988, 1996; Steffensmeier, Schwartz, Zhong, & Ackerman, 2005). However, that fact does not blunt the enduring impact of *Sisters in Crime* on criminology. As stated by Hartman and Sundt (2011), "The importance of Adler's work is not only, or even primarily, that it advanced a new hypothesis about crime, but that it brought gender and women to the forefront of our thinking" (p. 206).

We agree with Hartman and Sundt that the greatest legacy of *Sisters in Crime* is its attention to gender. However, the liberation hypothesis and its relative lack of support aside, we also see primary value in Adler's focus on gender vis-à-vis the theoretical concept of *opportunity*. More specifically, we believe her discussion of women's access to illegitimate opportunities for criminal offending reintroduced a theoretical mechanism that had largely been absent since the work of Cloward and Ohlin (1960). As such, Adler's work set the stage nicely for future theorizing about the intersection of gender, crime opportunity, and *criminal victimization*. In fact, within a few short years of the publication of *Sisters in Crime*, theories were developed that emphasized the idea that opportunity for victimization was created through public (liberated) lifestyles and activities. More specifically, these theories of victimization state that public lifestyles and activities increase the likelihood that individuals, as potential victims, will encounter motivated offenders looking for prey. From such a perspective, historical shifts in the overall lifestyles and activities of Americans were deemed key in understanding trends in victimization over time, with the idea being that liberated lifestyles create more opportunity for victimization (Cohen & Felson, 1979; Cohen, Felson, & Land, 1980). Further, within any one historical time period, lifestyles and activities were considered important in understanding differential risks of victimization across sociodemographic groups, including those defined by gender (Cohen, Kluegel, & Land, 1981; Hindelang, Gottfredson, & Garofalo, 1978). In particular, because women's lifestyles were typically less public than those of men, women were presumed to have fewer opportunities for encountering potential offenders and were thus at lower risk for experiencing victimization. With ideas such as these, opportunity theories of victimization took root, and they remain an important perspective in contemporary criminology.

In this chapter, we elaborate on theory and research addressing "gendered opportunity and victimization." Generally speaking, we use this term to refer to the various ways in which gender is related to opportunity for experiencing victimization—a scholarly line of inquiry that shares important commonalities with the core theme of Adler's work (i.e., her focus on opportunity for offending). In reviewing this line of inquiry, we consider multiple types of victimization (e.g., violent, sexual, property) in various domains (e.g., streets, cyberspace, schools). However, we do not discuss types of victimization that should have little connection to public activity (e.g., intimate partner violence, domestic violence).

Given this caveat, we discuss gendered opportunity and victimization over the course of four distinct sections: (1) a review of research examining gender-specific historical trends in rates of victimization; (2) a review of studies examining *mediating processes*—or the extent to which gender impacts individual victimization risk *indirectly*—through crime opportunity; (3) a review of research examining *moderation processes*—or the extent to which gender *interacts* with opportunity in affecting individual risk of victimization; and (4) a review of qualitative work on how gender shapes routine activities and pathways to victimization. We follow our review of previous work on each of these aspects of "gendered opportunity and victimization" with a discussion of suggested future directions for research in this area before concluding the chapter.

Gender, Opportunity, and Aggregate Trends in Victimization

Today, one of the most widely tested theories of victimization is routine activity theory. Simply put, this theory suggests that individuals' daily routine activities affect opportunities for victimization, with some activities generating more opportunities than others. As a starting point for explaining how routine activities produce opportunities for victimization, routine activity theory states that three elements for a crime event are necessary: (1) *a motivated offender*—someone inclined, willing, and able to commit the crime; (2) *a suitable victim or target*—a person or thing that allows the offender to fulfill criminal objectives; and (3) *absence of capable guardianship*—any persons or things that can discourage or prevent the crime (see, e.g., Cohen & Felson, 1979). Routine activity theory takes the first element—a motivated offender—as a given. In other words, the theory assumes there will always be people sufficiently motivated to commit crime. However, motivated offenders do not always have the opportunity to act on their motivation. Opportunity depends on the presence and accessibility of suitable victims or targets and the absence of capable guardianship.

Routine activity theory further suggests that such opportunity for victimization is affected by the patterns of activity that constitute everyday life (thus, *routine* activities). Public routine activities on the part of potential victims (i.e., those occurring outside the home)—such as going to school, going to work, shopping, dining out—are presumed to provide more opportunity for victimization than home-based activities. More specifically, public activity provides motivated offenders with an accessible supply of suitable, potentially unguarded targets. In short, public activity provides motivated offenders with the opportunity to victimize.

Routine activity theory was originally developed in an attempt to explain historical increases in crime rates in the United States between 1960 and the mid-1970s (see, e.g., Cohen & Felson, 1979; Cohen et al., 1980; M. Felson & Cohen, 1980). The theory's proponents argued that changing routine activities of Americans during this historical period created more opportunity for motivated offenders to come into contact with suitable targets (or victims) that were ineffectively guarded. Scholars highlighted the importance of many activities in which women, especially, were engaged. For example, they documented the growing rates of college enrollment among young women, the increasing movement of women (especially married ones) from the role of homemaker to employment outside the home, and the increasing number of single-person households in the United States. Such changes increased the likelihood that women would spend more time in public space, where they would be more exposed to and victimized by motivated offenders. Furthermore, with women earning greater income, there was generally more money available for the purchase of attractive durable consumer goods and the pursuit of leisure and entertainment among American households, thus further enhancing the supply of suitable targets available to be taken by motivated offenders encountered in public space.

The routine activity perspective had a clear implication for trends in aggregate rates of victimization: As women's routine activities become more public and more similar to those of men, men's and women's victimization rates should converge over time. In short, males and females today share increasingly similar daily routines and environments. Therefore, the large historical gap between their respective victimization risks should be narrowing. Accordingly, trends over time in *victimization* rates should be gendered along the lines of what Adler had proposed with respect to trends in *offending*.

Although there has been research debunking Adler's hypothesis about historical increases in female offending (e.g., Steffensmeier, 1978, 1980; Steffensmeier & Allan, 1988, 1996; but see Lauritsen, Heimer, & Lynch, 2009), generally much less work examines longitudinal trends in victimization rates. However, in recent years, some important research has addressed this issue. For example, Lauritsen and Heimer (2008) analyzed data from the National Crime Victimization Survey (NCVS), known as the National Crime Survey (NCS) in its early years, to "provide the first detailed description of how nonlethal violent victimization among women and men has changed over the past three decades" (p. 126). They compared victimization for women and men according to victimization type (i.e., the offense) and victim–offender relationship for the years 1973 to 2004. Overall, their analysis revealed that the gender gap in *robbery* victimization had remained stable, whereas that of *aggravated and simple assault* had narrowed over time, although there was some variation in that overall pattern depending upon whether stranger or nonstranger victimizations were considered. Lauritsen and Heimer noted that the overall narrowing of the gender gap for assault (stranger assault, specifically) was actually not a result of the fact that female rates of victimization had increased. Instead, it was a result of male rates declining more steeply than female rates over the course of the time series. In sum, this research shows little evidence of women's rates of stranger-initiated robbery and assault victimization rising over the time period in which women's opportunities in the public sphere had increased, and the implication of routine activity theory regarding a narrowing gender gap in victimization is not fully supported.

Gender, Opportunity, and Individual Victimization Risk: Mediation Processes

At the same time that routine activity theory was being developed, Hindelang et al. (1978) put forth their lifestyle-exposure theory of victimization. This theory suggested that the risk of being victimized varied by such demographic characteristics as gender, age, and race because demographic groups differed in the kinds of lifestyles that they lived. Thus, members of high-risk demographic groups (i.e., males, youth, Blacks), relative to low-risk demographic groups (i.e., females, elderly, Whites), spent more time in public (especially at night), more time away from family or household members, and more time in proximity to or associating with criminal offenders. As a result of these lifestyles, they encountered more opportunities to be victimized than those who stayed at home, were around family or household members, and interacted only with prosocial individuals. Eventually, scholars recognized the overlap between routine activity theory and lifestyle-exposure theory and merged them into a "lifestyle–routine activity theory," or L-RAT (e.g., Cohen et al., 1981; Miethe, Stafford, & Long, 1987). The resulting integrative perspective of L-RAT suggests that lifestyles and activities, as well as the opportunities for victimization that they create, vary across the contexts of space and time and across sociodemographic groups.

Thus, beyond implications for explaining trends over time in victimization rates by gender, L-RAT helps us understand why males and females differ in their risk of being victimized. Although the original L-RAT scholars noted that women's exposure to victimization opportunity was increasing since the early 1960s, they also observed that such exposure remained lower than that of men (e.g., Cohen et al., 1981; Hindelang et al., 1978). As such, gender was viewed as an important correlate of an individual's risk of criminal victimization, with females purportedly at *less* risk than men.

The key theoretical mechanism explaining persistent gender differences is lifestyle or routine activity. Gender thus has no direct effect on victimization. Rather, L-RAT theories presume that gender affects victimization risk only *indirectly through lifestyles and routines*. Males are more victimized than females only to the extent that they pursue riskier lifestyles and routines that lead them more often into criminogenic situations and interaction with more dangerous or antisocial associates. Hence, gendered opportunities for victimization are presumed to be created through a *mediating process* whereby gender affects lifestyles and routine activities, which, in turn, affect opportunity for and risk of victimization.

Researchers have assessed the mediation hypothesis through a two-stage estimation process. They first test the direct effect of gender on victimization to establish whether gender has a statistically significant effect on victimization (i.e., to see whether males are more victimized than females). In the second stage, they assess the effects of lifestyles and routines by including these measures, along with gender, in the analysis. If the direct effect of gender on victimization is reduced, this finding suggests that the lifestyle and routine activity measures are accounting for the gender–victimization relationship. Gender thus leads to victimization only because males and females engage in different lifestyles and routine activities. The effect of gender on victimization is therefore said to be indirect, or mediated by these measures. In contrast, if gender continues to have a direct effect, this finding would mean that the effect of gender on victimization is not the result of lifestyles and activities.

Over the past three decades, a handful of researchers have empirically tested the mediation hypothesis to better understand the direct and indirect relationships between gender and victimization among adolescents and the general population. First, several studies of adolescents have investigated whether the effect of gender on victimization is mediated by opportunity provided by lifestyles and routine activities. Jensen and Brownfield's (1986) study of a national survey of high school seniors who participated in Monitoring the Future and a probability sample of students enrolled in Foothills High School in Tucson, Arizona, were among the first to test whether lifestyle and routines mediated the gender–victimization relationship. Jensen and Brownfield tested whether self-reported deviant activities mediated the relationship between gender and two types of victimization, including property (e.g., theft, vandalism) and violent (e.g., robbery, threat, assault). Their findings across these two data sets were consistent: The direct effect of gender on either theft or violent victimization was reduced considerably once deviant behavior was controlled for in the multivariate analyses. Their findings also showed that noncriminal activities did not mediate the relationship between gender and victimization; that is, the relationship between gender and victimization was not attenuated "beyond that obtained when offense behavior is controlled" (Jensen & Brownfield, 1986, p. 97).

Extending Jensen and Brownfield's work, Lauritsen, Sampson, and Laub (1991) used longitudinal data from the first five waves of the National Youth Survey to understand the role of opportunity in victimization. Their findings are supportive of the idea that delinquent lifestyle—a measure combining the youth's reported involvement in predatory activities and the extent of the youth's involvement with delinquent peers—at least partially, if not fully, mediates the gender–victimization relationship. For example, once delinquent lifestyle was taken into account, the effect of gender in predicting assault victimization was reduced but remained significant across all waves. More complete mediation was observed in the estimation of robbery and larceny victimization. In three of the four waves studied, Lauritsen et al. found that the effects of gender on robbery and larceny were reduced to nonsignificance once delinquent lifestyle was controlled. Hence, the effects of gender on such victimization risks appeared to operate through delinquent lifestyle (i.e., the delinquent lifestyle measure completely mediated gender's effects on these types of victimization).

More recently, Henson, Wilcox, Reyns, and Cullen (2010) used a sample of high school students living in rural northern Kentucky to test whether nondelinquent and delinquent lifestyles and activities mediated the relationship between gender and minor and serious types of violent victimization. Their analyses yielded three general insights about the mediation mechanism linking gender and violent victimization. First, for minor violent victimization (e.g., pushing, slapping), gender's effect appeared largely indirect, operating primarily through delinquent lifestyle, as measured by participation in a variety of delinquent activities. Specifically, the negative effect of being female on minor violent victimization declined by almost 75% when the variable of delinquent lifestyle was controlled. Second, the negative effect of being female on serious violent victimization (e.g., threats or assaults with weapons) declined only about 10% when delinquent lifestyle was controlled, and it remained statistically significant. Third, controlling for a variety of nondelinquent routine activities did not reduce the effect of gender on victimization. Henson and his colleagues (2010) thus concluded that "females appear less vulnerable to minor violent victimization because they are less likely to be exposed to and involved in delinquency as part of their routine activities" (p. 321).

Popp and Peguero (2011) studied a sample of 10th-grade students who participated in the Education Longitudinal Study of 2002. They examined the interrelationships among gender, extracurricular routine activities, and school-based violent victimization (e.g., being threatened, being hit, or something taken by force) and property victimization (e.g., something stolen or purposively damaged property). They reported that nondelinquent extracurricular activities did *not* mediate the relationship between gender and either violent or property victimization. That is, once extracurricular activities were taken into account, the protective effect of female gender on either type of victimization remained statistically significant. These findings led Popp and Peguero to conclude that female students had a reduced risk of either violent or property victimization compared to males, even when taking into account their involvement in extracurricular activities.

Beyond studies of adolescents, researchers also have examined the mediation hypothesis using representative samples of the general population. In one of the first examples of such a study, Miethe and his colleagues (1987) employed data from the 1975 NCS to examine the relationship of gender to the risk of both violent (e.g., assault, robbery, and personal larceny) and property (e.g., burglary, household larceny, motor vehicle theft) victimization. They measured routine activities and lifestyles as the frequency of nighttime activity and whether an individual's major daily activity was outside the household. They reported conflicting findings on whether routine activities and lifestyles mediated the relationship between gender and violent victimization. Thus, the direct effect of gender on violent victimization was comparable in magnitude to the direct effect of nighttime activity. By contrast, the mediating effects of routine activities and lifestyles on the gender–property victimization relationship were supported. That is, gender differences in the likelihood of property victimization were eliminated once routine activities and lifestyles were taken into account.

Sampson and Lauritsen (1990) further illustrate how the mediating effects of lifestyles on the gender–victimization relationship may vary in magnitude across victimization type in general population samples. Their study relied on data from the 1982 and 1984 British Crime Surveys to examine each year separately. Their results indicated that deviant lifestyle partially mediated the relationship between gender and stranger violence, but it completely mediated the relationship between gender and acquaintance violence. That is, the direct effect of gender, although attenuated, was still statistically significant in the former types of violence but was attenuated to the point of nonsignificance in the latter type.

A recent study by Bunch, Clay-Warner, and Lei (2012), using a longitudinal data set created from the NCVS, found that males experienced more violent victimizations than females. This difference existed largely because males spent more evenings away from home than did females. Additionally, compared to women, males had a small yet statistically significant increased risk of theft victimization. This difference was also accounted for by their routine activities. Once again, males' greater tendency for going out at night increased their risk of theft victimization. In other words, night activity mediated the effect of gender on both violent and theft victimization.

Considered collectively, the existing research provides evidence that the gender–victimization relationship is often mediated by gender-based differences in lifestyles or routine activities. These lifestyles and routines affect the risk of victimization presumably because they affect the opportunity for victimization—that is, they affect the extent to which suitable, unguarded targets are available to motivated offenders. The research also suggests, however, that certain lifestyles and activities play a larger role in explaining why males tend to be more victimized than females. Specifically, it appears that delinquent behaviors for adolescents and nighttime activities for the general population mediate the gender–victimization relationship. Further investigations of the link between gender and opportunity, including longitudinal research designs and refined measures of lifestyles and routines, are the logical next steps to identifying and clarifying the theoretical processes underlying possible mediating effects of opportunity and advancing rigorous testing of the mediation hypothesis for different types of victimization with different samples of persons.

Gender, Opportunity, and Individual Victimization Risk: Moderation Processes

The mediation hypothesis discussed above has recently found company in an alternative mechanism for understanding the interrelationships among gender, opportunity, and victimization. This alternative mechanism is a *moderation hypothesis* whereby gender interacts with lifestyles and routine activities in affecting victimization. This moderation hypothesis suggests that the effects of lifestyle and routine activities differ across males and females. Thus, some lifestyles or activities might expose men to more victimization, whereas others might expose women to more victimization. In other words, the effects of lifestyles and activities are *moderated* by (or interact with) an individual's gender; they are *gender specific* rather than gender neutral in their impact. When conducting a study, empirical support for the moderation hypothesis can be demonstrated in one of two ways. First, moderation is demonstrated if males and females are analyzed separately in different statistical equations and the effects of particular lifestyles and activities on victimization differ across the gender groups. Second, moderation is demonstrated if the sample as a whole is analyzed and there are statistically significant interaction effects between gender and lifestyles and activities. The main effects of gender and lifestyles and activities would be controlled in the equation, and then interaction terms would be added (e.g., an interaction between gender and night activity). Significant interaction terms would suggest that the effects of lifestyles and activities were contingent upon gender.

A number of studies have examined the moderation hypothesis through one of the aforementioned types of empirical analysis. For example, in one of the earliest studies to focus on how gender moderates opportunity, Mustaine and Tewksbury (1998a) found that different lifestyles and activities were important when comparing the risk of victimization for male and female college students. Overall, the lifestyles and activities measured in this study were less successful at estimating females' risk of victimization than males'. The authors suggest that this may occur because, regardless of their lifestyles and activities, women are, by virtue of their gender, likely to be seen as attractive, opportunistic targets. Somewhat similarly, R. B. Felson and Burchfield (2004) found that drinking specifically enhanced the risk of physical and sexual assault victimization for males more so than for females. The authors presumed that this gendered effect was a result of males being especially provocative when drinking. Such a "provocation effect" was less important for explaining females' physical and sexual assault victimization.

Wilcox, Tillyer, and Fisher (2009) analyzed school-based theft and assault victimization among male and female subsamples of Kentucky youth. In contrast to the findings of Felson and Burchfield (2004), those of Wilcox and colleagues indicated that the effects of risky lifestyles and activities were more pronounced for females than for males. Putting a unique twist on the conclusions of Mustaine and Tewksbury (1998a), Wilcox et al. (2009) suggested that females' risk of being seen as attractive or suitable targets because of their gender actually served to increase the effects of risky lifestyles and activities. In another study using male and female subsamples of these same Kentucky youth, Tillyer, Wilcox, and Gialopsos (2010) conducted a gender-specific follow-up of two types of school-based sexual victimization—sexual harassment and unwanted sexual touching. For both types of sexual victimization, the findings replicated those reported for theft and physical assault by Wilcox et al. (2009): Lifestyle- and activity-related risk factors were significantly stronger predictors of victimization for females than for males. In both studies, a delinquent lifestyle (indicated by a student's criminal involvement) was a much stronger predictor of victimization for females than for males (see also Fineran & Bolen, 2006).

Subsequent studies on a variety of samples and a diverse array of victimization types have provided more of a mixed bag of evidence regarding the extent and nature of gender-specific effects of lifestyles and activities. For example, Popp and Peguero's (2011) analysis—discussed in the previous section on mediation effects— also examined whether gender interacted with extracurricular routine activities in the estimation of violent and property school-based victimization among adolescents, thus creating gender-specific risks of victimization at school. While Popp and Peguero found no evidence that the effect of gender was mediated by extracurricular activities, they did find that gender and activities were related to victimization through processes of moderation. However, the pattern of moderation was not consistent. For instance, Popp and Peguero found that participation in clubs and interscholastic sports provided significantly less risk of violent victimization for females than for males, but participation in intramural sports provided more risk for females than for males.

Similarly, Henson, Reyns, and Fisher (2013) found few differences in the effects of online routine activities on male versus female college students' risks of online interpersonal victimization; only two routines varied in their effects on online interpersonal victimization across males and females. However, these two routines appeared to interact with gender in conflicting ways. Specifically, the number of social network updates was more of a risk factor for females, but adding strangers as friends on social network sites was more of a risk factor for males.

In a longitudinal study of college students, Zaykowski and Gunter (2013) explored the effects of deviant activities (measured as assaultive behavior) on risk of assault victimization at two different time points: the same year in which they measured assault victimization (i.e., a concurrent measure) and one year prior (i.e., a lagged measure). Results indicated that the concurrent measure of deviant activities was positively related to assault victimization for both males and females. In other words, deviant activity during the course of one year was related to assault victimization during the course of that same year, and this effect was observed for both males and females. However, the effect was approximately 50% stronger for females. In contrast, the lagged measure was not related to victimization for either gender. This means that assault victimization during the course of one year was not predicted by deviant activity occurring in the prior year (see also Lauritsen et al., 1991).

Finally, several studies have found that nighttime activity is a stronger predictor of violent victimization for males than for females (R. B. Felson, 1997; R. B. Felson, Savolainen, Berg, & Ellonen, 2013; Miethe et al., 1987; Mustaine & Tewksbury, 1998b). In their study of Finnish adolescents, R. B. Felson et al. (2013) assessed whether the effect of night life (going out at night) on being victimized in a public setting was spurious by computing the effect of night life on victimization in other (nonpublic) settings. They concluded that most of the relationship between night activity and public victimization was spurious for females, but was causal for males.

Overall, then, the research has not yet identified clear patterns regarding the extent to which gender moderates the effects of lifestyles and activities on individual risk of victimization. Still, the existing evidence has shown that the "opportunity for victimization" can be substantially gendered, thus providing support for the moderation hypothesis. In other words, "what makes men and women vulnerable or attractive, or affects their levels of guardianship or exposure to motivated offenders, may differ in important ways" (Lauritsen & Carbone-Lopez, 2011, p. 556).

Gender, Opportunity, and Victimization: Qualitative Research

Qualitative research alone cannot describe longitudinal trends in the relationship among gender, opportunity, and victimization, nor can it evaluate the mediation and moderation processes at work in this relationship to the same degree as the quantitative studies reviewed above. However, qualitative data are useful in their ability to provide additional insight into the complex nexus among gender, opportunity, and victimization. Qualitative studies also are helpful in identifying productive areas for empirical and theoretical advancement in this topic. Extant qualitative research highlights several areas in particular that are important for making sense of the relationship among gender, opportunity, and victimization. These key areas are gendered routine activities and gendered pathways into crime and victimization.

Gendered Routine Activities

Several qualitative studies have examined the ways in which perceptions of women, in conjunction with their lifestyles and activities, can shape women's opportunity for sexual victimization. In their examination of female adolescent experiences with sexual aggression, Livingston, Hequembourg, Testa, and VanZile-Tamsen (2007) interviewed a community sample of 319 women. Findings from their study indicated that adolescent girls gratify the needs of some offenders through their female gender and younger age. As explained by Livingston et al., the target suitability of this population is also related to their being perceived by potential offenders as more vulnerable. Developmental factors such as their smaller size, sexual naiveté, lack of resistance strategies, inexperience with substance use, or reluctance to seek help for fear of social or disciplinary repercussions all play a role in adolescent girls' perceived vulnerability. The authors conclude that the risk of victimization for adolescent girls is increased through the interaction of the developmental factors and perceived vulnerability just described with lifestyle and environmental factors, such as increased socializing and family structure.

In Kavanuagh's (2013) analysis of interviews with 15 female sexual assault survivors from a larger parent study, the participants explained how routine activity factors that affect self-protection and engaging in risk management behaviors were important factors that impacted their experiences with sexual assault. Without excusing the behavior of their attackers, these women identified their own actions and behaviors that increased their risk of sexual victimization in the context of nightlife activities. Such factors included decisions that decreased guardianship (e.g., being preoccupied with text messaging, going to the bathroom alone) and that increased exposure to motivated offenders (e.g., attending events in crowded or poorly lit venues). They also cited the importance of target attractiveness—of simply being female—in such risky situations.

The findings from these studies highlight that, to some extent, gender can dictate an individual's lifestyle and routine activities, thereby impacting the degree of risk for sexual victimization. Gender also makes an individual a more or less attractive target for sexual victimization. In the case of young females, gender is an important factor in their being viewed by potential offenders as naive, powerless, and unlikely to resist victimization. Furthermore, women's actions in public places may increase the risk of victimization by creating opportunity for predation. Such qualitative findings add richness to the quantitative research discussed above, especially that which addresses the mediation hypothesis. In particular, the findings add more detail regarding how gender impacts lifestyles and perceptions of target attractiveness (from the vantage point of offenders), which, in turn, affect victimization risk.

Gendered Pathways

Qualitative work has demonstrated that women's pathways into criminal offending are distinct from those of men because, unlike men, women's pathways are substantially intertwined with their relationships to men, as well as with their victimization by men (e.g., Chesney-Lind, 1989; DeHart, 2008; Simpson, Yahner, & Dugan, 2008). In fact, qualitative work has suggested that gendered pathways to *offending* and gendered pathways to *victimization* are substantially interrelated. As such, gender-focused research into the victim–offender overlap can offer further insight into the nuanced relationship of gender and opportunity for both crime and victimization.

Jody Miller's qualitative research on female gang members is particularly suitable for examining how gender and opportunity for criminal involvement and victimization are intertwined. According to Miller (1998), gang participation exposes youth to opportunities for victimization in a highly gendered manner. Young female gang members can use their gender to decrease their risks of victimization by not participating in gang activities that are considered masculine, such as street fighting or committing crime. A major consequence, however, is that female members are not considered equal to males and may be exposed to greater risks of victimization within their gangs. The connection between delinquency and victimization is further illustrated by Miller's claim that many young women turn to gangs as a means to protect themselves from violence and mistreatment by their families and by other men in their lives. Nonetheless, gang involvement itself exposes these young women to increased victimization risks particular to the gang lifestyle. For example, young women are often physically assaulted during the initiation process or if they later break gang rules. Such qualitative work coincides well with previously discussed findings from quantitative tests of the moderation hypothesis. In particular, Miller's (1998) work provides richness to some of the findings from quantitative studies that delinquency is a significantly stronger predictor of victimization for women and girls as opposed to men and boys (Fineran & Bolen, 2006; Tillyer et al., 2010; Wilcox et al., 2009).

Miller's research also provides further information on the ways in which gender shapes the particular types of victimization female gang members are at risk of experiencing. As explained by Miller and Brunson (2000), girls' and boys' accounts suggest that both groups face a series of gender-specific victimization risks. Although young men are at greater risk for lethal violence, young female gang members most often face risks that are specifically tied to their perceived sexual vulnerability. For example, many male gang members in the study stated that the only purpose for females in gangs is to provide sex. Furthermore, girls who are initiated into gangs by being "sexed in," rather than being "beat in," must submit to any and all sexual demands or face expulsion.

The gender differences in gang members' victimization risks is further delineated by Miller and Decker (2001), who claim that female gang members' risks for criminal victimization are considerably less than males' risks. This claim is backed up by homicide data showing not only that young women are much less likely to be victims of gang homicide, but also that the vast majority of female gang homicide victims were not the intended targets of the attack. Such work can help make sense of the seemingly inconsistent evidence regarding the moderation hypothesis, as reviewed above (see R. B. Felson et al., 2013; Tillyer et al., 2010; Wilcox et al., 2009). Miller's work, in fact, suggests that gender will moderate the opportunity–victimization relationship differently, depending on the type of crime. Hence, the notion of gendered pathways involves not only the idea of unique effects on victimization across gender but also crime-specific gendered effects. For some types of crimes, being female will enhance the effects of opportunity on risk, whereas for other crimes, being male will enhance the effects of opportunity on risk.

Jody Miller's book *Getting Played* (2008) provides yet another example of how pathways to crime and victimization are intertwined and gendered. In this work, Miller's interviews with disadvantaged urban youth highlight the ways in which gender and *social ecological factors* combine to create different victimization risks for specific populations. According to Miller (2008), African American girls face victimization risks equal to those of African American boys and much higher than those of girls of other racial groups, which counters the conventional wisdom that females' victimization risks are consistently lower than those of males. Miller (2008) makes use of her data to examine the ways in which neighborhood conditions, social disorganization, and low social cohesion are linked to violence against the female youth she studied as well as women in general.

Using the same data, Cobbina, Miller, and Brunson (2008) reveal the ways in which gender and ecological contexts can interact to shape perceived victimization risks and risk management strategies differently for males and females. Young men's victimization risks are shaped by their greater participation in neighborhood life. This is reflected in their risk-avoidance strategies, which include staying within the boundaries of their own neighborhoods, not engaging in activities that might lead to retaliatory violence, and traveling in groups or with weapons. Neighborhood ecology also creates particular risks for young women. Public space is male dominated and is characterized by the sexualizing of interactions with young women (e.g., harassing language, unwanted touching), who are perceived as physically and psychologically weak. Young women's risk-avoidance strategies reflect this gender-specific risk and include avoiding public neighborhood spaces altogether and relying on the company of others, especially males, for protection.

This line of research by Miller and her colleagues demonstrates that gender, opportunity, and victimization not only are strongly related to larger social and neighborhood-level forces, but also do not have a static relationship across all subgroups. Such work, again, provides richness when viewed alongside findings from quantitative studies—specifically those revealing that opportunity-related risk factors and risk management are, in part, contextual, but that contextual influences operate differently across males and females (Lauritsen & Carbone-Lopez, 2011).

Gender, Opportunity, and Victimization: Looking Forward

The studies reviewed up to this point in the chapter imply several worthwhile directions for future research on the relationship among gender, opportunity, and victimization. Although an exhaustive review of such directions is beyond the scope of this chapter, several are discussed briefly below.

Domain-Specific Opportunity

It is important to examine the ways that gender, opportunity, and victimization vary across different public domains. In fact, the studies reviewed above were conducted in multiple specific domains beyond traditional public settings (e.g., neighborhood streets). For instance, Henson et al. (2013) demonstrated that males and females have different pathways to online victimization. Their data revealed that several differences in males' and females' types of online activity and security have created unique gender-specific opportunity structures for online victimization. Additionally, several studies have addressed the relationships among gender, activities, and victimization in school-based domains (e.g., Popp & Peguero, 2011; Tillyer et al., 2010; Wilcox et al., 2009). Another example of domain-specific research includes Wolff and Shi's (2009) examination of victimization within the prison system. This study demonstrates that victimization rates for female inmates may be roughly equivalent to those of males, but that rates are distorted by female inmates' greater likelihood to report victimization to authorities. Further consideration of these and other domains in future work could be helpful in making sense out of "inconsistent" findings across studies. Put simply, what constitutes opportunity, and how opportunity interrelates with gender, might also be dependent on the context, or domain, in which it is situated.

Multilevel Opportunity

Related to the need to focus on domain-specific opportunity, another important direction for future research is the continued exploration of gender, opportunity, and victimization from a multilevel perspective. Multilevel opportunity theory suggests that opportunity structures for victimization exist at various levels of analysis. For example, individual routine activities and lifestyles are important, but so are opportunity-related characteristics of the contexts, or domains, in which individuals are embedded—contexts such as places, streets, neighborhood settings, online networks, or prisons (Cobbina et al., 2008; Daday, Broidy, Crandall, & Sklar, 2005; Miller, 2008; Wilcox, Gialopsos, & Land, 2013; Wilcox, Land, & Hunt, 2003). Although a good deal of victimization research has examined victimization in relation to multilevel opportunity structures (e.g., Fisher, Sloan, Cullen, & Lu, 1998; Miethe & McDowall, 1993; Sampson & Wooldredge, 1987; Wilcox, Madensen, & Tillyer, 2007; Wilcox Rountree, Land, & Miethe, 1994), little work has layered considerations of gender on top of considerations of multiple contexts of opportunity (for exceptions, see Lauritsen & Carbone-Lopez, 2011; Tillyer et al., 2010). Combining a focus on gender with attention to multilevel opportunity would allow us to better contextualize the mediating and moderating processes regarding gender and opportunities for victimization reviewed herein.

More Qualitative Research

As evidenced by the studies reviewed earlier, qualitative research provides insight into the relationship among gender, opportunity, and victimization that sometimes reinforces the findings of quantitative data. However, this research can provide a distinct perspective and richness that cannot be captured by numerical data. Qualitative work thus often has the freedom to advance our understanding of complex topics by showing whether theoretical constructs have significance to the lived experiences voiced by individuals and by identifying new or underresearched avenues expressed by the subjects.

Importantly, qualitative research directly addresses Kruttschnitt's (1996) powerful critique of the status of gender and victimization research. As explained by Kruttschnitt, quantitative research has been instrumental in providing evidence of the stability in female rates of victimization and in activity-related risk factors for some types of victimization. Kruttschnitt maintains, however, that quantitative tests of L-RAT are inadequate for explaining the relationship between gender and other types of victimization (e.g., intimate partner violence). According to Kruttschnitt, quantitative studies are often unable to measure adequately the extent of men's and women's high-risk activities or whether particular activities took place with other persons or in situations that increase the likelihood of victimization. She also claims that L-RAT does not adequately address the intersection of race, gender, and victimization, nor does it adequately situate victimization risk within the life course. Kruttschnitt thus argues that the gender–crime–victimization literature is in dire need of new theoretical development and measurement advancement. Her suggestion is that qualitative research can provide fruitful directions for both of these needs. In other words, Kruttschnitt suggests that future quantitative research on the relationship between gender and victimization—including the theory that underlies such research and the measures used in such research—should be informed by qualitative work. We agree, and we suggest that the sort of quantitative and qualitative work reviewed here be used in conjunction with one another in mixed-methods research designed to inform theory development and to further understand the gender–opportunity–victimization nexus.

Conclusion

Building upon Freda Adler's famous work on gender, opportunity, and criminal offending, this chapter reviewed the key studies that address the interrelationships among gender, opportunity, and *victimization*. We focused on four strains of research: (1) work that examines historical trends in rates of victimization for males and females; (2) work that tests a mediation hypothesis whereby gender is related to individual victimization indirectly, through opportunity; (3) work that tests a moderation hypothesis that expresses an interaction between gender and opportunity in affecting individual victimization; and (4) qualitative research on the intersection of gender, opportunity, and victimization. Although Adler's work was not about gender and victimization per se, many themes in her work have carried over into the victimization literature.

In terms of trends in victimization, we reviewed recent findings showing little support for the idea that the gender gap in victimization—in which males have historically been at much greater risk—is closing over time. In short, it is closing only for some victimization types (e.g., stranger assault) and largely because male rates have declined more than female rates. Thus, research on the gender gap in victimization is not consistent with some ideas implied in Adler's work; increasing opportunities for women have not translated into growing rates of victimization for women in comparison to rates for men.

Regarding research that tests the relationship between gender and victimization as being mediated by opportunity, the findings thus far are supportive of Alder's core theme of considering the possible link between gender and opportunity. Although victimization research on the mediation hypothesis certainly does not support the liberation hypothesis per se, it does suggest that one of the reasons women have persistently lower rates of victimization than men is because they engage in less risky or opportunistic lifestyles and activities, especially delinquent lifestyles. From this perspective, opportunity certainly matters for understanding victimization, and opportunity is predicted by gender.

Research that examines the gender–opportunity–victimization nexus through the moderation hypothesis suggests that gender does not predict opportunity so much as it conditions opportunity. Hence, these studies challenge Adler's assumption that unisex explanations are at work. Research to date suggests that some forms of opportunity are more strongly related to female victimization, whereas other forms of opportunity are more strongly related to male victimization. Adding to this complexity is the fact that crime-specific and domain-specific effects have been observed.

Finally, qualitative work on the interrelationships among gender, opportunity, and victimization has supported (or been supported by) the mediating and moderating processes just reviewed. For example, supporting Adler's original contentions, findings from qualitative research reveal that gender can have a substantial impact on opportunities for both offending and victimization. In contrast, research also reveals that women's pathways into crime are especially linked with their victimization experiences and that women often turn to crime and experience victimization because of continued marginalization, rather than because of increased liberation.

In closing, some of Freda Adler's claims in her classic work, *Sisters in Crime*, have been shown to be correct. She was correct that women's liberation increased not only women's opportunities for work and education, but also their criminal opportunities. However, her hypothesis that this would result in women taking greater advantage of their opportunities for offending has not borne out over time. Further, as we explored here, women are not necessarily experiencing victimization with greater frequency. Although Adler's liberation hypothesis has not found substantial support, her groundbreaking book initiated research into the exploration of the interrelationships of gender, opportunity, and involvement in crime as an offender, victim, or both. She thus prompted myriad studies that have allowed a better understanding of this complex relationship, including those that examine the extent to which gender's effect on victimization is mediated by opportunity and those that examine the extent to which gender moderates opportunity in producing victimization. Greater sophistication in research design and measurement, as well as a better theoretical grounding through qualitative work, will doubtlessly advance our understanding of the gender–crime–victimization nexus.

References

Adler, F. (1975). *Sisters in crime: The rise of the new female criminal.* New York, NY: McGraw–Hill.

Adler, F. (1977). The interaction between women's emancipation and female criminality: A cross-cultural perspective. *International Journal of Criminology and Penology, 5,* 101–112.

Bunch, J., Clay-Warner, J., & Lei, M. (2012). Demographic characteristics and victimization risk: Testing the mediating effects of routine activities. *Crime and Delinquency.* Advance online publication. doi:10.1177/0011128712466932.

Chesney-Lind, M. (1989). Girls, crime, and woman's place: Toward a feminist model of female delinquency. *Crime and Delinquency, 35,* 5–29.

Cloward, R .A., & Ohlin, L. E. (1960). *Delinquency and opportunity: A theory of delinquent gangs.* New York, NY: The Free Press.

Cobbina, J. E., Miller, J., & Brunson, R. K. (2008). Gender, neighborhood danger, and risk-avoidance strategies among urban African-American youths. *Criminology, 46,* 673–709.

Cohen, L. E., & Felson, M. (1979). Social change and crime rate trends: A routine activity approach. *American Sociological Review, 44,* 588–608.

Cohen, L. E., Felson, M., & Land, K. C. (1980). Property crime rates in the United States: A macro-dynamic analysis, 1947–1977; with ex ante forecasts for the mid-1980s. *American Journal of Sociology, 86,* 90–118.

Cohen, L. E., Kluegel, J. R., & Land, K. C. (1981). Social inequality and predatory victimization: An exposition and test of a formal theory. *American Sociological Review, 46,* 505–524.

Daday, J. K., Broidy, L. M., Crandall, C. S., & Sklar, D. P. (2005). Individual, neighborhood, and situational factors associated with violent victimization and offending. *Criminal Justice Studies, 18,* 215–235.

DeHart, D. D. (2008). Pathways to prison: Impact of victimization in the lives of incarcerated women. *Violence Against Women, 14,* 1362–1381.

Felson, M., & Cohen, L. E. (1980). Human ecology and crime: A routine activity approach. *Human Ecology, 8,* 389–406.

Felson, R. B. (1997). Routine activities and involvement in violence as actor, witness, or target. *Violence and Victims, 12,* 209–221.

Felson, R. B., & Burchfield, K. B. (2004). Alcohol and the risk of physical and sexual assault victimization. *Criminology, 42,* 837–859.

Felson, R. B., Savolainen, J., Berg, M. T., & Ellonen, N. (2013). Does spending time in public settings contribute to the adolescent risk of violent victimization? *Journal of Quantitative Criminology, 29,* 273–293.

Fineran, S., & Bolen, R. M. (2006). Risk factors for peer sexual harassment in schools. *Journal of Interpersonal Violence, 21,* 1169–1190.

Fisher, B. S., Sloan, J. J., Cullen, F. T., & Lu, C. (1998). Crime in the ivory tower: The level and sources of student victimization. *Criminology, 36,* 671–710.

Hartman, J. L., & Sundt, J. L. (2011). The rise of feminist criminology: Freda Adler. In F. T. Cullen, C. L. Jonson, A. J. Myer, & F. Adler (Eds.), *The origins of American Criminology: Advances in criminological theory* (Vol. 16, pp. 205–220). New Brunswick, NJ: Transaction.

Henson, B., Reyns, B. W., & Fisher, B. S. (2013). Does gender matter in the virtual world? Examining the effect of gender on the link between online social network activity, security and interpersonal victimization. *Security Journal, 26,* 1–16.

Henson, B., Wilcox, P., Reyns, B. W., & Cullen, F. T. (2010). Gender, adolescent lifestyles, and violent victimization: Implications for routine activity theory. *Victims and Offenders, 5,* 303–328.

Hindelang, M. J., Gottfredson, M. R., & Garofalo, J. (1978). *Victims of personal crime: An empirical foundation for a theory of personal victimization.* Cambridge, MA: Ballinger.

Jensen, G. F., & Brownfield, D. (1986). Gender, lifestyles, and victimization: Beyond routine activity. *Violence and Victims, 1,* 85–99.

Kavanaugh, P. R. (2013). The continuum of sexual violence: Women's accounts of victimization in urban nightlife. *Feminist Criminology, 8,* 20–39.

Kruttschnitt, C. (1996). Contributions of quantitative methods to the study of gender and crime, or bootstrapping our way into the theoretical thicket. *Journal of Quantitative Criminology, 12,* 135–161.

Lauritsen, J. L., & Carbone-Lopez, K. (2011). Gender differences in risk factors for violent victimization: An examination of individual-, family-, and community-level predictors. *Journal of Research in Crime and Delinquency, 48,* 538–565.

Lauritsen, J. L., & Heimer, K. (2008). The gender gap in violent victimization. *Journal of Quantitative Criminology, 24,* 125–147.

Lauritsen, J. L., Heimer, K., & Lynch, J. P. (2009). Trends in the gender gap in violent offending: New evidence from the national crime victimization survey. *Criminology, 47,* 361–399.

Lauritsen, J. L., Sampson, R. J., & Laub, J. H. (1991). Conventional and delinquent activities: Implications for the prevention of violent victimization among adolescents. *Violence and Victims, 7,* 91–108.

Livingston, J. A., Hequembourg, A., Testa, M., & VanZile-Tamsen, C. (2007). Unique aspects of adolescent sexual victimization experiences. *Psychology of Women Quarterly, 31,* 331–343.

Miethe, T. D., & McDowall, D. (1993). Contextual effects in models of criminal victimization. *Social Forces, 71,* 741–759.

Miethe, T. D., Stafford, M. C., & Long, J. S. (1987). Social differentiation in criminal victimization: A test of routine activities/lifestyle theories. *American Sociological Review, 52,* 184–194.

Miller, J. (1998). Gender and victimization risks among young women in gangs. *Journal of Research in Crime and Delinquency, 35,* 429–453.

Miller, J. (2008). *Getting played: African American girls, urban inequality, and gendered violence.* New York: New York University Press.

Miller, J., & Brunson, R. K. (2000). Gender dynamic in youth gangs: A comparison of males' and females' account. *Justice Quarterly, 17,* 419–448.

Miller, J., & Decker, S. H. (2001). Young women and gang violence: Gender, street offending, and violent victimization in gangs. *Justice Quarterly, 18,* 115–140.

Mustaine, E. E., & Tewksbury, R. (1998a). Victimization risks at leisure: A gender-specific analysis. *Violence and Victims, 13,* 231–249.

Mustaine, E. E., & Tewksbury, R. (1998b). Specifying the role of alcohol in predatory victimization. *Deviant Behavior, 19,* 173–199.

Popp, A. M., & Peguero, A. A. (2011). Routine activities and victimization at school: The significance of gender. *Journal of Interpersonal Violence, 26,* 2413–2436.

Sampson, R. J., & Lauritsen, J. L. (1990). Deviant lifestyles, proximity to crime, and the offender–victim link in personal violence. *Journal of Research in Crime and Delinquency, 27,* 110–139.

Sampson, R. J., & Wooldredge, J. D. (1987). Linking the micro- and macro-level dimensions of lifestyle–routine activity and opportunity models of predatory victimization. *Journal of Quantitative Criminology, 3,* 371–393.

Schwartz, J., Steffensmeier, D. J., & Feldmeyer, B. (2009). Assessing trends in women's violence via data triangulation: Arrests, convictions, incarcerations, and victim reports. *Social Problems, 56,* 494–525.

Simpson, S. S., Yahner, J. L., & Dugan, L. (2008). Understanding women's pathways to jail: Analyzing the lives of incarcerated women. *Australian and New Zealand Journal of Criminology, 41,* 84–108.

Steffensmeier, D. J. (1978). Crime and the contemporary woman: An analysis of changing levels of female property crime, 1960–1975. *Social Forces, 57,* 566–584.

Stefffensmier, D. J. (1980). Assessing the impact of the women's movement on sex-based differences in the handling of adult criminal defendants. *Crime and Delinquency, 26,* 344–357.

Steffensmeier, D. J., & Allan, E. A. (1988). Sex disparities in arrests by residence, race and age: An assessment of the gender convergence/crime hypothesis. *Justice Quarterly, 5,* 53–80.

Steffensmeier, D., & Allan, E. (1996). Gender and crime: Toward a gendered theory of female offending. *Annual Review of Sociology, 22,* 459–487.

Steffensmeier, D., Schwartz, J., Zhong, H., & Ackerman, J. (2005). An assessment of recent trends in girls' violence using diverse longitudinal sources: Is the gender gap closing? *Criminology, 43,* 355–405.

Tillyer, M. S., Wilcox, P., & Gialopsos, B. M. (2010). Adolescent school-based sexual victimization: Exploring the role of opportunity in a gender-specific multilevel analysis. *Journal of Criminal Justice 38,* 1071–1081.

Wilcox, P., Gialopsos, B. M., & Land, K. C. (2013). Multilevel criminal opportunity. In F. T. Cullen and P. Wilcox (Eds.), *Handbook of criminological theory* (pp. 579–601). New York, NY: Oxford University Press.

Wilcox, P., Land, K. C., & Hunt, S. A. (2003). *Criminal circumstance: A dynamic, multicontextual criminal opportunity theory.* New York, NY: Aldine de Gruyter.

Wilcox, P., Madensen, T. D., & Tillyer, M. S. (2007). Guardianship in context: Implications for burglary risk and prevention. *Criminology, 45,* 771–804.

Wilcox, P., Tillyer, M. S., & Fisher, B. S. (2009). Gendered opportunity? Adolescent school-based victimization. *Journal of Research in Crime and Delinquency, 46,* 245–269.

Wilcox Rountree, P., Land, K. C., & Miethe, T. D. (1994). Macro–micro integration in the study of victimization: A hierarchical logistic model analysis across Seattle neighborhoods. *Criminology, 32,* 387–414.

Wolff, N., & Shi, J. (2009). Type, source, and patterns of physical victimization: A comparison of male and female inmates. *The Prison Journal, 89,* 172–191.

Zaykowski, H., & Gunter, W. D. (2013). Gender differences in victimization risk: Exploring the role of deviant lifestyles. *Violence and Victims, 28,* 341–356.

CHAPTER 11

The Neighborhood Context of Women's Experiences with Violent Crime

Sally S. Simpson and Candace Kruttschnitt[1]

Criminologists have long considered the role of the neighborhood in fueling delinquency and crime. In the United States, this work was spawned by the ecological studies of delinquency by Shaw and McKay (1942, 1969). Subsequent research in the 1970s and 1980s shifted the focus of this research in three ways: away from delinquency to criminal violence, away from neighborhoods to cities or higher levels of aggregation, and away from a limited set of causal variables that could be derived only from official data sources (Sampson & Lauritsen, 1994, p. 46). Findings from this research point to a common set of factors that appear to be related to community violence: poverty, residential mobility, family disruption, and population density (Sampson & Lauritsen, 1994, pp. 63–64).

At the beginning of the 21st century, scholars again returned to the study of "neighborhood effects" and began to address the questions of why and how factors like poverty and population density produce variations in violence across neighborhoods (Sampson, Morenoff, & Gannon-Rowley, 2002). Neighborhood ties, social control, collective efficacy, disorder, and routine activities have all been posited as important mechanisms that account for neighborhood disparities in crime (Maimon & Browning, 2010, 2012; Sampson, 2012; Sampson et al., 2002; Sampson, Morenoff, & Raudenbush, 2005).

Importantly, an implicit assumption in this research is that the same neighborhood-level mechanisms influence both men's and women's probability of encountering violent crime. As Lauritsen and Carbone-Lopez (2011) note, "most theories that focus on the relationship between neighborhood conditions and crime are similarly silent about potential gender differences in victimization risk factors primarily because victim's characteristics are not a key concern of the theory" (p. 542). This omission—this failure to bring gender into the study of neighborhoods and crime experiences—is problematic. We know that gender structures violent encounters not only by determining one's probability of victimization but also by determining the relational distance between the victim and offender. Simply put, although women may be, on average, less likely than men to be violently victimized, they are more likely than men to be victimized by someone they know, especially an intimate partner (Bachman & Saltzman, 1995; Harrell, 2012).

The reduced probability of women encountering violence from strangers in their neighborhoods, relative to their male counterparts, raises a number of significant questions: How important are neighborhood characteristics and interactions in women's experiences of violence? Do prior experiences with violent crime play a role in women's residential mobility? And does residential mobility have any effect on women's subsequent odds of encountering a violent crime?

In this chapter, we explore these issues. We start by reviewing what previous scholars have discovered about (1) the neighborhood characteristics that increase women's risks of violent victimization; (2) the neighborhood characteristics that increase women's risks of intimate-partner violence (IPV); and (3) the effects of residential mobility on subsequent violent encounters. We then introduce data gathered from a sample of jailed women in Baltimore City. The women reported their neighborhoods of residence for the 36 months prior to their incarceration. They also reported up to eight incidents of violent victimization perpetrated by a partner or a nonpartner. These data permit us to determine whether neighborhood characteristics are related to women's experiences of violent victimization, whether crime victimization or other factors motivated them to move to a new neighborhood, and whether the characteristics of their new neighborhood influence subsequent crime victimizations. As such, our chapter constitutes a review of and unique contribution to both the emerging research on the social–interactional factors related to neighborhood variations in violence and the emerging feminist perspective on gendered lives (Burgess-Proctor, 2014).

Neighborhood Context, Gender, and Violent Experiences

Neighborhood Characteristics Related to Women's Risk of Violence

Despite the recent growth in neighborhood-level research, most of this research focuses on criminal victimization (or other social problems) without considering how neighborhood characteristics may impact women differently from men. Sensitive to this issue, Harries and Kovandzic (1999) examined aggregate levels of assault and homicide involving female victims across various neighborhoods in Baltimore in the early 1990s. Their spatial analyses revealed striking differences between neighborhoods that had a high probability of violence against women and those that had a low probability; the former included a high percentage of (1) individuals living in poverty or extreme poverty, (2) African Americans, and (3) families headed by women with children. These findings mirror the early studies of aggregate predictors of variations in violent crime across metropolitan areas (Bursik, 1988), but they do not reveal much about the nature of the victimization women experienced.

Another attempt to draw women more directly into the "neighborhood-effects" literature focuses on the social disorganization paradigm by pointing to the effect of neighborhood groups in regulating offending. Wilcox Rountree and Warner (1999) explored whether the gendering of neighborhood ties affects variations in crime control. They found that only women's ties had a deterrent effect on crime, but that this effect was conditioned by the percentage of female households in a neighborhood: Women's ties were most effective in communities with the smallest proportion of female-headed households. Although these findings do not directly address women's odds of violent victimization, they have important implications for our understanding of the links between neighborhood disadvantage and gendered violence. Specifically, as recent ethnographic work on young women living in extremely disadvantaged urban communities shows, in the absence of male protection, young women are left to their own devices as they try to navigate the violence they find in their homes, neighborhoods, and schools (Jones, 2010; Miller, 2008). These experiences may have long-term effects, increasing the likelihood that they will encounter IPV in later life (Potter, 2006; Raghavan, Mennerich, Sexton, & James 2006). Disadvantage has also been shown to influence girls' probability of engaging in violence via their association with intimate peers who encourage violent behavior (see Zimmerman & Messner, 2010).

In summary, little is known about how neighborhood characteristics influence women's risks of violence. There is some evidence, however, that impoverished neighborhoods with a large proportion of female-headed single-parent households place women at greatest risk for violent victimization.

Neighborhood Characteristics Related to IPV

The bulk of the research on IPV focuses on the individual or situational attributes associated with IPV such as age, race, gender, socioeconomic status, and substance abuse. There is, however, an emerging body of research that directs attention to the community context in which IPV occurs. The findings from this research suggest that the neighborhood characteristics that predict other types of violent crime also predict intimate violence. Specifically, high concentrations of residential poverty, unemployed males, and female heads of household with young children spawn a disproportionate amount of intimate violence (Benson, Fox, DeMaris, & Van Wyk, 2003; Cunradi, Caetano, Clark, & Schaefer, 2000; Miles-Doan, 1998; O'Campo et al., 1995; Pearlman, Zierler, Gjesvik, & Verhoek-Oftedahl, 2003; Pinchevsky & Wright, 2012).

As this research on the neighborhood context of IPV has expanded, attempts to understand what might explain the association between neighborhood disadvantage and IPV have started to appear. This research draws on recent advances in social disorganization theory and, in particular, on the notions of collective efficacy and social support. Sampson, Raudenbush, and Earls (1997) advanced the construct of collective efficacy in an attempt to explain how the structural features of a neighborhood are linked to crime. Specifically, they argued that neighborhoods with greater social cohesion promote informal social control among their residents that, in turn, inhibits crime. Browning (2002) was perhaps the first scholar to examine whether collective efficacy could reduce rates of IPV under conditions of structural disadvantage. He found that collective efficacy significantly reduced IPV, and he argued that it may be a stronger source of community rates of IPV than the factor of structural disadvantage. Subsequent work by Wright and Benson (2011) also found that collective efficacy reduced rates of IPV. Unlike street crime, however, they found that collective efficacy could not account for the link between structural disadvantage and IPV.

Because neighborhoods vary in their levels of social support, scholars also have hypothesized that support could be an important neighborhood characteristic that mediates the effects of disadvantage on rates of IPV. Women in violent relationships who can turn to family and friends for assistance may be more likely to leave an abusive partner. The results of analyses of disadvantage, social support, and rates of IPV are, however, counterintuitive. Van Wyk, Benson, Fox, and DeMaris (2003) found that the relationship between neighborhood disadvantage and IPV was conditioned by social support (contact with others), such that support decreased IPV only in neighborhoods with low and medium levels of disadvantage and not in the most disadvantaged neighborhoods. Subsequently, Wright (2012) also found that the effect of social support (operating somewhat differently for family and friends) on IPV is reduced in disadvantaged neighborhoods.

In total, these findings repeatedly indicate that the most disadvantaged neighborhoods have the highest rates of IPV and that what we might consider important protective factors—collective efficacy and social support—are relatively ineffective in these disadvantaged contexts. These findings raise the question of what factors in disadvantaged neighborhoods might be uniquely important to the occurrence of partner violence as opposed to street violence or violence perpetrated by a stranger.

Importantly, Lauritsen and Cabone-Lopez (2011) examined this issue with the Area-Identified National Crime Victimization Survey. They found that, net of neighborhood disadvantage, four factors predicted IPV: young age, single parenthood, single without children, and a shorter time in their current home. Only two of these factors, however, significantly differentiated women's probability of encountering violence from an intimate partner rather than a stranger: age and single parenthood. The fact that length of residence in the current home did not substantially distinguish IPV from stranger violence is somewhat surprising because we might expect that women who have experienced more violence from an intimate partner would be more inclined to move. However, it may be that the experience of violent victimization, regardless of whether the perpetrator is an intimate or a stranger, impels women to move. This interpretation would be consistent with the contradictory findings pertaining to the effects of residential instability on women's probability of victimization by intimates and nonintimates. Specifically, some scholars find that residential instability produces more IPV (Benson et al., 2003), others find it has no effect (see, e.g., Browning, 2002; Miles-Doan, 1998), and still others find it associated with a greater risk of stranger violence, nonstranger violence, and IPV (Lauritsen & Schaum, 2004).

The findings on the relationship between neighborhood characteristics and rates of IPV are threefold. First, characteristics of disadvantaged neighborhoods, like poverty and a high proportion of female-headed households, are associated not only with high rates of violence between strangers but also with high rates of violence between intimates. Second, although both collective efficacy and social support have been shown to reduce rates of IPV, neither can explain the association between concentrated disadvantage and high rates of IPV. Third, because rates of IPV are affected by individual attributes as well as neighborhood attributes, it is important to consider whether the individual predictors of IPV differ from the predictors of nonintimate violence in disadvantaged neighborhoods. Younger women and single parents have a significantly greater risk of encountering IPV relative to stranger violence. The role residential changes play in IPV, however, remains unclear.

The Effects of Moving on the Risk of Violence

Residential instability can occur for a variety of reasons. People can be highly motived to move for positive reasons ("pull-outs"), such as the opportunity to get ahead or to live closer to family or other support networks. Conversely, they may be forced to move for negative reasons ("push-outs"), such as no longer being able to afford their housing, their neighborhood having deteriorated, or experiencing fear of crime or actual criminal victimization. We borrow these terms from Miller (1986), who used the terms pull-out and push-out to distinguish the primary mechanisms that lead young females to life on the streets (see also Daly, 1992). Evidence suggests that push-out factors are more salient than pull-out factors in why individuals desire to move—at least in the Moving to Opportunity (MTO) program, which is discussed below (Kling, Liebman, & Katz, 2007). Race may also condition the effect of perceived crime on mobility such that Whites who perceive more crime in their neighborhoods are more likely to move out and be replaced by Blacks, but Blacks moving out of a perceived higher crime rate neighborhood are rarely replaced by Whites (Hipp, 2010; Xie & McDowall, 2010).

The MTO experiment allowed low-income families in five cities (Baltimore, Boston, Los Angeles, New York, and Chicago) to participate in a housing program where they were randomly assigned to three groups: experimental, section 8, and control. The experimental group was given a "restricted" opportunity to relocate. Their vouchers could only be redeemed in parts of the city with extremely low poverty rates (10% or less). The section 8 group was offered housing vouchers with no restraints; they could move wherever they wanted to go. The control group was offered no vouchers to move. Analyses from all five cities revealed that adults who moved (the experimental and section 8 groups) all felt safer in their new neighborhoods but that moving to better neighborhoods (those with lower levels of poverty) did not produce notable long-term effects on the probability of being involved in violence (Kling et al., 2007; Kling, Ludwig, & Katz, 2005).

There were, however, significant gender effects in this outcome: Boys in the experimental group were less likely to be arrested for violent crimes, but they were more likely to be arrested for property crimes; girls in the experimental group had fewer arrests for both violent and property crimes than girls in the control group. Further, as Sharkey and Sampson (2010) note, these gender-specific findings contradict those found in the earlier Gautreaux program in Chicago that offered low-income families apartments throughout the city of Chicago. Boys in families that participated in the Gautreaux project that moved to the suburbs were less likely to be arrested for a variety of crimes (including violent offenses), but these effects did not emerge for girls who moved to the suburbs.

Although the MTO experiment focused on juveniles and the effect of changing neighborhoods on criminal offending, these findings raise important questions about how moving affects the probability of experiencing violence in a destination neighborhood, particularly when individuals are push-outs or motivated to leave a neighborhood because of their perceptions of disorder or their personal experiences with crime victimization. Using data from a subsample of adolescents (ages 9–12) from the Project on Human Development in Chicago Neighborhoods, Sharkey and Sampson (2010) examined whether residential moves between neighborhoods increase or decrease violence (e.g., violent activity, exposure to violence, and violent victimization). They found that (1) residential mobility within Chicago is associated with increases in all types of violence, whereas moving outside of the city reduces violent behavior and exposure to violence but has no significant effect on victimization; (2) there was no consistent interaction between moving and gender; and (3) the divergent violent trajectories could not be explained by just the characteristics of the destination neighborhoods; rather it was related to the "broader structure within which neighborhoods are embedded" (Sharkey & Sampson, 2010, p. 669).

Taken together, the findings from these divergent bodies of research raise a number of intriguing questions about the neighborhood context of women's experiences of violence. Poverty and single parenthood loom large in women's experiences of violence generally and within the context of their intimate relationships. However, it is unclear whether—and, if so, how—these factors are linked to the likelihood that women will move to another residence and neighborhood. It also remains unclear whether such a move would alter their odds of experiencing violence in their destination neighborhood. Sharkey and Sampson's (2010) research would suggest that the demographic characteristics of their destination neighborhood (racial and economic composition) should be less important to their subsequent experiences of violence than institutional resources and distance. But their research was confined to youths whose residential moves either facilitated or inhibited new peer networks because of their enrollment in school. For adult women, particularly economically disadvantaged women, it is unclear how much physical distance they can put between their old and new residential neighborhoods and, in some cases, their violent partners.

Understanding how neighborhoods influence women's violent encounters requires, therefore, that we are sensitive to initial neighborhood characteristics, relational variations in their violent encounters, reasons for moving, and the characteristics and experiences found in destination neighborhoods. In the next section, we use data from Baltimore to explore whether the landscape of the city, in particular the stratification of disadvantage by neighborhoods, affects the victimization experiences of a group of "high-risk" criminally involved women. As we consider the lives of these women, it is important to understand their circumstances as well as the decisions and choices they make regarding their living arrangements (Maher, 1997). Below, we describe who these women are, how we collected data from them, and what that information tells us about the gendered effects of neighborhoods on victimization.

Understanding the Gendered Effects of Neighborhoods: Implications From Baltimore

Studying Women's Victimization in Baltimore Neighborhoods

Research in Baltimore was undertaken as part of a larger study that examined adult women's experience of violence (Horney, Ferrero, Gartner, Kruttschnitt, & Simpson, 1999). Other research sites included Minneapolis and Toronto. The Baltimore data are useful for our purposes because violence, although rare in the general population, is relatively common among criminally involved populations. Therefore, we expected and found considerable levels of violence—both offending and victimization—reported by the Baltimore women.

The Baltimore data collection effort began in 2001. Interviews were conducted with 351 women who were serving time for a criminal offense or awaiting criminal adjudication, sentencing, or transfer to another facility. During the interview process, we collected demographic details such as age and race or ethnicity, information about childhood experiences, and specifics about romantic partners, employment, living conditions, criminality and victimization, and home address for the three-year period prior to their current incarceration. Because the address information can be linked to neighborhood data from the U.S. Census, it was possible to identify the characteristics of the neighborhoods where the women were living and assess whether neighborhood quality changed (for better or worse) if the women moved from one place to another within the city. We could also use self-reported partner and nonpartner victimization to see whether victimization (amount and type) was affected by mobility. Unlike other studies of residential mobility and crime, when our respondents reported changing addresses during the 36-month period before incarceration, we asked for their new address information *and* an explanation of why they changed residences.

As mentioned previously, if people are highly "motivated" to leave their current residence for a better living situation (pull-outs), we might expect them to settle in a community that has more positive opportunities (e.g., a job, closer to family, safer community) that might reduce the risk of nonpartner victimization. Conversely, forced movers (push-outs) may leave their residences because they have run out of money, are facing eviction, or are not getting along with roommates or a partner. These motivations may play out in opportunistic moves (staying with a friend or family member for a short time; finding cheaper options in the same area or a similar if not worse neighborhood) or highly constrained choices such as living on the streets. These new conditions could increase the risk of nonpartner victimization because the new neighborhood is apt to be less familiar and life on the streets creates more exposure to motivated offenders. Further, if leaving an abusive partner was cited as a reason for the move, the risk of subsequent partner violence might also be affected, although it is unclear how exactly it would affect future risk of IPV. Some studies suggest that leaving an abusive partner can increase the risk of victimization, at least for certain types of IPV such as intimate terrorism (Johnson, 2008). But other researchers have found that leaving a violent relationship is a successful self-help strategy that lowers the risk of IPV (Hamberger & Guse, 2005).

THE BALTIMORE WOMEN. The women who participated in the study were mostly African American with an age range of 18 through 55. Almost all were unmarried (86%) with children (81%). Consistent with their high-risk status, most of the women lacked a high school diploma, were irregularly employed, and reported substantial criminal and drug involvement with a previous arrest history (Slocum, Simpson, & Smith, 2005). Importantly, for this chapter, a large percentage of women moved at least once during the three years prior to the current incarceration—70%. Further, many could be classified as "chronic" movers—that is, changed addresses more than four times during the 36-month period—which likely signifies an unstable and transitory lifestyle.

NEIGHBORHOOD CHARACTERISTICS. We can use these data to examine whether neighborhood characteristics are associated with violent victimization and to describe what role, if any, moving has on victimization experiences. To do so, we first must consider the "typical" Baltimore neighborhood where the women lived prior to their incarceration. We tied individuals to neighborhoods by linking the home address provided by respondents to Census data. Then, using Census tract information, we classified neighborhood disadvantage according to levels of unemployment, poverty, public assistance, and educational attainment. We created maps that characterize the level of disadvantage using shades of white, black, and gray. Greater levels of disadvantage are displayed in darker colors. Lighter areas of the maps depict more privileged communities.

Map 11.1 displays all the home address locations of the women in the Baltimore study that we could geocode. As shown on the map, most addresses are concentrated in decidedly disadvantaged neighborhoods. This distribution remained relatively stable even when a change in address was reported. Stability was maintained, in part,

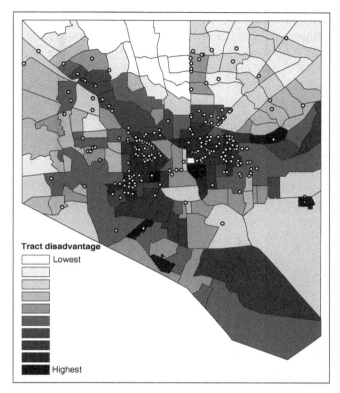

Map 11.1. Women's neighborhoods, by disadvantage

because most of the women who reported moving did *not* move out of the Census tract in which they were originally living (56%). Thus, mobility within the city for the Baltimore women tended to be restricted—occurring *within,* rather than *between,* neighborhoods. We think this has important implications for the level of victimization and relational variation in women's violent encounters. For instance, there may be little change in nonpartner victimization associated with mobility because the structural features of the neighborhood remain the same. Similarly, it may also be difficult for a victim to successfully escape a violent relationship if she is merely moving around the corner or to another block in the same neighborhood. This expectation is consistent with narrative descriptions of violent encounters the women provided to researchers. One of the Baltimore women, when asked to depict, in her own words, the nature and circumstances of partner violence, described how difficult it was to get away from her violent partner, although she was eventually successful.

> I tried to leave him, keep trying to leave him, because I don't want him back cuz he spit on me. And I just didn't want him back, and he kept thinking he could beat me up to make me stay. But I found somebody that was going to protect me, and I worked up enough courage to really leave, and he still harassed me until I moved away.

Relational Variation in Violent Experiences and Neighborhood Conditions

One thing is obvious from the Baltimore data: Violence, or its threat, permeates day-to-day life for these respondents. The women see and hear about violence in their communities and also are involved in such acts directly as offenders and victims. But there is notable variation in their experiences. Consistent with other studies, the risk of intimate-partner victimization is much greater than the risk of victimization by nonpartners. For instance, the average monthly number of IPV incidents reported is 1, but the range is great (0–62). The average number of nonpartner incidents is half that of IPV (0.5), with a much smaller monthly range (0–1.7).

Notably, the dispersion of these events by neighborhood does not substantially differ. Returning to our maps and comparing Map 11.2 (nonpartner victimization) with Map 11.3 (IPV), two important conclusions are apparent. First, more IPV is

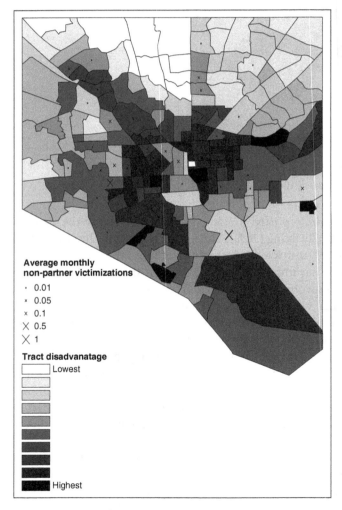

Map 11.2. Average monthly nonpartner victimization, by neighborhood disadvantage

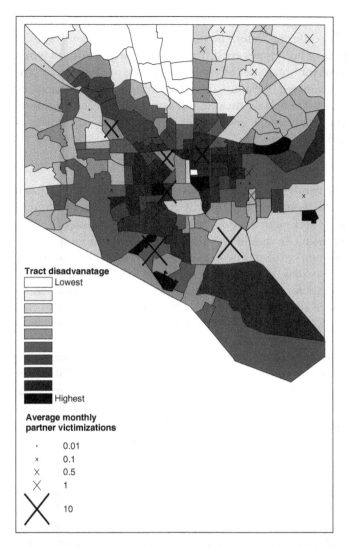

Tract disadvanatage

Lowest

Highest

Average monthly partner victimizations

.	0.01
×	0.1
X	0.5
X	1
X	10

Map 11.3. Average monthly partner victimization, by neighborhood disadvantage

reported within and across neighborhoods than nonpartner violence. This means that women in Baltimore are more likely to be victimized by individuals they are in relationships with than by nonpartners. Second, both IPV and nonpartner violence are not found only in disadvantaged neighborhoods. We can see these differences by comparing the location (by shading) and size of the X's depicted on the maps. Recall that disadvantage is shown by different shades of black, gray, and white. If there was an association between disadvantage and victimization, we would see X's concentrated mainly in the darkest areas of the maps. The size of the X's also indicate the average amount of victimization occurring per month. Neighborhoods that have more monthly victimization, on average, are shown with larger X's. Although the scale is different between Maps 11.2 and 11.3 (there is more partner than nonpartner victimization and thus the X's differ in scale), the distributions are relatively similar between maps. Victimizations of both types are diffused across neighborhood types. Thus, the distribution patterns for both types of victimization are not highly concentrated by neighborhood disadvantage. We confirmed these observations using more advanced statistical techniques. There is no meaningful association in the Baltimore data between neighborhood disadvantage and violent victimization—regardless of whether the women changed addresses.

Reasons for Moving

One of the weaknesses in the gender and neighborhood violence literature is that it does not take into account why people move. In light of the contradictory findings regarding residential mobility and victimization, we suggested that understanding the decision making behind the move should provide a better understanding of how neighborhoods influence women's violent encounters. As discussed previously, we suspected that women who pursued more positive opportunities (pull-outs) would have lower victimization risks (before and after moving) compared with those whose reasons for moving were more adverse (push-outs). One possible mechanism that would produce these differences is the destination neighborhood. Push-outs have fewer choices of where to go when they decide to move.

The first step we took to test our suspicions about the link between the reason for moving and victimization risk was to code the reasons given for moving into three main categories (pull-outs, push-outs, and release from a treatment or correctional facility). We then extracted leaving an abusive partner from the push-out category so that we could assess this type of move separately. We examined victimization levels, by partner and nonpartner, to assess whether the type of move changed victimization levels posttransition.

Given the population of women in the Baltimore sample, it should not be surprising that most who moved at least once during the three-year period before incarceration did so because of some adverse condition (51% were classified as push-outs). Another third (32%) moved to pursue positive opportunities (pull-outs); and the remainder (17%) changed addresses after completing some kind of drug or mental health treatment or correctional program. Women reported moving to "get away" from an abusive partner 18 times, or 3.2% of moves.

When we inspected whether the type of move was related to neighborhood characteristics, we did find some notable differences between pull-outs and the other movers. Specifically, pull-outs tended to move to much less disadvantaged areas.

We next examined whether the different reasons for moving affected postmove victimization levels. Here, two findings stood out: (1) Women who moved after they were released from a facility experienced an increased risk of IPV compared with push-outs; and (2) women who left an abusive partner effectively lowered their risk of IPV postmove compared with other push-outs. There was no association between type of move and changes in levels of nonpartner victimization. The risk of increased levels of IPV postfacility moves did not hold up to a more comprehensive analysis, but the decreased risk of IPV associated with leaving an abusive partner was a consistent outcome.

Perceptions of Neighborhood Safety

As noted earlier, the MTO experiments revealed that moving from a disadvantaged neighborhood to a new location increased the likelihood that the neighborhood would be seen as safe but had no effect on the probability of being involved in violence (Kling et al., 2007). We know from previous analyses that a substantial number of women did not move very far when they changed addresses; in fact, a majority stayed within the same Census tract when they moved. And yet, sociologists have pointed out that perceptions of community safety tend to be highly localized (within blocks of one's home, rather than an entire neighborhood) and that the general tendency is to perceive one's immediate neighborhood to be safe despite empirical evidence to the contrary (reducing cognitive dissonance; Garofalo, 1981). Feminist research, in contrast, stresses that women—who are more apt than men to be victims of sexual violence and IPV—often feel unsafe both in their communities and at home (Stanko, 1985).

Given this literature, we thought it would be useful to investigate whether perceptions of neighborhood safety were influenced by the reasons women gave for moving. Neighborhood safety was measured by asking the women how safe they thought it was for women and children to walk alone at night in their neighborhood. We asked this question every time a woman's address changed so we could compare pre- and postmove assessments. We discovered that, in stark contrast to the MTO experiments, moving generally lowered (not raised) perceptions of neighborhood safety. On the whole, women perceived their new environment to be less safe than their old neighborhood. However, this perception was conditioned by the type of move. Push-outs were substantially more likely to view their new neighborhood as less safe than other type of movers. In fact, perceptions of safety did not markedly change one way or the other for pull-outs or for women who transitioned after release from a facility.

Conclusion

Our study of incarcerated women in Baltimore contributes to the emerging research on neighborhood context and the gendering of violent crime victimization. We found that neighborhood disadvantage is unrelated to women's risk of both partner and nonpartner violence. Although this finding may seem counterintuitive, especially in light of the growing body of research that highlights the association between community disadvantage and IPV (Benson, Wooldredge, Thistlethwaite, & Fox, 2004; Harries & Kovandzic, 1999; Wright & Benson, 2011), we believe it comports well with (1) what we know about our sample and analyses and (2) the prior literature on residential mobility and victimization.

First, the majority of studies that have examined the relationship between neighborhood disadvantage and women's victimization have had a greater dispersion in types of neighborhoods within which they could explore this relationship and they did not look at movement across or within these neighborhoods. We did, and in so doing found that for the women in our sample, mobility within Baltimore was severely restricted and their moves tended to occur within, rather than between, neighborhoods. Our respondents are generally disenfranchised women (single heads of household, unmarried, irregularly employed with low educational attainment), and they tend to live in poorer neighborhoods. And thus when they do move, there is little change in neighborhood conditions. This is especially true for women who are forced, by economics or social conditions, to leave their homes. Even if they move within their current neighborhood tract, they still end up in places that feel less safe. If they leave their neighborhoods, they may also move away from family and other support networks, leaving them with little knowledge of the local area to keep them safe.

Second, these Baltimore women were highly transitory. Simpson and Joseph (2011) reported that 70% of the women moved at least once and 12.3% moved more than four times in a 36-month period. Prior research suggests that this kind of residential instability increases women's risks of violent victimization. Using data from the NCVS, Lauritsen and Schaum (2004) found that residential instability was associated with a greater risk of all types of violent victimizations—stranger, nonstranger, and intimate partner. Lauritsen and Carbone-Lopez (2011) also discovered that both IPV and stranger violence were predicted by a shorter time living in a current home. Using data from Chicago, Sharkey and Sampson (2010) observed that violence of all types increased with residential mobility within the city.

Beyond the constricted range of neighborhoods these women had available to them and the deleterious effects of residential mobility on victimization risk, we also know that many women reported involvement in high-risk activities that increase the likelihood of violent victimization. For instance, they (and their partners) used and sold illicit drugs. A substantial number also participated in the sex trade or other illicit activities (e.g., robbery) to earn income. Often, these activities were the source of arguments with partners—over money or drugs and because of jealously. Thus, the individual-level characteristics of the women and their involvement in illicit activities, coupled with the generally impoverished neighborhoods from which and to which they moved, increase their exposure to violent situations.

In conclusion, the state of knowledge about gender, crime, and neighborhoods is still evolving. Women's experiences—whether they are different from or similar to men's—have yet to take center stage in this literature. In this chapter, we reviewed this literature and then offered a more nuanced understanding of the key relationships using data from a group of high-risk women in Baltimore. Future research should explore the mechanisms of neighborhood disadvantage that place women and men at greater risk for violence and probe more deeply into the kinds of situations and circumstances that give rise to gendered victimization.

NOTE

[1]We gratefully acknowledge the contributions of Mariel Alper (doctoral student) and Patricia Joseph (M.A.), Department of Criminology and Criminal Justice, University of Maryland.

References

Bachman, R., & Saltzman, L. E. (1995). *Violence against women: Estimates from the Redesigned Survey*. BJS Special Report NCJ-154348. Washington DC: U.S. Department of Justice, Office of Justice Programs.

Benson, M. L., Fox, G. L., DeMaris, A., & Van Wyk, J. (2003). Neighborhood disadvantage, individual economic distress and violence against women in intimate relationships. *Journal of Quantitative Criminology, 19,* 207–235.

Benson, M. L., Wooldredge, J., Thistlethwaite, A. B., & Fox, G. L. (2004). The correlation between race and domestic violence is confounded with community context. *Social Problems, 51,* 326–342.

Browning, C. R. (2002). The span of collective efficacy: Extending social disorganization theory to partner violence. *Journal of Marriage and the Family, 64,* 833–850.

Burgess-Proctor, A. (2014). Feminist criminological theory. In G. Bruinsma & D. Weisburd (Eds.), *Encyclopedia of criminology and criminal justice*. New York, NY: Springer-Verlag.

Bursik, R. J. (1988). Social disorganization and theories of crime and delinquency: Problems and prospects. *Criminology, 26,* 519–552.

Cunradi, C. B., Caetano, R., Clark, C., & Schaefer, J. (2000). Neighborhood poverty as a predictor of intimate partner violence among White, Black and Hispanic couples in the United States: A multilevel analysis. *Annals of Epidemiology, 10,* 297–308.

Daly, K. (1992). Women's pathways to felony court: Feminist theories of lawbreaking and problems of representation. *Southern California Review of Law and Women's Studies, 2,* 11–52.

Garofalo, J. (1981). The fear of crime: Causes and consequences. *Journal of Criminal Law and Criminology, 72,* 839–857.

Hamberger, K., & Guse, C. (2005). Typology of reactions to intimate partner violence among men and women arrested for partner violence. *Violence and Victims, 20,* 117–129.

Harrell, E. (2012). *Violent victimization committed by strangers, 1993–2010*. Special Report BJS NCJ-239424. Washington, DC: U.S. Department of Justice, Office of Justice Programs.

Harries, K., & Kovandzic, E. (1999). Persistence, intensity, and areal extent of violence against women: Baltimore City, 1992 to 1995. *Violence Against Women, 5,* 813–828.

Hipp, J. R. (2010). The role of crime in housing unit racial/ethnic transition. *Criminology, 48,* 683–723.

Horney, J., Ferrero, K., Gartner, R., Kruttschnitt, C., & Simpson, S. S. (1999). *Women's experience of violence: Victimization and offending in the context of women's lives*. Project funded by National Consortium on Violence Research. Pittsburgh, PA: National Consortium on Violence Research.

Johnson, M. P. (2008). *A typology of domestic violence*. Boston, MA: Northeastern University Press.

Jones, N. (2010). *Between good and ghetto. African American girls and inner-city violence.* New Brunswick, NJ: Rutgers University Press.

Kling, J. R., Liebman, J. B., & Katz, L. F. (2007). Experimental analysis of neighborhood effects. *Econometrica, 75,* 83–119.

Kling, J. R., Ludwig, J., & Katz, L. F. (2005). Neighborhood effects on crime for female and male youth: Evidence from a randomized housing voucher experiment. *Quarterly Journal of Economics, 120,* 87–130.

Lauritsen, J. L., & Carbone-Lopez, K. (2011). Gender differences in risk factors for violent victimization: An examination of individual-, family-, and community-level predictors. *Journal of Research in Crime and Delinquency, 48,* 538–565.

Lauritsen, J. L., & Schaum, R. J. (2004). The social ecology of violence against women. *Criminology, 42,* 323–357.

Maher, L. (1997). *Sexed work: Gender, race, and resistance in a Brooklyn drug market.* Oxford, UK: Clarendon Press.

Maimon, D., & Browning, C. R. (2010). Unstructured socializing, collective efficacy, and violent behavior among urban youth. *Criminology, 48,* 443–474.

Maimon, D., & Browning, C. R. (2012). Adolescents' violent victimization in the neighborhood. *British Journal of Criminology, 52,* 808–833.

Miles-Doan, R. (1998). Violence between spouses and intimates: Does neighborhood context matter? *Social Forces, 77,* 623–645.

Miller, E. M. (1986). *Street woman.* Philadelphia, PA: Temple University Press.

Miller, J. (2008). *Getting played: African American girls, urban inequality, and gendered violence.* New York: New York University Press.

O'Campo, P., Gielen, A. C., Faden, R. R., Xue, X., Kass, N., & Wang, M. C. (1995) Violence by male partners against women during the child bearing year: A contextual analysis. *American Journal of Public Health, 85,* 1092–1097.

Pearlman, D. N., Zierler, S., Gjelsvik, A., & Verhoek-Oftedahl, W. (2003) Neighborhood environment, racial position and risk of police-reported domestic violence: A contextual analysis. *Public Health Reports, 118,* 44–58.

Pinchevsky, G., & Wright, E. M. (2012). The impact of neighborhoods on intimate partner violence and victimization. *Trauma, Violence and Abuse, 13,* 112–132.

Potter, H. (2006). An argument for Black feminist criminology: Understanding African American women's experiences with intimate partner violence using an integrated approach. *Feminist Criminology, 1,* 106–124.

Raghavan, C., Mennerich, A., Sexton, E., & James, S. E. (2006). Community violence and its direct, indirect, and mediating effects on intimate partner violence. *Violence Against Women, 12,* 1132–1149.

Sampson, R. J. (2012). *Great American city: Chicago and the enduring neighborhood effect.* Chicago, IL: University of Chicago Press.

Sampson, R. J., & Lauritsen, J. L. (1994). Violent victimization and offending. In A. J. Reiss, Jr., & Jeffrey A. Roth (Eds.), *Understanding and preventing violence* (Vol. 3). *Social influences* (pp. 1–114). National Research Council. Washington, DC: National Academies Press.

Sampson, R. J., Morenoff, J. D., & Gannon-Rowley, T. (2002). Assessing "neighborhood effects": Social processes and new directions in research. *Annual Review of Sociology, 28,* 443–478.

Sampson, R. J., Morenoff, J. D., & Raudenbush, S. (2005). Social anatomy of racial and ethnic disparities in violence. *American Journal of Public Health, 95,* 224–232.

Sampson, R. J., Raudenbush, S. W., & Earls, F. (1997). Neighborhoods and violent crime: A multilevel study of collective efficacy. *Science, 227,* 918–923.

Sharkey, P., & Sampson, R. J. (2010). Destination effects: Residential mobility and trajectories of adolescent violence in a stratified metropolis. *Criminology, 48,* 639–681.

Shaw, C. R., & McKay, H. D. (1942). *Juvenile delinquency and urban areas.* Chicago, IL: University of Chicago Press.

Shaw, C. R., & McKay, H. D. (1969). *Juvenile delinquency and urban areas* (Rev. ed.). Chicago, IL: University of Chicago Press.

Simpson, S. S., & Joseph, P. (2011). *Women on the move: Neighborhoods, mobility, and violence.* Paper presented at the Annual Meeting of the American Society of Criminology, Washington, DC.

Slocum, L. A., Simpson, S. S., & Smith, D. A. (2005). Strained lives and crime: Examining intra-individual variation in strain and offending in a sample of women. *Criminology, 43,* 1067–1110.

Stanko, E. A. (1985). *Intimate intrusions.* London, UK: Routledge & Kegan Paul.

Van Wyk, J. A., Benson, M. L., Fox, G. L., & DeMaris, A. (2003). Detangling individual-, partner-, and community-level correlates of partner violence. *Crime and Delinquency, 49,* 412–438.

Wilcox Rountree, P., & Warner, B. D. (1999). Social ties and crime: Is the relationship gendered? *Criminology, 37,* 789–814.

Wright, E. M. (2012). The relationship between social support and intimate partner violence in neighborhood context. *Crime and Delinquency.* Advance online publication. doi:0011128712466890.

Wright, E. M., & Benson, M. L. (2011). Clarifying the effects of neighborhood context on violence "behind closed doors." *Justice Quarterly, 28,* 775–798.

Xie, M., & McDowall, D. (2010). The reproduction of racial inequality: How crime affects housing turnover. *Criminology, 48,* 865–896.

Zimmerman, G. M., & Messner, S. F. (2010). Neighborhood context and the gender gap in adolescent violent crime. *American Sociological Review, 75,* 958–980.

PART V

Key Theoretical Issues

CHAPTER 12

Can the Gender Gap in Offending Be Explained?

Jennifer Schwartz and Darrell Steffensmeier

Why do women commit less crime than men? Is this still true in today's day and age? In current news stories, popular books, movies or television, and other information sources, we are told that women today are drinking more alcohol and doing it more frequently, more often getting into physical fights and otherwise in-flicting greater violence on others, and stealing or embezzling large sums of money, *just like men*. The typical story will reference a female increase or epidemic and draw on recent cultural exemplars before making broad claims about the *new* female offender.

A recent example is Martha Stewart, who has been described as the quintessen-tial 21st-century female offender, a powerful businesswoman led astray by power and greed. There are abundant examples of exceptional female criminals who gained a real niche in crime, both historically and today. Marm Mandelbaum, a prominent dealer in stolen goods in New York City in the 1850s–1860s, is arguably the most successful fence in U.S. history. As we explain later, notwithstanding her prominence in media accounts and current criminology textbooks, Martha Stewart is hardly in the same mold as Marm. Instead, Stewart profited very little and at best was only a minor player in the insider-trading conspiracy in which she was alleged to be involved.

Implicit or even explicit in these story lines is the potentially problematic "dark side" of gender equality. That is, as gender role "traditionalism" decreases or as women gain economic and political power, might they inevitably become more motivated and have greater opportunities to engage in serious crimes? To answer such questions requires a broader understanding of the sorts of factors that contrib-ute to historical gender differences in crime.

Criminologists have long recognized the existence of this *gender gap in offending*. When criminologists talk about the *gender gap,* they usually are referring to the differences in criminality between women and men.[1] Academics, policy makers, and the general public are curious to know whether their stereotypes of women offenders as victims acting in self-defense, as sneakier suspects who get away with it more, or as deviant women who buck gender norms are true. Of course, it is not that simple. Female crime is a complex phenomenon, as is men's crime, requiring complex *multivariate* explanations.

Another recurrent intellectual theme inquires whether women are committing more crime these days. Some are prone to think girls and women drink more, fight a lot now or more viciously, and steal larger sums of money from places of work. Many wonder whether advances of modern women have allowed women to "catch up" with men in terms of criminal offending or otherwise changed female offending patterns to be more similar to those of males. But what social factors generated a gender gap in offending to begin with? And what similarities or differences are there in female and male offending?

Scientifically, the gender gap in crime is an important topic because sex has one of the strongest connections with the likelihood of committing crime. And, gender is now understood to shape how, where, and why women and men carry out their offenses. This makes the gender gap in offending an important social fact to understand to better prevent crime. Better solutions to male offending may inhere in greater understanding of the factors that prevent more females from engaging in crime. A firm understanding of the social factors that contribute to the gender gap in criminal offending also is necessary to understand and predict change in the historical gender–crime relationship.

In this chapter, we first describe the gender gap in criminal offending and its variability across type of offense and other important factors. Then we set about to understand the origins of the gender gap in offending. To explain the gender gap, we draw on a middle-range theoretical approach that incorporates various sociological and criminological perspectives and draws on relevant empirical literature that pertains to gender and crime. The gendered paradigm of offending considers sex similarities and differences in women's and men's focal concerns, risk preferences, and crime opportunities as primary drivers of the crime gender gap. This perspective considers both preferences and willingness to commit crime as well as opportunities to do so. Finally, we consider whether the gender gap in offending is currently narrowing or what future direction it might take.

Notably, the gender gap in offending—including its size, its nature, and its possibly changing status—was at the core of Freda Adler's (1975) *Sisters in Crime.* Adler invited scholars to explore how the gendered nature of social roles and opportunities might shape participation in criminal behavior. Although her conclusions about the narrowing of the gender gap and the significance of gender equality as a main "cause" of change were overdrawn, her insights nonetheless contributed to sustained research on gender and crime in the ensuing decades.

The Gender Gap in Criminal Offending: What Needs to Be Explained?

Multiple data sources provide information on female offending and the gender gap. For example, the UCR program provides annual arrest statistics by sex for a variety of offense categories (e.g., homicide, theft, drinking/drugs). Other major sources, such as victimization surveys and self-report surveys, provide information about various forms of street or conventional crimes. A third source includes field and case studies as well as task force reports that provide information about criminal enterprises and crime organizations that is not available in UCR arrest statistics or other major traditional sources of crime data. To learn about a variety of serious forms of criminality that comprise the broader criminal landscape—such as corporate crime and arms smuggling—it is essential to look beyond the UCR and other traditional data sources. We will have more to say about these sources later.

Together, the above-mentioned sources show that the gender gap in crime is near universal: Throughout recorded history, for virtually all societies and subgroups and for nearly every crime category, females offend less than males. That is, fewer women than men offend and women tend to offend at lower rates than men for nearly all crime categories. The striking fact is that in the United States this past year, for example, 9 of 10 killers (or robbers) were men. In the largest corporate financial scandals, like those conspiracies associated with the financial collapse around 2009 and the ongoing Great Recession, almost 9 of 10 white-collar corporate criminals were male. When it comes to the most serious violent and lucrative property offenses, the gender gap tends to be rather large.

Yet there also are some perhaps surprising similarities across the two sexes. For example, nearly as many women as men drink alcohol, experiment with marijuana, and take prescription drugs in ways not prescribed. Further, almost as many girls as boys shoplift each year, and data indicate that females embezzle from work or other organizations nearly as often as men do. Women engage in minor violence almost as often as men, particularly when it comes to violence that is less injurious or occurs in more private settings. And prostitution has long been the purview of women. So, the gender gap can also be characterized as small to nonexistent when one considers lesser offenses.

The gender gap in offending is larger for more serious offenses and, as indicated above, narrower or even nonexistent for minor behaviors. These are among the most robust and consistent findings in criminology (Schwartz, Steffensmeier, Zhong, & Ackerman, 2009; Steffensmeier & Allan, 1996). And these findings seem to apply across subgroups in society, places, and historical time periods. In the United States, for example, the size of the gender gap and its tendency to vary with offense seriousness are similar among Whites, Blacks, and Hispanics. Studies on gender and crime in other nations demonstrate similar patterning and size of the gender gap for different types of offenses (Schwartz, 2014). We will return to the matter of change in the gender gap over time. Suffice it to say, for a long time in many places, men have substantially outnumbered women among society's most serious offenders.

Findings that show men have greater and more serious involvement in antisocial or health-averse behaviors are not confined to criminology. For example, studies of health-related behaviors (e.g., heavy drinking/alcoholism, suicide, accidental drowning) and traffic safety (e.g., fatalities/accidents/risky driving, seatbelt compliance, road rage) all show that men engage in dangerous or lethal behaviors more than women. Therefore, it is critical to address the question: *Why are there such profound gender differences in serious crime?*

At the same time, it is important not to ignore that, regardless of sex, most offending is of a minor nature. For example, the large majority (nearly three quarters) of both female and male offenders are arrested for drunk driving, larceny-theft, drug offenses, misdemeanor assault, public disorder, harassment, or criminal mischief (Schwartz & Steffensmeier, 2007). Female rates are lower for most of these offenses, with females being about one of every four or five drug, driving under the influence, or simple assault arrestees. However, female rates are nearly equal to male rates for larceny-theft, fraud, and embezzlement. Because the majority of crimes are lesser offenses, the majority of female and male crimes tend to be similar. Female and male offenders share similar background characteristics, including histories of abuse or other victimization, disadvantaged living circumstances, and poor educational and economic opportunities. Therefore, it is also *critical to address the marked gender similarity with more subtle gender differences when it comes to minor offenses.*

A second important and robust aspect of the gender–crime relationship is the concentration of women offenders in sex work versus that of males in sexual predation (e.g., sexual assault, abuse, pimping, or sex trafficking). Power differentials between women and men are starkly reflected in such crimes. Prostitution is perhaps the only offense for which women outnumber men, according to arrest statistics, yet this may speak more to U.S. society's *regulation* of women's sexuality compared to men's. Sexuality and romantic relationships are important pathways for women's entry and roles played in crime and in the criminal enterprise, yet these also tend to be limiting factors to female ascension in the criminal underworld. Premiums are placed on sexual attractiveness and youthfulness—advantages that tend to decline with age; by contrast, men's criminal capital tends to accrue with age and experience. Notably, women may sometimes be involved in more lucrative aspects of the sex trade as owners or managers, but the business end tends to be dominated by male entrepreneurs. And, of course, sexual abuse and sexual assault remain a threat or tool for female oppression. So, the gender gap is large for rape and sexual assault but the opposite for sex work.

A third important, yet understudied, aspect of the gender–crime relationship is men's predominance in more organized and professional criminal enterprises, which have the potential to be more lucrative and inflict more harm. There tend to be fewer women in organized criminal enterprises than in looser, less professional offending groups (Steffensmeier, 1983; Steffensmeier & Terry, 1986; Steffensmeier & Ulmer, 2005). Particularly in crimes organized for joint economic gain, sex segregation in offender groups is extensive. Most crime groups are composed of all males, or women are in the minority. There are far fewer crimes committed by groups of all females compared to all-male or mixed-sex groups, especially for larger scale property crimes or more violent offenses. Moreover, evidence suggests that when females are included in street gangs, economic corporate conspiracies, robbery groups, burglary rings, human trafficking networks, or drug trafficking enterprises, their participation tends to be marginal, derived from female-typical roles or gendered behavioral expectations, and compensated at a much lower rate, net their less central participation. Women in crime groups tend to be accomplices, are unlikely to share equally in the rewards, and may be called upon to use their sexuality or femininity to accomplish the crime, casting them in marginal roles (Steffensmeier, Schwartz, & Roche, 2013; Steffensmeier & Terry, 1986). Women sometimes do lead or play central roles in complex or highly organized schemes, and, of course, some women can and do engage in violent crimes with others using very physical means, but these instances are statistically more rare.

Importantly, whether women are included in the crime group depends in part on the tactics required and the environment in which the crime is to be carried out. The tendency toward in-group preferences (or out-group antipathy) and the reliance on sex typing in assessing the capabilities of potential female crime partners will be more intense when there is greater risk or environmental uncertainty, when force or fear rather than stealth or fraud is the modus operandi to accomplish the crime, when the group is organized for profit-oriented reasons, and when the group's organization is more complex and professionalized. In such circumstances, women are unlikely to be perceived as having attributes useful to the commission of the crime, or women are used in sex-typed ways that seem most efficient and effective to the enterprise. Thus, an important variation to understand in the gender gap is women's lower representation in more organized or professional forms of offending as well as their greater marginalization toward ancillary, marginal roles.

In summary, there are three exceptionally important nuances of the gender–crime relationship that must be well understood to address the question: Can the gender gap in offending be explained?

First, the gender gap is wider for more serious offenses but narrows as the offense becomes more common or less serious. Most crime is of the less serious nature, so the female and male offending populations share many similar background characteristics and motivators. Male involvement is much greater in society's most harmful crimes—that is, those that are: (1) lethal or entail threat to life and limb (e.g., murder, rape, kidnapping, genocide); (2) lucrative, involving greater financial or property loss; (3) undermining of the political or social order (e.g., corporate financial fraud conspiracies, local racketeering, and corruption); or (4) involving organized crime or networks (e.g., mafia, gangs, transnational crime organizations that smuggle arms, humans, drugs, counterfeit goods).

Second, sex work figures prominently in female criminal careers, whereas sexual predation is far more common among males. Sexuality provides entry into offending and is an important tool for women in executing (more serious or persistent) crimes. Sexual assault or victimization is a potent male tool of control.

Third, more lucrative or violent, professional, or organized forms of crime favor males but marginalize females' participation and roles in criminal enterprises. Female offending is more individualistic. Thus, women tend to be solo offenders or co-offenders in small, nonpermanent partnerships or to be temporary low-level operatives in more long-running criminal enterprises (e.g., drug distribution networks, human smuggling rings).

Understanding the Gender Gap in Offending: Traditional Theoretical Approaches

Although most theories of crime were developed by male criminologists with male offenders in mind, such traditional general theories seem also to apply to female offenders. Early evidence showed that women's and men's crime rates tended to parallel each other, so when male crime went up, female crime went up, and in places where male crime rates were high, female rates were also relatively high. This suggests the main sources of crime might overlap for females and males. Whereas traditional theories might have accounted for gender similarities, it was unclear whether gender-neutral theories would be useful to understanding gender differences. If gender-neutral factors influence the criminal behavior of both sexes, the gender gap would result from some balance of (1) *different exposure* of females to crime-causing risk factors versus crime-preventing protective factors and (2) *different effects* of risk factors on female versus male offending. We briefly review how major general crime theories have been applied to understand the gender gap in serious crime.

Approaches like anomie theory and conflict theory suggest that structural factors such as poverty and inequality, particularly in the face of societal emphasis on success and profits, underlie much of conventional crime. Consistent with these approaches, both male and female criminals come disproportionately from the ranks of the poor and disadvantaged. The main mechanism proposed in anomie theory is strain related to life circumstances. Earlier examinations using strain-based approaches would explain the gender gap in crime as a consequence of lesser strain experienced by women or, more commonly, the predominance of familial goals and lesser relevance of success and profit goals to women compared to men. More current strain approaches suggest that females and males may experience similar levels and types of strain, but express the effects differently. For example, females are more prone to internalize their problems and experience depression or other mental health problems, whereas males tend to externalize their problems, including in delinquent, violent, or criminal ways (Broidy & Agnew, 1997; Giordano, Schroeder, & Cernkovich, 2007).

Social process approaches such as differential association theory and labeling theory tend to explain conventional crime in terms of differential opportunities for the learning of criminal values and skills or in terms of self-fulfilling prophecy effects of labels imposed by social control processes. Such theories would explain the gender gap as a consequence of lower access by females to criminal learning opportunities or the greater consistency between male stereotypes and negative behavioral labels. Empirical research has consistently found that males have greater exposure to delinquent peers who provide motives and opportunities for crime and also that peers have a stronger impact on boys' than girls' offending (Faris & Felmlee, 2011; McCarthy, Felmlee, & Hagan, 2004; Mears, Ploeger, & Warr, 1998).

Control theory argues that weak social bonds account for much crime. Consistent with this approach, both male and female delinquents and criminals come disproportionately from families with abuse or neglect histories, have lower levels of academic achievement, or exhibit other evidence of having weak stakes in conformity. The gender gap would be explained by greater female socialization toward bonding behavior as well as closer monitoring of girls' behavior. Girls tend to have warmer, closer relationships with their families, which lead them to internalize conformity norms to a greater extent. As another important aspect of control theory, girls tend to be monitored more closely by family, with earlier curfews and more restrictions than their brothers (Booth, Farrell, & Varano, 2008; Bottcher, 2001).

Social disorganization and other place-based theories of offending investigate how negative social conditions impede informal social control, community organization efforts, and other social ties. Many of the place characteristics have similar effects on female and male crime rates, but some have moderately stronger effects on males, partially accounting for the gender gap (Schwartz, 2006; Steffensmeier & Haynie, 2000). That is, females may be more resilient to their social conditions or males may have a stronger tendency toward criminal adaptation to their social environment.

Although existing theories help understand female and male crime at a general level and each explains some part of the gender gap, they are less adept at explaining a number of persistent differences between female and male offending patterns. As previously described, females commit less serious crimes, whether against persons or property, and are less likely to participate in or to lead criminal groups. When involved with others, women typically act as accomplices to males, who both organize and lead the execution of crime; more organized and highly lucrative crimes are dominated overwhelmingly by males (Daly, 1989; Steffensmeier, 1983; Steffensmeier & Ulmer, 2005).

Additionally, females are far more likely than males to be motivated by relational concerns and to require a higher level of provocation before turning to crime. Situational pressures such as threatened loss of valued relationships or the need to help out a loved one play a greater role in female offending. The role of men in initiating women into crime—especially serious crime—is a consistent finding across research (Caputo, 2008; Miller, 1986; Steffensmeier & Terry, 1986). Similarly, "doing crime for one's kids or family" plays a greater role in female than male offending (Daly, 1994; Steffensmeier, 1983). Such findings also suggest that women are not necessarily less risk oriented than men, but that women's risk taking is less prone to lawbreaking and more protective of relationships and emotional commitments.

Further, although many factors are as predictive of female as of male offending, female offenders are more likely to have been victims of sexual abuse as children or adults, and they are more likely to have had records of neurological and other psychological problems (e.g., depression, substance abuse) (Belknap & Holsinger, 2006). Female felons nevertheless tend to be more conventional in other aspects of their life. Specifically, they are more likely to have greater responsibilities for children, commitment to education or job training, and legitimate sources of income and are thus more amenable to rehabilitation or reform (Daly, 1994; Steffensmeier, Kramer, & Streifel, 1993). These and other differences in female and male offending patterns often involve subtle issues of context that are not well explained by other theories and that are nearly invisible to quantitative analysis.

Not expressly taken into account by the general theories of crime are insights from recent feminist writings and perspectives about the profound significance of sex and gender in shaping human existence and behavior, including crime and the gender gap. These insights include the significance of gendered power relations, most notably, the impact of male power and oppression; the significance of "sexed" and "physical" bodies in shaping gender relations and opportunities; and the significance of gender in structuring "thinkable courses of action and identities" (Daly, 2006, p. 211). Highlighted as a central feature in our *gendered framework* discussed next, these and other aspects of gender and sexual stratification have even greater significance in the illegitimate than in the legitimate realms.

Understanding the Gender Gap in Offending: A Gendered Approach

A gendered approach recognizes the utility of general crime theories in identifying factors that increase the risk of criminal involvement (e.g., lack of control, differential association, strain). These theories, however, are limited because they do not take into account—as does a gendered approach—the ways in which profound differences in the lives of women and men shape the different patterns of female and male serious offending. The general crime theories thus shed little light on the specific ways in which gender differences in the type, frequency, and context of criminal behavior are shaped by differences in the lives of men and women. Most importantly, a gendered approach can address the large gender differences that exist for certain types of offenses—more violent, lucrative, or organized offenses—and can address other nuances of the gender–crime relationship. Yet a gendered approach also is quite different from gender-specific theories that propose that the causes of and pathways into crime are distinctly different for males and females. Indeed, a gendered theory ought to be useful for understanding and explaining both female *and* male offending.

We apply to criminality some key insights from sociological and feminist writings on gender. Gender operates at various levels to influence individual identities and behaviors, interactions among individuals, and even organizational processes or properties that affect sex-specific aggregate crime rates. For the individual, gender socialization is a potent source of one's sense of self and strongly shapes what behaviors or pathways are thought of as possible. Gender socialization is ongoing and the content changes with age, so one's "gendered self" may evolve or change over time. Gender is also composed of culturally agreed upon dimensions that are flexible, depending in part on the particular situational dynamics. Actors "do gender"—or behave in one of several culturally scripted ways to demonstrate (accentuate or down-play) gender—when interacting with others. These everyday actions in which gender is "accomplished" create and maintain gender (West & Zimmerman, 1987). Relevant here are self and others' notions of gender-appropriate actions or interactions, par-ticularly regarding deviance and crime. Finally, gender operates at a level much larger than the individual or even small group. Sex stratification is a prominent feature of social and economic life, characterizing families, economic labor markets, politics and government, the military, and so forth. The sex distribution within each of these institutions shapes the criminal opportunities of females and males.

We also draw on notions of power and control, which undergird feminist thought. Physical sex differences and historical power arrangements are such that males have tended to exert dominance over females. Sometimes this is expressed in paternalistic, protective ways, whereas in other instances, power, coercion, or physi-cal might is exercised by men on women. This understanding is implicit in our gen-dered approach. Nevertheless, we recognize that women and men exercise some measure of agency in the choices they make, which contributes to individual-level differences in outcomes.

Choice has to do with evaluating actions or options for satisfying values or desir-able ends, such as happiness or fulfillment, improved economic well-being or social status, physical or material security, or drive for excitement. Although values or ends exist within some hierarchy, the opportunity for an individual to exercise unfettered choice is unrealistic because persons typically must seek their ends in a world of limited means and through the instrumentality of an organized group. Choices are structured by not only internal limits (e.g., aspirations, moral concerns) but also external limits (e.g., physical and material means) that together shape the thinkable courses of actions as to what is likely or possible versus unlikely or impossible. People also take into account whether their choices produced the expected results as well as consequences of prior choices. Objective conditions are relevant in making judgments about possible courses of action, including the decision to engage in crime or deviance. The objective conditions pertain not only to external social fac-tors (e.g., time, energy, requisite skill, access to suitable co-offenders), but also to physical and biological facts (e.g., sexuality, physicality). Consequently, a give and take occurs in which individuals sacrifice some values or ends to satisfy others.[2]

Gender powerfully shapes, but does not determine, those courses of action that people see as possible or rewarding. Theoretical frameworks devised for the study of crime and deviance, and of female deviance specifically, ought to reveal how people take both subjective and objective conditions into account for making judgments about deviance by themselves and others. This pertains not only to external social facts but also to physical and biological facts. The framework we present next seeks to do that.

Our perspective considers how both motives and opportunities for crime are influenced by gender (Steffensmeier & Allan 1996; Steffensmeier et al., 2013). Gender differences in crime may be better understood by taking into account gender differences in (1) focal concerns and risk preferences and (2) access to criminal opportunity.

Gendered Focal Concerns and Risk Preferences

Gender differences in orientations toward crime stem largely from differing focal concerns ascribed to women and men. Norms disapproving of female deviance and crime originate from two focal concerns ascribed to women: nurturant role obligations encouraging the centrality of social relationships and cooperative, communalistic orientations; and female beauty and sexual or moral virtue. In contrast, the lesser taboos against male crime stem largely from focal concerns ascribed to men: individualistic orientations stressing autonomy and dominance or control; status and achievement in the public sphere combined with provider and protector role obligations in the private sphere encouraging competitiveness, decisiveness, and risk taking; and sexual access to and success with women. These focal concerns function as overarching cognitive schemas that shape gender ideologies, identities, and action and contribute to gender differences in moral orientations, in individual and collective identity, in risk preferences, and in femininity and masculinity imperatives. Gendered focal concerns also shape and are shaped by social interactions (i.e., doing gender) by guiding expectations and appraisals of others and self with regard to risk-taking and criminal behavior (Steffensmeier & Allan, 1996; West & Zimmerman, 1987). Behaviors—and potential behaviors—are accountable to and assessed by sex category.

Women are also restrained from engaging in seriously injurious criminal behavior because they are more likely to be socialized to an ethic of care—that is, to be more responsive to others' needs and to preserve family connections, traditions, and identities (Gilligan, 1982). Concern for others also manifests in women's greater reluctance to engage in behaviors that are clearly harmful to others. Overall, feminine cooperative behavior runs counter to lawbreaking. Men, on the other hand, are conditioned toward status seeking and socialized to be more independent and competitive. Thus, the separation between what is *feminine* and what is *criminal* is sharp, whereas the dividing line between what is *masculine* and what is "illegal" is often narrow. Although male sex role norms do not proscribe crime, risk taking and defying social convention are qualities more admired in men than in women. The saying is "boys will be boys," not "girls will be girls!" Whereas crime can be a resource for men to accomplish masculinity and increase status among peers, particularly in social locations lacking conventional means for economic success, it is hard to imagine that engaging in most crimes enhances femininity (Daly, 2006). By extension, men find it easier than women to justify illegal wrongdoing because law-violating behavior, especially for status-seeking or financial reasons, is more compatible with male focal concerns. Stereotypical masculine qualities align not only with committing business frauds, for example, but also with actions that might precipitate the fraud such as engaging in risky financial ventures or bad business deals and gambling, drinking, or sexual affairs.

Gendered focal concerns influence motivational and contextual differences in crime by contributing to gender-specific risk preferences and risk-taking styles and gendered responses to stress. The centrality of relational concerns to women shapes their law-violating behavior and allows them to be pulled into criminal involvements by men in their lives. Women are not less amenable to risk; rather their risk-taking tends to violate the law less and be more protective of emotional commitments. Women may take greater risks to establish or sustain valued relationships, whereas males take greater risks for status, power, monetary gain, or competitive advantage (Haynie, Steffensmeier, & Bell, 2007; Steffensmeier & Allan, 1996). Gendered focal concerns and risk preferences are reproduced in group and organizational settings.

Access to Criminal Opportunity

Access to criminal opportunity (e.g., skills, criminal associates, and settings) is strongly stratified by sex. Criminal opportunity presents itself or may be sought out in relation to our social networks, work settings, organizations or groups of which we are a part, and the routines of daily life (Steffensmeier, 1983, 1986; Steffensmeier & Ulmer, in press). Each of these contexts is strongly gendered and provides unique opportunities for crime. Two distinct opportunity structures are important for understanding female offending: (1) informal social networks and social processes that restrict and shape female access to criminal learning and performance structures (*opportunity via network access*); and (2) formal access making one situationally available or suitably located to participate in a scheme (*opportunity via situational position*) (Steffensmeier & Ulmer, in press).

Linkages exist between underworld and upperworld processes of *institutional sexism* and *homosocial reproduction* that exclude women from male networks, including those that carry out crime, and restrict criminally involved women to sex-typed roles. Institutional sexism—rules, prejudices, and stereotypes associated with gender, race, or other social characteristics—helps or hinders a person's potential enactment of various social roles. Any person who aspires to a role, whether criminal or noncriminal, will be restricted by the social definition of his or her preexisting status (Lemert, 1951). Through *homosocial reproduction*, or "like chooses like," sexism and male domination in the underworld—and in the upperworld—are perpetuated, particularly in more lucrative, high-risk arenas (Steffensmeier, 1983, 1986). Gender shapes opportunities for developing legitimate and illegitimate social networks within social groups, alliances with others, and organizations, lessening women's opportunities to form strong networks and develop trust among associates that facilitate collusion to carry out and cover up more dangerous, complex, or continual schemes.

Steffensmeier (1983, 1986) was the first to theorize about the role of sex segregation in the underworld as a framework for explaining the gender gap in crime and then offered support for it by way of qualitative interviews with a variety of male thieves and hustlers. Since then, an abundance of qualitative studies have built on Steffensmeier's seminal work on sex segregation in the underworld, documenting men's sexism toward women in economically driven crime networks that has limited and shaped female criminal involvement (e.g., Maher & Daly, 1996; Miller, 2001; Steffensmeier & Terry, 1986; Zhang, Chin, & Miller, 2007; see reviews in Miller, 2010; ; Schwartz, Conover-Williams, Clemons, forthcoming; Steffensmeier & Ulmer, in press).

The research supports Steffensmeier and Ulmer's assertion (2005): "Sex-segregation in the underworld . . . powerfully inhibits women's access to illicit-business work roles and in large part effectively forecloses their participation as high-level operators" (p. 221). Among men involved in illicit pursuits, women are seen as less likely to have criminal capital or valued traits and competencies, including trustworthiness, criminal capabilities, nerve to carry out the scheme, worthwhile social connections, and the mettle or ambition to profit highly. Not only are women less likely to be recruited for involvement in criminal schemes, but also they are less able to recruit others should they wish to orchestrate an illegal scheme. Opportunity via network access is restricted by gendered interactional processes.

However, women are not excluded entirely from serious crime and some women undoubtedly play important roles in criminal enterprise. Many underworld operators, although professing a preference not to work with females, sometimes have done so. Men are more likely to commit crimes with a woman in the following situations: (1) when a romantic or close personal *relationship* exists, (2) when an exceptional female has carved out a *niche* in the underworld, or (3) when there was *utility* in deploying a female for safety or profitability, such as where women create less suspicion, have access to helpful information or specialized skills, attract a more willing or less fearful clientele, or prevent missing out on a good opportunity when male accomplices are not available.

In one instructive example from Maher and Daly's (1996) ethnographic work on the hierarchy of an urban crack-cocaine drug market, women were rarely utilized as street-level sellers, more often playing lower level or offshoot roles (e.g., middle-women between male customers from outside the neighborhood and ethnic male drug dealers; sellers of condoms, clean works, sex work). However, when police presence was high, such as during crack-down periods, more women were employed because of their greater utility as street-level sellers (e.g., aroused lesser police suspicion) or were used as temporary fill-ins for recently incarcerated male operatives. Even so, women were compensated less than male dealers and, despite women's reliable work, they were still perceived by male dealers as unreliable, untrustworthy, and incapable of effectively conveying a threat. Maher and Daly concluded that the most important factor contributing to the observed patterns was underworld institutionalized sexism (p. 484).

Also consistent with Steffensmeier's theoretical framing, Zhang et al. (2007) interviewed 129 China-to-U.S. human smugglers about their involvement and found key differences in the extent of involvement and roles of women and men in criminal enterprise because of gender stratification in illicit enterprise. They concluded that gender stratification within illicit settings had created market niches, which some women could use to their advantage. Although human smuggling was predominantly male, women were more prevalent in roles or networks when opportunities arose from gendered assumptions that women smugglers would be more caring and prioritize the well-being of their clients, when risk of violence or detection was low, and when their actions could be rationalized in a way consistent with gendered expectations (e.g., as an altruistic act for family or friends).

Limits on female access to legitimate opportunities put further constraints on their criminal opportunities because women are less likely to hold jobs such as truck driver, dockworker, or carpenter that would provide opportunities for large-scale theft, drug dealing, fencing, and other illegal activities. In contrast, abundant opportunities exist for women to commit or to be caught and arrested for petty forms of theft and fraud, for low-level drug dealing, and sex-for-sale offenses. The scarcity of women in the top ranks of business and politics limits their chance for involvement in price-fixing conspiracies, financial fraud, and corruption (Steffensmeier et al., 2013). Like the upperworld, the underworld has its glass ceiling. If anything, women face even greater occupational segregation in underworld crime groups—whether syndicates or more loosely structured organizations (Steffensmeier, 1983; Steffensmeier & Ulmer, 2005). Just as in the legitimate world, women face discrimination at every stage, from selection and recruitment to opportunities for mentoring, skill development, and, especially, rewards.

Applying the Gendered Paradigm to Corporate Financial Fraud

Women in the United States have made some monumental gains at work. Women now comprise at least half the labor force and more women today are middle and upper managers in corporate America. It would seem opportunities now abound for women to engage in serious corporate crimes. In an article in the *American Sociological Review* (Steffensmeier et al., 2013), we drew out the implications of our gendered paradigm for understanding women's and men's corporate financial fraud involvement. We studied serious accounting malpractices like securities fraud, insider trading, and Ponzi schemes in America's public companies to find out just how involved women were in these conspiracies. The Corporate Fraud Task Force indicted 436 individuals involved in 83 such schemes during July 2002 to 2009. We read and recorded information from indictments and other documents or reports that described who was involved and what they did.

Based on the gendered paradigm, we expected women's corporate crime involvement to be much lower and more marginal than male involvement because women may be more averse to risky financial ventures, to abusing positions of organizational power, and to winning at all costs in economic matters and also because women may hold fewer top-level corporate positions that are conducive to illegal collusion or because they are excluded by male colleagues from crime groups and less able to recruit suitable partners to direct a conspiracy. In short, we predicted a large gender gap not only in traditional street crimes but also in corporate crime.

Gendered Focal Concerns and Risk Preferences

Women's ethical orientations act as controls or deterrents to corporate wrongdoing. Women tend to "do business" in ways that carry concern about environmental impacts and bring a more ethical perspective to the workplace (Beutel & Marini, 1995; Kodinsky, 2010). Corporate women more often than men use their organizational power to address issues of social responsibility and are more inclined than men to a business mind-set of making people a priority, not just profits (O'Fallon & Butterfield, 2005). Female executives tend to score more positively on measures of socialization, self-control, empathy, social involvement, and integrity (Collins, 1999).

Masculine focal concerns emphasizing competition and achievement at all costs may put men at greater risk than women in managerial positions for involvement in corporate crime (Daly, 1989). Research on entrepreneurship and management style finds that males are more inclined than women toward strategic, proactive risk-taking and aggressive, bold strategies in the face of uncertainty (O'Fallon & Butterfield, 2005). This is especially likely in masculine environments and criminal coalitions where males' risk-taking propensities exacerbate one another.

Males are more vulnerable to financial strain and loss of status and more likely to use criminal coping strategies in response to strain, whereas females are more at risk for criminal involvement because of personal relationships, including interpersonal and family-related strains, and gender-based discrimination, and are more likely to use less deviant coping strategies (e.g., self-harming behaviors, like drug or alcohol use) (Broidy & Agnew, 1997). Thus, gaining and protecting privileged status, economic power, and wealth incentivize males more than females to use illegal means. Women who commit business-related frauds like embezzlement tend to do so (or rationalize it) for reasons of protecting their families or valued relationships, whereas males tend to embezzle to protect their status as successful businessmen, rationalizing their crimes as stemming from "normal business practices" (Cressey, 1953/1973; Klenowski, Copes, & Mullins, 2011).

Despite enculturation into a male-dominated business environment, in general, female executives can be expected to feel guilt and find it more difficult to rationalize involvement in business-related frauds than their male counterparts. Along with differences in moral orientations and risk taking, men and women may also differ in how they view opportunities for corporate fraud. Women who move into top management may be deterred by their uniqueness and sense that they are watched more carefully than men in those positions (Benson & Simpson, 2009).

Criminal Opportunity

FORMAL ACCESS THROUGH POSITION. Statistics suggest women's opportunities to commit corporate crimes as top-level executives remain limited; however, women's opportunities for corporate crime opportunities as mid-level managers and supervisors have markedly increased (Catalyst, 2014). Census Bureau surveys indicate that women today are not only about as likely as men to be in the paid workforce but also strongly represented in corporate America in mid-level roles. Thus, women comprise about three quarters of all financial workers, occupy one half of all managerial, administrative, and professional positions, are the majority of technical and clerical "white-collar" workers, and are about half of all accountants, many as corporate professionals (Huffman, Cohen, & Pearlman, 2010). However, case studies of Fortune 500 companies find women comprise only about 15% of senior executives or board of director positions (Catalyst, 2014). It seems the number of women occupying the highest corporate positions remains low.

Available evidence also suggests that mid-level officials are as likely as top management to be involved in corporate wrongdoing and targeted for prosecution (Clinard & Yeager, 2006). Mid-level officials have considerable decision-making autonomy regarding investment, pricing, marketing, and production and they direct staff to carry out top management's objectives. Thus, opportunities for white-collar crimes via professional and managerial positions may be near equal for women and men.

INFORMAL NETWORK ACCESS. Organizational sex segregation literature suggests that even when women occupy higher level organizational positions, exclusionary practices limit women's involvement in predominantly male informal networks at work (Gorman & Kmec, 2009; Kanter, 1977). Crime research (discussed earlier) has also documented sex-segregated practices that limit and shape female involvement in underworld crime groups.

What We Found

Women corporate fraudsters were about as rare as female killers or robbers—less than 10% of those sorts of offenders. Of the 436 individuals indicted for corporate fraud, only 37 were women. Most of these frauds were complex enough to require co-conspiracy over several years and a criminal division of labor. Often, women were not included at all in these groups. When they were, women were nearly always in the minority, often alone, and most typically played rather small roles. The Enron conspiracy led to over 30 indictments; only 3 were women and each played a minor role. The 5 women indicted among 19 in the HealthSouth fraud were in accounting-related positions and instructed by senior personnel to falsify financial books and create fictitious records. Martha Stewart, rather than being the criminal mastermind of an insider-trading conspiracy, committed "one of the most ill-fated white-collar crimes ever" in which she saved just $46,000 after receiving a stock tip secondhand from her broker. Notably, the conspiracy's ringleader, Samuel Waksal (founder and chief executive officer of pharmaceutical company ImClone Systems), had first-hand prior knowledge of the Food and Drug Administration's decision not to approve the company's anticancer drug, unloaded as much stock as he could, and tipped off family members and (male) friends to unload their stock. But, Waksal did not tip off Stewart; she was not involved in the actual conspiracy.

Women were almost never the ringleader or even a major player in the fraud. Only one woman chief executive officer led a fraud—the smallest fraud we studied—and two women conspired with their husbands. Evidence suggested social barriers to women orchestrating these schemes, including difficulties in recruiting participants. One reason for women's low representation among the ringleaders and major players is perhaps because women are not as often in positions to lead these schemes. However, even when we compared women and men in similar corporate positions, women were less likely to play leadership roles in the fraud.

Moreover, the women benefited little from their illicit involvement. Over half of the women did not gain anything financially from their participation in the fraud, whereas half the men pocketed half a million dollars or more. The sex difference in illicit gains persisted even when we compared offenders in similar positions. Males profited much more. Women identified "gains" such as keeping one's job.

The extent of sex segregation that characterizes these serious financial schemes is striking, especially within the context of statistical gains made by women for less serious embezzlements and property crimes. For example, for the minor property offenses captured by official arrest statistics—larceny-theft, embezzlement, fraud, and forgery—women now comprise nearly half of such property offenders. We turn now more directly to the issue of identifying and understanding change in the gender gap in criminal offending.

Changes in the Gender Gap Over Time: What Needs to Be Explained?

It is the assumption of many today that women's crime must be catching up to men's crime as women continue to march toward equality. It certainly was the presumption of the first author before enrolling in graduate school. And long before that, in 1922, early U.S. criminologist Clarence Darrow (1922) made the statement,

> No doubt as woman enters the field of industry formerly monopolized by man, and as she takes her part in politics . . . the percentage of female criminals will rapidly increase. . . . As she takes her place with men she will be more and more judged as men are judged, and will commit the crimes that men commit. (p. 78)

Women may take on the same motives or risk preferences for crime—and may be presented with greater opportunities through social integration and inclusion in power or leadership arrangements.

At first, it seems extraordinarily logical that as girls and women come to engage in many of the same activities as males, they will in many ways "act like men," including committing serious crime. Freda Adler's (1975) *Sisters in Crime* made the argument that increased economic opportunities during the 1970s allowed women to follow natural proclivities to be as crime prone as men. Although "women have demanded equal opportunity in the fields of legitimate endeavors, a similar number of determined women have forced their way into the world of major crime such as white-collar crime, murder, and robbery" (Adler, 1975, p. 3). Adler argued that as women were climbing the corporate business ladder, they were making use of their "vocational liberation" to pursue careers in white-collar crime. As noted previously, Adler's work, and the dark side of liberation debate more generally, played a pivotal role in the dramatic increase in interest in female crime during the 1970s and continuing today.

Despite its intuitive logic, the increases in crime ostensibly associated with women's changing roles and positions in society have not materialized. We summarize systematic evidence on this debate, which shows little change in the historical gender–crime relationship. In general, statistics indicate that the gender gap in serious or more organized forms of offending has changed little, whereas the gap closes moderately between males and females for some minor forms of offending. We describe two periods—the 1960s/1970s, when female arrest rates increased more than male arrests for minor property crimes, and the 1990s/2000s, when female arrests for minor violence and substance abuse leveled off or declined less when male rates were steeply declining. Both instances help demonstrate two important points toward understanding gender gap trends in crime.

First, current crime data are lacking to sufficiently address the questions of whether and which changes in women's lives have spurred increases in offending. As previously discussed, the UCR provides some valuable information. Specifically, the UCR contains summary arrest data by sex and age, which is helpful for examining national trends in arrests over a long period of time for both male and female offenders.

Although these official police data have many advantages, two limitations bear mention. The first limitation is that the offense categories into which different kinds of arrests are grouped are broad. For example, the category of larceny-theft includes arrests for shoplifting an item worth $50 and for thefts of items worth much more. Offenses defined as a simple assault might range from arrests for such acts as a shove or spitting on a police officer to punching with a closed fist or even more harmful behavior. Further, because the offense categories are broad, they primarily measure minor behaviors because these offenses are more common. So, embezzlement or fraud arrests tend to be for low-yielding offenses rather than for major organized or long-running schemes. A second limitation pertains to the arrest data itself. Specifically, how many arrests occur could reflect not only the behavior of offenders (i.e., how frequently people break the law) but also the behavior of law enforcement officials (e.g., how much law enforcement targets low-level versus upper level drug operatives, domestic altercations versus street violence). To address both of these limitations, other sources of data that do not involve enforcement officials have been developed, including victimization surveys that ask respondents to disclose whether they have been victimized (and to tell about the nature of the offense and the characteristics of the offenders who perpetrated the act) and self-report surveys in which respondents are asked to disclose their involvement in various offenses. These sources provide an important reference point to disentangle any changes in arrest data resulting from offender behavior versus victim or law enforcement behavior (e.g., calling the police, making an arrest). However, these data also elicit mostly minor offenses, especially from self-reports.

Second, explanations of the gender gap must be multivariate. Any changes in the gender gap seem to be multicausal, meaning that some balance of changes in the nature of crime opportunity, social control, sex-segregating practices or structures, and economic marginality cause female and male crime trends to diverge. We explore these after outlining major gender gap trends based on empirical evidence.

Gender Gap Trends Over the 1960s and 1970s: Minor Property Crime

Initial evidence from the 1960s and 1970s seemed to point in favor of the view that women were becoming more involved in white-collar and other crimes, but there were inconsistencies. Adler (1975) used official arrest statistics to show that from the 1960s until the mid-1970s, women gained on men in arrests for fraud/forgery/embezzlement and larceny-theft (e.g., shoplifting). However, inconsistent with Adler's expectations, there was little evidence that women engaged in any more violence during this time (Steffensmeier & Cobb, 1982). No marked changes in female-to-male violence were identified in arrest data, self-reports of violence by adolescents over the 1960s (Canter, 1982), or victim reports on violent offenders over the mid-1970s (Hindelang, 1979).

Scholars also took issue with Adler's interpretation of the arrest data for fraud, forgery, and embezzlement as emblematic of the liberated female crook. Rather, arrest data more likely were composed of unemployed or marginally employed women who embezzled small sums of money as bank tellers, accountants, book-keepers, or treasurers; committed credit card or welfare fraud; bounced a check because of "insufficient funds"; and forged small checks on stolen accounts. Unfortunately, national arrest data were not sufficiently detailed to address such critiques directly. However, Daly's (1989) landmark study of women in white-collar crime confirms this (see also Holtfreter, 2005). Based on detailed presentence investigation reports on 1,342 offenders convicted of any fraud or nonviolent economic crime in a federal court (1976–1978), women comprised only 14% of all such offenders and just 5% committed significant white-collar crimes like antitrust, bribery, or securities fraud. Daly (1989) also found that women's financial profits were less than men's; more women than men were unemployed; and most employed women were clerical workers or in low-level positions. Economic marginality, rather than liberation or occupational mobility, matched the profile of most female offenders. Yet, data limitations have largely precluded the study of pink-collar crimes (i.e., low-level embezzlements or employee theft by women in female-dominated service or clerical jobs) or more serious white-collar crime in any depth.

A recent analysis, which draws on newly available arrestee data from the 2010 National Incident Reporting Based System and detailed UCR data from New York and Pennsylvania, confirms that fraud, forgery, and larceny arrests in official data do not reflect white-collar or occupational offending. Steffensmeier, Harris, and Painter-Davis (2012) break down the types of property crime and value of the property or money stolen for females and males arrested for larceny, fraud, or forgery. *First,* shoplifting alone accounted for about 70–75% of female larceny-theft arrests compared to about 55% for males; males were more likely to be arrested for theft from a motor vehicle, theft from a coin-operated machine, and purse snatching. Most larceny-thefts, regardless of arrestee's sex, were low value (90–95% were less than $100). *Second,* for fraud and forgery, check fraud alone (e.g., "bad checks" "insufficient funds") accounted for 65–70% of female arrests compared to about 50% of male arrests; nearly all of the remaining arrests (regardless of sex) were for theft of services (e.g., illegal cable hookup, subway "turnstile jumping"), credit card or ATM fraud, welfare fraud, and fraudulent hustles or swindles. Most fraud or forgery arrests involved misdemeanor charges and relatively small monetary loss (typically under $200 to $500).

Some embezzlement, whether committed by males or females, is lucrative, netting $100,000 or $1 million or more, and thus clearly is not a trivial matter. However, males tend to embezzle larger amounts than females, on average (Wright & Steffensmeier, 2011; Zietz, 1981). Likewise, some embezzlement is committed by upper level business or government officials, but most, especially that committed by women, is committed by low to mid-level employees, budget personnel, or office managers—such as bank tellers, bookkeepers, office managers, club treasurers, or secretaries. When one considers that women today occupy more than three quarters of all financial reporting or budget management positions, which provide opportunities for embezzling but also entail regular audits (i.e., high surveillance), it seems that male rates are much higher than female rates of embezzlement, all else being equal. Much embezzlement is not occupational at all, but instead involves a caretaker embezzling from an older person or an officer embezzling from club or association funds. Overall, it seems that female embezzlement is rather congruent with traditional female roles and focal concerns.

Gender Gap Trends for the 1990s and 2000s:
Minor Violence and Substance Abuse

By the mid-1990s, popular concern about women's crime shifted from property-related and white-collar offenses that ostensibly stemmed from female labor market advances to violence and aggression by young women who were readily adopting masculine ways of behaving. On a related note, girls' and women's binge drinking and problem-drinking behaviors such as drunk driving have been scrutinized as of late under these same assumptions about rising female involvement. Similar to earlier periods, the current concerns expressed over the emergence of a female crime wave—this time over violence and substance abuse instead of property crime—were fueled largely by uncritical interpretation of official arrest statistics. For assault and drunken driving, the gender gap in arrests narrowed substantially from the mid-1990s to at least the early 2000s. Other data sources, however, showed no change in the share of girls' or women's violence.

For example, based on UCR data, both aggravated assault and simple assault showed increased female representation, from about 15% of arrestees in 1980 to 25% by 2003. Yet, according to victims' reports on offender characteristics in the NCVS, girls' share of felony assault held steady at about 12% across two decades. Simple assault fluctuated more in the NCVS, but remained fairly steady between 15% and 20% through the 2000s. Furthermore, self-report data showed that fighting has actually decreased for both sexes. Male fighting declined from 50% to 40% and female fighting declined from 35% to 25% (Schwartz et al., 2009; Steffensmeier, Schwartz, Zhong, & Ackerman, 2005).

It does not seem that female crime rates have significantly increased since the 1970s. If any changes have occurred, they are confined to lower level offenses, such as simple assault and drunk driving. The evidence regarding trends in the gender gap for more serious violence is unequivocal, however: Women are not involved in any more violence than they used to be.

Thus, homicide gender-gap trends have remained consistent since the 1980s. Today, as was the case two to three decades ago, females comprise about 12% to 14% of all homicide offenders (versus about 17% to 18% in 1960). Suicide, which is serious violence turned inward and usually involving a gun, shows female involvement to be about 20% for the past two to three decades. Rape is overwhelmingly a male crime, as it was 20 to 30 years ago, despite some definition broadening. Specifically, the percentage of female offenders arrested for rape has remained consistent at 2% to 3%. The NCVS shows a similar stable pattern in female sexual assault. Also, imprisonment for violence shows an unchanged female percentage for violent index crimes (homicide, rape, robbery, and assault). From the mid-1980s to today, about 5% to 6% of newly admitted violent prisoners were female. Prison admissions include the most serious violent offenders and are a good marker of trends because of fewer changes in working definitions of serious violence. In-stock incarceration statistics also indicate an unchanged female percentage of violent offenders—about 3% to 4%. Moreover, any increases in female imprisonment were driven primarily by changes in drug policies that locked up low-level female operatives in drug networks.

The lack of evidence for a narrowing gender gap in serious violence is remarkable given the expectation that women's violence *must* have changed over time as well as the larger shifts in the social construction of "violence." The only offenses for which there seems to be *any* evidence of female-to-male increases are assault and, to a lesser extent, robbery. Scholars explain these changes as in large part the result of violence-prevention paradigms and crime-control policies that target minor sorts of offenses in private settings that are typical of female offending patterns (Miller, 2001; Schwartz et al., 2009; Steffensmeier et al., 2005). Recent declines in male violence may also be contributing to a larger female share of violence because the gender gap is a function of the movement of both female and male rates. In the case of robbery, greater female economic hardship and drug addiction may have pushed some women to commit robbery, often with male accomplices (Miller, 2001). Also, broader definitions of robbery and the practice of upcharging (e.g., a robbery charge for a shoplifter who resists being detained or runs away but is caught) likely have greater impacts on female's arrest rates than men's.

Young women's drunk-driving arrest rates almost doubled from 1980 to 2004, from 233 to 400 per 100,000 women (ages 18–20), increasing female representation from 9% to 20% of drunk drivers (Schwartz & Rookey, 2008). In contrast, self-reported "driving after having too much to drink" has remained about 25% female since the mid-1980s, according to the Centers for Disease Control's nationally representative Behavioral Risk Factor Surveillance System. Drunk-driving estimates from the highly reliable Fatality Analysis Reporting System, which records blood alcohol test results for drivers in fatal traffic accidents, shows the female percentage was 11% to 12% across the 1980s and is currently at 15%. The small increase is not significant according to time-series tests and is not as large as it is for arrests (Schwartz & Rookey, 2008). Thus, as for drinking, drunken-driving statistics based on sources independent of police decision making do not corroborate the relative female increases shown in arrest data.

Finally, liquor-law violations by boys have declined over the past 25 years (800 to 600 per 100,000 boys ages 10–18), but girls' arrest rates have increased somewhat (325 to 350 per 100,000 girls ages 10–18) (Zhong & Schwartz, 2010). Whereas the female percentage of liquor law *arrests* climbed from 16% in 1980 to 31% by 2005, during that time the female share of 12th graders self-reporting having one or more drinks in the past year remained even—at about 50%. Similarly, the female percentage for problem drinking patterns—frequent and heavy drinking on several occasions—has remained at or below 40% since 1980.

This discussion leads to two conclusions. First, these disparities in official sources (e.g., arrest data) versus unofficial sources (e.g., self-report data) suggest that girls' and women's violence and drinking patterns have not so much changed as social control policies have increasingly targeted female offending patterns. That is, what has changed is not so much females' involvement in these acts but that they are now getting arrested for them more often. Second, more serious violence and drinking behaviors remain male dominated, but for the past 25+ years, adolescent girls' drinking and minor aggressions have been about as prevalent as boys' drinking and minor aggressions.

Explaining Changes in the Gender Gap

Our most important conclusions with regard to gender gap trends in crime are that (1) the gender gap has been pretty stable for serious forms of crime; and (2) any gender gap changes have been for minor sorts of offending. What factors shape the persistent gender gap for serious crime and contribute to occasional shifts in minor crime? We highlight key factors that broadly affect motivations and opportunities for women (or men) to commit crime.

Economic Marginality of Women

One of the better predictors of criminal activity is economic hardship. If a larger segment of the female population faces greater economic insecurity today than previously, female property crime may rise. This is so although more women now enjoy greater freedoms, occupy formerly male-dominated professions, and have advanced to higher level professional positions. Rising rates of divorce, out-of-wedlock births, and female-headed households have aggravated the economic pressures on women. These circumstances have left females without male support and more child care and other caretaking responsibilities than they had three or four decades ago. Growing economic adversity increases the pressures to commit consumer-based crimes such as shoplifting, check fraud, theft of services, and welfare fraud, as well as sex hustling and low-level drug dealing. Drugs have profoundly shaped the contemporary underworld of crime, particularly the street crimes of the urban underclass. Addictions, abuses, and drugs amplify income-generating crime for both sexes, but more for females. In these and other crimes, the social marginality of women and traditional power arrangements are readily apparent.

Nature of Crime Opportunities Over Time and Space

Changes in the productive activities in American society have affected the nature of crime activities that its citizens encounter. Female and male offenders alike tend to gravitate toward activities that are readily available and within their skill sets, so the level and character of female and male crime will be strongly affected by the crime opportunities available and whether they are suited to female interests, abilities, and opportunities. Changing labor market participation by women is but one such change in the nature of female crime opportunities. Changing patterns of productive activity related to consumer goods, the credit economy, and welfare state also may create new opportunities for female crimes of theft and fraud.

Females have made large arrest gains in the kinds of nonviolent economic crimes that are likely to continue to persist in significance in the 21st century. These might include, for example, offenses made possible by the growth in credit-based currency and self-service marketing of goods (e.g., check fraud; shoplifting). Many of these crimes are within the reach of virtually everyone and are conducive to female involvement. Meanwhile, globalization and other broad transnational trends are likely to provide greater opportunities for male involvement, as in arms- or drug-smuggling enterprises.

Sex Segregation in the Underworld

Women are disadvantaged for selection into criminal groups, in the range of criminal pathways open to them, and in opportunities for tutelage, increased skills, and rewards through criminal enterprise. The blunt fact here is that virtually all crime arenas are male dominated or controlled, and "homosocial reproduction" assures males will most often choose other like males with whom to work in illicit enterprise. This male dominance is demonstrated in at least three ways: (1) most serious and lucrative criminal enterprises involve males as the perpetrators; (2) a masculine sub-culture surrounding crime prevails, as reflected in sex stereotyping, emphasis on physicality, and so forth; and (3) females typically act as accomplices to males, who both organize the crime and profit the most from it. Sex segregation in the under-world is a powerful force that shapes the level and nature of female involvement in co-offending and collective criminal enterprise.

Sex-segregated roles and practices appear to be pervasive across various forms of collective criminal enterprise, but important variability is also evident—depending on such things as the task environment of crime, the crime network or group's atti-tudes toward women, and perhaps most importantly the usefulness of women for carrying out or executing the criminal activity or business. Some criminal markets are less accessible to women than other markets, such as those that require violence or force versus coercion, involve greater risk or threat, are profit motivated, charac-terized by hierarchy, and demand a high degree of professionalization or skill. Within criminal groups and enterprise, the nature of activities or certain roles are sex typed so some may lend themselves more readily to females. It is likely that sex segregation and institutionalized sexism are even stronger in the underworld, in part because there is no affirmative action, no interest groups lobbying for change, and little bureaucracy with legitimate hiring processes.

Declines in Male Crime

One important contributor to the modern narrowing of the gender gap for certain crimes is steeper male declines rather than female increases in arrest rates. Men's crime rates (for certain crimes) were particularly high for a decade beginning in the mid-1980s, but have fallen steeply since about 1994. Women's crime rates also increased and then decreased, but male rates had much farther to fall after climbing higher, so the rebalancing of the gender gap is not all that surprising (widening the gender gap, then narrowing it). Similar social factors apparently underlie female and male offending, or the two trends would not follow each other's vicissitudes so closely. However, multiple factors driving down male rates more than female rates include deterrence policies and prevention programs targeted predominantly at male offending patterns and the civilizing effects of messages and policy initiatives focused initially and primarily on the unacceptability of men's violence against women. Also, some changes in the underworld may have impacted more on male crime levels. Male burglary, for example, has been declining since about 1980 because of shifts in the underworld away from burglary toward drug dealing as a more attractive money-making option, among other reasons.

Law, Policing, and Mobilization of Social Control
Changes in the gender gap, particularly those shown only in official data, are partly a function of changes in laws (definitions of crime), in policing (law in action), or in sanctioning or punishment that disparately affects females. In general, widening the arrest net to include lower level offenders will tend to make more visible women's offending patterns. Laws that broaden crime definitions, zero-tolerance enforcement policies, and extending the arm of the law into previously private settings are prone to disparately increase female visibility to law enforcement. This implies that some narrowing of the gender gap for minor offenses is artifactual.

Policing and enforcement policies and practices can also modify opportunities for crime. For example, crackdowns on active offenders can reduce the supply of co-offenders by targeting chronic male offenders and thus open up opportunities for females as temporary workers or low-level operatives in crime and drug networks.

Recommendations for Research and Theory Building

The study of female offending and the gender gap has advanced considerably over the past several decades. The debate spurred by the writings of Adler and others about the origins of the gender gap and effects of female liberation and emancipation on female arrest trends has contributed to alternative explanations that offer both a richer and probably a more accurate account of the phenomenon. However, although empirical evidence on recent trends in female offending suggests congruency with traditional gender relations and focal concerns, much about the gender gap in criminal offending remains unknown and speculative. Our recommendations for future inquiry and conceptualization on the gender gap in criminal behavior include the following.

Multifaceted Approach to Gender Roles
One thing that makes gender so difficult to study is that it is pervasive, yet dynamic and flexibly performed, depending upon the situation. There is both change and stability in gender roles (recently and over the past 100 years), depending on which aspect of women's and men's statuses is considered. Any inquiry into the gender–crime relationship may yield different interpretations depending on how gender equality, gender norms, and other gender-related variables are conceptualized and measured. There may be greater diversity in (female) gender roles and relations, but

core elements of the organization of gender have not changed much, if at all (Cotter, Hermsen, & Vanneman, 2011). The argument that the economic and occupational roles of women are rapidly changing and that the changes have substantially affected female offending and the gender gap ignores other structures of male domination and the ways in which gender and gender relations structure social life. Gender is constructed not only by roles but also by power relations. Moreover, as our earlier discussion clarified, the profound significance of sex or gender in contributing to *gendered lives and practices* is even greater in the underworld. There is an express need to recognize the intersectional nature of gender with other statuses, such as race, ethnicity, and age, and to recognize that change has occurred for some groups of women more than for others.

Development of More Diverse Databases on the Full Spectrum of Criminal Involvement

It is important to develop databases that better contextualize female offending and also that delve into the kinds of crime that are most harmful to society. We see the following as particularly useful.

First, localized studies of police and court reports on persons arrested or convicted are needed to provide a contextual understanding of the organizational management of crime and a detailed breakdown of the kinds of crime committed by women and men (especially within the broad UCR categories). These records typically include useful information on the circumstances leading to the crime, nature of one's involvement if there are co-offenders, and profits or outcomes.

Second, case studies are needed that examine the immediate context of the offense and the larger social setting of habitual female offending. Future scholars may follow the fine examples set by Eleanor M. Miller's (1986) study of street women, Jody Miller's research on girls and gangs (2001), Darrell Steffensmeier and Robert Terry's (1986) research on institutional sexism in the underworld among hustlers and thieves, and Gail Caputo's study (2008) of drug-addicted women who took up criminal occupations of shoplifting and sex work. Such studies (and many others) reveal the extent to which the lives of delinquent girls and women continue to be powerfully influenced by gender-related conditions of life.

Third, the most important next step is to develop databases that identify more serious forms of criminal offending, their sex distribution, and the nature of female involvement (if any). As noted previously, UCR arrest data mainly track minor or less serious forms of criminal offending. If one wants to learn about the sex distribution of more serious forms of criminality, one must look elsewhere. Moreover, if one wants to know about variability in women's criminal roles, enticements, rewards, and other details about involvement in criminal enterprise and co-offending relationships, official data are of limited use. It is crucial that databases be developed that better represent the kinds of crime and criminal offenders that are most harmful to society.

We take a step in this direction in our gender and corporate fraud study, in which we collected and coded information from a web-based repository on corporate crime created by the Department of Justice on Enron-era criminal indictments. Other possible data sources that could be mined include (1) archival case records maintained by a range of government agencies (e.g., Securities and Exchange Commission, Environmental Protection Agency); (2) indictments and prosecutions initiated by state and U.S. attorney offices; (3) archives and ad hoc databases on registered sex offenders, gang members, terrorist group members, outlaw biker members and associates, mafia groups and members, sea piracy, arms smuggling, human trafficking, and genocide; and (4) investigations initiated by local, national, and international agencies and by specialized task forces and law enforcement entities that are targeted at specific forms of criminality and criminal networks or enterprises.

Need for Middle-Range Theories

Clearly, any possible theory of gender and crime is complicated by (1) the complexity and diversity of crime activities of both males and females and of their relations to other correlates such as age, race, and social class and (2) ubiquitous social change, which compounds the problem tremendously not only in relation to changes in criminogenic conditions but also in reference to shifts in what a society defines or treats as being criminal.

The main aim, we believe, should be toward a middle-range rather than comprehensive theory of sex differences in crime, such as the conceptual framework we advanced and tested in the gender–corporate crime study (Steffensmeier et al., 2013; see also Steffensmeier, 1983; Steffensmeier & Allan, 1996). Built around the interplay of "gendered focal concerns," "gendered crime opportunities," and "gendered risk preferences," the theory arguably has wide applicability for looking at sex differences in other kinds of criminal behavior and for studying female offending and the gender gap more generally. Among its advantages, the framework helps to consider key ways in which women's routes to crime (especially serious crime) may differ from those of men; women's exclusion from the most lucrative crime opportunities; the role of physical and sexual differences in generating sex differences in crime, including women's ability to exploit sex as an illegal money-making service; the centrality of greater familial responsibilities and relational concerns among women and the manner in which these both shape and allow women to be pulled into criminal involvements by men in their lives; and the greater need of criminally involved women for protection from predatory or exploitative males. Last, the framework helps to consider the varying disadvantages that potential female offenders face in selection and recruitment into criminal groups, in the range of career paths opened by way of participation in these groups, and in opportunities for tutelage, increased skills, and rewards.

Distinguishing gender differences in crime opportunities, especially by linking them to gendered focal concerns and risk preferences, helps in particular to illuminate how social structure and culture influence sex differences in crime. They do so by making a particular pattern of differentiated options available to males and females for solving economic problems, seeking excitement, taking care of self and others, and so forth. They also create or provide constraints that influence the decision to adopt a particular criminal or legitimate option.

In the context of recent assertions and ongoing interest about changes in female crime and the gender gap, what might this conceptual framework suggest about 21st-century trends in female crime? Based on the framework and what is known currently about the gender gap in crime, we would expect for the foreseeable future that women will continue to select criminal behaviors congruent with traditional gender roles and focal concerns. That is, we would forecast that the three main patterns described earlier as characterizing the gender gap—both today and historically—will robustly persist. Specifically, we expect that (1) the gender gap will remain wide for serious offenses, while being small to nonexistent for some common or less serious offenses; (2) sex work and sexuality in collective crime activities will continue to figure prominently in female criminal careers, whereas sexual predation will continue to be much more common among males; and (3) lucrative or violent, professional, or organized forms of crime will continue to overwhelmingly favor male involvement but marginalize females' participation and roles in criminal enterprise. Female offending will continue to be mainly solo, as temporary accomplices or low-level operatives in more long-running criminal enterprises (e.g., drug distribution networks, human smuggling rings).

Last, we nonetheless also expect to find exceptional cases of female offenders who have established a niche and gained power in the underworld (as Marm Mandelbaum did in the 1850s). In the media and in some social science reports, these cases will almost surely generate notoriety and even speculation about the "rise" of a new female criminal with its linkage to changing gender roles. The task for criminologists and criminal justice policy makers will be to determine whether such cases are false (e.g., as with Martha Stewart), rare, or abundant enough to be a true marker of the times versus whether the three traditional gender-gap patterns remain as robust. This task is challenged by primary reliance on official data that mainly capture minor or less serious offenders. If current net-widening arrest practices continue, which target minor sorts of offenses that women are more prone to commit, continued narrowing of the gender gap may well be expected for some offenses. However, it is not likely that women's involvement in lucrative, organized, or violent crimes, covered in lesser known databases, will change all that much in the near future.

We suspect that women will continue to select criminal behaviors congruent with traditional female focal concerns and risk preferences and for which opportunities are more abundant. Like male offenders, they will gravitate to those activities which are most possible, within their skills, provide a satisfactory return given the options, and carry the fewest risks.

NOTES

[1]The term "gender" refers to socially constructed roles, behaviors, activities, and attributes that are considered appropriate for men and women (i.e., feminine, masculine). The term "sex" refers to the physical and biological characteristics that define men and women. We use *gender* unless we are referring to measured differences between men and women (i.e., sex differences).

[2]This conception does not necessarily presume rationality—people persist in patterns of action that are meaningless, terrific, or even destructive for long periods of time (p. 302). Rather, making a choice presumes at least some degree of moral reflection, practical deliberation, and intellectual calculation.

References

Adler, F. (1975). *Sisters in crime: The rise of the new female criminal.* New York, NY: McGraw–Hill.

Belknap, J., & Holsinger, K. (2006). The gendered nature of risk factor for delinquency. *Feminist Criminology, 1,* 48–71.

Benson, M. L., & Simpson, S. S. (2009). *White-collar crime: An opportunity perspective.* New York, NY: Routledge.

Beutel, A., & Marini, M. (1995). Gender and values. *American Sociological Review, 60,* 436–448.

Booth, J. A., Farrell, A., & Varano, S. P. (2008). Social control, serious delinquency, and risk behavior. A gendered analysis. *Journal of Research in Crime and Delinquency, 54,* 423–456.

Bottcher, J. (2001). Social practices of gender: How gender relates to delinquency in the everyday lives of high-risk youths. *Criminology, 39,* 893–932.

Broidy, L., & Agnew, R. (1997). Gender and crime: A general strain theory perspective. *Journal of Research in Crime and Delinquency, 34,* 275–306.

Canter, R. (1982). Sex differences in delinquency. *Criminology, 20,* 373–398.

Caputo, G. (2008). *Out in the storm: Drug-addicted women living as shoplifters and sex workers.* Boston, MA: Northeastern University Press.

Catalyst. (2014). *U.S. women in business.* Retrieved from http://www.catalyst.org/knowledge/us-women-business

Clinard, M. B., & Yeager, P. C. (2006). *Corporate crime.* New York, NY: The Free Press.

Collins, J. (1999). *Personality and value differences among male and female white-collar executives.* Paper presented at the Annual Meeting of the American Psychological Association, Boston, MA.

Cotter, D., Hermsen, J., & Vanneman, R. (2011). The end of the gender revolution? Gender role attitudes from 1977–2008. *American Journal of Sociology, 117,* 259–289.

Cressey, D. R. (1973). *Other people's money: A study in the social psychology of embezzlement.* Montclair, NJ: Patterson Smith. (Original work published in 1953.)

Daly, K. (1989). Gender and varieties of white-collar crime. *Criminology, 27,* 769–794.

Daly, K. (1994). *Gender, crime and punishment.* New Haven, CT: Yale University Press.

Daly, K. (2006). Restorative justice and sexual assault: An archival study of court and conference cases. *British Journal of Criminology, 46,* 334–356.

Darrow, C. (1922). *Crime: Its causes and treatment.* New York, NY: Crowell.

Faris, R., & Felmlee, D. (2011). Status struggles: Network centrality and gender segregation in the same and cross gender aggression. *American Sociological Review, 76,* 48–73.

Gilligan, C. (1982). *In a different voice: Psychological theory and women's development.* Cambridge, MA: Harvard University Press.

Giordano, P. C., Schroeder, R. D., & Cernkovich, S. A. (2007). Emotions and crime over the life course. A neo-meadian perspective on crime continuity and change. *American Journal of Sociology, 112,* 1603–1661.

Gorman, E., & Kmec, J. (2009). Hierarchical rank and women's organizational mobility: Glass ceilings in corporate law firms. *American Journal of Sociology, 114,* 1428–1474.

Haynie, D., Steffensmeier, D., & Bell, K. (2007). Gender and serious violence: Untangling the role of friendship sex composition and peer violence. *Youth Violence and Juvenile Justice, 5,* 235–253.

Hindelang, M. J. (1979). Sex differences in criminal activity. *Social Problems, 27,* 143–156.

Holtfreter, K. (2005). Is occupational fraud "typical" white-collar crime? A comparison of individual and organizational characteristics. *Journal of Criminal Justice, 33,* 353–365.

Huffman, M., Cohen, P., & Pearlman, J. (2010). Engendering change: Organizational dynamics and workplace desegregation, 1975–2005. *Administrative Science Quarterly, 55,* 255–277.

Kanter, R. M. (1977). *Men and women of the corporation.* New York, NY: Basic Books.

Klenowski, P. M., Copes, H., & Mullins, C. W. (2011). Gender, identity, and accounts: How white collar offenders do gender when making sense of their crimes. *Justice Quarterly, 28,* 46–69.

Kodinsky, R. (2010). Attitudes about corporate social responsibility. *Journal of Business Ethics, 91,* 167–181.

Lemert, E. M. (1951). *Social pathology: A systematic approach to the theory of sociopathic behavior.* New York, NY: McGraw–Hill.

Maher, L., & Daly, K. (1996). Women in the street-level drug economy: Continuity or change? *Criminology, 34,* 465–491.

McCarthy, B., Felmlee, D., & Hagan, J. (2004). Girl friends are better: Gender, friends, and crime among school and street youth. *Criminology, 42,* 805–836.

Mears, D., Ploeger, M., & Warr, M. (1998). Explaining the gender gap in delinquency: Peer influence and moral evaluations of behavior. *Journal of Research in Crime and Delinquency, 35,* 251–266.

Miller, E. M. (1986). *Street women.* Philadelphia, PA: Temple University Press.

Miller, J. (2001). *One of the guys: Girls, gangs, and gender.* New York, NY: Oxford University Press.

Miller, J. (2010). Steffensmeier, Darrell J.: Organization properties and sex segregation in the underworld. In F. T. Cullen & P. Wilcox (Eds.), *Encyclopedia of criminological theory* (pp. 883–885). Thousand Oaks, CA: Sage.

Miller, S. L. (2001). The paradox of women arrested for domestic violence: Criminal justice professionals and service providers respond. *Violence Against Women, 7,* 1339–1376.

O'Fallon, M., & Butterfield, K. (2005). A review of the empirical ethical decision-making literature. *Journal of Business Ethics, 59,* 375–413.

Schwartz, J. (2006). Family structure as a source of female and male homicide in the United States. *Homicide Studies, 10,* 253–278.

Schwartz, J. (2014). A "new" female offender or increasing social control of women's behavior? Cross-national evidence. *Feminist Studies, 39,* 790–821.

Schwartz, J., Conover-Williams, M., & K. Clemons. (forthcoming). Thirty years of sex stratification in crime partnerships and groups. *Feminist Criminology.*

Schwartz, J., & Rookey, B. (2008). The narrowing gender gap in arrests: Assessing competing explanations using self-report, traffic fatality, and official data on drunk driving, 1980–2005. *Criminology, 46,* 637–671.

Schwartz, J., & Steffensmeier, D. (2007). The nature of female offending: Patterns and explanation. In R. Zaplin (Ed.), *Female offenders: Critical perspective and effective interventions* (pp. 43–76). Boston, MA: Jones & Bartlett.

Schwartz, J., Steffensmeier, D., Zhong, H., & Ackerman, J. (2009). Trends in the gender gap in violence: Re-evaluating NCVS and other evidence. *Criminology, 47,* 401–425.

Steffensmeier, D. (1983). An organizational perspective on sex-segregation in the under-world: Building a sociological theory of sex differences in crime. *Social Forces, 61,* 1010–1032.

Steffensmeier, D. (1986). *The fence: In the shadow of two worlds.* Totowa, NJ: Rowman & Littlefield.

Steffensmeier, D., & Allan, E. (1996). Gender and crime: Toward a gendered theory of female offending. *Annual Review of Sociology, 22,* 459–487.

Steffensmeier, D., & Cobb, M. (1982). Sex differences in urban arrest patterns, 1934–79: Stability or change? *Social Problems, 29,* 37–50.

Steffensmeier, D., Harris, C. T., & Painter-Davis, N. (2012). *Dissecting UCR arrests for larceny and fraud using NIRBS and state-level crime databases: Are those arrested "white collar" or "ordinary offenders?* Paper presented at the 2012 Annual Meeting of the American Society of Criminology, Chicago, IL.

Steffensmeier, D., & Haynie, D. (2000). Gender, structural disadvantage, and urban crime: Do macrosocial variables also explain female offending rates? *Criminology, 38,* 403–438.

Steffensmeier, D., & Kramer, J., & Streifel, C. (1993). Gender and imprisonment decisions. *Criminology, 31,* 411–446.

Steffensmeier, D., Schwartz, J., & Roche, M. (2013). Gender and 21st century corporate crime: Female involvement and gender gap in Enron-era corporate frauds. *American Sociological Review, 78,* 448–476.

Steffensmeier, D., Schwartz, J., Zhong, H., & Ackerman, J. (2005). An assessment of recent trends in girls' violence using diverse longitudinal sources: Is the gender gap closing? *Criminology, 43,* 355–406.

Steffensmeier, D., & Terry, R. (1986). Institutional sexism in the underworld: A view from the inside. *Sociological Inquiry, 56,* 304–323.

Steffensmeier, D., & Ulmer, J. (2005). *Confessions of a dying thief: Understanding criminal careers and illegal enterprise.* New Brunswick, NJ: Aldine Transaction.

Steffensmeier, D., & Ulmer, J. (in press). Taking criminal opportunity seriously: An actor-centered approach. In F. T. Cullen, P. Wilcox, R. J. Sampson, & B. D. Dooley (Eds.), *Challenging criminological theory: The legacy of Ruth Rosner Kornhauser.* New Brunswick, NJ: Transaction.

West, C., & Zimmerman, D. H. (1987). Doing gender. *Gender and Society, 1,* 125–151.

Wright, L. S., & Steffensmeier, D. (2011). *What police reports tell us about male and female arrests for larceny, fraud, forgery, and embezzlement*. Paper presented at the Annual Meeting of the Pennsylvania Sociological Association Meetings, Mansfield, PA.

Zhang, S., Chin, K., & Miller, J. (2007). Women's participation in Chinese transnational human smuggling. *Criminology, 45*, 699–733.

Zhong, H., & Schwartz, J. (2010). Exploring gender-specific trends in underage drinking across adolescent age groups and measures of drinking: Is girls' drinking catching up with boys'? *Journal of Youth and Adolescence, 39*, 911–926.

Zietz, D. (1981). *Women who embezzle or defraud*. New York, NY: Praeger.

CHAPTER 13

Does Feminist Theory Matter?

Amanda M. Petersen, Emily J. Salisbury, and Jody Sundt

Open nearly any book on criminological theory or browse criminal justice texts in the library and you are bound to see chapters, sections, and even entire volumes dedicated to feminist theory. However, had you been a student in the same library 20 or 30 years prior, many of these writings would have been mysteriously absent from the shelves. It was not until the mid-1970s that feminist thought began to shape criminological research by introducing important questions and perspectives related to gender. Since that time, the influence of feminist theory has grown at an exponential pace. Still, many scholars do not account for gender in their research, new theories and policies are developed without sufficient attention to gender differences, and the experiences of men continue to dominate our understanding of crime and justice. More generally, others question the importance of feminist theory, arguing that it has little to offer the study of crime and justice or that it is a tangential field of study related solely to women's issues.

Those who value feminist theory appreciate the numerous ways that this perspective contributes to our understanding of crime and justice. Feminist theory not only is concerned with the experiences of women and girls, but also is broadly applicable. All theory—feminist or otherwise—matters in the social sciences for the ways that it informs the research process. Theory also guides what we think we ought to do after the research is finished. More specifically, theory matters in four unique ways.

First, theory helps us to ask better questions—ones that are meaningful, innovative, and relevant. Theory enables us to take on a certain perspective, or lens, and understand phenomena in light of this view. Without well-developed theory, we are less capable of asking questions that build coherent bodies of research connected by a common understanding of a given topic. Feminist theories, in particular, emphasize the influence of *gender* in social phenomena. And, as a consequence, feminist theories lead researchers to ask better questions about gender and gendered patterns.

Second, theory helps us interpret our observations. The same theoretical lens that helps us ask better research questions can also help us make sense of our data. Feminist theories provide insight into why gendered patterns occur and help us draw solid inferences about the meaning of these patterns.

Third, theory can inform the ways that we study questions. Some theoretical traditions value certain methodologies over others, which shapes not only the way that questions are asked, but also how researchers go about answering their questions. In addition, theories are linked to epistemological or ontological traditions—simply put, ways of knowing and worldviews—and are therefore concerned with the nature of knowledge and our ability to interpret and understand that knowledge. These traditions may also influence the methods used to study questions or the tools used to interpret findings. Although there is not one particular method or worldview that is required for feminist scholarship, a number of popular research traditions have emerged that are based on feminist theories, values, and objectives.

Fourth, theory matters because it suggests ways to solve problems. Most researchers are committed to building stronger bodies of knowledge in their specialty or field of interest. Although some research is conducted solely for the sake of understanding the social world, many people conduct research with the hope that their findings will be used to address an existing problem. There is a strong tradition among feminist scholars of activism or *praxis*—practicing one's ideals. As discussed in more detail below, feminists have promoted important criminal justice reforms.

In all of the ways that theory generally matters in the social sciences, feminist theory matters. These ideas are explored more fully below. We begin by considering the definition of feminist theories, noting that this idea is fluid and multifaceted. Next, we more thoroughly examine the unique ways that feminist theory can be a beneficial resource in asking questions about gender, interpreting gendered differences, studying research questions, and solving crime- and justice-related problems. We conclude by revisiting why feminist theory matters and illustrate the wide-ranging influence that feminist scholarship has had on our understanding of crime and justice.

What Are Feminist Theories?

Understanding feminist theory begins with an understanding of feminism. The term feminism is frequently associated with the various movements for women's liberation. bell hooks, a popular feminist theorist and cultural critic, captured this aspect of feminism when she wrote, "Feminism is a movement to end sexism, sexist exploitation, and oppression" (hooks, 2000, p. viii). However, what prompted and sprang from these movements was a way of thinking about the social world that people observed around them, particularly as it related to patriarchy, sexism, and gendered differences. Feminism, therefore, was defined by some not as an action or a specific set of propositions or rules, but as a perspective. For those who identify with feminism, these definitions are not exclusive, but complementary. This is one of the qualities that makes feminism difficult to define.

Some individuals who work to end sexism, sexist exploitation, and oppression do so because they identify as feminists. Daly and Chesney-Lind (1988) noted this idea when they wrote that feminism is "a set of strategies for social change" (p. 502) as well as "a set of theories about women's oppression" (p. 502). These theories evolved based on shifting societal conditions and the collective intellectual contributions of those who discuss and utilize the theories. For this reason, feminist thought not only changes over time, but also varies from person to person.

One common idea that connects most, if not all, feminist thought is that despite gender being a socially constructed idea, gender matters—politically, socially, culturally, historically, and individually. Feminist theory, therefore, is theory that takes into account the idea that gender matters. More specifically, a core assumption of feminist theory is that a woman's experience in the world is not the same as a man's experience. In the field of criminology and criminal justice, this reality means that questions about gendered differences in offending, criminal justice processes, victimization, and employment in criminal justice professions are at the forefront of feminist theory. Rather than applying a "gender-neutral" approach to theory, feminist theorists tend to inquire about, interpret, and at times seek to resolve these differences. Depending on the particular theorist, the use of feminist theory or perspective may be subtle or more overt. As noted above, the theoretical framework employed may influence the question that is asked, the way the findings are interpreted, the method used to study the question, or the approach to addressing the gendered differences highlighted in the research.

This variation can be clearly exemplified by the work of Freda Adler, who was among the first scholars to receive substantial attention for her work on the role of gender in criminological research. Adler's 1975 book, *Sisters in Crime: The Rise of the New Female Criminal*, is often the first work cited in any chapter on the history of feminist criminology and is discussed as the first major work to focus on gendered differences and gendered patterns in offending. Although Adler recognized a shift in female offending and sought to interpret her observations by theorizing about the effect that the women's movement had on gender roles in society, Adler prefers to first be seen as a scientist and does not identify strongly with feminist criminology (Hartman & Sundt, 2011). In contrast, other scholars, such as Meda Chesney-Lind, who focus on gender or utilize feminist theory in their criminological research, see their work as arising from a feminist perspective and identify strongly as feminist criminologists. Still other scholars fall somewhere between these two approaches. Some might see this lack of uniformity as problematic for the development of feminist theory. Yet, it can also be argued that this diversity significantly contributes to the expansion and popularization of feminist theory in criminology and criminal justice, making feminist theory *matter* in ways that would not be possible with an exclusive or rigid definition of feminism and feminist theory.

Asking Questions About Gender

Prior to the 1970s, there was little mention of women in the criminological literature. When female offenders were discussed, they were often identified as pathological deviants who were simply straying from their expected behavioral and biological roles as meek, passive, and maternal domestics or women were noted as inherently cunning because of their need to hide the pain associated with menstruation and fake orgasm (e.g., Lombroso & Ferrero, 1895/1920; Pollak, 1950; for a critique, see Smart, 1978). The study of crime and criminal justice was largely the study of why men sometimes committed crimes and how men behaved as actors in the criminal justice system. The women's movement of the 1960s and 1970s helped bring more women into academia and propelled feminist thought from the margins to a more central position in theoretical debates. Cultural assumptions that distorted views about women and girls, exaggerated the differences between males and females, or simply ignored gender altogether were rigorously challenged.

Female criminologists, such as Adler, started to ask questions specifically about women as offenders, victims, and criminal justice professionals drawing on their own gendered experiences and perspectives (Hartman & Sundt, 2011). Whereas previous research ignored gender, distorted its significance, or simply treated it as a "control variable," feminist theory focused on the lives of women and placed gender as a social phenomenon at the forefront of research projects—examining the *meaning* of gender. Adler's *Sisters in Crime*, although not specifically informed by feminist theory, gained particular notoriety as an illustration of this burgeoning body of women-centered research. Alternatively, Meda Chesney-Lind, who Adler cited as being a more accurate representation of a feminist criminologist than herself (Hartman & Sundt, 2011), identified her research as political and informed by feminist thought (Belknap, 2004), influencing the questions posed in her research.

One common trait of scholars like Adler and Chesney-Lind, as well as others who took on the study of women, crime, and gender in 1970s (e.g., Dorie Klein, Wilma Scott Heide, Rita Simon, Carol Smart), is that they asked unprecedented research questions that led to new interpretations of crime and the criminal justice system. For example, Freda Adler implicitly began her research by asking the question, "Why are women committing more crimes today than they have in the past?" Indeed, she observed that despite women committing far less crime than men, the female crime rate was increasing. Moreover, women seemed to be committing violent crime at a greater rate than they had in the past. Adler theorized that this change was the result of shifting gender roles caused by the women's movement of the 1960s and 1970s. As traditional social and psychological barriers between men and women were being broken down, Adler believed that women would be liberated from traditional feminine identity with its strong prohibition on deviance. Adler predicted that women's crime rates would continue to increase as women further redefined their roles in society and encountered more opportunity to commit crime, such as through employment in white-collar careers.

Forty years later, we know that Adler's prediction has not come to fruition and the gender gap is still firmly in root, even with more opportunities for women to engage in offending. However, just because Adler's conclusions were incorrect does not diminish the importance of her question and what it represented—a fundamental shift in the way offending was interpreted. Further, Adler's theory is recognized as part of the feminist criminological canon not because Adler identified as a feminist, but because her work pointedly examined why a gendered pattern in offending was occurring, as well as the interpretations associated with that pattern.

The areas in which researchers have utilized feminist theory to interpret gendered differences and patterns now go well beyond the work of Freda Adler. Below, we consider four areas that are particularly rich: feminist interpretations of offending, criminal justice processes, the criminal justice profession, and victimization.

Interpreting Offending

Feminist theories of offending begin with the idea that women and men, girls and boys, have fundamentally different life experiences that facilitate delinquent and offending behavior. The concept of gender itself is at the forefront in explaining why women commit far less crime and violence than men, why girls and women require more provocation than boys and men before committing violent acts, and why women's criminality is often related to prior traumatic experiences and unhealthy, abusive relationships. Indeed, feminist theories recognize the intersection between victimization and offending among justice-involved girls and women.

Feminist criminologists have focused primarily on a perspective of offending that recognizes the social, psychological, biological, cultural, and historical distinctions across gender. This approach, known as the pathways perspective, integrates the cumulative knowledge from feminist psychology (e.g., Jean Baker Miller, Carol Gilligan, Stephanie Covington), feminist sociology (e.g., Betty Friedan), feminist philosophy (e.g., Simone de Beauvoir), and gendered addiction research (e.g., Yih-Ing Hser, Nena Messina) into the understanding of female offending. By listening to female offenders' own stories about how they became involved in the criminal justice system, feminist criminologists began to see a pattern of experiences that was qualitatively different from the dominant, male-based etiological explanations of crime.

Consistently, data have shown that criminally involved women have life histories plagued with physical and sexual abuse, poverty, unhealthy intimate relationships, mental illness (i.e., depression, anxiety, posttraumatic stress disorder), and substance abuse. The feminist pathways approach seeks to explain how women often find themselves in a cycle of victimization that leads to offending behavior. One research study of women probationers in Missouri (Salisbury & Van Voorhis, 2009) found support for three commonly described pathways by women offenders in prior studies: (1) a "child abuse" pathway, which demonstrated that abuse during childhood led to mental illness and substance abuse; (2) a "relational" pathway, revealing that intimate relationships, characterized by a loss of personal power, were associated with women probationers' diminished self-efficacy, increased intimate-partner victimization, mental illness, and substance abuse; and (3) a "social and human capital" pathway that emphasized women probationers' lack of social support, dysfunctional intimate relationships, and low educational achievement. Each pathway increased the chances of women probationers' failure on community supervision and further penetration of the system through incarceration.

Importantly, feminist interpretations of offending are not limited to only understanding the experiences of girls and women. Indeed, if we are to understand how sex roles and gender norms influence the behavior of women through femininity, we must similarly understand how they affect the behavior of men through masculinity. More broadly, feminist scholars seek to explore how patriarchy influences the cultural forces surrounding femininity and masculinity. Although patriarchy is frequently referred to as the oppression of women by men, Carol Gilligan (2002) provides a deeper meaning, suggesting that patriarchy oppresses not only girls and women, but also boys and men, although in different ways.

> Patriarchy . . . literally means a hierarchy—a rule of priests—in which the priest, the *hieros*, is a father. It describes an order of living that elevates fathers, separating fathers from sons (the men from the boys) and placing both sons and women under a father's authority. (Gilligan, 2002, pp. 4–5, emphasis in original)

Within this framework, Gilligan (2002) further argues that sons do not become fathers (and part of the patriarchal order) until they embrace their masculinity while also letting go of their inherent femininity. Daughters, in contrast, cannot elevate beyond their femininity regardless of how much they might embrace their masculinity over their femininity. There is no elevation from daughter to mother in a patriarchal order because this transition is still from woman to woman (perhaps the reason why Gilligan excludes daughters from her definition altogether). In the case of either son or daughter, a profound sense of loss occurs: for the son, a loss of part of himself; for the daughter, a loss in having to hide part of herself. Thus, feminism is "understood not as a battle in the war between the sexes but rather a movement to transform a world in which both men and women suffer losses that constrain their ability to love" (Gilligan, 2002, p. 46). What it means to be a *man* versus what it means to be a *woman* are central ideas to the feminist approach of understanding both women's and men's offending and the distinctions that exist between them.

Interpreting Criminal Justice Processing

Feminist theory is often invoked when interpreting criminal justice responses to offending in two ways: when examining and explaining how the criminal justice system has traditionally responded to female crime and when theorizing and implementing gender-informed methods for responding to offending. The two interpretations are intertwined given that the shortcomings of a system that ignores gender have prompted the development of procedures and programs that place gendered differences and patterns at the forefront.

Feminist theorists have long pointed to patriarchy as the driving theoretical force in the criminal justice processing of women and girls. Patriarchy, the institutionalization of male dominance, is theorized to explain why women and girls are arrested for certain crimes more frequently than men and boys (e.g., Chesney-Lind, 1989; Kurshan, 1992). Under this approach, the criminal justice system is conceptualized as a social control mechanism that acts in place of an absent or defective form of familial control, especially targeting women for crimes that are sexual (e.g., prostitution), "unladylike" (e.g., drug use, theft), or resistant to male control (e.g., assault). Mandatory arrest policies, for example, often involve women in the criminal justice system for "assaults" that were committed in defense of abuse by a male intimate partner (Miller, 2005). These arrests increased assault rates among women, leading the public and media to view women and girls as increasingly violent and in need of enhanced social control.

Theories of patriarchy have influenced theories of judicial paternalism. One side of judicial paternalism theory proposes that judges may seek to monitor and punish girls who deviate from gendered norms under the façade of benevolence or fatherly care by criminalizing status offenses (Chesney-Lind, 1977). Oppositely, judicial paternalism has also been theorized to be responsible for leniency in the sentencing of female offenders. Daly (1989) found that the issue of parenthood complicates judicial paternalism. Judges may provide more lenient sentences to female offenders; however, this leniency is granted to women who are mothers so that their ability to act as a caretaker to their family is uninterrupted. Gruhl, Welch, and Spohn (1984) also found evidence of judicial leniency toward women, theorizing that parental role and head-of-household status may affect judicial decision making. The Gruhl et al. study also took the importance of race into consideration, acknowledging that gender may interact with race to produce different outcomes for women and men of different races. Race, gender, and class are the foundation of intersectional theories, which also predominate in interpretations of gender differences in criminal justice processing. Intersectionalities have become an important theoretical framework in the study of gender, especially when seeking to understand the unique disadvantage faced by poor Black women (e.g., Christian & Thomas, 2009; Richie, 1996; Sudbury, 2004).

Based on gendered differences and patterns, feminist theory has also informed interpretations of correctional policies, procedures, and programming. These interpretations are highly connected to interpretations of offending, given that a gendered interpretation of why someone offends is necessary to address gender differences among offenders. Theorists who seek to interpret the unique needs of men and women with feminist theory frequently turn to one of several theoretical traditions for guidance. Relational theories, developed by Gilligan (1982) and Miller (1976), suggest that women tend to find identity and self-worth through personal affiliations and relationships. Consequently, efforts to reduce offending in women would work toward "development of relationships that are mutual, caring and empowering" (Bloom, 1999, p. 23). Trauma theories acknowledge that women and girls experience and process trauma differently than men and boys, whereas holistic addiction theories interpret gender differences in substance abuse (Van Voorhis & Salisbury, 2013). Each of these theories has been instrumental in the development of correctional responses to crime that are gender informed and gender responsive, such as the use of gender-responsive risk or needs assessment, as well as programs that address trauma and addiction in female offenders.

Interpreting Experiences of Criminal Justice Professionals

Beyond influencing views on offending and responses to female crime, feminist perspectives have also begun to change the landscape of professionalism in criminal justice. Although the traditional, masculine culture still exists in most areas of the criminal justice system, with the exception of victim and nonprofit services, there has been a shift toward recognizing the benefits of a more feminized profession.

A clear illustration can be found in the legal mandates surrounding cross-gender supervision of male and female inmates. Despite the increased access to correctional employment opportunities for women throughout the 1970s, female officers were primarily limited to positions that supervised other women. As a result, female staff often lacked the work experience considered necessary to earn promotion to administrative positions. In 1982, female officers filed suit against the Michigan Department of Corrections alleging employment discrimination through restriction of duties based on gender. The U.S. District Court ruled in favor of the female officers by stating that inmates had no right to privacy because they were being observed unclothed or undressing by correctional staff, regardless of gender (*Griffin v. Michigan Department of Corrections*, 654 F. Supp. 690, 1982).

Although this case created opportunities for women to work in male facilities, men had long since been permitted to supervise female inmates without reservation. However, new case law supports the designation of exclusively female staff in positions that require pat downs, strip searches, urinalysis, and observation of women inmates in varying states of undress. In *Teamsters Local Union No. 117 v. Washington State Department of Corrections*, a U.S. District Court ruled a summary judgment in favor of the Washington State Department of Corrections that established 84 female-only staff positions at the two women's correctional institutions. The judgment was informed by feminist research uncovering the high rates of trauma and victimization experienced by women inmates, as well as the disproportionate number of male staff sexual assaults against female inmates.

The adoption of such female-only staff positions is also consistent with the broader effort by the U.S. Department of Justice, the National Institute of Corrections, and the Center for Effective Public Policy to support gender-responsive correctional practices in institutional settings. The Gender-Informed Program Assessment is designed to assist correctional facilities with a structured method of adhering to the principles of effective correctional intervention and gender-responsive practices. Broadly, the purpose of the assessment focuses on fostering the success of women inmate populations through creating a culture of safety and respect among inmates and staff. Facilities that choose to go through the Gender-Informed Program Assessment process will discover the importance of embracing the realities of women offenders, beginning with its leadership to the line staff. As more agencies begin to adopt gender-informed practices, the correctional profession and culture itself will likely shift further toward greater recognition that gender matters, not only for how we view offending and offenders, but also for how we view the correctional profession itself.

Interpreting Victimization

The victimization of women continues to be an important area of inquiry within feminist criminology. Traditional criminology never prioritized the victimization of women as a major line of study, in part because for much of the 20th century a woman was legally viewed as the property of her father or husband. Today, much of the knowledge amassed on intimate-partner abuse, stalking, domestic violence, rape, sexual assault, and sex trafficking is the result of feminist scholarly research.

For instance, one of the most recent advances in feminist interpretations of victimization is the redefinition of "rape" in the UCR published by the FBI. Feminist criminologists worked for decades to gain a more accurate definition—one that recognizes that rape does not require use of physical force and that victims and assailants could be either gender or the same gender. In 2012, the FBI adopted the modern version, defining rape as "penetration, no matter how slight, of the vagina or anus with any body part or object or oral penetration by a sex organ of another person, without the consent of the victim" (FBI, 2012).

Other interpretations of women's victimization place race at the center of study rather than solely gender. Potter (2006) proposed a Black feminist criminology to demonstrate that Black women's victimizations and offenses cannot be fully understood by classic feminist criminological theory because it was largely developed through the experiences of White women. Using intimate-partner abuse as an illustration, Potter (2006) argues that to truly grasp Black women's victimizations (and those of other minority and immigrant women), one must first learn how the sources of the abuse and reactions to it are affected by African American women's "place" in society. "Being at the least valued end of the spectrum for both race and gender places these women in a peculiar position not faced by Black men or White women" (Potter, 2006, p. 110).

As a result, Potter (2006) argued that the identities of African American women should be understood as complex and multidimensional around multiplicative forms of oppression as a result of their race, ethnicity, gender, class, nationality, and sexuality. Her efforts are not to "pathologize" Black women by recognizing the insidious traumas they face, but to highlight that not doing so only serves to deny the realities of Black women. For researchers to gain a true representation of Black women's victimization, we must realize that some African American women will choose to stay in abusive relationships out of fear of losing a father figure for their children (a reality in light of the overincarceration of young Black men in the United States) or to avoid stereotypical characterizations as just another single Black mother (Potter, 2004).

Potter's (2006) Black feminist criminology represented an effort to push both traditional (gender-neutral) and feminist explanations of victimization and offending forward. Her analytical strategy to construct knowledge in these areas by first beginning with conceptualizations of Black culture helps the discipline take on a fresh perspective. In turn, her work will likely inspire new research questions and interpretations beyond race and gender to include the culture of sexuality and sexual orientation.

Ways of Knowing

Among the important contributions of feminism is the way it has challenged traditional, male-centric models of knowing. Belenky, Clinchy, Goldberger, and Tarule (1986) were among the first to advance a model of cognitive development specifically informed by the experiences and views of girls and women. Their influential work, titled *Women's Ways of Knowing*, argued that the cognitive development of girls and women, specifically views about the sources, authority, and nature of knowledge, was different than that experienced by boys and men. Based on their interviews with 135 girls and women between the ages of 16 and 60, they identified five categories of cognitive development experienced by women: silence, received knowledge, subjective knowledge, procedural knowledge, and constructed knowledge. Each category represents a different belief about the relationship between the self and sources of knowledge or truth (Hofer & Pintrich, 1997).

Although the orientations toward knowledge identified by Belenky et al. (1986) had parallels with stages of cognitive development proposed by Perry (1970) based on a study of mostly male college students, they emphasized that women's ways of knowing—the sources of knowledge identified by women—were tied to self-concept and relationships with others. In particular, Belenky et al. drew a distinction between "connected knowing," or truth based on empathy and care, and "separate knowledge," or detached and impersonal truth based, for example, on critical thinking. As Belenky et al. assert, at the most advanced mode of thinking "[a]ll knowledge is constructed and the knower is an innate part of the known" (p. 137). According to this view, knowledge is contextual and is an integration of both objective and subjective experiences.

Works like those by Belenky and her colleagues (1986) help us think about where knowledge comes from, how we know, what counts as truth, and how our beliefs shape our answers to these questions. They also sensitize us to the ways that our experiences as "knowers" are shaped by our gender and self-concept. Theorists' self-concepts and their beliefs about where knowledge originates similarly influences how they conduct research. Research, after all, is one way that knowledge is created.

Two predominant scientific philosophies that guide research in criminology are positivism and social constructivism. Positivism is a belief that reality exists apart from human perceptions of that reality and that this knowledge can be acquired and understood through the human senses and objective research practices. This particular philosophy is associated with quantitative research methodologies. In contrast, social constructivism focuses on the subjective meaning of experiences. According to this view, knowledge develops through social interactions with others and is shaped by our cultural and historical backgrounds. Social constructivism is associated with qualitative research methodologies. Feminist scholars have challenged both views.

For example, feminists observed that the "truth" promoted in much of the positivist research was missing a key consideration—women—and, therefore, was not generalizable or objective knowledge. Feminist theorists such as Harding (1987) proposed the concept of "strong objectivity" as a way of reimagining objectivity to include an acknowledgment of social position as well as inclusion of marginalized individuals and groups as research practitioners and subjects (Hirsch & Olson, 1995). Researchers who saw the merits of this approach and valued many aspects of the positivist framework, particularly those who had gender- or woman-centered research agendas, began to identify as "feminist empiricists" (Leckenby, 2007).

Feminist empiricism has certainly not gone without critique, especially its continued use of positivist epistemology. Some critics are concerned that feminist empiricism is simply "adding women" to a faulty epistemology and "stirring." This argument assumes that true objectivity is not possible, especially when founded in a framework developed by a dominant group (i.e., male intellectuals). In response to these critiques, feminist-informed epistemologies have emerged. Similar to the notion that history is written by the victors, feminist standpoint epistemology is an "alternative way of knowing" (Smith, 1990, p. 20) that focuses primarily on understanding the world from the position of the oppressed (Brooks, 2007).

Feminist standpoint epistemology does not seek to reduce or control the influence of the social position of the researcher or research subjects, but seeks to use subjective experience to achieve greater understanding of the research topic. Particular attention is paid to interpreting the research topic from the position of those who experience it directly, especially those who may be disadvantaged by a specific social dynamic. The knowledge generated by this process is arguably more authentic than that which seeks to remove the lived experiences of those involved in the research project. This perspective maintains that the lived experience is a truer representation of how society operates than a "value-free," numerical analysis. For this reason, Harding (1987) describes feminist standpoint epistemology not as a perspective, but as an achievement. By this, Harding means that an action must occur—namely, an intellectual and political action—that shifts the understanding of the social world from the dominant perspective to the perspective of the oppressed.

Harding (1987) is quick to point out that although feminist empiricism and feminist standpoint epistemology have unique appeal, they are not inherently in conflict with one another. In fact, Harding emphasizes that it is not necessary to choose one epistemology or another, but to appreciate that they are in "dialogue with each other" (p. 186). Although these two epistemologies are discussed in great depth in feminist research texts, other epistemologies such as feminist postmodernism epistemology and culture-specific epistemologies also offer unique feminist-informed frameworks for understanding knowledge with important implications for research in the field of criminology and criminal justice.

Epistemologies, although interesting in their own right, also serve to influence methodologies, or the way that research is carried out, which are connected to the methods that are used in a study. Sprague (2005) describes methodology as "the terrain where philosophy and action meet" (p. 5) or the link between epistemology and method. A given epistemology will lead to decisions about what questions are asked and how data are collected, analyzed, interpreted, and presented, which are all based on one's beliefs about the discovery or creation of knowledge. For example, feminist empiricists tend toward a quantifiable research methodology in which an attempt is made to understand the social world through a research process that is representative of the population under study. This affects, for example, how the research sample is selected (randomly), what methods are used (quantitative), and how the results are analyzed (statistically). Alternatively, feminist standpoint epistemologists are more likely to favor a methodology that values contextual knowledge and, therefore, uses a nonrandom and theoretically driven sample, qualitative method, and open-ended data coding and interpretation.

In practice, scholars who conduct feminist-informed research may not adhere strictly to a specific scientific ideology or methodology, but take a pragmatic approach that allows the needs of the research project to dictate the most appropriate methodology. Frequently, researchers who have feminist-informed research practices integrate qualitative and quantitative methods into one research project. Mixed methods, as this strategy is often called, exists to use the strengths of one method to supplement the weaknesses of another (Morgan, 2014). Integrating methods is not inherently a feminist action, but can be one way of expressing feminist theory in the research process when used to addresses the weaknesses in any given epistemology (Leckenby & Hesse-Biber, 2007). Researchers who integrate methods in a single study, or who use both qualitative and quantitative methods independently in their work, may not identify strongly with one ideology, but value the ability to look at their research topic from a variety of angles. For these researchers, the research topic is the most influential factor in selecting the appropriate method, or methods, rather than a theory of knowledge (Creswell, 2013).

Ways of Solving Problems

Feminist theory not only informs the process of posing questions about, interpreting, and studying a given topic, but also, for many scholars, implies action. Even for researchers whose work is primarily concerned with understanding the social world as it relates to women and the construction of gender, the ultimate goal of such research is not only to understand, but also to change, the social conditions that create disadvantage and oppression. The connection between feminist theory and action is so prevalent that it is frequently acknowledged as being closely aligned with an advocacy or participatory worldview (e.g., Creswell, 2013). The personal values that each researcher brings to his or her work will influence how action-oriented research is described—as applied research, advocacy, activism, or something else—and such descriptions surely vary across the field. Additionally, the action that the researcher elicits varies by the individual or research project, resulting in a wide range of outcomes. Evaluation research, the creation of gender-informed policies and programs, the provisions of expert knowledge to organizations and governmental entities, and the dissemination of knowledge related to gendered patterns and differences are a sampling of the ways in which feminist theory is used to solve problems within and outside the criminal justice system.

Each year, the American Society of Criminology's Division on Women and Crime publishes a list of sessions of interest to be presented at the American Society of Criminology Annual Meeting. These sessions, which each have an emphasis on women or gender, encompass a wide variety of topics across the spectrum of criminological and criminal justice research. At the 2013 Annual Meeting, the Division on Women and Crime promoted over 120 sessions. Based on session titles alone, it appears that 27% of the sessions contained at least one presentation that was action oriented. This number is likely slightly higher, given that an applied or advocacy angle was at the center of certain research projects but not made apparent in the title. Sessions focused on problem solving in the area of victimization—such as domestic violence, human trafficking, and preventing and responding to sexual violence—were most common among the problem solving–oriented sessions. A smaller number of sessions addressed criminal justice responses to female offenders, and several discussed strategies for teaching gender and sensitive topics in the classroom. For one quarter of all gender-based presentations at a research-heavy conference to be action oriented is one way of demonstrating just how relevant feminist theory is to the field of criminology and criminal justice.

Examples of the use of feminist theory to solve justice-related problems are as vast and unique as the scholars and practitioners who seek to put gender at the center of their work. Although an endless number of illustrations are available, several recent and ongoing projects are notable for their scale and effect. The work of Stephanie Covington and Barbara Bloom at the Center for Gender and Justice, for example, is concerned with promoting and enhancing gender-responsive policies and programs in the criminal justice system (The Center for Gender and Justice, 2014). These women and their colleagues conduct research, provide training to practitioners and administrators in criminal justice settings in gender-related topics and treatment models, offer assessment of gender-responsive programming, and consult on a wide variety of gender-related topics. Although the center is a powerful example of this kind of problem solving, countless feminist-informed scholars offer these types of action-oriented services in their own states and communities.

The provision of expert testimony in the development and evaluation of policy is, although common across the field, especially significant with regard to feminist theory. For many feminist scholars, the wish for feminism to be inherently action oriented and the desire to share knowledge and create meaningful change are integral parts of the research process. Barbara Owen and her testimonials regarding prison rape and the treatment of female prisoners provide a noteworthy model of the effort to problem solve through education. On multiple occasions, Owen testified before the U.S. Department of Justice Office of Justice Program's Review Panel on Prison Rape (Office of Justice Programs, 2006, 2011). This panel, which convenes annually, is concerned with hearing evidence on the status of prison rape, in accordance with the Prison Rape Elimination Act of 2003. Owen's testimony as a prison sociologist, Prison Rape Elimination Act expert, and scholar of gender-responsive programs and policies provided a credible source of knowledge on how prison culture and staff training can influence the incidence of rape in prisons and jails that incarcerate women and girls, as well as how incarcerated women experience intimate relationships and victimization. Additionally, Owen acted as an expert consultant in the development of the United Nations Rules for the Treatment of Female Prisoners and Non-Custodial Measures for Women Offenders, also known as the Bangkok Rules, which were implemented in 2010 (United Nations Office of Drugs and Crime, 2009). These rules are informed by a feminist perspective and acknowledge that the needs of prisoners are gender specific and should be treated accordingly. The Bangkok Rules and the Prison Rape Elimination Act are themselves clear examples of how feminist theory can enhance the ability of individuals and organizations to solve problems. Owen's work toward both measures stands as an illustration of the actions that an individual can take to promote change.

A final example of how feminist theory has informed the way that problems related to crime and justice are solved is the invention and implementation of Girls Courts. Girls Courts are specialized courts that were developed with the intention of meeting the unique needs of female juveniles and were implemented in the State of Hawaii in 2004; in Orange County, California, in 2009; and in Harris County, Texas, in 2011 (Annie E. Casey Foundation, 2011; Makanui-Lopes, 2013; Superior Court of Orange County, 2013). In 2009, the Superior Court of California in Orange County also established a Boys Court, which is gender responsive to at-risk boys. Each of the aforementioned courts uses theories related to trauma, victimization, addiction, relationship, and empowerment to respond to delinquency, consistent with criminological and criminal justice feminist literature and theory. Similarly, criminal justice professionals such as Judge Christine Carpenter of the Circuit Judge of Division One in the 13th Judicial Circuit bring a trauma-informed perspective to their supervisory roles, as Judge Carpenter does in the Alternative Sentencing Courts in Columbia, Missouri (GAINS Center for Behavioral Health and Justice Transformation, 2013). The work of feminist scholars to integrate gender-informed and feminist theory into the research literature has certainly influenced the creation of these courts, and the work of individuals, such as that of Meda Chesney-Lind and her colleagues who consulted on the Hawaii Girls Court, provided a direct connection to the project (Davidson, Pasko, & Chesney-Lind, 2011).

Conclusion: Does Feminist Theory Matter?

Social psychologists define mattering as "the extent to which we make a difference in the world around us" (Elliott, Kao, & Grant, 2004, p. 339). People matter when others attend to them, invest in them, or rely on them. If this definition is applied to an idea, it is possible to ask whether feminist theory has made a difference and whether others are aware of the idea, think it is important, and rely on it. As demonstrated throughout this chapter, feminist theories have certainly mattered in the ways that scholars have asked questions about gender, interpreted their findings, studied questions, and solved problems. Freda Adler and her contemporaries brought issues surrounding gender into the study of crime and justice, prompting a wide range of scholarship across the criminological and criminal justice literature. Heidensohn (2012) goes so far as to say that given their scope, resiliency, and robustness, feminist theories are the most successful developments in the study of crime and justice in the second half of the 20th century.

To illustrate the extent to which feminist theory matters to criminology, we conducted an analysis of the influence of Adler's (1975) *Sisters in Crime* on the discipline. As one of the first studies to propose a social, rather than a biological, account of gender differences in criminal offending, Adler's work was a bellwether that signaled a new, vibrant area of inquiry. Today we can observe the wide-ranging influence of feminist criminology and questions about gender by exploring the frequency and location of citations to *Sisters in Crime*.

When scholars write about a topic, they provide citations to works that they drew upon or quoted. These works appear in the bibliographies of research articles, books, and reports. Databases such as Google Scholar cross-reference academic studies and make it possible to view the list of works that cite a particular study. Conducting a citation analysis of *Sisters in Crime* using Google Scholar revealed 1,070 citations. We exported these citations to a spreadsheet that made it possible to examine some basic patterns about when and where references were made to *Sisters in Crime*. Figure 13.1 illustrates the annual number of times that *Sisters in Crime* was cited from 1976 to 2013, excluding citations to websites. *Sisters in Crime* was cited an average of 25 times per year. These citations appeared in 331 books, book chapters, theses, and dissertations and in 634 research articles, government reports, and conference papers.

The influence of feminist criminology can also be estimated by examining the range of journals where citations to *Sisters in Crime* have appeared. Although *Sisters in Crime* has been widely referenced in criminal justice and criminological journals, Adler's study has also significantly influenced the study of sociology as indicated by

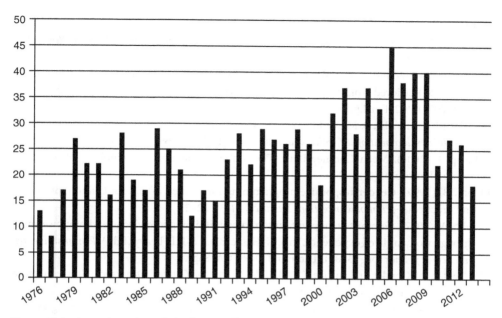

Figure 13.1. Annual number of citations to *Sisters in Crime*, 1976–2013 (n = 964)

the number of citations that appear in sociological journals. The reach of the work extends far beyond these disciplinary borders. *Sisters in Crime* has been cited in journals from a range of academic disciplines including economics, education, gender studies, history, international studies, law, literary criticism, political science, psychiatry, and psychology. The influence of *Sisters in Crime* has crossed international borders as well, with citations appearing in Canadian, British, Australian, German, Korean, Spanish-language, French, Chinese, Russian, Italian, and Swedish publications.

To place these numbers in context, a research article appearing in 1 of the top 20 journals in the discipline will be cited an average of 23 times over a five-year period (Google Scholar Metrics, 2014). Both the number of citations and the longevity of the influence of *Sisters in Crime* point to the sustained and widespread interest in and effect of feminist criminology.

Without doubt, feminist theory has made a difference in the scholarship and practice of crime and justice. And, a book or a course on criminology would be incomplete without feminist theories of crime. Whether feminist theory is widely valued and relied upon by academics, students, and members of the public is less clear, but this orientation has a strong and active set of champions. Perhaps the most important measure of whether a particular theory matters, however, is whether it continues to inspire new questions, stimulate debate, and even generate controversy. In this respect, feminist theory matters a great deal.

References

Adler, F. (1975). *Sisters in crime: The rise of the new female criminal.* New York, NY: McGraw–Hill.

Annie E. Casey Foundation. (2011). Harris county continues reforms. *Harris County JDAI, 3*(3), 1–4. Retrieved from http://www.co.harris.tx.us/hcjpd/JDAINewsletter/Newsletter%20 July%202011%20Final.pdf/

Belenky, M. F., Clinchy, B. M., Goldberger, N. R., & Tarule, J. M. (1986). *Women's ways of knowing: The development of self, voice, and mind.* New York, NY: Basic Books.

Belknap, J. (2004). Meda Chesney-Lind: The mother of feminist criminology. *Women and Criminal Justice, 15*(2), 1–23.

Bloom, B. (1999). Gender-responsive programming for women offenders: Guiding principles and practices. *Forum on Corrections Research, 11*(3), 22–27.

Brooks, A. (2007). Feminist standpoint epistemology: Building knowledge and empowerment through women's lived experience. In S. N. Hesse-Biber & P. L. Leavy (Eds.), *Feminist research practice: A primer* (pp. 53–82). Thousand Oaks, CA: Sage.

The Center for Gender and Justice. (2014). *The Center for Gender and Justice.* Retrieved from http://www.centerforgenderandjustice.org/

Chesney-Lind, M. (1977). Judicial paternalism and the female status offender: Training women to know their place. *Crime and Delinquency, 23*, 121–130.

Chesney-Lind, M. (1989). Girls' crime and woman's place: Toward a feminist model of female delinquency. *Crime and Delinquency, 35*, 5–29.

Christian, J., & Thomas, S. S. (2009). Examining the intersections of race, gender, and mass imprisonment. *Journal of Ethnicity in Criminal Justice, 7*, 69–84.

Creswell, J. W. (2013). *Research design: Qualitative, quantitative, and mixed methods approaches* (4th ed.). Thousand Oaks, CA: Sage.

Daly, K. (1989). Rethinking judicial paternalism: Gender, work–family relations, and sentencing. *Gender and Society, 3*, 9–36.

Daly, K., & Chesney-Lind, M. (1988). Feminism and criminology. *Justice Quarterly, 5*, 497–538.

Davidson, J. T., Pasko, L., & Chesney-Lind, M. (2011). She's way too good to lose: An evaluation of Honolulu's Girls Court. *Women and Criminal Justice, 21*, 308–327.

Elliott, G., Kao, S., & Grant, A. -M. (2004). Mattering: Empirical validation of a social–psychological concept. *Self and Identity, 3*, 339–354.

Federal Bureau of Investigation. (2012). *UCR program changes definition of rape: Includes all victims and omits requirement of physical force.* Criminal Justice Information Service, U.S. Department of Justice. Retrieved from http://www.fbi.gov/about-us/cjis/cjis-link/march-2012/ucr-program-changes-definition-of-rape/

GAINS Center for Behavioral Health and Justice Transformation. (2013). *Notes from the field: Judge Christine Carpenter on trauma-informed courts. Monthly Newsletter.* Retrieved from http://gainscenter.samhsa.gov/eNews/november13.html#first/

Gilligan, C. (1982). *In a different voice: Psychological theory and women's development.* Cambridge, MA: Harvard University Press.

Gilligan, C. (2002). *The birth of pleasure.* New York, NY: Knopf.

Google Scholar Metrics. (n.d.). *Top publications: Criminology, criminal law, and policing.* Retrieved from http://scholar.google.com/citations?view_op=top_venues&hl=en&vq=soc_criminologycriminallawpolicing/

Griffin v. Michigan Department of Corrections. (1982). 654 F. Supp. 690.

Gruhl, J., Welch, S., & Spohn, C. (1984). Women as criminal defendants: A test for paternalism. *Western Political Quarterly, 37,* 456–467.

Harding, S. G. (1987). *Feminism and methodology: Social science issues.* Bloomington: Indiana University Press.

Hartman, J. L., & Sundt, J. L. (2011). The rise of feminist criminology: Freda Adler. In F. T. Cullen, C. L. Jonson, A. J. Myer, & F. Adler (Eds.), *The origins of American criminology* (pp. 295–220). New Brunswick, NJ: Transaction.

Heidensohn, F. (2012). The future of feminist criminology. *Crime, Media, Culture, 8,* 123–134.

Hirsch, E., & Olson, G. A. (1995). Starting from marginalized lives: A conversation with Sandra Harding. *JAC: A Journal of Composition Theory, 15,* 193–225.

Hofer, B. K., & Pintrich, P. R. (1997). The development of epistemological theories: Beliefs about knowledge and knowing and their relation to learning. *Review of Educational Research, 67,* 88–140.

hooks, bell. (2000). *Feminism is for everybody: Passionate politics.* Cambridge, MA: South End Press.

Kurshan, N. (1992). Women and imprisonment in the U.S. In W. Churchill & J. Vander Wall (Eds.), *Cages of steel: The politics of imprisonment in the United States* (pp. 331–358). Washington, DC: Maisonneuve Press.

Leckenby, D. (2007). Feminist empiricism: Challenging gender bias and "setting the record straight." In S. N. Hesse-Biber & P. L. Leavy (Eds.), *Feminist research practice: A primer* (pp. 27–52). Thousand Oaks, CA: Sage.

Leckenby, D., & Hesse-Biber, S. N. (2007). Feminist approaches to mixed-methods research. In S. N. Hesse-Biber & P. L. Leavy (Eds.), *Feminist research practice: A primer* (p. 249–291). Thousand Oaks, CA: Sage.

Lombroso, C., & Ferrero, G. (1895/1920). *The female offender.* New York, NY: Appleton.

Makanui-Lopes, S. (2013). *Hawai'i Girls Court.* Retrieved from http://www.girlscourt.org/

Miller, J. B. (1976). *Toward a new psychology of women.* Boston, MA: Beacon Press.

Miller, S. L. (2005). *Victims as offenders: The paradox of women's violence in relationships.* New Brunswick, NJ: Rutgers University Press.

Morgan, D. L. (2014). *Integrating qualitative and quantitative methods: A pragmatic approach.* Thousand Oaks, CA: Sage.

Office of Justice Programs. (2006). *Hearings on rape and staff misconduct in U.S. prisons.* Represa, CA: U.S. Department of Justice. Retrieved from http://www.ojp.usdoj.gov/reviewpanel/pdfs_apr11/transcript_042611.pdf/

Office of Justice Programs. (2011). *Hearing on sexual violence by the Review Panel on Prison Rape.* Washington, DC: U.S. Department of Justice. Retrieved from http://www.ojp.usdoj.gov/reviewpanel/pdfs_apr11/transcript_042611.pdf/

Perry, W. G. (1970). *Forms of intellectual and ethical development in the college years: A scheme.* New York, NY: Holt, Rinehart and Winston.

Pollak, O. (1950). *The criminality of women.* Philadelphia: University of Pennsylvania Press.

Potter, H. (2004). *Intimate partner violence against African American women: The effects of social structure and Black culture on patterns of abuse.* Unpublished doctoral dissertation, University of Colorado–Boulder.

Potter, H. (2006). An argument for Black feminist criminology: Understanding African American women's experiences with intimate partner abuse using an integrated approach. *Feminist Criminology, 1,* 106–124.

Richie, B. (1996). *Compelled to crime: The gender entrapment of battered black women.* New York, NY: Routledge.

Salisbury, E. J., & Van Voorhis, P. (2009). Gendered pathways: A quantitative investigation of women probationers' paths to incarceration. *Criminal Justice and Behavior, 36,* 541–566.

Smart, C. (1978). *Women, crime, and criminology: A feminist critique.* New York, NY: Routledge.

Smith, D. E. (1990). *The conceptual practices of power: A feminist sociology of knowledge.* Boston, MA: Northeastern University Press.

Sprague, J. (2005). *Feminist methodologies for critical researchers: Bridging differences.* Walnut Creek, CA: AltaMira Press.

Sudbury, J. (2004). Women of color, globalization, and the politics of incarceration. In B. R. Price & N. J. Sokoloff (Eds.), *The criminal justice system and women: Offenders, prisoners, victims, and workers* (pp. 219–234). Boston, MA: McGraw–Hill.

Superior Court of Orange County. (2013). *Collaborative courts.* Retrieved from http://www .occourts.org/directory/collaborative-courts/

Teamsters Local Union No. 117 v. Washington State Department of Corrections. (2013). Document 39. Case No. C11-5760 BHS.

United Nations Office of Drugs and Crime. (2009). *Report on the meeting of the expert group to develop supplementary rules specific to the treatment of women in detention and in custodial and on-custodial settings.* Bangkok, Thailand. Retrieved from http://www.unodc.org/documents/commissions/CCPCJ_session19/UNODC_CCPCJ_EG3_2009_1eV1052017.pdf/

Van Voorhis, P., & Salisbury, E. J. (2013). *Correctional counseling and rehabilitation* (8th ed.). Cincinnati, OH: Anderson/Elsevier.

PART VI

Patriarchy, Masculinity, and Crime

CHAPTER 14

Masculinities and Crime

James W. Messerschmidt and Stephen Tomsen

It is no secret who commits the great majority of crimes. Arrest, self-report, and victimization data reflect that men and boys perpetrate more conventional crimes—and the more serious of these crimes—than do women and girls. And men have a virtual monopoly on the commission of syndicated, corporate, and political crime (Beirne & Messerschmidt, 2014). Criminologists have consistently advanced gender as the strongest single predictor of criminal involvement; consequently, studying men and boys provides insights into understanding the highly gendered ratio of crime in industrialized societies. Historically, the reasons for this highly gendered ratio of crime have puzzled researchers, officials, and commentators. Although criminal justice agencies focus heavily on detecting, prosecuting, and punishing the working-class, poor, and minority male offenders, it is apparent that high levels of recorded and reported offending reflect a real and pervasive social phenomenon of disproportionate male criminality. Since its origins at the end of the 1800s, criminology has experienced difficulty explaining the link between masculinity and crime, and research has often disregarded the link between criminal offending and maleness.

Much traditional criminological interest focused on why males, especially those from the working class, engaged in "dangerous" forms of crime (e.g., gang delinquency). Despite this near-exclusive interest in males rather than females, these discussions ignored how crime was connected to *masculinity* and how men and boys seek to attain power and status by displaying or constructing masculinity in various social contexts. According to Messerschmidt (1993), "Major theoretical works in criminology are alarmingly gender-blind. That is, while men and boys have been seen as the 'normal subjects,' the gendered content of their legitimate and illegitimate behavior has been virtually ignored" (p. 1).

Equipped with this "male norm" perspective, traditional criminologists proceeded to explore how crime is linked to a variety of factors (e.g., community disorganization, social learning, strain, lack of social bonds). In so doing, they failed to probe how crime is linked specifically to the *gender* of males, especially to nonpathological and widespread forms of masculine identity. The result has been a tendency to naturalize male offending and to revert to gender essentialism by explaining male wrongdoing as an inherent and presocial phenomenon to which men are drawn.

When they did consider gender, the earliest criminologists—such as Edwin Sutherland (1956 1947) and Albert Cohen (1955)—relied ultimately upon an essentialist "sex-role" framework to explain the relationship between masculinity and crime. That is, they presumed that a "natural" distinction existed between men and women, a distinction that led ineluctably to masculine men and feminine women. Accordingly, despite other substantive differences in their theories, these criminologists were united in arguing that certain innate or biological characteristics formed the basis of gendered social conditions—the male and female sex roles—that led to specific sexed patterns of crime. In other words, biogenic criteria allegedly established differences between men and women, and society culturally elaborated the distinctions through the socialization of sex roles. These sex roles, in turn, determined the types and amounts of crime committed by men and women and by boys and girls. Thus, for these early criminologists, the body entered criminological theory cryptically as biological differences between men and women (Messerschmidt, 1993).

Notwithstanding, early criminologists like Sutherland and Cohen can be credited for putting masculinity on the criminological agenda. These scholars perceived the theoretical importance of gender and its relation to crime, and they acted upon that awareness. However, their conclusions demonstrate the limitations one would expect from any prefeminist criminological work. Gender essentialism was the accepted doctrine of the day; it took modern feminism to dismantle that powerful "common-sense" understanding of gender. Rather than being gender blind then, Sutherland and Cohen simply had a different conception of gender than exists among criminologists today. The social and historical context in which they wrote embodied (1) a relative absence of feminist theorizing and politics and (2) an assumed natural difference between men and women. Accordingly, it should not be surprising that they advanced these types of theories.

This focus on biology by early criminologists also often viewed crime as a reflection of *defective* male and female bodies or identities (Gould, 1981). A range of subsequent accounts similarly disregarded the social link between crime and masculinity. These have included Marxist and leftist accounts that focused on class differences to explain crime and then either relied on biological sex differences to explain the gendered pattern of most criminal offending or said nothing about it (Bonger, 2003; Taylor, Walton, & Young, 1973).

The concentration on differences between male and female offenders was challenged in the 1970s by Freda Adler (1975), who assumed an undifferentiated sameness across gender constructions. In her view, because of the second wave of the women's movement, adolescent girls were becoming more masculine, and this led an increasing number of them to use "weapons and wits to establish themselves as full human beings, capable of violence and aggression as any man" (Adler, 1975, p. 15). For Adler (1977), because of "liberation," the "'second sex' had risen" (p. 101) by the mid-1970s and therefore adolescent girls became increasingly aggressive, violent, and masculine; that is, gender sameness (rather than difference) was now the order of the day.

Although the idea that alleged liberation results in increasing masculinity and thus violence on the part of adolescent girls (and women generally) was soundly criticized (Belknap, 2014), Adler's argument revealed that criminology did not at that time possess the theoretical language capable of representing violence by girls and women—criminology simplistically perceived girls' and women's violence from the perspective of violent acts by boys and men (Messerschmidt, 1995). Indeed, for societies that formally recognize only two genders, it follows that if an individual is not one (feminine) then she must be the other (masculine). In such a conceptualization, the only variation possible is an exchange of one gender for its "opposite"; there are no conceivable alternatives to the dichotomy of "male" and "female." Consequently, we should not be surprised at Adler's formulation. Even so, Adler drew attention to the fact that gender is not determined biologically, and therefore her argument inadvertently encouraged scholars to identify and examine possible masculinities by girls and women (as well as femininities by boys and men) and their relation to crime. Thus, the legacy of Adler's formulation has helped lead to conceptualizations of how girls' and women's crime may be related to both femininity and masculinity, depending on the social context.

Contemporary research on masculinities and crime concentrates on the social construction of masculinities by both boys and men *and* girls and women and on the "everyday" qualities of their aggressive and destructive forms. Since the 1980s, the shift to social constructionism has been a response to the wider reflection on gender and identity born of social movements including feminism, gay and lesbian activism, and sections of "the men's movement." In particular, research on violence against women has stressed the relationship between offending and everyday, often legitimated, constructions of manhood. In the academy, there has been a growth in research on male violence and a general expansion of research on masculinity (see Connell, Kimmel, & Hearn, 2005; Kimmel, 1987; Segal, 1990).

This chapter outlines the key modes of theoretical understanding of the links between crime and masculinity, gives an overview of the growing breadth of empirical studies and literature in this field, and finally reflects on the ongoing dilemma of the official and criminal justice responses to selectively criminalized masculinity that often merely exacerbate the bond between offending and male identity.

Hegemonic Masculinity

This new field owes much of its inspiration to the theoretical contributions by the well-known Australian sociologist Raewyn Connell (1987, 1995), who developed a key explanatory model of different forms of masculinity. Connell's concept of *hegemonic masculinity* has been defined not as a particular character type, but as an entire complex of historically evolving and varied social practices in societies that either legitimate or attempt to guarantee the shoring up of patriarchy and male domination of women. Hegemonic masculinity then is that form of masculinity in a particular social setting that structures gender relations hierarchically between men and women and among men. This relational character is central, in that it embodies a particular form of masculinity in hierarchical relation to a certain form of femininity and to various nonhegemonic masculinities. Arguably, hegemonic masculinity has no meaning outside its *relationship* to femininity—and nonhegemonic masculinities— or to those forms of femininity that are practiced in a complementary, compliant, and accommodating subordinate relationship with hegemonic masculinity. And it is the legitimation of this relationship of superordination and subordination whereby the meaning and essence of hegemonic masculinity are revealed. Moreover, any attainment or approximation of this empowered hegemonic form by individual men is highly contingent on the uneven levels of real social power in different men's lives.

The mostly ill-fated effort to attain hegemonic masculinity among millions of men with highly limited sources of social power is reflected in a distinct form that occurs among men and boys in situations of marginal social status (e.g., uncertain or low-paying employment, members of minority groups). This marginalized form is referred to as "protest masculinity" (Connell, 1995, p. 109). This concept has been used before by criminologists, and it is similar to how a psychoanalytic perspective would describe the concept of "masculine protest." It illuminates a particular kind of gender identity that is characteristic of men in a marginal social location. Like other men, they wish to claim that they exercise power and are in control in their lives. However, their masculine claim on power is contradicted by the reality that they are in a position of economic and social weakness. To openly display or prove their masculinity, they may overreact in a very hypermasculine and aggressive way by engaging in antisocial, violent, and criminal behavior. Frequently, "protest masculinity" is exhibited through overt misogyny, compulsory heterosexuality, and homophobia.

This model of "hegemonic" and other masculinities has been quite influential but also much contested in the social sciences, including criminology. For some liberal critics, this model may seem too closely tied to Marxist ideas about an overarching dominant ideology as a ruling set of oppressive masculine beliefs. Yet much of the critique has come from more radical and postmodern camps. Some critics have suggested that this model downplays social class and reflects a degrading view of working-class men as inherently violent and destructive (Hall, 2002). Jefferson (2002) suggests that this model results in a narrow view of masculinity as a set of personal attributes that are all negative. And Collier (1998) also argues that the model imprecisely offers a shifting notion of "masculinity" as comprising whatever it is that most men do in different contexts.

Contemporary Research on Masculinities and Crime

The criticisms discussed above have been soundly challenged (Connell, 2002; Connell & Messerschmidt, 2005; Messerschmidt, 1998). The concepts of hegemonic and marginalized masculinities have informed a rich and widening range of crimi-nological studies that examine the full spectrum of masculine offending. This basic idea has well withstood more than 25 years of research experience. Moreover, mul-tiple patterns of masculinity have been identified in numerous studies, in a variety of countries, and in different institutional and cultural settings. And it is a widespread research finding that certain masculinities are hegemonic, necessarily in *relation* to femininities and nonhegemonic masculinities. That the concept of hegemonic mas-culinity presumes the subordination of femininities and nonhegemonic masculini-ties is a process that has been well documented in many international settings (Connell & Messerschmidt, 2005).

Critical work in criminology has emphasized that masculinity helps to explain not only violent crime by less powerful men but also such diverse matters as motor vehicle offenses, theft, drug use and dealing, white-collar crime, and political crime. In the "new masculinities" approach, there is an emphasis on the relations between different masculinities, the causes and patterns of most criminal offending and victimization, and the broader workings of the wider criminal justice system of public and private policing, criminal courts, corrections, and prisons (Newburn & Stanko, 1994).

These scholars share the view that masculinities are plural, socially constructed, reproduced in the collective social practices of different men, and embedded in insti-tutional and occupational settings. Furthermore, masculinities are linked intricately with struggles for social power that occur between men and women and among dif-ferent men. They vary and intersect importantly with other dimensions of inequality. Messerschmidt's (1993, 1997, 2000, 2004, 2012) influential accounts of crimes as "doing masculinity"—to be understood within a structured action framework—incorporate differences of class, race or ethnicity, age, sexuality, bodies, and the com-mon concern with power. Because there are different forms of masculinity that are differently linked to the attainment of social power, crime itself is a means or social resource or practice to construct masculinity and analyses must balance consider-ation of structural forces and human agency. The following research examples draw out this central point.

Differences in masculinity that shape violence against women are a frequent topic of interest. For example, Kersten (1996) details cross-cultural evidence to illustrate an underlying link between masculine domination and a wide range of reported and unreported rapes, forms of sexual harassment, and coercion from both male strangers and acquaintances. Additionally, he stresses the national differ-ences in gender relations and evolving masculinities to argue that, although these assaults are related to a range of social and historical factors, they are higher in Australia (rather than Germany or Japan) because of its overtly aggressive public masculine culture. Such violence is viewed as a means of asserting or seeking a male identity that is increasingly under threat of change from new social forces. Likewise, the work of DeKeseredy and Schwartz (2005) has shown that for a variety of forms of male physical and sexual violence against women, the intent of the perpetrator often is to deploy violence as a means of presenting a particular type of dominating masculine image to himself, to the victim, and to his peer group. The work of Cruz (2003) shows similar masculine dynamics among gay men involved in domestic violence.

In a recent study of homicide and sexual assault of Asian women by stranger North American men, Park (2012) compares the motives of white men and non-Asian men of color as perpetrators. He found more similarities than differences between these two differing rapist-murderers; specifically, through this violence both construct Western masculinities as an assertion of their "right" to place and space in national and global hierarchies that are informed by "the West's deep hostility for, and admiration of, Asian men, nations and economies in the context of Western constructs of Asia rising and the Asia Pacific century" (Park, 2012, p. 493). In other words, through violence against Asian women, both White and non-Asian men of color, according to Park, are expressing their anxieties regarding alleged Western male decline in the face of the alleged "rising" Asian man. The surprising result, then, is that *both* White and non-Asian men of color uphold global White supremacy by asserting their violent masculine Western dominance of Asian women who allegedly are unprotected by "weak" Asian men.

A key analysis of the 1990s concluded that the typical "masculine scenarios" of most killings are disputes between men regarding insults and slights to personal honor or assaults directed at controlling female spouses and domestic partners (Polk, 1994). A detailed discussion of many incidents reflects the masculine and everyday forms of most fatal interpersonal violence. It appears the criminal defenses (particularly provocation) that are invoked by many accused have been generally unavailable to women who kill, which suggests a link with notions of masculine violence and a degree of respect in the criminal justice system and wider culture.

Research on antihomosexual killings has also suggested a masculine pattern in much of this violence and the official criminal justice system response to it (Tomsen, 2009). Antihomosexual killings occur within two general masculine scenarios. Typically, they comprise fatal attacks in public space that are perpetrated by groups of young males concerned with establishing a manly self-image and more private disputes with allegations of an unwanted homosexual advance by a perpetrator protecting a masculine sense of honor and bodily integrity through retaliatory violence. Thus, many hate crimes (racist attacks as well as violence directed at gay men, lesbians, and transgender people) are not a form of offending that is wholly distinct from other masculine violence (Tomsen, 2002). Other Australian research of international significance to the study of masculinities and crime includes a rich analysis of the local cultures of male violence and aggression and the exploitation of female sex workers in frontier mining settlements. Such masculine leisure practices are substantially condoned among company and political leaders as a seemingly inevitable aspect of the clustering of groups of men in harsh and homosocial environments to carry out the work that produces corporate profits and a large slice of national wealth (Carrington, McIntosh, & Scott, 2012).

In probably the best study to date on masculinities and street violence, Mullins (2006) presents an important account of how and why a specific form of hegemonic masculinity is embedded in the street life of St. Louis, Missouri. His analysis not only supports previous theoretical work on masculinity and street crime, but also extends that work by demonstrating that street-life hegemonic masculinity can be understood only in its relationship to subordinated "punk" masculinities—masculinities that likewise are constructed in the same street-life culture—and in relation to particular femininities in that street culture. Mullins's exposition of street violence is solid, confirming previous theoretical work that considerable violence among men in public settings results from masculinity challenges (Messerschmidt, 2000). Mullins explores how men within specific social situations come to view certain practices of other men as a threat to their masculinity, a threat that requires a culturally supported masculine response: physical violence. Moreover, he clarifies how such masculinity challenges can subsequently escalate, resulting all too often in the death of one or more of the male interactants.

Mullins's (2006) analysis adds two new and intriguing dimensions to our understanding of men involved in street violence. First, he presents an incisive discussion of interaction among street men and the various women in their lives. Previous work on masculinities and street crime unaccountably ignores this salient component of gender relations. Mullins, however, uniquely explicates that such men tend to construct *hegemonic* masculinities—or those masculinities that fashion power relations between men and women and among men—over women on the street or over those sharing domestic households. Second, Mullins examines one of the most underexplored areas of research on masculinities in general—the contradictions involved in masculine constructions. The author lucidly illustrates how the men in his study vacillated among multiple meanings of masculinity according to their interactional needs.

A recent study by Baird (2012) on gang violence and the construction of masculinity adds to Mullins's conclusions. Baird compared boys from poor neighborhoods who joined gangs with boys who did not. He found that masculinity plays an integral role as to why violence is perpetrated by male gang members and that the gang becomes an attractive offering for "doing masculinity" (Messerschmidt, 1993). Boys who did not join gangs were more likely to have family support that helped them adopt a "moral rejection" of gangs, crime, and violence, which contributed to these boys embracing alternative nongang and nonviolent forms of masculinity. Boys who joined gangs were less likely to adopt moral rejection, primarily because of growing up in dysfunctional families; they were also more likely to admire older gang members and perceive the gang as an attractive pathway to masculine construction.

Until quite recently, there has been scant analysis of masculine attitudes toward subjection to violence beyond the general finding that men as a group tend to be less fearful in relation to crime. Australian and European research within the new masculinities approach has studied the experience of confrontational violence by tracing the role of victimization in establishing power relations between men and the mixed effects on victims that both undermine and reinforce conventional ideas of masculinity (Stanko & Hobdell, 1993; Tomsen, 2005).

The narrow view that masculine crime solely comprises acts of physical violence has been balanced by accounts of gendered patterns of theft and economic, corporate, and political offending. An important early example of this view was an analysis of the particular masculine attractions that motor vehicle offending and thefts hold for many working-class boys (Cunneen, 1985; see also Cunneen & White, 1996). The broad potential of this explanation of nonviolent offending has been recognized in international studies; for example, an important interview study provides further understanding of the motivations and processes involved in the masculine magnetism to a range of nonviolent offending by exploring the group interactions and exchanges that precede collective offending—including robbery, burglary, and vehicle theft by groups of young risk-taking males (Copes & Hochstetler, 2003). As an example of one of these crimes—robbery—Contreras (2009) examined how male robbers manipulate the masculinity of male drug dealers they victimize by employing female accomplices to lure them—for example, by walking by and making "eyes"—and the drug dealers subsequently pursue the females and thereby are successfully set up to be robbed. Contreras argues that because drug dealers as "real men" consistently need to "prove" their *heterosexual* masculinity, they are mindlessly susceptible to female advances. Male robbers then construct a "superior" masculinity by such maneuvering of drug dealers' heteromasculinity and through the exploitation of female accomplices. Finally, a recent study of illegal but nonviolent graffiti artists found that such "writers" construct a particular masculinity through their outlaw art and thereby achieve masculine status and respect among male peers (Monto, Machalek, & Anderson, 2012). By practicing this particular form of art, these "outlaws" orchestrate a masculinity that is admired for its flamboyant and edgy set of aesthetics as well as for its daring, risky, and rebellious significance.

In an interesting examination of how masculinity is tied to social class through economic fraud committed by socially privileged men, the authors did not attempt to uncover the causes of the criminal behavior, but rather they analyzed how the offenders subsequently explained and justified their actions (Willott, Griffin, & Torrance, 2008). Specifically, during the interviews the sample of privileged men drew on particular masculine discourses to present a cohesive and plausible account of their offending behavior. For example, these men stated that they used the male breadwinner discourse (he is *the* economic "provider" for the family) but extended this notion to include employees and their families. That is, they described themselves as "normal men" who engaged in financial fraud unpretentiously to *provide* for their families and to *protect* their employees and their employees' families from economic ruin. In this sense, then, these professional men constructed themselves in a specific middle-class masculine way—they must shoulder more responsibility than working-class men who are simply providers for their families but not protectors of others.

The masculine seductions of criminal risk at higher levels of social class and privilege are apparent in a classic account of the 1985 *Challenger* disaster that seriously undermined confidence in the U.S. Space Shuttle program. The fatal decision to launch against strong evidence of equipment failure and the resulting crew deaths reflected the dominance of a particular managerial masculinity that valued risk and decisiveness and discounted human consequences (Messerschmidt, 2014).

Institutional crime by collective decision making or oversight does not fit the classic liberal notion of a single-reasoning criminal actor (presumed as well to be a man). These insights into the masculinity of corporate and economic crime might well inform the recent criminological interest in state crime. There is a range of major public institutional offending of concern to critical criminology—including internal and external official violence, paramilitary activity, and warfare—that also is deeply masculine, yet remains a fertile but mostly untouched field for researchers of this ilk. Destructive military masculinities have been of particular concern in recent discussions about the potential success of international peacekeeping efforts in a range of postwar settings (Breines, Connell, & Eide, 2000). And one of Messerschmidt's (2010) recent works—*Hegemonic Masculinities and Camouflaged Politics: Unmasking the Bush Dynasty and Its War Against Iraq*—investigates the orchestration of regional and global hegemonic masculinities through the speeches of the two U.S. Bush presidents—George H. W. Bush and George W. Bush—that contrast forms of communicative social action to "sell" the long-standing war against Iraq. In this study, Messerschmidt (2010) makes the case that there are evolving hegemonic masculinities. He then outlines how state leaders may appeal to particular hegemonic masculinities in their attempts to sell wars and thereby camouflage salient political and criminal practices that subsequently and significantly violated international law.

There also is the danger that destructive military masculinities enacted abroad will be transferred to the United States and other liberal democracies and shape gendered aspects of policing. This possibility has been signaled by a recent analysis of the growing use of lethal military weaponry, such as killer drones, for more routine use in domestic law enforcement settings. In particular, this illuminates the masculine attractions of such lethal "game-like" technology for police officers and officials and the need to recognize and contest the masculinity of related paramilitarism (Salter, 2014).

Discourse Analysis and Life-History Studies

Discourse analysis involves the study of communication—written, verbal, and visual—to reveal or "deconstruct" underlying messages or "meanings" embedded in "what is being said." The new crime and masculinities research has examined the discursive analysis of cultural representations (e.g., media) and has included a variety of ethnographic studies that seek out the viewpoints that inform masculine social action in relation to crime and criminal justice. The significance of a general vicarious masculine interest in violence, crime, and wrongdoing is evident from contributions made by researchers exploring the status of cultural meanings in a wide range of societies. Sparks (1996) has explained how popular Hollywood depictions of male heroism as a critical aspect of policing and law enforcement—in such films as *Dirty Harry, Lethal Weapon,* and *Total Recall*—shape and skew public understanding of crime and the law. Cavender (1999) has shown how masculine models were constructed differently in Hollywood feature films of the 1940s when compared with those of the 1980s. This is not just a matter of the characters written into the scripts. Practice at the local level—that is, the actual face-to-face interaction of shooting the film *as an actor*—ultimately constructs masculine fantasy models (in this case, "detectives") at the society-wide or regional level. And Aiello (2014) recently demonstrated how the six highest grossing American police movies discursively construct a "hotshot" form of police officer masculinity involving "solving the case," "rescuing the girl," and "getting the bad guy." Aiello then compared these Hollywood depictions of policing masculinity to police department–controlled websites of official recruitment materials and found that none of the hotshot masculinity practices matched the ideal police officer masculinity in the recruitment video material, which concentrated on being honorable, cooperative, and respectful of the law and the rights of citizens. Thus, Aiello concluded that the two different forms of discursive masculinity keep hidden the actual curriculum of police training and police work and their accompanying forms of masculinity (see Prokos & Padavik, 2002).

The tension between individual agency and objective factors experienced as the divide between human choice and external constraint in masculine criminal activity and the value of an insider understanding of that tension are evident in the fully ethnographic picture drawn by Bourgois's (2002) study of New York crack dealers from a deprived Puerto Rican neighborhood. The men studied by Bourgois struggled for masculine respect through their wrongdoing. Drug dealing, violence, and sexual assaults provided a distorted mirror of the limited empowerment that was won by male forebears in a traditional rural patriarchy, where protection and provision for women and families were vital aspects of gender dominance. Graphic snapshots of brutality, gang rapes, and other crimes and cultural detail gathered by painstaking and dangerous fieldwork fleshed out the racialized, criminal masculinities assumed by these young men.

The theme of masculine crime in deindustrialized settings has been pursued by Australian and British ethnographic researchers studying nighttime leisure and related offending and policing (Hobbs, Hadfield, Lister, & Winlow, 2003; Tomsen, 1997; Winlow, 2001). There are sensual attractions in the liminal "nighttime" economy for its many young participants and an allied official ambivalence toward the male aggression and disorder that characterize it. In Monaghan's (2002) insider account of "bouncing" in a study of private security officers working in nightclubs and pubs in city centers in southwest Britain, physicality and violent potential are transformed into workplace skills built on the importance of forceful bodies. The mixed official response to the economic benefits and social costs of the expanding night economy that fosters drunkenness, male conflicts, and disorder problems is evident also in the discomfort with, and reliance on, the aggressive masculinity of security officers instructed to maintain a semblance of public order.

The danger of this work generates hierarchies of male physical ability within private policing, especially reflected in the masculine contrasts between "hardmen," "shopboys" working security in retail stores, and "glass-collector types" who are less physically imposing and are unable to deal with the risks of violent encounters. The same masculine hierarchy inflects the positioning of the minority of women working in this occupation; they are either denigrated as unmasculine and physically incapable or, in fewer cases, given a marginal position in a masculine hierarchy.

This hierarchy is a specific form of masculinity that has global manifestations and corresponds with images from a general culture. It also seems to involve a form of private policing that is laxly regulated and that reproduces forms of masculine identity that are close to the original aggressive physicality of traditional, unreformed public policing. Given the fine line between legitimate force and actual assault, bouncing itself encapsulates a gendered identity at the edge of protest and official masculinities that criminal justice systems often express as tensions and convergence.

In a North American study, Anderson, Daly, and Rapp (2009) explored the relationship between masculinities and crime within the hip-hop and electronic dance music nightclub scenes. The authors found that respondents who revealed they contextually constructed masculinity "upward" through excessive alcohol use, heightened sexuality, competitiveness, and commercialization were those most frequently involved in nightclub crime. These males defined "clubbing" as a status-oriented and hedonistic endeavor in which they must "macho-up" to negotiate, thereby constructing a masculine performance that often simultaneously leads to crime.

The importance of life-history research to studies of crime and masculinity that seek out insider perspectives on offending has appeared in a range of recent accounts. Jefferson (1997) argued that researchers in this field should not ignore the unconscious and contradictory personal aspects of any criminal masculine identity. Obviously, he had in mind the lessons of his own life-history account of Mike Tyson that traces the evolution of a socially vulnerable boy into a champion athlete and convicted rapist and reveals the links between racial marginality and hypermasculine violence. Similarly, in one of Messerschmidt's (2000) recent studies, a dynamic interplay of hegemonic and other masculinities is demonstrated through discussion of the lives of youth assaultive and sexual offenders from working-class neighborhoods. This interplay occurs against the backdrop of different relations between the male body (whether mature, muscular, and strong or physically small and weak) and achievable masculinities in different criminal pathways (Messerschmidt, 2000; see also Messerschmidt, 2012).

Despite a recent attempt to challenge the notion that some girls or women in specific situations construct masculinities through criminal practices (Irwin & Chesney-Lind, 2008), the fact that gender is not determined biologically surely leads scholars to identify and examine possible *masculinities by women and girls* (and femininities by men and boys) and their relation to crime. There remains a necessity in the new masculinities criminological research to uncover girls' and women's relations to crime and violence and to determine whether such social action constructs masculinity or femininity.

Jody Miller's (2001, 2002) work is unique in this regard because her important book, *One of the Guys*, shows that certain gang girls identify with the boys in their gangs and describe such gangs as "masculinist enterprises": "To be sure, 'one of the guys' is only one part of a complex tapestry of gender beliefs and identities held by the gang girls I spoke with—and is rarely matched by gendered actions—but it remains significant nonetheless" (Miller, 2002, p. 442). Pointing out that gender inequality was rampant in the mixed-gender gangs of which these girls were members—such as male leadership, a double standard with regard to sexual activities, the sexual exploitation of some girls, and most girls' exclusion from serious gang crime—certain girls differentiated themselves from other girls through a construction of being "one of the guys." In other words, the notion "one of the guys" is not fashioned by being *similar* to boys (because of inequalities) but, rather, certain girls are *different* from other girls because they embrace a masculine identity. Miller's research contributes to the process of discovering differences among gang girls, especially regarding how the distribution of male and female members within particular gangs may impact gender construction. Moreover, her work helps point scholars in an important direction for discovering these differences and demonstrates how certain girls, like certain boys, can construct a masculine self through involvement in crime.

Similarly, in his book *Flesh & Blood*, Messerschmidt (2004) demonstrated through a study of adolescent assaultive violence that numerous gender constructions by violent girls were prevalent and that some girls "do" masculinity by in part displaying themselves in a masculine way, by engaging primarily in what they and others in their milieu consider authentically masculine behavior, and by outright rejecting most aspects of femininity.

In addition to eschewing possible masculinities by girls and women and femininities by boys and men, most writing on crime and masculinity concentrates on the *mind* while ignoring the *body*. Messerschmidt's (2012, 2014) work, however, highlights how violent boys *and* girls interact with and through their body. The interview data in his studies demonstrate that the body is not neutral in doing masculinity (or femininity) but, rather, is an agent of social practice: Often, the body initially constrained, yet eventually facilitated, gendered social action; it mediated and influenced future social practices. Given the social context, bodies could do certain things but not others—the bodies of these youth are "lived" in terms of what they can do. Consequently, for these youth doing masculinity (or femininity) is experienced in and through the body: Eventually they literally construct a different body and, thus, a new gendered self through their embodied everyday violent practices such as engagement in fights and sexual assault.

The life-histories approach has also been deployed to offer clues about questions raised by nonoffenders. Because crime is a ready resource for attaining masculinity, particularly among socially marginal or highly competitive groups of men, researchers wonder what this means for the masculinity of nonoffenders. Accordingly, British researchers have explored the subjective significance of "desistance" for male working-class offenders (Gadd & Farrall, 2004). Ending criminal offending and criminal careers is a puzzle for conventional criminology that the masculinities approach may help to unravel. By following the signposts in Jefferson's (1997) analysis of violence and the masculine unconscious and by balancing individual agency with structural determination (of the sort stressed in research on risk factors and life-course stages), these researchers conclude that desistance is a complex gendered process (Gadd & Farrall, 2004). A detailed discussion of life circumstances reveals the contradictory nature of this desistance. An apparent ending to criminality is shaped around heroic male discourses of redemption and protectiveness and the uncertain possibilities of male renunciation of actual or fantasized violence, the latter being more widespread and commonly shared by offenders and other males alike. Although Gadd and Farrall undoubtedly uncovered some of the reasons for desistance, more recently Carlsson (2013) showed how both persistence in and desistance from crime are imbued with age-specific notions of masculinity at different stages of the life course. For example, Carlsson found that at specific times in life (e.g., early adulthood), certain practices, such as having a good job or forming a family, become more important markers of masculinity than other practices, such as risk taking, which is more likely to center the self during the teenage years. Consequently, desistance from crime is clearly related to age-specific meanings of masculinity.

An additional value of insider understanding in accounts of masculine offending and nonoffending is signaled by a study of young Australian men and security officers involved in regular episodes of drinking violence and disorder (Tomsen, 2005). The point is that although the link between masculinity and criminality has been newly emphasized, researchers have minimal understanding of the means by which withdrawal from violence fits with a socially respected masculine identity. "Disengagement" is understood here as a process of situational decision making and withdrawal from conflicts and offending that may characterize a broad population of noncriminal men, rather than as any full "desistance" from a set criminal pathway and identity. Involvements in drinking-related public violence are tied to matters of male group status, the protection of honor in episodes involving insults and slights that must be addressed, and the collective pleasure of carnival-like rule breaking in public disorder. Yet an awareness of danger and a disengagement from occasions of conflict can fit with rational and restrained models of a masculine self. This may even be cultivated by public safety campaigns that provide an exaggerated belief that individual agency always prevails in avoiding violence.

Masculinities and Social Control

A growing number of studies in this new field explore the ties between masculinity and elements of the justice system: policing, courts, prisons, and probation. A close look at these studies suggests the contradictory relations that exist between criminal "protest" masculinities and "official" state masculinities in this sphere. Any full understanding of this evidence must consider the ways in which criminalized masculinities are produced in tension with the official forms of masculinity inscribed in policing and criminal justice systems. As Connell (1995) has suggested, dynamic relationships exist between hegemonic and other subordinated or marginalized forms of masculinity that produce different masculinities and gender politics within masculinity. The criminological implication is that social forms of masculinity linked to violence and offending are both produced and policed by aspects of the criminal justice system and state institutions.

In this sense, Hall's (2002) critique of hegemonic masculinity does usefully draw attention to the interrelation of different masculinities and how problematic conceiving the differences between hegemonic and potentially criminal protest masculinities has become for criminologists with an elastic use of these terms in some discussions of male criminality. Furthermore, the hypocrisy of commentators in this field to which he refers suggests that there remains an insufficient understanding of the condoning and cultivation of violent forms of masculinity by capitalist, imperial, and contemporary postcolonial nation-states. Moreover, masculine violence is deployed internally and externally in a range of state forms and is both legitimated and denounced in different historical and social circumstances (although see the earlier discussion of Messerschmidt's (2010) book as it begins to fill this research void).

The paradox of regulating criminalized masculinities with the formally law-abiding tough sexist and aggressive official masculinities of criminal justice systems is reflected in research on policing (Prokos & Padavic, 2002). For example, Nolan (2009) discussed the existence in policing of an "idiosyncratic construct of masculinity that privileges tacit conspiracies of silence" (p. 250), thereby validating heterosexuality, hierarchical regimentation, homosocial bonding, homophobia, and paternalistic misogyny among North American male police officers. And responses to criminal justice intervention that foster and reproduce masculinities with a direct or indirect relation to criminality are uncovered in other contemporary studies. Most notably, the general failure of prisons to deter crime or to rehabilitate inmates with any certainty is now informed by accounts of inmate masculinity, illustrating the sharp struggles over male power and status and the masculine hierarchies that characterize prison subcultures and the lives of incarcerated men.

An interview study with British prisoners suggests that a specific form of masculinity that is hard, aggressive, bullying, and conformist is a usual adaptation to prison (Jewkes, 2005). Prisons cause a dehumanizing impact that threatens personal identity through a climate of "mortification and brutality." This impact engenders a hard masculine social performance among inmates. Jewkes's analysis and related work on prison masculinities cogently suggest that aspects of the intervention process itself affirm destructive forms of male identity, to which criminal justice systems ostensibly are opposed to (Sabo, Kupers, & London, 2001; Whitehead, 2000, 2005).

This contradiction leads to a major conceptual problem for the new crime and masculinities paradigm because a critical analysis of masculine offending necessitates an understanding of the historically shifting and fluid way that destructive masculinities have been either condoned or denounced by policing and criminal justice systems. Moreover, this problem results in dilemmas for programs of punishment, correction, and crime prevention that may appear both to treat and to foster male criminality (Holland & Scourfield, 2000).

Feminists have been critical of the way in which male violence against women has been simultaneously denounced, yet condoned or ignored in the wider culture and in traditional "hands-off" police responses. Further examples of the mixed official reaction to male violence from the new literature on masculinity and crime concern the shifting historical responses to public violence and various forms of hate crime (Tomsen, 2002). In many of these cases, discouraged reporting, lax policing, and lenient sentences signal support for the generation of an aggressive masculinity in relation to public leisure and spaces. Male-on-male violence that results from this may be regarded as a minor public nuisance or an inevitable aspect of the social reproduction of appropriate masculinities.

Furthermore, violence and criminal offending by groups of men can also signal resistance against social hierarchy. Historical and cross-cultural scholarship has convincingly demonstrated that much male violence is an ambiguous form of protest or rebellion against social hierarchies based on social class, caste, and racial or ethnic differences. This research includes studies of disorder, unruly leisure, festivals, carnivals, and more direct acts of insubordination, including rallies and riots, as means of symbolic protest and collective cultural resistance to the moral values of ruling groups (Tilly, 2003). In fact, official and police concerns over collective male disorder that refer to a compelling need to protect the broader public are driven also by anxiety about the symbolic challenge to state, class, and racial authority that this disorder can comprise.

These different examples reflect the complexities of official reactions and the criminalization process in relation to different crimes and masculinities. Male crime is gendered crime; yet when commentators on the masculinity–crime nexus cannot acknowledge the link between the bulk of male offending and such other factors as social class and race, they risk inadvertently naturalizing male offending. This shortsighted view reinforces a widespread public belief in a common-sense opinion of masculinity as a force inevitably leading millions of men to involvement in crime and violence.

The dilemmas of problematic-gendered male offending and an overlapping criminalization process are evidenced in the debate raised by contentious crimes and their policing. For example, the ongoing concern in Australia over how to deal progressively with the issue of domestic and sexual assaults in indigenous communities has become increasingly public (HEREOC, 2006). In such cases, different forms of violence are related to particular racialized protest masculinities that reflect distinct histories of marginality resulting from the effects of migration and racial dispossession in a White Anglo-dominated culture.

The increasing casting of a wide net of social control recently was highlighted by Victor Rios (2012), who shadowed the everyday lives of 40 delinquent Black and Latino boys for three years in Oakland, California. Thirty of these boys had previously been arrested and they all lived in high-crime neighborhoods. Rios also interviewed another 78 boys from these same neighborhoods, and he concluded from the data generated that the social system of control in the lives of these boys impacts their future masculine and criminal behavior.

Rios (2012) introduced the concept of the *youth control complex*, or "a ubiquitous system of criminalization molded by synchronized, systematic punishment meted out by socializing and social control institutions" (p. 40). The youth control complex impacts the future outcome of these boys, Rios argues, through the combined effects of schools, families, businesses, residents, media, community centers, and the criminal justice system that "collectively punish, stigmatize, monitor, and criminalize young people in an attempt to control them" (p. 40). Through institutionalized mechanisms of social control, the ongoing developing masculinity of these boys is challenged through systems marking them as criminal. Indeed, the youth control complex involves both "material" and "symbolic" criminalization. For Rios, the former involves, for example, police harassment, exclusion from businesses and public recreation spaces, in-school detention rooms, and school suspensions; the latter includes, for example, surveillance, profiling, stigma, and degrading forms of interaction. Rios argues the result of the youth control complex is that these young men become adversarial toward society, they lose faith in its institutions, and they begin to resist it and build various resilient skills to cope.

Rios emphasizes that the youth control complex *collectively* impacts these boys because it is the sum of the punitive parts that is most damaging. Although it may seem trivial, if a boy is "called a 'thug' by a random adult, told by a teacher that he will never amount to anything, and frisked by a police officer, all in the same day, this combination becomes greater than the sum of its parts" (Rios, 2012; p. 40). And it is this sum that creates the condition for certain types of masculinity and crime. Rios demonstrates that for the most part, the youth control complex offers the boys meanings of masculinity that emphasize conformity to a subordinated racialized social status and, therefore, many of the boys find that the alternative to conformity is to become "hard"; that is, to survive on the street one must construct a hypermasculinity. Two examples of this specific type of masculinity are as follows:

> You can't act weak or you'll get taken out.
> I can't act like a bitch, . . . 'cause if I do, suckas will try to swoop up on me and take me out. So I gotta handle my business. (Rios, 2012, p. 131)

This hypermasculinity found embedded in the street culture is likewise reinforced through certain aspects of the youth control complex, especially institutions of the criminal justice system. For example, Rios (2012) observes that police officers frequently used "a brutal masculinity that inculcated a toughness, manliness, and hypermasculinity in the boys. This hypermasculinity often influenced the young men to perpetrate defiance, crime, and violence, sanctioning police to brutalize or arrest them" (p. 138). The result becomes a cycle whereby the boys practice a hypermasculinity on the streets, certain aspects of the youth control complex generate meanings supporting that notion of masculinity, and the boys are channeled into crime and the criminal justice system.

Conclusion

Research findings affirm the overall value in acknowledging the link between crime and masculinities and criminological understanding. It is now incumbent upon criminologists to move beyond the impasse generated by explanations of crime that either downplay male offending or focus on it to the exclusion of evidence of criminalization and other social factors. Criminalization is a common strategy in a contemporary era of post-left–new social movement activism toward crime that may dovetail with punitive law-and-order politics (Snider, 1998). This strategy can encourage a major expansion of police and prisons and the imposition of longer and often mandatory sentences, which erode any commitment to alternative punishments. Such harsh penalties will have the pernicious effect of net widening, mass incarceration, and punishment for vengeance sake, rather than reform or rehabilitation. And, of course, this strategy specifically targets and brutalizes poor, Black, and indigenous men, resulting in further divisive and negative impacts on their fragile communities.

Masculine crime may appear to be inevitable, even abhorrent. Yet there is scant progressive gain in simple essentialist understandings of male offending, a denial of human agency, or a cynical dismissal of substantial efforts to educate and promote diverse and nonviolent masculinities among marginalized boys and men. Being critically aware of the extent and effects of the criminalization process and its secondary effects in racist and class-divided societies requires a constant reflexivity in analyzing the masculinity–crime nexus.

References

Adler, F. (1975). *Sisters in crime: The rise of the new female criminal.* New York, NY: McGraw–Hill.

Adler, F. (1977). The interaction between women's emancipation and female criminality: A cross-cultural perspective. *International Journal of Criminology and Penology, 5,* 101–112.

Aiello, M. F. (2014). Policing the masculine frontier: Cultural criminological analysis of the gendered performance of policing. *Crime, Media, Culture, 10,* 59–79.

Anderson, T., Daly, K., & Rapp, L. (2009). Clubbing masculinities and crime: A qualitative study of Philadelphia nightclub scenes. *Feminist Criminology, 4,* 302–332.

Baird, A. (2012). The violent gang and the construction of masculinity among socially excluded young men. *Safer Communities, 11,* 179–190.

Beirne, P., & Messerschmidt, J. W. (2014). *Criminology: A sociological approach* (6th ed.). New York, NY: Oxford University Press.

Belknap, J. (2014). *The invisible woman: Gender, crime, and justice.* Belmont, CA: Wadsworth.

Bonger, W. (2003). Criminality and economic conditions. In E. McLaughlin, J. Muncie, & G. Hughes (Eds.), *Criminological perspectives: Essential readings.* London, UK: Sage. (Original published in 1916.)

Bourgois, P. (2002). *In search of respect: Selling crack in El Barrio.* New York, NY: Cambridge University Press.

Breines, I., Connell, R. W., & Eide, I. (Eds.). (2000). *Male roles, masculinities, and violence: A culture of peace perspective.* Paris, France: UNESCO.

Carlsson, C. (2013). Masculinities, persistence, and desistance. *Criminology, 51,* 661–693.

Carrington, K., McIntosh, A., & Scott, J. (2012). Globalization, frontier masculinities, and violence. *British Journal of Criminology, 50,* 393–413.

Cavender, G. (1999). Detecting masculinity. In J. Ferrell & N. Websdale (Eds.), *Making trouble: Cultural constructions of crime, deviance and control.* New York, NY: Aldine de Gruyter.

Cohen, A. K. (1955). *Delinquent boys: The culture of the gang.* New York, NY: The Free Press.

Collier, R. (1998). *Masculinities, crime and criminology: Men, heterosexuality, and the criminal(ised) other.* London, UK: Sage.

Connell, R. W. (1987). *Gender and power.* Sydney, Australia: Allen & Unwin.

Connell, R. W. (1995). *Masculinities.* St. Leonards, Australia: Allen & Unwin.

Connell, R. W. (2002). On hegemonic masculinity and violence: Response to Jefferson and Hall. *Theoretical Criminology, 6,* 89–99.

Connell, R. W., Kimmel, M., & Hearn, J. (Eds.). (2005). *Handbook of studies on men and masculinities.* Thousand Oaks, CA: Sage.

Connell, R. W., & Messerschmidt, J. W. (2005). Hegemonic masculinity: Rethinking the concept. *Gender and Society, 19,* 829–859.

Contreras, R. (2009). "Damn, yo—Who's that girl?" An ethnographic analysis of masculinity in drug robberies. *Journal of Contemporary Ethnography, 38,* 465–492.

Copes, H., & Hochstetler, A. (2003). Situational construction of masculinity among male street thieves. *Journal of Contemporary Ethnography, 32,* 279–304.

Cruz, M. (2003). "Why doesn't he just leave?" Gay male domestic violence and reasons victims stay. *Journal of Men's Studies, 11,* 309–323.

Cunneen, C. (1985). Working class boys and crime: Theorising the class/gender mix. In P. Patton & R. Poole (Eds.), *War/masculinity.* Sydney, Australia: Intervention.

Cunneen, C., & White, R. (1996). Masculinity and juvenile justice. *Australian and New Zealand Journal of Criminology, 29,* 69–73.

DeKeseredy, W. S., & Schwartz, M. D. (2005). Masculinities and interpersonal violence. In R. W. Connell, M. Kimmel, & J. Hearn (Eds.), *Handbook of studies on men and masculinities.* Thousand Oaks, CA: Sage.

Gadd, D., & Farrall, S. (2004). Criminal careers, desistance and subjectivity: Interpreting men's narratives of change. *Theoretical Criminology, 8,* 123–156.

Gould, S. J. (1981). *The mismeasure of man.* New York, NY: Norton.

Hall, S. (2002). Daubing the drudges of fury: Men, violence and the piety of the "hegemonic masculinity" thesis. *Theoretical Criminology, 6,* 35–61.

HEREOC. (2006). *Ending family violence and abuse in Aboriginal and Torres Strait Islander communities–Key issues.* Sydney, Australia: Australian Human Rights and Equal Opportunity Commission, June 2006.

Hobbs, D., Hadfield, P., Lister, S., & Winlow, S. (2003). *Bouncers: Violence and governance in the night-time economy.* Oxford, UK: Oxford University Press.

Holland, S., & Scourfield, J. B. (2000). Managing marginalised masculinities: Men and probation. *Journal of Gender Studies, 9,* 199–211.

Irwin, K., & Chesney-Lind, M. (2008). Girls' violence: Beyond dangerous masculinity. *Sociological Compass, 2,* 837–855.

Jefferson, T. (1997). Masculinities and crime. In M. Maguire, R. Morgan, & R. Reiner (Eds.), *The Oxford handbook of criminology.* Oxford, UK: Clarendon Press.

Jefferson, T. (2002). Subordinating hegemonic masculinity. *Theoretical Criminology, 6,* 63–88.

Jewkes, Y. (2005). Men behind bars: "Doing" masculinity as an adaptation to imprisonment. *Men and Masculinities, 8,* 44–63.

Kersten, J. (1996). Culture, masculinities and violence against women. *British Journal of Criminology, 36,* 381–395.

Kimmel, M. S. (Ed.). (1987). *Changing men: New directions in research on men and masculinity.* Newbury Park, CA: Sage.

Messerschmidt, J. W. (1993). *Masculinities and crime: Critique and reconceptualization of theory.* Lanham, MD: Rowman & Littlefield.

Messerschmidt, J. W. (1995). Managing to kill: Masculinities and the Space Shuttle *Challenger* explosion. *Masculinities, 3*(4), 1–22.

Messerschmidt, J. W. (1997). *Crime as structured action: Gender, race, class, and crime in the making.* Thousand Oaks, CA: Sage.

Messerschmidt, J. W. (1998). Review of the book *Masculinities, crime and criminology: Men, heterosexuality and the criminal(ised) other,* by R. Collier. *Theoretical Criminology, 3,* 246–249.

Messerschmidt, J. W. (2000). *Nine lives: Adolescent masculinities, the body, and violence.* Boulder, CO: Westview Press.

Messerschmidt, J. W. (2004). *Flesh & blood: Adolescent gender diversity and violence.* Lanham, MD: Rowman & Littlefield.

Messerschmidt, J. W. (2010). *Hegemonic masculinities and camouflaged politics: Unmasking the Bush dynasty and its war against Iraq.* Boulder, CO: Paradigm.

Messerschmidt, J. W. (2012). *Gender, heterosexuality, and youth violence: The struggle for recognition.* Lanham, MD: Rowman & Littlefield.

Messerschmidt, J. W. (2014). *Crime as structured action: Doing masculinities, race, class, sexuality, and crime* (2nd ed.). Lanham, MD: Rowman & Littlefield.

Miller, J. (2001). *One of the guys: Girls, gangs, and gender.* New York, NY: Oxford University Press.

Miller, J. (2002). The strengths and limits of "doing gender" for understanding street crime. *Theoretical Criminology, 6,* 433–460.

Monaghan, L. F. (2002). Hard men, shop boys and others: Embodying competence in a masculinist occupation. *Sociological Review, 50,* 334–355.

Monto, M. A., Machalek, J., & Anderson, T. (2012). Boys doing art: The construction of outlaw masculinity in a Portland, Oregon, graffiti crew. *Journal of Contemporary Ethnography, 42,* 259–290.

Mullins, C. W. (2006). *Holding your square: Masculinities, streetlife, and violence.* Portland, OR: Willan.

Newburn, T., & Stanko, E. (Eds.). (1994). *Just boys doing business? Men, masculinities and crime.* London, UK: Routledge.

Nolan, T. (2009). Behind the blue wall of silence. *Men and Masculinities, 12,* 250–257.

Park, H. (2012). Interracial violence, western racialized masculinities, and the geopolitics of violence against women. *Social and Legal Studies, 21,* 491–509.

Polk, K. (1994). *When men kill: Scenarios of masculine violence.* Melbourne, Australia: Cambridge University Press.

Prokos, A., & Padavic, I. (2002). "There oughtta be a law against bitches": Masculinity lessons in police academy training. *Gender, Work and Organizations, 9,* 439–459.

Rios, V. (2011). *Punished: Policing the lives of Black and Latino boys.* New York, NY: New York University Press.

Sabo, D., Kupers, T., & London, W. (Eds.). (2001). *Prison masculinities.* Philadelphia, PA: Temple University Press.

Salter, M. (2014). Toys for the boys? Drones, pleasure and popular culture in the militarisation of policing. *Critical Criminology, 22,* 163–177.

Segal, L. (1990). *Slow motion: Changing masculinities, changing men.* London, UK: Virago.

Snider, L. (1998). Towards safer societies: Punishment, masculinities and violence against women. *British Journal of Criminology, 38,* 1–39.

Sparks, R. (1996). Masculinity and heroism in the Hollywood "blockbuster": The culture industry and contemporary images of crime and law enforcement. *British Journal of Criminology, 36,* 348–360.

Stanko, E., & Hobdell, K. (1993). Assault on men: Masculinity and male victimization. *British Journal of Criminology, 33,* 400–415.

Sutherland, E. H. (1947). *Principles of criminology.* Philadelphia, PA: Lippincott.

Sutherland, E. H. (1956). Development of the theory. In A. Cohen, A. Lindesmith, & K. Schuessler (Eds.), *The Sutherland papers* (pp. 13–29). Bloomington: Indiana University Press. (Original published in 1942.)

Taylor, I., Walton, P., & Young, J. (1973). *The new criminology: For a social theory of deviance.* London, UK: Routledge & Kegan Paul.

Tilly, C. (2003). *The politics of collective violence.* Cambridge, UK: Cambridge University Press.

Tomsen, S. (1997). A top night: Social protest, masculinity and the culture of drinking violence. *British Journal of Criminology, 37,* 90–103.

Tomsen, S. (2002). Hate crimes and masculine offending. *Gay and Lesbian Law Journal, 10,* 26–42.

Tomsen, S. (2005). "Boozers and bouncers": Masculine conflict, disengagement and the contemporary governance of drinking-related violence and disorder. *Australian and New Zealand Journal of Criminology, 38,* 283–297.

Tomsen, S. (2009). *Violence, prejudice and sexuality.* New York, NY: Routledge.

Whitehead, A. (2000). *Rethinking masculinity: A critical examination of the dynamics of masculinity in the context of an English prison.* Unpublished doctoral dissertation, University of Southampton, England.

Whitehead, A. (2005). Man to man violence: How masculinity may work as a dynamic risk factor. *Howard Journal of Criminal Justice, 44,* 411–422.

Willott, S., Griffin, C., & Torrance, M. (2008). Snakes and ladders: Upper-middle class male offenders talk about economic crime. In S. Tomsen (Ed.), *Crime, criminal justice, and masculinities.* Burlington, VT: Ashgate.

Winlow, S. (2001). *Badfellas: Crime, tradition and new masculinities.* Oxford, UK: Berg.

CHAPTER 15

Male Peer Support Theory

Walter S. DeKeseredy and Martin D. Schwartz

It is an accepted part of the literature today that "the correlation between peer delinquency and delinquency is one of the most consistently demonstrated findings in delinquency research" as the result of "thousands of studies on the topic" (Zimmerman & Vasquez, 2011, pp. 1235–1236). Unfortunately, the bulk of this literature is gender blind and ignores violence against females. Despite this glaring oversight of one of the world's most compelling social problems, it is nonetheless true that *male peer support* is one of the most powerful determinants of why men use violence when interacting with women.

Originally developed by Walter DeKeseredy (1988a), the concept of male peer support is defined as the attachments to male peers and the resources that these men provide that encourage and legitimate woman abuse. Men (and women) are exposed to a wide variety of messages that support and oppose various behaviors, something that is at the core of much criminological theorizing. In the context of a world that is still heavily patriarchal, with regular and extensive social and media messages offering excuses and justifications for the exploitation and victimization of women, many men (and women) are concerned and confused by their relations with the opposite sex. *Male peer support theory* suggests that when some men seek the advice of their peers, they are given both encouragement and advice on how to abuse women who "talk back" or do not provide sex on demand. Research findings have shown that having friends who offer such advice is one of the most powerful determinants of whether a young male engages in physical or sexual assault of intimate partners.

Although we studied mostly college students, an international body of qualitative and quantitative research we recently reviewed (DeKeseredy & Schwartz, 2013) supports what Bowker (1983) said close to 30 years ago about all-male subcultures of violence:

This is not a subculture that is confined to a single class, religion, occupational grouping, or race. It is spread throughout all parts of society. Men are socialized by other subculture members to accept common definitions of the situation, norms, values, and beliefs about male-dominance and the necessity of keeping their wives in line. These violence-supporting social relations may occur at any time and in any place. (pp. 135–136)

Indeed, male peer pressure that perpetuates and rationalizes the sexual objectification of women and the sexual or physical abuse of them is found within a wide variety of communities of all ethnicities. Such peer influence has been reported, to name just a few, among African American men in Chicago (Wilson, 1996), among Puerto Rican drug dealers in East Harlem (Bourgois, 1995) and poor African American boys in St. Louis (Miller, 2008), on mostly White Canadian college campuses and their immediate surroundings (DeKeseredy & Schwartz, 1998a), in Canadian Francophone college communities (Schwartz & DeKeseredy, 2000), in U.S. college fraternities and athletic teams (Benedict, 1998; Burstyn, 2000; Forbes, Adams-Curtis, Pakalka, & White, 2006; Sanday, 1990), in rural Ohio and Kentucky (DeKeseredy & Schwartz, 2009; Donnermeyer & DeKeseredy, 2014; Websdale, 1998), and in rural New Zealand and rural South Africa (Campbell, 2000; Jewkes et al., 2006). There is also evidence of the emergence of pro-abuse male peer support groups in cyberspace, and many men who abuse women consume electronic forms of pornography with their male friends (DeKeseredy & Olsson, 2011; DeKeseredy & Schwartz, 2013).

The social world is multivariate and it is impossible to select a single social scientific factor and state that it accounts for all cases of woman abuse. Still, male peer support is a powerful explanation of a mechanism that contributes to much woman abuse in North America and beyond. The main objective of this chapter is to review the major theoretical work done on this topic over the past several decades.

The Roots of Male Peer Support Theory

Male peer support theory has expanded in the past 25 years far beyond its origins. Since it was first published in 1988, we have crafted seven variants of this theory and linked our theoretical development to rigorous qualitative and quantitative data analysis. With other scholars who have used the theory (e.g., Dragiewicz, 2008, 2011; Franklin, 2005; Franklin, Bouffard, & Pratt, 2012), we found that there are several sociological and social psychological processes by which patriarchal or violent peers motivate men to abuse and oppress women. The key within all of this work is the proposition that certain all-male peer groups encourage, justify, and support the abuse of women by their members.

Male peer support theories grew out of intellectual seeds planted in several places at York University, situated in Toronto, Canada, and at the 1987 American Society of Criminology meeting in Montreal where we first met. DeKeseredy developed the first rendition as part of his doctoral dissertation and was strongly influenced by social support theory, which is used by social psychologists to explain the role of social support in health maintenance and disease prevention. Their arguments are derived from a large empirical literature that shows that people with friends and family members who offer them psychological and material resources are healthier than persons with few or no supportive contacts (Caplan, 1974; Cassell, 1976; Cohen & Wills, 1985; Sarason & Sarason, 1985). Ellis (1988) and Hoff (1990) were the first researchers interested in violence against women to recognize social support theory's explanatory value and to reconceptualize it to suit their empirical and theoretical interests. Several years later, Cullen (1994) modified social support theory to show the broader criminological community how certain sociocultural factors insulate people from committing crimes, although he did not apply this theory to his collaborative work on the sexual victimization of college women.

Ellis (1988) turned social support theory upside down, and with his guidance DeKeseredy (1988a) shortly followed suit. As presented in Figure 15.1, social support—specifically, the role of male peers—is a major component of his original model. DeKeseredy argued that many men experience various types of stress in dating relationships, whose sources range from sexual problems to challenges to their perceived male authority. Some men try to deal with these problems themselves. Other men, however, turn to their male friends for advice, guidance, and various other kinds of social support. The resources provided by these peers may encourage and justify woman abuse under certain conditions. Furthermore, male peer support can influence men to victimize their dating partners regardless of stress.

There is some support for this model. Based on analyses of self-report data gathered from a convenience sample of 333 Canadian male undergraduates, DeKeseredy (1988b) found that social ties with physically, sexually, or psychologically abusive peers are strongly related to abuse among men who experience high levels of dating life-events stress. This finding supports a basic sociological assertion promoted by differential association and social learning theorists: that the victimization of women is behavior that is socially learned from interactions with others. As well, like Ellis's theory, DeKeseredy's account and data challenge traditional social support theory, which emphasizes only the beneficial features of social support (Heller & Swindle, 1983). Data gathered by us over the past 25 years confirm Vaux's (1985) claim that "social support may facilitate the resolution of problems or the management of distress, but there are no guarantees that such a resolution is free of cost" (p. 102). Even so, DeKeseredy's original model has some pitfalls, and we addressed them five years later by developing our modified male peer support model presented in Figure 15.2 (DeKeseredy & Schwartz, 1993).

Figure 15.1.   DeKeseredy's original male peer support model

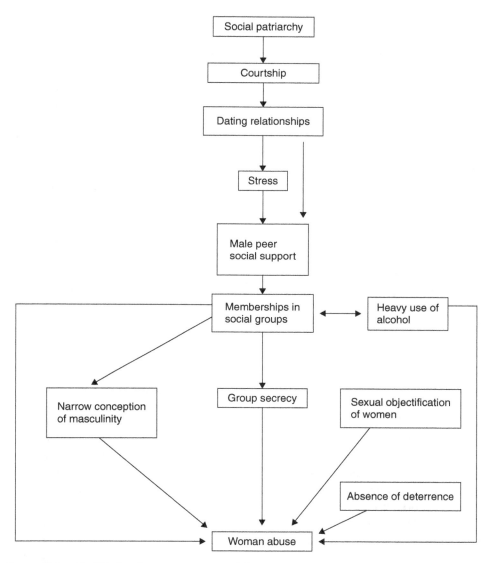

Figure 15.2. Modified male peer support model

We crafted Figure 15.2 six years after meeting each other at the 1987 Annual Meeting of the American Society of Criminology, based on our own criticism that Figure 15.1 was too focused on individual factors. Although it was strongly informed by feminist thought, it was still missing the recognition that there are many other related determinants, including broader social factors, that can motivate a man to abuse a woman. Of course, although we wanted to broaden the model substantially, we made no attempt or claim to explain every single variable that could be related to male peer support and the abuse of women.

In this newer model, we argued that there were four particularly important factors that needed to be added to Figure 15.1: the ideologies of familial and courtship patriarchy; alcohol consumption; membership in social groups (e.g., fraternities and sports teams); and the absence of deterrence (for a detailed explanation of this complex modified model, see DeKeseredy & Schwartz, 2013, and Schwartz & DeKeseredy, 1997). Whereas Figure 15.1 was informed by feminist thought, Figure 15.2 more specifically took into account various sociological factors (i.e., social forces) important to feminist theory. In particular, the modified model recognized how the broader social patriarchy acts as an ideology that justifies not only to men but also to many women why male superiority should reign in many fields and endeavors. Familial and courtship patriarchy is a subset of this thinking that describes domestic or intimate situations: who makes decisions, who drives, who pays for dinner, and who determines when to engage in sexual relations.

Figure 15.2 incorporated the same stressful situations in dating as Figure 15.1, but situates them in a much broader context, particularly on the college campus, of male social groups such as fraternities, sports teams, and single-sex dorms. Such organizations too often champion the objectification and exploitation of women through songs, newsletters, and group showings of pornography. Others teach that "no means yes" or that sex with women unable to give consent is acceptable. Many more simply provide a culture of sexual entitlement that raises both male expectations of "scoring" and worry and shame if a member were to allow a date to say no. More broadly, alcohol (or perhaps alcohol-soaked partying) also seems to be related to much sexual assault. Perhaps most important, there seems to be a lack of deterrence on virtually all college campuses because few men are ever punished for sexual or physical assault on women, and when they are, the punishments are mild. Few local prosecutors will push such cases, especially against athletes. The full theory is more complex than this, but the key point is that although society gives many messages that feminists have often termed a "rape culture," those who have friends that reinforce such messages are the ones most likely to become physical and sexual predators.

Figure 15.2 is superior to Figure 15.1, but it, too, has limitations. Perhaps the most salient is that although most of the individual elements have been repeatedly tested empirically, there have only been limited tests of the entire model. However, in their attempt to test the entire model on a single campus sample, Franklin et al. (2012) were able to offer empirical support. Unfortunately, given the complexity of some of the variables, it may not be possible to completely measure some of the core elements. The model may have more value as a heuristic or teaching model than as a predictive one. In other words, its greatest strength may lie in summarizing the complex relevant literature and proposing important ways to theorize and conceptualize male influence, rather than in mathematically isolating and predicting which men are most likely to abuse women.

Figure 15.2 also does not account for how social networks that favor and promote the abuse of women develop. Rather, it starts with the proposition that these groups already exist and discusses their role in woman abuse. Thus, one empirical question is whether pro-abuse social groups shape and mold men to learn these new behaviors or whether men who come to the university already holding such beliefs are attracted to these groups. This has long been a subject of some debate in dealing with such groups as fraternities: Do they "determine" beliefs and behavior or just provide a home for birds of a feather to flock together? For example, a central element of Sanday's (1990) theory of fraternity gang rape is that fraternity rituals mold this behavior. She argues that a young man comes to college and then goes through initiation ceremonies that involve the "transformation of consciousness": "By yielding himself to the group in this way, the pledge gains a new self" (p. 135). Warshaw (1988), in contrast, as well as some national representative sample survey data (e.g., DeKeseredy & Schwartz, 1998a), suggest that men with sexist ideologies seek out patriarchal all-male social groups so that they will receive support for their attitudes and behavior. The same problem applies to men in intimate relationships: We know that many men who abuse their intimate or ex-partners have strong social support networks, but not whether they were influenced by these groups to adopt new attitudes or whether these groups mainly serve to give support for already existing views (DeKeseredy & Schwartz, 2013).

The most common method of studying such questions about woman abuse with college students is with anonymous, self-report questionnaires given one time, in one place. This "one-shot" approach is excellent for documenting the existence of sexist male peer groups and the support resources they provide that encourage and justify male-to-female victimization. However, it tells us little, if anything, about the trajectory of individuals involved in sexist male homosocial networks.

One major solution to this problem could come from future researchers taking a longitudinal approach to the study of woman abuse in college, along the lines suggested and demonstrated by White and Humphrey (1997). With a longer term methodology, researchers may be able to get answers to such other unanswered questions as these:

- Do some members drop out of sexist male peer groups and rely on other means of social support to help "keep their women in line?"
- Do some members of a particular patriarchal male peer support group move on to join other (off-campus?) groups with similar values, beliefs, and practices?
- Do some all-male group members simply mature out of sexist peer groups as they get older and become employed? Do they then change their behavior?
- Are current or former members of sexist peer groups who get married or end up in cohabiting relationships more or less likely to be physically, sexually, and psychologically abusive?
- Do some men who join male peer groups eventually quit and then join again (DeKeseredy & Schwartz, 1998b, p. 91)?[1]

In addition to helping researchers answer the above questions, longitudinal research has another benefit. Many critics argue that surveys can misrepresent people or be misinterpreted. A longitudinal study that examines a large number of men over a long period of time with multiple measures of male peer support mitigates many of these criticisms (DeKeseredy & Schwartz, 1998b). Further, the validity of theoretical constructs is strengthened (White & Humphrey, 1997).

Contemporary Male Peer Support Theories

Since 1993, we have developed six more male peer support models, some of which were constructed with other colleagues. As well, we have long since departed from theorizing woman abuse in college populations, but the original model in Figure 15.1 and the modified male peer support model featured in Figure 15.2 continue to be the backbone of all of our newer male peer support offerings, as well as those developed by colleagues with different substantive interests. For example, using Figure 15.2, Sinclair (2002) studied incarcerated White adolescents to show how peer culture can promote the abuse of girls in the same way that the model theorizes for college campuses. Franklin (2007) used the model to explain how the police subculture operates to oppress women in policing. She constructed a visual model similar to that in Figure 15.2.

One thing all of our contemporary perspectives have in common is that they are integrated theories. In other words, they bring together several bodies of knowledge. It is to our last attempt to explain college woman abuse that we briefly turn to first. Space limitations preclude us from offering in-depth reviews of all our more recent theoretical efforts, but the key elements of most of them are made explicit.

A Gendered Social Bond/Male Peer Support Theory of University Woman Abuse

Near the start of the new millennium, despite calls for integrated woman abuse theories (e.g., Jasinski, 2001; Miller & Wellford, 1997), only a few scholars made any such attempts. Additionally, few woman abuse theorists attempted to engage the major theoretical contributions of mainstream criminologists. In 2001, together with social work scholar Alberto Godenzi (see Godenzi, Schwartz, & DeKeseredy, 2001), we addressed these two issues. Taking as a starting point that gender-blind and conservative theories have some value, Hirschi's (1969) social bond theory was integrated with insights from feminist theory, male peer support theory, and other critical criminological perspectives. The goal was to create not a formal new theory but rather a heuristic designed to show the value of adding feminist insight to gender-blind theory.

It may seem odd for feminists like us to draw from Hirschi's (1969) work on juvenile delinquency. Although he does report that this exclusion is "difficult to justify," in his influential *Causes of Delinquency*, Hirschi states in a footnote that "in the analysis which follows, the 'non-Negro' becomes 'White,' and the girls disappear" (Hirschi, 1969, p. 35). Following this, the vast majority of studies of social bond theory used all-male samples.

Our model, however, shows that consensus or middle-range theories, such as Hirschi's, that have been sharply attacked for ignoring gender may still have useful theoretical constructs that can be combined with critical insights. We turn Hirschi upside down with the argument that attachment and involvement with conventional peers may in fact promulgate violence against women on college campuses when it is noted that conventional institutions are patriarchal and part of a rape culture. University groups (e.g., social fraternities, sports teams) may (although this is far from universal) enforce adherence through homophobia and group pressure while promoting a hypermasculine culture that encourages men to use coercion and force to increase their scorecard of sexual encounters.

Our gendered social bond/male peer support perspective, like Hirschi's, is a theory of conformity. We argue that college women are abused by men "in numbers that would numb the mind of Einstein" (Lewis, as cited in Vallee, 2007, p. 22). Survey research done over the past 30 years consistently shows that at least one of every four North American female undergraduates has been sexually assaulted by a male partner or acquaintance, using a broad definition (DeKeseredy & Schwartz, 2013). Recalling Katz's (2006) claim that "it takes a village to rape a woman" (p. 149), these numbers suggest that sexual assault is virtually normative on college campuses. Perhaps this is too much of an overstatement, but it might be useful to conceptualize men who do not engage in woman abuse as being the deviants.

Because they are not following the mandates of the popular rape culture, we can conceive of these nonabusive men as having a bond to the dominant social order that is weak or broken. Somewhat like Agnew's (2011) attempt to build a unified criminology, we had an interest in, as Rock (1992) suggests, ending "the criminological cold war and the facile ideological oppositions of the 1970s and 1980s" (p. xi). Our main objective, however, was to provide an integrated theory of conformity that attempts to explain why men who belong to patriarchal peer groups engage in woman abuse and other sexist practices. Our formulation suggests that abuse is a by-product of the men's attempt to maintain a social bond with a conventional or traditional social order marked by gender inequality (Mooney, 1996; Young, 1999).

Beyond the College Campus

Until 2002, virtually all work on male peer support dealt with the influence of college men on other college men. Even so, as stated at the start of this chapter, it definitely thrives in many other places. We always suspected such male peer support existed off the college campus, but it was not until 1996 that we started moving toward examining the male peer group dynamics that extend beyond academic settings and their immediate surroundings. The starting point was William Julius Wilson's (1996) influential book *When Work Disappears: The World of the New Urban Poor*. Here, in the chapter titled "The Fading Inner-City Family," Wilson says:

> Males especially feel pressure to be sexually active. They said that all members of their peer networks brag about their sexual encounters and that they feel obligated to reveal their own sexual exploits. Little consideration is given to the implications or consequences of sexual matters for the longer-term relationship. (p. 99)

Wilson's work, and other research done by members of the New Chicago School (e.g., Sampson, Raudenbush, & Earls, 1997), influenced us to team up with two colleagues to conduct the first Canadian study of the relationship among poverty, joblessness, and crime in Canadian public housing (DeKeseredy, Alvi, Schwartz, & Tomaszewski, 2003). The woman abuse data generated by the project helped spawn our economic exclusion/male peer support model later developed at Ohio University and presented in Figure 15.3 (DeKeseredy & Schwartz, 2002).

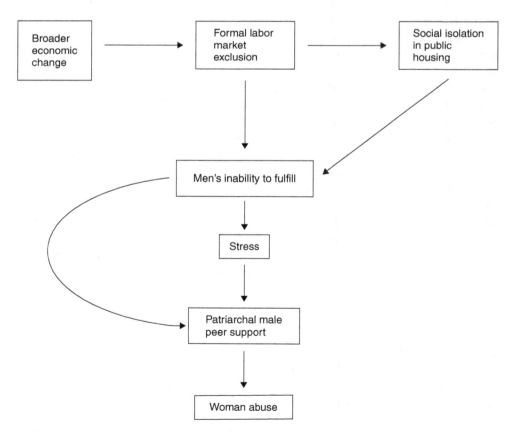

Figure 15.3.   Economic exclusion/male peer support model

Some women are at higher risk of being abused by their marital or cohabiting partners than are other women. Why do female public housing residents experience more violence than women in the general population? The theoretical model described in Figure 15.3 argues that recent major economic transformations (e.g., the shift from a manufacturing to a service-based economy) displaces working-class men and women (and they continue to do so today), who often end up in public housing and other "clusters of poverty" (Sernau, 2001). Men who have been socialized to believe that it is a man's job to be the "breadwinner" find themselves not only unemployed but also completely without any prospects of legitimate employment. They attribute their inability to advance not to the failure of the broader economic structure to provide equitable opportunity but to their own personal failure to measure up to events in their lives. This sense of failure and the stress it engenders has been described by Cobb and Sennett (1993) as a "hidden injury" of the class structure in North America. It also has a hidden injury to women. Because "their normal paths for personal power and prestige have been cut off" (Raphael, 2001, p. 703), the resulting stress leads economically marginalized men to seek social support from male peers with similar problems, which, in turn, promotes woman abuse and other highly injurious forms of gender violence.

The economic exclusion/male peer support model fills several gaps in the theoretical literature on woman abuse, but it is not a predictive model and it can be improved. For instance, consistent with the other male peer support theories reviewed here and elsewhere (see DeKeseredy & Schwartz, 2013), it does not specifically address whether members of patriarchal male peer support groups are intentionally recruited into these alliances or whether they gravitate to such groups as a way of selectively attempting to sustain or receive support for their earlier acquired values and behavior. Also, it does not specify that men may interact with and be influenced by peers who live away from public housing. Another point to note is that like every other male peer support model, racial or ethnic variations in male peer support dynamics remain to be more deeply examined. Nevertheless, as stated previously, there is evidence of pro-abuse male peer support in some U.S. inner-city communities of color and in some Puerto Rican neighborhoods (e.g., Bourgois, 1995; Miller, 2008; Wilson, 1996).

Guided by Figure 15.3 and data from our Canadian public housing study (DeKeseredy et al., 2003), we developed and tested the social and economic exclusion model of separation/divorce woman abuse in public housing (DeKeseredy, Schwartz, & Alvi, 2008). We also recently created a new left realist gendered subcultural theory (DeKeseredy & Schwartz, 2010). They are too complex to summarize here, but reflect our strong commitment to linking macro-level forces with microsocial factors, a path we started down in 1993. However, more recently we took somewhat of a radical departure from the bulk of our theoretical work and turned our attention to key factors associated with the abuse of rural women. Not surprisingly, one of these factors is male peer support.

The Rural Context

After decades of neglect, a growing number of scholars are now examining issues of crime and criminal justice in rural contexts. Collectively, rural studies reviewed by Donnermeyer and DeKeseredy (2014) show that rural communities are not less criminogenic than urban areas, a discovery that challenges conventional wisdom. In fact, rural rates may be higher than urban rates in particular types of rural places and for specific kinds of crime (Donnermeyer, 2012). For example, Rennison, DeKeseredy, and Dragiewicz (2012) found that rural separated or divorced women were markedly more likely to be sexually assaulted than similar urban women. Nevertheless, until the creation of Figures 15.4 and 15.5 (DeKeseredy, Rogness, & Schwartz, 2004; DeKeseredy, Donnermeyer, Schwartz, Tunnell, & Hall, 2007), rural research on woman abuse was underdeveloped theoretically. In fact, the same can be said about any type of rural crime research, and what did exist prior to our offerings was dominated by place-based perspectives, such as social disorganization theory (Donnermeyer & DeKeseredy, 2014).

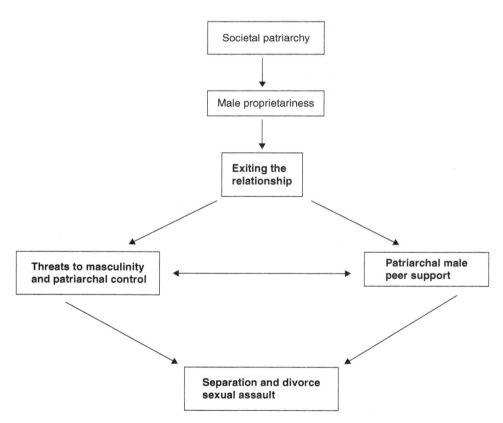

Figure 15.4.   A feminist/male peer support model of separation and divorce sexual assault

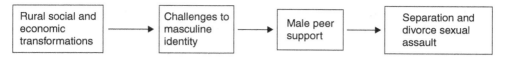

Figure 15.5. A rural masculinity crisis/male peer support model of separation and divorce sexual assault

Why do men sexually assault partners who want to leave or who have left them? Until we conducted our study of such victimization in rural southeast Ohio (DeKeseredy & Schwartz, 2009), there were no research answers to this question. The bulk of the empirical work on separation or divorce assault, regardless of whether it is qualitative or quantitative, had been done in urban areas, such as Boston and San Francisco. Furthermore, the extant literature focused on lethal and nonlethal physical violence (for reviews of this literature, see Brownridge, 2009; DeKeseredy et al., 2004; DeKeseredy & Schwartz; 2009; Hardesty, 2002), rather than sexual violence.

Heavily informed by perspectives offered by DeKeseredy and Schwartz (1993, 2002), Ellis and DeKeseredy (1997), Rogness (2003), and Wilson and Daly (1992) and developed with the help of McKenzie Rogness, Figure 15.2 situates separation or divorce within the larger context of societal patriarchy. Nevertheless, a constant such as this cannot be used to explain variations in the frequency and severity of male sexual assaults on women who want to or who have left them (Ellis & DeKeseredy, 1997). In other words, if we live in a patriarchal society that promotes "male proprietariness," why then do some men sexually assault during or after the relationship ends, whereas most others do not? One answer is that data generated by studies using differing patriarchal ideology scales all indicate that there are variations in male proprietarieness (DeKeseredy et al., 2004), which is "the tendency [of men] to think of women as sexual and reproductive 'property' they can own and exchange" (Wilson & Daly, 1992, p. 85). Proprietariness refers to "not just the emotional force of [the male's] own feelings of entitlement but to a more pervasive attitude [of ownership and control] toward social relationships [with intimate female partners]" (Wilson & Daly, 1992, p. 85).

Many women resist or eventually will resist their spouse or cohabiting partner's proprietariness in a variety of ways, such as arguing, protesting, and fighting back if they have been abused (DeKeseredy & Schwartz, 2009; Sev'er, 2002). There are also many women, although the precise number is unknown, who defy men's control by exiting or trying to exit a relationship and this may involve emotional separation, obtaining a separate residence, or starting or completing a legal separation or divorce. Emotional separation, a major predictor of a permanent end to a relationship, is defined as a woman's denial or restriction of sexual relations and other intimate exchanges.[2] Emotionally exiting a relationship can be just as dangerous as physically or legally exiting one because it, too, increases the likelihood of male violence and sexual abuse (Block & DeKeseredy, 2007; McFarlane & Malecha, 2005).

Regardless of how a woman does it, her attempt to leave or her successful departure from a sexist relationship challenges male proprietariness, but exiting alone cannot account for sexual assault. For example, many abusive patriarchal men have male friends with similar beliefs and values and these peers reinforce the notion that women's exiting is a threat to a man's masculinity (DeKeseredy & Schwartz, 2002). As well, many members of patriarchal peer groups view wife beating, rape, and other forms of male-to-female victimization as legitimate and effective means of repairing "damaged patriarchal masculinity" (Messerschmidt, 1993; Raphael, 2001). Not only do these men verbally and publicly state that sexual assault and other forms of abuse are legitimate means of maintaining patriarchal authority and control, but also they serve as role models because many of them physically, sexually, and psychologically harm their own intimate partners (DeKeseredy & Schwartz, 2013).

In short, patriarchal male peer support contributes to the perception of damaged masculinity and motivates sexually abusive men to "lash out against the women . . . they can no longer control" (Bourgois, 1995, p. 214). Another point to consider is that if a patriarchal man's peers see him as a failure with women because his partner wants to leave or has left him, he is likely to be ridiculed because he "can't control his woman" (DeKeseredy et al., 2004). Thus, like many college men who rape women, he is attempting to regain status among his peers. Similar to other men who rape female strangers, acquaintances, or dates, the sexual assaults committed by men during or after the process of separation or divorce may have much more to do with their need to sustain their status among their peers than either a need to satisfy their sexual desires or a longing to regain a loving relationship (Godenzi et al., 2001).

Figure 15.4 guided our study of separation or divorce sexual assault in rural Ohio and it received some empirical support (see DeKeseredy & Schwartz, 2009). Also, Figure 15.4 informed the construction of Figure 15.5, which is referred to as a rural masculinity crisis/male peer support model of separation or divorce sexual assault. Although Figure 15.4 is heavily influenced by feminist and male peer support theory, it does not address key rural social problems, such as the disappearance of work and the loss of family farms. Thus, we and our colleagues built on Figure 15.4 by focusing on these and other factors that enhance a sociological understanding of separation or divorce sexual assault, masculinities, and the U.S. rural gender order (DeKeseredy et al., 2007).

Major social and economic transformations occurring throughout U.S. rural communities described by DeKeseredy et al. (2007) and others (e.g., Donnermeyer & DeKeseredy, 2014) are fueling increases in nonviolent crime and a myriad of other social problems such as suicide, poverty, and male responses to the termination of intimate relationships (Donnermeyer, 2012; Hogg & Carrington, 2006; Jensen, 2006). Even so, regardless of the methods used to study these issues, it is also essential to theorize them and to put gender at the forefront of the analysis. The theoretical model presented in Figure 15.5 is heavily influenced by critical criminological thought and does not reduce gender to an afterthought or to a control variable in a regression equation. Moreover, it is a rare attempt to explain the plight of a group of women who have historically suffered in silence. Indeed, if battered lesbians, women of color, and female members of other ethnic or racial groups have been delegated to the margins by mainstream criminology (Sokoloff & Dupont, 2005), the same can be said about socially and economically excluded rural women who endure harms such as those identified here.

Obviously, we do not provide a detailed description of Figure 15.5, but it is important to keep in mind that in addition to being critical and to bringing marginalized women's experiences to the center of criminological analysis, Figure 15.5 responds to some of the problems in the state of male peer support theory and to research that must be done in the future. Chief among these limitations is the question of whether there are regional variations in male peer support for sexual assault and other types of woman abuse (DeKeseredy & Schwartz, 1998b). There has been little empirical work on men outside the mostly White, middle-class confines of large university campuses; further research thus should be conducted to determine whether the experiences of other male subgroups—for example, working-class men of the same age in rural communities—are the same. As well, to the best of our knowledge, except for DeKeseredy et al.'s (2004) model, there has been no other previous attempt to apply male peer support theory to any type of abuse during separation or divorce sexual assault. Thus, Figure 15.5, like some of the other theories reviewed in this chapter (e.g., Figure 15.3), moves male peer support research and theorizing beyond the limited realm of academic settings and focuses on a very high-risk relationship status category. Moreover, it addresses the fact that rural women's individual experiences are parts of a larger set of economic and social structural factors (Donnermeyer & DeKeseredy, 2014; Donnermeyer, Jobes, & Barclay, 2006).

Moving Forward

Dragiewicz (2011) concluded in her review of the scholarly evidence of patriarchal support for violence against women that:

> studies have documented the influence of patriarchal peer support for men's violence against women at the mesosystem level in a variety of contexts, including studies of battered wives, dating violence, batterer narratives, campus sexual assault, separation assault, and woman abuse in representative random samples. (p. 113)

The mesosystem is a level of influence included in ecological models of violence (Carlson, 1984; Heise, 1998; World Health Organization, 2002). Other levels included are individual, interpersonal, community, and culture. Dragiewicz further asserts that:

> The mesosystem is the most important part of the ecological model because it describes the cumulative interaction of all the other levels upon a person. The

mesosystem describes an individual's experience in context: it captures, for example, the interaction between an individual's personal history of abuse, experienced in the context of a specific relationship, which the individual has access to particular resources in a community and cultural context that shapes his or her interpretation of events and perception of available resources. (p. 20)

Unfortunately, male peer support for woman abuse is essentially ubiquitous and has a long history. The data gathered to date and reviewed by us elsewhere (DeKeseredy & Schwartz, 2013) tell us much, but there are still many unanswered questions and new avenues to explore. Chief among the problems in the state of male peer support theory and research is the question of how male peer support groups form or come together. Additionally, future work on male peer support and woman abuse on campus must address new types of intimacy. Dating has certainly changed today and we have recently seen a significant shift from dating to "hooking up" on college campuses. In fact, "hook-up culture" dominates the lives of today's college students (Freitas, 2013). Hooking up is an ambiguous term and it means different things to different students. Generally, the phrase refers to a casual sexual encounter (with no promise of commitment) ranging from kissing to sexual intercourse (Bogle, 2008).

Although the relationship between pornography and woman abuse is highly complex (Jensen, 2007), a growing body of research indicates that male peer support is part of the equation (DeKeseredy & Olsson, 2011; DeKeseredy & Schwartz, 2013), especially on college campuses. Still today, what Kanin (1985) refers to as "hypererotic" subcultures are endemic to postsecondary institutions. Here the members have high expectations of having sex and end up feeling disappointed or angry if women reject their advances. This subculture is heavily influenced by a combination of the new hook-up culture and pornography. What Dines (2010) states below sounds similar to Kanin's male peer support theory:

Given the increasing prevalence of hooking up in the culture, especially on college campuses, these men's perceptions that other guys seem to have no problem finding sex is not completely inaccurate. Where they seem to lose touch with reality is in the degree to which they assume this is the norm. In the porn world of never-ending sex, every interaction with a woman—be it a student, a doctor, a maid, a teacher, or just a stranger—ends up sexualized. Add to this the stories that men regale each other about their latest conquest, stories that often sound like the porn movie they just watched, and you have constructed a world of constant male access to every woman a man meets. When the real world doesn't play out like this, then anger and disappointment make sense. (p. 89)

More research, especially quantitative work, is needed on the relationship between hooking up and male peer support. As well, although there is a large literature on genocidal sexual violence in countries such as Rwanda and Bosnia-Herzegovina

(Kuehnast, de Jonge Oudratt, & Hernes, 2011), male peer support theory has thus far not been applied to this atrocity but would be helpful because male bonding is an integral part of combatant socialization (Wood, 2011).

Questions we asked 15 years ago remain unanswered (DeKeseredy & Schwartz, 1998b). Are White men more or less likely than African American, Native American, or Hispanic males to join and be influenced by all-male collectives? Are working-class and unemployed men more or less likely than privileged male undergraduate students to receive pro-abuse male peer support? Another thing we do not know is the extent to which peer violence is related to woman abuse within interracial couples. This, however, is not surprising, because male-to-female violence in intimate heterosexual interracial relationships of all sorts is an understudied topic (Renzetti, 2011).

Elliott Currie (2009) reminds us that "The burden of violent crime . . . is not shared equally around the globe. It is heavily concentrated in some societies, and some places and people within those societies" (p. 4). It is only logical to assume, then, that male peer support is likely to be stronger in some societies and in some places and people within those societies. Even so, there is no conclusive evidence to support this hypothesis. Hence, male peer support studies need to move in yet another new direction: comparative research.

Other recommendations for further theoretical and empirical work could easily be presented here and are offered in our book *Male Peer Support and Violence Against Women: The History and Verification of a Theory* (DeKeseredy & Schwartz, 2013). We hope that future North American studies will respond to our suggestions, but in the meantime, women who are currently being abused by men who belong to patriarchal subcultures of violence cannot afford to sit back and hope that researchers and theorists develop greater insight into pro-abuse male social networks. Something must be done now to help curb the alarming rates of woman abuse uncovered by decades of survey research. As Dawn Currie (1995) put it nearly 20 years ago, "Research alone does not result in social change. Social transformation is the consequence of a number of inter-related activities which often require lobbying, the development of policy initiatives, consultation, etc." (p. 44).

NOTES

[1]These questions are heavily informed by Sanchez-Jankowski's (1991) gang research and by the questions raised by Connell's (1995) suggestions on the nature of how men negotiate their masculinity through the lifespan.

[2]This is a modified version of Ellis and DeKeseredy's (1997) definition of emotional separation.

References

Agnew, R. (2011). *Toward a unified criminology: Integrating assumptions about crime, people, and society.* New York: New York University Press.

Benedict, J. R. (1998). *Athletes and acquaintance rape.* Thousand Oaks, CA: Sage.

Block, C. R., & DeKeseredy, W. S. (2007). Forced sex and leaving intimate relationships: Results of the Chicago women's health risk study. *Women's Health and Urban Life, 6,* 6–24.

Bogle, K. A. (2008). *Hooking up: Sex, dating, and relationships on campus.* New York: New York University Press.

Bourgois, P. (1995). *In search of respect: Selling crack in El Barrio.* New York, NY: Cambridge University Press.

Bowker, L. H. (1983). *Beating wife-beating.* Lexington, MA: Lexington Books.

Brownridge, D. A. (2009). *Violence against women: Vulnerable populations.* New York, NY: Routledge.

Burstyn, V. (2000). *The rites of men: Manhood, politics, and the culture of sport.* Toronto, Ontario: University of Toronto Press.

Campbell, H. (2000). The glass phallus: Pub(lic) masculinity and drinking in rural New Zealand. *Rural Sociology, 65,* 532–536.

Caplan, G. (1974). *Social systems and community mental health.* New York, NY: Behavioral Publications.

Carlson, B. E. (1984). Causes and maintenance of domestic violence: An ecological analysis. *Social Services Review, 58,* 569–587.

Cassell, J. C. (1976). The contribution of the social environment to host resistance. *American Journal of Epidemiology, 104,* 107–123.

Cobb, J., & Sennett, R. (1993). *The hidden injuries of class.* New York, NY: Norton.

Cohen, S., & Wills, T. A. (1985). Stress, social support, and the buffering hypothesis. *Psychological Bulletin, 98,* 310–357.

Connell, R. W. (1995). *Masculinities.* Berkeley: University of California Press.

Cullen, F. T. (1994). Social support as an organizing concept for criminology: Presidential address to the Academy of Criminal Justice Sciences. *Justice Quarterly, 11,* 527–559.

Currie, D. H. (1995). *Student safety at the University of British Columbia: Preliminary findings of a student safety study.* Vancouver, British Columbia: University of British Columbia.

Currie, E. (2009). *The roots of danger: Violent crime in global perspective.* Upper Saddle River, NJ: Prentice Hall.

DeKeseredy, W. S. (1988a). Woman abuse in dating relationships: The relevance of social support theory. *Journal of Family Violence, 3,* 1–13.

DeKeseredy, W. S. (1988b). *Woman abuse in dating relationships: The role of male peer support.* Toronto, Ontario: Canadian Scholars' Press.

DeKeseredy, W. S., Alvi, S., Schwartz, M. D., & Tomaszewski, E. A. (2003). *Under siege: Poverty and crime in a public housing community.* Lanham, MD: Lexington Books.

DeKeseredy, W. S., Donnermeyer, J. F., Schwartz, M. D., Tunnell, K. D., & Hall, M. (2007). Thinking critically about rural gender relations: Toward a rural masculinity crisis/male peer support model of separation/divorce sexual assault. *Critical Criminology, 15,* 295–311.

DeKeseredy, W. S., & Olsson, P. (2011). Adult pornography, male peer support, and violence against women: The contribution of the "dark side" of the internet. In M. Vargas Martin, M. Garcia-Ruiz, & A. Edwards (Eds.), *Technology for facilitating humanity and combating social deviations: Interdisciplinary perspectives* (pp. 34–50). Hershey, PA: IGI Global.

DeKeseredy, W. S., Rogness, M., & Schwartz, M. D. (2004). Separation/divorce sexual assault: The current state of social scientific knowledge. *Aggression and Violent Behavior, 9*, 675–691.

DeKeseredy, W. S., & Schwartz, M. D. (1993). Male peer support and woman abuse: An expansion of DeKeseredy's model. *Sociological Spectrum, 13*, 394–414.

DeKeseredy, W. S., & Schwartz, M. D. (1998a). *Woman abuse on campus: Results from the Canadian National Survey.* Thousand Oaks, CA: Sage.

DeKeseredy, W. S., & Schwartz, M. D. (1998b). Male peer support and woman abuse in postsecondary school courtship: Suggestions for new directions in sociological research. In R. K. Bergen (Ed.), *Issues in intimate violence* (pp. 83–96). Thousand Oaks, CA: Sage.

DeKeseredy, W. S., & Schwartz, M. D. (2002). Theorizing public housing woman abuse as a function of economic exclusion and male peer support. *Women's Health and Urban Life, 1*, 26–45.

DeKeseredy, W. S., & Schwartz, M. D. (2009). *Dangerous exits: Escaping abusive relationships in rural America.* New Brunswick, NJ: Rutgers University Press.

DeKeseredy, W. S., & Schwartz, M. D. (2010). Friedman economic policies, social exclusion, and crime: Toward a gendered left realist subcultural theory. *Crime, Law and Social Change, 54*, 159–170.

DeKeseredy, W. S., & Schwartz, M. D. (2013). *Male peer support and violence against women: The history and verification of a theory.* Boston, MA: Northeastern University Press.

DeKeseredy, W. S., Schwartz, M. D., & Alvi, S. (2008). Which women are more likely to be abused? Public housing, cohabitation, and separated/divorced women. *Criminal Justice Studies, 21*, 283–293.

Dines, G. (2010). *Pornland: How porn has hijacked our sexuality.* Boston, MA: Beacon Press.

Donnermeyer, J. F. (2012). Rural crime and critical criminology. In W. S. DeKeseredy & M. Dragiewicz (Eds.), *Routledge handbook of critical criminology* (pp. 290–302). London, UK: Routledge.

Donnermeyer, J. F., & DeKeseredy, W. S. (2014). *Rural criminology.* London, UK: Routledge.

Donnermeyer, J. F., Jobes, P., & Barclay, E. (2006). Rural crime, poverty, and community. In W. S. DeKeseredy & B. Perry (Eds.), *Advancing critical criminology: Theory and application* (pp. 199–218). Lanham, MD: Lexington Books.

Dragiewicz, M. (2008). Patriarchy reasserted: Fathers' rights and anti-VAWA activism. *Feminist Criminology, 3*, 121–144.

Dragiewicz, M. (2011). *Equality with a vengeance: Men's rights groups, battered women, and antifeminist backlash.* Boston, MA: Northeastern University Press.

Ellis, D. (1988). Post-separation woman abuse: The contribution of social support. *Victimology, 13*, 439–450.

Ellis, D., & DeKeseredy, W. S. (1997). Rethinking estrangement, interventions and intimate femicide. *Violence Against Women, 3*, 590–609.

Forbes, G. B., Adams-Curtis, L. E., Pakalka, A., & White, K. B. (2006). Dating aggression, sexual coercion, and aggression-supporting attitudes among college men as a function of participation in aggressive high school sports. *Violence Against Women, 15*, 441–455.

Franklin, C. A. (2007). Male peer support and the police culture: Understanding the resistance and opposition of women in policing. *Women and Criminal Justice, 16*, 1–25.

Franklin, C. A., Bouffard, L. A., & Pratt, T. C. (2012). Sexual assault on the college campus: Fraternity affiliation, male peer support, and low self-control. *Criminal Justice and Behavior, 39*, 1457–1480.

Freitas, D. (2013). *The end of sex: How hookup culture is leaving a generation unhappy, sexually unfulfilled, and confused about intimacy.* New York, NY: Basic Books.

Godenzi, A., Schwartz, M. D., & DeKeseredy, W. S. (2001). Toward a gendered social bond/male peer support theory of university woman abuse. *Critical Criminology, 10*, 1–16.

Hardesty, J. L. (2002). Separation assault in the context of postdivorce parenting: An integrative review of the literature. *Violence Against Women, 8*, 597–621.

Heise, L. L. (1998). Violence against women: An integrated, ecological framework. *Violence Against Women, 4*, 262–290.

Heller, K., & Swindle, R. W. (1983). Social networks, perceived social support and coping with stress. In R. E. Feiner, L. A. Jason, J. N. Moritsugu, & S. S. Farber (Eds.), *Preventive psychology: Theory, research and practice* (pp. 87–103). New York, NY: Pergamon.

Hirschi, T. (1969). *Causes of delinquency.* Berkeley: University of California Press.

Hoff, L. A. (1990). *Battered women as survivors.* New York, NY: Routledge.

Hogg, R., & Carrington, K. (2006). *Policing the rural crisis.* Sydney, Australia: Federation Press.

Jasinski, J. L. (2001). Theoretical explanations for violence against women. In C. M. Renzetti, J. L. Edleson, & R. K. Bergen (Eds.), *Sourcebook on violence against women* (pp. 5–22). Thousand Oaks, CA: Sage.

Jensen, L. (2006). At the razor's edge: Building hope for America's rural poor. *Rural Realities, 1*, 1–8.

Jensen, R. (2007). *Getting off: Pornography and the end of masculinity.* Cambridge, MA: South End Press.

Jewkes, R., Dunkle, K., Koss, M. P., Levin, J. B., Nduna, M., Jama, N., & Sikweyiya, Y. (2006). Rape perpetration by young rural South African men: Prevalence, patterns, and risk factors. *Social Science and Medicine, 63*, 2949–2961.

Kanin, E. J. (1985). Date rapists: Differential sexual socialization and relative deprivation. *Archives of Sexual Behavior, 14*, 219–231.

Katz, J. (2006). *The macho paradox: Why some men hurt women and how all men can help.* Naperville, IL: Sourcebooks.

Kuehnast, K., de Jonge Oudraat, C., & Hernes, H. (Eds.). (2011). *Women and war: Power and protection in the 21st century.* Washington, DC: U.S. Institute of Peace.

McFarlane, J., & Malecha, A. (2005). *Sexual assault among intimates: Frequency, consequences, and treatments.* Washington, DC: U.S. Department of Justice.

Messerschmidt, J. W. (1993). *Masculinities and crime: Critique and reconceptualization.* Lanham, MD: Rowan & Littlefield.

Miller, J. (2008). *Getting played: African-American girls, urban inequality, and gendered violence.* New York: New York University Press.

Miller, S. L., & Welford, C. F. (1997). Patterns and correlates of interpersonal violence. In A. P. Cardarelli (Ed.), *Violence between intimate partners: Patterns, causes, and effects* (pp. 16–28). Boston, MA: Allyn & Bacon.

Mooney, J. (1996). Violence, space and gender. In N. Jewson & S. MacGregor (Eds.), *Transforming cities* (pp. 100–115). London, UK: Routledge.

Raphael, J. (2001). Public housing and domestic violence. *Violence Against Women, 7*, 699–706.

Rennison, C. M., DeKeseredy, W. S., & Dragiewicz, M. (2012). Urban, suburban, and rural variations in separation/divorce rape/sexual assault: Results from the national crime victimization survey. *Feminist Criminology, 7*, 282–297.

Renzetti, C. M. (2011). Economic issues and intimate partner violence. In C. M. Renzetti, J. L. Edleson, & R. K. Bergen (Eds.), *Sourcebook on violence against women* (2nd ed., pp. 171–187). Thousand Oaks, CA: Sage.

Rock, P. (1992). The criminology that came in from the cold. In J. Lowman & B. D. MacLean (Eds.), *Realist criminology: Crime control and policing in the 1990s* (pp. ix–xiv). Toronto, Ontario: University of Toronto Press.

Rogness, M. (2002). *Toward an integrated male peer support model of marital rape in the United States.* M.A. thesis. Department of Sociology and Anthropology, Ohio University. Athens, Ohio.

Sampson, R. J., Raudenbush, S. W., & Earls, F. (1997). Neighborhoods and violent crime: A multilevel study of collective efficacy. *Science, 277*, 918–924.

Sanchez-Jankowski, M. (1991). *Islands in the street: Gangs and American urban society.* Berkeley: University of California Press.

Sanday, P. R. (1990). *Fraternity gang rape.* New York: New York University Press.

Sarason, I. G., & Sarason, B. R. (1985). *Social support: Theory, research, and applications.* The Hague, The Netherlands: Martinus Nijhof.

Schwartz, M. D., & DeKeseredy, W. S. (1997). *Sexual assault on the college campus: The role of male peer support.* Thousand Oaks, CA: Sage.

Schwartz, M. D., & DeKeseredy, W. S. (2000). Aggregation bias and woman abuse: Variations by male peer support, region, language and school type. *Journal of Interpersonal Violence, 15*, 555–565.

Sernau, S. (2001). *Worlds apart: Social inequalities in a new century.* Thousand Oaks, CA: Pine Forge Press.

Sev'er, A. (2002). *Fleeing the house of horrors: Women who have left abusive partners.* Toronto, Ontario: University of Toronto Press.

Sinclair, R. L. (2002). *Male peer support and male-to-female dating abuse committed by socially displaced male youth: An exploratory study.* Doctoral dissertation. Ottawa, Ontario: Carleton University.

Sokoloff, N. J., & Dupont, I. (2005). Domestic violence: Examining the intersections of race, class, and gender—An introduction. In N. J. Sokoloff (Ed.), *Domestic violence at the margins: Readings on race, class, gender, and culture* (pp. 1–13). New Brunswick, NJ: Rutgers University Press.

Vallee, B. (2007). *The war on women.* Toronto, Ontario: Key Porter.

Vaux, A. (1985). Variations in social support associated with gender, ethnicity, and age. *Journal of Social Issues, 41*, 89–110.

Warshaw, R. (1988). *I never called it rape.* New York, NY: Harper & Row.

Websdale, N. (1998). *Rural woman battering and the justice system: An ethnography.* Thousand Oaks, CA: Sage.

White, J. W., & Humphrey, J. A. (1997). A longitudinal approach to the study of sexual assault: Theoretical and methodological considerations. In M. D. Schwartz (Ed.), *Researching sexual violence against women: Methodological and personal perspectives* (pp. 22–42). Thousand Oaks, CA: Sage.

Wilson, M., & Daly, M. (1992). Til death do us part. In J. Radford & D. E. H. Russell (Eds.), *Femicide: The politics of women killing* (pp. 83–98). New York, NY: Twayne.

Wilson, W. J. (1996). *When work disappears: The world of the new urban poor.* New York, NY: Knopf.

Wood, E. J. (2011). Rape is not inevitable in war. In K. Kuehnast, C. de Jonge Oudraat, & H. Hernes (Eds.), *Women & war: Power and protection in the 21st century* (pp. 37–64). Washington, DC: U.S. Institute of Peace.

World Health Organization. (2002). *World report on violence and health: Summary.* Geneva, Switzerland: Author.

Young, J. (1999). *The exclusive society.* London, UK: Sage.

Zimmerman, G. M., & Vasquez, B. E. (2011). Decomposing the peer effect on adolescent substance use: Mediation nonlinearity, and differential nonlinearity. *Criminology, 49,* 1235–1273.

PART VII

Women, Justice, and Corrections

CHAPTER 16

Gender and Criminal Justice Processing

Nicholas Corsaro, Jesenia M. Pizarro,
and Sandra Lee Browning

A great deal of the discussion in *Sisters in Crime Revisited* has focused on disentangling the circumstances, complexities, contexts, and social constructions related to female criminality. In this chapter, we focus primarily on legalistic and systems approaches by specifically analyzing how the criminal justice system operates in terms of legislating, arresting, prosecuting, and incarcerating offenders—particularly when gender (and subsequent intersections of race with gender) often operates as a point of divergence in offender processing. In terms of reported offending and victimization rates, males and females engage in distinctive criminal offending patterns in that males are overrepresented for violent crimes, whereas females are overrepresented in specific status-based offenses such as prostitution (Steffensmeier, 1993). Disproportionate rates of offending by gender and race typically withstand rigorous empirical scrutiny; however, unraveling why such patterns exist and whether there is consistent variation in female as well as minority-female criminal justice processing is the primary focus of this investigation.

In this chapter, we first review trends in criminal justice processing over time that account for gender and race delineations. We then illustrate how these trends in processing are likely influenced (although not always explained) by gender differences in serious criminal offending by providing a specific review of the most serious and well-documented type of violent crime: homicide. Next, we appraise how laws, the enforcement of law (i.e., police-driven arrest decisions), criminal incidents reported, and official crime data are socially constructed and appear to be disproportionately applied across various contexts involving different demographic groups beyond what would be expected based on offending differences. More specifically, we examine how written legislation, selective police enforcement, courtroom decisions, and corrections-based differences are seemingly influenced by gender and race. We conclude by illustrating that there is no one component of the criminal justice system where race and gender seem to matter most. However, when reviewing the criminal justice system from a more holistic standpoint, we clearly see a multiplicative race–gender effect across the various justice systems.

A Review of U.S. National Trends Over Time

National population estimates show that females outnumbered males in the United States in terms of sheer numbers by roughly 2% to 5% each year from 1980 through 2011 (Bureau of Justice Statistics, 2013a). However, men committed more Part I violent crimes (i.e., assaults, robberies, rapes, and homicides), at a ratio of 7:1, when compared to violent offenses committed by females. Interestingly, Figure 16.1 presents data from the NCVS indicating that, since 2000, the rate of violent crime victimizations by gender became relatively comparable between men and women (Bureau of Justice Statistics, 2013a). Males in the early 1990s were 33% more likely to be victims of violent crimes than were females; however, between 2008 and 2011, the victimization difference ratio approached roughly 8%. Although male and female victimizations became more proportional, the predominant perpetrators of violence have continued to be male offenders, with a considerably higher arrest-to-population ratio for males (4.3:100,000) than for females (1.3:100,000) from 2008 through 2011.

Figure 16.2 illustrates that males have been between three to four times more likely to be arrested than females over the past 30 years (Bureau of Justice Statistics, 2013b). However, arrest disparities have become considerably closer since 2000

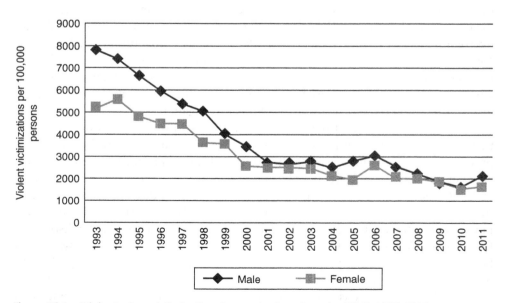

Figure 16.1. Violent crime victimizations by gender based on the NCVS, 1993–2011

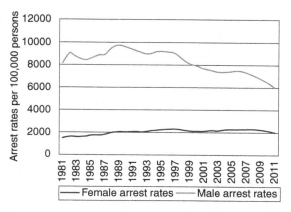

Figure 16.2.   Overall U.S. arrest rates by gender, 1980–2011

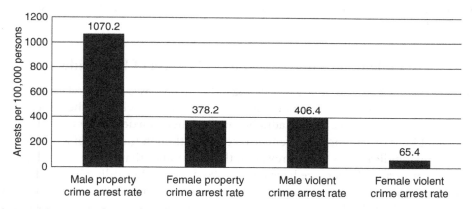

Figure 16.3.   Arrests by gender, 1980–2011

because of a sizable reduction in male arrest rates and a modest, steady increase in female arrest rates. The types of incidents where females have been more represented in arrests are related to property, drug, and vice offenses.

In terms of arrests by offense type across the intersections of gender and race, Figure 16.3 shows that males have been roughly three times more likely than females to be arrested for property crimes (1,070.2 male arrests per 100,000 compared with 378.2 female arrests per 100,000) between 1980 and 2011 and more than six times more likely to be arrested for violent offenses (406.4 male arrests per 100,000 compared to 65.4 female arrests per 100,000) during this same period (Bureau of Justice Statistics, 2013b).

Rates of arrest have been disproportionately higher for Blacks compared to Whites from 1980 to 2011 for both property crimes and violent crimes. Arrest rates for Blacks for property crimes was three times higher (1,773.2 arrests per 100,000) than that for Whites (575 arrests per 100,000). The Black violent crime arrest rate (780.4 arrests per

100,000) was also much higher than the White violent crime arrest rate (156.5 arrests per 100,000) over the past 30 years (Bureau of Justice Statistics, 2013b).

Thus, we see through detailed examinations of victimization, offense, and arrest data that specific crime incidents (i.e., violent offenses) are more likely to be perpetrated by various demographic groups (males relative to females and Blacks relative to Whites). We might expect, then, some disparity by gender and race in who is officially processed (e.g., who is arrested or imprisoned) based simply on these differences in the commission of crimes (e.g., more men than women will be sent to prison because men commit more serious offenses). However, if gender and race differences in official processing are greater than involvement in crime would predict, then this would be evidence of bias, if not discrimination. As we will see, official processing introduces cumulative and multiplicative biases that result in gender and racial differences above and beyond what offense patterns would produce. There is perhaps no better illustration of violent offense and processing distinctions that is captured more accurately than homicide incidents (because unlike many other offenses, most homicides are reported or discovered by police officials).

Violent Offense Processing: The Case of Homicide

Studies that have examined the processing of homicide cases as they relate to gender and race have focused on two outcomes: (1) "clearance"—whether the police make an arrest in a case, and (2) "court adjudication"—whether a defendant is found guilty and what kind of sentence an offender receives. Although the body of research centering on adjudication is more prevalent, the few studies that have explored gender and race in terms of clearance have found mixed results. Regarding homicide clearance, previous studies have noted that incidents involving White victims are more likely to be cleared relative to cases with minority victims (Addington, 2006; Lee, 2005; Litwin & Xu, 2007; Regoeczi, Jarvis, & Riedel, 2008). Conversely, several studies have found that race and ethnicity variables do not have a significant impact on clearance (Addington, 2006; Jiao, 2007; Puckett & Lundman, 2003) or even that cases involving minority victims have higher clearance rates (Trussler, 2010). In terms of gender, the bulk of research suggests that homicides involving females as victims are more likely to have their cases cleared (Lee, 2005; Regoeczi et al., 2008). Several previous studies, however, found null effects for victim sex (Addington, 2006; Litwin & Xu, 2007; Wellford & Cronin, 1999; Wolfgang, 1958). Criminologists explain these findings by observing that cases involving Whites and females are easier for the police to investigate. Specifically, homicides involving Whites and women more often occur within the victim's residence and are carried out with personal weapons, which increase the likelihood of law enforcement coming across physical evidence. Additionally, these incidents tend to involve an assailant who is known to the victims and their family. This could in turn increase the odds for investigators to find potential witnesses and to hold prior event information (e.g., an ex-partner had threatened to kill a female victim) that can serve to facilitate the investigation.

To date, approximately a dozen studies have focused on the adjudication in the courts of homicide incidents generally, as opposed to research concentrating on specific types of cases, such as those that might lead to the death penalty (see Auerhahn, 2007a, 2007b; Baumer, Messner, & Felson, 2000; Dawson, 2004; Farrell & Swigert, 1978, 1986; Franklin & Fearn, 2008; Garfinkel, 1949; Johnson, Wingerden, & Nieuwbeerta, 2010; Swigert & Farrell, 1976, 1980; Wolfgang, 1958). Garfinkel was one of the first scholars to examine the issue of homicide adjudication and sentencing. He found in this early study that homicide incidents involving a White victim and a Black assailant elicited severe court charges such as murder in the first degree and, once convicted, the sanction was lengthier than those involving Black victims. As such, the findings in Garfinkel's study foreshadowed subsequent research findings that the race of the victim is a significant determinant in the arrest, prosecution, conviction, and sentencing of the offender. Regardless of their race and ethnicity, offenders who victimize Whites are significantly more likely to be arrested, prosecuted, convicted, and sentenced more harshly than those who victimize Blacks or any other minorities (Kingsnorth, Lopez, Wentworth, & Cumming, 1998; Smith, Visher, & Davidson, 1984; Sorensen & Wallace, 1999; Spohn, 2000).

Later studies have also found a relationship among gender, age, and social economic status with court outcomes such as charging, conviction, and sentencing (e.g., Farrell & Swigert, 1978, 1986; Farrell and Swigert, 1978; Wolfgang, 1958). Specifically, these studies reported that Black young males of low socioeconomic status were charged more harshly in homicide cases than Whites, females, older individuals, and those from higher economic strata. These findings were especially pronounced when cases involved victims with opposite demographic and social characteristics. Studies within the past two decades have both confirmed and expanded upon earlier research. Baumer et al. (2000) examined the effect of victim characteristics on the preadjudication, adjudication, and sentencing procedures in 33 U.S. counties. Similar to earlier research, they discovered that non-White male defendants were more likely to be processed and that defendants accused of murdering non-Whites were less likely to receive a conviction or the most serious indictments. Conversely, those accused of murdering females were more likely to be convicted and received harsher punishments than those accused of murdering males. They also found that prior criminal involvement mattered during the court process, in that defendants with a prior criminal history received harsher punishments when compared to those without such a history. Interestingly, offenders convicted of murdering a victim who provoked the incident received less severe punishments.

Researchers have also found a relationship between the victim–offender relationship and court outcomes (Auerhahn, 2007a, 2007b; Dawson, 2004). Dawson's examination of 24 years of data on homicides in Toronto, Canada, found that intimate-partner homicide (IPH) cases were less likely to receive a first-degree murder charge, or even to be sent to trial, when compared to stranger homicide incidents. Further, when IPH cases were sent to trial and a conviction was reached, the sentence length was significantly shorter than for non-IPH cases. Auerhahn's (2007a) more current examination of IPH and non-IPH cases in Philadelphia suggests that gender mediates this relationship. Thus, incidents involving a male assailant and a female victim were adjudicated for the most serious charge and received the harshest sanctions, whereas incidents involving female assailants and male victims culminated in lesser charges and sanctions. Recent research also suggests interactions between the demographics and prior criminal histories of victims and offenders. For example, Auerhahn's (2007b) study suggests the existence of a "Black/Hispanic criminal stereotype" that attributes violence, aggression, blameworthiness, and dangerousness implicit to Black or Hispanic male suspects. Such stereotypes may lead to disproportionate court outcomes.

In the most recent study in the area, Johnson et al. (2010) examined covariates of the sentencing recommendation and outcome of approximately 1,300 Dutch homicides that occurred between 1993 and 2004 to assess the generalizability of U.S. research findings in an international context. Uniquely, this study tested the effect of numerous case variables such as incident location, modus, and motive. Their findings converge with studies conducted in the United States. Thus, similar to the United States, they discovered that prior convictions positively affected the sentencing outcome of cases. Male offenders who killed female victims received harsher sentences than those who killed males, and females were sentenced to shorter incarceration terms than males. Immigrants, too, received harsher sentences than Dutch nationals. Age was also a significant covariate because offenders who were either very young or old received less harsh punishment. Unlike U.S. research, however, they did not find evidence of interactions between the demographic characteristics of offenders.

In terms of case variables, Johnson et al. (2010) found that weapon type, incident location, and homicide type were important in determining case outcomes. That is, offenders convicted of homicides carried out with guns, occurring in public locales, and involving nonintimates received harsher penalties. Thus, the intersection of the offender, the victim, and the situational circumstances of the encounter plays a tremendous role in processing distinctions, even for the most serious and violent crimes with a high reliability in its measurement (i.e., a missing person, the presence of a victim).

Further in-depth examinations of criminal justice practice illustrate processing differences (arrests, prosecutions, and incapacitation-based services) across these demographic groups that are not solely a product of distinctions in overall offending patterns. Indeed, unique patterns are observed at various phases of the criminal justice system between male and female suspected offenders and between White and non-White suspects.

Behavioral Legislation

A criminal justice systems approach focuses on enforcing and processing individuals who are in violation of the criminal law. Without the presence of a law, there can be no unlawful offender who is subject to a criminal justice response (e.g., arrest, trial, conviction, incarceration). To assess the process of legal definitions and the enforcement of such definitions, we take a social constructionist approach. This approach shows how groups (such as gender and racial groups) differ in their language, knowledge, and interpretation of everyday life (Berger & Luckman, 1966). At issue is whose interpretation or "construction" of reality is taken as normal and controls what occurs in society. Related to the intersection of the criminal law and gender (as well as race), laws can be (and often are) disproportionally applied to different demographic groups. According to the sociologist Donald Black (1976), the quantity of law will vary with the social rank and power of the individual. Individuals of higher social rank (as measured by numerous social indicators, including social class, race, and gender) have more law available to them—law that can be used to take decisive action in their favor while applying less law and less punitive sanctions to their criminal transgressions.

Some feminist critics (e.g., Daly & Chesney-Lind, 1988) have suggested that the study of crime and justice processing is androcentric (i.e., is framed by male experiences and understandings of the social world). From this viewpoint the question is, why do gender-based laws exist and how do subsequent contacts with criminal justice agencies differ between males and females? Nagel and Hagan (1983) illustrate that there is historical evidence of either a chivalrous or a paternalistic justice system. Chivalry is more closely associated with servitude toward females (i.e., pedestal placement and preferential treatment), whereas paternalism is focused more on protecting and educating the powerless. From either framework, the protector becomes an influential source of social control where decisions are believed to be made "in the female's best interest." However, there is a price that comes with the "so-called benefits of chivalry" (Moulds, 1980, p. 133). The price of chivalry is that women are often viewed as being emotional, fragile, indecisive, and childlike and thus less accountable for their actions. However, chivalry is extended only to women who behave in nonaggressive stereotypical gender roles; those who deviate from the prescribed roles are more likely to receive harsher criminal sanctions throughout the system (Farnworth & Teske, 1995; Franklin & Fearn, 2008; Grabe, Trager, Lear, & Rauch, 2006; Visher, 1983). For example, a female who is questioned by a police officer who argues she committed an offense because she was a victim of circumstances beyond her control is more likely (from this perspective) to become a beneficiary of more lenient justice than a female who similarly admits responsibility for her actions, but fails to plead for help or present herself as a victim.

There are also multiple illustrations of androcentric legislation and subsequent application of the law. For example, promiscuity and prostitution are offenses for which women (relative to men) are almost exclusively prosecuted. Hewitt and Mickish (1983) examined official handling of prostitution cases between 1900 and 1920 within Indiana, and they found that there were nearly equal numbers of males and females arrested, tried, and convicted for prostitution. However, beginning in the 1920s, sexual offenses such as promiscuity and prostitution began to be attributed to sexual status associated with female deviance. Thus, although males and females

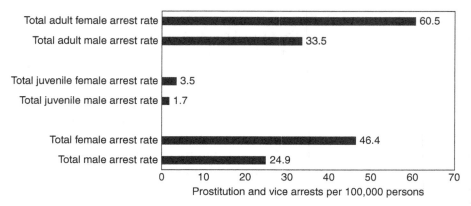

Figure 16.4.   Prostitution and vice crime arrest averages by males and females, 1980–2011

both engage in compensation-based voluntary sex, females are more likely to be charged with promiscuous sexual behavior offenses than are their male counterparts. This distinction has continued through the present time. As seen in Figure 16.4, between 1980 and 2011, the average rate of arrests for prostitution and vice offenses was much higher for all females (60.55 arrests per 100,000 persons) relative to males (33.55 arrests per 100,000 persons); importantly, a similar 2:1 female:male arrest ratio was found for both juveniles and adults (Bureau of Justice Statistics, 2013b).

Similarly, status offenses such as "running away from home" are gender neutral in the written law, although they are applied quite differently for male and female juveniles who come into contact with the juvenile justice system (Chesney-Lind & Shelden, 1998). More contemporary research has reaffirmed that "protectionist policies" have continued to reflect a paternalistic approach to female status offenders (Bishop & Frazier, 1992). Between 1980 and 2009, juvenile females were arrested for running away from home 40% more than juvenile males (Bureau of Justice Statistics, 2013c). Simpson (1989) refers to such distinctions as "gendered justice"—which certainly can be found beyond standard legislative creation. Next, we will examine how gendered justice typically operates through policing and law enforcement responses to victimization.

Policing and the Influence of Gender and Race

The police are the catalyst agency for the entire criminal justice system. According to studies using survey research data, police officers report that they make decisions to arrest suspects based on both (1) the nature and seriousness of an offense and (2) how an offender behaves when confronted by an officer (Moyer, 1981). A comprehensive examination of the policing literature shows that how police officers actually behave, as well as who they arrest, is shaped by neighborhood context, gender, and race. These factors affect police decisions even after controlling for offense seriousness and prior suspect arrest history.

Thus, classic policing research indicates that officers typically behave differently across neighborhood contexts. Werthman and Piliavin (1967) demonstrated that neighborhood environments shape officers' perceptions regarding appropriate levels and types of responses to illicit activity. Studies have since shown that police are more likely to use aggressive force in highly distressed and high-crime communities (Terrill & Reisig, 2003). Compared to those living in middle-class communities, residents in poor neighborhoods also are more likely to report that police officers' demeanor and use of language are more curt and abrasive (Weitzer, 1999). An additional problem is underpolicing, a problem that occurs when officers fail to respond quickly to calls for police assistance, investigate crimes, and be responsive to crime victims. Klinger (1997) argues that the police are less responsive in poor urban neighborhoods because they believe that certain crimes are normal in these communities and they view victims in such contexts as less deserving of police attention. Extensive evidence shows that police officer discretion, actions, and behaviors vary across contexts.

Since the 1970s, the police-led "war on drugs" has channeled disproportionate attention of law enforcement to specific groups. The Los Angeles Police Department introduced military tactics in the war on drugs (Bass, 2001). Comparative studies show much of the national focus has been to address problems with youth, gang, and gun offending (i.e., violent crimes disproportionately involving young, male offenders). However, females (and in particular females of color) have also been subjected to consistent discretionary police concentration.

Weitzer and Tuch (2002) found that 73% of the Black men in their sample reported having experiences with racial profiling compared to 38% of Black women. Friedman, Lurigio, Greenleaf, and Albertson (2004) reported that 73% of young men and 45% of young women had been stopped by the police and that African American youths were more likely than other racial groups to report physical abuse during police contacts. Likewise, Brunson and Miller (2006) discovered that 83% of the young Black men in their sample reported prior experiences of being previously harassed or mistreated by police compared with 43% of Black female respondents. However, Brunson and Miller illustrate that reported police harassment by young Black females often differs from that reported by young Black males. Specifically, young Black females indicate officers tend to ask similar questions across both males and females (e.g., why are you walking on the street at night, where are your parents, what have you been doing?), but typically elucidate to females they are only asking specific questions to provide protection. However, should females challenge this proactive and chivalrous approach, they will be considerably more likely to be treated as suspects.

Specific research on race, age, and demeanor of suspects indicates that Black suspects are more likely to be arrested than are White suspects (Browning, Cullen, Cao, Kopache, & Stevenson, 1994; Lundman, Sykes, & Clark, 1978). This disparity is not specific to Black males. In particular, the war on drugs has also resulted in the arrest and conviction on drug charges of an unprecedented number of Black women and in an 828% increase in their incarceration between 1986 and 1991 (Bush-Baskette, 1998). Despite similar rates of drug use and drug selling across racial lines, Black woman are far more likely than White women to be imprisoned for violating drug laws. The inequities in drug law enforcement were examined in the 2008 Human Rights Watch report, *Targeting Blacks: Drug Law Enforcement and Race in the U.S.* Blacks comprised more than half (53.5%) of prison drug convictions and were more than 10 times more likely than Whites to be in prison for a drug conviction. Black women were 4.8 times more likely than White women to be in prison for a drug offense (Human Rights Watch, 2008).

In an attempt to unravel the situational determinants that explain arrest patterns, Smith and Visher (1981) found that police are more likely to arrest suspects when victims are present and when a criminal offense is more severe. Additionally, their research indicates that police appear to be more likely to apply formal sanctions against persons of disadvantage (i.e., people living in disadvantaged neighborhoods and, in particular, Black suspects residing in distressed communities). In essence, police work involves controlling the population, and aggressive suspects who directly challenge police authority are more likely to be arrested (Klinger, 1994; Van Maanen, 1974). This challenge to police authority may be a real challenge or it could be based on an interpretation by law enforcement officials. Finally, Robinson and Chandek (2000) found that domestic violence incidents with Black female victims were less likely to result in arrest than were incidents involving White female victims. Thus, chivalrous explanations of decision making likely guide police behaviors differently depending on the race of the suspect or victim.

Visher (1983) shows that police seemingly use different standards in their arrest decisions for female and male suspects. When dealing with males, police typically respond to a variety of situational interactions (e.g., demeanor and respect toward authority beyond legal factors such as offense seriousness). However, suspect demeanor is not the only extralegal determinant of police decision making. When dealing with females, arrest decisions appear to be made on the basis of individual factors, rather than situational cues. According to Visher's research, chivalrous treatment at the stage of arrest depends upon a larger set of gender expectations where female suspects who violate typical middle-class standards of traditional female characteristics and behaviors (e.g., White, older, and submissive) are not afforded chivalrous treatment during arrest decisions and, young, Black, or hostile women receive little preferential treatment regardless of demeanor. With respect to violent offenses, police officers appear to hold behavioral expectations of Black females that contradict traditional stereotypes of females in chivalrous relationships. Comparatively, older White women who are calm and deferential toward the police are more likely to be granted leniency.

In summary, police behavior and officer decision making are influenced by broader societal (e.g., the war on drugs and violence), organizational, and individual influences. At an aggregate level, many police agencies prioritize violent and drug-related offenses—particularly in highly distressed and marginalized communities.

Certainly, patterns of criminal offending explain a large proportion in the variation around rates of arrest. However, individual and event characteristics, such as suspect demeanor and conformity to stereotypical attributes, also have been shown to significantly impact police officer decision making in terms of arrests.

Courtroom Processing

Two primary circumstances exist in which courtroom processing has been the focus of numerous studies: pretrial decisions (e.g., release prior to and during the trial) and sentencing on conviction. Across these different trial phases, conflict theorists contend that the relative power of an individual (or group of individuals) is an important determinant when examining court decision outcomes (Black, 1976). Certainly, the specific influences of gender and race on official processing in courtrooms is not always clear because there are so many factors to take into consideration. A more complete explanation appears to support the conclusion that courtroom personnel (particularly prosecutors and judges) focus heavily on preconceived gender-role identification in decision making.

Attribution theories can serve to explain these patterns. These theories begin with the assumption that courtroom actors are under pressure to dispose of cases efficiently and effectively, but find this task difficult because they have limited time and resources and lack enough information about the cases they are processing (Albonetti, 1991). Consequently, to decrease their uncertainty about cases, they attempt to classify cases based on decision-making schemas drawn from prior experiences and social and courtroom customs. In doing so, they adopt stereotypes based on courtroom and social mores that dictate what a "normal" case or offender should look like (see Sudnow, 1965). What is considered normal is often based on racial, gender, and class stereotypes of criminality. These stereotypes may lead to lenient or harsher punishment. But the key point is that the sanctions reflect not only what offenders do but also the interpretive lenses that judges and other court personnel use to decide the defendants' fate.

Extending this line of inquiry, Steffensmeier and his colleagues have developed "focal concerns theory" (see, e.g., Steffensmeier & Demuth, 2000; Steffensmeier, Ulmer, & Kramer, 1998). This perspective posits that court actors consider three key issues when making decisions: (1) blameworthiness and culpability; (2) dangerousness and community protection; and (3) individual or organizational practical constraints. Blameworthiness and culpability take into account both the victim's and the offender's role in the crime. For example, an offender is considered less blameworthy if the victim precipitated the incident by physically attacking the offender. The criminal history of the victim is also an important variable in the assignment of blameworthiness on offenders. That is, the more dangerous the victim appears, the less culpable and blameworthy the offender. On the other hand, attribution of dangerousness and community protection takes into account the amount of risk the offender poses to society. This assessment often incorporates the offender's criminal history and other characteristics that may be considered "risky," such as the serious-ness and heinousness of the offense. Finally, individual or organizational constraints refer to extralegal factors, such as courtroom work group relationships, number of pending court dockets, court resources, and local prison capacity. As will be seen in the following, these types of factors have been found to shape how gender and other factors affect court decisions.

Historically, women have not been prosecuted and convicted for more serious violent crimes such as robbery, burglary, assault, and auto theft that are typically committed by males. Women have been more likely to engage in and be prosecuted and convicted for property crimes and misdemeanors, although still at a low ratio when compared to male offenders. Between 2000 and 2009, for every one female convicted in federal court, roughly eight males were convicted (Bureau of Justice Statistics, 2013c). Again, however, the key question is whether these differences in court processing reflect only differences in behavior (e.g., men commit more crimes than women) or whether processing is also shaped by other factors that reflect the race, class, and age status of offenders (not just what offenders do, but who they are). In this regard, several representative research agendas merit attention.

Nagel and Hagan (1983) theorized that women are less likely to be detained prior to trial (i.e., protected when only accused of a criminal transgression), prose-cuted fully to conviction, and unfavorably treated in plea negotiations and sentenc-ing (i.e., punished more severely if convicted for violating gender expectations). Based on a systematic review of the literature, they found that women were more likely to fare better in pretrial decisions with respect to males, in that they were more likely to be released on recognizance (with little evidence of distinctions in bail amounts). In a pretrial release study conducted in London, Eaton (1987) found that men and women in traditional families (i.e., women who were married and men who were married and had dependents) were more likely to be released prior to and during the trial phase. Thus, familial roles likely influence pretrial decisions made by judges.

Earlier research focusing on judicial discretion found that the defendant's race was associated with harsher sentences. However, research has not always been clear on this point. Spohn, Gruhl, and Welch (1982) found that Black defendants received more severe sentences than White defendants largely because of serious offense his-tory differences. That is to say, once prior offense severity was accounted for in their analysis, sentence lengths handed out by the courts were no longer different between Blacks and Whites. Research that focuses on gender differences in sentencing also indicates inconsistent findings. Atkinson and Newman (1970), as well as Hagan, Hewitt, and Alwin (1979), found that female defendants receive more lenient sen-tences; comparatively, Hagan, Nagel, and Albonetti (1980) and Unnever, Frazier, and Henretta (1980) found no significant effect of gender on sentencing once offense severity and prior criminal history control variables were incorporated into the anal-yses. However, Datesman and Scarpitti (1980) found that Black females relative to White females were given more severe dispositions than Black males relative to White males. Miethe and Moore (1986) found that race, gender, and age are likely to interact with other variables in terms of influencing sentence severity. In short, the literature provides vastly inconsistent conclusions regarding sentencing factors associated with gender and race, likely because of a race and gender intersection rather than a simple bivariate association.

Steffensmeier et al. (1998) were among the first to examine the intersection among race, gender, and age on sentencing, taking into account important legal factors. They found the following: Seriousness of offense committed and defendant's prior criminal record had the largest influences on sentences received. However, race, gender, and age retained their significant relationship with sentence length even after important controls were accounted for in the analyses. Specifically, they found that males (relative to females) and younger offenders (relative to older offenders) were sentenced more harshly, even when taking other control variables into account. Among males, younger Black defendants were sentenced to harsher sentences than were younger Whites, but this race effect diminished among older White and Black male offenders. Comparatively, among females, race effects were persistent across all ages; younger as well as older Black females were sentenced to harsher sentences than were White females of all ages.

Recent scholarship highlights the importance of examining unique and consistent departures from sentencing guidelines (rules used to guide sentences for specific offenses, taking into account criminal history) as a potential locus of unwarranted sentencing disparity. Mustard's (2001) study on sentencing departures found, after including perhaps more exhaustive controls than any previous study, that large differences in the length of sentence exist on the basis of race, gender, education, income, and citizenship (p. 311). These disparities continue to emerge despite explicit statements in the sentencing guidelines that these characteristics should not affect the sentence length. He specifically found that Blacks and males receive longer sentences and are less likely to receive "no prison" when that option is available. Further, compared to Whites and females, Blacks and males are more likely to receive more punitive departures and less likely to receive less punitive departures than are Whites and females.

But what makes these patterns in the sentencing data emerge? Daly (1989) found that women who were parents or wives (i.e., "family-based" variation) had a significant impact at both pretrial release and the sentencing of Black, White, and Hispanic men and women. Daly (1989) contends that family-based justice appears in the criminal court because gender divisions of labor and family–state relationships constrain the court from treating defendants "equally." Also, interviews with judges conducted in Steffensmeier et al.'s (1998) focal concerns study show that judges make attributions regarding offender blameworthiness, danger, risk of recidivism, and practical consequences related to the capacity of the criminal justice system. Consistent with this perspective, recent research has uncovered interaction effects among the demographics and prior criminal histories of victims and offenders. For example, Auerhahn's (2007b) study of homicide offenders found a significant three-way interaction among being Black or Hispanic, being under the age of 25, and prior criminal history—which she called the "Black/Hispanic criminal stereotype" (Auerhahn, 2007b, p. 293). The interaction suggested that Black/Hispanic males under the age of 25 who had a prior criminal history at the time of the homicide received, at minimum, a sentence length that was significantly longer than that received by offenders who did not exhibit this combination of characteristics. Similarly, Franklin and Fearn (2008) recently reported that young male assailants with criminal histories received longer sentences than females, older assailants, and those who had not been convicted of a felony prior to the homicide. Their findings also suggest that the murderers of victims who are traditionally not considered worthy, either because they had a prior criminal involvement or because they provoked the incident, elicited less severe sanctioning.

In summary, for several decades, scholars interpreted the consistently lower sentences of females (relative to males) as evidence of a chivalry (protection) effect of the courts and indicated that judges were more likely to view women offenders as "passive, sensitive, dependent, weak, conformist, gentle, and domesticated" (see Lotz & Hewitt, 1977, p. 45). This viewpoint is overly simplistic when reviewing the specific literatures that examine the intersection of gender and race on courtroom processing. Based on lengthy interviews conducted with judges, Daly (1989) illustrated that above all else, courtroom actors attempt to protect families and children. Courtroom officials worry about "breaking up families" and "punishing innocent family members" (e.g., causing unnecessary strain and affecting the psychological development of children). Caregiving labor is perhaps more important to courts than economic support. Indeed, it appears that sentencing in courts corresponds with family-based attributes. In this circumstance, the courts operate as a microcosm of broader society by reinforcing gender-based notions of responsibility with regard to child-rearing practices, although this effect is more pronounced for White women than for women of color (who, it appears, are not afforded similar considerations, at least compared to White women).

Incarceration, Probation, and Parole

Correctional systems operate independently from police and courtroom systems; however, the decisions made at those phases of the criminal justice system directly impact the various correctional agencies. Just as pollutants introduced in a river upstream have a cumulative effect on water quality downstream, biased decision making by police and courts, related to factors such as gender and race, adversely impacts the decisions that are available to administrators in correctional processing. As the prison historian Nicole Rafter (1990) stated, "partiality toward Whites contributed to development of a bifurcated system, one track custodial and predominantly Black, the other reformatory and reserved mainly for Whites" (p. 155).

Although imprisoned less than either Black or White men, Black women have historically been imprisoned in far greater numbers than White women. According to the Bureau of Justice Statistics (2013c), the number of African American women under correctional supervision—incarcerated, on probation, or on parole—exceeded the number of White women (260 per 100,000 population for Black females compared with 90 per 100,000 population for White females). Comparatively, the Black:White imprisonment ratio for women is 9:1.

Belknap (2001) notes there are structural and historical reasons why women have been neglected in the correctional system, which have created tremendous gaps in risk, quality of treatment, and offender reentry processes (p. 156). First, women comprise a small proportion of the total jail and inmate population compared to men. Second, women are not incarcerated for violent and more serious offenses (with higher social costs) relative to men. Their relative lack of incarceration has come at a high cost.

Traditionally, convicted women have been more likely to be sent to reformatories (rather than prisons), all in hopes of reforming their perceived waywardness and teaching them to embrace "proper" gender roles (Feinman, 1983). Also to reinforce traditional gendered roles, women are far more likely to be cited for minor rule infractions than male inmates (McClellan, 1994). Examples include citations for possessing "contraband" such as an extra pillowcase, failing to eat all of the food during a meal, or talking out of line—all actions that rarely receive formal sanctions in male institutions. Searches (in particular vaginal searches) for contraband are typically performed by correctional officers instead of by medical staff, which have been shown to correspond to tearing, bleeding, and infections (Mann, 1984). Belknap (2001) illustrates another source of gender inequality. Although reformatory-style housing appears to be less intimidating on the exterior when compared to prisons that house male inmates (e.g., less likely to have rows of barbed wire fencing or armed guarded towers), the interior conditions for female reformatories are considered far worse—including lack of access to mental and physical care and more deplorable living conditions.

Between 1990 and 2000, the rate of women imprisoned in the United States increased at nearly double the rate of the increase of imprisoned men (Covington & Bloom, 2003). This growth in female imprisonment was triggered in large part by the war on drugs, which had a disquieting effect on the incarceration of females generally and on Black females in particular. Daly (1994) notes such growth was linked to drug cases where "gender-blind" mandatory sentencing was often invoked (i.e., where judges are required to impose specific sentences regardless of the circumstances of an event). By concentrating on drugs and potentially suppressing judicial discretion, a disproportionate trend in prison growth impacted Black women more so than White women. More specifically, Bush-Baskette (1998) illustrates that Black females were incarcerated for drug offenses at an increased rate three times that of White females between the 1980s and 1990s. In terms of race alone, an even more disproportional pattern of incarceration exists for Black males compared to White male inmates (Tonry, 1995). Notably, during this same period, Tonry reports that drug usage rates were higher for Whites relative to Blacks for marijuana, cocaine, and hallucinogens. Thus, criminal justice processing, and in particular the incarceration of offenders, seemingly focused more on Black males relative to White males and Black females relative to White females.

One challenge with offender processing is that corrections officials should screen, classify, and assess offenders' risks relative to their needs (i.e., deficits that lead to crime) and provide treatment and programming accordingly (Gendreau, 1996). Gender differences in the risk and need levels of men and women are often ignored because few states have incorporated objective classification instruments to address female offenders' needs (Van Voorhis & Presser, 2001). In this case, gender-neutral classification is oriented toward male offenders' needs and risks because of their disproportionate representation in prisons. Covington and Bloom (2003) illustrate how correctional programming for female offenders has been based on profiles of male pathways to criminality. Programs, policies, and services that focus on the overwhelming number of men in the criminal justice system often fail to identify options that are gender responsive and culturally responsive in terms of women's needs.

One of the ironies from a gendered-justice viewpoint is that roughly two of three incarcerated women are primary caregivers of children living with them, compared with less than 50% of males who reported having children live under their care prior to incarceration. However, most institutions that house females are located in remote rural areas that are inaccessible to families, adding further strain on the mother–children relationships that is an inevitable consequence of female incarceration. Ironically, Belknap (2001) states that "prisons have unabashedly programmed female offenders into their 'proper' gender roles as wives and mothers but simultaneously make few or no provisions for them to maintain contact with their youngest children" (p. 179). Finally, women have had less access to education and vocational opportunities. Belknap notes that more educational programs are needed to help women deal with histories of prior physical and sexual abuse. Thus, gender reinforcement (with few provisions for child rearing and support) combined with limited vocational, educational, and training services has been consistently reinforced in prison contexts.

Similar to men, most women who are released from jail or prison are likely to return to the same disadvantaged neighborhoods and problematic conditions without having received the appropriate services to address their underlying problems (Morash, Bynum, & Koons, 1998). Richie (2001) posits that women released from incarceration need comprehensive programs, treatment, empowerment programs, ex-offender peer group support, mother–child programs, and intermediate sanctions (rather than simple parole violations equating to loss of parole status) to most effectively reduce their risk of recidivism.

For women released into community supervision, Cobbina (2010) found that women probationers and parolees perceived family and social support as the most critical factor in successful community reentry. Parole officers have also been found to be a critical dimension for women offenders when their relationship is characterized by trust and respect, which makes it possible for women to work to solve their reentry problems with their supervising officers (Skeem, Louden, Polaschek, & Camp, 2007). Also, women immersed in a high-quality relationship with an intimate partner had a lower risk of recidivism; by contrast, partner relations had a less overall impact on male parolees (Cobbina, Huebner, & Berg, 2012). It appears that intimate partners were a protective factor against recidivism for women (and less so for men), whereas peer deviant association was a risk factor for male recidivists (and less so for females). The findings also suggest that females often have strong familial attachments and are typically reluctant to bring shame on their families (Mullins & Wright, 2003); therefore, they are seemingly more responsive to informal, familial social controls (Giordano, Cernkovich, & Rudolph, 2002).

Conclusion

Freda Adler (1975) theorized that the liberation movement would lead to changes in female-oriented criminal behavior and that as women's opportunities in the workplace increased, so too would women's engagement in illegal activity. Although this change in *overall offending* patterns did not happen as theorized, patterns of *arrest*, *conviction*, and *incarceration* have considerably narrowed (particularly in the past 20 years) between men and women. However, the social processes that best explain these empirical patterns are hardly based on notions of liberation. Thus, an understanding of system processing must account for differences in offending patterns as well as patterns of treatment across gender (and race).

As indicated in this chapter, research suggests that differences exist in police processing, court adjudication, and correctional treatment across genders. Specifically, women and men appear to have distinct and unique experiences when going through the criminal justice process. There have been multiple explanations for these differences in processing, including paternalism and chivalry hypotheses, distinct offending patterns among the genders and racial groups, and the modus of the crimes they commit. This is perhaps best exemplified with one of the most serious and well-documented violent crimes—that is, homicide.

Homicide victimization and offending is not randomly distributed among the population, but some groups are more likely to be involved in these incidents than others. Males, young adults, African Americans, and those that live criminal lifestyles are disproportionately represented among victims and offending populations compared with those who do not exhibit these characteristics (Pizarro, Zgoba, & Jennings, 2011). Relative to males, females are less likely to be represented in acts of lethal violence. When females are involved in an act of lethal violence, they are more likely to be victims than offenders.

A comparison of the genders also suggests that the modus of incidence (e.g., who the victim is, place of the crime, motives for the act) involving females differs from that involving males (Pizarro, DeJong, & McGarrell, 2010). Research suggests that female violence is often influenced by gender norms (Steffensmeier & Allen, 1996;

Steffensmeier & Haynie, 2000a, 2000b). Their acts of lethal violence often tend to involve their children or their intimate partners, whereas acts committed by males are more likely geared toward acquaintances and strangers. Research has also shown that women who commit acts of violence against their intimate partners are more likely to act in response to fear for their safety and self-defense (Kruttschnitt, Gartner, & Ferraro, 2002; Websdale, 1999). Specifically, they are abused by their intimate partners and feel helpless and trapped. As a result, they either resort to homicide to end the abusive relationship or engage in the act in self-defense while being physically abused by their partners. Additionally, on average, women who victimize their offspring are often acting out of helplessness and fear of continued abuse, fear of failing as a mother, or psychiatric episodes such as extreme depression (Harris, Hilton, Rice, & Eke, 2006; Schwartz & Isser, 2007). Indeed, Oberman and Meyer (2008) found that women who murdered their children were victims of abuse or neglect themselves, whether in their childhood or by their significant others. Other explanations involve psychiatric episodes such as postpartum depression and Munchausen syndrome by proxy (Wilczynski, 1997; Schwartz & Isser, 2007; Firstman & Talan, 1997). In contrast, incidents involving males are more likely to occur in public streets and be motivated by disputes, gangs, drugs, and robberies. Conversely, when women kill they are likely to be acting alone and to be responding to a victim-initiated attack (Jensen, 2001). These incident characteristics can explain recent research findings that suggest that females receive lesser charges and sanctions when they are arrested and adjudicated in homicide incidents (Auerhahn, 2007b).

What is true in homicide appears to hold true across multiple offense categories, requiring a broader explanation of behavior. Miller and Mullins (2006) argue that theoretical criminology has traditionally operated on two distinct (yet somewhat parallel) perspectives. First, many criminological theories have ignored women completely by focusing either implicitly or exclusively on male patterns of participation in crime. Second, other theories have been developed around gender-specific beliefs that there are fundamental differences between men and women (e.g., men are instrumental, women are relational; men are aggressive, women are passive). Not surprisingly, these overly restrictive and reductionist explanations of human understanding have led to theoretical inaccuracies; however, a broader concern from a practical standpoint is that influential actors in various phases in the criminal justice system also make decisions in gender-restrictive ways. Miller and Mullins ultimately contend that theoretical criminology should take a middle-range approach by understanding gender is complex, which influences behavior (such as offender processing) in context-specific ways.

Across police, courts, and corrections, it is our position that there is a critical distinction between "gendered justice" and "justice which accounts for gender" under relevant circumstances. Gendered justice here refers to biased and prejudicial actions made by criminal justice officials based upon preconceived notions regarding how women should behave and act in ways that reinforce traditional gender stereotypes. However, justice, which accounts for gender specifically, accounts for individuals' needs, such as parental considerations (both men and women, although more likely to be women) and training and vocational services. Based on our review of the empirical literature, we believe there are recurring themes observed in traditional criminal justice processing (and these same patterns also include components that focus on race): First, when criminal justice processing is explicitly *gender specific*, it tends to operate in a patriarchal fashion that reinforces stereotypes and creates distinct disadvantages for females who are immersed in the justice system. When patriarchy occurs, the motivation is typically focused on male dominion and gender expectation reinforcement under the guise of protection—that is, to protect society from males and to protect females from society. The best illustration of a patriarchal approach to female offenders often occurs in sex-based incidents.

Belknap (2001) documents the historical developments of statutory rape laws, where the age of eligible consent rose from as young as age 7 in the early 1900s to 16 to 18 years old by the 1920s for females; no such law was developed for males, however. Additionally, police seem to place higher emphasis on sexual activity of females (prostitution arrests) than arresting consensual male partners also engaged in illicit illegal sexual activity, as evidenced in the patterns of prostitution arrests. DeFleur (1975), Smith and Visher (1981), and Visher (1983) also illustrate that police officers are less likely to arrest women who act in sex-role stereotypical ways (i.e., deferential, feminine, in search of protection). Minority women are least likely to receive chivalrous police processing compared to White women, thus indicating sex-by-race distinctions in patterns of processing as well. Indeed, the literature indicates that *gender specific* typically means *selective* enforcement, prosecution, and correctional processing.

Second, *gender-neutral* approaches to processing typically operate on standards derived from male offending patterns, which more often than not create a disproportionate strain on female offenders (and in particular females of color). Illustrations of gender-neutral policies and practices include the war on drugs that has led to exponential increases in arrests, prosecutions, and incarceration rates from the 1980s onward, as well as mandatory sentencing laws and simplistic government policies that focus extensively on offender punishment. Are females receiving *more equal treatment* in the criminal justice system today than was the case in years past? Our analysis of trends in incarceration suggests that if more equal treatment means more equitable incarceration, the answer is a definitive yes. Many more women offenders are likely to be incarcerated now than at any previous time in U.S. history, and the criminal justice system appears to be more willing to imprison women (Bloom & Chesney-Lind, 2000). Covington and Bloom (2003) perhaps articulate this process most eloquently, noting,

> as a result of prisoners' rights litigation based on the parity model, women offenders are being swept up in a system that appears to be eager to treat women equally, which actually means *as if they were men*. Since this orientation does not change the role of gender in prison life or corrections, female prisoners receive the worst of both worlds. (p. 4, emphasis in original)

Thus, completely ignoring gender in criminal justice processing certainly does not lead to heightened levels of liberation but rather to disproportionate strain on females caught up in the male-dominated system.

Finally, we contend that there are pragmatic circumstances when *gender could and should* be taken into account in a *systematic* and *documented manner* within criminal justice processing. Andrews and Bonta (2010) developed the risk, need, and responsivity principles to understand the effectiveness of correctional-based programs to better reduce offender recidivism through treatment. These types of actuarial assessment tools are used to classify prisoners in terms of criminogenic needs and guide treatment accordingly. As we have seen, correctional programming for female offenders has been based on profiles of male criminality. Correctional administrators and program providers should specifically develop gender-responsive curricula and training programs that incorporate this knowledge (Covington & Bloom, 2003). The strongest actuarial risk tools are those that take into account individual criminogenic risks; and policies that are most practical make responses available at a rate that calibrates with offenders' needs.

In terms of approaches to criminal justice processing that take gender into account, a 1995 study of female prisoners in California showed that 80% of the respondents were mothers, the majority of whom were single mothers who averaged two children and for whom they were the primary caregiver prior to their arrest (Owen & Bloom, 1995). Likewise, an additional study of female inmates found that 80% of women prisoners had experienced some form of abuse, either as children or as adults (Bloom, Chesney-Lind, & Owen, 1994). Individual risk identification and responses are at the center of effective correctional program and treatment strategies (Andrews & Bonta, 2010). Although there is evidence that courtroom officials attempt to account for family circumstances in offender processing, these patterns tend to occur haphazardly and inconsistently (particularly when race of the offender is added to the equation). A more comprehensive approach is necessary for gender and race equity, fairness, and utility.

The various agencies that comprise the criminal justice system (i.e., legislators, juvenile justice, police, courts, and correctional agencies) as well as the practitioners who work within it do not function in a social vacuum; indeed, the system of criminal justice often reflects the structure, ideas, and concerns of the society within which it operates. Men and women engage in different crimes and are processed differently. However, our research shows variation in processing resulting from differences in *illegal patterns of behavior* is not the full story in terms of *processing distinctions*.

References

Addington, L. A. (2006). Using National Incident-Based Reporting System murder data to evaluate clearance predictors: A research note. *Homicide Studies, 10,* 140–152.

Adler, F. (1975). *Sisters in crime: The rise of the new female criminal.* New York, NY: McGraw–Hill.

Albonetti, C. (1991). An integration of theories to explain judicial discretion. *Social Problems, 38*, 247–267.

Andrews, D. A., & Bonta, J. (2010). *The psychology of criminal conduct* (5th ed.). New Providence, NJ: Anderson.

Atkinson, D. N., & Neuman, D. A. (1970). Judicial attitudes and defendant attributes: Some consequences for municipal court decision-making. *Journal of Public Law, 19*, 68–87.

Auerhahn, K. (2007a). Adjudication outcomes in intimate and non-intimate homicides. *Homicide Studies, 11*, 213–230.

Auerhahn, K. (2007b). Just another crime? Examining disparity in homicide sentencing. *Sociological Quarterly, 48*, 277–313.

Bass, S. (2001). Policing space, police race: Social control imperatives and police discretionary decisions. *Social Justice, 28*, 156–176.

Baumer, E. P., Messner, S. P., & Felson, R. B. (2000). The role of victim characteristics in the disposition of murder cases. *Justice Quarterly, 17*, 281–307.

Belknap, J. (2001). *The invisible woman: Gender, crime, and justice* (2nd ed.). Belmont, CA: Wadsworth.

Berger, P. L., & Luckman, T. (1966). *The social construction of reality: A treatise in the sociology of knowledge.* Garden City, NY: Anchor.

Bishop, D. M., & Frazier, C. E. (1992). Gender bias in juvenile justice processing: Implications of the JJDP Act. *Journal of Criminal Law and Criminology, 82*, 1162–1186.

Black, D. (1976). *The behavior of law.* New York, NY: Academic Press.

Bloom, B. E., & Chesney-Lind, M. (2000). Women in prison: Vengeful equity. In Roslyn Muraskin (Ed.), *It's a crime: Women and justice* (pp. 66–73). Upper Saddle River, NJ: Prentice Hall.

Bloom, B. E., Chesney-Lind, M., & Owen, B. (1994). *Women in California prisons: Hidden victims of the war on drugs.* San Francisco, CA: Center on Juvenile and Criminal Justice.

Browning, S. L., Cullen, F. T., Cao, L., Kopache, R., & Stevenson, T. J. (1994). Race and getting hassled by the police: A research note. *Police Studies, 17*, 1–12.

Brunson, R. K., & Miller, J. (2006). Gender, race, and urban policing: The experience of African American youths. *Gender and Society, 20*, 531–552.

Bureau of Justice Statistics. (2013a). *Measuring the prevalence of crime with the National Crime Victimization Survey.* Retrieved from http://www.bjs.gov/index.cfm?ty=pbdetail&iid=4759/

Bureau of Justice Statistics. (2013b). *Arrest data analysis tool.* Retrieved from http://www.bjs.gov/index.cfm?ty=datool&surl=/arrests/index.cfm/

Bureau of Justice Statistics. (2013c). *New releases.* Retrieved from http://www.bjs.gov/index.cfm?ty=dctp/

Bush-Baskette, S. R. (1998). The war on drugs as a war against Black women. In S. L. Miller (Ed.), *Crime control and women* (pp. 185–194). Thousand Oaks, CA: Sage.

Chesney-Lind, M., & Shelden, R. G. (1998). *Girls, delinquency, and juvenile justice.* Belmont, CA: Wadsworth/Thomson Learning.

Cobbina, J. E. (2010). Reintegration success and failure: Factors impacting reintegration among incarcerated and formerly incarcerated women. *Journal of Offender Rehabilitation, 49*, 210–232.

Cobbina, J. E., Huebner, B. M., & Berg, M. T. (2012). Men, women, and postrelease offending: An examination of the nature of the link between relational ties and recidivism. *Crime and Delinquency, 58,* 331–361.

Covington, S. S., & Bloom, B. E. (2003). Gendered justice: Women in the criminal justice system. In Barbara E. Bloom (Ed.), *Gendered justice: Addressing female offenders* (pp. 3–24). Durham, NC: Carolina Academic Press.

Daly, K. (1989). Neither conflict nor labeling nor paternalism will suffice: Intersections of race, ethnicity, gender, and family in criminal court decisions. *Crime and Delinquency, 35,* 136–168.

Daly, K. (1994). *Gender, crime, and punishment.* New Haven, CT: Yale University Press.

Daly, K., & Chesney-Lind, M. (1988). Feminism and criminology. *Justice Quarterly, 5,* 497–538.

Datesman, S. K., & Scarpitti, F. R. (1980). *Women, crime, and justice.* New York, NY: Oxford University Press.

Dawson, M. (2004). Rethinking the boundaries of intimacy at the end of the century: The role of victim–defendant relationship in criminal justice decision making over time. *Law and Society Review, 38,* 105–138.

DeFleur, L. B. (1975). Biasing influences on drug arrest records: Implications for deviance research. *American Sociological Review, 40,* 88–103.

Eaton, M. B. (1987). The question of bail: Magistrates' responses to applications for bail on behalf of men and women defendants. In P. Carlen & A. Worral (Eds.), *Gender, crime and justice* (pp. 95–107). Philadelphia, PA: Open University Press.

Farnworth, M., & Teske, R. H. C. (1995). Gender differences in felony court processing: Three hypotheses of disparity. *Women and Criminal Justice, 6,* 23–44.

Farrell, R. A., & Swigert, V. L. (1978). Legal disposition of inter-group and intra-group homicides. *Sociological Quarterly, 19,* 565–576.

Farrell, R. A., & Swigert, V. L. (1986). Adjudication in homicide: An interpretive analysis of the effects of defendant and victim social characteristics. *Journal of Research in Crime and Delinquency, 23,* 349–369.

Feinman, C. (1983). Historical overview of the treatment of incarcerated women: Myths and realities of rehabilitation. *The Prison Journal, 63,* 12–26.

Firstman, R., & Talan, J. (1997). *The death of innocents: A true story of murder, medicine, and high-stake science.* New York, NY: Bantam Books.

Franklin, C. A., & Fearn, N. E. (2008). Gender, race, and formal court decision-making outcomes: Chivalry/paternalism, conflict theory, or gender conflict? *Journal of Criminal Justice, 36,* 279–290.

Friedman, W., Lurigio, A. J., Greenleaf, R., & Albertson, S. (2004). Encounters between police officers and youths: The social costs of disrespect. *Journal of Crime and Justice, 27,* 1–25.

Garfinkel, H. (1949). Research note on inter- and intra-racial homicides. *Social Forces, 27,* 369–381.

Gendreau, P. (1996). Offender rehabilitation: What we know and what needs to be done. *Criminal Justice and Behavior, 23,* 144–161.

Giordano, P. C., Cernkovich, S. A., & Rudolph, J. L. (2002). Gender, crime, and desistance: Toward a theory of cognitive transformation. *American Journal of Sociology, 107,* 990–1064.

Grabe, M. E., Trager, K. D., Lear, M., & Rauch, J. (2006). Gender in crime news: A case study test of the chivalry hypothesis. *Mass Communication and Society, 9,* 137–163.

Hagan, J., Hewitt, J. D., & Alwin, D. F. (1979). Ceremonial justice: Crime and punishment in a loosely coupled system. *Social Forces, 58,* 506–527.

Hagan, J., Nagel, I. H., & Albonetti, C. (1980). The differential sentencing of white-collar offenders in ten federal district courts. *American Sociological Review, 45,* 802–820.

Harris, G. T., Hilton, N. Z., Rice, M. E., & Eke, A. W. (2006). Children killed by genetic parents versus stepparents. *Evolution and Human Behavior, 28,* 85–95.

Hewitt, J. D., & Mickish, J. (1983). Prostitution during the Progressive era: The Middletown experience. *Wisconsin Sociologist, 24,* 99–111.

Human Rights Watch. (2008). *Targeting blacks: Drug law enforcement and race in the U.S.* Washington, DC: Humans Right Watch.

Jensen, V. (2001). *Why women kill: Homicide and gender equality.* Boulder, CO: Rienner.

Jiao, A. Y. (2007). Explaining homicide clearance: An analysis of Chicago homicide data 1965–1995. *Criminal Justice Studies, 20,* 3–14.

Johnson, B. D., Wingerden, S. V., & Nieuwbeerta, P. (2010). Sentencing homicide offenders in the Netherlands: Offender, victim, and situational influences in criminal punishment. *Criminology, 48,* 981–1018.

Kingsnorth, R., Lopez, J., Wentworth, J., & Cumming, D. (1998). Adult sexual assault: The role of racial/ethnic composition in prosecution and sentencing. *Journal of Criminal Justice, 26,* 359–371.

Klinger, D. A. (1994). Demeanor or crime? Why "hostile" citizens are more likely to be arrested. *Criminology, 32,* 475–493.

Klinger, D. A. (1997). Negotiating order in patrol work: An ecological theory of police response to deviance. *Criminology, 35,* 277–306.

Kruttschnitt, C., Gartner, R., & Ferraro, K. (2002). Women's involvement in serious interpersonal violence. *Aggression and Violent Behavior, 7,* 529–565.

Lee, C. (2005). The value of life and death: Multiple regression and event history analyses of homicide clearance in Los Angeles County. *Journal of Criminal Justice, 33,* 527–534.

Litwin, K. J., & Xu, Y. (2007). The dynamic nature of homicide clearances: A multilevel model comparison across three time periods. *Homicide Studies, 11,* 94–114.

Lotz, R., & Hewitt, J. D. (1977). The influence of legally irrelevant factors on felony sentencing. *Sociological Inquiry, 47,* 39–48.

Lundman, R. J., Sykes, R. E., & Clark, J. P. (1978). Police control of juveniles: A replication. *Journal of Research in Crime and Delinquency, 15,* 74–91.

Mann, C. R. (1984). Race and sentencing of female felons: A field study. *International Journal of Women's Studies, 7,* 160–172.

McClellan, D. S. (1994). Disparity in discipline of male and female inmates in Texas prisons. *Women and Criminal Justice, 5,* 71–97.

Miethe, T. D., & Moore, C. A. (1986). Racial differences in criminal processing: The consequences of model selection on conclusions about differential treatment. *Sociological Quarterly, 27,* 217–237.

Miller, J., & Mullins, C. W. (2006). *The status of feminist theories of crime.* In F. T. Cullen, J. P. Wright, & K. R. Blevins (Eds.), *Taking stock: The status of criminological theory—Advances in criminological theory* (Vol. 15. pp. 217–250). New Brunswick, NJ: Transaction.

Morash, M., Bynum, T. S., & Koons, B. A. (1998). *Women offenders: Programming needs and promising approaches.* Washington, DC: National Institute of Justice.

Moulds, E. F. (1980). Chivalry and paternalism: Disparities of treatment in the criminal justice system. In S. K. Datesman & F. R. Scarpitti (Eds.), *Women, crime, and justice* (pp. 277–299). New York, NY: Oxford University Press.

Moyer, I. L. (1981). Demeanor, sex, and race in police processing. *Journal of Criminal Justice, 9,* 235–246.

Mullins, C. W., & Wright, R. (2003). Gender, social networks, and residential burglary. *Criminology, 41,* 813–840.

Mustard, D. B. (2001). Racial, ethnic, and gender disparities in sentencing: Evidence from the U.S. federal courts. *Journal of Law and Economics, 44,* 285–314.

Nagel, I. H., & Hagan, J. (1983). Gender and crime: Offense patterns and criminal court sanctions. *Crime and Justice: A Review of Research, 4,* 91–144.

Oberman, M., & Meyer, C. L. (2008). *When mothers kill: Interviews from prison.* New York: New York University Press.

Owen, B., & Bloom, B. E. (1995). Profiling women prisoners: Findings from national surveys and a California sample. *The Prison Journal, 75,* 163–185.

Pizarro, J. M., DeJong, C., & McGarrell, E. F. (2010). An examination of the covariates of female homicide victimization and offending. *Feminist Criminology, 5,* 51–72.

Pizarro, J. M., Zgoba, K. M., & Jennings, W. (2011). Assessing the interaction between offender and victim criminal lifestyles and homicide type. *Journal of Criminal Justice, 39,* 367–377.

Puckett, J. L., & Lundman, R. J. (2003). Factors affecting homicide clearances: Multivariate analysis of a more complete conceptual framework. *Journal of Research in Crime and Delinquency, 40,* 171–193.

Rafter, N. H. (1990). *Partial justice: Women, prisons, and social control.* New Brunswick, NJ: Transaction.

Regoeczi, W. C., Jarvis, J., & Riedel, M. (2008). Clearing murders: Is it about time? *Journal of Research in Crime and Delinquency, 45,* 142–162.

Richie, B. E. (2001). Challenges incarcerated women face as they return to their communities: Findings from life history interviews. *Crime and Delinquency, 47,* 368–389.

Robinson, A. L., & Chandek, M. S. (2000). The domestic violence arrest decision: Examining demographic, attitudinal, and situational variables. *Crime and Delinquency, 45,* 18–37.

Schwartz, L. L., & Isser, N. K. (2007). *Child homicide: Parents who kill.* Boca Raton, FL: Taylor & Francis.

Simpson, S. S. (1989). Feminist theory, crime and justice. *Criminology, 27,* 605–631.

Skeem, J. L., Louden, J. E., Polaschek, D., & Camp, J. (2007). Assessing relationship quality in mandated community treatment: Blending care with control. *Psychological Assessment, 19,* 397–410.

Smith, D. A., & Visher, C. A. (1981). Street-level justice: Situational determinants of police arrest decisions. *Social Problems, 29,* 167–177.

Smith, D. A., Visher, C. A., & Davidson, L. A. (1984). Arrest equity and discretionary justice: The influence of race on police arrest decisions. *Journal of Criminal Law and Criminology, 75,* 234–249.

Sorensen, J., & Wallace, D. H. (1999). Prosecutorial discretion in seeking death: An analysis of racial disparity in the pretrial stages of case processing in a Midwestern county. *Justice Quarterly, 16,* 559–578.

Spohn, C. C. (2000). *Thirty years of sentencing reform: The quest for a racially neutral sentencing process.* Washington, DC: National Institute of Justice, U.S. Department of Justice.

Spohn, C. C., Gruhl, J., & Welch, S. (1982). The effect of race on sentencing: A re-examination of an unsettled question. *Law and Society Review, 16,* 72–88.

Steffensmeier, D. (1993). National trends in female arrests, 1960–1990: Assessment and recommendations for research. *Journal of Quantitative Criminology, 9,* 411–441.

Steffensmeier, D., & Allan, E. (1996). Gender and crime: Toward a gendered theory of female offending. *Annual Review of Sociology, 22,* 459–487.

Steffensmeier, D., & Demuth, S. (2000). Ethnicity and sentencing outcomes in U.S. federal courts: Who is punished more harshly? *American Sociological Review, 65,* 705–729.

Steffensmeier, D., & Haynie, D. (2000a). Gender, structural disadvantage, and urban crime: Do macrosocial variables also explain female offending rates? *Criminology, 38,* 403–438.

Steffensmeier, D., & Haynie, D. (2000b). The structural sources of urban female violence in the United States: A macrosocial gender-disaggregated analysis of adult and juvenile homicide offending rates. *Homicide Studies, 4,* 107–134.

Steffensmeier, D., Ulmer, J., & Kramer, J. (1998). The interaction of race, gender, and age in criminal sentencing: The punishment cost of being young, Black, and male. *Criminology, 36,* 763–798.

Sudnow, D. (1965). Normal crimes: Sociological features of the penal code in a public defender's office. *Social Problems, 12,* 255–276.

Swigert, V. L., & Farrell, R. A. (1976). *Murder, inequality, and the law: Differential treatment in the legal process.* Lexington, MA: D. C. Health.

Swigert, V. L., & Farrell, R. A. (1980). Speedy trial and the legal process. *Law and Human Behavior, 4,* 135–145.

Terrill, W., & Reisig, M. D. (2003). Neighborhood context and police use of force. *Journal of Research in Crime and Delinquency, 40,* 291–321.

Tonry, M. (1995). *Malign neglect: Race, crime, and punishment in America.* New York, NY: Oxford University Press.

Trussler, T. (2010). Explaining the changing nature of homicide clearance in Canada. *International Criminal Justice Review, 20,* 366–383.

Unnever, J. D., Frazier, C. E., & Henretta, J. C. (1980). Race differences in criminal sentencing. *Sociological Quarterly, 21,* 197–205.

Van Maanen, J. (1974). Working the street: A developmental view of police behavior. In H. Jacob (Ed.), *The potential for reform in criminal justice* (pp. 93–130). Beverly Hills, CA: Sage.

Van Voorhis, P., & Presser, L. (2001). *Classification of women offenders: A national assessment of current practices.* Washington, DC: National Institute of Corrections.

Visher, C. A. (1983). Gender, police arrest decisions, and notions of chivalry. *Criminology, 28,* 5–28.

Websdale, N. (1999). *Understanding domestic homicide.* Boston, MA: Northeastern University Press.

Weitzer, R. (1999). Citizen perceptions of police misconduct: Race and neighborhood context. *Justice Quarterly, 16,* 819–846.

Weitzer, R., & Tuch, S. A. (2002). Perceptions of racial profiling: Race, class, and personal experience. *Criminology, 40,* 435–456.

Wellford, C., & Cronin, J. (1999). *Analysis of variables affecting the clearance of homicides: A multistate study.* Washington, DC: Justice Research Statistics Association.

Werthman, C., & Piliavin, I. (1967). Gang members and the police. In D. J. Bordua (Ed.), *The police: Six sociological essays* (pp. 56–98). New York, NY: Wiley.

Wilczynski, A. (1997). *Child homicide.* London, UK: Greenwich Medical Media.

Wolfgang, M. E. (1958). *Patterns in criminal homicide.* Philadelphia: University of Pennsylvania Press.

CHAPTER 17

Understanding the Female Prison Experience

Mary K. Stohr, Cheryl Lero Jonson, and Jennifer L. Lux

M any scholars agree that women offenders differ from their male counterparts not only in terms of behavior, but also in areas related to mental health, substance abuse, family, and medical concerns. Additionally, there is widespread agreement that the characteristics and needs associated with institutional adjustment manifest themselves differently for women than for men. Adler (1975) recognized these differences and similarities between the genders in her seminal work *Sisters in Crime*. The purpose of this chapter is to review the history of the incarceration of women and to take stock of what is known about how females experience prison and adapt to life within it. Common risk factors for female offenders (e.g., substance abuse and mental health issues) are discussed in light of the unpredictable and difficult behaviors that derive from such high-risk areas of need. Finally, we conclude with a call for more research to better understand the prison experience for women. We argue that future efforts should focus on assisting women to reduce their risks and meet their needs so that they might become *sisters in success* rather than *sisters in crime*.

It's a Man's World: Even in Prisons

Just as in society, in prison, women have been defined by their "otherness" (Cullen, Jonson, and Stohr, 2014; see also Alder, 1975). Women have often been seen as less powerful and ascribed less status in society, and these characteristics have permeated the prison walls (Adler, 1975). Women in prison, because of their low numbers compared to their male counterparts, have historically been viewed as less worthy of attention. Instead, they became a forgotten population, with their unique needs and issues virtually ignored (Belknap, 2006; Butler, 1997; Holsinger, 2013; Rafter, 1992; Sokoloff, 2005).

Incarcerated women have traditionally been placed in correctional systems designed for men and modeled after patriarchal ideals in that men and their circumstances and needs were valued over women and their circumstances and needs. Prior to 1840, when women first entered the correctional system, they were housed alongside men. Women and men were not always separated, even in work assignments. For instance, in Tennessee in the early part of the 19th century, males and females were sent together to work on railroads and in coal mines (Rafter, 1992). However, as the decades passed, females began to be segregated from their male counterparts. Rafter (1992) describes the four stages of the segregation of females from males in the penal system.

First, females were included as part of the general population of inmates. To achieve some form of segregation, females were placed in individual cells or a group would be placed together in a large room. Because only one room was assigned for women, it was often overcrowded and the inmates were not classified by the seriousness of their offense or behavior (Rafter, 1992). The second phase involved females being segregated into separate sections or areas within the male institution. Thus, a certain floor, attic, or similar space would be devoted to housing female inmates. The third stage saw the construction of a particular building on the grounds of a male correctional complex to house female offenders. Consequently, males and females were on the same grounds, but not housed under the same roof (Rafter, 1992). In both the second and the third stages, female inmates were often supervised less, thus leaving them vulnerable to victimization from one another and correctional officers. Eventually, a fourth phase commenced in 1873 with the construction of the Indiana Reformatory for Women. The Indiana Reformatory was the first adult female correctional facility that was built upon its own grounds and not associated with a male facility.

Although segregating the sexes helped alleviate some issues (e.g., privacy, sexual assault from male inmates), this practice created additional burdens for female offenders to bear. Furthermore, patriarchal ideals still were a dominant force in these female-only institutions. As Rafter (1992) poignantly states, the segregation of females from males in the correctional system resulted in women becoming "much and unfortunately neglected" (p. 10). Because of the low numbers of women inmates, many officials—including chaplains and physicians—did not view it as worth their time to visit the female areas of the institutions. The special needs of women were often neglected because attention did not seem warranted. Thus, although segregation of the sexes was undertaken with good intentions, it had many latent consequences. Women were defined as the "other" or as second-class citizens in the prison world, just as they were in the wider world at this time (Adler, 1975; Holsinger, 2014).

As will be discussed in further detail, women come to prison with a host of unique needs that must be addressed. Women in prison are more likely than their male counterparts to have medical needs, mental health issues, and substance-abuse problems, to have been victims of sexual and/or physical abuse, and to have children living with them at the time of their incarceration (Hagan & Coleman, 2001; Holsinger, 2014; McDaniels-Wilson & Belknap, 2008; Mumola, 2000; Mumola & Karberg, 2006; Proctor, 2009; The Sentencing Project, 2007; Stohr & Walsh, 2012). Many programs that seek to address these various issues, such as drug treatment, mental health care, and educational and vocational programming, are often severely lacking in female institutions (The Sentencing Project, 2007). Thus, unlike their male counterparts, women are more likely to reenter communities with the needs and issues they imported into the institution having never been addressed.

Furthermore, it is important to understand that subjecting males and females to the exact same penal conditions and correctional treatment options may not result in equal treatment for the sexes (Holsinger, 2014). Gender differences, because of existing inequalities and gendered socialization, influence how men and women respond to these experiences (Adler, 1975; Holsinger, 2014, p. 89). Thus, true equality can only be achieved if these gender differences are fully understood and taken into account when securing and treating male and female correctional populations.

Striving for Equality for All . . . Even in Prison Populations

More than 108,000 mothers, daughters, sisters, nieces, and wives are in state and federal prisons on any given day (Carson & Golinelli, 2013). Although this number pales in comparison to the more than 1.4 million fathers, sons, brothers, nephews, and husbands incarcerated, it still represents a large number of women residing behind the walls of a prison. And this number has risen substantially over the past 30 years. In 1980, a mere 15,118 women were housed behind bars. Fast forward to 2010 and that number had risen to 112,797, a 646% increase (Callahan, 1986; Guerino, Harrison, & Sabol, 2010). This increase in the female prison population is a full 1.5 times higher than the increase experienced by men in the past three decades (Guerino et al., 2010), which has resulted in females constituting a larger percentage of the prison population than ever before. Yet from 1925 to roughly 1980, females only comprised approximately 3% to 4% of the total prison population (Minor-Harper, Marbrook, Baldea, & Stanford, 1986). Today, women account for approximately 7% of the prison population (Guerino et al., 2010). With their rising numbers in the penal system, the unique needs and challenges faced by women can no longer be ignored or seen as peripheral to the needs of incarcerated men (Adler, 1975; Belknap, 2003).

The War on Drugs and the Latent War on Women

Why are female faces becoming more prominent in our nation's penal institutions? One answer is the war on drugs, which has dramatically increased the number of people behind bars by birthing many "get-tough" policies (Clear, 1994; Currie, 1998; Lynch, 2007; Zimring, 2001). Although this organized and long-lasting fight against drugs has increased the number of men incarcerated, this battle has had especially detrimental effects on female offenders (Mauer & King, 2007). The impact of harsh mandatory minimum sentencing policies for drug offenses demanding long and severe sentences has also been felt by women, with minority woman taking the brunt of the incarcerative blow (Mauer & Huling, 1995).

Specifically examining the influence of drug offenses on increasing incarceration rates, Blumstein and Beck (1999) discovered that 43% of the increase in women's incarceration has been because of drug offenses, as opposed to 28% of the growth of men's incarceration. One explanation could be the role women play in the drug trade. Because women in the drug trade are often couriers or drug runners, they are highly visible and vulnerable to arrest by law enforcement and subjected to mandatory minimum drug laws (Holsinger, 2014; Sokoloff, 2005). Furthermore, as stated by Holsinger, "women's low status in low-level positions in the drug world means that they do not have access to intelligence that could assist them in prosecutorial bargaining" (p. 91). Thus, women are often on the drug trade's front lines in the war on drugs, and, in turn, suffer disproportionately as the war's causalities.

When examining the prison population, it is apparent that women are overwhelmingly incarcerated for low-level nonviolent and drug offenses compared to their male counterparts. In 2012, one quarter of females in state prisons were incarcerated for drug offenses and 27.8% were behind bars for a property offense, with roughly one third serving time for a violent offense. In contrast, more than 50% of men were incarcerated for a violent offense, with only 17.7% and 16.2% of men serving for a property or drug offense, respectively (Carson & Golinelli, 2013).

As stated previously, although the war on drugs has clearly affected females in general, minority women have especially felt the impact of the war's harsh policies. Between 1986 and 1991, there was a 241% increase in White women's incarceration for drug offenses (Mauer & Huling, 1995). Although a 241% increase in incarceration in five short years is astonishing, this increase pales in comparison to that experienced by minority women. Hispanic women saw an increase of incarceration for drug offenses of 328% during the same five-year period. An even more dramatic increase was experienced by African American women, with prison sentences for drug offenses increasing by 828% between 1986 and 1991 (Mauer & Huling, 1995).

The war on drugs, with its associated get-tough policies, had one other major impact on female imprisonment. The use of mandatory minimums moved discretion away from judges, forcing them to give required prison terms to people who would normally have been given nonincarcerative, community-based sanctions (Faris & Miller, 2010). Raeder (1995) explicitly described the impact of mandatory minimum sentences on women by stating this policy "subverted the earlier nonincarcerative model of female sentencing" (p. 157). Prior to this get-tough movement, women were often diverted from prison and instead given probation or other community-based alternatives; when they were sentenced to prison, they were given shorter sentences than their male counterparts (Raeder, 1995). However, the war on drug's push to punish those involved with strict and harsh sanctions in essence killed the alleged chivalry some have argued existed in the criminal justice system; consequently, the war has contributed to the increase of women found in our penal institutions.

The Pressure to Conform to Conduct Expectations for Women and Girls

Why Women Question Authority in Prisons More Than Men

The biological and social construction literature is not clear on why this is so, but women in prisons and jails seem less likely to keep quiet about the needs or injustices they experience during incarceration, at least at the hands of other inmates, than are men in similar circumstances. One of the authors first noted this phenomenon in the 1980s when speaking to colleagues at a male prison who had previously worked in a female facility. To a man (and they were all men who had this background at this time), these prison staff claimed that they would rather work in a male prison than in a female one. When queried as to why that might be, their explanation for this preference was that the women were "too mouthy" or would not hesitate to come right up to the officer and complain about every little thing. The male inmates, on the other hand, were much less likely to behave in this manner. Years later, when this author was engaged in a national study of women's jails and interviewing the administrators of five of them, all males and a female lieutenant, they also noted that the women were more likely to "rat out" or tell on another inmate right in front of that inmate (Stohr & Mays, 1993). The jail administrators claimed that female inmates would not hesitate to complain to male and female staff about other staff or the operation of the facility itself.

If true, this finding that women are more likely to question authority, even in a prison or jail setting where formal authority of staff is absolute and victimization by other inmates is a real possibility, might in part be explained by Adler's (1975) work. From *Sisters in Crime* we learned that women and girls were empowered by feministic conceptions of their rights vis-á-vis others and were unbowed by assertions and trappings of authority. In her prologue to the book, Adler wrote in 1975 that:

> the phenomenon of female criminality is but one wave in this rising tide of female assertiveness—a wave which has not yet crested and may even be seeking its level uncomfortably close to the high-water mark set by male violence. (p. 1)

Adler noted the rising assertiveness in the conventional sphere of women and believed that feminism was one explanation for it.

Additional explanations for the willingness of women to assert themselves and to question authority, perhaps more than men in correctional facilities, might also include the relative safety of women's prisons versus men's; the more verbal nature of women versus men (perhaps as a social construction or a biological determinism); the greater need for services and programming that women have vis-á-vis men; and the past abuse by authority figures, which might make the women more likely to see the fallibility of such personages. Women's facilities, in total, are by all accounts much less likely to be violent environments than are men's facilities (Belknap, 2001; Owen, 2006). Physical violence is rare and less likely to involve a weapon. Organized violence is often nonexistent. Given this fact, the complaints of females regarding their incarceration or the behavior of other inmates, even right in front of a fellow inmate, becomes much more understandable because females know they are less likely to be punched in the nose by other inmates than would be true for a male inmate making the same sort of complaint (Owen, 1998, 2006).

The claim that women are more "verbal" than men has been made by nonfeminists as a means of dismissing their dialog and trivializing women as gossips or nags or as "bitchy" wives in need of control by their husbands. For instance, "nags," or women who dared to speak up in their medieval European communities about their needs and abuse, could be subjected to a "scolds brace," a device that would prevent a wife from talking. Her husband might also authorize that she be dunked a few times in a body of water to further teach the lesson that she should not be a nag or a "gossip" (Earle, 1896; Walker, 1979). Of course, men were not similarly abused for the same behavior. Currently in the lexicon of popular music we find that women are referred to as bitches, a sexist and degrading reference, and they are told to shut up and endure their own abuse (e.g., The Rap Up, 2013). As a side note, it is no coincidence that all of the negative terms listed here, and many more, which cannot be remarked on in polite company, are gendered in their historic and current application to females. Women who were too free with their speech were punished and exhorted to be passive and nonaggressive in their speech and behavior (the traditional female sphere according to Adler, 1975).

But the old prejudice might have a grain of truth in it: not that women's speech is more laden with gossip or nagging, but that women talk more than men, especially in the private sphere of the family and friends and, since the advent of feminism, in the public sphere as well, as they enter professions and politics. If it is true that women are at least as verbal as men in the free world and have more license to be so in the incarcerated world because they are not as fearful of violence, then this might also explain why women are more likely to assert themselves in a correctional environment.

Another reason why women might be more willing to state their needs in a correctional environment is that they have more needs than men in the same environment. And women are less likely to have those needs met. As mentioned previously, historically women in prisons were incarcerated with men, where they were more likely to be abused, or, by the latter half of the 19th century, in rooms attached to largely male facilities where males were the focus and the services and supervision of women were scant (Dix, 1967; Rafter, 1992; Stohr & Walsh, 2012). In such places and in the academic literature on women's plight in corrections, women were often forgotten or ignored because their relatively small numbers and lack of societal importance did not warrant attention (Belknap, 2003).

Women are more likely to have medical needs than men (Mallicoat, 2012; Stohr & Walsh, 2012). They are more likely to be prescribed psychotropic drugs than men, presumably because they experience more mental health problems (Gray, Mays, & Stohr, 1995; Morash, Haarr, & Rucker, 1994). They are more likely to have been subjected as children and adults to physical and sexual abuse than male inmates (Belknap, 2001; Blackburn, Mullings, & Marquart, 2008; Owen, 1998). They are more likely to have drug or alcohol problems before entering prisons or jails (Stohr & Walsh, 2012). They are more likely to have had custody of their children than men and therefore to miss the presence of their children more (Henriques, 1996). All of these realities mean that women and girls in prisons and jails have some of the same programming needs in terms of treatment and job training, although they might be less likely to have them met because of their numbers, location in the state, and gender; but they also have greater physical and mental health care and familial needs than incarcerated men. Perhaps it is the existence of these unmet and greater needs that spurs women to be more verbal in that their demands be met because, in some cases, their lives and their children's lives depend upon it.

Or perhaps it is because incarcerated women and girls have a greater history of victimization than incarcerated men and boys. Men and boys are victims of more crime generally, but women and girls are victimized by violent crimes such as rape, sexual assault, and domestic violence, which most men in the free world do not experience (Fisher, Daigle, & Cullen, 2010; Truman, Langton, & Planty, 2013). Much of this violent victimization of women and girls occurs at the hands of male family members, some of whom are in "authority" roles, such as fathers, stepfathers, grandfathers, and uncles. This fact may lead women and girls to be less intimidated by and give less respect to others in positions of authority, as well as to challenge those in authority positions more.

Attempts to Gain Conformity in Female Conduct

The control of women's behavior and speech has been an enduring theme throughout human history, but particularly for Western countries in the past 3,000 to 5,000 years as civilizations formalized their traditions, laws, and religions (Lerner, 1986). Ironically, the rise of patriarchy or the valuing of men and boys over women and girls occurred in tandem with the rise of democracy in ancient Greek city-states and later in the Roman polity. As democracy spread in these civilizations, it was only applied to male citizens, usually only propertied ones, and certainly not to women who were considered either *property of* their male relatives or too childlike and inferior of mind to be trusted with the suffrage (Lerner, 1993; Stohr, 2014).

This view of women and girls as weak, dependent, and childlike, whose sphere was more appropriately in the home, was reflected in the historical practice of their confinement in sections of men's prisons and the first women's prisons (as mentioned previously). Once separate women's prisons were developed, they were subjected to some of the same strictures (e.g., enforced silence was attempted in early women's prisons) as early men's facilities, with the additional consideration that women who commit crime were "doubly deviant" because they had offended both against societal rules and against expectations for their gender (Belknap, 2003). This flouting of gendered expectations was to be remedied by the imposition of stricter controls over women's speech, dress, and behavior in prisons (Mallicoat, 2012). The focus was on ladylike behavior that was more reflective of the dichotomous conception of women as either the "madonna" or the "whore." Women who committed crimes were relegated to the latter category, but the effort with prison programming and controls was to transform female prisoners into madonnas who practiced ladylike behavior (Rafter, 2013). Their training was for domestic positions, which it was thought befit their lower class and female status.

One's class and race, along with gender, certainly influenced how women were treated in prisons and jails in the United States. As with men, the vast majority of women incarcerated throughout the history of prisons and jails in this country have been poor (Welch, 2004). Except for the most serious of crimes or infamous crimes, the rich were able to avoid incarceration or the crimes they committed were not subject to it. With regard to race, prior to the Civil War, most of the relatively few women who were incarcerated were White, although after the war, and particularly in the South, prisons were used as a means of reinstituting slavery for African Americans (Oshinsky, 1996; Young, 2001). As discussed previously, the onset of the war on drugs in the 1980s led to a significant increase in the incarceration of minority group members and of women.

Although the women's movement, which Adler (1975) so aptly defines in her work, did lead to better overall treatment of incarcerated women, the attempts to control and mold women into "ladies" continues in the prisons and jails of today. These efforts are evident in the limited programming available to women in prisons, its "pink-collar" and thus poor paying content, and the increased sanctions women experience for using foul language or challenging a rule (Lindquist, 1980). In related research published in 2008, Gover, Perez, and Jennings found that women's misconduct in prison stems from different causes than men's and is best addressed in a different way than it is for men. Their findings were that women with longer sentences, who perceived staff as more caring and who felt safer in prison, were less likely to "act out." Of course, past and current attempts to force women and girls into gender-specific roles while incarcerated are in direct conflict with Adler's (1975) societal prescription for a more liberated female and certainly would not be perceived as "caring" behavior by those women studied by Gover and her colleagues.

Coping and Adaptation in Women's Prisons

The upshot of the preceding discussion is that women bring along a whole basketful of problems when they enter correctional institutions (Owen, 2006). As mentioned previously, they typically have a history of neglect or of physical or sexual abuse, with the collateral mental health ailments and substance abuse that accompany such issues. Their physical health is often fragile because of their inattention, substance abuse, poverty, homelessness, and gynecological issues (Gilfus, 2006). They are more often mothers who are separated from children they were caring for prior to incarceration (Dalley, 2003; Owen, 2006). Because most states have only one or two women's prisons, which are located at some distance from the cities where most offenders reside, separation from families, friends, and the communities they are familiar with is more acute for women (Belknap, 2001). Further, women face a prison system that was constructed and operated for, and mostly by, males. Old ideas about what it means to be a lady and patriarchy linger on in available programming and some staff attitudes, all of which color the incarceration experience of women (Belknap, 2001; Owen, 2006; Schram, 2003). Moreover, women suffer the same pains of imprisonment that Sykes (1958) identified for men more than 50 years ago—namely the deprivation of liberty, autonomy, goods and services, heterosexual relationships, and security. Given all of these issues, problems, and unmet needs, what are these women to do? The answer is, of course, they adapt to their environment and cope with the situation they face.

In her now classic study of a women's prison, titled *In the Mix: Struggle and Survival in a Women's Prison*, Owen (1998) reviews the various ways that women adjust and therefore cope with the incarcerative elements they face. Their mode of adaptation, as one would expect, is tempered by their past, their present, and their conception of a future. It is also undoubtedly shaped by their needs. Therefore, research spanning almost 50 years (i.e., Ward & Kassebaum, 1965) would indicate that some female inmates will form pseudo-families to fill the loss they experience from separation not only from their children, but also from their mothers, fathers, husbands or wives, boyfriends or girlfriends, sisters, grandparents, and other close relatives (Pollock, 2002). Close inmate associates of the women will take on these familial roles relative to her (e.g., mother, sister) or will adopt her into the already established family to fill a given role. Although rarely remarked upon in discussions of male prisons, the first author of this chapter observed a less structured version of familial roles in men's prisons. Thus, some younger inmates referred to their elders as "dad"; older inmates referred to younger ones they were close to as "son"; and still other inmates referred to fellow inmates they were friends with as "brother." These families, particularly in female prisons, not only meet emotional needs but also provide goods and services, security, companionship, or intimate relationships. The formation of such families by women in prisons has long been described by scholars as a means incarcerated women use to try to alleviate the pains of imprisonment described above.

Unlike male inmates, imprisoned women do not engage in gang activity as a means of coping (Owen, 1998; Pollock, 2002). Nor is race a divisive issue in such prisons. Some early research (e.g., Giallombardo, 1966) identified set roles for women inmates in their subculture, much like in men's prisons. Such roles might include a woman who acted more as an outlaw in the environment by engaging in the black market, another who is more likely to abide by the rules, or yet another who eschews the inmate subculture and focuses on just doing her time so that she will be let out on her release date. More recent scholarly work has not noted clear roles as part of a subculture (Owen, 1998). Women do have identifiable inmate leaders in their prison subculture, and these women tend to be characterized as younger, African American, gregarious, and more likely to be engaged in homosexual activity (Pollock, 2002). But they are less likely to be in organized gangs or other such groupings as in men's prisons. This lack of organization may explain why women's prisons have a less vibrant black market and thus why female inmates have less access than male inmates to illegal goods to purchase (e.g., cigarettes, alcohol, drugs).

If they are self-aware regarding their past and hope to have a better future, Owen (1998) notes that women in prison will also try to adapt by choosing a low-key existence in the prison. They will try to avoid "the mix" of drugs and abusive relationships while inside so as not to return to them when released. Such women will consciously stay out of the places in the prison, as well as away from the people in the prison, where low-grade crimes and conflicts occur, such as the yard and the dining hall.

Such women may look for a programming or work niche that gives them the skills to avoid dangerous and injurious relationships and that will allow them to provide financially for their families in a prosocial way once released (Owen, 1998). Unfortunately, despite lawsuits to increase the amount and quality of programming for women in prisons, there are fewer services available for women inmates than there are for men. Further, the drug and alcohol treatment programs that are available tend to be modeled after what is provided for males—even using male examples, male pronouns, and confrontational approaches to teaching that are less successful with women (Owen, 2006).

Having said this, the studies of vocational programming in women's prisons that have been conducted over the past several decades indicate that there is more and better vocational training than there used to be in women's prisons (see, e.g., Chapman, 1980; Glick & Neto, 1977; Morash et al., 1994; Simon & Landis, 1991; Weisheit, 1985). Even so, these programs often still retain a traditional focus on "women's" work (e.g., sewing, food service, domestic work, secretarial, cosmetology) and less on nontraditional and better paying "men's" work (e.g., welding, carpentry, computer programming, plumbing, graphics/painting, masonry) (Schram, 2003). The lead author of this paper recently (2012) witnessed an example of such gender disparity in programming (although at a southwestern juvenile detention facility and not at a prison per se). She observed programming where the 4 girls in the facility were allowed to spend their time making bead bracelets for their afternoon activity, whereas the 30 or more boys were treated to a high school history lesson from an outside instructor.

In any event, most incarcerated women are involved in some form of programming. These activities might include one or more of the following: institutional maintenance or service (e.g., the kitchen, laundry work, cleaning the facility); schooling to earn a general educational development certificate or high school diploma; work programs (e.g., sewing); drug or alcohol treatment; and parenting training

(Pollock, 2002). Some private companies have contracted with women's prisons to provide jobs and free-world wages that exceed any payment given to an inmate for typical prison work. Examples of these private-company jobs include data entry, reservation call-in work, and eyeglass lens grinding (Pollock, 2002).

Female-Specific Risk/Need Factors and Subsequent Adaptation to the Institution

As briefly mentioned in the previous section, female offenders have historically been overlooked in the literature, most likely because of their lower rates of criminal behavior and their lesser value and "other" status as a result of patriarchy. More recently, however, women are gaining increased attention from researchers, policy makers, and corrections staff because rates of offending for this group have steadily increased, with more women sentenced to prison today compared to previous decades (Guerino et al., 2010). This research is important because it sheds light on many issues that otherwise would have gone unnoticed by criminal justice scholars. Particularly relevant for this chapter is the literature on offender risk/needs factors and whether such criminogenic factors are the same across gender.

Two distinct criminological camps exist in the literature concerning risk/needs factors and gender—a gender-neutral perspective and a gender-specific perspective. First, the gender-neutral perspective stems from personality and cognitive social learning theories, which is the basis for the Canadian psychologists' risk, need, and responsivity model (Andrews & Bonta, 2010; Andrews, Bonta, & Hoge, 1990; Andrews, Bonta, & Wormith, 2006). The Canadians and other scholars in this camp argue that crime varies among individuals depending on how they are rewarded or punished for unlawful behavior, whether their peers model procriminal or anticriminal behavior, and whether the individual is attached to conventional institutions (e.g., home, school, work). Subsequently, these factors interact with one another to lead someone to engage or not engage in criminal activities. Even further, once these factors are taken into account, demographic variables, such as race, gender, and social class, will have minimal effects on whether the individual commits a crime.

Men Are From Mars, Women Are From Venus

The risk, need, and responsivity model has had a considerable impact on the field of corrections over the past decade and continues to be used as a framework for establishing evidence-based practices throughout the world. As is common with any correctional paradigm or theoretical approach, however, the model has not been without its critics, especially as it applies to female offenders. Specifically, feminist scholars argue against the application of the gender-neutral approach because it is believed that the processes and risk factors underlying criminal behavior differ across gender (Chesney-Lind & Pasko, 2004).

From this viewpoint, the gender-neutral literature ignores the rates of occurrence and the impact of characteristics that are associated more with female offenders (i.e., it ignores the different pathways women take that lead them to prison). As discussed in the preceding section, compared to men, women are more likely to have custody of their children, have higher incidences of mental health problems, and have more physical health difficulties (Bloom, Owen, & Covington, 2003). In addition, national surveys have shown that offenders across both genders have issues with substance abuse; however, women in prison tend to have higher rates of drug use than men (Harlow, 1999).

Much like other chapters in this volume (see, e.g., Chapter 6 by Leanne Fiftal Alarid and Emily M. Wright), Daly's (1992, 1994) research, as well as that of other feminist scholars, (e.g., Salisbury & Van Voorhis, 2009), has helped us to better understand female offenders' unique trajectories into crime (e.g., patterns of abuse, trauma, drug addiction, and poor relationships). Specifically, these studies have shown us that women's criminal development and reoffending "are based on factors either (a) not typically seen with men, (b) typically seen with men but in even greater frequency with women, or (c) seen in relatively equal frequency but with distinct personal and social effects for women" (Salisbury & Van Voorhis, 2009, p. 543).

Gender-Responsive Treatment

Although there appear to be different opinions and recommendations when it comes to risk and needs for female inmates, most would agree that cognitive–behavioral interventions work for changing offender behavior, regardless of gender (or correctional setting; see, e.g., Covington & Bloom, 2006; Dowden & Andrews, 1999). Two issues are important to consider when ruminating about treatment and programming for female offenders.

First, some scholars (e.g., Matthews & Hubbard, 2008) have noted that the structure of cognitive–behavioral intervention groups may need to be modified. For example, a typical cognitive–behavioral intervention group is very structured, with an emphasis on reviewing the previous group lesson, introducing a new topic, and rehearsing the new skill or behavior. Given that women are more emotional and conversational than men, however, it has been suggested that some flexibility be built into the group protocol to allow for conversation between participants. The goal of this flexibility is to allow for a more supportive environment and encourage positive feedback (Latessa, Listwan, & Koetzle, 2013).

Second, as with any correctional treatment group, establishing a therapeutic alliance between group members and the individual client, as well as between group members and facilitator(s), is important, especially for female offenders. Within the alliance, respect and trust are established, which can substantially affect how successful someone is both in the group setting and beyond. Even further, the alliance is typically initiated by the staff who lead the group; thus, facilitators and staff must create a supportive and caring environment (Miller & Rollnick, 1991).

Women-Centered Corrections:
A Paradigmatic Shift From "Other" to Us

Female-Centered Prison

The evidence is clear in this evidence-driven discipline of criminal justice/criminology: Women have too often been accorded second-class citizenship in the world of prisons and in the wider world (Adler, 1975). Moreover, female inmates' needs and responsivity to programming differ from that of male inmates for the reasons delineated previously. Therefore, it is time again to resurrect the push for women- and girl-centered correctional facilities. We write "resurrect" because this idea is not new; it was instituted by some of the first pioneering female wardens of women's prisons (Hawkes, 1998; Yates, 2002).

What is called for now, in this postmodern and evidence-focused world of corrections, is a reconstituting of those original female-centered prisons so that they fit what we know to be true today. So we begin our discussion of the model female-centered prison with this provision: Women's (and men's) prisons should house only serious, repeat, and dangerous offenders because prison should be a *last resort*, when all other attempts to redirect a criminal pathway have been thwarted or when the person has committed a crime so egregious they must pay their debt to society with their confinement. A female-centered prison today would have a feminist, rather than a patriarchal focus, meaning that women's needs and their reality would be kept in mind as the inmates are managed and as programming and its delivery are constructed (Adler, 1975). Being female in such a prison would be valued and the realities females face, which differ from male realities, would be recognized, understood, and appreciated.

The Implementation Problem Answered

As many studies have demonstrated when trying to develop a utopian dream, the road is rocky and littered with implementation problems (Rothman, 1980). Either the idea is ill conceived or the theory is deficient. Staff sabotage organizational changes and policy delivery efforts because they do not understand or agree with them. Funding does not materialize as promised. Key leaders leave the organization and are not replaced with someone with the same passion, drive, and buy-in to the program. The ideas and their implementation flounder further on the rocks of disinterest or ineptitude of staff or the distracting passing fancy of a new idea or initiative. Along with these possible, and seemingly likely, implementation obstacles, women's prison reform must incorporate a true understanding of their clients as Adler (1975) was searching for in her seminal work. Women in prisons and jails are not just offenders-lite, or males without the same degree of violence in most of their offending. Instead, as we established in this chapter, and as Adler wrote in her book, women offenders truly differ from men. Hence, their prisons should reflect who women are, how they made it to the prison door, and what gender-specific and -sensitive ways would be best employed to see that once released, they do not come back.

What we propose here is not a theoryless idea, but one that would be grounded in the well-developed and conceived theory of feminism as described by Adler (1975) and others (Daly & Chesney-Lind, 1988). To ensure this feminist understanding and value are paramount in our female-centered prison, staff (from the warden down to the correctional officers) would need to be selected carefully for intelligence and sensitivity on gender issues and then trained extensively and continuously so they understand the special needs and overarching feminist focus for women in such a prison. Training on feminism and the way that women inmates' pathways take them to and from criminality would better prepare staff to assess needs and then supervise and facilitate the custody and treatment of women. Staff would need to embrace a human-service role in reference to their female charges, one Jurik (1985) identified as a preference of female staff in men's prisons and one that focuses on the provision of goods and services for inmates, referrals and advocacy for and of inmates, assisting inmates with their adjustment, and participating in helping networks with other staff to help inmates (Johnson, 2002).

Furthermore, the policies and procedures and the specific ways in which women are treated in the prison would need to be reexamined and reconfigured so that, as much as possible within the confines of a prison, they reflect a female-centered facility that is responsive to their needs. Related to this retooling of the policies and procedures manual would be the development of assessment tools that fit women (as discussed previously). These assessment tools would measure the risk, needs, and responsivity of women and move the women to programming developed to fit them. Treatment and programming that reflect a woman's real-world needs such as job training, education, mental health, addictions, victimization in relationships, parenting practices, and other related issues would need to be developed and delivered so women in prisons can leave as soon as possible and as fully developed and productive citizens.

R-E-S-P-E-C-T Is Key

Implicit in the operation of the female-centered and feminist prison would be R-E-S-P-E-C-T! Aretha Franklin was right when she sang the song by this name: People, including women in women's prisons (as with men in men's prisons), need and deserve respect to fully function as mature adults. Too often people in prisons are demonized and denigrated so they come to believe they are less than human and are not capable of functioning as mature adults in the wider world. As a result, they may cling to the old irresponsible and destructive behaviors of the past that harmed them and everyone in their orbit (Johnson, 2002; Owen, 1998). Because the vast majority of women inmates will reenter their communities at some point in their lives, some 90+% (Petersilia, 2003), it is vital for inmate families and the communities the women return to, as well as for the women themselves, that they come to see themselves not only as people who have erred, but also ultimately as people who are deserving of respect and who treat others with respect, whether in their relationships with significant others, family members, employers, and other community members.

Prisons, then, and our female-centered prison in particular, must give women the opportunity to understand their humanity and their worth. Society must do what it must to construct an environment where they are respected and given the opportunity to treat others similarly. This can be done explicitly through programming that showcases feministic conceptions of womanhood and how it manifests itself in women's lives—how alternate paths are available for women, dependent on the choices they make. Or respectful treatment and values might be implicit in work, education, and religious programs that recognize women's worth and are worthwhile, providing women with the training and tools they need to find or create a prosocial niche while in prison and a prosocial environment once they leave it.

Reentry and the Need for Social Support

Along with respect, reentry is another watchword in corrections these days (Petersilia, 2003). It is not enough to have a female-centered prison if the world women return to is destructive and oppressive. Women who were involved in the mix of drugs and alcohol, deficient or destructive relationships, and criminal engagement before their incarceration will need help in reentry to the community to ensure that they do not return to the antisocial environment (Owens, 1998). Reentry to the community from a female-centered prison would then involve not only all of the efforts to address needs and deficiencies while in prison, but also planning with outside families, friends, and community organizations to help link women with the social support they need to become fully functioning citizens and human beings (Cullen, 1994; Petersilia, 2003). This would mean that the prison employs outreach specialists who assess where women are in terms of their risk and needs before they reenter the community and ensure contacts and arrangements are made for housing, jobs, child visitation or custody, health care, and supervision (if she will be paroled), which will make transition to the community a likely success.

Once in the community, of course, female offenders will need assistance from the community corrections officer, health and human services personnel, or a collection of people in the public and private sectors to ensure the transition goes smoothly. This process is more likely to "work" if several agencies devote some staff time to this process and if there is a coordinator or one person who can be the contact person to provide referrals to services, advice, and other assistance as needed by the women.

Conclusions: Moving From Sisters in Crime to Sisters in Success

In her highly influential work *Sisters in Crime*, famed criminologist Freda Adler (1975) makes the startling claim that at their essence women and men are more similar than dissimilar. At the time, this was an unsettling claim for some because it was supportive of the nascent feminist movement; it was an alternate claim to the one being bandied about at the time and since, which proposed that women and men are so different in their preferences, beliefs, and behavior (i.e., Venus versus Mars) that they not only *represent* dissimilar planets, but may as well be *on* different planets. Instead, Adler assumed a supposition of similarity and thought that, if accorded sufficient opportunity, women would engage in as much crime as men: hence the title of her book, *Sisters in Crime.*

Although greater engagement in crime, particularly traditionally masculine crimes that would indicate women were truly liberated, did not occur as Adler had predicted, she was correct in her claim that women and men are at base similar. Research on women and men in corrections as clients and as workers has borne out this claim (Andrews & Bonta, 2010; Cullen, Link, Wolfe, & Frank, 1985; Hemmens, Stohr, Schoeler, & Miller, 2002; Jurik & Halemba, 1984; Lovrich & Stohr, 1993). Such research has found that they have the same needs and similar perceptions about security, employment, housing, respect, love, and fulfillment and that their behavior is motivated by these needs. As we have noted in this chapter, women's risks and needs in the correctional environment and in communities do differ from men's to some extent, but many are the same; they are not on different planets so much as in alternate neighborhoods.

To fashion correctional environments that "fit" women, however, the difference in needs and risks must be recognized and addressed. In this chapter we have discussed how this might be done and how it might affect the conduct and care of these women while incarcerated. In the end, if we want female offenders to be successful in meeting their needs in a prosocial fashion while incarcerated or when they transition to communities or, in other words, become *sisters in success*, then we need to provide them with the correctional environment, the tools, and the services to help them achieve that end. True liberation for such women will come when they are on a prosocial pathway of their choosing that provides a better life for them and safer communities for all of us.

References

Adler, F. (1975). *Sisters in crime: The rise of the new female criminal.* New York, NY: McGraw–Hill.

Andrews, D. A., & Bonta, J. (2010). *The psychology of criminal conduct.* New Providence, NJ: Anderson.

Andrews, D. A., Bonta, J., & Hoge, R. D. (1990). Classification for effective rehabilitation: Rediscovering psychology. *Criminal Justice and Behavior, 17,* 19–52.

Andrews, D. A., Bonta, J., & Wormith, S. J. (2004). *The Level of Service/Case Management Inventory (LS/CMI).* Toronto, Ontario: Multi-Health Systems.

Andrews, D. A., Bonta, J., & Wormith, S. J. (2006). The recent past and near future of risk and/or need assessment. *Crime & Delinquency, 52,* 7–27.

Belknap, J. (2001). *The invisible woman: Gender, crime and justice* (2nd ed.). Belmont, CA: Wadsworth/Thomas Learning.

Belknap, J. (2003). Responding to the needs of women prisoners. In S. Sharp & R. Muraskin (Eds.), *Female prisoners in the United States: Programming needs, availability, and efficacy* (pp. 93–106). Upper Saddle River, NJ: Prentice Hall.

Belknap, J. (2006). *The invisible woman: Gender, crime, and justice* (3rd ed.). Cincinnati, OH: Wadsworth.

Blackburn, A. G., Mullings, J. L., & Marquart, J. W. (2008). Sexual assault in prison and beyond: Toward an understanding of lifetime sexual assault among incarcerated women. *The Prison Journal, 88,* 351–377.

Bloom, B., Owen, B., & Covington, S. (2003). *Gender responsive strategies: Research, practice, and guiding principles for women offenders.* Washington, DC: National Institute of Justice.

Blumstein, A., & Beck, A. J. (1999). Population growth in U.S. prisons, 1980–1996. In M. Tonry & J. Petersilia (Eds.), *Crime and justice, prisons* (Vol. 26, pp. 17–62). Chicago, IL: University of Chicago Press.

Butler, A. M. (1997). *Gendered justice in the American west: Women prisoners in men's penitentiaries.* Urbana: University of Illinois Press.

Callahan, C. (1986). *Women in prison: Does the justice system do them justice?* Anchorage: Alaskan Women's Commission.

Carson, E. A., & Golinelli, D. (2013). *Prisoners in 2012: Advance counts.* Washington, DC: U.S. Department of Justice, Bureau of Justice Statistics.

Chapman, J. (1980). *Economic realities and female crime.* Lexington, MA: Lexington Books.

Chesney-Lind, M., & Pasko, L. (2004). *The female offender: Girls, women, and crime.* Thousand Oaks, CA: Sage.

Clear, T. R. (1994). *Harm in American penology: Offenders, victims, and their communities.* Albany: State University of New York Press.

Covington, S., & Bloom, B. (2006). Gender responsive treatment and services in correctional settings. *Women and Therapy, 29,* 1–8.

Cullen, F. T. (1994). Social support as an organizing concept for criminology: Presidential address to the Academy of Criminal Justice Sciences. *Justice Quarterly, 11,* 527–559.

Cullen, F. T., Link, B., Wolfe, N., & Frank, J. (1985). The social dimensions of correctional officer stress. *Justice Quarterly, 2,* 505–533.

Cullen, F. T., Jonson, C. L., & Stohr, M. K. (2014). *The American prison: Imagining a different future.* Los Angeles, CA: Sage.

Currie, E. (1998). *Crime and punishment in America.* New York, NY: Metropolitan Books.

Dalley, L. P. (2003). Children of imprisoned mothers: What does the future hold? In J. Joseph & D. Taylor (Eds.), *With justice for all: Minorities and women in criminal justice* (pp. 121–136). Upper Saddle River, NJ: Prentice Hall.

Daly, K. (1992). Women's pathways to felony court: Feminist theories of lawbreaking and problems of representation. *Southern California Review of Law and Women's Studies, 2,* 11–52.

Daly, K. (1994). *Gender, crime, and punishment.* New Haven, CT: Yale University Press.

Daly, K., & Chesney-Lind, M. (1988). Feminism and criminology. *Justice Quarterly, 5,* 497–538.

Dix, D. (1967). *Remarks on prisons and prison discipline in the United States.* Montclair, NJ: Patterson Smith. (Original work published in 1843; revised ed. published in 1845.)

Dowden, C., & Andrews, D. A. (1999). What works for female offenders: A meta-analysis. *Crime and Delinquency, 45,* 438–452.

Earle, A. M. (1896). *The curious punishments of bygone days.* Port Townsend, WA: Loompanics Unlimited. Retrieved from http://www.gutenberg.org/files/34005/34005-h/34005-h.htm/

Faris, J., & Miller, J. (2010). Family matters: Perceptions of fairness among incarcerated women. *The Prison Journal, 90,* 139–160.

Fisher, B. S., Daigle, L. E., & Cullen, F. T. (2010). *Unsafe in the ivory tower: The sexual victimization of college women.* Thousand Oaks, CA: Sage.

Giallombardo, R. (1966). *Society of women: A study of women's prison.* New York, NY: Wiley.

Gilfus, M. E. (2006). From victims to survivors to offenders: Women's routes of entry and immersion into street crime. In L. F. Alarid & P. Cromwell (Eds.), *In her own words: Women offenders' views on crime and victimization* (pp. 5–14). Los Angeles, CA: Roxbury.

Glick, R., & Neto, V. (1977). *National study of women's correctional programs.* Washington, DC: U.S. Government Printing Office.

Gover, A. R., Perez, D. M., & Jennings, W. G. (2008). Gender differences in factors contributing to institutional misconduct. *The Prison Journal, 88,* 378–403.

Gray, T., Mays, G. L., & Stohr, M. K. (1995). Inmate needs and programming in exclusively women's jails. *The Prison Journal, 75,* 186–202.

Guerino, P., Harrison, P. M., & Sabol, W. J. (2010). *Prisoners in 2010.* Washington, DC: U.S. Department of Justice, Bureau of Justice Statistics.

Hagan, J., & Coleman, J. P. (2001). Returning captives of the American war on drugs: Issues of community and family reentry. *Crime and Delinquency, 47,* 352–367.

Harlow, C. W. (1999). *Prior abuse reported by inmates and probationers.* Washington, DC: U.S. Department of Justice, Bureau of Justice Statistics.

Hawkes, M. Q. (1998). Edna Mahan: Sustaining the reformatory tradition. *Women and Criminal Justice, 9,* 1–21.

Hemmens, C., Stohr, M. K., Schoeler, M., & Miller, B. (2002). One step up, two steps back: The progression of perceptions of women's work in prisons and jails. *Journal of Criminal Justice, 30,* 473–489.

Henriques, Z. W. (1996). Imprisoned mothers and their children: Separation–reunion syndrome dual impact. *Women and Criminal Justice, 81,* 77–95.

Holsinger, K. (2014). The feminist prison. In F. T. Cullen, C. L. Jonson, & M. K. Stohr (Eds.), *The American prison: Imagining a different future* (pp. 87–110). Thousand Oaks, CA: Sage.

Johnson, R. (2002). *Hard time: Understanding and reforming the prison* (3rd ed.). Belmont, CA: Wadsworth.

Jurik, N. C. (1985). Individual and organizational determinants of correctional officer attitudes towards inmates. *Criminology, 23,* 523–539.

Jurik, N. C., & Halemba, G. (1984). Gender, working conditions and the job satisfaction of women in a non-traditional occupation: Female correctional officers in men's prisons. *Sociological Quarterly, 25,* 551–556.

Latessa, E. J., Listwan, S. J., & Koetzle, D. (2013). *What works (and doesn't) in reducing recidivism.* Waltham, MA: Anderson.

Lerner, G. (1986). *The creation of patriarchy.* New York, NY: Oxford University Press.

Lerner, G. (1993). *The creation of feminist consciousness: From the Middle Ages to eighteen-seventy.* New York, NY: Oxford University Press.

Lindquist, C. A. (1980). Prison discipline and the female offender. *Journal of Offender Counseling Services and Rehabilitation, 4,* 305–318.

Lovrich, N. P., & Stohr, M. K. (1993). Gender and jail work: Correctional policy implications of perceptual diversity in the work force. *Policy Studies Review, 12,* 66–84.

Lynch, M. J. (2007). *Big prisons, big dreams: Crime and the failure of America's penal system.* New Brunswick, NJ: Rutgers University Press.

Mallicoat, S. (2012). *Women and crime: A text/reader.* Thousand Oaks, CA: Sage.

Matthews, D. J., & Hubbard, B. (2008). Reconciling the differences between "gender-responsive" and the "what works" literatures to improve services for girls. *Crime and Delinquency, 54,* 225–258.

Mauer, M., & Huling, T. (1995). *Young black Americans and the criminal justice system: Five years later.* Washington, DC: The Sentencing Project.

Mauer, M., & King, R. S. (2007). *Uneven justice: State rates of incarceration by race and ethnicity.* Washington, DC: The Sentencing Project.

McDaniels-Wilson, C., & Belknap, J. (2008). The extensive sexual violation and sexual abuse histories of incarcerated women. *Violence Against Women, 14,* 1090–1127.

Miller, W. R., & Rollnick, S. (1991). *Motivational interviewing: Preparing people to change addictive behavior.* New York, NY: Guilford Press.

Minor-Harper, S., Marbrook, M., Baldea, M., & Stanford, J. (1986). *State and federal prisoners, 1925–85.* Washington, DC: U.S. Department of Justice, Bureau of Justice Statistics.

Morash, M., Haarr, R., & Rucker, L. (1994). A comparison of programming for women and men in U.S. prisons in the 1980s. *Crime and Delinquency, 40,* 197–221.

Mumola, C. J. (2000). *Incarcerated parents and their children.* Washington, DC: U.S. Department of Justice, Bureau of Justice Statistics.

Mumola, C. J., & Karberg, J. (2006). *Drug use and dependence, state and federal prisoners, 2004.* Washington, DC: U.S. Department of Justice, Bureau of Justice Statistics.

Oshinsky, D. M. (1996). *Worse than slavery: Parchman Farm and the ordeal of Jim Crow justice.* New York, NY: The Free Press.

Owen, B. (1998). *In the mix: Struggle and survival in a women's prison.* Albany: State University of New York Press.

Owen, B. (2006). The context of women's imprisonment. In A. V. Merlo & J. M. Pollock (Eds.), *Women, law, and social control* (pp. 251–270). Boston, MA: Pearson.

Petersilia, J. (2003). *When prisoners come home: Parole and prisoner reentry.* New York, NY: Oxford University Press.

Pollock, J. M. (2002). *Women, prison and crime* (2nd ed.). Belmont, CA: Wadsworth.

Proctor, J. (2009). The impact imprisonment has on women's health and health care from the perspective of female inmates in Kansas. *Women and Criminal Justice, 19,* 1–36.

Raeder, M. S. (1995). The forgotten offender: The effect of the sentencing guidelines and mandatory minimums on women and their children. *Federal Sentencing Reporter, 8,* 157–162.

Rafter, N. H. (1992). *Partial justice: Women, prisons, and social control* (2nd ed.). New Brunswick, NJ: Transaction.

Rafter, N. H. (2013). "Much and unfortunately neglected" women in early and mid-nineteenth century prisons. In M. K. Stohr & T. Walsh (Eds.), *Corrections: A text/reader* (2nd ed., pp. 54–67). Thousand Oaks, CA: Sage.

The Rap Up. (2013). *11 rap songs to disrespect women to.* Retrieved from http://therapup .net/2009/04/11-rap-songs-to-disrespect-women-to/

Rothman, D. J. (1980). *Conscience and convenience: The asylum and its alternatives in progressive America.* Boston, MA: Little, Brown.

Salisbury, E., & Van Voorhis, P. (2009). Gendered pathways: A quantitative investigation of women probationers paths to recidivism. *Criminal Justice and Behavior, 36,* 541–566.

Schram, P. J. (2003). Stereotypes and vocational programming for women prisoners. In S. F. Sharp (Ed.), *The incarcerated woman: Rehabilitative programming in women's prisons* (pp. 17–28). Upper Saddle River, NJ: Prentice Hall.

The Sentencing Project. (2007). *Women in the criminal justice system: Briefing sheets.* Washington, DC: Author.

Simon, R., & Landis, J. (1991). *The crimes women commit and the punishment they receive.* Lexington, MA: Lexington Press.

Sokoloff, N. J. (2005). Women prisoners at the dawn of the 21st century. *Women and Criminal Justice, 16,* 127–137.

Stohr, M. K. (2014). Women and the law. In A. Walsh & C. Hemmens (Eds.), *Law, justice and society* (3rd ed., pp. 318–346). New York, NY: Oxford University Press.

Stohr, M. K., & Mays, G. L. (1993). *Women's jails: An investigation of offenders, staff, administration and programming.* Washington, DC: National Institute of Corrections, Jails Division.

Stohr, M. K., & Walsh, T. (2012). *Corrections: The essentials.* Thousand Oaks, CA: Sage.

Sykes, G. M. (1958). *The society of captives: A study of a maximum security prison.* Princeton, NJ: Princeton University Press.

Truman, J., Langton, L., & Planty, M. (2013). *Criminal victimization, 2012.* Washington, DC: U.S. Department of Justice, Bureau of Justice Statistics.

Walker, L. E. (1979). *The battered woman.* New York, NY: Harper & Row.

Ward, D., & Kassebaum, G. (1965). *Women's prison: Sex and social structure.* Chicago, IL: Aldine–Atherton.

Weisheit, R. (1985). Trends in programs for female offenders: The use of private service agencies as service providers. *International Journal of Offender Therapy and Comparative Criminology, 29,* 35–42.

Welch, M. (2004). *Corrections: A critical approach* (2nd ed.). Boston, MA: McGraw–Hill.

Yates, H. M. (2002). Margaret Moore: African American feminist leader in corrections. *Women and Criminal Justice, 13,* 9–26.

Young, V. D. (2001). All the women in the Maryland State Penitentiary: 1812–1869. *The Prison Journal, 81,* 113–132.

Zimring, F. (2001). Imprisonment rates and the new politics of criminal punishment. In D. Garland (Ed.), *Mass imprisonment: Social causes and consequences* (pp. 145–149). Thousand Oaks, CA: Sage.

CHAPTER 18

A Gendered Theory of Offender Rehabilitation

Paula Smith and Sarah M. Manchak

The number of incarcerated offenders in the United States has increased dramatically since the 1970s, with the population of inmates in prisons and jails currently exceeding 2.2 million (Glaze & Herberman, 2013). When probation and parole are considered, the total number of individuals under some form of correctional supervision is slightly less than 7 million (Glaze & Herberman, 2013). As might be anticipated, a considerable amount of academic work has been dedicated to understanding this era of mass incarceration and community control (see Abramsky, 2007; Gottschalk, 2006; Lynch, 2007; Simon, 2007; Tonry, 2004). Several authors have cautioned that the growth of the correctional enterprise has created an organizational crisis as large numbers of offenders are processed through the criminal justice system (see Feeley & Simon, 1992; Simon, 1993). At its worst, this situation has led to a "new penology" in which the larger social purposes of corrections—such as offender rehabilitation—are abandoned to attend to the daily, pragmatic activities associated with managing large correctional populations. In the best case scenario, a premium is placed on those correctional administrators who can confront challenging organizational conditions (e.g., overcrowding and large caseloads) while fostering a safe environment for the delivery of human services (see DiIulio, 1987).

One group for whom correctional population growth is notably pronounced is women. The criminal justice system in the United States has experienced a tremendous influx of female offenders. To illustrate, the number of female offenders increased by nearly 50% between 1990 and 2009, whereas the population of male offenders has grown at only half this rate (Glaze, 2010). Furthermore, males accounted for 86% of the correctional population in 1990, but this figure decreased to 82% in 2009 (Glaze, 2010). In comparison, the number of adult females in prison increased an average of 4.6% per year between 1995 and 2005, compared to less than

3% for adult males during this same time period (Hartney, 2007). As a result, although men still account for the vast majority of offenders served in the correctional system, the increasing number of female offenders demands attention.

In this context, the current chapter begins by presenting the leading approach to offender rehabilitation, which is often referred to as the risk–need–responsivity model (RNR). This model argues that the predictors of crime are the same for males and females and thus that the principles for effective rehabilitation generalize across both sexes. In other words, it can be considered "gender neutral," or "generalist." Next, the chapter discusses how this generalist view has been challenged by scholars who argue that men and women differ in the pathways that lead them to crime. This "gender-specific" perspective thus argues that correctional treatment should differ for male and female offenders. As an alternative to these competing perspectives, we present a third view—a "gender-informed" theory—that is both evidence based and draws the best features from the generalist and gender-specific approaches.

The RNR Model

Over the past two decades, a model has emerged that is now considered one of the leading approaches to offender treatment: the RNR model (Cullen, 2013). This approach is often referred to as the "Canadian model" because it was invented by a group of Canadian psychologists, the most prominent of which were Donald Andrews, James Bonta, and Paul Gendreau. For our purposes, the RNR model is important because it is a generalist (or gender-neutral) perspective, arguing that males and females are amenable to the same rehabilitative services.

As the name implies, the RNR model is composed of three main parts: the risk principle, the need principle, and the responsivity principle. Before we discuss these principles in kind, we first present the models' underlying theoretical perspective, which is called the psychology of criminal conduct. Next, we offer a brief history of the development of this model. Then, we present the RNR principles, how they apply to offender rehabilitation for men and women alike, and the empirical evidence supporting this assertion.

The Theoretical Framework of the RNR Model

The sheer number of offenders involved in the correctional system underscores the need for more effective assessment and intervention strategies. The RNR model represents a powerful correctional paradigm in this regard (Andrews & Bonta, 2010; see also Cullen & Jonson, 2011; Smith, 2013). Within this context, the term *paradigm* refers to an all-encompassing way of conducting science within a set of agreed-upon theoretical ideas (Masterman, 1970; see also Kuhn, 1962). This phrase is employed purposefully here to highlight that the RNR model integrates coherently criminological knowledge, prescriptions for the content of treatment, and the technology for delivering interventions.

The RNR model incorporates an explanation of offender behavior often referred to by its advocates as "the psychology of criminal conduct." The RNR model thus directly connects general psychological and criminological theories to a specific theory of effective correctional programming, which is often referred to in the treatment literature as the "principles of effective correctional intervention" (Andrews, 1995; Gendreau, 1996; Gendreau, Cullen, & Bonta, 1994). To explain crime, the psychology of criminal conduct integrates concepts from social learning, cognitive, and personality theories, all frameworks that are supported by literally thousands of studies. It contends that the fundamental sources of human behavior are general; that is, they are the same for everyone—whether criminal or noncriminal, male or female. Specifically, actions (1) are preceded by thoughts (i.e., cognitions or attitudes) and (2) are also influenced by prior learning experiences, current supportive associations, and personality factors (i.e., traits and temperament).

Moreover, the RNR model, informed by the psychology of criminal conduct, has culminated in the development of numerous practical innovations that can be used by those delivering treatment to offenders. These include validated instruments that assess (1) an offender's risk for recidivism and the factors that must be addressed to reduce that risk and (2) the extent to which correctional programs are implemented appropriately and demonstrate fidelity to treatment principles (called the Correctional Program Assessment Inventory) (see Andrews & Bonta, 2010).

A Brief History of the RNR Paradigm

In 1974, Robert Martinson reviewed 231 evaluations of correctional treatment programs and concluded that "with few and isolated exceptions the rehabilitative efforts that have been reported so far have had no appreciable effect on recidivism" (p. 25). He further stated that "we haven't the faintest clue about how to rehabilitate offenders and reduce recidivism" (p. 48). Previous scholars have aptly noted that his message became an instant cliché and exerted a tremendous impact on the field of corrections, because it was delivered during a time of social and political tension, especially in the United States (see Cullen & Gendreau, 1989; Gendreau, Goggin, French, & Smith, 2006). Moreover, his message provided the rationale needed to proliferate the use of incarceration and punitive sanctions during the "get-tough" era of the 1980s and beyond (Simon, 1993).

In response to Martinson's (1974) proclamation that "nothing works" to reduce recidivism, scholars addressed the issue of whether evaluation studies of treatment programs really showed that *all* treatment programs were ineffective in reducing recidivism. To analyze his data, Martinson used a narrative review where studies of programs were described individually and their overall effects were counted or tallied up (Cullen & Gendreau, 1989; Gendreau & Ross, 1979, 1987; Palmer, 1975). This approach, however, has several important methodological weaknesses. For example, once studies are described, what percentage must show positive effects to conclude that a treatment was effective? One scholar might conclude that the "treatment glass" was half full, whereas another might define it as half empty. Further, as a qualitative assessment, a narrative review cannot easily account for differences across treatments (e.g., techniques used, underlying theoretical model). Thus, the Canadian scholars turned to new, more exacting tests of what works: the meta-analysis.

Using the technique of meta-analysis, researchers can quantitatively synthesize available evaluation studies to compute the overall statistical relationship, or "effect size," of interventions on reoffending (Andrews et al., 1990; Davidson, Gottschalk, Gensheimer, & Mayer, 1984; Dowden & Andrews, 1999a, 1999b; French & Gendreau, 2006; Garrett, 1985; Gendreau, Goggin, Cullen, & Andrews, 2000; Izzo & Ross, 1990; Landenberger & Lipsey, 2005; Lipsey, 1992; Lipsey & Wilson, 1998; MacKenzie, 2000; Mayer, Gensheimer, Davidson, & Gottschalk, 1986; Pearson, Lipton, Cleland, & Yee, 2002; Wilson, Bouffard, & MacKenzie, 2005). In essence, meta-analysis involves collecting all primary studies on a specific topic, coding the studies to record the effect size—that is, the statistical association that one variable (such as the treatment program) has on another variable (such as recidivism). It also is possible to code information on potential "moderators," which are variables that may affect the direction or strength of this effect (e.g., type of treatment; integrity of treatment delivery, and strength of the research study design). The resulting data can then be aggregated across studies to calculate statistically the average treatment effect. This effect is usually reported as a number (e.g., .20) along with a confidence interval (e.g., the true effect is between .14 and .26) (see Lipsey & Wilson, 2001; Rosenthal, 1991). Today, quantitative synthesis through meta-analysis is the review method of choice in most disciplines and has been applied extensively to the corrections literature (Smith, Cullen, & Latessa, 2009).

Meta-analysis, supplemented by narrative reviews, generated the evidence to refute the notion that nothing works and instead identified the most effective approaches to offender treatment. Thus, in an early and now-classic narrative review, Palmer (1975) pointed out that Martinson and his colleagues had overlooked many positive instances of treatment effectiveness. He suggested that a much better question was "which methods work best for which type of offenders under what conditions?" (Palmer, 1975, p. 150). Notably, McGuire (2013) reported that more than 100 quantitative reviews of offender treatment have been published to date, and the main findings have been replicated with remarkable consistency (see also Lipsey & Cullen, 2007). The key conclusion is that across all evaluation studies, correctional interventions have been found to reduce recidivism. In short, rehabilitation works.

The existing meta-analyses also produced another salient finding that has important implications for the treatment enterprise. They showed that the effects of treatment programs were *heterogeneous*. This means that with regard to lowering recidivism, some programs achieved large reductions, some achieved modest reductions, some had no effects, and some actually made offenders worse (especially interventions that were punitively oriented, such as boot camps). Why might this variation in effectiveness occur? Notably, the Canadian psychologists provided a compelling answer: The more programs adhered to the RNR principles of effective correctional interventions, the more successful they were in diminishing reoffending (i.e., in a meta-analysis, they achieved a higher treatment effect size).

The Principles of Effective Intervention: The RNR Model

As psychologists, the Canadian scholars rooted their treatment model on a general theory of human behavior, which they called the psychology of criminal conduct. As mentioned, the RNR model involves the practical application of psychological and criminological theories to changing antisocial behavior in the form of planned interventions. The empirical evidence indicates that to be effective in reducing recidivism, correctional treatments must attend to three basic principles: (1) deliver the most intensive interventions to higher risk offenders (*the risk principle*), (2) target dynamic (i.e., changeable) risk factors—referred to in the model as "criminogenic needs" (*the need principle*), and (3) employ cognitive–behavioral treatment modalities (*general responsivity principle*) while adjusting the mode and style of service delivery to match key offender characteristics (*specific responsivity principle*). These principles form the core of the RNR model in corrections. Given their importance, they each merit further discussion.

THE RISK PRINCIPLE. The term *risk factor* refers to measurable aspects of offenders and their circumstances that predict whether they will engage in future criminal behavior (see Andrews & Bonta, 2010; Gendreau, Little, & Groggin, 1996). Risk factors are divided into two types. "Static" risk factors cannot be changed by a correctional treatment (e.g., past criminal history); "dynamic" risk factors can potentially be changed by treatment (e.g., antisocial attitudes, antisocial peers, substance abuse) (Gendreau et al., 1996).

The *risk principle* specifies *who should be targeted* for treatment and has two components: assessment and matching. First, the classification of offenders should be based on an actuarial measure of risk factors (Andrews & Bonta, 2010). In the past, the assessment of risk was based on an official's personal judgment regarding the offender's likelihood to recidivate. In contrast to this "clinical" method, an "actuarial" assessment is based on the use of a survey instrument that includes statistically significant predictors of recidivism. Such assessments yield a numerical score that indicates an offender's risk of reoffending. Typically, offenders are classified as low, medium, or high risk. Research now clearly shows the advantages of using actuarial assessments to measure risk for future recidivism over clinical approaches (Barbaree, Seto, Langton, & Peacock, 2001; Harris, Rice, & Quincy, 1993; Harris, 1994; Hoffman, 1980; Hoge & Andrews, 1996; Lowenkamp, Holsinger, & Latessa, 2001; Shields & Simourd, 1991). At present, correctional agencies have access to a wide range of actuarial measures to assist with the accurate identification of offender risk level (Bechtel, Lowenkamp, & Latessa, 2007; Flores, Lowenkamp, Smith, & Latessa, 2006; Gendreau, Goggin, & Smith, 2002; Lowenkamp, Holsinger, Brusman-Lovins, & Latessa, 2004; Shields & Simourd, 1991).

Second, the intensity and duration of services should match the level of offender risk (Andrews & Bonta, 2010). After offenders are assessed and classified, case management activities should be used to adjust the intensity and duration (i.e., dosage) of treatment an offender receives. This intervention should depend on the offender's risk level. Specifically, the results of meta-analyses have consistently found that higher risk offenders derive the most benefit from treatment. In fact, treatment programs targeting higher risk samples reduced recidivism by 7% more than programs targeting lower risk offenders (Andrews & Bonta, 2010). From a theoretical viewpoint, this pattern of findings makes good sense. Higher risk offenders are, by definition, likely to possess a greater number of—and more severe—criminogenic needs and therefore require a higher dosage of intervention. In contrast, participation in intensive treatment services can increase the failure rates of lower risk samples by disrupting protective factors and exposing these clients to their higher risk counterparts (see Lowenkamp, Latessa, & Smith, 2006; Smith & Gendreau, 2007).

THE NEED PRINCIPLE. The *need principle* provides guidance about *what should be targeted* for treatment. In this model, dynamic risk factors are referred to as "criminogenic needs" because they are deficits that, unless fixed, will result in criminal behavior. Similar to medicine, the logic is that the causes of a problem—whether illness or the propensity to offend—must be treated if individuals are to be "cured" and not continue to have the problem in question. The need principle thus underscores that correctional programs must target the dynamic risk factors associated with criminality to reduce the risk for future recidivism (Andrews, 1989; Andrews, Bonta, & Hoge, 1990; Gendreau, 1996). According to the research, there are a handful of criminogenic needs that most robustly predict criminal behavior and therefore are the most important treatment targets. These include antisocial attitudes, antisocial associates, antisocial personality traits (e.g., impulsivity, sensation seeking, lack of empathy, aggression/hostility, poor self-regulation), family and marital relationships, substance abuse, educational or vocational achievement, and use of leisure time (Gendreau et al., 2002, 1996; Hoge & Andrews, 1996; Simourd & Andrews, 1994; Zamble, 1993).

Of note, research has also shown that there are a range of *noncriminogenic factors* that are often mistakenly viewed as appropriate correctional program targets. However, these factors do not predict recidivism (Dowden & Andrews, 1999a; Gendreau et al., 1996). Examples of such inappropriate targets include self-esteem, mental health issues, vague emotional problems, physical activity, bonding among antisocial peers, and fear of punishment. If the wrong factors are focused on in treatment, the intervention either will be ineffective or will increase the risk of recidivating.

THE RESPONSIVITY PRINCIPLE. The *responsivity principle* has important implications for *how correctional treatment should be delivered*. To again use a medical analogy, an illness will only be cured if the correct treatment is prescribed. The medicine must be capable of curing the illness; that is, it must be "responsive" to the condition it is intended to change. In the same way, correctional treatments will only work if they are capable of changing the criminogenic needs that lead offenders to recidivate. They must be responsive to the condition leading offenders to return to crime.

Responsivity can be subdivided into two key components: *general responsivity* and *specific responsivity*. First, general responsivity refers the selection of treatments that will reduce recidivism across offenders. Thus, when having to decide which rehabilitation modality to use in a program, what should practitioners do? Notably, the empirical research has consistently found that the most effective interventions are based on cognitive–behavioral and social learning models of treatment (Andrews et al., 1990; Antonowicz & Ross, 1994; Baro, 1999; French & Gendreau, 2006; Garrett, 1985; Gendreau & Ross, 1987; Izzo & Ross, 1990; Lipsey, Chapman, & Landenberger, 2001; Mayer et al., 1986; for a review, see also Andrews & Bonta, 2010; Smith, 2013). The logic behind the use of this approach is that cognitive–behavioral techniques are most conducive to how most individuals learn new behaviors. The use of modeling, rehearsal, and reinforcement is coupled with helping offenders understand the linkages among their thoughts, emotions, and behaviors.

In a recent summary of the meta-analytic findings in the corrections literature, Smith et al. (2009) found that 73% of effect size estimates (or 16 of 22) for cognitive–behavioral interventions were greater than $r = .15$. Similarly, Andrews and Bonta (2010) reported that cognitive–behavioral treatment programs produced 19% greater reductions in recidivism in comparison with nonbehavioral treatment programs. Notably, interventions that emphasize incapacitation and deterrence are also less effective than human service and treatment strategies (Dowden & Andrews, 1999b; Gendreau et al., 2000; Jonson, 2010; Lipsey, 2009; MacKenzie, 2000), and employing ineffective (Dowden & Andrews, 1999b; Lowenkamp, 2004) strategies or poorly implemented effective strategies (Andrews & Dowden, 2005; Barnoski, 2004) can actually *increase* the likelihood of recidivism.

Second, the specific responsivity principle refers to the need to deliver treatments in a way that is attuned to the individual differences of offenders. Thus, although all offenders should receive cognitive–behavioral therapy as an overall treatment approach (general responsivity), how the program is undertaken could differ depending on the individuals in the program (specific responsivity). In short, this principle acknowledges that not all individuals respond to treatment the same way; therefore, corrections practitioners should match the style and mode of services to key offender characteristics (Cullen, Gendreau, Jarjoura, & Wright, 1997). For example, offenders with lower intelligence levels might respond better in a highly structured program with staff who can relate to their style of thinking. Similarly, offenders who lack motivation may first need to undergo treatment that can increase their motivation and commitment to treatment. Likewise still, offenders with mental illness may need symptom stabilization before they can effectively engage in correctional treatment. Other common specific responsivity concerns may include transportation issues, language barriers, ethnicity or cultural issues, and lack of housing.

It should be reiterated that none of these responsivity concerns is strongly correlated with future recidivism. As such, correctional programs are unlikely to have an appreciable impact on criminal behavior if these factors are targeted to the exclusion of criminogenic needs of offenders (Andrews & Bonta, 2010). In contrast, if a program ignores important responsivity issues (e.g., acute mental illness), then the likelihood of successful completion is low and, in turn, diminishes treatment effectiveness. In comparison with the other principles, fewer outcome studies rigorously assessing the specific responsivity principle have been published to date (see Andrews & Bonta, 2010; Smith et al., 2009).

Perhaps the most crucial issue to discuss in this chapter, in particular, is how the RNR model considers the issue of gender. We will address this issue in more detail shortly, but two comments will help to frame this issue. First, the model's advocates are clear in arguing that male and female offenders will respond similarly to effective treatments because their risk factors are the same (Andrews & Bonta, 2010). For example, in line with the general responsivity principle, they would recommend that regardless of gender, offenders receive cognitive–behavioral interventions. Second, gender might play a role in specific responsivity. Although the research is not extensive, men and women might respond differently to how a treatment is delivered (Andrews & Bonta, 2010).

Although the RNR model has robust empirical support, considerable debate remains in the field of corrections about the extent to which the principles of effective intervention are applicable to female offenders (see Andrews & Bonta, 2010; Blanchette & Brown, 2006). Indeed, the vast majority of offenders in the criminal justice system are men and, as a result, the preponderance of the research involves samples of male offenders. Feminist scholars have raised concerns about the generalizability of these findings to female offenders, however. According to this viewpoint, women have different pathways to criminal behavior, and therefore their needs differ from those of men (Bloom, Owen, & Covington, 2003; Daly, 1994; Reisig, Holtfreter, & Morash, 2006). In the next section, we discuss the opposing gender-neutral and gender-specific perspectives and introduce a newer perspective that marries the two: the gender-informed perspective.

What Works With Female Offenders: Competing Perspectives

As this discussion suggests, two distinct perspectives on the treatment of female offenders have long been debated in the literature (see Daigle, Cullen, & Wright, 2007; Hubbard & Matthews, 2008): the *generalist* approach (also called *gender-neutral*) and the *gender-specific* approach. As noted in the previous section, there is an abundance of empirical evidence to support offender rehabilitation in general, as well as the principles of effective intervention in particular (see Gendreau, 1996; McGuire, 2013; Smith et al., 2009). At the same time, the vast majority of these research findings have involved samples that have included only male offenders. How much they apply to female offenders thus remains in question.

Again, the Canadians' RNR model embraces the generalist approach, arguing that the principles of effective intervention are applicable to both male and female offenders (e.g., Andrews & Bonta, 2010; Dowden & Andrews, 1999a). According to this perspective, the empirical status of the RNR model as a correctional paradigm is largely attributable to the fact that the underlying theories represent *general models of human behavior*. The basic tenets of cognitive, behavioral, and social learning theories have been applied extensively to a wide array of target behaviors in a variety of target populations—including criminal behaviors. Hence, it is reasonable to hypothesize that the principles of effective intervention are also applicable to special populations of offenders, including females. Instead, as noted, gender is viewed only as a potentially important specific responsivity factor (see Andrews & Bonta, 2013).

In contrast, advocates of the gender-specific approach assert that the available empirical literature is limited in important ways and does not adequately reflect the experiences of women in the criminal justice system (see Bloom et al., 2003; Chesney-Lind, 2000; Covington & Bloom, 2007; Hannah-Moffat, 2004; Salisbury, Van Voorhis, & Spiropoulos, 2009; Ward & Brown, 2004). More recently, a third perspective has emerged as a handful of authors have attempted to merge the basic concepts from both perspectives into a more coherent theoretical model, referred to as the *gender-informed approach* (see Blanchette & Brown, 2006; Gehring, Van Voorhis, & Bell, 2010; Giordano, Deines, & Cernkovich, 2006; Hubbard & Matthews, 2008). Each of these approaches will be compared and contrasted in the next section to consider implications for the identification of risk and need factors, the assessment and classification of offenders, and the implementation of effective correctional treatment for women.

Identifying the Predictors of Criminal Behavior

The generalist approach contends that the predictors of crime and recidivism are essentially the same for males and females; that is, the proximal causes of criminality are general rather than gender specific (for supportive meta-analytic evidence, see Dowden & Andrews, 1999a; Gendreau et al., 1996; Hubbard & Pratt, 2002; Moffitt, Caspi, Rutter, & Silva, 2001; Simourd & Andrews, 1994). According to this viewpoint, gender is important, but only to the extent that it shapes how males and females acquire common risk factors. To reiterate, previous empirical research has repeatedly demonstrated similarities in the causes of crime across gender (Moffitt et al., 2001; Simons, Miller, & Ainger, 1980; Smith & Paternoster, 1987).

In contrast, gender-specific theorists contend that these more traditional approaches omit experiences—and thus risk factors—that are unique to women. Thus, they point to distinct differences by gender in socialization, development, and economic marginalization as the primary explanations for the gender differences in risk factors (Chesney-Lind, 1989; Daly, 1992, 1994; Reisig, Holtfreter, & Morash, 2002). For example, Covington and Bloom (1999) argued that "the philosophy of criminogenic risk and needs does not consider factors such as economic marginalization, the role of patriarchy, sexual victimization, or women's place in society" (p. 3).

These unique life-course trajectories that lead to criminal offending are referred to as *gendered pathways* (Daly, 1992, 1994; for a summary, see Miller & Mullins, 2006). To illustrate, Chesney-Lind (1989, 1997) has advanced the idea that the pathways to criminal justice involvement differ across genders. Specifically, her work has suggested that girls' exposure to the criminal justice system is often a result of attempts to escape an abusive situation (e.g., sexually assaulted by a stepparent), which then leads to basic survival strategies involving criminal behaviors, as well as to depression and substance use (Chesney-Lind, 1997; Chesney-Lind & Shelden, 2004). Furthermore, she contends that status offenses (e.g., running away) are far more likely to be criminalized in girls versus boys, and that the high rate of substance abuse among female offenders often represents an attempt to self-medicate the pain and trauma associated with past abuse and victimization (Chesney-Lind, 2000). As such, more females are incarcerated than warranted, given the level of actual threat posed to the public. Once incarcerated, most of these female offenders fail to receive the services required to address their unique needs.

Several studies seem to suggest that women and men do, in fact, differ in their pathways into crime. Daly (1992) analyzed the presentence investigations of 40 women for a federal court to also develop a framework for women's pathways to criminal involvement. The resultant framework included a variety of "nontraditional" criminogenic needs and highlighted the role of childhood abuse, domestic violence, drug addiction, and economic marginalization in female criminality. Similarly, Funk (1999) compared the predictors of recidivism in a sample of male and female juvenile probationers. In support of the pathways theory, significant relationships were found among abuse, gender, and delinquency. Specifically, Funk found that the relationship between abuse and offending was much stronger for females ($r = .41$) than for males ($r = .03$). A similar pattern of findings was later supported by Hubbard and Pratt (2002), as well as Belknap and Holsinger (2006).

Daigle et al. (2007) also investigated the predictors of male and female delinquency using national-level longitudinal survey data and compared risk factors from traditional criminological theories with those from life-course and feminist theories. The results indicated that some predictors were similar between males and females (e.g., victimization), whereas others were unique (e.g., depression). Overall, Daigle and her colleagues concluded that general theories of crime may not be able to fully address the predictors of delinquency because some variables were, in fact, uniquely predictive of female offending.

More recently, Salisbury and Van Voorhis (2009) evaluated 313 female probationers to test how three unique pathways to female offending were related to recidivism. This study represents one of the few quantitative studies to date that examines the pathways model. Information was gathered through gender-specific risk/need assessments and surveys. Salisbury and Van Voorhis found empirical support for the following three pathway models: (1) the *childhood victimization path model* in which women are victimized as children, contributing to past and current mental illness and substance abuse; (2) the *relational path model* in which dysfunctional adult relationships lead to victimization, which in turn impacts the likelihood of poor self-efficacy, mental illness, and substance abuse; and (3) the *social and human capital path model* in which education deficits and problematic family relationships contribute to decreased self-efficacy as well as financial and employment problems. Each pathway was correlated with reincarceration in the probationers studied.

Finally, Brennan, Breitenbach, and Dieterich (2010) examined the characteristics of 718 incarcerated females and also found support for unique pathways to female offending. Their results identified a total of eight distinct gendered pathways to crime (which were then collapsed into four general pathways to crime): (1) *normal women*, or lower risk, higher need, drug-involved females; (2) *marginalized "socialized" female offenders*, or those afflicted by substance abuse, vocational or educational deficits, poverty, homelessness, and social isolation; (3) *serious, chronic, violent women offenders*, or high-risk, high-need, chronic offenders with mental health issues, antisocial personality traits, and histories of victimization; and (4) *lifelong victimization women offenders*, or those with high stress, childhood victimization extending to adulthood, addiction, and retaliatory violence. They further argue that these pathways encompass both "traditional" predictors of crime (e.g., antisocial attitude, antisocial personality traits, substance abuse) and factors typically categorized as gender-specific factors (e.g., victimization history, economic marginalization, mental illness).

In sum, there is reason to believe that the risk factors for future recidivism are more similar than different across genders, but many of the pathway models have provided preliminary support for the notion that some needs are unique for women. It is important to emphasize, however, that few quantitative studies directly comparing male and female samples have been conducted. This information is critical to more precisely answer the question of whether the proximal causes of criminal behavior are similar or different across genders.

Measuring Risk for Future Recidivism

Feminist scholars have questioned the validity of actuarial tools used to classify women (Bloom, 2000; Funk, 1999; Holtfreter & Cupp, 2007; Reisig et al., 2006) and have expressed concerns about the misclassification of females (Van Voorhis & Presser, 2001). The construct of gendered pathways has important implications for offender assessment and, ultimately, for treatment. If females predominantly engage in criminal behaviors for gender-specific reasons (e.g., sexual abuse, depression), then many commonly used composite risk measures—which assume the generality of crime causation—would not contain these risk factors and thus would not be predictive of recidivism in female offenders. Consistent with the notion that females have unique pathways to criminal behavior, many feminist scholars have argued that interventions designed for male offenders should not be capriciously applied to females. As a consequence, many feminists have rejected the applicability of RNR or classification instruments to female offenders (Bloom, 2000; Funk, 1999; Holtfreter & Cupp, 2007; Reisig et al., 2006).

Two studies have examined how well a leading RNR-informed measure of risk, the Level of Service Inventory-Revised (LSI-R; Andrews & Bonta, 1995), works with women. In the first, Holtfreter Reisig, and Morash (2004) found that economic marginalization was highly correlated with recidivism in female offenders and that the LSI-R was no longer predictive for women once this variable was controlled. As a consequence, they concluded that the LSI-R does not adequately account for the economic marginality that is so common among female offenders. Relatedly, Manchak, Skeem, Douglas, and Siranosian (2009) found that different risk factors contributed to the predictive utility of the LSI-R for women and men. Specifically, although the financial risk factor predicted recidivism for both groups, its salience was much more pronounced for female offenders in predicting recidivism. Notably, the financial factor was the *only* factor that remained significant for women once other risk factors were statistically controlled for.

Subsequently, Reisig et al. (2006) conducted a study involving 235 female offenders under community supervision in Minnesota and Oregon. They compared the ability of the LSI-R to predict recidivism for those offenders who committed crimes for gender-neutral reasons (i.e., economic motivation) versus gender-specific reasons (i.e., prostitution, abuse and neglect, and drug-connected women). Their analysis revealed that the LSI-R predicted recidivism for economically motivated offenders, but it often misclassified offenders who entered crime through gendered pathways. It should also be noted, however, that the economically motivated offenders comprised only a quarter of the sample. Nevertheless, Reisig et al. (2006) noted that there was a clear "cause for concern" (p. 400) because the LSI-R endangers public safety and misallocates treatment resources by underclassifying some offenders (especially drug-connected females) and overclassifying others. In short, Reisig et al. (2006) concluded that the LSI-R might be appropriate to assess male offenders, but not female offenders. Finally, Holtfreter and Cupp (2007) conducted a recent literature review of 11 studies on the predictability of the LSI-R for women. They concluded that this tool is better able to predict more extreme forms of recidivism, which are relatively rare for women. They cautioned that correctional administrators who rely too heavily on this tool with women could be misguided.

By contrast, a number of other studies on the use of actuarial risk assessments with female offenders have arrived at the opposite conclusion. For example, Lowenkamp et al. (2001) explored the validity of the LSI-R for men and women, as well as the role of childhood abuse in predicting risk. The results indicated that the LSI-R accurately predicted recidivism for both males and females. Furthermore, they found that although women were more likely to report abuse, history of physical or sexual abuse failed to predict recidivism once risk was controlled using the LSI-R (see also Vose, Lowenkamp, Smith, & Cullen, 2009). More recently, Smith et al. (2009) conducted a meta-analysis to examine the predictive validity of the LSI-R. The results included 27 effect sizes and a sample of more than 14,000 offenders and yielded a moderate effect size ($r = .35$) with recidivism. Moreover, this correlation was not statistically different from the average effect size for their male counterparts.

An additional primary study on the relevance of the risk principle with female offenders merits discussion here. Lovins, Lowenkamp, Latessa, and Smith (2007) conducted an evaluation of community-based correctional programs. Interestingly, higher risk females who participated in residential programs had a lower adjusted probability of rearrest of .46 relative to an adjusted probability of .66 for the comparison group, which received community supervision. In contrast, lower risk women had a rearrest probability of .18 relative to just .06 for the control group. Thus, higher risk women who participated in residential treatment had a lower probability of recidivism relative to a comparison group, whereas lower risk women increased in likelihood of rearrest after exposure to the same treatment. These findings support the notion that the risk principle is applicable to female offenders.

Implications for Correctional Treatment Programs

Does one gender derive more benefit from treatment that is consistent with cognitive–behavioral principles? To answer this question, we first look to meta-analyses on the effectiveness of cognitive–behavioral interventions with general samples (i.e., nonoffenders, mental health outcomes) and offending samples (i.e., criminal outcomes). Unfortunately, whereas it is well-established that cognitive-behavioral treatment generally outperforms most other therapeutic approaches across nonoffender samples (Butler, Chapman, Forman, & Beck, 2006) and across offender samples (Andrews et al., 1990; Dowden & Andrews, 1999a, 1999b; Dowden & Andrews, 2000; Hanson, Bourgon, Helmus, & Hodgsin, 2009; Landenberger & Lipsey, 2005; Lipsey, 2009), little is known about the differential effects of cognitive-behavioral treatments by gender.

To illustrate, in their review of 16 meta-analyses across nearly 10,000 subjects and 332 studies, Butler and his colleagues (2006) concluded that very few meta-analyses have actually examined the role of gender on the effectiveness of cognitive-behavioral treatments for a variety of psychological problems and disorders (e.g., anxiety, depression, obsessive–compulsive disorder, bulimia) and even one type of criminal behavior, namely sex offending. Similarly, Landenberger and Lipsey (2005) could not directly examine the interaction between gender and cognitive-behavioral treatment on offender outcomes across 58 studies of adult and juvenile offenders. They argued that this would be difficult to do, given that most studies were "all male or predominantly male" (Landenberger & Lipsey, 2005, p. 464). However, they did conclude that the gender composition of samples showed no relationship to effect sizes.

Two relevant individual studies have directly tested the effects of gender in predicting outcomes among individuals in cognitive–behavioral programs. In one study, Pelissier, Camp, Gaes, Saylor, and Rhodes (2003) examined the effectiveness of a prison-based cognitive–behavioral intervention in reducing recidivism and drug use for 1,842 male and 473 female offenders with substance use problems over a three-year period postrelease from prison. Here, the results indicated that women were less likely to relapse into substance use (35% vs. 50%) and reoffend (25% vs. 44%) than men. Interestingly, however, receiving treatment had an effect on whether male inmates recidivated. This finding did not hold for the women in the sample; treatment and nontreatment samples of women did not significantly differ in their recidivism rates.

Similarly, Hubbard (2007) examined the clinical and criminal outcomes (program completion, arrest, and reincarceration) of 344 men and 102 women participating in cognitive–behavioral programming across four different treatment sites in Ohio. Following participants for approximately a year and a half, she found that although there were no differences between men and women in terms of program completion, women were significantly less likely to be arrested and reincarcerated.

Given these findings, what can be concluded about gender differences in general responsivity? In short, very little. Few studies examine whether women do better or worse than men in cognitive–behavioral correctional treatment. The studies that do examine this question seem to suggest that (a) women who participated in cognitive–behavioral therapy recidivate at lower rates than their male counterparts and (b) treatment does not seem to matter for women. The first finding is not surprising. It is well established that women are slightly less likely to recidivate to begin with. For example, rates of recidivism (i.e., rearrest) among women are approximately 10% lower than those of men (57.6% vs. 68.4%) (Langan & Levin, 2002).

The second conclusion may be more questionable. It may be that treatment does not have as pronounced effects for women as it does for men, but replication and more rigorous tests of this assumption are needed. It is unclear, for example, whether the women in Pelissier et al.'s (2003) treatment group were receiving high-quality treatment that showed fidelity to cognitive–behavioral principles. Without this information, it would be premature to conclude that treatment is not useful for women.

Perhaps these two conclusions can be better reconciled with consideration of some specific responsivity issues that may place women at an advantage, both for succeeding in treatment and for being less likely to recidivate in general. At least two studies have shown that female offenders are higher in motivation for treatment than male offenders (Messina, Burdon, Hagopian, & Prendergast, 2006; Stanton-Tindall et al., 2007). Additionally, women may be more receptive to correctional treatment because they have better interpersonal skills and different cognitive styles than men (see Bennett, Farrington, & Huesman, 2005). In short, the factors that place women in a better position to benefit from treatment may also place them in a position to have better criminal justice outcomes than men. Nevertheless, more research is certainly needed to determine how men and women may (or may not) engage in and respond to cognitive–behavioral interventions differently.

Still, there is substantial evidence that cognitive–behavioral therapy is a superior model for the treatment of offenders (Andrews et al., 1990; Dowden & Andrews, 1999a; Izzo & Ross, 1990; Lipsey, 1992). At present, there is little direct evidence to suggest that women would not benefit from cognitive–behavioral correctional interventions as well as men. Although other approaches have been put forth as more appropriate or conducive to female offenders (e.g., feminist, relational, holistic models), no known empirical data demonstrate that these approaches are any more effective at reducing recidivism among female offenders than cognitive–behavioral therapies (Blanchette & Brown, 2006; Worell, 2001).

It is important to note that Dowden and Andrews (1999a) found evidence that the RNR principles do in fact apply to women as well as men. In their meta-analysis of 26 studies, they found that programs targeting higher risk women produced a reduction in recidivism of 19%, whereas those targeting lower risk women were associated with a 4% increase. In addition, the findings suggested meaningful differences in the average treatment effect for programs that targeted primarily criminogenic needs ($r = .26$) versus those that targeted noncriminogenic needs ($r = .04$). Finally, Dowden and Andrews (1999a) found that female programs using a cognitive–behavioral approach were more effective at reducing recidivism among participants.

Scholars who embrace the generalist perspective acknowledge that the needs of female offenders do differ from those of males and also recognize that issues such as low self-esteem, mental illness, victimization, and poverty are common among female offenders (see Andrews & Bonta, 2010). These needs, however, tend to be viewed as *specific responsivity issues* or barriers to treatment success, rather than primary treatment targets aimed at reducing recidivism (Andrews & Bonta, 2010). Feminists, in contrast, argue that issues such as victimization or poverty should be addressed as a central program element as it is related directly to criminality among women (Bloom et al., 2003).

Merging the Perspectives

Several recent attempts to merge key concepts from both the generalist and the gender-specific perspectives have been published in the literature (Blanchette & Brown, 2006; Gehring et al., 2010; Giordano et al., 2006; Hubbard & Matthews, 2008). This growing body of academic work represents an important advancement in articulating a gendered theory of offender rehabilitation. To illustrate, Giordano and her colleagues (2006) have argued that the either/or dichotomy between the generalist and the gender-specific viewpoints is unnecessary. These perspectives are not necessarily fundamentally incompatible or mutually exclusive, but rather can be integrated in a manner that embraces the similarities and differences across genders.

Blanchette and Brown (2006) published what is arguably one of the most balanced and integrated considerations of the topic to date. They challenged one of the key criticisms levied by feminist researchers against the general responsivity principle by arguing that cognitive–behavioral treatment in no way "dehumanizes" female offenders. In fact, the adoption of treatment models consistent with the best available evidence ensures that women and girls have access to the highest quality interventions possible. This assertion is consistent with the viewpoint of some leading feminist scholars (see Worell & Remer, 2003).

Blanchette and Brown (2006) provide several core recommendations based upon their review of the empirical literature. First, they advise against the strict application of gender-neutral *or* gender-specific theories of female criminality. Instead, they promote *gender-informed theories* that operationalize theoretical constructs to account for gender differences. For example, social control theory—which focuses on the role of marital attachment and employment—should incorporate additional constructs to account for female bonding, such as attachment to children (Blanchette & Brown, 2006).

Second, they call for gender-informed assessment models that build upon the work of the Canadian school, such that the principles of effective classification can be more carefully applied to women. At the same time, they caution that gender-specific issues, such as *relative risk for reoffending*, should be incorporated into assessment strategies to minimize the likelihood of overclassification.

Third, Blanchette and Brown (2006) provide a persuasive rationale for the development of actuarial assessment tools that are designed and validated for this special population of offenders. To illustrate, Van Voorhis and Presser (2001) conducted a national survey of state prisons and determined that 36 states had not validated their classification system on female inmates. As a result, Van Voorhis and her colleagues have developed a series of gender-responsive instruments designed to increase the predictability of mainstream risk assessments, as well as to identify the criminogenic needs specific to female offenders (Van Voorhis, Wright, Salisbury, & Bauman, 2010). They have designed both a "trailer" that can be added to an existing risk/need tools, such as the LSI-R, and a stand-alone tool for the assessment and classification of female offenders (the Women's Risk Needs Assessment). Quantitative data from probation, prison, and prerelease samples in different states informed the development of these gender-responsive tools.

Notably, the results suggested that both "traditional" criminogenic needs (e.g., criminal history, education, employment and antisocial associates) and gender-responsive factors (e.g., depression or anxiety, psychotic symptoms, parental stress and victimization) were predictive of future adjustment and recidivism. In particular, the gender-responsive scales produced correlations between .27 and .34, whereas the so-called gender-neutral scales were associated with correlations ranging from .16 to .36. However, when these gender-neutral and gender-responsive factors were combined, the overall predictive validity of the instrument was considerably improved (Van Voorhis et al., 2010).

Fourth, Blanchette and Brown (2006) proposed a reformulation of the general responsivity principle as it relates to female offenders to incorporate gender-specific best practices. One such example of a gender-responsive cognitive–behavioral program developed specifically for female offenders is *Moving On* (Van Dieten, 2010). This program incorporates motivational interviewing, cognitive–behavioral strategies, and relational theory to target needs specific to female offenders. Gehring et al. (2010) evaluated the effectiveness of this intervention in a sample of 190 probationers. Successful program completers had significantly lower rates of recidivism (arrest, conviction, and incarceration) over the matched comparison cases, with differences between the groups ranging from 10% to 13%. This study lends support to the generalist notion that cognitive–behavioral interventions apply to women as well as men, but also supports the feminist perspective that females benefit from an intervention designed to address gender-specific needs.

As a final note, considerable overlap is likely to exist between many of the program elements identified from the "what works" literature and the recommendations emanating from gender-informed advocates. For example, Koons, Burrow, Morash, and Bynum (1997) conducted a nationwide survey of expert and offender perceptions of program elements leading to successful outcomes for female offenders. The results affirmed that many of the same program characteristics described by the Canadians within the RNR framework are also likely relevant within the context of effective interventions with female offenders (e.g., warm and dedicated staff, a range of treatment targets, prosocial modeling, structured and individualized programming, skill acquisition, and brokerage).

Conclusion

The approaches for managing and treating female offenders vary widely. Proponents of the generalist perspective have argued that the RNR model is based on general theories of human behavior and thus is applicable to female offenders. Accordingly, gender should not affect the selection of the treatment modality (general responsivity), although it might be a relevant specific responsivity factor that should be considered in choosing the style and means of service delivery. In contrast, proponents of the gender-specific approach have contended that the pathways to criminal behavior differ substantially across genders and the assessment and treatment of female offenders should differ from those used with male offenders. More recent attempts have been made to integrate the key findings from these divergent perspectives in an effort to further advance a gendered theory of correctional rehabilitation.

Taken together, what does the existing body of literature tell us about the RNR model and gender? First, it is apparent that little is yet known about how men and women respond differentially to cognitive–behavioral correctional treatment. In theory, humans—regardless of age, race, or gender—learn in very similar ways: from observation, modeling, and reinforcement. However, the level of complexity of an individual's specific responsivity profile can certainly impact the ability to understand and effectively participate in such treatment. At present, we simply do not have enough knowledge about how men and women perform in cognitive–behavioral treatment and how this is impacted by specific responsivity issues that may or may not vary across gender.

Second, responsivity issues experienced by women can be both protective and problematic. Although women are more likely to have lower self-esteem, greater trauma histories, and higher incidence of mental illness than men, they also seem to demonstrate somewhat better motivation for treatment and possess social and cognitive abilities that may make them more amenable to cognitive–behavioral interventions.

Third, although women may present with more complex specific responsivity profiles, this does not inherently make women "riskier." Even in the presence of more, or more serious, responsivity concerns—such as mental illness (Abram, Teplin, & McClelland, 2003; Steadman, Osher, Robbins, Case, & Samuels, 2009; Teplin, 1990; Zlotnick, Clarke, Friedman, Roberts, & Melnick, 2008), abuse histories (Harlow, 1999; Messina et al., 2006), and poor self-esteem (Kling, Hyde, Showers, & Buswell, 1999)—women are no more likely than men to recidivate (Messina et al., 2006; Pelissier et al., 2006). These specific responsivity issues, however, can impact other more proximal outcomes (e.g., treatment involvement, drug relapse) that may have longer term, distal consequences. Given the paucity of research in this area, more investigation is certainly warranted. Additionally, future research must better explore the complex relationship (e.g., potential mediation, moderation) among specific responsivity, general responsivity, and criminal outcomes.

In conclusion, the issue of responsivity and gender is one that is perhaps the least well-understood and most underresearched principle of the RNR model. Extant research does signal that the role of gender in general responsivity, specific responsivity, and the interaction of the two is important to examine. A clear understanding of these issues is yet nascent, and there are ample avenues for researchers to pursue within this particular topic.

References

Abram, K. A., Teplin, L. A., & McClelland, G. M. (2003). Comorbidity of severe psychiatric disorders and substance use disorders among women in jail. *American Journal of Psychiatry, 160,* 1007–1010.

Abramsky, S. (2007). *American furies: Crime, punishment, and vengeance in the age of mass incarceration.* Boston, MA: Beacon Press.

Andrews, D. A. (1989). Recidivism is predictable and can be influenced: Using risk assessments to reduce recidivism. *Forum on Corrections Research, 1*(2), 11–17.

Andrews, D. (1995). The psychology of criminal conduct and effective treatment. In J. McGuire (Ed.), *What works: Reducing reoffending* (pp. 35–62). Chichester, West Sussex, UK: Wiley.

Andrews, D. A., & Bonta, J. (1995). *The Level of Service Inventory-Revised user's manual.* Toronto, Ontario: Multi-Health Systems.

Andrews, D. A., & Bonta, J. (2010). *The psychology of criminal conduct* (5th ed.). New Providence, NJ: Anderson.

Andrews, D. A., Bonta, J., & Hoge, R. D. (1990). Classification for effective rehabilitation: Rediscovering psychology. *Criminal Justice and Behavior, 17,* 19–52.

Andrews, D. A., & Dowden, C. (2005). Managing correctional treatment for reduced recidivism: A meta-analytic review of programme integrity. *Legal and Criminological Psychology, 10,* 173–187.

Andrews, D. A., Zinger, I., Hoge, R. D., Bonta, J., Gendreau, P., & Cullen, F. T. (1990). Does correctional treatment work? A clinically relevant and psychologically informed meta-analysis. *Criminology, 28,* 369–404.

Antonowicz, D. H., & Ross, R. R. (1994). Essential components of successful rehabilitation programs for offenders. *International Journal of Offender Therapy and Comparative Criminology, 38,* 97–104.

Barbaree, H. E., Seto, M. C., Langton, C. M., & Peacock, E. J. (2001). Evaluating the predictive accuracy of six risk assessment instruments for adult sex offenders. *Criminal Justice and Behavior, 28,* 490–521.

Barnoski, R. (2004). *Outcome evaluation of Washington State's research-based programs for juvenile offenders* (Document No. 04-01-1201). Olympia, WA: Washington State Institute for Public Policy.

Baro, A. L. (1999). Effects of a cognitive restructuring program on inmate institutional behavior. *Criminal Justice and Behavior, 26,* 466–484.

Bechtel, K., Lowenkamp, C. T., & Latessa, E. (2007). Assessing the risk of re-offending for juvenile offenders using the youth level of service/case management inventory. *Journal of Offender Rehabilitation, 45*(3–4), 85–108.

Belknap, J., & Holsinger, K. (2006). The gendered nature of risk factors for delinquency. *Feminist Criminology, 1,* 48–71.

Bennett, S., Farrington, D. P., & Huesmann, L. R. (2005). Explaining gender differences in crime and violence: The importance of social cognitive skills. *Aggression and Violent Behavior, 10,* 263–288.

Blanchette, K., & Brown, S. L. (2006). *The assessment and treatment of women offenders: An integrative perspective.* West Sussex, UK: Wiley.

Bloom, B. (2000). Beyond recidivism: Perspectives on evaluation of programs for female offenders in community corrections. In M. McMahon (Ed.), *Assessment to assistance: Programs for women in community corrections* (pp. 107–138). Lanham, MD: American Correctional Association.

Bloom, B., Owen, B., & Covington, S. (2003). *Gender responsive strategies: Research, practice, and guiding principles for women offenders.* Washington, DC: U.S. Department of Justice.

Brennan, T., Breitenbach, M., & Dieterich, W. (2010, Spring). Unraveling women's pathways to serious crime: New findings and links to prior feminist pathways. *Perspectives: The Journal of the American Probation and Parole Association, 4*(2), 35–47.

Butler, A. C., Chapman, J. E., Forman, E. M., & Beck, A. T. (2006). The empirical status of cognitive–behavioral therapy: A review of meta-analyses. *Clinical Psychology Review, 26,* 17–31.

Chesney-Lind, M. (1989). Girls' crime and woman's place: Toward a feminist model of female delinquency. *Crime and Delinquency, 35,* 5–29.

Chesney-Lind, M. (1997). *The female offender: Girls, women, and crime.* Thousand Oaks, CA: Sage.

Chesney-Lind, M. (2000). *Women and the criminal justice system: Gender matters* (Topics in Community Corrections Annual Issue). Washington, DC: National Institute of Corrections.

Chesney-Lind, M., & Shelden, R. G. (2004). *Girls, delinquency, and juvenile justice* (3rd ed.). Belmont, CA: Wadsworth.

Covington, S. S., & Bloom, B. E. (1999, November). *Gender-responsive programming and evaluation for women in the criminal justice system: A shift from what works? to what is the work?*

Paper presented at the Annual Meeting of the American Society of Criminology, Toronto, Ontario, Canada.

Covington, S. S., & Bloom, B. E. (2007). Gender responsive treatment and services in correctional settings. In E. Leeder (Ed.), *Inside and out: Women, prison, and therapy* (pp. 9–34). Binghamton, NY: Haworth Press.

Cullen, F. T. (2013). Rehabilitation: Beyond nothing works. In M. Tonry (Ed.), *Crime and justice in America, 1975 to 2025—Crime and justice: A review of research* (Vol. 42, pp. 299–376). Chicago, IL: University of Chicago Press.

Cullen, F. T., & Gendreau, P. (1989). The effectiveness of correctional rehabilitation: Reconsidering the "nothing works" debate. In L. Goodstein & D. L. MacKenzie (Eds.), *The American prison: Issues in research and policy* (pp. 23–44). New York, NY: Plenum Press.

Cullen, F. T., Gendreau, P., Jarjoura, G. R., & Wright, J. P. (1997). Crime and the bell curve: Lessons from intelligent criminology. *Crime and Delinquency, 43,* 387–411.

Cullen, F. T., & Jonson, C. L. (2011). Rehabilitation and treatmentcorrections programs. In J. Q. Wilson & J. Petersilia, *Crime and public policy* (pp. 293–344). New York, NY: Oxford University Press.

Daigle, L. E., Cullen, F. T., & Wright, J. P. (2007). Gender differences in the predictors of juvenile delinquency: Assessing the generality-specificity debate. *Youth Violence and Juvenile Justice, 5,* 254–286.

Daly, K. (1992). Women's pathways to felony court: Feminist theories of lawbreaking and problems of representation. *Southern California Review of Law and Women's Studies, 2,* 11–52.

Daly, K. (1994). *Gender, crime and punishment.* New Haven, CT: Yale University Press.

Davidson, W. S., Gottschalk, R., Gensheimer, L., & Mayer, J. (1984). *Interventions with juvenile delinquency: A meta-analysis of treatment efficacy.* Washington, DC: National Institute of Juvenile Justice and Delinquency Prevention.

DiIulio, J. J. (1987). *Governing prisons: A comparative study of correctional management.* New York, NY: The Free Press.

Dowden, C., & Andrews, D. (1999a). What works for female offenders: A meta-analytic review. *Crime and Delinquency, 45,* 438–452.

Dowden, C., & Andrews, D. A. (1999b). What works in young offender treatment: A meta-analysis. *Forum on Corrections Research, 11*(2), 21–24.

Dowden, C., & Andrews, D. A. (2000). Effective correctional treatment and violent reoffending: A meta-analysis. *Canadian Journal of Criminology, 42,* 449–467.

Feeley, M. M., & Simon, J. (1992). The new penology: Notes on the emerging strategy of corrections and its implications. *Criminology, 30,* 449–474.

Flores, A. W., Lowenkamp, C. T., Smith, P., & Latessa, E. J. (2006). Validating the level of service inventory-revised on a sample of federal probationers. *Federal Probation, 70*(2), 44–48.

French, S. A., & Gendreau, P. (2006). Reducing prison misconducts: What works! *Criminal Justice and Behavior, 33,* 185–218.

Funk, S. J. (1999). Risk assessment for juveniles on probation: A focus on gender. *Criminal Justice and Behavior, 26,* 44–68.

Garrett, C. J. (1985). Effects of residential treatment on adjudicated delinquents: A meta-analysis. *Journal of Research in Crime and Delinquency, 22,* 287–308.

Gehring, K. S., Van Voorhis, P., & Bell, V. R. (2010). "What works" for female probationers? An evaluation of the Moving On program. *Women, Girls, and Criminal Justice, 11*(1), 6–10.

Gendreau, P. (1996). The principle of effective intervention with offenders. In A. T. Harland (Ed.), *Choosing correctional options that work: Defining the demand and evaluating the supply* (pp. 117–130). Thousand Oaks, CA: Sage.

Gendreau, P., Cullen, F. T., & Bonta, J. (1994). Intensive rehabilitation supervision: The next generation in community corrections? *Federal Probation, 58*(1): 72–78.

Gendreau, P., Goggin, C., Cullen, F. T., & Andrews, D. A. (2000). Effects of community sanctions and incarceration on recidivism. *Forum on Corrections Research, 12*(2), 10–13.

Gendreau, P., Goggin, C., French, S., & Smith, P. (2006). Practicing psychology in correctional settings. In A. K. Hess & I. B. Weiner (Eds.), *The handbook of forensic psychology* (3rd ed., pp. 722–750). Hoboken, NJ: Wiley.

Gendreau, P., Goggin, C., & Smith, P. (2002). Is the PCL-R really the "unparalleled" measure of offender risk? A lesson in knowledge cumulation. *Criminal Justice and Behavior, 29*, 397–426.

Gendreau, P., Little, T., & Goggin, C. (1996). A meta-analysis of the predictors of adult offender recidivism: What works! *Criminology, 34*, 575–607.

Gendreau, P., & Ross, B. (1979). Effective correctional treatment: Bibliotherapy for cynics. *Crime and Delinquency, 25*, 463–489.

Gendreau, P., & Ross, R. R. (1987). Revivification of rehabilitation: Evidence from the 1980s. *Justice Quarterly, 4*, 349–407.

Giordano, P., Deines, J., & Cernkovich, S. (2006). In and out of crime: A life course perspective on girls' delinquency. In K. Heimer & C. Kruttschnitt (Eds.), *Gender and crime: Patterns in victimization and offending* (pp. 17–40). New York: New York University Press.

Glaze, L. E. (2010). *Correctional populations in the United States, 2009* (NCJ No. 231681). Washington, DC: U.S. Department of Justice, Bureau of Justice Statistics.

Glaze, L. E., & Herberman, E. J. (2013). *Correctional populations in the United States, 2012* (NCJ No. 243936). Washington, DC: U.S. Department of Justice, Bureau of Justice Statistics.

Gottschalk, M. (2006). *The prison and the gallows: The politics of mass incarceration in America.* Cambridge, UK: Cambridge University Press.

Hannah-Moffat, K. (2004). Losing ground: Gendered knowledges, parole risk, and responsibility. *Social Politics, 11*, 363–385.

Hanson, R. K., Bourgon, G., Helmus, L., & Hodgson, S. (2009). The principles of effective correctional treatment also apply to sexual offenders: A meta-analysis. *Criminal Justice and Behavior, 36*, 865–891.

Harlow, C. W. (1999). *Prior abuse reported by inmates and probationers.* Washington, DC: U.S. Department of Justice, Bureau of Justice Statistics.

Harris, G. T., Rice, M. E., & Quincy, V. L. (1993). Violent recidivism of mentally disordered offenders: The development of a statistical prediction instrument. *Criminal Justice and Behavior, 20*, 315–335.

Harris, P. M. (1994). Client management classification and prediction of probation outcome. *Crime and Delinquency, 40*, 154–174.

Hartney, C. (2007). *The nation's most punitive states for women.* Retrieved from http://www .nccdglobal.org/sites/default/files/publication_pdf/factsheet-women.pdf

Hoffman, P. B. (1980). Revalidating the salient factor score: A research note. *Journal of Criminal Justice, 8,* 185–188.

Hoge, R. D., & Andrews, D. A. (1996). *Assessing the youthful offender: Issues and techniques.* New York, NY: Plenum Press.

Holtfreter, K., & Cupp, R. (2007). Gender and risk assessment: The empirical status of the LSI-R for women. *Journal of Contemporary Criminal Justice, 23,* 363–382.

Holtfreter, K., Reisig, M. D., & Morash, M. (2004). Poverty, state capital, and recidivism among women offenders. *Criminology and Public Policy, 3,* 185–208.

Hubbard, D. J. (2007). Getting the most out of correctional treatment: Testing the responsivity principle on male and female offenders. *Federal Probation, 71*(1), 2–8.

Hubbard, D. J., & Matthews, B. (2008). Reconciling the differences between the "gender-responsive" and the "what works" literatures to improve services for girls. *Crime and Delinquency, 54,* 225–258.

Hubbard, D. J., & Pratt, T. C. (2002). A meta-analysis of the predictors of delinquency among girls. *Journal of Offender Rehabilitation, 34,* 1–13.

Izzo, R. L., & Ross, R. R. (1990). Meta-analysis of rehabilitation programs for juvenile delinquents: A brief report. *Criminal Justice and Behavior, 17,* 134–142.

Jonson, C. L. (2010). *The impact of imprisonment on reoffending: A meta-analysis.* Unpublished doctoral dissertation, University of Cincinnati, OH.

Kling, K. C., Hyde, J. S., Showers, C. J., & Buswell, B. N. (1999). Gender differences in self-esteem: A meta-analysis. *Psychological Bulletin, 4,* 470–500.

Koons, B. A., Burrow, J. D., Morash, M., & Bynum, T. (1997). Expert and offender perceptions of program elements linked to successful outcomes for incarcerated women. *Crime and Delinquency, 43,* 512–532.

Kuhn, T. (1962). *The structure of scientific revolutions.* Chicago, IL: University of Chicago Press.

Landenberger, N. A., & Lipsey, M. W. (2005). The positive effects of cognitive–behavioral programs for offenders: A meta-analysis of factors associated with effective treatment. *Journal of Experimental Criminology, 1,* 451–476.

Langan, P. A., & Levin, D. J. (2002). *Recidivism of prisoners release in 1994.* Washington, DC: U.S. Department of Justice, Bureau of Justice Statistics.

Lipsey, M. W. (1992). Juvenile delinquency treatment: A meta-analytic inquiry into the variability of effects. In T. Cook, H. Cooper, D. Cordray, H. Hartmann, L. Hedges, R. Light . . . F. Mosteller (Eds.), *Meta-analysis for explanation* (pp. 83–127). New York, NY: Russell Sage Foundation.

Lipsey, M. W. (2009). The primary factors that characterize effective interventions with juvenile offenders: A meta-analytic overview. *Victims and Offenders, 4,* 124–147.

Lipsey, M. W., Chapman, G. L., & Landenberger, N. A. (2001). Cognitive behavioral programs for offenders. *Annals for the American Academy of Political and Social Science, 578,* 144–157.

Lipsey, M. W., & Cullen, F. T. (2007). The effectiveness of correctional rehabilitation: A review of systematic reviews. *Annual Review of Law and Social Science, 3,* 297–320.

Lipsey, M. W., & Wilson, D. B. (1998). Effective intervention for serious juvenile offenders: A synthesis of research. In R. Loeber & D. P. Farrington (Eds.), *Serious and violent juvenile offenders: Risk factors and successful interventions* (pp. 313–345). Thousand Oaks, CA: Sage.

Lipsey, M. W., & Wilson, D. B. (2001). *Practical meta-analysis.* Thousand Oaks, CA: Sage.

Lovins, L. B., Lowenkamp, C. T., Latessa, E. J., & Smith, P. (2007). Application of the risk principle to female offenders. *Journal of Contemporary Criminal Justice, 23,* 383–398.

Lowenkamp, C. T. (2004). *Correctional program integrity and treatment effectiveness: A multi-site, program-level analysis.* Unpublished doctoral dissertation, University of Cincinnati, OH.

Lowenkamp, C. T., Holsinger, A. M., Brusman-Lovins, L., & Latessa, E. J. (2004). Assessing the inter-rater agreement of the level of service inventory revised. *Federal Probation, 68*(3), 34–38.

Lowenkamp, C. T., Holsinger, A. M., & Latessa, E. J. (2001). Risk/need assessment, offender classification, and the role of childhood abuse. *Criminal Justice and Behavior, 28,* 543–563.

Lowenkamp, C. T., Latessa, E. J., & Smith, P. (2006). Does correctional program quality really matter? The impact of adhering to the principles of effective intervention. *Criminology and Public Policy, 5,* 575–594.

Lynch, M. (2007). *Big prisons, big dreams: Crime and the failure of America's penal system.* New Brunswick, NJ: Rutgers University Press.

MacKenzie, D. L. (2000). Evidence-based corrections: Identifying what works. *Crime and Delinquency, 46,* 457–471.

Manchak, S. M., Skeem, J. L., Douglas, J., & Siranosian, M. (2009). Does gender moderate the predictive utility of the Level of Service Inventory-Revised (LSI-R) for serious violent offenders? *Law and Human Behavior, 36,* 425–442.

Martinson, R. (1974). What works?—Questions and answers about prison reform. *National Affairs, 35,* 22–54.

Masterman, M. (1970). The nature of a paradigm. In I. Lakatos & A. Musgrave (Eds.), *Criticism and the growth of knowledge* (pp. 59–90). Cambridge, UK: Cambridge University Press.

Mayer, J. P., Gensheimer, L. K., Davidson, W. S., & Gottschalk, R. (1986). Social learning treatment within juvenile justice: A meta-analysis of impact in the natural environment. In S. Apter & A. Goldstein (Eds.), *Youth violence: Program and prospects* (pp. 24–38). Elmsford, NY: Pergamon.

McGuire, J. (2013). "What works" to reduce re-offending: 18 years on. In L. A. Craig, L. Dixon, & T. A. Gannon (Eds.), *What works in offender rehabilitation* (pp. 20–49). Malden, MA: Wiley.

Messina, N., Burdon, W., Hagopian, G., & Prendergast, M. (2006). Predictors of prison-based treatment outcomes: A comparison of men and women participants. *American Journal of Drug and Alcohol Abuse, 32,* 7–28.

Miller, J., & Mullins, C. W. (2006). The status of feminist theories in criminology. In F. T. Cullen, J. P. Wright, & K. R. Blevins (Eds.), *Taking stock: The status of criminological theory—Advances in criminological theory* (pp. 217–249). New Brunswick, NJ: Transaction.

Moffitt, T. E., Caspi, A., Rutter, M., & Silva, P. A. (2001). *Sex differences in antisocial behavior: Conduct disorder, delinquency, and violence in the Dunedin Longitudinal Study.* Cambridge, UK: Cambridge University Press.

Palmer, T. (1975). Martinson revisited. *Journal of Research in Crime and Delinquency, 12,* 133–152.

Pearson, F., Lipton, D., Cleland, C., & Yee, D. (2002). The effects of behavioral/cognitive–behavioral programs on recidivism. *Crime and Delinquency, 48,* 476–496.

Pelissier, B. M. M., Camp, S. D., Gaes, G. G., Saylor, W. G., & Rhodes, W. (2003). Gender differences in outcomes from prison-based residential treatment. *Journal of Substance Abuse Treatment, 24,* 149–160.

Reisig, M. D., Holtfreter, K., & Morash, M. (2002). Social capital among women offenders: Examining the distribution of social networks and resources. *Journal of Contemporary Criminal Justice, 18,* 167–187.

Reisig, M. D., Holtfreter, K., & Morash, M. (2006). Assessing recidivism risk across female pathways to crime. *Justice Quarterly, 23,* 384–405.

Rosenthal, R. (1991). *Meta-analytic procedures for social research* (Rev. ed.). Newbury Park, CA: Sage.

Salisbury, E. J., & Van Voorhis, P. (2009). Gendered pathways: A quantitative investigation of women probationers' path to incarceration. *Criminal Justice and Behavior, 36,* 541–566.

Salisbury, E. J., Van Voorhis, P., & Spiropoulos, G. V. (2009). The predictive validity of a gender-responsive needs assessment: An exploratory study. *Crime and Delinquency, 55,* 550–585.

Shields, I. W., & Simourd, D. J. (1991). Predicting predatory behavior in a population of young offenders. *Criminal Justice and Behavior, 18,* 180–194.

Simon, J. (1993). *Poor discipline: Parole and the social control of the underclass, 1890–1990.* Chicago, IL: University of Chicago Press.

Simon, J. (2007). Rise of the carceral state. *Social Research: An International Quarterly, 74,* 471–508.

Simons, R. L., Miller, M. G., & Aigner, S. M. (1980). Contemporary theories of deviance and female delinquency: An empirical test. *Journal of Research in Crime and Delinquency, 17,* 42–57.

Simourd, L., & Andrews, D. A. (1994). Correlates of delinquency: A look at gender differences. *Forum on Corrections Research, 6*(1), 26–31.

Smith, D. A., & Paternoster, R. (1987). The gender gap in theories of deviance: Issues and evidence. *Journal of Research in Crime and Delinquency, 24,* 140–172.

Smith, P. (2013). The psychology of criminal conduct. In F. T. Cullen & P. Wilcox (Eds.), *The Oxford handbook of criminological theory* (pp. 69–88). New York, NY: Oxford University Press.

Smith, P., Cullen, F. T., & Latessa, E. (2009). Can 14,737 women be wrong? A meta-analysis of the LSI-R and recidivism for female offenders. *Criminology and Public Policy, 8,* 183–208.

Smith, P., & Gendreau, P. (2007). The relationship between program participation, institutional misconduct and recidivism among federally sentenced adult male offenders. *Forum on Corrections Research, 19*(1), 6–10.

Stanton-Tindall, M., Garner, B. R., Morey, J. T., Leukefeld, C., Krietemeyer, J., Saum, C. A., & Oser, C. B. (2007). Gender differences in treatment engagement among a sample of incarcerated substance abusers. *Criminal Justice and Behavior, 34,* 1143–1156.

Steadman, H. J., Osher, F. C., Robbins, P. C., Case, B., & Samuels, S. (2009). Prevalence of serious mental illness among jail inmates. *Psychiatric Services, 60,* 761–765.

Teplin, L. A. (1990). The prevalence of severe mental disorder among male urban jail detainees: Comparison with the Epidemiologic Catchment Area Program. *American Journal of Public Health, 80,* 663–669.

Tonry, M. (2004). *Thinking about crime: Sense and sensibility in American penal culture*. Oxford, NY: Oxford University Press.

Van Dieten, M. (2010). *Moving On: A program for at-risk women*. Ottawa, Ontario: Orbis.

Van Voorhis, P., & Presser, L. (2001). *Classification of women offenders: A national assessment of current practices*. Washington, DC: U.S. Department of Justice, National Institute of Corrections.

Van Voorhis, P., Wright, E. M., Salisbury, E., & Bauman, A. (2010). Women's risk factors and their contributions to existing risk/needs assessment: The current status of gender-responsive supplement. *Criminal Justice and Behavior, 37,* 261–288.

Vose, B., Lowenkamp, C. T., Smith, P., & Cullen, F. T. (2009). Gender and the predictive validity of the LSI-R: A study of parolees and probationers. *Journal of Contemporary Criminal Justice, 25,* 459–471.

Ward, T., & Brown, M. (2004). The good lives model and conceptual issues in offender rehabilitation. *Psychology, Crime and Law, 10,* 243–257.

Wilson, D. B., Bouffard, L. A., & MacKenzie, D. L. (2005). A quantitative review of structured, group-oriented, cognitive-behavioral programs for offenders. *Criminal Justice and Behavior, 32,* 172–204.

Worrell, J. (2001). Feminist interventions: Accountability beyond symptom reduction. *Psychology of Women Quarterly, 25,* 335–343.

Worell, J., & Remer, P. (2003). *Feminist perspectives in therapy: An empowerment model for women*. Chichester, UK: Wiley.

Zamble, E. (1993). Expanding the recidivism inquiry: A look at dynamic factors. *Forum on Corrections Research, 5*(3), 27–30.

Zlotnick, C., Clarke, J. G., Friedmann, P. D., Roberts, M. R., & Melnick, G. (2008). Gender differences in comorbid disorders among offenders in prison substance abuse treatment programs. *Behavioral Sciences and the Law, 26,* 403–412.

INDEX

Academy of Criminal Justice Sciences, 31
Accomplished femininity, 133
Activity spaces, 165–67
Actuarial assessment, 375, 382, 386
Adams, H., 18
Add Health. *See* National Longitudinal Study
    of Adolescent Health
ADHD (attention deficit hyperactivity
    disorder), 49
Adjudication. *See* Court adjudication
Adler, Freda, 3–14, 67–68, 76, 78, 87, 103,
    106–7, 118, 173, 174, 176, 177, 178,
    180, 181, 182, 183, 192, 204, 205, 230,
    245, 246, 252, 341
    career path of, 5–7
    criticisms of work/theories, 9–11,
      189–90, 283
    on female assertiveness, 355
    feminist criminology influenced by, 18,
      23–25, 26–30, 31, 35–36, 262,
      263–64, 274–75
    importance of questions asked by, 263–64
    legacy of, 12
    liberation hypothesis of (*see* Liberation/
      emancipation hypothesis)
    masculinity hypothesis of, 5, 9,
      29–30, 282–83
    rebuttals to theories of, 27–30
    self-identification as a scientist, 262
    theories of applied to prisoners, 351, 355,
      356, 358, 363, 364, 365–66
Adler, Patricia, 117
Adolescence. *See also* Boys; Delinquency;
    Girls
    biosocial perspective on, 54–57
    delayed-onset pathway theory on, 72–73, 75

residential mobility and, 214
taxonomy of offending theory on,
    70–71, 72, 73
victimization and, 194–95
Adolescence-limited (AL) offenders, 70–71,
    72, 73, 75, 111
Adornment thesis, 20
Adrenocorticotropic hormone, 46, 53
Advances in Criminological Theory (series), 12
Affiliation networks, 164–67
Afghanistan, 88
Africa, 181
African American(s)
    criminal justice processing and, 327–28, 329
    delayed-onset model on, 75
    gender gap and, 231
    residential mobility and, 213
African American boys, 166, 201, 296, 303
African American females
    crime patterns in, 33
    criminal justice processing and, 266,
      333–34, 336–37, 338–40
    felony offending in, 111, 112–13
    feminist criminology on, 31, 33, 268–69
    the glass ceiling and, 178
    incarceration of, 338–40, 354, 358, 359
    neighborhood context, violence, and,
      210, 216
    sentences of, 7, 336–37
African American girls, 95
    delinquency in, 166
    feminist criminology on, 32
    in gangs, 131, 133
    incarceration of, 96
    physical aggression in, 58–59
    victimization risk in, 201